A Web-Based Introduction to Programming

A Web-Based Introduction to Programming

Essential Algorithms, Syntax,
and Control Structures Using PHP, HTML,
and MariaDB/MySQL

Fifth Edition

Mike O'Kane

CAROLINA ACADEMIC PRESS

Durham, North Carolina

Library of Congress Cataloging-in-Publication Data

Names: O'Kane, Mike, 1953- author.
Title: A web-based introduction to programming : essential algorithms, syntax, and control structures using PHP, HTML, and MariaDB/MySQL / by Mike O'Kane.
Description: Fifth edition. | Durham, North Carolina : Carolina Academic Press, LLC, [2021] | Includes index.
Identifiers: LCCN 2021035347 (print) | LCCN 2021035348 (ebook) | ISBN 9781531022105 (paperback) | ISBN 9781531022112 (ebook)
Subjects: LCSH: Computer software—Development. | Internet programming. | Computer programming—Web-based instruction. | PHP (Computer program language) | XHTML (Document markup language)
Classification: LCC QA76.76.D47 O43 2021 (print) | LCC QA76.76.D47 (ebook) | DDC 005.3—dc23
LC record available at https://lccn.loc.gov/2021035347
LC ebook record available at https://lccn.loc.gov/2021035348

Carolina Academic Press
700 Kent Street
Durham, North Carolina 27701
(919) 489-7486

www.cap-press.com

Printed in the United States of America.

To my dear mother and father,
thank you for the love and light that you bestowed on us.

Contents

Preface

The problem I have tried to solve with this textbook is, quite simply, how to effectively introduce general programming concepts to students who have never programmed before. Perhaps like me, you have found yourself frustrated by textbooks that try to cover too much too fast, make inappropriate assumptions about what a student already knows, or take sudden leaps in complexity when providing examples and exercises.

I believe that the purpose of an introductory programming course is to help students gain confidence and develop their understanding of basic logic, syntax, and problem-solving. They do not need to learn all aspects of a language or even learn best practices—these are topics for the next course level. The question is: how to provide the kind of hands-on experience that supports active learning without overwhelming the beginning student with too much syntactical and programmatic detail?

I have tried many approaches over the years before settling on a Web-based strategy, using PHP, CSS, and HTML to develop small, interactive Web applications. This approach has proved very successful. Many students report how much they enjoy the course, how much they have learned, and how well the material has served them in subsequent courses and in their professional life. Some have even indicated that the approach positively changed their opinion of programming as a career and course of study, which is most gratifying.

The book focuses on the primary challenges that face beginning students: an appreciation of language syntax (especially when working between different languages, such as PHP, HTML, CSS, and MySQL); fundamental concepts and structures; common algorithmic requirements; problem-solving and debugging; and perhaps most important, confidence to explore and experiment. There is no intention to provide a complete coverage of HTML, CSS, PHP, MySQL, or OOP, although all of these are introduced in some detail, and the PHP coverage is quite extensive. As a language, PHP offers the programmer some alternative coding choices (such as use of the print or echo construct, or a choice between double quotes or single quotes); in these cases the book follows some arbitrary conventions in order to minimize differences between PHP syntax and the syntax of other widely used languages, and to facilitate explanation of topics such as escape characters and concatenation. Similarly a simple client/server model is followed throughout in order to develop familiarity with this type of design. A summary of these conventions is included in Chapter 16 (More About PHP). The last chapter in the book (Where to Go From Here) provides some guidance on next steps, with brief overviews of useful tools, version control systems, Javascript and other languages, OOP, IDEs and frameworks, and potential areas of study and career paths. The textbook appendices are designed to support students in need of additional assistance on various topics, and the textbook Web site provides installation guides, "Hints and Help" FAQs to help with chapter exercises, and hands-on tutorials on a range of general-purpose tools considered essential for any beginning student (including Using the Command Line, FTP, phpMyAdmin, Security and Validation, and Version Control with Git and GitHub).

Intended Audience

The book is designed to serve:

- Instructors teaching introductory programming, programming logic and design, or Web programming courses, who want a textbook that engages students, integrates multiple languages, and provides a foundation for subsequent courses, but avoids overwhelming beginners with too much syntactical detail or program complexity.
- Traditional and online students taking a first course in programming, programming logic and design, or Web programming.
- Web designers, graphic artists, technical communicators, and others who find that their work increasingly requires some degree of programming expertise, and need an effective, hands-on introduction.
- Others who wish to learn the basics of programming, either for personal interest, or to explore the possibility of a career in this field.

Note that solutions to quizzes and exercises are only available to verified course instructors.

Approach

The book takes a fairly novel approach, allowing students to learn program logic and design by developing a large number of small Web-based applications. Students love working with the Web, and this approach has other important benefits:

- Important concepts such as client/server design, server-side processing, and interface-driven code modules can be introduced in the form of working applications, and then applied in hands-on exercises.
- Students not only learn the essential control structures and syntax of a programming language, but also learn to use a markup language (and associated style sheets), and a database query language to access and query a

database. This makes sense in today's programming environment where these languages are routinely used in combination to develop a networked application.

- The material is relevant to students across a range of disciplines: Computer Science, Information Systems, Technical Communications, Network Systems, Digital Media, Web Technologies, Mobile Applications, Database Programming, and other technology-related fields.
- The focus on hands-on problem-solving and fundamental structures prepare students for next-level, language-specific courses such as PHP, Python, Java or C++, as well as Web design and database courses, without replicating a great deal of material, while the syntax covered here is generally consistent with these and other languages.

The book makes use of a programming language (PHP), a scripting language (HTML), a style sheet language (CSS), and a database query language (MariaDB or MySQL), but does not attempt to provide a complete overview of these languages. Instead, students learn sufficient syntax to convert requirements into working applications using basic programming structures, arithmetic and logical expressions, user interfaces, functions, data files, and SQL queries. The focus remains on basic concepts, logic and design, algorithm development, and common programming procedures. The book provides context throughout, explaining why each topic is important, and referring students to related career paths.

Although the book focuses on Web-based applications, there is NO requirement for a network-based programming environment. The book uses a fully functional but standalone Apache Web server (the open source xampp distribution provided by the Apache Friends group) that students can easily install on on their Windows, macOS, or Linux computer. Students can begin programming in HTML, PHP and MariaDB or MySQL in literally minutes, and can work in any location with no Internet connection.

Features

Each chapter begins with clearly stated learning outcomes. Each topic is introduced using examples of simple program requirements that are first developed as algorithms and interfaces and then realized in working code. Code statements and control structures are explained step by step.

Different programming topics are treated in separate chapters. Even topics that are commonly combined, such as counting loops and event-controlled loops, or numerically indexed and associative arrays, have their own chapters so that students have the chance to develop and apply their understanding of each separately.

Each chapter includes quizzes that have been carefully developed to test the student's understanding of the chapter's learning outcomes. The questions have been tested extensively in the classroom.

Three different types of coding exercise are provided at the end of each chapter:

- **Fixit** exercises provide small programs that include a single error of some kind. These exercises help students improve their problem-solving ability, test their understanding of key concepts, and develop tracing and debugging skills.
- **Modify** exercises provide working programs that must be modified to perform a somewhat different or additional function. These exercises help students determine how and where to add new code, and test their ability to read and understand existing code.
- **Code completion** exercises allow students to apply concepts and tools covered in the chapter by developing new applications. These exercises test the student's ability to: understand requirements, develop algorithms, and produce working code. The code completion exercises follow consistent themes that are developed throughout the book, so that students can more readily appreciate the value of new functionalities that they learn in each chapter.

Templates for each exercise contain partially completed code so students don't waste time typing (and debugging) code that is not relevant to the problem at hand. The templates also help instructors to streamline the grading process.

All of the textbook code samples and exercise templates can be downloaded from the companion Web site, and added to the Web server's **htdocs** folder. Students can complete the exercises simply by opening, editing, and saving the appropriate files, and viewing the results in any Web browser, using the **localhost** URL. Assignments can be turned in simply by zipping and submitting the appropriate chapter folder.

Resources for Instructors

As previously mentioned, the textbook Web site provides a range of resources for students. The Web site also provides support for verified instructors, including test banks, presentation material, and quiz and code solutions. The Web site can be found at:

https://www.mikeokane.com/textbooks/wbip/

One or more of the tutorials on the Web site may serve as additional teaching resources for some instructors and courses (much of this material is also provided in textbook appendices but the online versions will be updated, and can be downloaded and edited):

- A short **Command Line** tutorial covers common file addressing and file management and navigation commands.

- An **Introduction to FTP** provides instructions to install an FTP client and run the FTP server that is included in the xampp installation. Students can use this to learn the basic process of exchanging files with a remote server. This tutorial can also be used in combination with the book exercises, for example if the coursework is to be completed on a remote server.

- A **phpMyAdmin** tutorial provides a quick tour of this interface, enough to get students started submitting SQL queries and managing databases, table, and user acounts. This tutorial can be used to provide more extensive coverage of database queries and management, once students have completed Chapter 14.

- A **Version Control** tutorial explains the purpose and general terminology of version control, introduces **git** and **GitHub**, and includes hands-on instructions designed to show student how to use these products, singly and in combination. Note that Version Control is introduced in Appendix G in the book, and students are referred to this tutorial. Some instructors may wish to require students to use these tools throughout the course, at least for online backup and recovery.

- A tutorial to introduce **Regular Expressions** is also being considered at this time and may be available by the time of publication.

Appendix E in the book provides important information regarding security and validation, and is a must-read for students who choose to work with a "live" online Web server.

Changes to the Fifth Edition

This fifth edition of the textbook includes: extensive revisions, corrections, and additions to all chapters that will hopefully improve understanding in areas where students tend to struggle; a more general introduction to file and folder management in Chapter 2 that gives equal coverage for Windows, macOS and Linux users; a combination of the HTML <label tag> and additional CSS in Chapter 4 to align content in HTML forms; greater use of the trim() function to clean input, especially when reading text files; a more structured approach to input validation and security in Chapter 8; increased coverage of superglobal arrays in Chapter 12; a new Chapter 16 to explain a range of additional PHP operators, structures and functions (including data and time functions), and explain conventions used in the book; a new Chapter 17 to cover additional HTML (form elements, lists, quotations and citations, HTML entities, and the use of <DIV> and <SPAN> tags); an expanded Appendix B, providing more detail regarding file addressing schemes and the use or absolute and relative addresses; a new Appendix C introducing navigation and management at the command line; a new Appendix E to describe basic security and validation procedures, and introduce regular expressions; a new Appendix F that introduces File Transfer Protocol (FTP), and includes a short tutorial; a new Appendix G that introduces version control with Git and GitHub, and refers students to an extended tutorial on the textbook Web site; a new Appendix H that introduces phpMyAdmin and includes a short a tutorial. Standalone, hands-on versions of most appendices are available on the textbook Web site, giving students and instructors greater flexibility in the way they are used.

Chapter Overview

Chapter 1: Introducing Computer Programming. Students learn the relationship between machine language and high-level languages, and review common tasks that computer programs typically perform. The work of a programmer is described, and the software development cycle is explained. The chapter highlights and briefly summarizes design approaches such as algorithm development, interface design, client/server design and object-oriented programming. Different programming languages are identified, and the distinction is made between interpreted and compiled languages, and between markup and programming languages. Standalone and network applications are also contrasted.

Chapter 2: Client/Server Applications—Getting Started. This chapter prepares students for the hands-on work they will perform in subsequent chapters. File types and local and Internet file addressing schemes are explained. Instructions are provided to install, run, and test the required software. Students are shown how to create, store, and run a number of sample applications in order to become familiar with the process of using a text editor, saving files, running the Web server, and viewing the results in a Web browser.

Chapter 3: Program Design—from Requirements to Algorithms. The general characteristics and requirements of effective instructions are explored, using human and program examples. Students walk through the process of reviewing simple requirements, creating input, processing, and output (IPO) charts, designing the interface, and developing solution algorithms. The chapter introduces sequence, selection and repetition instructions, variables and assignment operations, and arithmetic and logical expressions.

Chapter 4: Basics of Markup—Creating a User Interface with HTML. This chapter introduces the topic of data rendering, and provides a brief overview and history of Hypertext Markup Language (HTML). Commonly used HTML tags are explained, and the student is shown how to apply these to create and organize simple Web pages. Cascading style sheets are introduced, using a sample style sheet that is used throughout the course. Students also learn how to create and format HTML forms to obtain user input that will be processed by server side PHP scripts.

Chapter 5: Creating a Working Program—Basics of PHP. This chapter teaches sufficient PHP language syntax to process user input received from HTML forms, perform simple arithmetic, and produce formatted HTML output. In the process, students learn to code arithmetic expressions, use standard operators, variables, and functions, concatenate strings, and identify and fix syntax and logical errors.

Chapter 6: Persistence—Saving and Retrieving Data. This chapter explains the difference between persistent and transient data, and introduces text file processing as well as basic database concepts. Students learn to: open, read, write, and close text files; work with multiple files; parse lines of data that contain multiple values separated by some kind of delimiter.

Chapter 7: Programs that Choose — Introducing Selection Structures. This chapter introduces selection control structures and demonstrates the use of algorithms to solve problems requiring simple selection. Students learn the use of IF and IF..ELSE structures, Boolean expressions, relational operators, truth tables, string comparisons, and testing procedures.

Chapter 8: Multiple Selection, Nesting, ANDs and ORs. This chapter develops examples from Chapter 7 to handle problems associated with input validation and more complex requirements. Students explore the use of Boolean operators and compound Boolean expressions, nested selection structures, chained IF..ELSEIF..ELSE selection structures, and multiple but independent selection structures.

Chapter 9: Programs that Count — Harnessing the Power of Repetition. This chapter introduces loop structures with a focus on count-controlled FOR loops. Students learn how to refer to the counting variable within the loop, and how to use loops to generate tables, crunch numbers, accumulate totals, find highest and lowest values in a series, count and sum selected values from a file of records, and display bar charts.

Chapter 10: "While NOT End-Of-File" — Introducing Event-Controlled Loops. This chapter introduces WHILE loops and demonstrates the use of the priming read and the standard algorithm to process files of unknown length. The student is shown how WHILE loops can be used to perform various operations on a list of data values, and how a file of records can be processed and searched for specific records or field values.

Chapter 11: Structured Data — Working with Arrays. This chapter introduces numerically-indexed arrays, and shows how arrays can be used to store, access, and update a group of related data values. The use of the FOR loop to process arrays is explained, and various array-processing algorithms are demonstrated.

Chapter 12: Associative Arrays and Web Sessions. This chapter introduces associative arrays. Students learn how to use associative arrays as lookups, and gain a better understanding of the $_POST array and the way that data is received from HTML forms. Other superglobal arrays are introduced and students learn to combine Web forms and the code to process the forms in a single page. Web sessions are introduced, and students learn how to use the $_SESSION array to maintain session data between applications.

Chapter 13: Program Modularity — Working with Functions. This chapter demonstrates the importance of program modularity and introduces functions and include files. Students learn to write their own functions, build libraries of related functions, and call stored functions from different applications as needed.

Chapter 14: Connecting to a Database — Working with MySQL. This chapter introduces MySQL/MariaDB and the construction and application of databases queries. The relationship between relational databases and SQL is explained, along with the purpose and syntax of common queries (SELECT, INSERT, UPDATE and DELETE). Students learn to write code to open and close database connections, submit queries, handle errors, perform simple joins, and process query results.

Chapter 15: Introduction to Object-Oriented Programming. This chapter introduces Object-Oriented Programming. Examples show how simple object classes are
designed, how class variables are encapsulated and accessed by class methods, how objects are instantiated and used in applications, and how classes can be inherited by
other classes. An overview of basic OO terminology is provided.

Chapter 16: More About PHP. This chapter "fills in" some important topics that
were left out of the preceding text in order to avoid too much complexity. Topics include: an extended PHP function list, PHP data types, shortcut operators, WHILE..DO
loops, the SWITCH statement, multi-dimensional arrays and ragged arrays, date and
time functions. The chapter also clarifies some of the conventions followed in the book
(file and variable names, use of quotes, print versus echo statement, etc).

Chapter 17: More About HTML. Chapter 17 adds to the HTML that was described
in Chapter 4, with special attention to Web forms, quotes and citations, lists, images,
HTML entities, and use of <DIV> and <SPAN> containers.

Chapter 18: Where to Go From Here. This chapter offers ten suggestions for next
steps (these include the textbook tutorials, use of Git and GitHub for version control,
Javascript and other languages, OOP, IDEs and frameworks, community engagement,
and consideration of career options).

The textbook also includes a number of useful appendices as follows:

Appendix A introduces data representation, and shows how binary values can store
data for a wide range of purposes.

Appendix B provides help with file addressing schemes (including relative and absolute addresses).

Appendix C introduces the use of the command line, and includes a short list of
common Windows and macOS/Linux command equivalents.

Appendix D provides debugging help for students having trouble identifying and
resolving PHP code errors.

Appendix E provides material to address security issues (XSS attacks) and input
validation, and includes a brief introduction to regular expressions.

Appendix F explains the purpose of the **File Transfer Protocol** (FTP) and provides
a short hands-on guide to install an FTP client, run a local FTP server (included in the
xampp installation), and use the client to transfer files between a local file system and
remote server.

Appendix G provides an introduction to **Version Control Systems** using Git and
GitHub, and references an extensive tutorial on the textbook Web site.

Appendix H provides a brief introduction to **phpMyAdmin**, and includes a short
hands-on tutorial.

Acknowledgments

This textbook could not have been created without the generous help and support of many others. In particular I want to thank Constance Humphries for her invaluable technical advice, proof-reading, and development of video tutorials! My sincere thanks to Scott Sipe, Beth Hall, Susan Trimble and all at Carolina Academic Press for their supportive style, professionalism and experience. Thanks to all those instructors who have used the book and provided invaluable comments and corrections, and especially to Charlie Wallin at Asheville-Buncome Technical Community College, who has taught with the book since its inception and consistently provided invaluable feedback and suggestions, and Fred Smartt, who helped to field-test the first edition. Thank you to my co-workers and the administration at A-B Tech, for fostering such a wonderful teaching and learning environment in an institution that truly cares. And thanks most of all to all of the students who have learned with me and sometimes in spite of me as this book evolved in the classroom. A particular thank you to A-B Tech students Uma Benson, Jean-Jacques Maury, and Kenneth Stanley, who all voluntarily provided me with carefully compiled lists of corrections that were incorporated into the fourth edition. Their engagement with the material and concern for future students is greatly appreciated. Any remaining errors or inconsistencies are of course my own.

Lastly, a huge thank you to Kai 'Oswald' Seidler, Kay Vogelgesang, and all those who have contributed to the Apache Friends Project, and who continue to deliver and support the XAMPP distribution. So many of us owe you our great appreciation for your generosity of spirit!

About the Author

Mike O'Kane holds a master's degree in Systems Science (specializing in Advanced Technology) from Binghamton University. He has over twenty years' experience teaching computer science courses, most recently at Asheville-Buncombe Technical Community College in North Carolina. He also has extensive practical experience in the use of technology for learning, having worked at IBM as a short-course developer, NC State University as an Instructional Coordinator, and the University of North Carolina system as the first Executive Director of the UNC Teaching and Learning with Technology Collaborative. He has a passion for developing effective instructional content, and learning environments that promote rather than hinder student learning.

A Web-Based Introduction
to Programming

Chapter 1

Introducing Computer Programming

Intended Learning Outcomes

After completing this chapter, you should be able to:

- Describe the purpose of the microprocessor's instruction set.
- Explain the relationship between the instruction set and machine language.
- List some common tasks that computer programs perform.
- Describe what programmers do.
- Summarize the stages of the software development cycle.
- Explain the importance of writing and communications for programmers.
- Explain the relationship between high-level programming languages and machine language.
- Distinguish between the purpose of a compiler and an interpreter.
- Explain the difference between standalone and network applications.
- Explain the difference between programming languages and markup languages.

Introduction

Welcome! If you have never programmed before, this book is for you. By the time you complete the chapters and exercises, you will have a good grasp of the basic logic and design of computer programs. The book is designed to teach common programming syntax and control structures in a manner that will prepare you for further study in this field, and provide you with sufficient expertise to develop small, interactive Web applications, using a combination of the HTML markup language and PHP programming language. You will also be introduced to the CSS stylesheet language, and the SQL database query language.

To get started, in this first chapter we will explore the general process of programming and define some important term and practices. Don't be too concerned if some of the topics don't make complete sense yet. Your understanding will deepen as you work through the chapters and develop your own applications.

What Is a Computer Program?

A computer is a **programmable machine**. Computers perform all kinds of tasks by reading and executing different **computer programs**, or **software**. Each program contains instructions to direct the computer's operating system and hardware for a specific purpose. Every computer includes a **microprocessor**, which contains the computer's **instruction set**. The instruction set defines all of the basic commands (known as **opcodes**) that the computer can execute. These opcodes are very low-level activities such as adding numbers, moving a data value from one location to another, or comparing two values. The commands that execute the opcodes constitute the computer's **machine language**. Your programs work with the computer's operating system to issue commands to the microprocessor, so a computer program is essentially a set of instructions that tell the microprocessor to execute machine language opcodes in a particular sequence in order to deliver a spreadsheet, a game, a Web browser, a video, an email program, or some other service. If you've ever wondered why some software runs on one computer but not another, it is because different computers have different microprocessors and instructions sets, requiring different versions of a program.

Although different computer programs serve quite different purposes, all programs share some important characteristics. Here are some common tasks that any computer program might typically perform:

Provide interactive environments for users: programs may use text-based input/output or Graphical User Interfaces (GUI's) to interact with users. Interfaces may include graphics, animations, audio, video, and other multimedia features.

Read and write data: programs may access, create, modify or delete data that is stored in files and databases.

Perform numerical calculations: programs can add, subtract, multiply, divide, and compare numbers, and can combine these operations to perform much more complex calculations.

Perform comparison operations: programs can validate, convert, search, sort, compare, and replace data, including numerical, text, and other data types.

Communicate with other programs and devices: programs may exchange data with other programs, cameras, scanners, remote services (such as Internet-based or other networked services), satellites, cell phones, ATM machines, etc.

Control hardware: programs can control robots, satellites, aircraft, automobiles, printers, and other computers.

A single computer program may perform any combination of these operations. For example a computer game may look up player and game information in a file or database, provide an interactive multimedia environment for the player to play the game, perform numerical calculations, and communicate with programs running on other computers to allow multi-user play over the Internet. Similarly a payroll program may perform text-processing operations (such as validation and conversion), query and modify a database, perform numerical calculations, and send checks to a printer. What this means is that, as a programmer, you will want to know how to write programs that might include any or all of these operations.

What Do Programmers Do?

Programmers write program code, right? Well, actually programmers do a lot more than write code. One of the things that makes programming an attractive career is that this work requires an appealing combination of what used to be termed **right-brain** (creative, problem-solving, brain-storming) and **left-brain** (logical, linear, sequential) activities. There are a variety of career paths within the field, so if you have a general aptitude you have a good chance of finding work suited to your personal interests. For example if you like to work with people you may find yourself drawn to software design, interface development, usability, or training. If you prefer to work with data, you may prefer server-side application development, object design, or database administration. And if you are a visual and creative person you may be drawn to graphic design, animation, and media development.

Let's walk through the major stages in software development which will demonstrate the range of skills that programmers need in order to be successful in their work. Here we will simply summarize these steps so don't be concerned if this appears a little abstract right now. We will learn how to apply these steps to develop a working application in Chapter 3.

1. Evaluation of Requirements

In order to develop an effective software application we first need to determine the program's requirements. This usually requires careful reading and listening, asking questions, and careful documentation. Understanding and documenting requirements takes time and skill. A common mistake that beginning (and not just beginning) programmers make is to rush this important step in order to begin coding. Rushing the requirements phase can actually be very costly in terms of time, money and even professional relationships. So learn to go slowly and carefully when you are presented with a requirements document or when you first meet with a client. The more time you spend analyzing your program requirements (and asking questions if you are unsure about anything), the more easily the solution will appear. Remember: the most important skills a programmer needs at this phase are to listen, read, ask questions, document carefully, and communicate effectively with clients, managers, and other programmers.

2. Application Design

Once the requirements have been agreed, the work of designing the application can begin. This may be a one-person job, in the case of a small application, or may involve a design team. A design is often based on a **design pattern**. Design patterns offer well-tested templates that reflect best practices and effective strategies to meet common requirements. The application design document should also include a reference to the necessary data sources and formats, and specify the testing (**data validation**) needed to ensure that all input and output will be both secure and valid.

Unless your requirements are quite simple, your application design will most likely consist of multiple code segments or **modules**, each of which can be developed separately. There are many advantages to a modular approach. Each module can be developed and tested **separately**, often by different programmers or programming teams. The modules can be developed **concurrently** which speeds up development time. This approach also allows each module to be developed by different programmers with the most **suitable skills**. And a modular approach promotes **reusability**: once they have been developed, some of the more useful modules can be shared by many different applications. Modular design includes the development of testing procedures to test that each module will perform as expected when it is coded.

Client/server design is an essential feature of many applications, including Web applications. A **client** application, such as a Web browser, provides an interface to the user and waits for the user to request a service, for example by clicking on a link or menu option, submitting a form, or typing a URL. The client application then calls a **server** application to process the request and send back a response. When the client application receives the response this is presented to the user and the process repeats. You participate in a client/server interaction every time you use your Web browser to connect to Web-based services.

For example, Figure 1-1 shows the screens for a very simple client/server application to calculate an employee's pay based on their hours worked and hourly wage. This example provides the user with two Web pages. When you type the URL to request the first page, the Web browser sends a request to the appropriate Web server, which sends back the data to display the page. The first page contains a form. When the user clicks the "Get Your Wage Report Now" button, the Web browser sends a second request to the Web server that includes the data that the user has entered into the form. The server executes a program that has been developed especially to process this data. This program generates the content for the second page, which the server sends back to the browser for display to the user.

In this book you will develop many small client/server applications similar to the example described above.

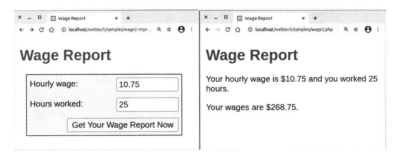

Figure 1-1: A simple client/server interaction

Object-Oriented Programming (OOP) provides another important modular design approach. OOP allows programmers to share and reuse code very effectively and to design applications in a very structured and logical fashion, reducing costs and simplifying long term maintenance. Chapter 15 provides an introduction to OOP.

Whether your programs are simple or complex, it helps greatly to stay away from a computer in the early phases of application design! Explore your design ideas using a pen and paper, sticky notes, a white board, even the backs of napkins! If you go to work as a programmer, you will find that this is how software design teams usually work. The reason is simple: using disposable materials prevents you from becoming too invested in any particular approach too quickly and encourages brainstorming and creativity. You will find that sketching out ideas on paper before you start coding will help you think things through and save you time in the long run. Once you have a clear idea of what to do you will be ready to develop your algorithms and application structure.

Important skills for software designers are creative thinking, organization, familiarity with data structures, a background in object-oriented programming, writing documentation, and experience with client-server programming and interface design.

3. Algorithm Development

Once you have a general design for your application, it is time to develop **algorithms** for each code module that the application will need. An algorithm is simply a set of clearly written, unambiguous instructions that have been developed to perform a task of any kind. Algorithms are a critical component of software design, often written in **pseudocode**, a mix of English and programming language syntax that programmers can easily understand. You will learn to develop algorithms using pseudocode in Chapter 3. The actual work of coding an application is ideally a fairly straightforward process of converting a carefully developed algorithm into a specific programming language.

The skills required for these activities include careful attention to detail, logical thinking, documentation (writing), and general programming experience.

4. Application Coding

This is the activity that is usually associated with programming! The algorithm for each program module is coded into a programming language. Each module is then carefully tested before the modules are assembled to produce the complete application. The most important skill required for coding is knowledge of the appropriate programming language, but programmers are expected to have the experience to develop code efficiently, test thoroughly, find and fix errors (debugging) and document the code so that other programmers can refer to the documentation as needed.

It should be noted that application "coding" may also include media production, graphic and interface design, database development, and incorporation of other components. If the programmer or team is lacking any of the required skills then this work may be out-sourced.

Application coding requires proficiency with programming languages and other technical skills, and also patience, thoroughness, and careful attention to detail.

5. Application Testing

Testing is a continuous process throughout the development cycle. While the development team must always test to find and correct **coding errors** ("bugs"), it is also important to test for **usability**. A development team may produce a terrific and thoroughly tested product that nevertheless turns out to be a disaster when distributed to end users. Why? Because the users may find the interface confusing, or the features may not match their needs or expectations. Usability testing brings users into the development process. At the minimum this will consist of followup meetings with the client, to present mock-ups of the interface and features in order to obtain approval before significant application development takes place. In the case of larger applications, usability experts may observe users working with the product to expose weaknesses and deficiencies. Testing is a continuous process: even after distribution, procedures for error reporting and feedback should be available, with urgent fixes (**patches**) applied as needed, and other improvements incorporated into the next major version.

Testing takes a great deal of patience, attention to detail, and thoroughness. Usability testing requires good listening skills, careful observation, and (if you are the programmer) humility! It's very easy for any programmer to be so focused on his or her own design that the needs of the user become secondary. If you notice yourself getting impatient with a user who cannot figure out how to use your product, or who wants the software to perform differently, then it's probably time to step back, pay attention to the user's concerns, and reconsider your own design assumptions.

6. User Support, Training, Software Maintenance

So now you have a complete and well-tested application. The development process does not end there! The software must be maintained, for example: errors (bugs) will be found that must be corrected; users will suggest additions and improvements; changes to hardware and operating systems may necessitate software updates. You will also need to develop online or printed manuals and other documentation to support your users, and you may need to deliver some form of training. User support and training is a career path for those who like to use technology, provide help desk support, and present technical information to users.

Important skills include: confidence and experience to communicate with both technical and non-technical people; ability to develop and present training materials; patience and sensitivity (and sometimes a sense of humor!) when responding to user questions, complaints and concerns.

The Software Development Life Cycle

Taken together these activities constitute the software development life cycle:

- Evaluation of requirements
- Application design
- Algorithm development
- Application coding
- Application testing and usability
- User support, training, software maintenance

This is not a precise list—in reality these various stages may not be so neat and sequential, and you will see somewhat different versions of this process in every programming textbook and in every workplace. Development teams may implement these various stages differently. But no matter how these stages are defined, no part of the development cycle should be treated carelessly. As you gain experience as a programmer you will more fully appreciate the special characteristics and importance of every step. And perhaps you can already see how the field of software design and development attracts people with a range of different skills, backgrounds, interests, and aptitudes.

The Importance of Writing and Communicating

In addition to the obvious need for technical training, writing and communication skills are frequently mentioned as important skills for software designers and developers. Documentation is critical to software development and wherever your own career path takes you in the field of software design and development, you will need to be able to write carefully and communicate effectively. Clients, designers and managers must refer to well-written documents that clearly define requirements, design and code specifications. Everyone involved in the development process must listen carefully and communicate effectively with one another. Programmers must document their working code so that other programmers can easily read and modify it (often the programmer who develops a piece of code will **not** be the programmer who is asked to make changes for the next version). Programmers may be expected to give presentations to clients or to their team. The testing phase also requires extensive documentation that indicates what tests were applied, the results of these tests, and how problems were resolved. Software users will need manuals and training materials. Lastly all maintenance procedures must be documented so that a complete record is always available regarding the current state and history of the software.

Version Control Systems

Version Control Systems (VCS) offer standard and widely used tools and procedures that help software developers to design, manage, and document their work at all stages of the software development life cycle. See **Appendix G** for additional information about VCS.

What Are Programming Languages?

Earlier we explored what a computer program **is**, and what programmers **do**, but what about programming **languages**? What is a programming language and why are there so many different languages?

As we have seen, a computer program is a sequence of instructions that direct the computer's microprocessor to execute commands that are available in the microprocessor's instruction set. These **low level** commands are expressed in **machine language** and are very basic, for example to add numbers, or copy a value from one memory location to another. It would be extremely time-consuming to write instructions in the 0s and 1s of machine language, and this code would be very error-prone and difficult to debug, maintain, or modify.

Instead of using machine language directly, we develop programs using **high-level programming** languages. Examples of current high-level languages are C++, C#, Java,

PHP, Python, and Ruby. Examples of older high-level languages are C, Ada, BASIC, COBOL, Fortran, Pascal, and perl (older does not necessarily mean no longer used — many applications written in older languages are still in widespread use, and programmers are still needed to maintain and even update these programs).

A high-level programming language consists of a set of special words, symbols and operators that a programmer uses to write program instructions. These instructions are often referred to as the program's **source code** and the process of writing source code is often simply called **coding**. High-level languages are quite easy for programmers to learn, and applications written in these languages can be developed very quickly and efficiently. However the computer can only understand machine language, so once a program has been written in a high-level language, the code must then be translated into machine language instructions. There are actually two approaches to translating high-level code to machine language, either by **compiling** the code or by **interpreting** the code. The approach depends on the programming language that you are using.

Compilers and Interpreters

Some programming languages are **compiling** languages. This means that the entire source code for a program is converted (or compiled) into an executable file by special software known as a compiler. The executable file that is produced by the compiler contains the necessary machine language instructions to perform the required task. Once a program has been compiled into an executable file, the source code is no longer required to run the program. End users of the program simply receive the executable file. Of course, the programmers keep the source code in order to perform updates and produce new versions. Usually when you purchase standalone software from a store you are buying an executable program that has been compiled. Two advantages of compiled programs are:

- Compiled programs tend to run faster.
- The end user does not have access to the source code (and so cannot change the program).

Since a compiler generates an executable file containing the machine language instructions for a specific microprocessor and operating system, the source code must be compiled separately for different platforms (Windows, macOS, Linux, etc). Also, each time the source code is modified, the new version must be compiled again to produce a new executable file. The new executable file must then be distributed to the end users.

Other programming languages are **interpreted** languages. Execution of programs written in interpreted languages is dependent on a special program known as an **interpreter**. An interpreter reads through the source code, converting the instructions into machine language and executing them as it does so. Because of this, both the interpreter **and** the source code are needed **every time that the program is executed** since no executable file is created for later use. One advantage of this approach is that the same source code can be used on any computer: computers running Windows, macOS, or Linux operating systems can each use their own language interpreter to translate the source code into their own specific machine language.

A disadvantage of using an interpreter is that in most cases we do not want to deliver the actual source code to the end user of the software. But this approach works very well for network-based programs, such as Web applications, since these programs are not distributed to end users. In these cases, the source code is located on a Web server and executed each time a request is submitted by a client application, such as a Web browser. The source code can be modified quickly and easily on the Web server with no need to recompile and redistribute the software every time a change is made. **PHP** is an example of an interpreted programming language that is widely used to develop server-based Web applications.

Some languages provide both compiling **and** interpreting options, and some languages actually **combine** compiling with interpreting stages to achieve greater efficiency and platform independence. A notable example is the **Java** language. Java applications are compiled "up to a point" to produce an "almost executable" version in the form of **byte code** that incorporates many of the efficiencies of the compilation process, and then Java interpreters are provided for different platforms so that the same byte code can be distributed for execution on any machine (Windows, macOS, Linux, etc.) in order to achieve platform independence.

So Many Languages!

As computer technology evolves, new programming languages are continually developed to take advantage of the latest hardware and software design strategies. For example new languages were developed to implement the functionality of object-oriented programming, while others have been developed to facilitate client/server application development. There are literally thousands of different programming languages and often a computer programmer is expert in only a few of these. While each programming language has its own special syntax and characteristics, most languages are very similar in their overall characteristics and functionality, and use the same basic logical structures to write instructions. We will learn about these common characteristics as we work through this book. A programmer who is familiar with the general logic of programming, and who has experience coding in one or two languages can usually learn new languages quite quickly.

Standalone and Network Applications

Computer programs can be designed for use on individual machines (as standalone applications), or across networks (as network applications).

A **standalone application** is designed to provide a complete service on the local computer, usually the computer sitting on the user's desk. Standalone applications do not require any network connectivity, interacting only with the computer's operating system and other **utility software** on the local machine. If a new version of the application becomes available, or if updates are required, these must be also installed on every user's computer. Examples of standalone software are traditional word-processing and spreadsheet applications, image-processing software, some games, etc. Increasingly even applications that execute locally incorporate some level of network connectivity, if only to report bugs or obtain updates or help files.

Network applications are programs that run partly or entirely on remote computers, linked to the user across a network of some kind. The more traditional network application was simply installed on a single host computer and then accessed by many users remotely. Today most network applications are **client/server**, consisting of any number of component programs that work together across a network. Some components of a client/server application can be installed on a local computer, and perform as **client** programs. Other components of a network application are installed on network servers and perform as **server** programs. The server-based components respond to requests from client components of the application as needed. At the minimum the client component usually provides the user interface that allows the user to submit information and view the results, while the server component does most of the processing.

You are using a client/server application whenever you use your Web browser. The Web browser performs as a local client component, providing your user interface and allowing you to send requests to server programs all over the world. So you are using a client/server application whenever you use your Web browser to obtain information, shop online, or play an online game. Other common examples of client/server applications are smart phone apps, ATM's, and e-mail programs.

Markup Languages

So far we have discussed the purpose of **programming** languages. As you now know, the purpose of a programming language is to allow a programmer to write instructions that **process** data. In other words, programming languages are used to perform operations that read or modify existing data or generate new data for some purpose (for example to calculate wages, convert temperatures, or keep track of a game player's score).

Another type of language is a **markup language**. Markup languages are often used in conjunction with programming languages, but have a very distinct purpose. The purpose of a **markup language** is to provide markup instructions that simply **describe** data or indicate how data is to be **formatted** (or **rendered**). Markup languages are defined for a wide range of purposes, for example your word-processing program uses a markup language to save formatting instructions with your document as you type a report or letter. The markup language that is used to render data for display by Web browsers is Hypertext Markup Language (HTML).

Combining Markup and Programming Languages

In this course, you will learn the basics of programming by developing small, Web-based client/server applications using a programming language known as **PHP**, one of the most widely used programming languages for this type of application. Since you will use a Web browser to display your program output, you will also learn the basics of the HTML markup language to format your application input and output for display in your browser window.

Additional Learning Material

See **Appendix A** for an introduction to data representation, binary data, and file formats.

See **Appendix G** to learn more about version control systems.

Check the other appendices, and also the textbook Web site to discover other tutorials that may be useful as you work through this book and develop your skills. The Web site also provides chapter-by-chapter **Hints and Help** pages with answers to frequently asked questions from students as they work through the exercises.

Summary

A computer is a programmable machine. The computer's microprocessor includes the computer's **instruction set** which defines all of the basic commands that the computer can execute. Each command is known as an opcode, and the language to express these commands constitutes the computer's **machine language**.

A **high level programming language** consists of a set of special words, symbols, and operators that together provide a grammar that a programmer uses to write instructions. These instructions are known as **source code** and the work of programming is often referred to as **coding**.

Once a program has been coded in a high level language it must be converted into machine language in order to be executed by a computer. If the language is a compiler-based language the entire source code is converted (**compiled**) into an executable version, copies of which are then distributed for use. If the language is an **interpreted** language, the source code is executed one line at a time by a language interpreter. This means that the source code is needed every time the program is executed. This approach is effective for Web-based applications since a single copy of the code can be maintained and executed on a Web server, with no need to distribute copies to individual users. **PHP** is an example of an interpreted language that is often used to develop Web applications.

All programs combine similar components to achieve their purpose. These components might include: graphical interfaces; read/write operations; numerical operations; text-processing, communication with other programs; control of hardware.

A software designer/developer requires a range of skills that combine creative problem-solving and logical thinking. Writing and communication are important skills that are often not associated with this field.

Version control software provides a useful management tool for all stages of application development.

Software development includes a number of stages: evaluation of requirements; application design; algorithm development; application coding; application and usability testing; user support, training, software maintenance. Since development is usually a continuous refinement process these stages are not clearly defined.

Some programs are designed to function as standalone applications, which means that they are installed locally and do not need access to other networks. A copy of a standalone application is required for every user. Network applications run over networks. A single network application can be installed on one computer and accessed across a network by many users.

An increasingly important type of network application is a **client/server** application, where **client** programs on local computers send requests across a network to **server** programs running on remote computers. These requests are processed and results returned to the client. A common example is a Web-based client/server application where a user's Web browser performs as a client to request services from server applications throughout the world.

Markup languages are not the same as **programming** languages. Programming languages provide instructions to **process** data. Markup languages provide tags to **describe** or format (**render**) data. The markup language that is used to render data for Web pages is Hypertext Markup Language (HTML).

In this course you will learn to develop simple Web applications using the PHP programming language and HTML markup language.

Chapter 1 Review Questions

1. A web application is an example of:
    a. Object-Oriented Programming
    b. Client/server design
    c. A microprocessor
    d. A standalone application

2. A program that requires the source code each time that it executes is using which method to convert the source code to machine language?
    a. A compiler
    b. An interpreter

3. Which approach is better when evaluating software requirements?
    a. Determine the requirements as quickly as possible in order to move on to the design and coding phases.
    b. Take time to analyze and clarify the application requirements.

4. What is the purpose of usability testing?
    a. Ensure that there are no code errors
    b. Ensure that the application runs on Windows, macOS and Linux
    c. Ensure that the application meets the needs and expectations of users
    d. Ensure that developers have the necessary skills

5. What language is often used to write algorithms?
    a. Markup language
    b. Pseudocode
    c. High-level programming language
    d. Machine language

6. Which language does the computer actually understand when it executes instructions for a program?
    a. Markup language
    b. High-level programming language
    c. Pseudocode
    d. Machine language

7. What is the computer's instruction set?
    a. The set of all programming languages that a computer can understand
    b. The set of all software that is currently available on the computer
    c. The basic set of commands that a computer can execute
    d. The rules for using a high-level programming language

8. What is source code?
    a. Programming instructions written in a programming language
    b. Program instructions that have been compiled into machine language
    c. The code used to identify text characters from languages all over the world
    d. The code used to identify memory addresses

9. What does an executable file contain?
    a. Programming instructions written in a programming language
    b. Program instructions that have been compiled into machine language.
    c. Formatted text
    d. An audio image

10. Which term applies to an application model where one program calls another program in order to have some task performed?
    a. Client/server
    b. Standalone program
    c. Instruction set
    d. An algorithm

11. What does an interpreter do?
    a. Reads and executes source code, one line at a time
    b. Converts source code into an executable file.
    c. Sends data from one program to another
    d. Converts and displays text that has been marked up

12. What does a compiler do?
    a. Reads and executes source code, one line at a time
    b. Converts source code into an executable file
    c. Sends data from one program to another
    d. Converts and displays text that has been marked up

13. When you use your Web browser to access information you are working with
    a. A client/server application
    b. A standalone application

14. What is an algorithm?
    a. A set of instructions to meet a requirement of some kind
    b. An executable file
    c. Program instructions that have been compiled into machine language
    d. Programming instructions written in a programming language

15. Which of the following is **not** a feature of modular application design?
    a. Concurrent development of each module
    b. Reusable code
    c. Separate testing of each module
    d. Less time needed to evaluate requirements

16. What category of language is used to describe or format data?
    a. Markup language
    b. High-level programming language
    c. Pseudocode
    d. Machine language

17. What languages will you learn in this course?
    a. C++ and HTML
    b. XML and Java
    c. PHP and FORTRAN
    d. PHP and HTML

18. Which is the correct order for these stages in the software development life cycle?
    a. Application coding, application design, algorithm development
    b. Application design, algorithm development, application coding
    c. Algorithm development, application design, application coding
    d. Algorithm development, application coding, application design

19. Is a Web browser a client application or a server application?
    a. Client
    b. Server

20. What type of application runs entirely on your own computer?
    a. Client/server
    b. Networked
    c. Web-based
    d. Standalone

Chapter 2

Client/Server Applications — Getting Started

Intended Learning Outcomes

After completing this chapter, you should be able to:

- Explain how Web programs function as client/server applications.
- Identify the content of a file by referring to the file extension.
- Locate local files using your computer's file addressing scheme.
- Locate remote files using the Internet Protocol (IP) addressing scheme.
- Use the localhost domain to access a standalone Web server.
- Identify the languages we will use in this course.
- Identify the software you will need to complete the hands-on work.
- Install the required software.
- Create, save and open an HTML document that is stored on a local Web server.
- Create, save and run a PHP file that is stored on a local Web server.
- Create, save and run an interactive Web application consisting of an HTML document that includes a form, and a PHP application that processes the form.

Introduction

This chapter will prepare you for the hands-on activities that you will perform as you work through the subsequent chapters of this book. First we will review **client/server** design with a focus on Web-based applications. Next we will look at how files and folders are organized and located, using **local** addresses based on **disk drives**, and **Internet** addresses based on **domain names**. This is important since you will need to be careful to save files to the correct locations on your disk drive, and then open these files in your Web browser using the correct Internet address.

You will also install the server software that you need to work through the textbook and complete the exercises. This is a very straightforward procedure and you will be able to test that your server is running correctly by running some sample programs.

Once the server has been installed you will have the option to install a text editor, then you will be asked to type in a few small programs, save them, and run them using your Web browser. The code for these programs is provided. The idea is not to learn to develop programs (that comes later), but to simply learn the general process of using an editor to create code, saving your files to the correct location under your Web server, running the server, and then testing that your programs work correctly.

Client/Server Design in Web Applications

In a client/server design, client programs send requests to server programs to perform a task of some kind, just as you might ask someone else to do something for you. The server receives the request from the client and responds appropriately. The server program resides on a networked computer and can respond to hundreds, thousands, or millions of client requests; consider an online shopping site that receives requests from customers all over the world every minute. An important advantage of client/server design is that software updates are applied on the servers without requiring any changes on the client computers.

Client/server applications are delivered world-wide across the **Internet**, and are also used to provide services to users of private networks (known as **intranets**) within an organization or company.

A Web application is a familiar example of an Internet-based client/server design. In the case of Web applications, the client program is a Web browser. The Web browser runs on a user's personal or office computer. Each time the user enters a URL, or clicks on a link on a Web page, or clicks a Submit button after entering data into a Web form, the browser sends the user's request. The request is transmitted across the Internet to the appropriate Web server. The Web server receives and processes the request, then sends back a response for the browser to display to the user. Web servers may be located anywhere on the Internet and can accept requests from any client that has Internet access (Figure 2-1). In order to process each request, the server program may communicate with other programs or access databases or files. This is a very efficient design since it allows the user to obtain all kinds of useful services without installing special software on their local computer. Instead the user uses their Web browser to execute programs that are located on remote servers.

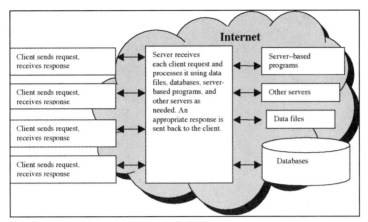

Figure 2-1: Overview of client/server design

In order to develop Web-based applications we must create files that contain the necessary instructions for our Web pages and programs, and store these files on a Web server. The server can then process the files as needed in response to requests.

In this course you will run a Web server on your **local** computer so that you can develop applications without having to connect to a server located on the Internet. In other words, your Web server will actually be located on the same computer as your Web browser, but it will behave exactly like a Web server running on the Internet. This approach allows you to keep all your work on your local computer or USB drive, and saves you the expense of setting up an account with an Internet Service Provider (ISP). Note that, if you prefer, you can also do all the work in this book using an Internet-based Web server; in that case you will need to transfer your files to and from the server in order to edit them.

Even though your Web server will run on your local computer, it will still function as though it were running on the Internet. You will need to be careful to save your files to the correct folder locations so that your Web server can find them, and you will also need to provide the correct Web addresses (URLs) for these files when you wish to view them in your Web browser. Web addresses are different from the addresses of files and folders used by your computer's operating system so let's review how files and folders are organized on disks, and then learn how files can be located using each of these addressing schemes.

Working with Files and Folders

Files are used to store data, all kinds of data. A file may contain text, images, videos, word-processing documents, programs, etc., but each file may only contain one type of data. The **file extension** usually indicates the format of the data that is stored in the file. This is very useful since the format indicates what type of program is needed to process the file. For example, a file with a **.jpg** extension contains image data stored using the **jpeg** image format, and can be opened by any image-viewing or image-processing program that can read this format. A file with an **.mp3** extension contains an MP3 audio file that can be handled by any MP3 player. A file with a **.zip** extension contains data that has been compressed using the ZIP compression scheme. To create zip files, or extract data from these files, you will need zip utility software.

Text files contain plain text (characters that can be typed on your keyboard). Text files can be viewed and edited using any text editing software. Files that contain plain text are often saved with a .txt extension. Often however, text files are given special extensions to indicate the specific purpose of the text that is stored in the file. In this course you will use a number of different extensions for your text files, as follows:

- **Plain text** files, using a **.txt** or **.dat** extension, will be used to store simple data for use by your programs. For example you might create a file named **scores.txt** that contains a list of student scores.
- **HTML** files, using an **.html** extension, will be used to store the markup instructions for Web pages. Our Web pages will include forms to allow the user to enter information that will be submitted for processing by our programs. For example you might create a text file named wages.html that contains a Web page with a form for the user to submit their hours worked and hourly wage.
- **CSS** files, using a **.css** extension, will be used to store style sheet specifications that define how our HTML code is to be rendered on the Web page.
- **PHP** files, using a **.php** extension, will be used to store the source code for PHP programs. Our PHP programs will usually receive information from the user or look up data in files in order to perform useful processing operations and generate output. For example you might create a text file named **wages.php** that contains the source code to receive wage information from a Web page, then calculate and display the pay.

Since these are all text files we can **create** and **modify** the content using any text editor. However since these files contain text to serve different purposes, the file extension indicates what software is required to **process** the content of each file. A file with an **.html** extension is usually opened by a **Web browser**, since Web browsers are designed to interpret .html files and display the contents as Web pages. A file with a **.php** extension can only be executed as a set of PHP instructions if it is opened by a **PHP code processor**. A PHP code processor is included with the Web server that you will install as you work through this chapter.

Files are usually organized into **folders** for ease of management, and files and folders are stored on **portable** or **fixed** disks that are accessed through **disk drives** connected to computers. You can access files on disks located in **local** drives that are attached to your personal computer. You can also access files on disks in **remote** disk drives, attached to computers that are connected to your computer through a network such as the Internet. No matter where the drive is located, in order to locate a specific file on a disk, you need to be able to refer to it using some kind of **file addressing scheme**.

File and Folder Addresses

Your computer's File Manager software allows you to point and click your way through your files and folders to find or open any file that you might wish to work with. Every file and folder on your computer has a unique address that is based on its name and its location in the overall folder structure, and as a programmer, it is important to be able to reference a file's location by providing its unique **file path** or **file address**. These locations and the method of addressing them will vary depending on which operating system you are using. Are you running a version of Windows? Do you have a Mac running a version of OS X. Or are you running a flavor of Linux? Let's consider all three.

File and Folder Addresses under Windows

If you are a Windows user then you probably know that your file system is separated into different disk drives, with each drive identified by a letter. For example your root hard drive (or perhaps the root partition on your hard drive), is usually identified by the letter **C:** while other drives such as a second hard drive, or portable drives, such as USB drives, are identified by other letters such as **D:** or **E:** or **F:** and so on. (In case you're wondering, the letters **A:** and **B:** are not used since they were originally associated with floppy disk drives, which are now obsolete.) Windows provides a tree structure for folders, with some folders located at the root of the drive, and others located inside those folders and so on. Your Windows C: drive will usually be the drive that contains standard Windows folders such as **System**, and **Program Files**, and **Users**, so we can easily determine the address of each folder. For example C:\Users is the address of a folder named **Users** that is located at the root of the C: drive, while C:\Users\sarah\ **Documents** is the address of a folder named **Documents** that is located inside a folder named **sarah**, that is located inside the **Users** folder, which is at the root of the C: drive. We can also determine the unique address of files that are located inside these folders, for example, if a file named **my-story.txt** is stored inside the **Documents** folder, its address will be **C:\Users\sarah\Documents\my-story.txt**. Note that Windows uses the back slash \ as a separator to separate each folder in the file system address.

The **Users** folder will contain folders for each user account on your computer. Your own account folder contains the folders that are available for your personal use, such as **Desktop**, **Documents**, **Downloads**, and **Pictures**, and every other user on your computer has their own version of these folders. You can add, delete, rename, copy, or move folders to suit your own purposes.

You usually work with the file system using a File Manager called **File Explorer** (it used to be called Windows Explorer). File Explorer provides a graphical interface that makes it easy to view, navigate and manage the files and folders on your computer. Use **File Explorer** now to explore your file system, in particular look at the files and folders inside your own account folder under the **Users** folder just to get a feel for how the system works and where files are located. Can you determine the address of a particular file by referring to the file name and folder structure?

File and Folder Addresses under macOS

If you are a macOS user (whichever version of OSX you are using) then your root hard drive is usually identified by the name **Macintosh HD** while other drives such as a second hard drive, or portable drives, such as USB drives, will have other names. macOS provides a tree structure of folders, with some folders located at the root of the drive, and others located inside those those folders and so on. Your **Macintosh HD** drive will usually be the drive that contains standard macOS folders such as **Applications** and **System** and **Users**, so we can easily determine the address of each folder. For example **/Users** is the address of a folder named **Users** that is located at the root of the drive, while **/Users/sarah/Documents** is the address of a folder named **Documents** that is located inside a folder named **sarah**, that is located inside the **Users** folder, which is at the root of the drive. We can also determine the unique address of files that are located inside these folders, for example, if a file named **my-story.txt** is stored inside the **Documents** folder, its address will be **/Users/sarah/Documents/my-story.txt**. Note that macOS uses the forward slash / as a separator to separate each folder in a file system address, and the first / indicates the root of the drive.

The **Users** folder will contain folders for each user account on your computer. Your own account folder contains the personal folders that are available for your own use, such as **Desktop**, **Documents**, **Downloads**, and **Pictures**, and every other user on your computer has their own version of these folders. You can add, delete, rename, copy, or move folders to suit your own purposes.

You usually work with the file system using a File Manager called **Finder**. Finder provides a graphical interface that makes it easy to view, navigate and manage the files and folders on your computer. Use Finder now to explore your file system, in particular look at the files and folders inside the **Applications** folder, and also explore your own account folder under the **Users** folder just to get a feel for how the system works and where files are located. Can you determine the address of a particular file by referring to the file name and folder structure?

File and Folder Addresses under Linux

If you are a Linux user you can visualize the entire file system as a tree structure with a single root, represented by the forward slash /. Linux provides a standard set of folders at the root level, and each folder is designed for a specific purpose. For example **/home** is the address of the folder that contains the accounts of different users, and **/home/sarah/Documents** is the address of a folder named **Documents** that is located inside a folder named **sarah**, that is located inside the **home** folder, which is at the root of the file system. You can also determine the unique address of files that are located inside these folders, for example, if a file named **my-story.txt** is stored inside the **Documents** folder, its address will be **/home/ sarah/Documents/my-story.txt**. Note that Linux uses the forward slash / as a separator to separate each folder in a file system address, and the first / indicates the root of the file system.

The **home** folder will contain folders for each user account on your computer. Your own account folder contains the personal folders that are available for your own use, such as **Desktop, Documents, Downloads**, and **Pictures**, and every other user on your computer has their own version of these folders. You can add, rename, delete, move and copy folders to suit your own purposes.

As a Linux user you will be using one of the many available File Managers, such as **Nautilus, Konqueror, Krusader**, or **Midnight Manager**. Each provides a graphical interface that makes it easy to view, navigate, and manage the files and folders on your computer. Use your File Manager now to explore your file system, in particular look at the files and folders inside the your own account folder under the **home** folder just to get a feel for how the system works and where files are located. Can you determine the address of a particular file by referring to the file name and folder structure?

More About Managing Files and Folders

This is just a very brief introduction to file systems but you should now be able to (a) locate a file or folder on your computer just by knowing its address, and (b) identify the address of a file or folder if you know its location on a drive. For more on files and folders, Appendix B explains more about file management and file addresses, and Appendix F introduces the File Transfer Protocol (FTP) which is used to transfer files between computers connected to the Internet.

Files and Folders on the Internet

You have just reviewed the addressing scheme used by your local operating system. You also need to have some understanding of the addressing scheme that is used for files and folders that are located on the Internet, in the "cloud".

All Internet addresses are formed using the IP (Internet Protocol) addressing scheme. An IP address provides information about a networked device. We use IP addresses to connect to services provided by Web servers throughout the world, but fortunately most of us never have work directly with IP addresses since they consist of numerical sequences. Instead we use **domain names**, for example **www.irs.gov**, **www.w3schools.com**, or **www.youtube.com**. Each domain name is associated with a specific IP address. Apart from ease of use, domain names also make it easy to relocate a Web site to a different Web server: we just point the domain name to the new IP address.

Just as a root folder on our local computer serves as the root of a system of files and folders, so a domain name serves as the root folder of a system of files and folders on a Web server. The address of a specific file on a Web server is known as a **URL** (Uniform Resource Locator). The URL consists of the Web server's domain name followed by the path from the root folder to the file. So for example the URL **https://www.w3schools.com/html/html_intro.asp** specifies a file named **html_intro.asp** that is located in a folder named **html**, that is located in the root folder of the Web server that is identified with the domain name **www.w3schools**. Note that URL addresses use the forward slash to identify folder names, similar to macOS and Linux.

Often we write URLs without specifying a file name at the end. For example, if we were to type **https://www.php.net/license/** into our Web browser's address box, we would actually receive a file even though we did not include a file name. That's because Web servers are configured to add default file names to URLs if none is provided. For example if a Web server is configured to open a file named index.php by default, then the URL **https://www.php.net/license/** would actually access a file in the **license** folder named **index.php** using the address **https://www.php.net/license/index.php**.

Naming Conventions for
Files and Folders

As a Web applications developer you will create files and folders that will be referenced in URLs. Here are four widely accepted conventions for naming your files and folders for Web applications. These are followed by most Web programmers, and actually they work well as naming conventions for ALL your files and folders.

Use descriptive names that describe the content of a file or folder: For example, let's say you have a page that displays a tax report for the tax year 2016. In that case **tr16.html** is not a meaningful file name, but **tax-report-2016.html** is very descriptive. At the same time be careful not to use **too** simple a name such as just **tax-report.html**; that name may look good right now, but then what will you call the file for next year's tax report? Best to come up with a consistent approach to your file names that will work over time; remember that once your files are online it's not easy to change their names because other Web sites may have already linked to them using the existing file name. We've all followed links on a Web page only to discover the file no longer exists, which often indicates that the name has been changed.

Avoid very long file names: this may seem to contradict the first rule, but avoid making your file and folder names unnecessarily long. In other words, choose a name like **tax-report-2016.html** rather than **final-version-of-tax-report-for-year-2016.html**. Apart from less typing, this also reduces the risk that your URL might be shortened if it is referenced from another site such as a blog. A blog might automatically reduce the address to something like **http://mywebsite/tax-reports/final-ver...html** where the file name has been shortened. Although the link itself will still work fine, if someone wants to copy the URL and paste it, they won't get the entire URL. Shorter names avoid this problem. So it's a compromise: make your file names descriptive but still keep them as short as possible. Avoid unnecessary words and also avoid connecting words like "the" and "of" in your names.

Use hyphens and never spaces in your file and folder names: We've become used to using spaces in our file and folder names because Windows, macOS, and even Linux allow spaces. Even so, spaces are not a good idea for files that will be used on the Web. Web browsers can have trouble with spaces and so can search engines. For this reason, use **hyphens** to separate words in your file and folder names instead of spaces. That's why our tax example uses **tax-report-2016.html** and not **tax report 2016.html**. Similarly use hyphens instead of underscores. For example avoid **tax_report_2016.html**. That's because the underscore is harder to read especially in a link that is already entirely underlined.

Use lower-case and not upper-case letters: Some Web programmers use a mix of upper- and lower-case letters. It's a bad idea because file names are case sensitive on many systems, such as Linux, so **tax-report-2016.html** will be treated as a different file than **Tax-Report-2016.html**. If you and your users know that all files are lower-case only, it greatly reduces the risk of broken links or mis-typed URLs.

Working with a Local Web Server

You are going to learn the fundamentals of program logic and design by developing Web applications using a Web server installed and running on your local computer. This means you won't need an account on a "live" Web server provided by a Web hosting service. It also means that the application that you develop won't be publicly visible on the Web. Working locally is actually quite a standard practice for professional Web development since it allows a programmer to develop and test a application privately before moving it to a public Web site. As a student it also provides additional benefits: you don't need to pay for a service provider and you can even do your work without an Internet connection. Although the Web server will be installed locally, in all other respects it will perform exactly as an Internet-based server. The Web server will receive requests from your Web browser, process these requests and respond appropriately. Your programs and files will be stored and accessed locally, however, if you were to copy these to a Web server located on the Internet, your applications would perform in exactly the same way across the Web. The required software is easily installed and easy to use.

The IP address of your standalone Web server will be **127.0.0.1** and the domain name will be **localhost**. This is a special non-unique IP address and domain name that allows you to reference your own computer instead of connecting to the **Internet**. So for example, in order to run a program named **my-web1.php** which is in a folder named **samples**, in a folder named **webtech** on your local Web server, you would type the URL:

>   **http://localhost/webtech/samples/my-web1.php**

Actually, if you type that URL into your Web browser's address box right now you will get a message that the page cannot be displayed! That's because you are trying to connect to a Web server that is not actually running, which means that the localhost domain is not available. Once you install and run the Web server (later in this chapter) this URL will work.

(NOTE: While this section explains how you can do all your work using a local server on your own computer, you are of course free to use a Web hosting service to run your programs on a "live" online Web site if you prefer to do that. In that case you will need to use **FTP** (File Transfer Protocol) software to transfer files between your own computer and a remote Web server. **Appendix F** provides a short hands-on introduction to FTP.) You will also need to make your applications thoroughly **secure: Appendix E** is a must-read to learn some basic security steps to follow when developing applications online.

What Languages Will I Use?

You will develop your Web programs using the following languages:

HTML (Hypertext Markup Language) provides the **markup instructions** that you will use to create and format the Web pages that display the user interface for your Web applications. You will use HTML to display headings, paragraphs, forms, tables, buttons, and images. Since this is a course in logic and design you will not learn everything there is to know about the HTML language. Nevertheless you will learn sufficient HTML to asily extend your skills in subsequent courses or personal research. Everything you learn will be based on current HTML standards.

CSS (Cascading Style Sheets) allows you to assign specific formatting to your HTML markup that will control the way this code will display in your Web browser. This book will teach you just enough CSS to understand the basic concept of a style sheet and apply some minimal formatting to your HTML pages.

PHP (PHP Hypertext Preprocessor) is a **programming language** that you will use to write server-based programs that process user requests by performing calculations, validating input, making decisions, reading data from files or databases, writing output to files or databases, returning results to the user, etc. This course covers sufficient PHP to teach basic programming logic and design as well as many important aspects of software development. This will prepare you for subsequent programming courses in PHP or other current programming languages.

SQL is a database query language that will be introduced later in the book. SQL allows you to work with database management systems, an important data source for many online applications. **MariaDB** is a recent community-developed branch of the **MySQL** database management system; MariaDB is included with your Web server. **HTML, CSS, PHP, SQL, and MariaDB** are all free technologies.

Let's look at an example to demonstrate how you will use these languages together to create a simple Web application. Figure 2-2 shows the same example of a simple client/server application that you reviewed in Chapter 1.

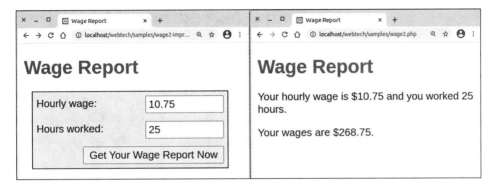

Figure 2-2: Client/Server Example using HTML, PHP, and CSS

Let's examine this application more carefully. These are two Web pages. The first Web page is generated from HTML code located in an **.html** file on a Web server. If you request this file (for example by typing the URL in your Web browser's address box), the Web server will send this code to your browser to be displayed. The HTML code in this file has been designed to display a Web page that contains a heading, a form with two prompts, two input boxes, and a Submit button.

When the user enters the requested input and presses the "Get Your Wage Report Now" button, the browser sends your input (10.75 and 25 in this case) back to the server with a request to process a second file that contains PHP code. The code in the PHP file provides instructions to: (1) receive the data submitted from the first Web page; (2) calculate a wage based on this input; (3) generate a new HTML page to display the results. The second Web page is created by this PHP code and the server returns this to the Web browser for display to the user.

The appearance of the text in both pages is defined by the instructions provided by a CSS stylesheet. We will explore this example in much more detail in the chapters that follow.

What Software Will I Need?

To complete your hands-on activities, you will need the following software:

- A **text editor** to create HTML, CSS, and PHP files.
- A **Web browser** to submit requests to the Web server and display the Web pages that are returned for display.
- A **Web server** that can process requests sent to the **localhost** domain.

Read the following sections carefully and follow the instructions to install the necessary software for your computer. Once you have the software installed you will be ready to create and test some sample applications.

Installing a Text Editor

You will need to install a text editor to create and modify your HTML and PHP code. You can use any text editor and there are many free editors available for Windows, Macintosh, and Linux. Some text editors contain special features that you will find useful as a programmer, for example code indentation, line numbering, and search and replace functions. Additionally a text editor that recognizes HTML and PHP will automatically apply different colors to special words, tags, and other syntactical elements of your code, which makes it easier to identify typing errors.

If you are using Windows, consider **Notepad++** (**https://notepad-plus-plus.org/**) which is designed for programmers and provides lots of useful features. Note: do not confuse **Notepad++** with **Notepad,** a very simple and not very useful editor that comes with the Windows operating system.

Macintosh users might consider **BBEdit**, a highly regarded text editor that can be found at: **https://www.barebones.com/products/bbedit/.**

Linux users might like **Kate, which provides a wide range of plugins and supports multiple programming languages. Kate is also available for Windows and macOS (https://kate-editor.org/en-gb/).**

The editors mentioned above are all easy to install and use. If you are willing to take more time to learn them, a number of more sophisticated editors that are especially designed for programming have versions for Windows, macOS or Linux, for example **Atom**, **Visual Studio Code**, and **Brackets**. It's probably better to consider using one of these once you have some experience.

For most users the default settings for your text editor installation will be fine. Take some time to get used to the basic operations to use your editor – you will have a chance to do this later in the chapter when you create some simple applications. Don't try and learn everything—you can explore the full functionality of your editor as you gain experience.

IMPORTANT NOTE: do not use a word-processor (such as MS Word) to create and edit your code. You need to save your code as plain text files.

Installing One or More Web Browsers

You need a Web browser to view the examples and your own programs. Any major browser should be fine and you will already have at least one browser already installed on your computer. Professional developers like to use two or three browsers so that they can test their Web sites more thoroughly. You are encouraged to work with multiple browsers for this reason but this is **not** required for the material in this textbook.

If you want to install additional browsers, **Mozilla Firefox** is an excellent and freely available browser that is available for Windows, macOS or Linux. **Apple Safari** is another great browser available for macOS and Windows. And you might also consider

Google Chrome for Windows, macOS or Linux. In all cases, installation is simple and for most users the default installation settings will be fine.

Installing Your Web Server

You must also install a Web server that will process your PHP code and deliver Web pages to your browser. We will use a free standalone distribution of open source software that includes the Apache Web server. This distribution, named **xampp**, has been been compiled by the Apache Friends project. Versions of xampp are available for Windows, macOS, and Linux. The textbook Web site contains complete instructions to download and install this software, along with a custom **webtech** folder that contains the sample and coursework files you will use with this textbook. Instructions and download files can be found at:

   https://www.mikeokane.com/textbooks/wbip/support.php

The installation documents also explain how to **run** and **stop** your Web server, how to test your Web server to be sure that it is working correctly, and how to resolve any installation problems. The material that follows assumes that you have successfully installed and tested your Web server, that you have at least one Web browser, and that you have a text editor to create and edit your program code.

Follow the instructions on the textbook Web site to install your Web server now. You will need to have the server installed, tested and running in order to complete this chapter. The instructions on the Web site will also help you to test your Web server and troubleshoot any problems.

Using Your Web Server

Now that you have installed and tested your Web server, let's learn how to use the server to run and test some Web applications! First start the Web server if you have not already done so. Now open any Web browser and type the following URL in the address window:

   http://localhost/webtech

Your installation is configured so that this URL will open a Web page (see Figure 2-3) that will help you to use this textbook. If this page displays then your Web server is running successfully. As you will see, the page provides links that make it easy for you to view and work with the samples and coursework files that are discussed in each chapter. Note that your Web server must be running in order for you to view this page (or to view any page with a URL that begins **http://localhost**). If you were to stop your Web server, this URL would no longer work and your browser would report a connection error.

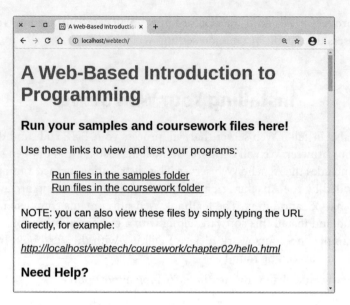

Figure 2-3: http://localhost/webtech

Let's run a simple program from the samples folder. Click the "Run files in the samples folder" link, and then click welcome.html from the list of files that appear. This should bring up a welcome page with an interactive form for you to complete (see Figure 2-4).

Figure 2-4: http://localhost/webtech/samples/welcome.html

Try completing the form and the press the "Submit the Form" button. If a second welcome screen appears with a response to your submission, then everything is installed correctly and working fine.

Using URLs with Your Web Server

Every file on the Web has a unique URL, or Web address. The **URL** consists of a domain name, followed by the folders and a file name that indicate the location of the particular file on the server. Our local Web server has the domain name **localhost** and this domain name points to the **htdocs** folder (which is in the folder that contains your installation).

Earlier you opened the file **welcome.html** from your **samples** folder. Open the file again and this time notice the URL in your browser's address window:

http://localhost/webtech/samples/welcome.html

All of the URLs of files located on your Web server will begin **http://localhost** because **localhost** is the domain name of your local server. But how does the Web server know where to find the **welcome.html** file in order to send the contents of the file to your Web browser?

The answer is that, by default, the Web server looks in the **htdocs** folder of your Web server installation in response to any URL that begins **http://localhost**. In other words the URL **http://localhost** is associated with the **htdocs** file folder on your drive, and in case you're wondering, the name **htdocs** is a shortened version of "hypertext documents". Use your File Manager to locate the **htdocs** folder in your Web server installation.

So if the URL is **http://localhost/webtech/samples/welcome.html** then the Web server will process the file named welcome.html that is located in the folder **htdocs/webtech/samples**. Use your File Manager to find this file on your disk—can you find it?

Be sure that you understand this. Each URL that begins **http://localhost/webtech** refers to a file on your Web server that is located under the **htdocs/webtech** folder and if you were to change the contents of any file inside this folder and then save your changes, the new version of the file would be displayed if you were to type the URL of the file in your Web browser.

As another example let's look at a file in your **coursework** folder. Type the URL **http://localhost/webtech** and choose the **coursework** folder. Now click **chapter02** and choose **hello.html**. This page displays a short introductory message about the kind of work you will do for each chapter (see Figure 2-5.).

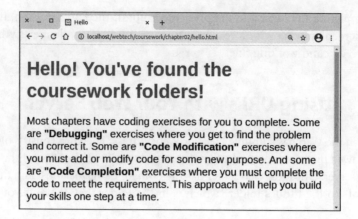

Figure 2-5: http://localhost/webtech/coursework/chapter02/hello.html

Note that the URL for this file is:

http://localhost/webtech/coursework/chapter02/hello.html

Can you use your File Manager to locate this file on your disk?

We will keep all our work files in **two** folders under the **htdocs\webtech** folder. The **samples** folder will contain all of the sample files referenced in the textbook. Try opening some of these programs in your browser now. You will notice that many files are listed in pairs with the same name but two different extensions (**.html** and **.php**). In these cases, click the **.html** files rather than the **.php** files to see what they do (the **.html** files display Web pages with forms that are used to "drive" the PHP programs). The **coursework** folder contains sub-folders for each chapter, and each chapter folder contains the files for your code exercises. If you were to try opening these files you will find that many of them do not work correctly or generate errors—that's because they contain code that you will complete yourself as you work through the chapters.

To summarize, always remember to first **start** your Web server **before** you attempt to run your programs, and always **stop** the Web server and then **exit the Control Panel** once you have completed your work. The URL to your programs will always begin with **http://localhost/** and this should be followed by the names of any subfolders, followed by the name of the file that you wish to open. To avoid typing the complete URLs, you can just type **http://localhost/webtech** (see Figure 2-3) and then click through the links to open the file you want to view.

Always Use URLs to Run Your Web Applications!

As you probably know you can use your File Manager to find a file on your computer and then open it just by clicking on the file name. That's because your operating system associates the file **extension** of a file with a default application that can handle that file type. For example, files with **.doc** and **.docx** extensions are usually associated with the **MS Word** application, which is why MS Word runs and opens the file when you click a file with one of these extensions. Your computer usually associates **.htm** and **.html** extensions with your Web browser, so if you click a file with one of these extensions the file will be displayed by your Web browser. **The page will display whether or not your Web server is running because you have opened it directly from your file system.**

This is a problem because if you don't use your Web server to open your Web applications, they will not be processed by the Web server. Your **.html** pages will still display correctly because your Web browser knows how to display HTML files. But if you try to submit a form or if you click a **.php** file you will have trouble because .php files **must** be processed by the Web server before they can be displayed correctly by the browser. Since we are working with a combination of .html and .php files, whenever you want to run your applications, you **must always first** run the Web server and **then view your .html and .php files by connecting to the Web server, using** a URL that begins with the **localhost** domain.

To understand this better, let's try running a Web application without using a URL, just to see what happens.

Use your File Manager to navigate to the **samples** folder on your drive. Double-click the file named **add-two-numbers.html**. A Web browser will probably start up, open the file and display the Web page (see the first screenshot in Figure 2-6). This page looks fine, but notice the file path that is displayed in the browser's address window, which in Windows will be something like like this (on macOS and Linux it will be only slightly different):

file://C:/xampp/htdocs/webtech/samples/add-two-numbers.html

Because you used our File Manager to open the file, you will see a file path in the address window that begins **file://** rather than a URL that begins **http://localhost**. That tells you that you are not connecting to the file through your Web server, which means you cannot process the form. If you type in two numbers and click the "Tell me the Sum" button, you will see something unexpected. You may see something similar to the second screenshot in Figure 2-6, or you may see something different, perhaps an error message, or possibly a blank page. Whatever is displayed, you will not see the expected page displaying the sum of the two numbers.

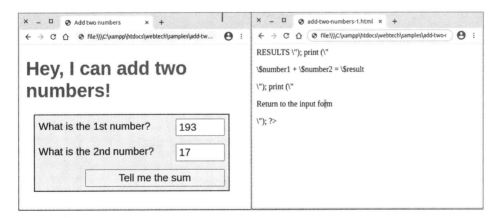

Figure 2-6: Opening a file using your File Manager instead of using a URL

This doesn't make much sense! What is happening is that when the "Tell me the Sum" button was clicked, rather than sending the request to the Web server, the Web browser simply opened a file named add-**two-numbers.php** which contains the PHP instructions to process the form. The problem is that your Web browser has no ability to execute PHP instructions; your Web **server** includes the PHP processor that is necessary to execute PHP code. The only way to access the Web server from your Web browser is to request these files using URLs that begin with the domain name **localhost.**

So the correct way to view your .html and .php files is to always, first, start the Web server if it is not already running, and then provide the URL to open the appropriate file. For example to correctly run the add-two-numbers application, use the URL:

> **http://localhost/webtech/samples/add-two-numbers.html**

Go ahead and do this to see that the application now works as expected. (see Figure 2-7).

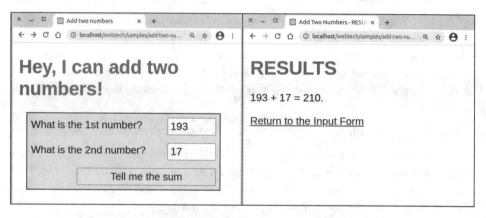

Figure 2-7: Opening a file using a URL beginning with http:/localhost

Where to Save Your Work Files

You will create and edit your HTML and PHP work files in the chapter folders under the **htdocs\webtech\coursework** folder of your xampp installation. These files will produce small Web applications. You will use a text editor to develop the code for these files and then save them. It is important that you save these files in the correct location so that the Web server can find them when you type in the URL. Once you are ready to test your applications, be sure that the Web server is running and then use your Web browser to run your programs. The URL for your files will be:

> **http://localhost/webtech/coursework/chapterXX/yyy**

where chapterXX is a chapter number (for example **chapter02**) and yyy is the name of a specific file, for example **my-first.html**. To avoid typing the entire URL, you can just type **http://localhost/webtech** and then click the links on that page to obtain the appropriate folder and file.

The Importance of Frequent Backups

Always keep a recent backup of your **webtech** folder on a separate disk or in cloud storage or even zipped in an email folder. It is also good practice to back up your work files every time you make major changes. If your drive crashes, you can reinstall the Web server on a new drive and then copy the backup of your **webtech** folder into the **htdocs** folder of your new installation. Take your backups seriously — there is nothing worse than losing hours, days, or weeks of hard work.

Creating an HTML Document

In order to get started, you will first create a simple HTML document, store it on your server and then send a request to open the document from your client Web browser. Don't be concerned about understanding this document right now — you will learn about HTML in Chapter 4.

Open your text editor. Type in the text for **my-first.html**, but write your name instead of "YOUR NAME", write today's date instead of "TODAY'S DATE", and write something about yourself to replace the words "WRITE ABOUT YOURSELF HERE":

```
<!-- Author: YOUR NAME
   Date:     TODAY'S DATE
   File:     my-first.html
   Purpose:  HTML Practice
-->
<html>
<head>
  <title>HTML Example</title>
</head>
<body>

  <h1>My Web Page</h1>

  <p>Hi! My name is <strong>YOUR NAME</strong>. Let me tell you a
  little bit about myself ... </p>

  <p>WRITE ABOUT YOURSELF HERE</p>

</body>
</html>
```

Code Example: my-first.html

(Figure 2-8) shows how your text might look using the Kate text editor on Linux.

Figure 2-8: Using a text editor to create my-first.html

When you are finished save the file with the name **my-first.html** in your **htdocs\webtech\coursework\chapter02 folder.** Be sure to save the file in the correct folder location with an .html extension.

The file has now been stored on the Web server. You can now submit a request to view this file from your Web browser. Start your server if it is not already running. Now type the following URL in your browser's address box:

http://localhost/webtech/coursework/chapter02/my-first.html

When the browser submits this request, the Web server receives the URL and locates the file (my-first.html). Since the file has an .html extension, the server simply sends the file contents back to the Web browser for display. Web browsers are designed to read HTML documents and treat any HTML tags as formatting instructions. You will learn more about this in the next chapter. Your HTML page should look similar to the screenshot in (Figure 2-9).

Figure 2-9: my-first.html screenshot

If the link to **my-first.html** does not work either your file name is different or the file is not in the correct location, or the Web server is not running.

If you wish to make changes to your document, simply edit your code in your text editor. Be sure to save your changes before viewing the file again and be sure to **refresh** the page in your Web browser otherwise your browser may continue to display the previous version.

Congratulations! You have just created a simple Web page, stored it on your Web server, then accessed the page from a client application (your Web browser)!

Creating a PHP Program

Now let's create a simple PHP program. Don't be concerned about understanding this document right now—you will learn about PHP in Chapter 5. Type the code listing for **myFirst.php** in your preferred text editor exactly as written except type your name instead of "YOUR NAME" and today's date instead of "TODAY'S DATE". Note that you can copy and paste code from **my-first.html** to save some time:

```
<!-- Author: YOUR NAME
   Date:    TODAY'S DATE
   File:    my-first.php
   Purpose: PHP Practice
-->
<html>
<head>
   <title>First PHP Example</title>
</head>
<body>

   <h1>Circle Calculation</h1>

   <?php
     $radius = 15.75;
     $area = pi() * pow ($radius 2);
     $circumference = 2 * pi() * $radius;

     print("<p>A circle with a radius of $radius has an area of
       $area and a circumference of $circumference.</p>");

     print("<p>That's all that I have been designed to tell
       you!</p>");

   ?>
</body>
</html>
```

Code Example: my-first.php

When you are finished save the file with the name **my-first.php** in your **htdocs\ webtech\coursework\chapter02 folder**. Be sure to save the file in the correct folder location with a .php extension.

Be sure your Web server is running. Now view this in your browser by typing the following URL:

> **http://localhost/webtech/coursework/chapter02/my-first.php**

When the browser submits this request, the Web server receives the URL and locates the file (my-first.php). Since the file has a .php extension, the server runs a PHP processor to execute any PHP code in the file and assemble a new HTML document. Once the PHP has been completely processed, the newly created HTML document is sent back to the Web browser for display. Your page should look something like the screenshot in Figure 2-10. We will learn more about this process in later chapters.

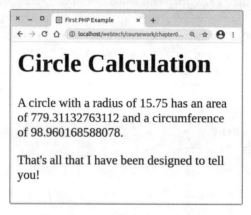

Figure 2-10: my-first.php screenshot

The text may wrap differently depending on the size of your browser window. If the link to **my-first.php** does not work as expected, you may have used the wrong file name, or saved the file in the wrong location. Or you may have forgotten to start your Web server. Or you may receive an error message, something like this:

```
Parse error: parse error, unexpected T_VARIABLE in
C:\xampp\htdocs\webtech\coursework\my-first.php on line 15
```

That means you have a syntax error in your PHP code. Programming languages such as PHP require a very precise syntax. There is a good chance that you may mistype something and this may generate an error message. Compare your code carefully with the example and see if you can find the errors. Once again remember to save your changes and remember to refresh the browser window to view your revised program.

Congratulations! You have just created a simple PHP program, stored it on your local Web server, and accessed it from a client (your Web browser)!

Creating an Interactive HTML and PHP Program

That last example displays information concerning a circle with a radius of **15.75**. We could improve the utility of this application by allowing the user to enter **any** radius. Next we will create a new version of this application that consists of two documents. The first (named **circle.html**) will be an HTML document that contains a form so that the user can submit a radius and submit this for processing. The second document (named **circle.php**) will contain a PHP program that receives the radius and calculates and displays the circumference and area of the circle. Here is the code for **circle.html** (once again don't be concerned about the details of this code right now, in this chapter you are just learning the general procedure, the code will be fully explained in the following chapters):

```
<!-- Author: YOUR NAME
  Date:     TODAY'S DATE
  File:     circle.html
  Purpose:  PHP Practice
-->
<html>
<head>
  <title>Circle Calculation</title>
</head>
<body>

  <h1>Circle Calculation</h1>

  <form action="circle.php" method="post">
    <p>What is the radius of the circle?
    <input type="text" size="20" name="radius"></p>
    <p><input type="submit" value="Tell me the area and
      circumference"></p>
  </form>
</body>
</html>
```

Code Example: circle.html

When you are finished save the file with the name **circle.html** in your **htdocs\ webtech\coursework\chapter02** folder. Be sure to save the file in the correct folder location with an .html extension.

The file has now been stored on the Web server. You can now submit a request to view this file from your Web browser. Just type the following URL in your browser's address box:

http://localhost/webtech/coursework/chapter02/circle.html

If you do this the document will display in your browser. Assuming that you typed everything correctly, you will see that it contains a Web page with a form (see the first screenshot in Figure 2-11).

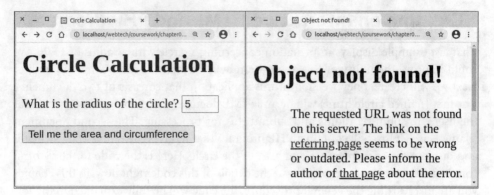

Figure 2-11: circle.html screenshot, and the result when the Submit button is clicked

If you enter a radius into the text box and click the "Tell me the area and circumference" button, you will get an error message, similar to that shown in the second screenshot in Figure 11.

That's because the form on this Web page is designed to send the radius to a program named **circle.php** in order for it to be processed. The problem is that we haven't created the **circle.php** program yet! So let's do that right now!

Here is the code for **circle.php**:

```php
<!-- Author: YOUR NAME
   Date:      TODAY'S DATE
   File:      circle.php
   Purpose: PHP Practice
-->
<html>
<head>
   <title> Circle Calculation</title>
</head>
<body>

   <h1>Circle Calculation</h1>

   <?php
      $radius = $_POST['radius'];
      $area = pi() * pow ($radius, 2);
      $circumference = 2 * pi() * $radius;

      print("<p>A circle with a radius of $radius has an area of
         $area and a circumference of $circumference.</p>");
   ?>
   <p><a href="circle.html">Calculate another circle?</a></p>

</body>
</html>
```

Code Example: circle.php

When you are finished save the file with the name **circle.php** in your **htdocs\ webtech\coursework\chapter02 folder**. Be sure to save the file in the correct folder location with a .php extension.

Now you should be able to use your form correctly. Open your Web document again and type the URL to open circle.html (**not** circle.php):

> http://localhost/webtech/coursework/chapter02/circle.html

Type a radius into the text box and click the "Tell me the area and circumference" button. This time you should see a new page that displays the area and circumference of a circle with the radius that you submitted (see Figure 2-12).

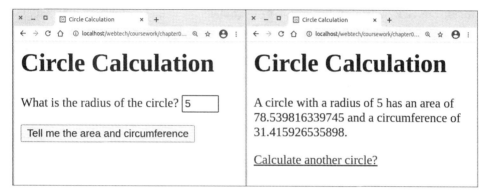

Figure 2-12: my-first.html screenshot

Note that you can click the "Calculate another circle?" link to return to the first page.

Congratulations! You have now created a simple Web application that consists of two files: the first file, circle.html, provides an input form and submit button; the second file, circle.php, contains the code to process the input from the form and display the result.

Do not be concerned about how these documents actually work at this point. The purpose of the current exercise is to give you practice using a text editor to type HTML and PHP code, saving your documents to the correct location on your disk, making corrections as needed, and viewing your applications in a Web browser using the correct URL. In the following chapters you will learn how to design and create Web applications that include HTML pages with forms and PHP programs that process these forms.

Additional Learning Material

The textbook Web site provides instructions to download and install your standalone Web server on your **Windows, macOS**, or **Linux** computer.

The **Chapter 2 Hints and Help** pages on the textbook Web provides answers to FAQs from previous students as they work through the chapter.

Appendix B provides more on the subject of files and folders, file navigation, and relative and absolute file addresses. **Appendix C** introduces you to working from the command line.

You will find it helpful to run your Web server while working through each chapter. That way you can use your Web browser to view the examples in the samples folder as you read about them, and you can also experiment with them, using your text editor to make changes. If you ever need to get back to the original version of a file in the samples folder, copies of the originals are provided in the **COPIES_OF_ORIGINAL_SAMPLES_FILES** folder, which is included in your **webtech.zip** download.

If you plan to do your work on a remote (live) Web server, you will need to be comfortable using **FTP** (File Transfer Protocol) to transfer your files. **Appendix F** provides a short tutorial, with instructions to install and use an FTP client. Check the textbook Web site for the latest version of the tutorial. You will also need to make your applications secure; read **Appendix E** to learn more about this important topic; the appendix will direct you to a tutorial on the textbook Web site that will provide you with additional guidance and useful code samples.

Version control software provides an effective and professional way to backup and manage your work. **Appendix G** introduces this topic; if you are just getting started, you will have plenty to learn right now so review this at a later stage. On the other hand, if you already have some familiarity with the material in these early chapters, consider reviewing Appendix G now to decide if you want to incorporate git and GitHub into your work process.

Summary

Client/Server applications are designed so that client-based software such as Web browsers can submit requests to server-based programs such as Web servers for processing. This makes it easy for large numbers of client programs to make use of common services. Another advantage is that new software installations and updates to existing software are performed on the server without requiring changes to the client computers. Client/server applications are used world-wide across the **Internet**, and are also used to deliver services on private **intranets**.

Web-based applications are developed by creating the required code in files and storing these on a Web server. Client applications, usually Web browsers, can submit requests to the server to process these files and return the results. When a server receives a request for an **.html** file, it simply locates and opens the file and returns the document for display by the Web browser. When a server receives a request for a **.php** file, it first processes the PHP instructions in the file and then returns the new HTML document that is generated. The Web server must be running in order for a client to submit requests.

Files usually include file extensions to indicate the data format that is stored in the file. Files can only be processed by programs designed to work with the file format. Text files can be opened by any text editing program, and sometimes contain text that requires specialized processing. In this course you will work with text files using various file extensions. Files with a **.txt** extension will be used to store data such as student scores or wage information. Files with an **.html** extension will contain HTML markup code for display in a Web browser. Files with a **.php** extension will contain PHP code that is processed by a PHP processor running on a Web server.

You can use your File Manager software to locate files and folders within the file system used by your operating system (Windows, macOS, or Linux). Every file and folder has a unique address or file path, based on a tree system, and it's important for a programmer to know how to reference a file using its unique address. Windows addresses use the back slash \ to separate folder names (for example **C:\Users\sarah\Documents\my-story.txt**), whereas macOS and Linux use the forward slash / (an example of a macOS address is **/Users/sarah/Documents/my-story.txt**, and a similar Linux address might be **/home/sarah/Documents/my-story.txt**).

Under the Internet addressing scheme, the root folder location on a Web server is referenced by a domain name, for example **w3schools.com**. The complete address to a specific file is known as a URL (Uniform Resource Locator) and consists of the domain name followed by the path from the root folder to the file, for example **https://www.w3schools.com/html/html_intro.asp**. Note that Internet addresses use the forward slash to identify folder names, similar to macOS and Linux.

In this chapter you learned how to install, start, and stop a local Web server with instructions provided on the textbook Web site. A local Web server has a special IP address (**127.0.0.1**) and the domain name is always **localhost**, which references the root folder of your Web server, usually a folder named **htdocs**. So the URL will always begin **http://localhost**, followed by the path to the specific file that you want to view. For example **http://localhost/webtech/coursework/chapter02/circle.html** refers to a file named **circle.html** which is located in the **chapter02** folder in the **coursework** folder in the **webtech** folder which is in the **htdocs** folder under your Web server installation.

You also learned how to create and modify HTML and PHP code using a text editor; how to save these files to your Web server; and how to view the results in a Web browser. Always be sure your Web server is running before trying to view your files in your Web browser, and always use the correct URL beginning with **http://localhost** to view the files. If you just click a file listed in your File Manager you will not get the expected result; you must connect to the Web server to process the files correctly and the way to do this is to use your Web browser and provide the correct URL. Also remember to re-save your file after you make any changes, and refresh your browser window if these changes don't appear when you try to view the file again.

Chapter 2 Review Questions

1. Consider the following Windows address: **D:\CourseMaterial\Coursework\wage1.html** Which statement is true?
   a. The file is stored in a folder named wage1.html
   b. The file is stored in a folder named Coursework
   c. The file is stored in a folder named CourseMaterial
   d. The file is stored in a folder named D:
   e. This address does not specify a file

2. Consider the following Windows address: **D:\CourseMaterial\Coursework\wage1.html**
   What is the name of the file?
   a. wage1.html
   b. Coursework
   c. CourseMaterial
   d. D:
   e. This address does not specify a file

3. Consider the following Windows address: **D:\CourseMaterial\Coursework\wage1.html**
   Where is the CourseMaterial folder located?
   a. Inside wage1.html
   b. Inside the Coursework folder
   c. On the D: drive
   d. It is not possible to tell from this address
   e. The address is incorrect

4. What type of address is this? D:\CourseMaterial\Coursework\wage1.html
   a. Internet address
   b. Local file system address

5. What is wrong with the following URL?
   http:\\www.w3.org\markup\guide\style.html
   a. Internet addresses must use the forward slash / as a separator
   b. The file name is in the wrong location
   c. The domain name is the wrong location
   d. The file name is missing
   e. The drive letter is missing

6. What is wrong with the following URL?
   http://www.w3.org/style.html/markup/guide/
   a. Internet addresses must use the back slash \ as a separator
   b. The file name is in the wrong location
   c. The domain name is the wrong location
   d. The file name is missing
   e. The drive letter is missing

7. Which component of a client/server application processes a PHP file?
    a. Client
    b. Server

8. What does HTML stand for?
    a. Highly Technical Markup Language
    b. Host Translated Markup Language
    c. Hypertext Markup Language
    d. Hands-on Technical Markup Language
    e. Hyper Transitional Markup Language

9. What is HTML?
    a. A markup language used to provide formatting instructions for text
    b. A programming language used to process input, perform calculations and other operations, and generate output
    c. An addressing scheme for URLs
    d. A name for a button on a user interface
    e. A form used to validate user input

10. What is PHP?
    a. A markup language used to provide formatting instructions for text
    b. A programming language used to process input, perform calculations and other operations, and generate output
    c. An addressing scheme for URLs
    d. A name for a button on a user interface
    e. A form used to validate user input

11. What is the domain name of the Internet address that you will use to access Web pages delivered by your standalone server?
    a. localhost
    b. www.w3.org
    c. webtech
    d. samples
    e. welcome.html

12. Where should you save the html and php files that you create for this course?
    a. Anywhere on your disk is fine
    b. In the correct chapter folder under xampp\htdocs\webtech\coursework\
    c. In the correct chapter folder under xampp\webtech\htdocs\coursework\
    d. In the correct chapter folder under xampp\webtech\coursework\
    e. In the correct chapter folder under xampp\coursework\

13. Which folder is divided into chapters?
     a. samples folder
     b. coursework folder

14. Which one of the following files can be found in your samples folder?
     a. getting-started.html
     b. getting-started.php
     c. course-web-site.html
     d. quote-generator.html
     e. quote-generator.php

15. In your samples folder there is a file named temp-converter1.php. What should you
     do to run this program and find out what it does?
     a. Open the file using your File Manager
     b. Run your local Web server and then type the url
        http://localhost/webtech/samples/temp-converter1.php
        in your browser window.
     c. Run your local Web server and type **http://localhost/webtech** in your
        browser window, then click on **samples** and then click on
        temp-converter1.php.
     d. Either of the last two procedures will work but not the first one

16. In your samples folder, what happens if you run quote-generator.php in your
     browser window?
     a. The browser displays the same quote every time you run it.
     b. The browser displays a different quote each time you run it.
     c. The browser displays a different presidential quote each time you run it.
     d. The browser asks you to input a quote.

17. Which of the following file types does NOT appear in the samples folder?
     a. .bmp
     b. .html
     c. .jpg
     d. .php
     e. .txt

18. What is the correct URL for your my-first.php document?
     a. http://localhost/webtech/coursework/chapter02/my-first.php
     b. http://webtech/coursework/chapter02/my-first.php
     c. http://localhost/coursework/chapter02/my-first.php
     d. http://webtech/chapter02/my-first.php
     e. http://localhost/my-first.php

19. In the samples folder, if you open welcome.html and submit the information but leave the first name and last name boxes blank, what does the resulting Web page display (among other things)?
    a. ERROR—INPUT IS MISSING!
    b. ERROR—YOU MUST ENTER YOUR FIRST NAME AND LAST NAME!
    c. Welcome!
    d. Welcome Whoever You Are!
    e. Welcome! You must enter your first name and last name!

20. In the samples folder, what is the difference between wage1.html and wage2.html?
    a. wage1.html allows you to input your hours worked and hourly wage but wage2.html does not
    b. wage2.html allows you to input your hours worked and hourly wage but wage1.html does not
    c. wage1.html allows you to input your name but wage2.html does not wage2.html allows you to input your name but wage1.html does not
    d. There is no difference between wage1.html and wage2.html

Chapter 2 Code Exercises

The exercises for this chapter are simply intended to ensure that (a) you have your software installed and working correctly, and (b) you are comfortable with the process of creating, editing and running your Web applications. Note that the Students page on the textbook Web site includes **Hints and Help** pages for the exercises in this and every chapter; these pages provide answers to students' most commonly asked questions. Refer to these first if you are not sure about the requirements of an exercise. or if you get stuck.

1. First be sure that you have installed your Web server. Now start your server. If you have any problems when you do this, first review the steps to install and run your Web server before you assume there is a problem with your installation. Refer to the **Installation Problems** guide on the textbook Web site at:

    https://www.mikeokane.com/textbooks/wbip/support.php

2. With your Web server started, open a Web browser and type the URL:

    http://localhost/webtech/samples/art-gallery.html

    You should see a Web page that displays a "Welcome to the Art Gallery" heading and allows you to choose an artist from a drop down list. If you do not see this and receive an error message instead, first be sure that you typed the URL correctly. If you still receive an error, then (a) your webtech folder was not included in your installation (use your File Manager to ensure that this folder is located in your **htdocs** folder), or (b) your server is not running (the server may not be running if you also get an error message when you type the URL **http://localhost** in your browser address window), or (c) your server was not installed correctly (this may be the case if you received an error message when you started the server. Make a careful note of all error messages and anything else that might be useful, then refer to the **Installation Problems** guide on the textbook Web site for help.

3. Assuming that the artGallery page is displayed, select an artist and then click the "Show me an Artwork" button. An artwork should now be displayed along with some additional information. If you do not see this, check the URL in your Web browser's address window. If the URL begins with **file://** then you are not using the right URL and you are not connecting to the Web server. Go back and use the correct URL. Remember that, to connect to your Web server, your URLs must **always** begin **http://** and in this case the URL should be:

    http://localhost/webtech/samples/art-gallery.html

4. If the art-gallery application performed successfully then you are ready to work. To become familiar with the procedure that we will follow throughout this textbook, use your text editor as directed in this chapter to create **my-first.html, my-first.php, circle.html**, and **circle.php** and save these files in the **chapter02** folder of your coursework folder if you have not already done this. Test each of these by running

your Web server, opening a Web browser, and typing the appropriate URLs. You may need to fix some of your code but eventually each program should run as described in the chapter. **Do not bypass this exercise.** You need to be comfortable creating and running your applications and using your Web server in order to work through this book.

Chapter 3

Program Design —
From Requirements to Algorithms

Intended Learning Outcomes

After completing this chapter, you should be able to:

- Describe important characteristics of successful instructions.
- Identify sequence, selection and repetition structures.
- Identify key elements of a simple requirements document.
- Develop an Input, Processing, Output (IPO) chart based on a simple requirements document.
- Develop a user interface design based on a simple requirements document.
- Write instructions in the form of an algorithm using pseudocode.
- Describe the purpose of variables and assignment operations.
- Write simple arithmetic and boolean expressions.

Introduction

In chapter 2 you wrote some code in the HTML and PHP languages in order to get used to the general process of developing and running Web applications using your standalone Web server. Before beginning to learn these languages, in this chapter we will take a step back to consider the general nature of instructions, and learn how to evaluate requirements in order to design and develop a working application.

A computer program is a sequence of instructions written in a programming language to meet a set of requirements. As a programmer you must learn to write clear and accurate instructions since a computer has no way to guess your intentions or ask for clarification. The process of developing instructions for a computer application is not so different from giving instructions to people. We will therefore begin this chapter by reviewing some important characteristics of human instructions and see how these apply to software design.

We will then work through the design process required to develop some simple Web applications, including the application that was presented in Chapter 2.

As you work through this chapter you will acquire some useful tools to evaluate program requirements and learn to write instructions in the form of **pseudocode** in order to create an **algorithm**. By the end of the chapter you will be ready to learn how to convert instructions into a programming language in order to produce a working application. Take time to think about what you are learning in this chapter. You may be impatient to start coding but the ideas presented here are fundamental to the work of software design and application development.

What Are Instructions?

How many times have you been asked to provide instructions? Perhaps you have given directions, or instructed someone to use a machine, repair something, play a game, cook some food, or perform a calculation? Perhaps you have had to write down these instructions. And how many times have you tried to follow someone else's instructions, to install a printer, perform a task at work, assemble a child's toy, replace a filter, repair a faucet, use a new tool, play a game, bake a cake, learn to swim, or submit an assignment? How often have you been frustrated by instructions that are poorly worded or that miss some vital piece of information, for example when the assembly instructions for that new toy you bought for your child don't clearly explain exactly how the parts should fit together?

We all follow instructions many times every day, sometimes instructions that we learned a long time ago, sometimes instructions that are new to us. It takes skill to design and write instructions that are clear and understandable. This skill is not very well recognized or rewarded, and the instructions that we try to follow are often not as good as they might be. We pay quite a high price for this. When we use poorly written instructions we may be unable to complete a task, or we may damage something, or we may need to request clarification. The same applies to the instructions that make up a computer program. A poorly written program may generate high costs in terms of money, stress, and time.

Common Characteristics of Instructions

A computer program delivers a set of instructions to the computer to perform a task of some kind. These instructions must of course be in a form that the computer can understand, but instructions of all kinds share certain characteristics, whether intended to be performed by human beings or by a computer. For example when we are asked for directions, we are being asked to deliver a set of instructions. Look at the street map in Figure 3-1 and imagine that someone has just asked you for directions to the library from the corner of Queen Street and Martin Luther King Boulevard (in this example, Rose Avenue and Sycamore Lane are one-way streets while the other streets are two-way streets).

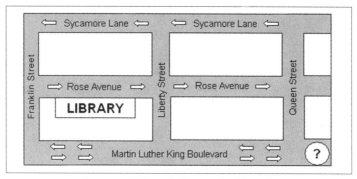

Figure 3-1: How do I get to the library?

Before you begin to design a solution for this or any problem, always take time to be sure that you completely understand the problem requirements. Exactly what is being asked? Consider this carefully and ask questions until you are sure what is needed with no assumptions on your part. For example, which library is this person looking for? We might assume the local library on Rose Avenue when he or she is completely unaware of that library and was actually asking for directions to the main city library a few miles away! Is this person walking or driving? If walking then the one-way streets don't matter. If you do misunderstand the requirements then your instructions may be terrific but they will solve the wrong problem! Asking questions helps ensure that you fully understand the requirements. This applies to instructions of any kind: understanding requirements is important when giving directions and important when developing computer programs.

Once you have a clear idea of the requirements, you can develop a solution and provide instructions. Here is one example of instructions that give directions to the library:

If you are driving: turn right on Queen Street. Continue on Queen Street for two blocks, then turn left on Sycamore Lane. Continue on Sycamore Lane for two blocks then turn left on Franklin Street. Drive one block then turn left on Rose Avenue. The library is on your right.

If you are walking: Walk one block along Martin Luther King Boulevard then turn right on Liberty Street. Walk one block and turn left on Rose Avenue. The library will be on your left.

A good set of instructions will be **understandable, correct, unambiguous**, and **efficient**. When we develop set of instructions we should measure them against each of these criteria before being satisfied with our work.

Instructions must be understandable.

Instructions must use terms and language that are understandable to the person (or computer) that is receiving them. In order to give effective instructions we must use a recognizable language. It is not useful to give directions in French if the person receiving them does not speak French! And an instruction to "turn right at the intersection with the sycamore tree" is not useful if the person does not know what a sycamore tree is.

Similarly, in order to write instructions that a computer can execute we must learn the terms and grammar of a programming language so that our instructions can be interpreted correctly. Programming instructions that do not use the programming language correctly are said to contain **syntax errors**. A computer cannot execute a program that contains syntax errors.

Instructions must be correct.

This may seem obvious but it is easy to make a mistake even when giving simple directions. For example we may say "turn right" when we meant to say "turn left". For this reason we should be careful to test our instructions very carefully before we apply them. Not only must each individual instruction be correct, but the entire set of instructions must also be **ordered** correctly. If you change the order of the sentences in your directions to the library then the individual might never reach the library.

In computer programming, instructions that are **understandable** but not **correct** are said to contain **logical errors**. The computer can execute the instructions but will not perform as expected. This is actually a more dangerous type of error than a syntax error. In the case of a syntax error, the program cannot execute so that it is obvious that there is a problem. In the case of a logical error the program executes and it may not be clear that it is doing something wrong, for example performing a calculation incorrectly.

Instructions must be unambiguous.

If you just say "turn on Queen Street" instead of "turn right on Queen Street", the instruction will be ambiguous since the person will not know which way to turn. Ambiguous instructions create uncertainty and the individual who is carrying out the instructions must either ask for clarification or else make their own decision.

A computer cannot interpret an ambiguous instruction so ambiguous instructions are treated as another kind of syntax error that prevents a program from executing.

Instructions must be efficient.

We can provide very understandable, correct and unambiguous directions that are not very efficient. For example when asked for directions to the library, you could respond as follows:

If you are driving: turn right on Queen Street. Continue on Queen Street for two blocks, then turn left on Sycamore Lane. Drive one block, then turn left on Liberty Street. Continue on Liberty Street for two blocks then turn right on Martin Luther King Boulevard. Drive one block then turn right. Take the next right on Rose Avenue. The library is on your right.

These instructions are understandable, correct and unambiguous but they are not as efficient as the previous set of instructions. Now consider the following directions to the library:

Go to the airport. Fly to Paris, France. Stay in Paris until you find someone to marry. Get married then move to Italy. Find a job and stay for three years. Then fly back here. At the airport hail a taxi and ask the driver to bring you to the library. The taxi driver will know where it is.

These instructions may be understandable, correct and unambiguous but they are certainly not very efficient (although they may make for an interesting life)!

Last, here is a set of instructions that are more efficient than any of the instructions that have been provided so far:

Continue along Martin Luther King Boulevard for two blocks then turn right. Take the next right on Rose Avenue. The library is on your right.

It is important to recognize that, for many problems, you cannot know whether or not your solution uses the most efficient instructions that could be applied. Often there may be any number of acceptable solutions. Some of these will be more efficient than others, while some will be quite similar to others in terms of efficiency. If you look at the map again you will see that there are many ways to get to the library. If you really think about it you will realize that there are actually an **infinite** number of ways to get to the library!

This is an important point because many beginning programmers think that there is a "right answer" to a programming requirement when in fact there are many possible solutions. Different programmers are likely to solve the same problem in different ways. A good programmer knows this and is always ready to consider a different approach. As you become more skilled your solutions will become more efficient. Programmers often work in teams to brainstorm and consider many different solutions before deciding on a particular approach. Even so, since we are always working under time constraints, we often discover more efficient solutions after our software application is already in production. This is one of the reasons that new software versions are released.

It is also important to notice that efficiency can mean different things to different people. In the case of the library, somebody who is disabled may benefit by taking a backstreet route to the library with less obstacles, while somebody else might want a route that takes them past the Post Office. Similarly, good software designers take account of the needs of different types of users when developing effective instructions. They also take account of the systems on which the programs will execute. For example a programmer may need to decide whether to use instructions that make the least use of memory, instructions that perform the fastest, or instructions that provide the most user-friendly interface.

Sequence, Selection and Repetition Structures

The directions to the library included instructions like "turn right on Queen Street", "If you are driving", and "Continue on Queen Street for two blocks". You may be surprised to learn that most algorithms are written using combinations of just three basic structures: **sequential** statements, where each instruction simply follows the next and is executed in order; **selection** statements, where the decision to execute a block of one or more instructions depends on the result of a test of some kind (such as "if you are driving"); and **repetition** (or loop) statements, where a block of one or more instructions is **repeatedly** executed as long as a test of some kind is true (such as "keep driving on Queen Street until you have driven two blocks"). Each of these is a major programming topic and will be explored in different chapters in the book, but here is a worked program example just to give you a feel for how these different structures are used when developing an algorithm.

Sequential Statements

Here is an example of four sequential instructions from a program that calculates weekly pay:

```
get hoursWorked
get hourlyWage
weeklyPay = hoursWorked * hourlyWage
display weeklyPay
```

In this example each instruction is executed in order. The hours worked and hourly wage are retrieved from the user (or from a file or some other source), and then the weekly pay is calculated and displayed.

Adding a Selection Statement

Here is an example where the algorithm is modified to include a selection statement:

```
get hoursWorked
get hourlyWage
IF hoursWorked > 40
    regularPay = 40 * hourlyWage
    overtimePay = (hoursWorked — 40) * (hourlyWage * 1.5)
    weeklyPay = regularPay + overtimePay
ELSE
    weeklyPay = hoursWorked * hourlyWage

display weeklyPay
```

In this example a selection statement has been added after the first two sequential instructions. The test condition of the selection statement is "**IF hoursWorked > 40**". If this test is **true** (in other words, if the hours worked are greater than 40) that means the employee worked overtime and so the indented block of **three** instructions is executed: the pay for the first 40 hours is calculated, followed by the calculation of the overtime pay, and these are then added together to determine the total pay. The program then jumps **past** the ELSE block of instructions and moves on to the next program instruction, which displays the weekly pay. However if the test is **false** (in other words if the hours worked are **not** greater than 40) then this first block of indented instructions is skipped entirely and the program jumps to the single instruction in the ELSE block, where the weekly pay is calculated with no overtime to consider, and then jumps to the next instruction that follows the selection structure, which displays the weekly pay.

In this example, indentation is used to indicate which instructions are included in the IF and ELSE blocks. Either block can contain any number of instructions, depending on the requirements. Note also that the last instruction in this algorithm (**display WeeklyPay**) is not part of the selection structure and is executed whether the test result is true or false.

Adding a Repetition (Loop) Statement

Here is an example that shows how a loop statement might be used to process the pay of ten employees instead of just one

```
count = 1
WHILE count <= 10
    get hoursWorked
    get hourlyWage
    weeklyPay = hoursWorked * hourlyWage
    display weeklyPay
    count = count + 1
```

In this example, a variable named **count** is first assigned the value **1**. The program then encounters a repetition statement, controlled by a test condition: **count <= 10**. This test is **true** (since count currently contains 1, which is less than or equal to 10) so the five instructions in the block are executed in order: the first four instructions calculate and display an employee's pay, and the last instruction adds 1 to the count variable, which now has the value **2**. Since this is a loop, the program then returns to the loop heading and the loop condition is tested again. The test is still **true**, since 2 is less than or equal to 10, so the block of five statements is executed again: another employee's pay is calculated and displayed, and the count is increased to **3**. The program will continue to loop and calculate weekly pay for different employees until, after 10 repetitions, the value of **count** increases to **11**. When that happens and the program returns to the loop test, the test is **false**, since 11 is **not** less than or equal to 10, so the program skips past the block of loop instructions and jumps to whatever statement comes next.

You can easily see the power of a repetition statement: if there were 1000 employees, the programmer only has to change 10 to 1000 to process the pay for all of them.

Combining Sequential, Selection, and Repetition statements

So far you have seen that blocks of sequential instructions can be contained within selection statements and also within loop statements, but these statements can be combined in any way that serves the requirements. Here is a more complete version of the weekly pay algorithm, this time including the selection statement within the loop statement:

```
count = 1
WHILE count <= 10
   get hoursWorked
   get hourlyWage
   if hoursWorked > 40
      regularPay = 40 * hourlyWage
      overtimePay = (hoursWorked — 40) * (hourlyWage * 1.5)
      weeklyPay = regularPay + overtimePay
   else
      weeklyPay = hoursWorked * hourlyWage
   display weeklyPay
   count = count + 1
```

The pay for ten employees is processed just as in the previous example, but this time each employee's weekly pay may or not include overtime pay, depending on the number of hours he or she has worked.

Take a few minutes to work through this last example just to understand the logic. This is just a first look at sequential and repetition statements, intended to introduce the general concept. You won't be expected to use these statements until chapters 7, 8, 9, and 10, where they will be explained in far more detail.

A Programming Example

Let's look at the steps you will take to develop instructions for a simple computer program that only requires sequential statements. Here are the requirements for the circle application that you created in Chapter 2:

Circle requirements:

Write a program that asks the user for the radius of a circle. The program should calculate the circle's circumference and area, and display the radius, circumference and area.

These are simple requirements but we will use them to introduce the process of developing an application.

First we will want to consider the requirements carefully to be sure that we understand them. Are you clear about what this program needs to do?

As you get started it helps to evaluate your requirements in terms of input, processing and output. **Inputs** are the data values that the program must **receive** in order to perform its task. Processes are the operations, or actions, that the program must **perform** on the data. **Outputs** are the data values that the program **delivers** before it terminates.

Look over your application requirements carefully. What input is required? Are the inputs to come from the user? From a file or database? From a combination of sources? What outputs are required? Are the outputs to be displayed on the screen? Sent to a printer? Looking over our circle requirements, we can see that the program requires the radius of a circle as input, and this will be provided by the user. The output will be the radius, area and circumference and this will be displayed to the user.

Now identify the actions that must be performed. These will indicate the instructions that your program must execute. In our circle requirements, the actions are "ask the user for the radius of a circle", "calculate the circle's circumference", "calculate the circle's area", "display the radius", "display the circumference", and "display the area".

If you cannot clearly determine the required inputs, processing and outputs from the requirements you've been given, you will want to request clarification. It is never a good idea to guess the requirements that were intended!

Creating an Input, Processing, Output (IPO) chart

It might help you to write the program's inputs, processes and outputs as a list or table, often referred to as an **Input/Processing/Output (IPO) chart**. For example here is an IPO chart for your circle requirements:

```
IPO listing for circle:
Inputs:  radius
Processing:
    receive the radius from the user
    calculate the area
    calculate the circumference
    display the radius, area and circumference
Outputs:   radius, area and circumference
```

(Note that, while an IPO chart can provide a helpful template as you get started with simple applications like the ones we will work on in this book, a real world application will require more comprehensive tools; see **Additional Learning Materials** at the end of this chapter.)

Designing the User Interface

Once we have an idea of the inputs, outputs and processes, the next step is usually to design the user interface. Designing the interface helps us to plan our algorithms since it is common to design different parts of a program (the program modules) around each screen of an interface. Different interfaces can mean quite different approaches to the application design so it's a good idea to sketch out some different ideas for your interface before settling on a specific solution. This is often referred to as **storyboarding**. Figure 3-2 shows the proposed design for our circle calculation interface.

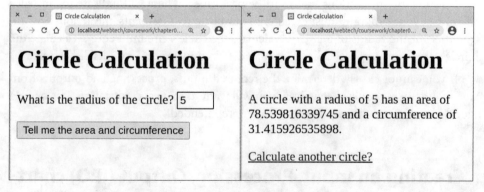

Figure 3-2: Interface design for circle program

This design could simply be sketched out using a pencil and paper. For this application we have designed two screens. The first screen is a Web page that provides a heading, prompt, input box to obtain the user input (the radius), and a submission button. When the submission button is pressed, the data is submitted and processed by a program that performs the calculations and generates a second Web page containing the output.

This is a basic client/server design: the client submits a request, based on user input, and the server receives and processes the request, then generates a response which is sent back to the client to be displayed to the user.

For more complex applications, the design phase is extensive. Programs will be broken down into a large number of different modules and screens. The work of software design is usually undertaken by senior programmers while junior programmers develop the design into working code.

Once you have a clear idea of your interface, it is often useful to go back to your customer and review the requirements. That's because people can often think more clearly about what they want when they begin to see what the product will look like. Frequently customers will clarify their needs once they see your proposed interface design.

Developing an Algorithm

An **algorithm** is the general term used to describe a set of instructions that perform a task of some kind. When we design an application we usually write our algorithms in a rather stylized form of English that is easy for a programmer to convert into any programming language. We call this style of writing **pseudocode** since it is "half-way" between English and actual program code. There are no precise rules for writing instructions in pseudocode; you will quickly get a feel for a style that works for you.

We designed our circle program in two components so we will develop the algorithm for each component separately. Here are the instructions for the first screen (circle.html) that provides a form for the user:

```
circle.html algorithm:
   Prompt the user for radius
   Get the radius
   Submit the radius to circle.php for processing
END
```

In this pseudocode example we use a combination of Prompt and Get instructions to indicate each input that the application needs to receive from the user. The **Prompt** instruction tells the programmer that the user must be provided with a message in order to know what to do. The **Get** instruction tells the programmer to provide some way for the input to be received (for example the user must be provided with an input box or a drop-down list or some other way to select a radius).

We also use a **Submit** instruction to indicate that, once the input has been received, it must be submitted to **circle.php** (the program that will process the radius).

Here is an algorithm for the PHP program (**circle.php**) that processes the radius submitted by the user, performs the required calculations, and displays the results:

```
circle.php algorithm:
   Receive the radius from circle.html
   area = PI * square (radius)
   circumference = 2 * PI * radius
   Display radius, area, circumference
END
```

This program uses a **Receive** instruction to tell the programmer that code will be required to receive the radius from **circle.html**. The next two instructions indicate the code that is needed to calculate the area and circumference. The **Display** instruction tells the programmer that code is required to display the results. This program contains input (the data received from the form), processing (the calculations), and output (the values that are displayed to the user).

These algorithms are not written in any specific programming language, and do not tell the programmer exactly what to do. They can include English words like "Prompt", "Get", "Display" and "Submit", and code-like instructions such as "circumference = 2 * PI * radius". That's why this is referred to as pseudocode, since it combines English language statements with statements that are quite similar to actual programming code. The pseudocode provides the programmer with a general design and step-by-step outline for the application so that he or she can more easily write the real code that will meet the requirements of the algorithm. Note that the programmer who develops the general design and algorithms may or may not be the same person who develops the actual code, and also note that there are no standard English words to use when developing algorithms; "Prompt", "Get", "Receive", "Display", and "Submit" could be other words as long as the instructions are clear. We will use these particular words in our algorithms and exercises throughout this book just to help you get started.

The order of these instructions is important! Instructions in a computer program are executed one at a time, in the order that they are encountered. Consider the following instructions:

```
circle.php algorithm:
   area = PI * square (radius)
   Receive the radius from circle.html
   Display radius, area, circumference
   circumference = 2 * PI * radius
END
```

Clearly the area cannot be calculated before the radius has been received! And the circumference cannot be displayed before the circumference has been calculated!

Variables, Assignments and Expressions

Look at the two calculations in our algorithm:

```
area = PI * square (radius)
circumference = 2 * PI * radius
```

These statements contain **program variables, assignments** and **arithmetic expressions.** These are all new concepts so let's look at each in turn.

Variables

As humans, when we receive a piece of information, we store it in our memory and then retrieve it later when we need it. That's true even if we need it only a second later (for example when someone tells us his or her name, and we immediately use their name when we reply). The strange thing about human memory is that we don't actually know exactly where in our memory we store each piece of information. Which raises the question — how do we know where to find it? Don't think about that too much, you may lose your amazing memorization skills!

Just like humans, computer programs must store any piece of data in memory so that the program can access it later, even if "later" means the very next instruction! But a computer program must have a way to find each piece of information that has been stored. Unlike human memory, every storage location in a computer's memory is identified by a unique numeric address. Rather than refer to these addresses directly, programming languages allow programmers to create **variables.** Each variable has a name that represents the location in memory where a specific data value is stored. We use the variable name to refer to this location.

In our **circle.php** algorithm we indicate three variables, named **radius, area,** and **circumference.** Each of these names represents a memory location. The value that is received from the user is stored in the variable (or memory location) named **radius.** The instruction **area = PI * square (radius)** tells the program to multiply the value of PI by the square of the value that is stored in **radius, and to assign the result to a variable named area.** The instruction **circumference = 2 * PI * radius** tells the program to multiply 2 by the value of PI by the value stored in **radius,** and to assign the result to a variable named **circumference. Note that the = sign is not used to indicate equality (as in a mathematical equation) but to signify assignment of a value to a variable, which will be explained in more detail in the next section.** The instruction **Display radius, area, circumference** tells the program to display the values that are stored in these three memory locations.

Variable names should be meaningful so that the name clearly indicates the type of value that the variable contains. Often a single English word is not sufficient to accomplish this and a variable name might contain multiple English words. However programming languages cannot allow spaces in variable names since this will create ambiguity (is it one variable or two?). Programmers therefore follow certain naming conventions to combine multiple English words into a single variable name. The most common conventions are:

- Use underscores between each English word in a variable name to represent the spaces, for example **hourly_wage** and **hours_worked**.
- Use an uppercase letter to begin each English word in a variable name, for example **hourlyWage** and **hoursWorked**. This approach is termed **camelback**, or **camel case,** notation.

PHP programmers follow either convention, however programmers in most current languages use camelback notation and that is the convention that we will follow in this book.

Another important naming convention is that the **first** letter of a variable name should always be lower-case, so for example use **hourlyWage** and not **HourlyWage**.

Named Constants

Most programming languages also allow the programmer to define names for fixed, or **constant**, values that can then be used in other statements throughout the program. For example let's say you need to refer to a sales tax rate a number of times throughout your code. You could specify the actual sales tax every time, for example **0.07**, or you could first assign this value to a **named constant**, for example **SALES_TAX = 0.07** and then refer to SALES_TAX every time you need to use the tax rate. But what's wrong with just using 0.07 directly in your code? If you use SALES_TAX you are prepared in case the tax changes. What if the tax changes to .08? Now you can just change SALES_TAX = 0.08 and the next time you run your program all the statements that use SALES_TAX will work with the new value. But why not just run a search to find all the 0.07's in your code and replace them with 0.08? That can be very dangerous: what if the value 0.07 was used somewhere in your code for some other purpose than the sales tax? That value would be changed too, which would lead to incorrect results.

Named constants are often written using all upper-case letters, with underscores to separate multiple English words in the name. This makes it easier to distinguish between named constants and variables.

Assignment Operations

An instruction to store a value in a variable is known as an **assignment operation**, or **assignment statement**. In an assignment statement, the variable that is to **store** the value is placed on the **left** side of the **assignment operator**, which is usually represented by the = sign. The value (or the expression that will produce the value) that is to be stored in the variable appears on the right side of the assignment operator. The statements **area = PI * square (radius)** and **circumference = 2 * PI * radius** are examples of assignments statements. Here are some more examples of assignment statements just to show how literal numeric values and values stored in variables can be combined in assignment statements in any way that serves the requirements of a particular program:

```
hourlyWage = 15.75
weeklyPay = hourlyWage * 40
hoursWorked = 25
weeklyPay = hourlyWage * hoursWorked
hourlyWage = hourlyWage + 1.05
```

The first statement assigns **15.75** to a variable named **hourlyWage**. The second statement multiplies the value stored in **hourlyWage** by **40**, and assigns the result to a variable named **weeklyPay**. The third statement assigns **25** to a variable named **hoursWorked**. The fourth statement multiplies the value stored in **hourlyWage** by the value stored in **hoursWorked** and assigns the result to the **weeklyPay** variable. The fifth statement is especially interesting: it adds **1.05** to the value stored in **hourlyWage** and assigns the result to **hourlyWage!** The same variable appears on both sides of the assignment operator! This should remind you that these are assignment statements not mathematical equations. The expression on the right side of the asignment operator is evaluated first and the result is then assigned to the variable on the left side of the assignment operator. So if **hourlyWage** previously contained the value **15.75**, the expression adds **1.05** to **15.75** and the result (**16.80**) is then assigned to **hourlyWage**. In other words this statements changes the value in **hourlyWage** from **15.75** to **16.80**, a wage increase!

Remember: in an assignment statement, the variable that is to receive a value is always placed on the **left** of the assignment operator, and the **value** to be stored (or the **expression** that generates this value) is located on the **right** hand side of the assignment operator.

Arithmetic and Logical Expressions

An **arithmetic expression** is simply an arithmetic operation that generates a numeric result. For example, 2 + 3 is an arithmetic expression and so is (2 + 3) * **20**. When writing computer programs, arithmetic expressions can also include the names of variables that are being used to store numbers. So **hourlyWage * hoursWorked** is an arithmetic expression. We can also write arithmetic expressions that combine variables and literal numbers, for example **hourlyWage * 40**.

Logical expressions (also called **Boolean** expressions) allow us to **compare** values, for example **hoursWorked < 40** is a **logical** expression that tests whether the value stored in **hoursWorked** is less than **40**. Unlike arithmetic expressions, which have a numeric result, logical expressions have a **true** or **false** result. We will explore the use of both arithmetic and logical expressions in later chapters.

A Smoking Calculator

Now consider the requirements for a program that will conduct a short smoking survey and give the person who is taking the survey some feedback concerning their smoking history:

Smoking requirements:

Write a program that prompts the user for their first and last names, the number of years they have smoked and daily average number of cigarettes they have smoked during this time. Calculate the approximate number of cigarettes they have smoked in their life by multiplying the number of years they have smoked by 365 by the daily average. The program should display all of the input data and the total in a short report.

Here is an IPO listing, developed from the requirements:

```
IPO listing for Smoking:
   Inputs:      first name, last name, years smoked, average
                   smoked daily
   Processing:  Obtain the four inputs from the user
                Calculate the total smoked
                Display the outputs
   Outputs:      last name, first name, years smoked,
                average smoked daily, total smoked
```

Figure 3-3 shows the interface design.

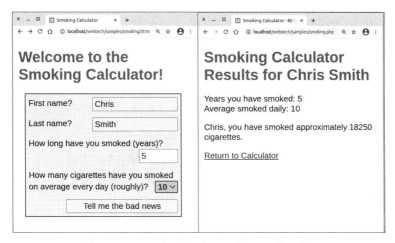

Figure 3-3: Interface for the Smoking application

Here is the algorithm for the first screen (an HTML document named **smoking.html** that contains the form that is displayed to obtain the user inputs):

```
smoking.html algorithm:
   Prompt for firstName
   Get firstName
   Prompt for lastName
   Get lastName
   Prompt for yearsSmoked
   Get yearsSmoked
   Prompt for smokedDaily
   Get smokedDaily
     Submit firstName, lastName, yearsSmoked, smokedDaily to
     smoking.php
END
```

Here is the algorithm for the PHP program (**smoking.php**) that processes the input from the form and generates the second page:

```
smoking.php algorithm:
   Receive firstName, lastName, yearsSmoked, smokedDaily from
     smoking.html
   totalSmoked = yearsSmoked * 365 * smokedDaily
   Display firstName, lastName, yearsSmoked, smokedDaily,
     totalSmoked
END
```

Once again our algorithms do not give exact details of how the instructions are to be coded. They simply indicate the overall design and outline the steps that must be performed. The details will be developed by the programmer who converts the algorithm into a specific programming language.

Coding the Application

Once you have developed your algorithms to meet a set of requirements, you are ready to code your application. The following chapters will take you step-by-step through the process of creating Web pages that include forms to receive user input, and writing PHP applications that process user input and generate results. As you work through each chapter you will learn additional procedures and control structures that will enable you to handle increasingly sophisticated requirements.

Additional Learning Material

The topics introduced in this chapter will be developed and expanded upon as you work through the book. The **Chapter 3 Hints and Help** pages on the textbook Web site provides answers to FAQs from previous students as they work through the end-of-chapter exercises.

While this chapter makes use of Input-Processing-Output (IPO) charts to review simple requirements, **Chapter 18** provides short introductions to more professional application design tools such as **integrated development environments (IDEs)**, **frameworks**, and **design patterns**.

Summary

A computer program delivers a set of instructions to the computer to perform a task of some kind. These instructions must be in a form that the computer can understand.

Instructions of all kinds share certain characteristics, whether intended to be performed by human beings or by a computer. A good set of instructions will be **understandable**, **correct**, **unambiguous**, and **efficient**. When we develop a set of instructions we should measure them against each of these criteria.

Computer instructions that are **understandable** but not **correct** are said to contain **logical errors**. Computer instructions that are not **understandable** (or **ambiguous**) are said to contain **syntax errors**.

Instructions may be **understandable** and **correct** but still may not be **efficient**.

A computer program is basically capable of three types of instruction: input, processing, and output. With smaller applications, it can be useful to develop IPO (Input,

Processing, Output) charts in order to better understand requirements. **Inputs** are the data values that the program needs to **receive** in order to perform its task. **Processes** are the actions or operations that the program must **perform. Outputs** are the data values that the program must **deliver** before it terminates.

It is common to design different parts of a client/server program (the program modules) around each screen of an interface.

An algorithm is a set of instructions to meet a set of requirements. Algorithms are constructed using combinations of three basic structures: **sequential statements, selection statements**, and **repetition (or loop) statements.**

Programmers usually write algorithms in a rather stylized form of English known as **pseudocode.** Algorithms written in pseudocode can easily be translated into a specific programming language (such as PHP) to create a working application.

Computer programs use **variables** to store data while the program is running. A variable references the address of a memory location where a data value is stored. The value can be accessed or modified within a program by using the variable name.

Variables names should be meaningful. We will use **camelback**, or **camel case**, notation for variable names that incorporate multiple English words (in this notation an upper-case letter is used to begin each English word). By convention the first letter of a variable name is always lower-case.

Names for **constant** values (values that are not to be changed by the program) are usually written in all upper-case letters, with English words separated by underscores. These names are usually referred to as **named constants.**

An **assignment** operation is used to store a value in a variable. The syntax for an assignment operation requires that the variable name appears to the **left** of the **assignment operator.** The assignment operator is often represented by the = symbol. The value (or expression that generates the value) that is to be stored in the variable appears to the **right** of the assignment operator, and is evaluated first; the result is then assigned to the variable on the left of the assignment operator.

An **arithmetic expression** is an arithmetic operation that generates a numeric result. Arithmetic expressions can include the names of variables that are being used to store numbers. Arithmetic expressions can also combine variables and literal numbers.

A **logical expression** (also called a **Boolean** expression) **compares** values, and generates a **true** or **false** result.

Chapter 3 Review Questions

1. Consider the following instructions carefully. What is wrong?

   Prompt for startingOdometerReading
   Get startingOdometerReading
   Prompt for endingOdometerReading
   Get endingOdometerReading
   Display distanceTraveled
   distanceTraveled = endingOdometerReading – startingOdometerReading

   a. The instructions are not efficient
   b. The instructions are not correctly ordered
   c. The instructions are ambiguous
   d. The instructions are not understandable
   e. There is nothing wrong with these instructions

2. Consider the following instructions carefully. What is wrong?

   Face the audience
   Place your left leg forward
   Hold out your right hand over your head
   Extend your hand out from your shoulder

   a. The instructions are not efficient
   b. The instructions are not correct
   c. The instructions are ambiguous
   d. The instructions are not understandable
   e. There is nothing wrong with these instructions

3. In programming, instructions that are not understandable because they do not use the language correctly are said to contain:
   a. Logical errors
   b. Sequential statements
   c. Syntax errors
   d. Iteration statements
   e. Sequential statements

4. In programming, instructions that are understandable but not correct are said to contain:
   a. Logical errors
   b. Sequential statements
   c. Syntax errors
   d. Iteration statements
   e. Selection statements

5. Which of the following questions needs to be more specific in order to answer it correctly?
    a. What is the sum of 23 and 45?
    b. Can you tell me your age?
    c. Which traffic light color means STOP?
    d. Can you tell me how to get to the store?
    e. What was the year of the first moon walk?

6. Consider the following instructions carefully. What is wrong?

    Take your rental car key to the parking lot
    Try all the cars until you find the car it fits — that's your rental car

    a. The instructions are not efficient
    b. The instructions are not correctly ordered
    c. The instructions are ambiguous
    d. The instructions are not understandable
    e. There is nothing wrong with these instructions

7. What is an algorithm?
    a. Instructions with input
    b. Instructions that are always repeated one or more times
    c. A set of clearly written, unambiguous instructions to perform a task
    d. Instructions that combine English with the structure and syntax of programming languages
    e. A statement that decides whether or not to execute a block of instructions based on a test of some kind.

8. What is pseudocode?
    a. Instructions with input
    b. Instructions that are always repeated one or more times
    c. A set of clearly written, unambiguous instructions to perform a task
    d. Instructions that combine English with the structure and syntax of programming languages
    e. A statement that decides whether or not to execute a block of instructions based on a test of some kind.

9. What is a selection statement?
    a. Instructions with input
    b. Instructions that are always repeated one or more times
    c. A set of clearly written, unambiguous instructions to perform a task
    d. Instructions that combine English with the structure and syntax of programming languages
    e. A statement that decides whether or not to execute a block of instructions based on a test of some kind.

10. How many assignment operations do you see in this algorithm?

    age = 20
    yearsToRetire = 65 − age
    Display yearsToRetire

    a. 0
    b. 1
    c. 2
    d. 3
    e. 4

11. How many **different** variables do you see in this algorithm?

    age = 20
    yearsToRetire = 65 − age
    Display yearsToRetire

    a. 0
    b. 1
    c. 2
    d. 3
    e. 4

12. What will be displayed if this algorithm is executed?

    age = 20
    yearsToRetire = 65 − age
    Display yearsToRetire

    a. 0
    b. 20
    c. 45
    d. 65
    e. 20, 45 and 65

13. This loop is designed to process 5 students. What is the purpose of the loop?
    Set count to 1
    WHILE count <= 5
        call in the next student
        ask the student for their GPA
        IF the student's GPA is greater than 3.2
                Congratulate the student
        Add 1 to the count
    a. Calculate the average GPA
    b. Congratulate all the students
    c. Ask each student their name
    d. Congratulate students with a GPA of 3.2
    e. Congratulate students with a GPA greater than 3.2

14. This loop is designed to process 5 students. What is the purpose of the loop?

       Set count to 1
       WHILE count <= 5
             call in the next student
             congratulate the student
             ask the student for their GPA
             Add 1 to the count
    a. Calculate the average GPA
    b. Congratulate all the students
    c. Ask each student their name
    d. Congratulate students with a GPA of 3.2
    e. Congratulate students with a GPA greater than 3.

15. This loop is designed to process 5 students. What is the purpose of the loop?

       Set count to 1
       Set totalGPA to 0
       WHILE count <= 5
             call in the next student
             ask the student for their GPA
             add the GPA to the totalGPA
             Add 1 to the count
       Divide the totalGPA by the count
    a. Calculate the average GPA
    b. Congratulate all the students
    c. Ask each student their name
    d. Congratulate students with a GPA of 3.2
    e. Congratulate students with a GPA greater than 3.2

16. How many inputs are included in the following requirement?

REQUIREMENT: *Write a program that asks the employee for their age. The program must subtract the age from 65, and display the age, followed by the number of years left to retirement.*

    a. 0
    b. 1
    c. 2
    d. 3
    e. 4

17. How many outputs are included in the following requirement?

REQUIREMENT: *Write a program that asks the employee for their age. The program must subtract the age from 65, and display the age, followed by the number of years left to retirement.*

---

    a. 0
    b. 1
    c. 2
    d. 3
    e. 4

18. Which variable name is an example of **camelback** notation?
    a. sales commission
    b. salesComission
    c. sales_commission
    d. SALESCOMISSION
    e. salescommission

19. What type of operation is used to store a value in a variable?
    a. Assignment statement
    b. Logical expression
    c. Arithmetic expression
    d. Sequential statement
    e. Repetition (loop) statement

20. What type of operation is used to compare two values?
    a. Assignment statement
    b. Logical expression
    c. Arithmetic expression
    d. Sequential statement
    e. Repetition (loop) statement

Chapter 3 Code Exercises

In Chapter 3 we learn how to analyze requirements and develop algorithms. Most of our Web-based applications will contain two components: an HTML document that contains the form to receive the user input and a PHP program that processes the input received from the form. These exercises will help you to develop algorithms for each component.

Your Chapter 3 code exercises can be found in your **chapter03** folder. This folder is included in your customized XAMPP installation at the following location:

htdocs\webtech\coursework\chapter03

Type your name and the date in the **Author** and **Date** sections of each file as you work on each exercise.

NOTE: You are not required to create working programs using HTML and PHP for these exercises, we will get to that in the following chapters. You won't need to run your Web server, you only need to **fix**, **modify**, or **create** the **algorithms** in pseudocode, as described in this chapter. Each of the exercises is provided in the **chapter03** folder as a text file. The Students page on the textbook Web site includes **Hints and Help** pages for the exercises in this and every chapter; these pages provide answers to students' most commonly asked questions. Refer to these first if you are not sure about the requirements of an exercise. or if you get stuck.

Debugging Exercises

Your **chapter03** folder contains a number of "fixit" text files. Each file contains an algorithm that has an error of some kind. Open the file in a text editor and read the comment section in the file to see what to do to fix them.

Code Modification Exercises

Your **chapter03** folder contains a number of "modify" text files. Each file contains an algorithm that needs to be modified to meet a revised requirement. Open the file in a text editor and read the comment section in the file to see what to do to modify them.

Algorithm Creation Exercises

1. Develop the algorithms for **paint-estimate.html** and **paint-estimate.php** based on the following requirements:

---

*Requirements for **paint-estimate**: Write a Web-based application for the King Painting company. The page provided by paint-estimate.html should ask the user for the length, width and height of a room. These inputs will be submitted to paint-estimate.php for processing.*

This program will use these inputs to perform a series of calculations: the area of each of the two long walls, the area of each of the two wide walls, the area of the ceiling, and the total area of the ceiling and the four walls combined. The program should then calculate the cost of paint, cost of labor, and the total cost, based on the following charges: a gallon of paint costs $17.00 and covers 400 square feet; labor costs 25.00 an hour and it takes 1 hour to paint every 200 square feet. The program should output the length, width, height, and total area of the room, followed by the paint cost, labor cost, and the total cost.

*For example if the user inputs 20, 15 and 8 for the length, width and height, the area of each of the two long walls will be 20 * 8 = 160, the area of each of the two wide walls will be 15 * 8 = 120. The area of the ceiling will be 20 * 15 = 300. The area of the four walls and ceiling combined will be 160 + 160 + 120 + 120 + 300 = 860.*

*The coverage will be 860/400 = 2.15, and the paint cost will be 2.15 * 17.00 = 36.55. The labor will be 860/200 = 4.3 hours, and the labor cost will be 4.3 * 25.00 = 107.50. The total cost will be 36.55 + 107.50 = 144.05.*

2. Develop the algorithms for **software-order.html** and **software-order.php** based on the following requirements:

*Requirements for **software-order**: Write a Web-based application that allows a customer to order any number of copies of your amazing SaveTheWorld software. The page provided by software-order.html should ask the user for the number of copies and the required operating system. These inputs will be submitted to software-order.php for processing.*

This program should calculate: the subtotal for the order (each copy sells for 35.00); a 7% tax (which is 0.07 times the subtotal); the shipping and handling charge, which is 1.25 for each copy; and the total cost (the subtotal plus the shipping/handling charge plus the tax). The program should display the operating system, the number of copies ordered, the sub-total, the tax, the shipping/handling, and the total cost.

*For example if the user inputs 5 copies, the subtotal will be 5 * 35.00 = 175.00, the tax will be 12.25, the shipping/handling will be 6.25, and the total cost will be 193.50.*

3. Develop the algorithms for **travel.html** and **travel.php** based on the following requirements:

Requirements for travel: Write a Web-based application that allows a customer to order a package trip to Rome. The page provided by travel.html should ask the user for the number of people traveling and the number of nights to reserve. These inputs will be submitted to travel.php for processing.

This program should calculate: the cost of the airline tickets ($875 per person), the cost of the hotel ($110 a person for each night), and the total cost. The program should display the number of people traveling, the number of nights, the cost of the airline tickets, the cost of the hotel, and the total cost.

For example if the user inputs 2 travelers for 4 nights the air travel will cost 2 * 875 = 1750 and the hotel cost will be 2 * 110 * 4 = 880, for a total cost of 2630.

4. Develop the algorithms for **game-intro.html** and **game-intro.php** based on the following requirements:

Requirements for game-intro: Write a Web-based application that allows a player to create a game character and purchase some experience, health, and supplies before the game begins. The page provided by game-intro.html should ask for a character name, character type, the number of experience tokens to be purchased, number of health tokens to be purchased, and number of supply tokens to be purchased. These inputs will be submitted to game-intro.php for processing.

This program should calculate the cost of the purchases in gold pieces. Every 10 health tokens costs 1 gold piece. Every 2 experience tokens costs 1 gold piece. Every 25 supply tokens costs 1 gold piece. For now, don't worry about the total evaluating to a fractional number of gold pieces (for example the total may be 8.5 gold pieces). The program should display the character's name and type, the number of each token purchased, and the total cost.

For example if the player purchases 20 health tokens, 10 experience tokens, and 25 supplies tokens, the cost will be 20 / 10 + 10 / 2 + 25 / 25 = 2 + 5 + 1 = 8 gold pieces.

5. Develop the algorithms for **event.html** and **event.php** based on the following requirements:

Requirements for event: Write a Web-based application that processes a ticket request for a performance. The page provided by event.html should ask the user for a name, phone number, and number of tickets. These inputs will be submitted to event.php for processing. This program should calculate the cost of the tickets ($35.00 each). For example if the user requests 10 tickets the cost will be 10 * 35, which is 350.

The program should display the name, phone number, number of tickets, and cost of the tickets.

6. Develop algorithms for **fuel-cost.html** and **fuel-cost.php** based on the following
    requirements:

---

*Requirements for fuel-cost: Write a Web-based application that will calculate and
display the fuel costs for a trip. The page provided by fuel-cost.html should ask the
user for his or her car's usual fuel consumption (mpg), the miles traveled, and the
fuel cost per gallon. These inputs will be submitted to fuel-cost.php for processing.
This program should calculate and display the cost of the trip based on these inputs.
For example if the user submits 20 as the mpg, 100 as miles traveled, and 3.00 as the
cost per gallon the program would calculate the cost as 100 / 20 * 3.00 which is
$15.00. You are only required to write the algorithms. You will write the code in
chapters 4 and 5.*

Chapter 4

Basics of Markup — Creating a User Interface with HTML

Intended Learning Outcomes

After completing this chapter, you should be able to:

- Explain the purpose of markup languages.
- Identify the three technologies that enabled the creation of HTML.
- Identify the basic protocols of the Internet and World Wide Web.
- Create a simple Web page using common HTML tags and attributes, including titles, paragraphs, headings, emphasized text, links to other pages, and images.
- Create an HTML table to display a list in columns and rows.
- Explain the purpose of style sheets.
- Create and modify a simple Cascading Style Sheet (CSS).
- Use external and internal stylesheets, and apply inline styles.
- Explain the purpose of HTML forms and the role of a form's **action** attribute.
- Create simple HTML forms that include labels, text boxes, drop down lists and submit buttons.
- Explain the role of the **name** attribute to submit HTML form input for processing.

Introduction

All information that you read has an appearance, whether it appears in a book, on a Web site, on a screen, on a poster or a package, or anywhere else. The term commonly used for defining the appearance of information is **rendering**. Consider what you are reading right now. How is the text rendered? Are you reading it on a printed page? On a screen? As a Web page? As an audio stream? How is the text **structured**, is it organized into headings, paragraphs, tables, etc? And how are these structures **styled**? Do you see different font types and sizes, colors, spacing, bold, italic, etc? What do you think about the rendering decisions that have been made, and how would you have rendered the text differently? Could it be rendered in different ways for different people (for example to serve the needs of readers with certain health conditions or impairments), or to display correctly on different devices (such as tablets, or smart phones)?

Most of this book is designed to teach you how to write Web-based computer programs that perform useful tasks by processing data in different ways (for example scientific or financial calculations, online searches, database lookups, reports, or interactive games). Processing data will require learning a programming language (PHP), and you will start do that in Chapter 5. However your PHP programs also need to interact with the user via Web pages, so you must first learn how to display information that the user can view on the screen and respond to. In this chapter you will learn to use a **markup language** and a **style sheet language** to define the appearance of information when it is displayed on a Web page.

Markup languages are used to define how text is to be structured when it is presented to the user, and the standard markup language for Web pages is **HTML**, or Hypertext Markup Language. In this chapter you will learn how to use HTML markup tags to create **elements** such as headings, paragraphs, tables, interactive forms, and hyperlinks for display on a Web page. You will also learn how to use a **style sheet** language called **CSS**, or Cascading Style Sheets, which is used to define the **appearance** of your HTML elements by specifying fonts and font-sizes, colors, bold and italic, spacing and positioning, etc). Although this textbook is not designed to teach you HTML and CSS in detail, it will provide a basic introduction that will prepare you for further study.

By the end of this chapter you will have the tools you need for Chapter 5, when you will begin learning PHP, and start coding Web-based applications.

A Short History of HTML

Hypertext Markup Language (HTML) is a markup language that is widely used to specify how data is to be rendered by a **Web browser**. HTML was developed from an idea into a language between 1989 and 1991, and the first Web browsers appeared in 1993 (they were named **lynx** and **Mosaic**). HTML made use of three existing technologies: **SGML**, **hyper-text**, and the **Internet**.

SGML

The general syntax of HTML was based on an existing markup language known as **SGML (Standard Generalized Markup Language)**. SGML was developed in the 1970s and is still used mainly in publishing fields to manage and deliver large and complex documents. Many of the original tags used in HTML markup are actually a subset of the much more extensive markup instructions defined by SGML. The syntax of HTML has evolved greatly since 1991. The latest version of HTML is named HTML5, and includes features to handle audio and video, 2D drawing, local storage, form controls, and new elements to handle specific page content.

Hypertext

Hypertext was invented in the 1940s. Hypertext is basically the idea of providing links through words and phrases within a document to obtain additional resources that are not contained in the document itself. This allows information to be interrelated on a global scale, and for users to explore an infinitely rich and multi-dimensional information landscape.

The Internet

The Internet was developed in the 1960s and allows computers to establish connections with other computers world-wide. Once connected, computers can communicate using various Internet protocols, or services. Essential Internet services include **ftp (File Transfer Protocol)** to transfer files, **telnet** to issue commands on a remote computer, **ping** to test the availability of a remote server, and **mail** to send and receive messages. In order to process HTML documents, a new Internet protocol was added: **http (Hypertext Transmission Protocol)**. The http protocol allows the transfer of formatted text and multimedia that can be rendered and displayed by Web browsers. The addition of http to the Internet created the **World Wide Web**. When you specify **http://** or https:// at the start of your URL, you are telling the browser that the data that is being requested is to be handled as a Web page.

Introducing HTML Tags

Markup languages define a set of **markup tags** that are combined with plain text to indicate how the text is to be structured and displayed. A text file that combines plain text with HTML markup tags is called an HTML document and usually has an **.html** extension. HTML tags are relatively few in number and follow some simple rules. Let's begin with a hands-on example. The file **my-web1.html** is located in your **samples** folder. Figure 4-1 shows what you will see if you open this page in your Web browser. First be sure that your Web server is running and then open **my-web1.html** by typing the following URL in your browser's address window:

http://localhost/webtech/samples/my-web1.html

Figure 4-1: my-web1.html

This information for this page is stored in the **my-web1.html** file which contains a combination of text and markup instructions (HTML code). When the Web browser opens the file, it displays the text according to the markup instructions. Let's look at the content of **my-web1.html**. The file is located in the following folder (the exact location of the **htdocs** folder depends on where you installed your software):

htdocs\webtech\samples\my-web1.html

Open this file in your text editor and look at the code.

```
<!DOCTYPE html>

<!-- Author: Mike O'Kane
     Date: August 13, 2013
     File: my-web1.html
     Purpose: HTML Example - introducing some basic HTML tags
-->
<html>
<head>
  <title>HTML Example</title>
</head>
<body>
  <h1>My First Web Page</h1>

  <p>Hi! My name is <strong>Mike</strong>. Let me tell you
  a little bit about myself.</p>
  <p>I enjoy hiking, kayaking, painting, writing, coding, and
gardening. And teaching of course!</p>

</body>
</html>
```

Code Example: my-web1.html

The first thing to notice about this file is that some of the text in the file is enclosed in < and > characters and this enclosed text is not displayed when you view the file in a browser. Any text that appears between < and > symbols in an HTML file is interpreted as an **HTML markup instruction**, commonly referred to as an **HTML tag**. These tags specify how the text in the document is to be rendered by the browser.

Before we look at each tag in detail, first look over the entire file and notice that the tags usually occur in pairs, for example <html> and </html>, <head> and </head>, <title> and </title>, <body> and </body>, <h1> and </h1>, <p> and </p>, <strong> and </strong>. These are opening and closing tags for each markup instruction and the closing tag for each markup instruction includes a / forward slash. Any text that appears between a pair of tags is formatted according to the tag's purpose. The opening tag indicates where a format starts to apply, and the closing tag indicates where the format no longer applies. For example <p> indicates the beginning of a paragraph and </p> marks the end of the paragraph, whereas <strong> marks the beginning of bold formatting and </strong> indicates the end of the bold formatting.

Also note that some tags are **nested** inside others, in other words the opening and closing tags for one instruction can be located **inside** the opening and closing tags of other instructions. In this example the pair of <title> tags are nested inside the <head> tags, a pair of <strong> and </strong> tags are nested inside a pair of <p> and </p> tags, and these, and other, tags are all nested inside the <body> tags, while both the <head> and <body> tags are nested inside the <html>tags.

Now let's examine the purpose of each tag in **my-web1.html**:

The DOCTYPE Declaration

The very first line in the file is <!DOCTYPE html>. This is a special declaration that tells the browser which version of HTML is being used. This particular DOCTYPE declaration is used to specify HTML5. The DOCTYPE declaration should always appear as the first line of your HTML files, before any other text in the file.

Comment Tags

The <!-- and --> tags are special symbols that tell the browser that any text within these tags is to be treated as a **comment**. Comments are not part of the content that is displayed by the browser—the browser ignores everything that appears between the <!-- and the --> tags. Comment sections are used to provide important information that can be read by programmers who may need to maintain or modify the file contents. Comments are a form of **documentation**, which is an important component of every software project and a part of every programmer's job. In **my-web1.html**, the comment section includes the programmer's name, the date the file was created, the name of the file and the purpose of the file.

IMPORTANT NOTE: to save space, the DOCTYPE and comment sections will not be shown in the code examples throughout the remainder of this book, however these sections are included in the sample files on your disk.

HTML Tags

The <html> and </html> tags simply indicate the beginning and end of the HTML data in the file. The HTML data within these tags is located inside two major sections, the <head> and the <body> sections.

Head Tags

Certain tags can be included between the **<head>** and **</head>** tags in order to provide information about the page as a whole. In this example, we use the **<head>** section to produce a page title using the **<title>** and **</title>** tags. In this case the title is "**HTML Example**". Can you see where this is displayed when you view the page? Right—it shows up in the **title bar** at the top of the window.

Body Tags

Everything that you want to actually display in the browser window must be located between the **<body>** and **</body>** tags.

Heading Level Tags

The <h1> and </h1> tags are used to indicate a Heading Level 1. You can set various heading levels in HTML, with Level 1 as the highest level. You can specify headings anywhere in your document as needed. Note that the text that appears between these tags is displayed as a heading.

Paragraph Tags

The <p> and </p> tags are used to indicate the beginning and end of paragraphs. Notice that you can use these tags as often as you want, for every paragraph in the page.

Strong Tags

The **** and **** tags are used to indicate bold text. Once again these tags can be used as often as needed in an HTML document.

Ignoring White Space

A web browser ignores **white space** (except single spaces between words) when formatting an HTML document for display. **White space** refers to any multiple spaces, new lines, tabs or indentations that were used to create the file. All of these are simply rendered as single white spaces. The browser applies paragraphs, indents, and other formats to your Web page based on the HTML tags only. To understand this, take a look at the code for **my-web2.html** (in your samples folder). This code is the same as **my-web1.html** except that the <p> and </p> tags have been removed. Now view this in your Web browser. Even though the text is organized into paragraphs in your editor window, it is no longer displayed as paragraphs in the browser! That's because the browser only displays a paragraph when it finds a <p> tag.

More HTML Tags

Let's add a few more tags so that we can include images and links to our Web page. Take a look at **my-web3.html** in your **samples** folder (see Figure 4-2).

Figure 4-2: my-web3.html

Here is the code for **my-web3.html**:

```
<!DOCTYPE html>

<html>
<head>
   <title>HTML Example</title>
   <link rel="stylesheet" type="text/css" href="sample.css">
</head>
<body>
   <h1>My First Web Page</h1>

   <img src="okane-pic.jpg" alt="image of Mike">

   <p>Hi! My name is <strong>Mike</strong>. Let me tell you
   a little bit about myself.</p>

   <p>I enjoy hiking, kayaking, painting, writing, coding,
   and gardening. And teaching of course!</p>

   <p>Here are some useful Web sites for this course:</p>

   <p><a href="https://www.w3c.org">The World Wide Web
   Consortium</a><br>
   <a href="https://www.php.net">PHP Home Page</a><br>
   <a href="https://www.w3Schools.com">W3Schools - Programming
      Tutorials</a><br></p>
   <p><a href="welcome.html">Welcome to the course!</a><br>
   <a href="quote-generator.php">Quote for the day</a><br></p>

</body>
</html>
```

Code Example: my-web3.html

As you can see, there are new features on this page, that require a number of new tags in the code. Let's review these in order of appearance (the **<link>** tag in the **<head>** section will be explained later in this chapter, in the style sheets section).

Image Tags

Look at the following line:

```
<img src="okane-pic.jpg" alt="image of Mike">
```

The **<img>** tag allows you to include images in your Web document. Many HTML tags can include **attributes** that provide additional specifications that are to be applied to the tag, and professional HTML developers need to become familiar with the various attributes that can be applied to each tag. Attributes are listed **inside** the opening tag, and each attribute has the general form **attribute** = **"value"**. In this example, the <img> tag includes two **attributes**. The first attribute is the **src** attribute which is used to indicate the name and location of the image. The image file is named **okane-pic.jpg**. Since this file is located in the same folder as **my-web3.html**, the attribute is simply src = "okanc-pic.jpg". If the image was storcd in a sub-folder named **images** inside the current folder, the attribute would be src = "images/okane-pic.jpg" (these are examples of **relative file addresses**, since the path to the image is **relative** to the current folder location). You can also refer to an image located anywhere on the Web, for example src = "https://www.mikeokane.com/images/okane-pic.jpg". See **Appendix B** to learn more about relative and absolute addresses.

The second attribute is the **alt** attribute which is used to indicate what text to display if the browser is not capable of displaying images, so **alt** = **"image of Mike"** specifies that the message "image of Mike" can be used as an alternative to the image. Consider someone who is visually impaired who may be viewing your Web page with software that reads the contents of the page aloud. Since the software cannot display the image, it reads the message from the **alt** attribute instead.

Anchor Tags

Look at the following line:

```
<a href="https://www.w3c.org">The World Wide Web Consortium</a>
```

Now this looks interesting! This is the **anchor** tag, which allows you to place links on your page to other Web pages. The <a> tag includes an **href** attribute which is used to indicate the URL that the link points to. The text between the <a> and </a> tags contains the phrase that appears on the current page — if the user clicks this text the browser submits a request for the page indicated in the **href** attribute and displays this page when it is received. Note that this example provides an **absolute address** — a complete URL to another Web page.

Just as when using the <img> tag, you can also specify **relative addresses** — links to other pages on the same Web site as the current page. The simplest example of a relative address is the address of a file in the same folder. In this case, you can simply provide the file name, for example the last two of the five anchor tags listed in **my-web3.html** provide links to files in the same folder as **my-web3.html**. The first of these is <a href = "welcome.html">Welcome to the Course!</a>. Since the **welcome.html** file is in the same folder as **my-web3.html**, only the file name is provided. The second of the relative links is <a href = "quote-generator.php">Quote for the day</a>. Note that this link specifies a PHP program named **quote-generator.php** in the same folder. See **Appendix B** to learn more about relative and absolute addresses.

Break Tags

Did you notice the <br> tag? This is a line break. It simply tells the browser to move to the next line before displaying whatever comes next. This is a little unusual because there is no closing tag. Under the current HTML standard, tags that do not require any text between the opening and closing tag can simply omit the closing tag. You may have noticed that the <img> tag is another tag that can be used without a closing tag since it does not require text between the opening and closing tags.

Introducing HTML Tables

Web designers often use **HTML tables** to align output neatly in rows and columns. HTML tables are created using the following tags:

<table> and </table> indicate the beginning and end of the entire table.

<tr> and </tr> indicate the beginning and end of each **row** in the table (**tr** stands for **table row**)

<td> and </td> indicate the beginning and end of each **column** in a row (**td** stands for **table data**).

<th> and </th> indicate column **headings** (**th** stands for **table heading**). By default, table headings are usually displayed centered and in bold.

Let's compare two web pages, first without, and then with tables in order to see the difference. The document **annual-temps1.html** displays a list of average monthly temperatures for the city of Asheville, North Carolina, but the information for each month is simply displayed on separate lines **without** using an HTML table. Here is the code for **annual-temps1.html**:

```
<html>
<head>
   <title>Weather data with NO table</title>
<link rel="stylesheet" type="text/css" href="sample.css">
</head>
<body>
   <h1>Monthly Temperatures</h1>
   <h2>Asheville, North Carolina</h2>
   <p>(This table displays the monthly averages)</p>
   <p>
   January: 25.8 (low) - 45.9 (high) <br>
   February: 28.0 (low) - 50.0 (high) <br>
   March: 34.9 (low) - 57.7 (high) <br>
   April: 41.8 (low) - 66.5 (high) <br>
   May: 50.6 (low) - 73.5 (high) <br>
   June: 58.3 (low) - 80.0 (high) <br>
```

```
    July: 62.7 (low) - 83.3 (high) <br>
    August: 61.8 (low) - 81.7 (high) <br>
    September: 55.4 (low) - 76.0 (high) <br>
    October: 43.3 (low) - 67.1 (high) <br>
    November: 35.3 (low) - 57.4 (high) <br>
    December: 28.8 (low) - 49.3 (high) <br>
    </p>
  </body>
</html>
```

Code Example: annual-temps1.html

(Note the use of the <h1></h1> and <h2></h2> tags to display the headings, and the <br> tag to provide line breaks.)

This document is displayed as the first screen shot in Figure 4-3. You will see that the information does not line up very nicely.

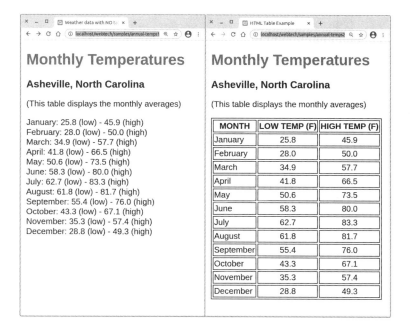

Figure 4-3: annual-temps1.html and annual-temps2.html screenshots

The document **annual-temps2.html** contains the same information but this time formatted using an HTML table. This document is displayed as the second screenshot in Figure 4-3. Clearly the layout looks **much** better!

Here is the HTML code for **annual-temps2.html**—notice the use of the table tags.

```
<html>
<head>
  <title>HTML Table Example</title>
  <link rel="stylesheet" type="text/css" href="sample.css">
</head>
<body>
  <h1>Monthly Temperatures</h1>
  <h2>Asheville, North Carolina</h2>
  <p>(This table displays the monthly averages)</p>
  <table>
    <tr> <th>MONTH</th>
         <th>LOW TEMP (F)</th>
         <th>HIGH TEMP (F)</th>
    </tr>
    <tr> <td>January</td>
         <td class="center">25.8</td>
         <td class="center">45.9</td>
    </tr>
    <tr> <td>February</td>
         <td class="center">28.0</td>
         <td class="center">50.0</td>
    </tr>
    <tr> <td>March</td>
         <td class="center">34.9</td>
         <td class="center">57.7</td>
    </tr>
    <tr> <td>April</td>
         <td class="center">41.8</td>
         <td class="center">66.5</td>
    </tr>
    <tr> <td>May</td>
         <td class="center">50.6</td>
         <td class="center">73.5</td>
    </tr>
    <tr> <td>June</td>
         <td class="center">58.3</td>
         <td class="center">80.0</td>
    </tr>
    <tr> <td>July</td>
         <td class="center">62.7</td>
         <td class="center">83.3</td>
    </tr>
```

```
    <tr> <td>August</td>
        <td class="center">61.8</td>
        <td class="center">81.7</td>
    </tr>
    <tr> <td>September</td>
        <td class="center">55.4</td>
        <td class="center">76.0</td>
    </tr>
    <tr> <td>October</td>
        <td class="center">43.3</td>
        <td class="center">67.1</td>
    </tr>
    <tr> <td>November</td>
        <td class="center">35.3</td>
        <td class="center">57.4</td>
    </tr>
    <tr> <td>December</td>
        <td class="center">28.8</td>
        <td class="center">49.3</td>
    </tr>
  </table>
</body>
</html>
```

Code Example: annual-temps2.html

The entire table is identified using the <table> and </table> tags. Each row is identified using the <tr> and </tr> tags. The column headings are identified using the <th> and </th> tags. The weather data to be displayed in each column is identified using the <td> and </td> tags: the first column in each row is left aligned and displays the month, the second column is center-aligned and displays the low temperature, and the third column is also center-aligned and displays the high temperature.

You may notice that some of the <td> tags are actually written <td class="center"> and that in these cases the displayed text is centered in the column. Also notice that the <head> section of our file includes a new statement: <link rel="stylesheet" type="text/css" href="sample.css">. We will learn how these two features work together to add special formatting to the tags in the section on style sheets later in this chapter.

Other HTML Tags

HTML includes a wide range of tags for different formatting purposes, and each tag may be customized by a large number of attributes. It is not our goal to provide a comprehensive overview of HTML. You are learning just enough to be able to write Web applications that implement your algorithms. You will learn more HTML tags later in this chapter and **Chapter 17** provides additional tags and HTML references.

Introducing Style Sheets

A Web browser decides how to display any Web page based on your use of HTML tags to define the structure of your text as headings, paragraphs, tables, etc. But these tags do not explicitly tell the browser just how these different elements are to appear on the screen. For example, what font should be used to display text in a paragraph? What font size? What color? What about the text in an <h1>heading, how should this appear? Take another look at Figure 4.1: when you opened the **my-web1.html** document, the browser made all of these decisions for you, applying default styles for each tag. But what if you want to override those default styles and decide for yourself the appearance of all the different elements on your Web page? For example how can you tell the browser to display your <h1> heading using the **Arial** font, colored **red**, in **bold**, with a size of **18 point**, similar to **annual-temps1.html** and **annual-temps2.html**?

We control the appearance of our HTML documents using a style sheet language known as **CSS**, which stands for Cascading Style Sheets. One way to do this is by creating a separate text file, with a .css extension, that contains CSS instructions. This is known as an **external style sheet**, and once created, this file can be referenced in your HTML document so the Web browser will know to check it when deciding how to display the Web page. Note that any number of HTML documents can refer to the same CSS file, so they will all be displayed with the same styles, which is often what you will want when developing a number of pages for the same Web site. Also, when you change a style in the CSS file, the change will be reflected on all the Web pages that are using that style sheet, which gives us a very powerful tool for updating and maintaining Web pages and Web sites.

The instructions in a .css file must be written using the CSS syntax, and the best way to introduce this is to look at an example. A style sheet named **sample.css** is included in your **samples** folder and this style sheet is used to determine the appearance of most of the Web pages displayed in this book (the files in your samples and coursework folders). To get started let's look at the first lines in the file:

```
body    { background: white }
          font-family: Arial, Helvetica, Sans-serif; }
h1   { font-size:18pt; color:red; font-weight:bold; }

h2   { font-size:12pt;   color:black; font-weight:bold; }

p { font-size:10pt;       color:black; }

p.alert  { font-style: italic; color:red;}

table, th, td { font-size:10pt; color:black; border:1px solid
black;}

td.center{ text-align:center;}
```

Code Example: The sample.css style sheet

The first thing you will notice is that this is very different from a HTML document! A CSS file is basically a lookup that the browser uses to determine what styles are required for specific HTML elements. As you look though this list, note that the name of each HTML element appears on the left and does not include the < and > symbols that you use when marking up your HTML documents (for example the CSS specifies **body** and not **<body>**, **h1** and not **<h1>**). Each of these element names is followed by a list of one or more styles that you wish to be applied to that particular element, and the list is enclosed between opening and closing curly braces { and }. Within the list, each style definition consists of a **property** and a **value**, separated by a **colon**, and each of these **property:value** pairs is separated by a **semi-colon**. Each property indicates a specific style that is to be formatted (for example **background**, or **font-family**, or **font-size**, or **color**), and the associated value indicates the format that is to be applied to that property. So for example if you look at the **body** listing you can see that, first, a **background** property is defined and set to the value **white**, and then a **font-family** property is defined, except in this case **three** values are provided (**Arial, Helvetica, sans-serif**), which tells the browser to choose whichever of these fonts is available for use (more on this below). Moving on to the **h1** element, **font-size:18pt** indicates the font size of these headings should be 18 point, **color:red** indicates that the color should be red, and **font-weight:bold** indicates that the headings should be displayed in bold. Note that the names of CSS properties and their possible values are all specified in the CSS language so you must know the correct names and values, and type them exactly; the browser will ignore any instructions that it cannot interpret.

You will recall that some tags are **nested** inside others in your HTML document, for example, headings, paragraphs, and tables are all nested between the opening and closing <body and </body> tags. The CSS sets the background of the body element to white, and this value will apply to the background of all of the nested elements, **unless, that is, your CSS assigns a different background color to any of these elements.** For example, your **h1** headings will also display with a white background, but if you added

background:yellow to your list of **h1** property:value pairs, your **h1** headings would then display with a yellow background. The same applies to the font-family which is defined in the **body** element: the selected font will be used by all the nested elements (headings, paragraphs, tables, etc) unless the font-family is redefined for any of these elements. This is one reason for the word **Cascading** in "Cascading Style Sheets": styles can "cascade" down to apply to nested elements, except where these elements re-define the style.

Specifying Fonts

You will notice that the font-family specification is a little different from the others; it provides three different values (**Arial**, **Helvetica**, and **sans-serif**), separated by commas. That's because by default the browser uses fonts provided by your desktop (either your operating system came with them, or you installed them yourself). Different operating systems provide different fonts, so your preferred font might not be available to the user's Web browser. The solution is to list a "family" of acceptable fonts, separated by commas; the Web browser will then select the first font in the list that your desktop can provide. The last option should always be a generic font, in this case **sans-serif** just tells the browser to use any sans-serif font that it can find. An example of a family of serif fonts might be **"Times New Roman"**, **Georgia**, **serif**, and monospace fonts might be **"Courier New"**, **Courier**, **monospace**. Note that font names that include spaces are enclosed in double quotes.

(You can avoid the problem of unavailable desktop fonts by instead choosing a **"Web font"**. A Web font is a font that is delivered by a Web server, so it is available no matter what desktop is being used (see the **Additional Learning Materials** section at the end of this chapter.)

Defining the Same Properties for Multiple Elements

One of the listings in sample.css defines the same properties for three different elements all at once (**table**, **th**, and **td**). Since the properties for these all require the same values, it is easier to list all three elements together, separated by **commas**. In case you are wondering, the **border** property is used to set the type of border that is to be used for the table: borders can have different widths, types of line, and colors. Note also that if the border property was defined for the table element but **not** for the **th** or **td** elements, the border would then appear around the whole table but not between the columns and rows within the table (which may be what you want in some circumstances).

Defining Different Styles for the Same HTML Element

Sometimes you may want to format the same tag differently in different parts of your document. For example, perhaps you want the text in **some** paragraphs on your Web pages to stand out because they are intended to alert the user about something important. You decide to call these paragraphs "alert" paragraphs and you want to display them in **red** and **italic**. The <**p**> tag can include a **class** attribute to identify that a particular paragraph needs special attention of some kind. For example, here's how we might identify certain paragraphs that will display "alert" messages:

```
<p class="alert">Be sure to save your files before you close
down the computer!</p>
```

Now that you have identified these paragraphs in your HTML code using the class attribute, you can include special formatting instructions in your style sheet for these special paragraphs as follows:

```
p.alert { font-style: italic; color:red; }
```

We add the name that we created to identify these special paragraphs to the **p** selector, using a period as a separator. As a result, any text inside paragraphs tags that include the **class="alert"** attribute will be displayed in red and italics. Note that the **p.alert** listing inherits the values of properties that were previously defined in the **p** listing, so there is no need to define those again, except for the **color property**, since this needs to be given a different value.

The **class** attribute can be applied to a number of other HTML tags for similar purposes. Refer back to the HTML code for **annual-temps2.html**. This page uses the sample.css style sheet and you will notice that some of the <td> tags are written <td class="center">. If you refer to your sample.css file you will see that it includes the formatting instruction:

```
td.center {text-align:center;}
```

This instruction specifies that the content of <td> tags with a class attribute "center" will be centered.

Selecting Colors for Fonts and Backgrounds

Some of the listings in sample.css specify colors by name. Most browsers recognize a lengthy list of color **names** that you can use when specifying colors, however only sixteen names are accepted as completely standard (these are: aqua, black, blue, fuchsia, gray, green, lime, maroon, navy, olive, purple, red, silver, teal, white, and yellow). Many more (over 16 million) colors can be referenced using each color's unique sequence of three 2-digit hexadecimal values. Each pair of digits defines the strength of one of the primary colors of light, red, green and blue (or RGB), in that order, with **00** indicating the lowest value for each of these colors and **FF** (which is the hexadecimal representation of the decimal value **255**) representing the highest possible value. So for example the color named **red** can be represented by **#FF0000** (full red with no green or blue), while **cyan** is **#00FFFF** (full blue and green with no red), and magenta is **#FF00FF** (full red, no green, full blue). Don't worry though, you don't have to learn or remember over 16 million hexadecimal color values! Use the Web to lookup HTML color charts and obtain the hexadecimal value that you need.

Here is how we would add an entry in our style sheet to format our paragraph text to Arial (or Helvetica), 10pt, with the color set to #302B54 (presidential blue):

```
p { font-family:Arial, Helvetica; font-size:10pt; color:#302B54; }
```

Referencing a Style Sheet in Your HTML Document

We will examine the rest of the **sample.css** file later in this chapter, when we learn how to create HTML forms. Before we do that, let's learn how to tell the Web browser to refer to an external style sheet when displaying the Web page. If you refer back to **my-web3.html** you will see an additional line in the <**head**> section

```
<head>
   <title>HTML Example</title>
   <link rel="stylesheet" type="text/css" href="sample.css">
</head>
```

The line <**link rel="stylesheet" type="text/css" href="sample.css"**> uses the <**link**> tag to tell the browser that an external style sheet is to be referenced in order to determine how to handle the tags in this document. The **href** attribute indicates that this style sheet is called **sample.css**, and that the style sheet is located in the same folder as the current document (since no file path or URL is specified).

You will want to include this line in the <head> section of every .html and .php file that you develop in this course, exactly as it is written here, in order to apply the **sample.css** instructions to the HTML tags in these files. You are welcome to copy and modify **sample.css** for your purposes. Don't change the copy in the **samples** folder however, that way you can always refer back to it if you need the original version.

Just for fun, let's see what happens if we apply a different external sheet to the same Web page. Open **my-web5.html** in your browser (be sure the web server is running). This file is exactly the same as **my-web3.html** except that it uses a style sheet named funky.css. Quite a difference! Compare the content of the **funky.css** file with sample.css.

Applying the Same Style Sheet to Multiple Pages

If the same external style sheet is referenced by a number of different HTML pages, changes to the style sheet will change the appearance of all of those pages, even an entire Web site. Since **sample.css** is referenced by almost all of the files in the samples and coursework folders, any changes that you make to sample.css will change the appearance of all those files when viewed in a Web browser. For example if you change the **body** listing in sample.css from {**background: white**} to {**background: gray**} then every HTML page that refers to sample.css will display with a gray background. Try it if you like, just be sure to change the background back to white when you are done.

Note that CSS style sheets that need to be accessed by multiple pages may be located in a different folder (and sometimes even on a different Web site entirely). See the **Additional Learning Materials** section a the end of this chapter to learn more about using **relative** and **absolute** file addresses to locate these files.

Cascading Style Sheets are very powerful and provide extensive tools to customize the overall appearance of Web pages at a very detailed level, so that a page can be designed exactly the way you want. There are lots of other properties and values that can be assigned to HTML elements, for all kinds of purposes. For example CSS allows you to define different behaviors for different sections of a page, lay out elements across the page, fine-tune widths, heights, spacing, padding and alignments. You only have to look at all the different designs for Web pages and Web sites to get a feel for what CSS can do. Major Web design platforms such as WordPress provide a large range of different style sheets and customization tools that make it easy to manage and customize both large and small Web sites.

Don't Feel Overwhelmed

As you can see there is lot to consider when developing CSS and hopefully this gives you some idea of the general procedure. Don't feel too overwhelmed: in this textbook we will just use the basic CSS introduced in this chapter in order to give our Web a applications a certain look and feel; you are not expected to do more than use the examples provided to complete the textbook exercises, or make minor changes in order to experiment a little.

Next you will learn a few more HTML tags that are used to generate interactive Web forms, along with the remaining CSS styles in sample.css, which will be applied to these new tags.

Interactive User Interfaces

A program that interacts with a human user requires a **user interface**. User interface design is a career within the software industry. This type of work appeals to people who combine an understanding of logic and software design with sensitivity to the ways that different people think and respond. The field attracts people from a range of backgrounds including graphic design, digital media, psychology, anthropology, technical communications, and computer programming.

A **graphical user interface** usually provides a fairly standard set of visual components that allow the user to make choices and enter data using the mouse or keyboard. Web-based interfaces often make use of **HTML forms** to provide the user with input options such as **submit** and **reset buttons, prompts** and **text input boxes, password boxes, drop down lists, radio buttons** and **check boxes.** When the user completes the form and presses the Submit button, the browser submits the input from the form to a server-based program for processing. The program processes the input and generates a new Web page containing a suitable response. This new page is returned to the user's Web browser for display. This is an example of a client/server application.

We will now learn how to create HTML documents that contain forms for user input. In later chapters we will learn to write the programs (using the PHP language) that process the input from these forms and generate an appropriate response to the user.

Creating HTML Forms

The simplest HTML form contains nothing more than a **submit button** that the user can click in order to have some task performed. When the button is clicked the request is sent to a server which executes the program that the form specifies. The program performs the task and usually generates a new Web page containing the results of the operation. This new page is returned to the browser for display to the user.

Consider the following program requirements:

Wage1 requirements:
Write a program that allows the user to submit a request to calculate the weekly pay and display the hours worked, hourly wage, and weekly pay for an employee who works 19 hours and earns $15.75 an hour.

For this program we will develop two documents. The first (**wage1.html**) will display a form containing a Submit button. When the user clicks this button the form will generate a request to the server to run a PHP program (**wage1.php**) that performs the calculation, then generates a Web page that displays the requested information. Figure 4-4 shows the screens for this application.

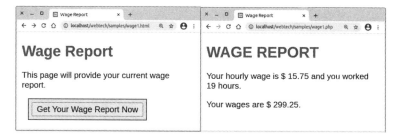

Figure 4-4: wage1.html and wage1.php screenshots

Here is the algorithm for the **wage1.html** document that displays the form:

```
wage1.html algorithm:
   Display Submit button to execute wage1.php
END
```

And here is the algorithm for the program (**wage1.php**) that processes the request:

```
wage1.php algorithm:
   hourlyWage = 15.75
   hoursWorked = 19
   wage = hourlyWage * hoursWorked
   Display hourlyWage, hoursWorked, wage
END
```

In this chapter we are only concerned with creating the **wage1.html** document that displays the form. In Chapter 5 we will learn how to create the **wage1.php** program that performs the processing.

In your samples folder you will find the **wage1.html** file. In order to view this form first be sure that your **Web server** is running and then open **wage1.html** by typing the following URL in your browser's address window:

http://localhost/webtech/samples/wage1.html

The form in **wage1.html** document simply provides a message and a Submit button with no additional input required from the user. If you press the **"Get Your Wage Report Now"** button a PHP program called **wage1.php** executes, and this program generates a second page.

Here is the HTML code for **wage1.html**:

```
<html>
<head>
  <title>Wage Report</title>
  <link rel="stylesheet" type="text/css" href="sample.css">
</head>
<body>
  <h1>Wage Report</h1>
  <p>This page will provide your current wage report.
  <form action="wage1.php" method="post">
    <input class = "submit" type="submit" value="Get Your
Wage Report Now">
  </form>
  </p>
</body>
</html>
```

Code Example: wage1.html

As you can see most of the tags in this document are similar to those you have already seen. What is new is the section containing a <**form**> tag and an <**input**> tag:

```
<form action="wage1.php" method="post">
  <input class="submit" type="submit" value="Get Your Wage
Report Now">
</form>
```

The <**form**> tag includes two attributes:

> **action** = "**wage1.php**"—the **action** attribute indicates the action that the Web server is to take when this form is submitted. Here the action specifies that a program named **wage1.php** is to be processed when the **Submit** button is pressed. In this example the **wage1.php** file is assumed to be in the same folder as **wage1.html** since only the file name is provided.

> **method** = "**post**"—the method attribute specifies the manner in which any user input is passed to the receiving program. Two methods may be used: "post" and "get". Without getting into details here, in this course we will always specify **method** = "**post**" in our forms (this provides greater security and allows larger amounts of data to be submitted).

Between the <**form**> and </**form**> tags is an <**input**> tag:

```
<input class="submit" type="submit" value="Get Your Wage Report
  Now">
```

This defines the **submit** button. Since the button is a component of the form, the <**input**> tag **must** be located between the beginning and ending <**form**> tags. This <**input**> tag includes three attributes:

class = "submit" – The class attribute is a CSS reference, telling the browser that this input element is to be formatted according to the style that has been defined for **input.submit** (we will learn more about this shortly, when we explore the settings in **sample.css** for all the form tags).

type = "submit" — the type attribute is used to specify what type of input is to be provided. **type** = "submit" tells the browser that this is a **submit** button. When this button is pressed the action specified in the <**form**> tag is passed back to the Web server to be processed (this particular form will submit a request to run the **wage1.php** program).

value = "Get Your Wage Report Now" — the **value** attribute tells the browser what message to display on the **Submit** button. You can provide any message you wish.

Note that the <input> tag does not need a closing tag.

Using HTML Forms to Obtain User Input

The form that we created in **wage1.html** does nothing but provide a submit button to run the **wage1.php** program. Since **wage1.php** requires no special input, we do not actually require a form to run the program. We could run **wage1.php** directly simply by typing the URL in the browser's address window, or by providing a link from a Web page. More often, you will use forms to write programs that require **user input**. Consider the following requirement:

Wage2 requirements:

Write an application that allows the user to submit their hours worked and hourly wage. The program should calculate the weekly pay and display the hours worked, hourly wage, and weekly pay.

Figure 4-5 shows a page design for a Web application that meets these requirements.

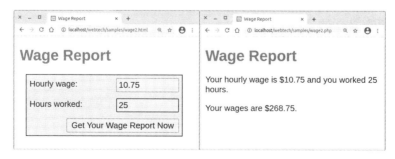

Figure 4-5: wage2.html and wage2.php screenshots

What is different from the Wage1 application?

The previous application generated a wage report based on an hourly wage of **$15.75** and **19** hours worked. That program was executed by a form that simply contained a submit button. This new version is much more powerful. The form provided by **wage2.html** includes input boxes that allow the user to enter **any** hourly wage and number of hours worked. Once the user enters the required data into the form, he or she presses the Submit button and the input is sent to **wage2.php** for processing. Here are the algorithms for **wage2.html** and **wage2.php**:

```
wage2.html algorithm:
   Prompt user for hourly wage
   Get hourlyWage
   Prompt user for hours worked
   Get hoursWorked
   Submit hourlyWage, hoursWorked to wage2.php
END

wage2.php algorithm:
   Receive hourlyWage, hoursWorked from wage2.html
   weeklyWage = hourlyWage * hoursWorked
   Display hourlyWage, hoursWorked, weeklyWage
END
```

Here we are only concerned with learning how to create the form in **wage2.html**. In Chapter 5 we will learn how to write the programming code for **wage2.php**. Here is the code for **wage2.html**:

```html
<html>
<head>
  <title>Wage Report</title>
  <link rel="stylesheet" type="text/css" href="sample.css">
</head>
<body>
  <h1>Wage Report</h1>
  <form action="wage2.php" method="post">
  <label>Hourly wage:
    <input type = "text" size = "10" name = "hourlyWage">
      </label>
  <label>Hours worked:
    <input type = "text" size = "10" name =
"hoursWorked"></label>
    <p><input class = "submit" type = "submit" value = "Get
Your Wage Report Now">
</form>
</body>
</html>
```

Code Example: wage2.html

Compare this form with the form in **wage1.html**. The **action** attribute specifies **wage2.php** as the program that is to process the form when the submit button is pressed. There are now four **<input>** tags. Note that all four tags are located between the **<form>** and **</form>** tags. This is required since they are all components of the form. Let's look at the purpose of each <input> tag in turn:

```
<label>Hourly wage
<input type="text" size="10" name="hourlyWage">
</label>
```

This piece of code is designed to display a **prompt** to the user, followed by a **text input box** that allows the user to type his or her response to the prompt. The HTML <label> tag is used to indicate a prompt, and notice that the opening <label> tag appears before the prompt, and the closing </label> tag appears **after** both the prompt **AND** the input element, so that the <input> tag is nested **inside** the opening and closing <label> tags.

The <input> tag contains three attributes:

type = **"text"**—tells the browser that this input tag is intended to display a text box to receive user input.

size = **"10"**—tells the browser how wide the text box should be.

name = **"hourlyWage"**—tells the browser what name to associate with the data that the user enters into the text box. This is VERY IMPORTANT. Whatever name you provide here will be passed to the program that will process the input (in this case wage2.php). Each input from the form will be uniquely identified by the name that you provide using the name attribute. Your names should not include spaces or begin with a number.

```
<label>Hours worked:
<input type="text" size="10" name="hoursWorked">
</label>
```

This **<input>** tag provides another textbox. A prompt is included before the text box so that the user knows what to type (**"Hours worked:"**). The data that the user enters into this textbox will be associated with the name **hoursWorked**. Note that this name must be different than the name provided for the first text box so that each value entered by the user will be submitted with a different name. Also notice that the names are **meaningful** and relate to the purpose of the input.

You may be wondering why the closing </label> tag appears **after** the <input> element and not **before**, after all the </label> tag indicates the end of the prompt message. Nesting the input box element **inside** the label ensures that the input box is directly associated with the label. That means that the input box will become **active** (allowing the user to type text in the box), if the user clicks anywhere in the prompt or the input box. That can be helpful for people using touch screens, or who are less agile with their fingers. Additionally, people who are using assistive technologies may have a screen reader, which will then read out the label text if the user activates the input box.

```
<input class = "submit" type="submit" value="Get Your Wage
Report Now">
```

This input tag defines a submit button, just like the submit button in **wage1.html**. In this example, the button contains the message "**Get Your Wage Report Now**". When the button is pressed the **wage2.php** program will be executed since this is the action indicated in the **action** attribute of the **<form>** tag.

Problems with Form Submission

If the Web server cannot process the action that your form has requested, you will receive an error message. For example if you specify a **.php** file and the server cannot find the file you would get a message similar to the following (the actual message depends on which browser you are using):

> **Not Found The requested URL /htdocs/webtech/samples/wage2.php was not found on this server.**

Often you will develop your HTML forms before you develop the PHP programs that process them. If you were to display **wage2.html** and press the submit button before **wage2.php** had been created you would receive an error message. You will also get an error if you press the submit button and the name of the **.php** program has been mistyped in the **<form>** tag, or if the path to the **.php** program is incorrect.

Drop Down Lists

So far we have seen how to create **text boxes** and submit buttons in your HTML forms. There are other ways to obtain user input. For example **drop down lists** allow the user to choose a value from a pre-defined list. Let's consider a form that allows the user to rate dogs and cats as pets. The user is asked to give ratings of **0** to **5** to indicate their preference for each animal. Of course we could just use textboxes to get these ratings but that would allow the user to enter anything! What if the user types 10 or "dogs are best!" instead of a rating from 0 to 5?

In order to be sure that the user can only enter numbers from **0** to **5** we can use a drop down list that only lists these six numbers. The use of a drop down list **constrains** the user in order to ensure valid input.

Figure 4-6 shows the interface provided by **compare-pets.html**.

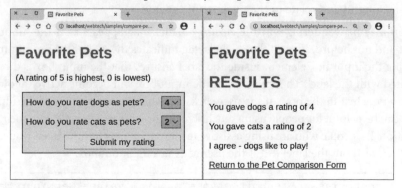

Figure 4-6: compare-pets.html and compare-pets.php

In order to specify drop down lists in our forms we use the <select> and </select> tags to specify a drop down list and <option> and </option> tags to specify each value within the list. Here is the code for **compare-pets.html**:

```html
<html>
<head>
  <title>Favorite Pets</title>
  <link rel="stylesheet" type="text/css" href="sample.css">
</head>
<body>

  <h1>Favorite Pets</h1>

  <form action="compare-pets.php" method="post" >

  <label>How do you rate dogs as pets (5 is highest rating,
    0 is lowest)?
    <select name="dogRating">
    <option>5</option>
    <option>4</option>
    <option>3</option>
    <option>2</option>
    <option>1</option>
    <option>0</option>
    </select></label>
    <label>How do you rate cats as pets (5 is highest rating,
    0 is lowest)?
    <select name="catRating">
    <option>5</option>
    <option>4</option>
    <option>3</option>
    <option>2</option>
    <option>1</option>
    <option>0</option>
    </select></label>
    <input class = "submit" type="submit" value="Submit my
      rating">
  </form>
</body>
</html>
```

Code Example: compare-pets.html

This example contains two drop down lists, and each list is enclosed in <select> and </select> tags. A <label> tag appears before the opening <select> tag, followed by a prompt that asks the user to give a rating, and note that the closing </label> tag is located after the closing </select> tag. Note also that each <select> tag includes the attribute **name,** similar to input text boxes. In the <select> tag for the first drop down list, the attribute **name** = "**dogRating**" specifies that the name **dogRating** will be associated with the specific value that the user selects from the list of options. Similarly **catRating** is the name specified for the value selected from the second list.

Within the <select> and </select> tags, we include as many <option></option> tags as we need, one for each option that we wish to appear in the list. In this case the options are all numbers, but they can also be text, for example if you wanted the user to choose a movie from a drop down list, each option could be a different movie title.

Combining Textboxes and Drop Down Lists

Now let's create an HTML page (**smoking.html**) that obtains the input needed for a program that conducts a short smoking survey (Figure 4-7).

Figure 4-7: smoking.html

We will use text boxes for the first and last names and number of years, but we will use a drop down list for the number of cigarettes smoked daily. This is to provide a limited number of options (0, 1, 2, 5, 10, 20, 30, 40) to simplify the survey and so that the user does not have to figure this out too carefully.

When the **submit** button is pressed, input data will be submitted to a program named **smoking.php** for processing. Here is the code for **smoking.html**:

```
<html>
<head>
  <title>Smoking Calculator</title>
  <link rel="stylesheet" type="text/css" href="sample.css">
</head>
<body>
  <h1>Welcome to the Smoking Calculator!</h1>
  <form action="smoking.php" method="post" >

    <label>First name?
    <input type="text" size="15" name="firstName">
    </label>

    <label>Last name?
    <input type="text" size="15" name="lastName">
    </label>

    <label>How long have you smoked (years)?
    <input type="text" size="5" name="yearsSmoked">
    </label>

    <label>How many cigarettes have you <br>
    smoked on average every day (roughly)?
    <select name="smokedDaily" >
      <option>0</option>
      <option>1</option>
      <option>2</option>
      <option>5</option>
      <option>10</option>
      <option>20</option>
      <option>30</option>
      <option>40</option>
    </select></label>

    <input class = "submit" type="submit" value="Tell me the
    bad news">
</form>
</body>
</html>
```

Code Example: smoking.html

Other Types of Input

There are other ways to receive user input in HTML forms: **password boxes** (which show only asterisks when the user types), **text areas** (for larger text entries), **radio buttons**, and **checkboxes**. See **Chapter 17** for references to these and other HTML tags.

CSS Layout and HTML Forms

Earlier in this chapter you learned how to use CSS properties and values to set the appearance of **individual** HTML elements, such as headings and paragraphs and tables. CSS also allows you to define the **layout** of these elements **in relation** to one another on the Web page. Elements can be arranged **inline** so that they flow from left to right across the page, or stacked like separate **blocks**, one above the other on the page (like paragraphs). Elements on the same "line" can be made to **float** to the left or right of other elements on the same line. Elements can also have **borders** around them, different **background** colors, different **font** settings, different **heights** and **widths**, **padding**, and so on. Page layout is an important and quite complex CSS topic that is mostly beyond the scope of this book. We will introduce some general concepts here by applying a few CSS properties to ensure that the elements in our HTML forms are laid out nicely and aligned with one another. You will not be expected to develop your own CSS layouts; just use the settings in **sample.css** for all of your exercises, whenever forms are required. **Chapter 17** provides some useful resources if you would like to experiment further.

Let's use the following requirements to layout our HTML forms:

- The entire form should be surrounded by a border so that it stands out.
- Each label (prompt) should appear to the left of the associated input or select element.
- All the labels should line up neatly on the left side of the form (left-aligned).
- All the input and select elements should line up neatly on the right (right-aligned).
- The label widths should be set to 400px, so that longer text will wrap rather than extend all the way across the page.
- The labels, and also the submit button, should have 5px margins around them so that there is some space between them and the form border and other form elements.
- The Submit button should be right-aligned and appear below the labels.

You have already examined the first lines of **sample.css**, now let's look at the remaining lines, which will layout your forms to meet these requirements (these are provided for your interest but you can skip this section if you prefer; you are not expected to make changes to the sample.css file):

```
select { font-size:10pt; font-weight: bold; color:blue; back-
ground: lightBlue }
option { font-size:10pt; color:black; background: silver}
form      {
                display: inline-block;
                margin-left:10px;
                background: #e6ecff;
                border:1px solid black;
          }
label    {
                font-size:10pt; color:black;
                clear: left;
                float: left;
                width: 400px;
                margin: 5px;
                line-height:18px
          }
input, select
          {
                float: right;
                width: auto;
          }
input.submit
          {
                clear: left;
                float: right;
                width: 180px;
                margin: 5px;
          }
```

The first two selectors listed here are **select** and **option**, both associated with drop down lists. The settings for **select** will control the appearance of the box that displays the currently selected option from the drop down list. The value that appears in this box will appear as **bold**, **10 pt.**, and **blue**, with a **light blue** background. The settings for **option** will control the appearance of the items that are displayed in the drop down list; these will appear as black with a silver background.

The **form** listing in **sample.css** defines the overall layout for the form. The form will be slightly indented (10px) from the left side of the page, with a black border, and a pale blue background (color value #e6ecff). The **display** property determines how the form element, and the elements nested inside the form, will appear in relation to one another. The value inline-block specifies that the nested elements will flow **across** the page from left to right (as long as there is enough space, if there is not, they will wrap to the next line), and that each element can be set to its own height and width. This is how we ensure that the labels and input boxes will appear next to each other rather than one above the other. However this setting means that **all** of the labels and input boxes in the form will line up across the page in one continuous flow! Fortunately we can apply the clear property to end this left-to-right flow each time a new label is to be displayed (see below).

The **label** selector sets the **size** and **color** for the label text, assigns a **width** of **240px**, and an all-round **margin** of **5px**, which is applied **within** the form margin so that each label is given a little distance from the edge of the form and from other form elements. The **clear:left** setting ensures that every label will appear on a new line since the value **left** indicates that a break in the flow should occur before this element is positioned. The **float** property is used to indicate the relative alignment of an element in the flow of elements across the page, and **float:left** indicates that the label text will be floated towards the left. Since our flow consists of just a label and an input box, or a label and a drop down list, this means that each label will be aligned to the left in the form. The line-height property nudges the vertical position of the prompt text so that it will be vertically centered with respect to the input box that follows.

The next listing sets **input** and **select** to float to the **right**, so our text input boxes and drop-down lists will be floated towards the right among the flow of elements where they appear (just as the labels will be floated to the left). Setting width to **auto** ensures that these elements will be assigned the full width available (after the labels) which effectively means that these elements will be right-aligned in the form.

Next we set the **submit** selector. The submit button is a type of **input** element, but we have already provided style settings for the input element, to position our input text boxes. We want to position our submit buttons differently than our text input boxes, which is why we used the **class** attribute in our HTML code to identify them with the name "submit" (**class="submit"**). That allows us to specify the settings for submit using the selector **input.submit**. Just as with our labels we use the **clear** and **float** properties to ensure that our submit buttons will appear on a new "line" and floated to the **right**. We also set the **width** of these buttons to **180px**, and an all-round **margin** of **5px**.

As you can see, page layout is a fairly complex and time-consuming process. Many Web developers use tools to do this work, often in the form of standard templates that they can use as-is, or tweak to fit their needs.

Internal and Inline Style Sheets

The **sample.css** example describes an **external style sheet**, but CSS styles can also be specified directly **inside** your actual HTML document, either in the **head** section of the document, as an **internal style sheet**, or even inside a single occurrence of an HTML tag, in the **body** of your document, as an **inline style**. There are very good reasons to combine the use of external, internal, and inline style settings. For example you might want to use the styles defined in **sample.css** for all your textbook exercises, but want to "over-ride" some of these settings for a specific exercise (perhaps change some properties of <h1> and <p> elements on a single page). Or you might even want to apply different values to some properties in a single HTML tag in your document, for example the color of just one paragraph.

Internal style sheets are placed in the <head> section of an HTML document, and these settings apply to all the elements within the document (except when over-ridden by a style that has been defined for a single element). Here's an example of an internal style sheet that specifies that <h1> headings in the document should be blue, and that paragraph text should be blue and 12pt:

```
<head>
  <title>CSS Example</title>
  <link rel="stylesheet" type="text/css" href="sample.css">
  <style>
    h1{color:blue; }
    p {color:blue; font-size:12pt;}
  </style>
</head>
```

Note that the head section **also** references the **external** style sheet **sample.css**, and that this style sheet is referenced **before** the internal style sheet. This is important because the style sheets are prioritized by the order in which they are read by the browser, with the most recent having highest priority. The internal style sheet settings will be prioritized over settings in the external style sheet (sample.css) because the browser reads the internal style sheet **after** having already read sample.css. All the style settings in sample.css will still apply to the document except for the specific values that the **internal** style sheet applies to the **h1** selector's **color** property, and the **p** selector's **color and font-size** properties.

Now let's say you want to change the text color of just a single paragraph in this HTML document. **Inline styles** use an element's **style** attribute to apply values to properties, for example:

```
<p style="color:green;">Hey I'm a green paragraph!</p>
```

The browser always applies the **last** value that it reads for an element's property. Inline styles are read as the browser is working through the <body> section of the document, having already reading any external and internal style sheets, so the inline styles have higher priority. All settings that are not defined as external, internal, or inline style, will be displayed using the browser's default CSS settings, since these have the lowest priority of all.

Just one more consideration: recall that sample.css includes a definition for the **p.alert** selector, which species that any paragraph that includes the **class="alert"** attribute will display as **red** and **italic**. So what happens to a paragraph that includes this attribute **as well as** a style attribute that defines the color to be green? For example:

```
<p class="alert" style="color:green;">Help! Am I red or
green?</p>
```

The answer in this case is **green**, simply because the style attribute appears **after** the class attribute and so it is the last **color** value to be read by the browser. The paragraph will also display as italic since that was the last value applied to the **font-style** property.

Once again there is no requirement to use internal or inline styles as you work through this book but you may find them useful. By now you should have a picture of styles "cascading" through these different CSS sources, and that explains why these are referred to as **Cascading** Style Sheets.

Additional Learning Materials

When linking to Web pages, images, style sheets, and other files, you will need to indicate the location of these files. **Appendix B** will help you understand the difference between **relative and absolute file addresses**, and learn how to apply these.

Chapter 17 introduces a number of other HTML elements that you may find useful, including other form elements (radio buttons, check boxes, text areas, hidden fields, and reset buttons), different kinds of lists, quotations and citations, and <DIV> and <SPAN> containers (used to layout pages and apply styles to different page sections). The use of images as background, and clickable images are described, and Web fonts and HTML **entities** are also explained.

The **Chapter 4 Hints and Help** pages on the textbook Web site provides answers to FAQs from previous students as they worked through the end-of-chapter exercises.

Summary

All information has an appearance. The term used for organizing and formatting information is **rendering**.

Markup languages provide syntax for instructions to render information for a specific purpose. Hypertext Markup language (HTML) is a markup language developed for the Web, that makes use of Standard Generalized Markup Language (SGML), Hypertext, and the Internet. A new Internet protocol named **http** was created to handle the transfer and processing of HTML documents, and this addition created the World Wide Web.

HTML uses a syntax of **tags** and **attributes** to render information for display in a Web browser. HTML tags come in pairs, for example <**p**> and </**p**>, which open and close a format around the text that is to be formatted. In cases where no text is required between the opening and closing tag, the closing tag can be omitted (for example the opening and closing break tags <**br**></**br**> can be simplified to <**br**>). Attributes appear inside opening tags and provide additional specifications concerning the tag. Useful tags include the <**img**> tag for including images, the <**a**> (anchor) tag for adding hypertext links, and the table tags (<**table**>, <**tr**>, and <**td**>) for tables with rows and columns.

Style sheets make it easy to separate standard design specifications from individual pages so that the same specifications can be applied to multiple documents. Style sheets can also be used to render the same document in different ways for different purposes. Style sheets follow their own syntax; an HTML element (called a **selector**) appears on the left, followed by a list of **property:value** pairs that define different styles for the element. Each property and value is separated by a **colon**, for example, **color:red**, and each pair is separated by a **semi-colon**. The entire list of property:value pairs for a selector is enclosed in opening and closing curly brackets { and }, for example **h1** {**color:red; font-size:18pt** }

Interactive **user interfaces** allow users to control a program and provide any input needed for processing. Web interfaces can make use of HTML forms to obtain user input and submit this input to be processed by programs running on a Web server. The <**form**> tag includes an **action** attribute to indicate the program that is to process the form input.

The simplest Web form contains a button to submit the form with no additional input needed. Forms can contain **submit buttons**, **labels** (to prompt the user for input), **text input boxes, password boxes, drop down lists, radio buttons** and **check boxes**. Each input field must be associated with a unique name, using the **name** attribute, since this is how the program that receives the form data will identify each input.

Drop down lists constrain the choices of the user in order to ensure valid input.

The **sample.css** file in the samples folder provides an example of an **external style sheet**, and sets the styles that are used extensively throughout the book, including styles to layout HTML forms. An external CSS must be referenced in the <**head**> section of an HTML document that intends to use it. You will not be required to develop your own style sheets, you can use the sample.css file for your exercises.

CSS styles can be specified in **external style sheets**, **internal style sheets** (in the <**head**> section of a document), and **inline** (within an individual HTML element in the <**body**> section of a document).

Chapter 4 Review Questions

1. Which word refers to the process of organizing and formatting text to appear a certain way?
   a. Rendering
   b. Compiling
   c. Interpreting
   d. Browsing
   e. Algorithm

2. Which is the earliest markup language?
   a. HTML
   b. SGML

3. Which of the following Web browsers was the first to appear?
   a. Mosaic
   b. Internet Explorer
   c. AOL
   d. Netscape
   e. Mozilla Firefox

4. Which of the following statements is true?
   a. The http protocol added the Internet to the World Wide Web
   b. The http protocol added the World Wide Web to the Internet

5. What symbols are used to indicate the beginning and end of a comment in HTML?
   a. <!--and-->
   b. /* and */
   c. <comment> and </comment>
   d. <html> and </html>
   e. <head> and </head>

6. What is the purpose of a **comment**?
   a. Instructions to the Web browser showing how text is to be displayed
   b. Instructions to mark the beginning and end of the HTML document
   c. Instructions to emphasize certain text on the page
   d. Documentation intended for someone viewing the page in a Web browser
   e. Documentation intended for someone reading the file—not displayed by the browser

7. How many **columns** will be displayed by this table?

```
<table>
<tr><td>France</td><td>Paris</td></tr>
<tr><td>England</td><td>London</td></tr>
<tr><td>Italy</td><td>Rome</td></tr>
</table>
```

    a. 1
    b. 2
    c. 3
    d. 4
    e. 5

8. How many paragraphs will the following HTML code display?

```
<p>This is a <strong>test</strong>of your understanding of
HTML tags. </p><p>I wonder how many paragraphs this block of
text will display?</p><p>I wonder ... </p>
```

    a. 1
    b. 2
    c. 3
    d. 4
    e. 6

9. What is white space?
    a. Text that is included in comment sections
    b. Multiple spaces, tabs, blank lines, blank areas or indentations in a text document
    c. The text that is not included inside HTML tags
    d. The text that is included inside HTML tags
    e. All areas of a Web page background that are colored white

10. What does the following code achieve? <img src = "test.jpg" alt="Test image">
    a. Displays an image stored in a file named test.jpg or else displays the message "Test image" if the browser is configured not to display images
    b. Displays an image stored in a file named test.jpg with the message "Test image" below the image.

11. Which of the following is an example of an anchor tag that is using an **absolute** address?
    a. \<a href="welcome.html">Welcome!\</a>
    b. \<a href="welcome.php">Welcome!\</a>
    c. \<a href="http://www.w3c.org/welcome.html">Welcome!\</a>

12. Which of the following is an example of an anchor tag that is using a **relative** address?
    a. \<a href="welcome.html">Welcome!\</a>
    b. \<a href="http://localhost/webtech/samples/welcome.html">
            Welcome!\</a>
    c. \<a href="http://www.w3c.org/welcome.html">Welcome!\</a>

13. What is the purpose of the \
 tag?
    a. It renders text as bold
    b. It renders text as brown
    c. It renders text as bright red
    d. It creates a brown background
    e. It creates a line break

14. What does **CSS** stand for?
    a. Cascading Style Sheet
    b. Character Style Sheet
    c. Consistent Style Sheet
    d. Character Syntax Specification
    e. Character Symbolic Standard

15. What is the purpose of an external CSS style sheet?
    a. Provides a standard style that can be applied to multiple HTML documents
    b. Provides a standard style that can be only be applied to a single HTML document

16. Which of the following will correctly create a form that contains a Submit button, and will run a program named test.php when the Submit button is pressed?
    a. <form action="submit" method="post">
       <input class="submit" type=" test.php" value="submit">
       </form>
    b. <form action="test.php" method="post">
       <input class="submit" type="submit" value="submit">
       </form>
    c. <input class="submit" type="submit" value="submit">
       <form action="test.php" method="post">
       </form>
    d. <form action="test.php" method="post">
       </form>
       <input class="submit" type="submit" value="submit">
    e. <form action="post" method="test.php">
       <input class="submit" type="submit" value="submit">
       </form>

17. Look at the following form. What is the name of program that will be executed when this form is submitted?

```
<form action="calc.php" method="post" >
<label>What is your answer?
<input type="text" size="20" name="someInput"></label>
<input class="submit" type="submit" value="Process The
Form">
</form>
```

    a. calc.php
    b. post
    c. someInput
    d. submit
    e. Process The Form

18. Look at the following form. What type of input is the form using to receive the user's age?

```
<form action="calculate.php" method="post">
<label>What age are you?
<select name="age">
<option>Less than 18</option>
<option>18 - 65</option>
<option>Above 65</option>
</select></label>
<input class="submit" type="submit" value="Submit">
</form>
```

   a. Input Box
   b. Drop Down List
   c. No input

19. Look at the following form. What type of input is the form using to receive the user's age?

```
<form action=" calculate.php" method="post">
<label> What age are you?
<input type="text" size="5" name="age"></label>
<input class="submit" type="submit" value="Submit">
</form>
```

   a. Input Box
   b. Drop Down List
   c. No input

20. What is wrong with this HTML code segment? <h1>This is a test <h1>
   a. The first <h1> tag should be </h1>
   b. The second <h1> tag should be </h1>
   c. Both <h1> tags should be </h1>
   d. The code should be <h1 This is a test /h1>
   e. Nothing is wrong with this code

Chapter 4 Code Exercises

Your Chapter 4 code exercises can be found in your **chapter04** folder. This folder is included in your customized XAMPP installation at the following location:

htdocs\webtech\coursework\chapter04

Type your name and the date in the **Author** and **Date** sections of each file as you work on each exercise.

Note that you are NOT required to create working programs using PHP for these exercises, we will get to that in the following chapters You only need to develop HTML pages, as described in this chapter. When comparing your work to the screen shots, don't worry if your pages wrap differently since the screen shots are designed to fit the textbook pages. The Students page on the textbook Web site includes **Hints and Help** pages for this and every chapter; these pages provide answers to students' most commonly asked questions. Refer to these first if you are not sure about the requirements of an exercise. or if you get stuck.

Debugging Exercises

Your **chapter04** folder contains a number of **fixit** files. Each file contains code with an error of some kind. Open the file in a text editor and read the comment section in the file to see what to do to fix them.

Code Modification Exercises

Your **chapter04** folder contains a number of **modify** files. Each file contains code with a comment section that indicates a revised requirement. Your job is to modify the code in each file to meet the new requirements.

Code Completion Exercises

1. You are developing a small Web site for a team of house painters: John and Mary King. The file **king-painting.html** already contains the text to display a home page but it has not been formatted. Add the HTML code to this file to render the page as shown in Figure 4-8 (note that the words "customized" and "high quality" are bold, the address does not include any blank lines, and the link on this page should link to a file named **paint-estimate.html**).

Figure 4-8: king-painting.html

2. Create an HTML document named **paint-estimate.html** based on the input requirements outlined in the paint-estimate exercise at the end of Chapter 3. Use label and input elements to create the form. The form should be designed to execute a program named **paint-estimate.php** (you will have a chance to code this at the end of the next chapter). The three input fields should be named **roomLength**, **roomWidth**, and **roomHeight**. Note that clicking the Submit button will generate an error since **paint-estimate.php** does not exist yet.

Figure 4-9 shows how your form should appear.

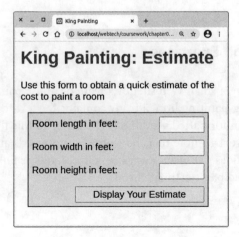

Figure 4-9: paint-estimate.html

3. Imagine you have developed an excellent educational computer game called **SaveTheWorld**. Create an HTML document named **software-order.html** based on the input requirements outlined in the software-order exercise at the end of Chapter 3. The form should be designed to execute a program named **software-order.php** (**you will have a chance to code this at the end of the next chapter**). Use a drop down list to obtain the choice of operating system (Linux, macOS, Windows), and a textbox for the number of copies. The name for the drop down selection should be **os**, and the name for number of copies should be **numCopies**. Figure 4-10 shows the layout for your form.

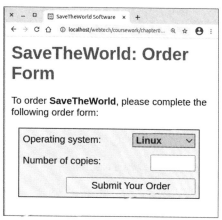

Figure 4-10: software-order.html

4. Create an HTML document named **travel.html** based on the requirements outlined in the travel exercise at the end of Chapter 3. The form should be designed to execute a program named **travel.php** (you will have a chance to code this at the end of the next chapter). Use text boxes for the two input fields. The names for the two fields should be **numTravelers** and **numNights**. Figure 4-11 shows the layout for your form.

Figure 4-11: travel.html

5. Create an HTML document named **game-intro.html** based on the requirements outlined in the game-intro exercise at the end of Chapter 3. The form should execute a program named **game-intro.php** (you will have a chance to code this at the end of the next chapter). The form should allow the user to type a **name** for the character, choose the **type** of character from a drop down list (Dwarf, Elf, Human, or Wizard), choose the number of **health tokens** to be purchased from a drop down list (0, 10, 20, or 30), choose the number of **experience tokens** to be purchased from a drop down list (0, 2, 4, 6, 8, or 10), and choose the number of **supply tokens** to be purchased from a drop down list (0, 25, 50, 75, or 100). The form should be designed to execute a program named gameIntro.php. Use these names for the input fields: **charName, charType, healthTokens, expTokens, supplyTokens.** Figure 4-12 shows how the form should appear but feel free to play with the exact appearance of the form and if you prefer you can come up with your own character types.

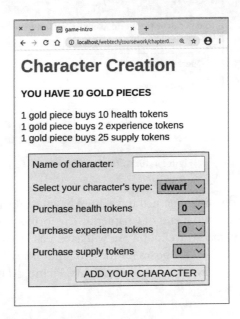

Figure 4-12: game-intro.html

6. Your **chapter04** folder contains a folder named **story**. The **story** folder contains three .html pages named **scene1.html, scene2.html,** and **scene3.html.** Open scene1.html in your Web browser and click the links provided until you see how the three scenes work together. Figure 4-13 shows two of the scenes. Now look at the code for these three files.

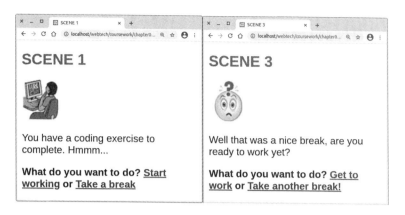

Figure 4-13: scene1.html and scene3.html

Come up with a story of your own. Change the three scenes and add one or two more scenes to make it interesting. Your scenes could constitute an adventure, a series of quiz questions, a journey, a collection of family photos, or something that only your imagination can come up with! If you need some clipart, a good site for free images is: **https://openclipart.org/**

Your images may be larger than those shown in the example, but keep them small enough so that the user does not need to scroll down to see the entire page. Also, whatever images you use, make them consistent in size so that your scenes do not jump around each time you click on a new page. Have fun!

7. Your **chapter04** folder contains a folder named **maze**. This folder provides the file for a simple maze game: **maze.jpg**, and 17 .html files named **maze0.html**, **maze1.html**, **maze2.html**, etc. **maze0.html** provides the entrance to the maze and displays a map of the maze (see Figure 4-14). The maze consists of 16 locations. **maze1.html** is the upper left location, **maze2.html** is the location to right (east) of **maze1.html**. **maze5.html** is the location below (to the south of) **maze1.html**, and so on. Each file displays a different location in the maze, from left to right, top to bottom. The goal of the player is get to Maze 13.

    View **maze0.html** in your Web browser to get started. As you move through the maze you will discover that there is a problem—four of the files need to be completed: **maze3.html**, **maze7.html**, **maze11.html**, **maze12.html**. These files are missing links to connect them to the rest of the maze. Your job is to complete these files so that the game can be completed. You can figure out what to add to these files by looking at the code for the other .html files, and referring to the map. Feel free to change **maze13.html** to achieve a more interesting ending!

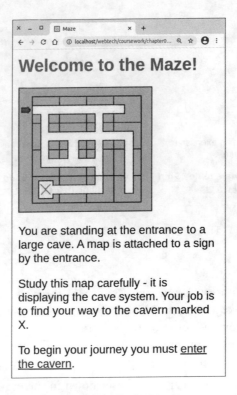

Figure 4-14: maze0.html

8. Complete the code in **event.html** based on the input requirements outlined in the event exercise at the end of Chapter 3 (see Figure 4-15). Be sure to save this to your **chapter04** folder. The event.html page should use an <h1> heading at the top and a paragraph to describe the performer. You can choose the performer and write a short description. Follow this with an <h2> tag to display a heading "To Purchase Tickets" followed by a form that requests a first name, phone number, and number of tickets (the prompt for number of tickets should also indicate that the tickets are $35 each). Use the names firstName, phone, and numTickets for these inputs. The form should be designed for submission to event.php which you will create in the next chapter. Run your Web server and test that this page displays correctly by opening a Web browser and using the URL:

    http://localhost/webtech/coursework/chapter04/event.html

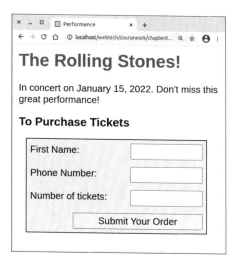

Figure 4-15: event.html

9. Complete the code in **fuel-cost.html** so that it meets the input requirements outlined in the fuel-cost exercise at the end of Chapter 3 (see Figure 4-16). Be sure to save this to your chapter04 folder. Use these names for your form inputs: mpg, miles, costPerGallon. Run your Web server and test that this page displays correctly by opening a Web browser and using the URL:

http://localhost/webtech/coursework/chapter04/fuel-cost.html.

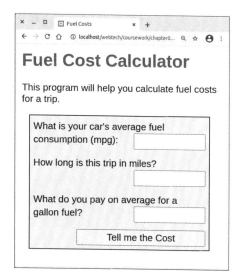

Figure 4-16: fuel-cost.html

Chapter 5

Creating a Working Program — Basics of PHP

Intended Learning Outcomes

- Distinguish between markup languages and programming languages.
- Develop .php files that combine PHP instructions with HTML tags.
- Write PHP instructions that correctly apply basic PHP syntax.
- Create and use variables in PHP instructions.
- Write instructions that use the $_POST array to receive input from an HTML form.
- Create expressions that perform basic arithmetic in PHP.
- Create expressions that use common PHP functions to perform calculations.
- Use print statements to generate HTML output from PHP code.
- Use the PHP number_format() function to format numeric output.
- Use the concatenation operator in print statements, to include values generated by PHP expressions, functions, and control structures.
- Explain the difference between syntax errors and logical errors.

Introduction

In Chapter 3, you learned how to read program requirements, design an interface, and develop program instructions in the form of **algorithms**. In Chapter 4, you learned to use HTML markup tags in order to create Web pages that include forms to obtain input from the user. It is now time to learn how to use a **programming language** to write code that is capable of retrieving this user input, processing data, and generating results. We will use the PHP programming language.

You may be confused concerning the difference between HTML and PHP. Why are you learning two languages anyway? Recall that HTML is a markup language and not a programming language. HTML is used to display or **render** data. We have learned how to use HTML tags for this purpose. Programming languages, on the other hand, are used to **process** data, for example, perform arithmetic operations, compare values, make decisions, store or retrieve data, display results, etc.

For example, you can use HTML to **display** a form that will submit someone's hourly wage and the hours worked but you cannot use HTML to **process** this input. You need a programming language to **retrieve** the hourly wage and hours worked that was submitted by the form, **multiply** these numbers to calculate the weekly pay, and **generate** new HTML to display the results. These are **data processing** operations.

Programming languages like PHP allow you to write processing instructions that make use of variables, assignment operations, arithmetic and logical expressions and input/output operations. In this chapter you will learn sufficient PHP syntax to perform basic data processing. In later chapters you will build on these skills to develop applications that can work with files and databases, perform tests, and repeat instructions. Appendix D will help you debug your code when you run into problems.

Why PHP?

Why use PHP when there are so many other programming languages to choose from? Programming languages are often classified as either **system** programming languages or **scripting** languages. The more traditional system programming languages (such as C, C++, C#, and Java) are usually **compiled** to run on different operating systems; programs written in these languages usually run faster, and are often intended for larger scale development and distribution. Scripting languages, such as PHP, Javascript, Python and Ruby, are usually **interpreted**; these languages are widely used for client/server applications that often consist of multiple short scripts that each perform small single-purpose processing tasks. (Review Chapter 1 for an explanation of the difference between compiled and interpreted languages.)

PHP is especially designed for use with HTML to develop Web applications. Learning to program with PHP will serve anyone interested in developing proficiency in Web programming since a high percentage of Web sites around the world are written in this language. PHP is also quite easy to learn which makes it ideal for learning the basics of programming. And since the general syntax is quite similar to many other programming languages, your experience with PHP will prepare you for learning these languages.

Working with HTML and PHP

You have learned to develop HTML pages with forms designed to obtain user input and submit this input to PHP programs for processing. Now it's time to develop those PHP programs! Let's start with the first wage example that we developed in Chapter 4. Here again are the algorithms for **wage1.html and wage1.php:**

```
wage1.html algorithm:
  Display Submit button to execute wage1.php
END
```

```
wage1.php algorithm:
  hourlyWage = 15.75
  hoursWorked = 19
  weeklyWage = hourlyWage * hoursWorked
  Display hourlyWage, hoursWorked, weeklyWage
END
```

Remember that algorithms are not computer programs; they are just a way to think through and plan the steps needed to create a working application. Algorithms are written in **pseudocode**, a mix of English words and code-like instructions. The only requirement for **wage1.html** is to display a Submit button that will execute wage1.php when it is clicked. We developed this in Chapter 4, using an HTML form, as follows:

```
<form action="wage1.php" method="post">
<input class = "submit" type="submit" value="Get Your Wage
Report Now">
</form>
```

The algorithm for **wage1.php** describes the instructions needed to calculate and display a weekly wage, based on a number of hours worked and an hourly wage. These instructions include calculations, which require the use a programming language. Here's how these instructions are actually written in the PHP language:

```
<html>
<head>
  <title>Wage Report</title>
  <link rel="stylesheet" type="text/css" href="sample.css">
</head>
<body>
  <h1>WAGE REPORT</h1>
  <?php
    $hourlyWage = 15.75;
    $hoursWorked = 19;
    $wage = $hourlyWage * $hoursWorked;

    print("<p>Your hourly wage is $$hourlyWage and you worked
      $hoursWorked hours.</p>");

    print("<p>Your wages are $$wage.</p>");
  ?>
</body>
</html>
```

Code Example: wage1.php

The first thing to notice is that this file contains a lot of HTML! PHP files can include sections of HTML code as well as sections of PHP code, however these sections are processed differently, and the PHP sections must be clearly identified. Your PHP code **must always** be located between PHP tags:

```
<?php
   ... php code is here ...
?>
```

If you include PHP code outside the PHP tags, this code will be treated as plain text and will simply be displayed on the Web page instead of being executed!

Similarly, HTML code and plain text **cannot** be directly included **inside** the PHP tags; only PHP code is allowed between <?php and ?>. If you include anything that is not PHP code between the PHP tags, an error message will be generated when the file is processed. Note that the wage1.php code is divided into three sections: first some HTML code, then a PHP section (between the <?php and ?> tags), and then two more lines of HTML.

How a .php File is Processed

When the PHP processor opens a .php file, it begins to dynamically build a new Web page that will be sent back to the user's browser to be displayed to the user. Whenever the processor encounters HTML code, this is added to the new page exactly as it is written. When the processor encounters a PHP section, the PHP instructions are processed. If you want to add output to the new page from **inside** a PHP section, you must do this using PHP **print** or **echo** statements. To understand this, let's see how **wage1.php** is processed.

As the processor works through **wage1.php**, the first lines in the file are standard HTML:

```
<html>
<head>
   <title>Wage Report</title>
   <link rel="stylesheet" type="text/css" href="sample.css">
</head>
<body>
   <h1>WAGE REPORT</h1>
```

These lines are simply directly added to the new page that is being generated.

The processor then reaches the <?php tag. The processor recognizes all statements between the <?php and ?> as PHP programming instructions that must be executed line by line. So the PHP instructions in **wage1.php** are:

```php
<?php
  $hourlyWage = 15.75;
  $hoursWorked = 19;
  $wage = $hourlyWage * $hoursWorked;
  print("<p>Your hourly wage is $$hourlyWage and you worked
    $hoursWorked hours.</p>");
  print("<p>Your wages are $$wage.</p>");
?>
```

Note that there are five instructions (or **program statements**), separated by semi-colons. **Every PHP instruction must end with a semi-colon.** Let's examine this code one instruction at a time.

```php
$hourlyWage = 15.75;
```

The first PHP instruction creates a variable named $hourlyWage and stores 15.75 in this variable. **In PHP all variable names must begin with a $ sign.** The = sign is the **assignment operator**, and so this is an instruction to assign the value 15.75 to $hourly-Wage. Another way of saying this is that 15.75 is **stored** in the variable $hourlyWage (remember that a variable is simply a user-defined name for a storage location).

```php
$hoursWorked = 19;
```

The second PHP instruction creates a variable called $hoursWorked and assigns the value 19 to this variable.

```php
$wage = $hourlyWage * $hoursWorked;
```

The third PHP instruction multiplies the value stored in $hourlyWage by the value stored in $hoursWorked, then stores the result in a new variable called $wage (so when executed this instruction will multiply **15.75** by **19**, and store the result, **299.25**, in **$wage**).

```php
print("<p>Your hourly wage is $$hourlyWage and you worked
  $hoursWorked hours.</p>");
```

This instruction uses the PHP **print** statement. Recall that HTML code cannot be directly included **inside** a PHP section, and PHP code cannot be included **outside** PHP sections. However we often need to create HTML code inside a PHP section in order to display values that our PHP has processed. Here we want to display a paragraph that contains the hourly wage and hours worked.

The PHP **print** statement allows us to generate HTML output inside our PHP sections. In this case the statement will add the following to the new Web page: "**<p>Your hourly wage is $**", followed by the value stored in **$hourlyWage**, followed by " **and you**

worked ", followed by the value stored in **$hoursWorked**, followed by " **hours.</p>**".
In other words this print instruction is putting together five pieces of data: there are
three literal character strings and the contents of two variables.

If you are wondering why "**$$hourlyWage**" includes two $ symbols, the first $ sym-
bol is intended to be actually displayed as part of the output, while the second $ symbol
is part of the variable name **$hourlyWage**.

The variable **$hourlyWage** contains the value 15.75 and the variable **$hoursWorked**
contains the value 19, so this print instruction will generate the following string and
add this to the text that is already part of the new HTML page:

```
<p>Your hourly wage is $15.75 and you worked 19 hours.</p>
```

The fifth PHP instruction also uses a print statement to generate output:

```
print("<p>Your wages are $$wage.</p>");
```

In this case, the statement is used to add a paragraph that includes the value stored in
the $wage variable. The statement generates the string "**<p>Your wages are $**", followed
by the value stored in the variable **$wage**, followed by the string "**.</p>**". Since the vari-
able **$wage** contains the value **299.25**, the actual output that is added to the new HTML
page is:

```
<p>Your wages are $299.25.</p>
```

That is the last PHP instruction but it is not the end of the wage1.php file. So far the
processor has constructed a new page that contains the HTML from wage1.php that
preceded the <?php tag, and the text that was generated **inside** the PHP section by the
two print statements. The processor now adds the remaining two lines of HTML that
are located **after** the PHP section:

```
</body>
</html>
```

Now that the processor has processed the entire file the new HTML page contains the
following:

```
<html>
<head>
  <title>Wage Report</title>
  <link rel="stylesheet" type="text/css" href="sample.css">
</head>
<body>
  <h1>WAGE REPORT</h1>
```

```
    <p>Your hourly wage is $15.75 and you worked 19 hours.</p>
    <p>Your wages are $299.25.</p>
</body>
</html>
```

Code Example: HTML output generated by wage1.php

The Web server now sends this page content back to the Web browser to be displayed to the user. Notice that there is **no** PHP code in this page. There is only the HTML code that was provided in **wage1.php**, combined with the HTML code that the PHP section generated when the **print** statements were processed.

Important Features of Client/Server Programs

To help understand this, let's review, without getting into much detail, the process by which a PHP program executes and generates a new Web document.

When the **submit** button on an HTML form is pressed, an action is submitted to a Web server. If the action specifies a PHP program the Web server looks for the requested **.php** file and processes the content of the file line by line in order to generate a new page to send back to the browser. Any text in the **.php** file that is located **outside** **<?php** and **?>** tags is added to the new document exactly as it is written. Each time that the processor finds a PHP code section in the file, this section is processed and if the code includes any **print()** instructions, the output from these instructions is added to the new page. When the end of the file is reached, the new page is sent back to the browser for display.

The two screens in Figure 5-1 show the original HTML document (**wage1.html**) that contains the form used to execute **wage1.php**, and the new document that is created on the server when **wage1.php** is processed and that is returned to the client.

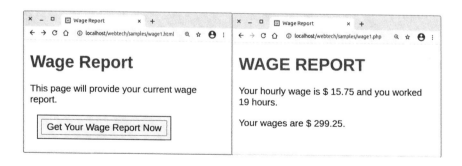

Figure 5-1: wage1.html and wage1.php screenshots

What is exciting about this is that, while **.html** files are **static** files that are stored on the Web server and the content is simply sent to the Web browser on request, **.php** files are **dynamic**. These files are also located on the Web server but when a **.php** file is requested the file is **processed**. As a result of the processing a new page is created and sent to the Web browser. The content and appearance of this document will depend on the PHP instructions in the file and, as you will see, may be different each time a user submits a request.

This is how Web sites provide you with information that is customized to your request. PHP is not the only language that can be used for this purpose. Dynamic web pages can be generated using any number of scripting languages. The process is very similar in all cases.

Consider two very important characteristics of client/server programming. First, the PHP program is located on a server, not on the user's computer. There is no need to install any software on the user's computer other than the Web browser. This means that software does not need to be distributed and that only a single copy is needed. This code can be easily maintained and modified with no need to change anything on the user's computer. Second, note that the user cannot access the PHP code. If the user clicks the **Page Source** option that can usually be found in a Web browser's **Developer** menu option, he or she will only see the HTML code for the page that was sent back to the server. So the PHP code is **secure** and cannot be viewed or modified by the end user.

Receiving Input from a Form — wage2.php

Now let's convert our Wage2 example — recall that this example included user input. Here are the algorithms for **wage2.html** and **wage2.php**:

```
wage2.html algorithm:
   Prompt user for hourly wage
   Get hourlyWage
   Prompt user for hours worked
   Get hoursWorked
   Submit hourlyWage, hoursWorked to wage2.php
END
```

```
wage2.php algorithm:
   Receive hourlyWage, hoursWorked from wage2.html
   weeklyWage = hourlyWage * hoursWorked
   Display hourlyWage, hoursWorked, weeklyWage
END
```

First let's review the code for wage2.html (this contains the HTML form that allows the user to input values for the hourly wage and hours worked):

```
<html>
<head>
  <title>Wage Report</title>
  <link rel="stylesheet" type="text/css" href="sample.css">
</head>
<body>
  <h1>Wage Report</h1>
  <form action="wage2.php" method="post">
    <label>Hourly wage:
    <input type="text" size="10" name="hourlyWage"></label>
    <label>Hours worked:
    <input type="text" size="10" name="hoursWorked"></label>
    <input class="submit" type="submit" value="Get Your Wage
    Report Now">
  </form>
</body>
</html>
```

Code Example: wage2.html

Note that this form (see Figure 5.2) is designed to receive input from the user in text boxes, and that the names given to these boxes are **hourlyWage** and **hoursWorked**. The values that are entered by the user will be associated with these names and submitted for processing by **wage2.php** when the Submit button is pressed.

Now let's look at the PHP code in the **wage2.php** file:

```
<html>
<head>
  <title>Wage Report</title>
  <link rel="stylesheet" type="text/css" href="sample.css">
</head>
<body>
  <h1>Wage Report</h1>

  <?php
    $hourlyWage = $_POST['hourlyWage'];
    $hoursWorked = $_POST['hoursWorked'];

    $wage = $hourlyWage * $hoursWorked;

    print("<p>Your hourly wage is $$hourlyWage and you worked
      $hoursWorked hours.</p>");

    print("<p>Your wages are $$wage.</p>");
  ?>
</body>
</html>
```

Code Example: wage2.php

Note that this program is very similar to **wage1.php** except that **wage2.php** does not contain the first two assignment statements that were included in **wage1.php**:

```
$hourlyWage = 15.75;
$hoursWorked = 19;
```

Instead, **wage2.php** includes the following two statements:

```
$hourlyWage = $_POST['hourlyWage'];
$hoursWorked = $_POST['hoursWorked'];
```

Recall that each of two text boxes in the form provided by **wage2.html** included a **name** attribute. The name of the first text box was **hourlyWage** and the name of the second text box was **hoursWorked**. When the form is submitted, the server receives these two names along with the values that the user typed into each text box. The server provides this information to the PHP program in a structure known as a **$_POST** array. The detailed structure of the $_POST array will be explained in Chapter 12. For now, you only need to understand how to use the $_POST array to retrieve values from HTML forms.

The $_POST array contains every value that was sent to the server when the user submitted the form. Each value is identified by the name that was specified in the form's input field. For example if the name used in the form's input field was 'hourlyWage' then the value is stored in **$_POST['hourlyWage']**. So the PHP program can obtain any of the submitted values simply by referencing the $_POST array, using the name of the appropriate input field. In our example we assign each value from the $_POST array to a PHP variable for use in subsequent program statements, for example we assign the value received from the "hourlyWage" text box to a variable named $hourlyWage.

Whenever your PHP program needs to obtain values that were submitted from an HTML form using the "post" method, your code will need to include statements that extract the values from the **$_POST** array. Be careful to use the correct syntax. The name **$_POST** must be followed by square brackets containing the name of the appropriate form field in single or double quotes. The name of the form field should not begin with a $ sign since this is not a PHP variable name.

It is not actually necessary to assign the value from the $_POST array to a variable that has the same name. You can use any variable names that you want, for example **$employeeWage = $_POST['hourlyWage'];** would work just as well as **$hourlyWage = $_POST['hourlyWage'];**. In that case, of course, the variable **$employeeWage** would then need to be used throughout the remainder of the program instead of $hourlyWage.

Now that the values have been received from the form and stored in **$hourlyWage** and **$hoursWorked**, the third line of PHP code simply multiplies the values stored in these two variables and stores the result in the **$wage** variable, similar to **wage1.php**:

```
$wage = $hourlyWage * $hoursWorked;
```

The program then generates text to be added to the new HTML page.

```
print("<p>Your hourly wage is $$hourlyWage and you worked
   $hoursWorked hours.</p>");

print("<p>Your wages are $$wage.</p>");
```

These statements are identical to those used in **wage1.php**.

To see what happens here, let's just assume that the user had submitted **10.75** for an hourly wage and **25** for hours worked. These values were transmitted to the server and provided to our program in the $_POST array; the PHP program assigned these to the variables $hourlyWage and $hoursWorked, and the result of multiplying these values was assigned to $wage. By the time the processor reaches the two print statements, the values stored in **$hourlyWage**, **$hoursWorked** and **$wage** will be **10.75, 25** and **268.75** respectively. So the print statements will insert the following into the new HTML page:

```
<p>Your hourly wage is $10.75 and you worked 25 hours.</p>
<p>Your wages are $268.75.</p>
```

The entire new page will therefore look like this:

```
<html>
<head>
  <title>Wage Report</title>
  <link rel="stylesheet" type="text/css" href="sample.css">
</head>
<body>
  <h1>WAGE REPORT</h1>
  <p>Your hourly wage is $10.75 and you worked 25 hours.</p>
  <p>Your wages are $268.75.</p>
</body>
</html>
```

Code Example: HTML output generated by wage2.php

The actual values for the hourly wage, hours worked and wage will of course depend on the values for the hourly wage and hours worked that were entered by the user.

Figure 5-2 illustrates a sample interaction using these user inputs.

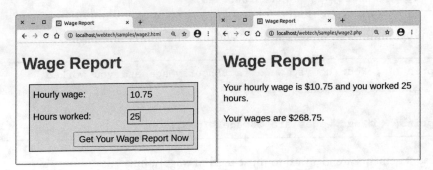

Figure 5-2: wage2.html and wage2.php screenshots

Processing the Smoking Survey — smoking.php

Now let's code the Smoking Calculator program. Here are the algorithms for smoking.html and smoking.php:

```
smoking.html algorithm:
   Prompt for firstName
   Get firstName
   Prompt for lastName
   Get lastName
   Prompt for yearsSmoked
   Get yearsSmoked
   Prompt for smokedDaily
   Get smokedDaily
   Submit firstName, lastName, yearsSmoked, smokedDaily to
     smoking.php
END
```

```
smoking.php algorithm:
   Receive firstName, lastName, yearsSmoked, smokedDaily from
smoking.html
   totalSmoked = yearsSmoked * 365 * smokedDaily
   Display firstName, lastName, yearsSmoked, smokedDaily,
totalSmoked
END
```

Here is the code for **smoking.html**:

```html
<html>
<head>
  <title>Smoking Calculator</title>
  <link rel="stylesheet" type="text/css" href="sample.css">
</head>
<body>
  <h1>Welcome to the Smoking Calculator!</h1>
  <form action="smoking.php" method="post" >

    <label>First name?
    <input type="text" size="15" name="firstName"></label>

    <label>Last name?
    <input type="text" size="15" name="lastName"></label>

    <label>How long have have you smoked (years)?
    <input type="text" size="5" name="yearsSmoked"></label>

    <label>How many cigarettes have you smoked on average
    every day (roughly)?
    <select name="smokedDaily">
      <option>0</option>
      <option>1</option>
      <option>2</option>
      <option>5</option>
      <option>10</option>
      <option>20</option>
      <option>30</option>
      <option>40</option>
    </select></label>

    <p><input class="submit" type="submit" value="Tell me the
    bad news">
    </form>
    </body>
    </html>
```

Code Example: smoking.html

Recall that this form contains four input fields. Three of these are text boxes, named firstName, lastName and yearsSmoked. The fourth is a drop down list, named smoked-Daily. When the Submit button is pressed the input from these fields will be passed to the Web server for processing by smoking.php.

Here is the code for smoking.php:

```
<html>
<head>
   <title>Smoking Calculator - RESULTS</title>
   <link rel="stylesheet" type="text/css" href="sample.css">
</head>
<body>
<?php
   $yearsSmoked = $_POST['yearsSmoked'];
   $smokedDaily = $_POST['smokedDaily'];
   $firstName = $_POST['firstName'];
   $lastName = $_POST['lastName'];

   $totalCigarettes = $yearsSmoked * 365 * $smokedDaily;

   print ("<h1>Smoking Calculator Results for
      $firstName $lastName</h1>");
   print("<p>Years smoked: $yearsSmoked<br>");
   print("Average number of cigarettes smoked daily:
      $smokedDaily</p>");
   print ("<p>$firstName, you have smoked approximately
      $totalCigarettes cigarettes.</p>");

   print ("<p><a href=\"smoking.html\">Return to Calculator
      </a></p>");
?>
</body>
</html>
```

Code Example: smoking.php

The server receives the names of the form fields firstName, lastName, yearsSmoked and smokedDaily, as well as the values that the user entered into these fields, and delivers these to the PHP program in the $_POST array. The program retrieves the values from the $_POST array and assigns these to PHP variables by referencing the names of the form's input fields:

```
$yearsSmoked = $_POST['yearsSmoked'];
$smokedDaily = $_POST['smokedDaily'];
$firstName = $_POST['firstName'];
$lastName = $_POST['lastName'];
```

The next PHP instruction multiplies the value stored in $yearsSmoked by 365 by the value stored in $smokedDaily and stores the result in a new variable $totalCigarettes:

```
$totalCigarettes = $yearsSmoked * 365 * $smokedDaily;
```

The remaining statements create text that becomes part of the new HTML document.

Note that in this example a print() statement is used to create the heading:

```
print (" <h1>Smoking Calculator Results for $firstName
    $lastName</h1>");
```

This heading must be included in the PHP section because it displays the last and first names and these are stored in PHP variables **$firstName** and **$lastName**. We can only refer to PHP variables **within** our PHP code section, and we can only generate HTML within PHP code sections using a PHP **print()** statement.

Figure 5-3 shows a sample interaction. The second screen shows the document created by **smoking.php** after processing data submitted from the form supplied by **smoking.html**.

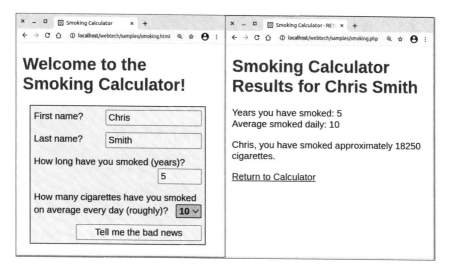

Figure 5-3: smoking.html and smoking.php screenshots

Using Fewer print() Statements

The smoking.php code contains **six** print statements, and each of these statements contains the output for a single heading or paragraph. This is not actually necessary; a single print statement can be used to provide output for any combination of text and HTML elements. For example the first three print statements in smoking.php could be written as a single print statement:

```
print ("<h1>Smoking Calculator Results</h1>for $firstName $last-
Name</h1><p>Years smoked: $yearsSmoked<br>Average number of cig-
arettes smoked daily: $smokedDaily</p>");
```

Using more or fewer print statements makes no difference with regard to the execution of the program, more print statements are used in the textbook examples just to make them more readable as you read through the code.

PHP — General Guidelines and Syntax

You are now ready to develop PHP code to process input from your own forms. First let's review some important guidelines and syntax rules to help you get started writing PHP.

Every PHP statement must end with a semi-colon

If you leave out a semi-colon the processor will generate an error message.

Variable names must follow PHP naming rules

The first character of a PHP variable name must always be a $ sign.

The second character must be a letter a–z, A–Z, or else an underscore.

After the first two characters, any combination of numeric digits and other characters are allowed. **However spaces are not allowed anywhere in a variable name.**

Here are some examples of **valid** variable names:

```
$userName
$employee1
$averageSalary
```

Here are some examples of **invalid** variable names:

```
$My Salary (spaces are not allowed)
$1stProgram (2nd character cannot be a digit)
salary3 (1st character must be a $)
```

PHP is case-sensitive

For example variables named **$salary**, **$Salary** and **$SALARY** will be considered to be three entirely different variables! So be careful not to mistype the name of a variable when you refer to it more than once — copying and pasting variable names helps to avoid this problem.

Variable names should be meaningful

The use of meaningful variable names makes it easy for another programmer to understand how a variable is being used. For example, **$averageSalary** and **$userPassword** are good variable names because it is obvious what they are being used for. However **$c1** and **$hgTER34** are poor variable names because it is not clear what they might contain.

The first letter of a PHP variable name should be lower-case

By convention in PHP the first letter in a variable name is lower-case. Underscores or upper-case letters are included in the variable if it contains multiple English words, for example, **$distanceToMoon** or **$distance-to-moon**. Notice that either of these are much easier to read than **$distancetomoon**. Using an uppercase letter to begin each English word within a variable name is referred to as **camelback**, or camel case, notation. In this book we follow the common convention of using camelback notation to separate English words in variable names, for example **$distanceToMoon**, and hyphens to separate English words in file names, for example **distance-to-moon.php**.

PHP variables are created the first time that they appear in the code

In PHP a variable is created the first time that the variable name appears in the code. You can create as many variables as you need. Once a variable has been created, your code can refer to it as often as necessary. If a numeric variable is used in a calculation or **print()** function before it has been assigned a value, the processor automatically assigns the value 0 to the variable. This can lead to trouble! Here's an example where the programmer mistypes a variable name:

```
$hourlyWage = 15.75;
$hoursWorked = 19;
$wage = $hourlyWage * $housrWorked;
```

In this example the value stored in **$wage** will be 0. Why? Because **$hoursWorked** has been mistyped as **$housrWorked** in the last statement. The processor thinks that this is a new variable and since it has no value it is assigned 0, and this is used in the calculation. The best protection against mistyping variable names is to copy and paste and avoid retyping a variable name! It is also important to test your programs carefully to ensure your calculations are working correctly.

PHP allows you to mix data types

PHP assumes that you know what you are doing with your variables and this can get you into trouble if you're not careful. For example PHP will allow the following:

```
$firstName = "Mary";
$age = 30;
$result = $firstName * $age;
```

The third statement appears to multiply the character string "Mary" by 30! In fact the processor sets the integer value of **$firstName** to 0 in order to perform the calculation so the result is that 0 is stored in the **$result** variable. It is up to you to protect your code against these type of errors. Later we will look at ways to validate input to help avoid these problems.

Variables can receive data from forms

As you saw in the **wage2.php** example, when form data is submitted to a PHP program for processing, the server provides a **$_POST** array which contains the values submitted to the form, indexed by the names of the form's input fields. These values can be extracted from the **$_POST** array by referencing the appropriate field name (for example **$_POST['hourlyWage']**). In this textbook we will make it a practice to assign all of the values received in the **$_POST** array to PHP variables with the same name as the form names, although this is not necessary.

Values are assigned to variables using the assignment operator

As we saw in our examples, assignment statements are used to store values in variables. Assignment statements use the = sign as an **assignment operator**. The syntax is always in the form

```
<variable> = expression;
```

where the variable on the left of the assignment operator will receive a value. The expression on the right side of the operator will be calculated and the resulting value assigned. Note that the expression is evaluated **before** a value is assigned to the variable on the left of the assignment operator. The following examples are all valid assignments:

```
$retailPrice = 20.56;
$tax = $retailPrice * 0.07.
$total = $retailPrice + $tax;
$firstName = "Mary";
$lastName = "Jones";
$fullName = "$firstName $lastName";
```

In the last statement the **$fullName** variable receives the string contained in **$firstName** followed by a space followed by the string contained in **$lastName**.

Values stored in variables can be replaced by new values

You can replace the value that is stored in a variable, for example:

```
$retailPrice = 20.56;

(... other code here ...)

$retailPrice = 75.50;
```

In this example, 20.56 is stored in **$retailPrice**, then later on the program 75.50 is stored in the same variable. Before this second assignment, **$retailPrice** contains **20.56**, but after this statement **$retailPrice** contains **75.50** and the previous value is lost.

A variable can appear on BOTH sides of an assignment

You can also modify the value stored in a variable and store the result back into the same variable, replacing the old value. This can be very useful, for example, when we need to accumulate a total:

```
$total = 225.25;
$nextPurchase = 14.75;
$total = $total + $nextPurchase;
```

In this example, 225.25 is stored in **$total**, then **14.75** is stored in **$nextPurchase**. The next statement adds the value stored in **$total** to the value stored in **$nextPurchase**, and stores the result back into **$total**. So **$total** now contains the value **240.00** and the previous value (**225.25**) has been lost.

Using the same variable on both sides of the = operator can be confusing at first since you are probably used to using the = operator in **mathematical equations**. In mathematics a statement like $x = x + 5$ doesn't make any sense. But in programming the = operator is used for **assignments**; it is simply an instruction to **store** the result of the expression on the right into the variable on the left, so $x = x + 5$ is a perfectly valid assignment which simply states: **add 5 to the value currently stored in x and store the result back into x** (which will replace the value previously stored in x).

We often find it useful to use a variable to count something, for example the number of students who are registering for a class. For example, if we are using a variable named **$numberOfStudents**, every time a new student registers we could **increment**, or add 1 to, the value already stored in this variable with the statement:

```
$numberOfStudents = $numberOfStudents + 1;
```

In other words, add 1 to the number already stored in $numberOfStudents, and assign this new value to the variable (which will replace the previous value).

This operation is so common that most languages, including PHP, provide a **shortcut** increment operator ++. So the last statement can simply be written

```
$numberOfStudents++;
```

which means add 1 to the value currently stored in the **$numberOfStudents** variable.

Similarly variables are often used to count **down**, or **decrement**. So if a student leaves the class we can decrement the value currently stored in **$numberOfStudents** as follows:

```
$numberOfStudents = $numberOfStudents - 1;
```

Or we can simply use the decrement operator:

```
$numberOfStudents--;
```

Note that the increment and decrement **shortcut** operators must not include spaces. A complete list of PHP shortcut operators can be found in Chapter 16.

Special note: assigning different data types to a variable

If you have previous experience programming in other languages, you may be surprised to learn that PHP variables do not need to be declared as a specific data type before they can be used. PHP determines the appropriate data type for a variable at the time that a value is assigned or used in an expression. Chapter 16 discusses the significance of data types in more detail.

Arithmetic Expressions

Let's look more carefully at arithmetic expressions. The **arithmetic operators** are:

+	(addition)	-	(subtraction)
*	(multiplication)	/	(division)
%	(modulus)		

When the processor encounters an arithmetic expression, **multiplication** and **division** operations are evaluated first in order from left to right, then **addition** and **subtraction** operations are evaluated in order from left to right. For example 1 + 2 * 3 - 4 first evaluates to 1 + 6 - 4 which evaluates to 7 - 4 which evaluates to **3**.

Parentheses can be used to change the **precedence** of operations in an expression. Any part of the expression that is enclosed in parentheses is evaluated first. For example (1 + 2) * (3 - 4) evaluates to 3 * (3 - 4) which evaluates to 3 * -1 which evaluates to **-3**.

If parentheses are nested the expressions inside the innermost parentheses are evaluated first, followed by the expressions inside the next innermost parentheses, and so on. For example (1 +2) * (3 / (4 - 1)) evaluates to (1 +2) * (3 / 3) which evaluates to (3) * (3 / 3) which evaluates to 3 * 1 which evaluates to **3**.

Arithmetic can include any combination of literal values and variables, for example the following calculation includes two variables and the literal value **40** (note that this assumes that **$hourlyWage** and **$deductions** have already been assigned values otherwise **0** will be assigned to **$weeklyWage**!):

```
$weeklyWage = ($hourlyWage * 40) - $deductions;
```

The **modulus operator** % is a **division** operator that calculates the **remainder** of a division. For example the result of **5 % 3** is **2** since 3 divides into 5 once with a remainder of 2. Similarly the result of **15 % 4** is **3** since 4 divides into 15 three times with a remainder of 3. Finding the remainder of a division can be useful for lots of real-world problems; for example if you have a piece of wood that is 60" inches long, and you cut it into 24" sections, you can calculate the length of wood that is left over using 60 % 24 (since 24 divides into 60 twice with a remainder of 12, the result is 12"). You can also use the modulus operator to test if a number divides into another perfectly, since this would have a result of 0 (for example 60 % 12 is 0 since 12 divides into 60 5 times with a 0 remainder).

Using Arithmetic Functions

Most programming languages, including PHP, provide a number of useful arithmetic **functions**. A function provides pre-written code to perform a useful task. Most programming languages provide a library of standard functions that can be called as needed by your programs. In a later chapter you will also learn how to create your own functions.

Functions do not just simplify the programmer's task. By using functions that have already been developed and thoroughly tested, the programmer does not run the risk of introducing errors by writing new code unnecessarily. It is considered good programming practice to always use existing functions when these are available. This practice aligns with the general principle of **reusability**.

In most languages, including PHP, functions are represented in code statements by specifying the function name followed by a pair of parentheses. If the function requires any arguments (values that the function needs in order to perform its task) then these are included within the parentheses in the order that the function expects. Multiple arguments must be separated by commas.

Here is a list of some common arithmetic functions in PHP, along with examples of their use:

pow()

The **pow()** function is used to raise a value to an exponent, for example **pow(2, 3)** will calculate the value of 2 cubed, while **pow(5, 17)** will calculate the value of 5 to the power of 17. The pow() function requires two arguments, the value to be raised, followed by the exponent. Variables can be used as arguments, so for example if you want to square the value stored in **$number** and store the result in a variable named **$square**, you could write:

```
$square = pow($number, 2);
```

and if you wanted to raise the value stored in **$number** by the value stored in **$exponent** and store the result in a variable named **$result**, you could write:

```
$result = pow($number, $exponent);
```

pi()

The **pi()** function simply delivers an accurate value for PI. If you need to use PI in a calculation this is a much better approach than typing in a value directly. For example if the radius of a circle is stored in **$radius**, you could calculate and store the circumference as follows:

```
$circumference = 2 * pi() * $radius;
```

To calculate the area you could use the **pi()** and **pow()** functions in your expression:

```
$area = pi() * pow($radius, 2);
```

Note that, unlike the pow() function, the pi() function does not have any arguments. The parentheses are still required however to indicate that pi() is a function.

round()

The **round()** function can be used to round a number to the nearest integer value. For example **round(3.8)** will generate the value **4**, while **round(3.2)** will generate the value **3**. The **round()** function can also be directed to round off to any number of places by adding a second argument that indicates the required number of decimal places, for example **round(3.828, 2)** will generate the value **3.83**.

ceil()

The **ceil()** function is similar to the **round()** function except that it always rounds up for positive numbers or down for negative numbers. For example **ceil(3.8)** will generate the value **4**, while **ceil(3.2)** will also generate the value **4**. This is useful for certain calculations. Consider a program that must calculate the number of gallons of paint needed to paint a wall at the rate of 200 square feet a gallon. If we divide the area of the wall by 200 we always want the result to be rounded up in order to know how many gallons of paint we need to purchase, for example:

```
gallonsOfPaint = ceil($wallArea / 200);
```

floor()

The **floor()** function is also similar to the **round()** function except that it always rounds down for positive numbers or up for negative numbers. For example **floor(3.8)** will generate the value **3**, while **floor(3.2)** will also generate the value **3**. This is useful for certain calculations. Consider a program that contains a variable **$months** and that the value in this variable needs to be broken down into years and months. If we divide **$months** by 12, we will get the number of years, but this may include a decimal value (for example if **$months** contains 28, this will generate **2.33333..**). We round down to the actual number of years using the **floor()** function, and then we use the modulus operator to figure the number of months left over:

```
$years = floor($months / 12);
$monthsLeftOver = $months % 12;
```

The first statement uses the floor() function to obtain the number of years; this will be the number of months divided by 12, rounded down to the nearest whole number. The second statement uses the modulus operator to calculate the number of months left over; this will be the remainder after dividing the value stored in **$months** by 12. For example if **$months** contains 28, $years will contain 2 (the rounded down result of dividing 28 by 12), and **$monthsLeftOver** will contain 4 (the remainder from dividing 28 by 12). You can use this approach to do all kinds of conversions, for example from inches to feet and inches (or even from inches to yards, feet, and inches, although this would require additional calculations, which you might want to try and work out for yourself).

sqrt()

The **sqrt()** function will return the square root of a value. For example sqrt(16) will generate a value of 4.

rand()

The **rand()** function can be used to generate a random number in any range. For example **rand(1, 10)** will generate a random number between 1 and 10. If **rand()** is used with no arguments, it will generate a decimal value between 0 and 1. Random numbers are useful for many purposes and are often used in simulations and games.

Chapter 16 includes a much more extensive list of standard PHP functions.

White Space in PHP Files

The PHP processor ignores white space (extra blank spaces, tabs, new lines) except in output statements. That means that the previous code examples could be written much less neatly! For example, **wage1.php** could be written like this:

```
<html><head>        <title>Wage Report</title><link rel
="stylesheet" type="text/css" ref
="sample.css"></head><body><h1>WAGE REPORT</h1><?php $hourlyWage =
15.75; $hoursWorked = 19; $wage
= $hourlyWage * $hoursWorked; print("<p>Your hourly wage is
$hourlyWage." and you worked $hoursWorked hours.</p>");
print("<p>Your wages
are $$wage.</p>");?></body></html>
```

This code will actually produce the same results as the previous version but obviously this is much harder to read and that is why we type in our code neatly!

There are two important reasons to write code neatly using a standard layout. First you will often need to refer back to your own code in order to make corrections or modifications. Second, other programmers may also need to reference your code, for example, if you are part of a team, or if someone else takes over your role when you get promoted. A programmer can lose significant time trying to read poorly written code. Many software companies require their programmers to follow certain conventions in code layout and documentation.

Generating Character Strings from PHP

As we saw in our three code examples, a **.php** file is often used to dynamically generate a return page in response to a request from a user. The **.php** file can contain sections of HTML code and sections of PHP code. The processor assembles the new page by working through the **.php** file line by line. Whenever it reads a section of HTML, this is added to the new page exactly as it appears in the **.php file**. Whenever it finds a section of PHP code, the processor processes the PHP instructions. If the PHP code includes **print**() statements, the output from these statements is added to the new page.

The syntax we are using for the **print**() statement is:

```
print (" ... your HTML output here ...");
```

The parentheses and the choice to use double quotes (are actually optional in PHP but we will use them in this book so that our syntax is more consistent with other languages). You can place any character string that you wish to output between the quotes. A character string is simply a sequence of characters that can be read as text. For example "How are you?" is a character string, and so is "123 Main Street" and "Please enter your first name: " and "Italy" and "dfge+%*?f12&". In fact the text of this book is also one very long character string! Character strings can include HTML tags, so for example "<p>Hello, how are you today?</p>" is a character string that includes opening and closing paragraph tags. That means that we can include strings that contain

HTML tags in our print statements and these tags will be added to the return document along with the other text in the string.

PHP also allows you to include variables within the quotes as part of your character string, in which case the value of the variable is displayed, for example:

```
print ("<p>Hello, $firstName, how are you today?<p>");
```

Be careful! Remember to include the $ symbol before your variable name, otherwise the PHP processor will think your variable name is just part the character string that is to be displayed! For example, consider this version of the previous print statement:

```
print ("<p>Hello, firstName, how are you today?<p>");
```

Since there is no $ to indicate a variable, this statement will simply assume that the word "firstName" is part of the string and display this word literally (try it).

If you require spaces, commas, periods or symbols (such as the $ symbol) to appear before or after the value of the variable in your output, be sure to include these in your character strings!

Including Double Quotes in Character Strings

Although it is not always required in PHP, most programming languages require you to indicate character strings in your code by enclosing them in quotes. This allows the language processor to distinguish between literal text that is to be treated as-written, and text that is part of the actual programming code. In this book we follow the standard convention of enclosing character strings in double quotes since that is a requirement for most languages. But using double quotes to surround our literal strings creates a problem: what if you need to display a double quote as **part** of the character string itself? If you need to include a double quote in your output, you must use \" instead of ". The **back slash** character tells the print statement that this quote is to be included as part of the character string, otherwise the processor will assume that the double quote indicates the end of the character string. For example:

```
print("<p>I said \"How are you today?\"</p>");
```

will generate:

```
<p>I said "How are you today?"</p>
```

The back slash is known as an escape character and is used to print a number of special characters (not just the double quote) that would otherwise be difficult to output. The use of escape characters is covered in more detail in the next chapter.

You can include HTML tags in your print() statements. For example:

```
print("<p>Your wages are $$wage.</p>");
```

You can also include HTML tags with attributes in your print() statements but remember to use \" when typing your attribute values since these are enclosed in double quotes. For example:

```
print("<a href=\"someFile.html\">Return to someFile</a>");
```

NOTE: PHP allow you to use either single OR double quotes to surround character strings. This means that you can use single quotes around a string that contains double quotes, in which case you no longer need to use \" in your string. Similarly, a string that contains a single quote can be surrounded by double quotes. There are also some difference in the way that strings are handled when enclosed in single or double quotes. For consistency, double quotes are used throughout this textbook, see **Chapter 16** for a more detailed comparison of single and double quotes.

Using the number_format() Function to Display Numbers to a Specific Number of Places

Often you want your program's numeric output to be formatted to display a specific number of decimal places. For example an employee's pay is a dollar amount and should always be displayed to exactly two places. However a calculation to multiply an hourly wage by hours worked may generate a value that contains more or less than two decimal places. For example if a variable named $wage contains 250.50, this would display as 250.5, and if it contained 250.576 this would display as 250.576. The **number_format()** function allows you to display a value to your preferred number of places without changing the value itself. For example **number_format($wage, 2)** will generate a character string with the value of the **$wage** variable rounded to two places, so if the variable contains **250.5**, this will generate "250.50", and if the variable contains **250.576**, this will generate "250.58", which is what we want. The **number_format()** function takes two arguments: a value and the number of decimal places to be displayed. The actual value stored in **$wage** is not changed and will remain 250.576.

This last point is worth stressing: number_format is used to **display** a value to a certain number of places but does not change the value itself. This is important, for example if the precise amount of daily rainfall is stored in a variable named **$dailyRainfall** as **1.26734** inches, you might want to use number_format to display this on a weather page to just one decimal place (**1.3** inches), using **number_format($dailyRainfall, 1**), but you would not want the actual rainfall amount stored in dailyRainfall (**1.26734**) to change, since this may be needed for other rainfall calculations.

Be careful not to confuse the number_format() function with the round() function. Whereas number_format() generates a new **character string** to **display** a number to a certain number of places, the round() function generates a new **numeric** value that has been rounded for use in **arithmetic calculations**. So for example **round(1.2, 2)** will return the value **1.2**, which may be useful for a calculation but does not provide a string formatted to 2 decimal places.

Including Calls to PHP Functions inside PHP Print Statements

We can use PHP functions such as number_format() in our print statements but we need to be careful how we do this. At first glance you might think that instead of:

```
print("<p>Your wages are $$wage.</p>");
```

you could simply use the following

```
print("<p>Your wages are $number_format($wage, 2).</p>");
```

But this will **not** work since PHP will assume you want to display the character string "number_format" exactly as written, as part of the output text, so, for example, if **$wage** contains the value **250.5**, this will display:

```
<p>Your wages are $number_format(250.5, 2).</p>");
```

This is definitely **not** what we want! We want PHP to understand that we are calling the **number_format()** function in order to round and display the value stored in **$wage** to 2 places.

To accomplish this, we must **separate** the call to the function from the literal character strings in our print statement. We do this as follows:

```
print("<p>Your wages are $".number_format($wage, 2).".</p>");
```

We need to consider the syntax of this statement carefully. This **print** statement now consists of three items: a character string ("**<p>Your wages are $**"), followed by a call to the **number_format()** function, followed by another character string ("**.</p>**"). The two character strings are enclosed in quotes to indicate that these contain literal text, while the call to the **number_format()** function is **not** enclosed in quotes to indicate that this is a PHP instruction that must be executed in order to obtain a value. There are periods between the two character strings and the call to the **number_format**() function. These periods are required and tell the **print** statement to **join** these three items (the first character string, the string returned by the call to the function, and the remaining character string) to create a single complete string that combines these. This process of combining a number of strings into a single string is termed **string concatenation.**

String Concatenation and the Concatenation Operator

In PHP the strings to be concatenated must be connected by periods and the period is known as the **concatenation operator** (some other languages use the + operator instead of the period as the concatenation operator). Concatenation is very useful to programmers since it is often important to add different strings together. We have just seen that it is necessary if you need to combine literal strings with a string produced by a call to a PHP function such as number_format(). Here is an example using the PHP pow() function:

```
print("<p>The cube of 34 is ".pow(34, 3)."</p>");
```

What if your program needs to create a string that contains a person's full name by joining the content of a variable that already contains a first name with a space, followed by the content of a variable that contains a last name? Look at this statement:

```
$fullName = $firstName." ".$lastName;
```

If **$firstName** contains "**Chris**" and **$lastName** contains "**Smith**", **$fullName** now contains "**Chris Smith**". Do you see the importance of the " " string in this concatenation of strings? Without it, **$fullName** would contain "**ChrisSmith**" with no space between the two names.

What if you need to display a complete address from variables that already contain the various parts of the address?

```
print("<p>I live at ".$streetAddress.", ".$city.", ".
    $state." ".$zip."</p>");
```

Look at this example carefully to see how commas and spaces are included in the address. You might also find it more useful to assign the complete address to a variable first and then display this variable:

```
$address = $streetAddress.", ".$city.", ".$state." ".$zip;
print("<p>I live at ".$address."</p>");
```

The advantage here is that you can now refer to the complete address elsewhere in your code since it has been stored in a variable.

You may be wondering why are we using concatenation in these last two examples since we can just refer to variables directly in character strings, for example:

```
print("<p>I live at $address</p>");
```

This is true, however in most programming languages, variables can never be included directly inside literal character strings and must **always** be concatenated. For this reason, some PHP programmers consider it good practice to **always** concatenate their variables, for example:

```
print("Hello, ".$firstName.", how are you today?");
```

instead of:

```
print("Hello, $firstName, how are you today?");
```

and

```
print("<p>Your hourly wage is $".$hourlyWage." and you worked
    ".$hoursWorked." hours.</p>");
```

instead of:

```
print("<p>Your hourly wage is $$hourlyWage and you worked
    $hoursWorked hours.</p>");
```

In this textbook, the variables are often included directly in literal character strings to keep the code samples as simple as possible.

The PHP Echo Statement

In addition to the **print** statement that has been applied in this book, PHP also offers the **echo** statement. The two are almost identical in operation, for example:

```
print ("Hello, $firstName, how are you today?");
```

could be written:

```
echo "Hello, $firstName, how are you today?";
```

This book uses the print statement with parentheses and double quotes simply because this is closer to the syntax of output statements in other languages. See chapter 16 for an explanation of the differences between print and echo.

Multiple PHP Sections

You can include as many PHP sections in your document as you want, as long as each PHP section contains only PHP instructions. The processor simply processes each PHP section that it finds, and adds any output from the **print** statements to the new HTML document that is being constructed. A .php file might contain many small PHP sections sandwiched between HTML code.

You can even place your **<?php** and **?>** at the very beginning and very end of the document! In that case ALL of the HTML code would have to be generated using **print** statements! However since it is easier to type HTML directly whenever you can, the more common practice is to mix PHP sections with HTML sections, and use print statements only when some HTML output **must** be generated by PHP code (for example when the HTML includes values from PHP variables, functions, or control structures). You will get a feel for this as you develop your own code. Always ensure that your HTML sections contain only text and HTML tags, and that any text and HTML that is generated in your PHP sections is coded inside print statements.

Finding Syntax Errors

Syntax errors are errors that prevent the processor from running the program. If the PHP processor is unable to understand an instruction it will generate an error message and stop executing. For example, you may forget semi-colons, mistype a variable name, include HTML within a PHP section without using a **print**() statement, refer to a variable or function outside a PHP section, forget to close a PHP section with ?>, etc.

Don't think it is unusual if you create a number of errors, or if you find it difficult to find some errors. The process of debugging code is an important and normal part of programming. **Appendix D** will help you find and resolve many common errors, and hopefully save you some frustration. Also the **Hints and Help** pages on the textbook Web site provide chapter-by-chapter help with problems you might encounter when working on the code exercises. It is also common practice to ask other programmers to look over your code; often a fresh eye can quickly identify an error that you've been staring at for hours!

Finding Logical Errors

Often the most difficult errors to find are **logical errors**. Logical errors occur when the program executes but does not work as expected. For example the program may generate incorrect output. Logical errors can be the result of inaccurate arithmetic expressions, statements that are out of order, or the wrong variables in expressions or print statements. In PHP, errors may also occur as a result of incorrect variable names since if you mistype a variable name, the processor just creates a new variable with your "new" name.

The only way to catch logical errors is to test your program carefully. Review your program requirements and consider what tests may be needed to ensure that your program is running correctly. When a program requires user input, run it with various input values so that you can check the results.

When we add selection and loop structures we will need to test code much more thoroughly — this will be covered in later chapters.

Additional Learning Materials

Chapter 16 provides more help with topics such as **short cut operators**, **string concatenation**, choosing between the PHP **print** and **echo** statements, the use of **single** and **double** quotes in strings, problems with "**smart**" quotes, as well as other topics related to later chapters. Chapter 16 also explains the conventions used in this book, so these are not confused with required PHP syntax.

Chapter 16 also explains PHP **data types**, and provides a more extensive list of PHP **functions**.

Appendix D will help you **debug** your exercises, listing a number of the most common errors that you are likely to encounter.

The **Chapter 5 Hints and Help** pages on the textbook Web site provides to FAQs from previous students as they worked through the end-of-chapter exercises.

Summary

PHP is a programming language that allows you to convert your algorithms into working Web programs. A PHP file may contain a combination of HTML code and PHP code. When the file is processed, the PHP processor reads the file line by line and generates a new page. Any HTML code is written directly into the new page. Any PHP code sections are processed and if these generate output from **print**() statements, this output is inserted into the new page. The print statements can include any combination of text, HTML tags and values from PHP variables and expressions. When the processor reaches the end of the file, the content of the new page is returned to the Web browser.

Every PHP statement ends with a **semi-colon**.

PHP variable names begin with a **$** symbol, followed by an alphabetic letter or underscore, followed by any combination of alphanumeric characters and underscores (some other characters are also allowed).

PHP is **case-sensitive**.

The **assignment** operator is used to assign values to PHP variables. The value of the expression on the right side of the assignment operator = is stored in the variable on the left side of the assignment operator.

Variables can be included in arithmetic expressions.

Parentheses change the **precedence of operations** in arithmetic expressions.

Standard PHP functions can be called as needed to perform a range of operations. Functions are called using the function **name** followed by **parentheses**. A function may require one or more arguments in order to perform its task.

The **number_format**() function is used to display a value to a certain number of places.

Character strings, variables and values returned by PHP functions such as number_format() can be joined together by a process known as **concatenation**, using the **concatenation operator** (which is a period in PHP).

A PHP program can receive input from an HTML form. The values from the form are submitted along with the names specified in the form for each input field. The server passes these values and the names to a PHP **$_POST** array. Each value can be extracted from the $_POST array by specifying the appropriate name.

Syntax errors will prevent the processor from processing PHP code and will generate error messages that must then be debugged.

Logical errors will not be caught by the processor and will not generate error messages. These are errors in the logic of the program and require testing to find.

Chapter 5 Review Questions

1. PHP is an example of a:
   a. System programming language
   b. Scripting language

2. Which statement is true?
   a. HTML files can contain HTML tags, text and PHP code
   b. PHP files can contain PHP code but not HTML tags
   c. PHP files can contain HTML tags, text and PHP code
   d. PHP files can contain PHP code and text but not HTML tags
   e. PHP files can contain HTML tags but no PHP code

3. Where must the PHP code be located inside a .php file?
   a. Between <?php and ?>
   b. Between <php> and </php>
   c. Between <? and ?>
   d. Between <php? and ?php>
   e. Between <php?> and </? >

4. Every PHP statement must end with:
   a. A period .
   b. A closing bracket >
   c. A double quote "
   d. A semi-colon ;
   e. An equals sign =

5. PHP variables must begin with:
   a. A lower-case letter
   b. An upper-case letter
   c. Either a lower-case letter or an upper-case letter
   d. A number
   e. A dollar sign $

6. Which one of the following is an acceptable name for a PHP variable?
   a. $this one
   b. thisOne
   c. this1
   d. $thisOne
   e. $1ofThese

7. Which one of the following correctly stores the result of 15 * 25 in a PHP variable?
   a. $result = 15 * 25;
   b. 15 * 25 = $result;
   c. result = 15 * 25;
   d. 25 * 15 = result;
   e. 15 * $result * 25;

8. What HTML code is generated after the following statements are executed?

```
$wage = 230.75;
print ("<p>Your wages are wage</p>");
```

   a. <p>Your wages are 230.75</p>
   b. <p>Your wages are 230.75;</p>
   c. <p>Your wages are $230.75</p>
   d. <p>Your wages are </p>
   e. <p>Your wages are wage</p>

9. Look at the following HTML form, then decide which one of the following statements is correct.

```
<form action="zip-it.php" method="post">
<label>Please enter your zip code:
<input type="text" size="20" name="zipCode"></label>
<input class="submit" type="submit" value="Submit your zip
    code">
</form>
```

   a. When the processor executes zip-it.php, the zip code submitted by the user can be extracted from $_POST['zip-it']
   b. When the processor executes zip-it.php, the zip code submitted by the user can be extracted from $_POST['$zip-it']
   c. When the processor executes zip-it.php, the zip code submitted by the user can be extracted from $_POST['zipCode']
   d. When the processor executes zip-it.php, the zip code submitted by the user can be extracted from $_POST['$zipCode']
   e. When the processor executes zip-it.php, the zip code submitted by the user can be extracted from $_POST['zip code']

10. The following HTML form passes a value to sleepy-time.php with the name sleep-Hours. Which PHP statement would correctly receive this value and assign it to a PHP variable named $sleepHours?

```
<form action="sleepy-time.php" method="post">
<label>How many hours do you sleep each night:
<input type="text" size="20" name="sleepHours"></label>
<input class="submit" type="submit" value="Can I sleep
now?">
</form>
```

     a. $_POST[$sleepHours] = 'sleepHours';
     b. $_POST['sleepHours'] = $sleepHours;
     c. sleepHours = $_POST[$sleepHours];
     d. $sleepHours = $_POST['sleepHours'];
     e. $sleepHours = $_POST[$sleepHours];

11. What is wrong with the following PHP code segment?

```
$discount = 2.50;
$itemCost = 10.50;
$reducedCost = $itemCost - $discount;
print ("<p>REDUCED FOR QUICK SALE!!
    Your cost is only $$itemCost!</p>");
```

     a. The first and second statements are in the wrong order
     b. The second and third statements are in the wrong order
     c. The third and fourth statements are in the wrong order
     d. The wrong variable is included in the print statement
     e. The value stored in $reducedCost will be 10.50 when it should be 8.00

12. What is wrong with the following PHP code segment?

```
$discount = 2.50;
$reducedCost = $itemCost - $discount;
$itemCost = 10.50;
print ("<p>REDUCED FOR QUICK SALE!!
    Your cost is only $$reducedCost!</p>");
```

     a. The first and second statements are in the wrong order
     b. The second and third statements are in the wrong order
     c. The third and fourth statements are in the wrong order
     d. The wrong variable is included in the print statement
     e. The value stored in $reducedCost will be 10.50 when it should be 8.00

13. What is wrong with the following PHP code segment?

```
$discount = 2.50;
$itemCost = 10.50;
$reducedCost = $itemCost - $Discount;
print ("<p>REDUCED FOR QUICK SALE!!
        Your cost is only $$reducedCost!</p>");
```

    a. The first and second statements are in the wrong order
    b. The second and third statements are in the wrong order
    c. The third and fourth statements are in the wrong order
    d. The wrong variable is included in the print statement
    e. A variable name has been mistyped.

14. What value is stored in $savings after these three PHP instructions are executed?

```
$savings = 500.00;
$deposit = 200;
$savings = $savings + $deposit;
```

    a. 200.00
    b. 500.00
    c. 700.00
    d. 1200.00
    e. Error! you cannot use the same variable on both sides of the = operator.

15. What value is stored in $result after this PHP instruction is executed?

```
$result = 2 + 3 * 5 - 1;
```

    a. 14
    b. 16
    c. 20
    d. 24
    e. 28

16. What value is stored in $result after this PHP instruction is executed?

```
$result = (2 + 3) * (5 - 1);
```

    a. 14
    b. 16
    c. 20
    d. 24
    e. 28

17. The value 2.4 will be stored in $gallonsNeeded after these three PHP instructions are executed. Which PHP function should you use to figure out how many gallon cans of paint you will need to buy (hint: you would need 3 cans)?

```
$areaToPaint = 1200;
$coveragePerGallon = 500;
$gallonsNeeded = $areaToPaint / $coveragePerGallon ;
```

    a. $gallonCansNeeded = round ($gallonsNeeded);
    b. $gallonCansNeeded = floor ($gallonsNeeded);
    c. $gallonCansNeeded = ceil ($gallonsNeeded);
    d. $gallonCansNeeded = pow ($gallonsNeeded);
    e. $gallonCansNeeded = sqrt ($gallonsNeeded);

18. What HTML code will the following print statement generate?

```
print("<p>She said \"You're hired!\" </p>");
```

    a. She said \"You're hired!\"
    b. <p>She said \"You're hired!\" </p>
    c. She said "You're hired!" </p>
    d. <p>She said "You're hired!" </p>
    e. You cannot include quotes in a print statement!

19. The arithmetic is wrong in the following PHP statement (it should be **65 - $age**). Is this a syntax error or a logical error?

```
$yearsToRetire = $age - 65;
```

    a. Syntax error
    b. Logical error

20. The following print statement is missing a closing quote. Is this a syntax error or a logical error?

```
print ("<p>I guess I have an error - I'm melting!</p>);
```

    a. Syntax error
    b. Logical error

Chapter 5 Code Exercises

Don't be surprised if you find these exercises a little frustrating as you get used to PHP syntax. Don't feel bad if you struggle to get your programs working—this is a normal part of the programming process and all programmers experience it. Developing the algorithms first helps minimize the pain! It is always a good idea to take your time, step away from the computer if you get stuck, come back and look through your code carefully. Remember that the Students page on the textbook Web site includes **Hints and Help** pages for the exercises in this and every chapter.

Your Chapter 5 code exercises can be found in your **chapter05** folder. This folder is included in your customized XAMPP installation at the following location:

htdocs\webtech\coursework\chapter05

Type your name and the date in the **Author** and **Date** sections of each file as you work on each exercise.

Debugging Exercises

Your **chapter05** folder contains a number of "fixIt" files. Each of these files contains PHP code that has an error of some kind. The type of error is indicated in the comment section of each file. You will need to run each program in order to see the errors, and to debug and test the code to see if it works correctly. For example to run **fixit1.php**, first run the Web server, then use the URL:

http://localhost/webtech/coursework/chapter05/fixit1.php

Code Modification Exercises

Your **chapter05** folder contains a number of "modify" files. Each pair of files contains HTML and PHP code that needs to be modified to meet a requirement. The requirements are included in the comment section of each file. Modify the algorithms as specified, being careful to make changes to the .html and .php files as directed. You will need to run each program in order to test your changes. For example to run **modify1.html**, first run the Web server, then use the URL:

http://localhost/webtech/coursework/chapter05/modify1.html

Code Completion Exercises

1. Create a PHP program named **paint-estimate.php** based on the processing requirements outlined in the **paint-estimate** exercise at the end of Chapter 3. The complete code for **paint-estimate.html** has been provided in the **chapter05** folder, along with some code for **paint-estimate.php** to save you some time. Your job is to add the

necessary PHP code to **paint-estimate.php**. Be careful to use the same names and case to receive the input values from **paint-estimate.html**.

IMPORTANT: Use the **ceil()** function to round up the number of gallons of paint needed to cover the room to the next whole number, and also to round up the number of hours of labor. You can't buy gallons in fractions, and we will assume the labor is paid in hourly increments. Also use the **number_format()** function to display your currency outputs to two decimal places.

In order to test your code, you will need to start your Web server if it is not already running, and then open **paint-estimate.html** in a browser window (be sure you are using a URL and not a Windows address). Enter test input into the form, and then submit for processing by **paint-estimate.php**. Use the sample data listed in the exercise at the end of Chapter 3 to test your results (room length = 20, room width = 15, room height = 8). Using this sample data, since you have rounded up the paint coverage, your paint cost will now be 3 * 17.00 = 51.00, and your labor cost will now be 5 * 25 = 125.00, so the total cost will be 176.00.

2. Create a PHP program named **software-order.php** based on the processing requirements outlined in the **software-order** exercise at the end of Chapter 3. The complete code for **software-order.html** has been provided in the **chapter05** folder, along with some code for **software-order.php** to save you some time. Your job is to add the necessary PHP code to **software-order.php**. Be careful to use the same names and case to receive the input values from **software-order.html**.

In order to test your code, you will need to start your Web server if it is not already running, then open **software-order.html** in a browser window (be sure you are opening the file using a URL and not a Windows address). Enter test input into the form, and then submit for processing by **software-order.php**. Use the sample data listed in the exercise at the end of Chapter 3 to test your results.

3. Create a PHP program named **travel.php** based on the processing requirements outlined in the travel exercise at the end of Chapter 3. The complete code for **travel.html** has been provided in the **chapter05** folder, along with some code for **travel.php** to save you some time. Your job is to add the necessary PHP code to **travel.php**. Be careful to use the same names and case to receive the input values from travel.html.

In order to test your code, you will need to start your Web server if it is not already running, then open **travel.html** in a browser window (be sure you are opening the file using a URL and not a Windows address). Enter test input into the form, and then submit for processing by **travel.php**. Use the sample data listed in the exercise at the end of Chapter 3 to test your results.

4. Create a PHP program named **game-intro.php** based on the processing requirements outlined in the game-intro exercise at the end of Chapter 3. Review those requirements carefully since they explain the required user input and the necessary calculations. The complete code for **game-intro.html** has been provided in the **chapter05** folder, along with some of the code for **game-intro.php** to save you

some time. Your job is to add the necessary PHP code to **game-intro.php**. Be careful to use the same names and case to receive the input values from **game-intro.html**.

In order to test your code, you will need to start your Web server if it is not already running, then open **game-intro.html** in a browser window (be sure you are opening the file using a URL and not a Windows address). An example of the output is shown in Figure 5-4, based on the name **Webtech**, character type **Elf, 20** health tokens. **10** experience tokens, and **25** supply tokens. Note that the character's name and type should be displayed in the heading, and the cost in this case should be **8 gold pieces.**

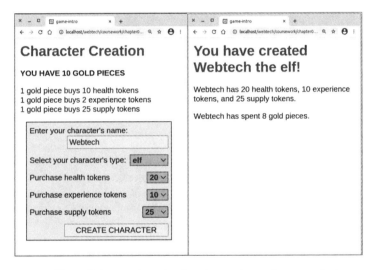

Figure 5-4: game-intro.html and game-intro.php screenshots

5. Copy your **event.html** file from your chapter04 folder to your chapter05 folder. Now create a PHP program named **event.php** based on the processing requirements outlined in the event exercise at the end of Chapter 3. Test your code by starting your Web server if it is not already running, opening a Web browser, and entering the URL:

    http://localhost/webtech/coursework/chapter05/event.html

    Enter any test input into the form, and then submit for processing by event.php. For example if you enter 10 for the number of tickets the program should display a total cost of 350.

6. Copy your **fuel-cost.html** file from your chapter04 folder to your chapter05 folder. Now create a PHP program named **fuel-cost.php** based on the processing requirements outlined in the **fuel-cost** exercise at the end of Chapter 3. Test your code by

starting your Web server if it is not already running, opening a Web browser, and entering the URL:

http://localhost/webtech/coursework/chapter05/fuel-cost.html

Enter 20 as the mpg, 100 as miles traveled, and 3.00 as the cost per gallon. This should generate a result of 15.0. Test two or three times using numbers of your own and make sure that the program is working correctly.

Chapter 6

Persistence —
Saving and Retrieving Data

Intended Learning Outcomes

After completing this chapter, you should be able to:

- Distinguish between transient and persistent data.
- Describe the advantages of a client/server design that includes remote data storage.
- Contrast the use of text files with a RDBMS for data storage.
- List the basic operations that can be performed on a text file.
- Utilize the fopen(), fgets(), trim(), and fclose() functions to read data from a text file.
- Utilize the fopen(), fputs(), and fclose() functions to write data to a text file.
- Recognize and utilize escape characters in text output.
- Utilize the fopen(), fputs(), and fclose() functions to append data to a text file.
- Explain the process of parsing a character string that contains a data record.
- Utilize the explode() and list() functions to parse a character string.
- Apply PHP file-handling functions to process multiple files.

Introduction

In order to be useful, a program must usually receive input, perform processing tasks, and generate output. So far our programs have received input from HTML forms submitted by the user, and generated output in the form of new HTML pages to be viewed by the user. The pages containing the forms and the pages displaying the program's response constitute a **user interface**.

171

Input and output is not restricted to interactions with a user. Programs may also interact with all kinds of local or remote **devices and applications** in order to perform tasks such as: controlling a piece of hardware (such as a camera, microphone, printer, or robot), performing a transaction (for example with a banking or shopping application), receiving updates, exchanging messages, or working with databases and files.

In order to interact with any device, a program must typically: (1) open a connection; (2) perform the required input and/or output operations; and (3) close the connection.

In this chapter you will learn to distinguish between temporary (transient) data and data that is stored (persistent data), and compare the use of text files and databases for persistent data storage. You will learn the basic operations needed to process text files, and implement these operations using PHP file-handling functions to read, write and append text files located on a Web server. You will also learn how to extract (parse) multiple data values from a single line that has been read from a text file.

The Difference Between Persistent and Transient Data

As human beings, we receive and generate data of all kinds every moment of our lives, eating, sleeping, walking, talking, listening, making phone calls, working, playing. Much of this data is not recorded and is easily forgotten. For example, you may be out walking and someone asks you for directions. You respond with appropriate instructions. No record is kept and so the data associated with this event is lost.

Other kinds of data is not lost. If you read a book or listen to a CD, or make a list, you are working with data that you (or someone else) can access again at a later date. That's because the data is **stored** in some form or another.

In the world of computing, data that is used and then forgotten is known as **transient** data. More precisely transient data refers to data that is produced while an application is running and lost when the application ends. Keyboard input and display output are examples of transient data because keyboards and monitors do not "remember" the data once it has been transmitted. Data that is stored in a program's variables is also transient since variables are created while an application is running and disappear when the application ends. Input that is received as a stream of data from devices such as a microphone or satellite or scanner is also transient. Similarly output that sends data to a dynamic Web page is transient.

Data whose life extends beyond the lifetime of any of the programs that process it is known as **persistent data**. Persistent data is **stored** so that it can be accessed and modified by programs as needed. Persistent data is commonly stored in files and databases, located on fixed disks, optical disks, tapes, or other storage media. If your application reads data from a storage medium, or writes data to a storage medium, then the application is working with persistent data.

Many programs work with a combination of transient and persistent data. For example, you might write a program that asks the user for information of some kind and then stores the information in a file for later use. In this case the user inputs and screen displays may be considered transient data, while the data that the program writes to the file is persistent since it will remain in the file after the program ends. Or you may write a program that reads data from a file, then displays the information to the user. In this case the input is derived from persistent data stored in the file, and the output to the screen is transient data.

Persistent data stored in files or databases may be used by many different programs, for many different purposes. Consider a data file that contains weekly timesheet data for employees (for example the first name, last name, hours worked and hourly pay for each employee). Four different programs might process this file for different purposes. Program **A** might allow a clerical worker to type an employee's timesheet information into a form, then add this information to the timesheet file. Program **B** might read all the timesheets in the timesheet file, calculate the weekly wage for each employee, and print paychecks. Program **C** might read the timesheet file and develop useful statistics for a payroll manager (for example the total wages, the average wage, highest wage, lowest wage, etc). Program **D** might provide a planning tool (for example the program might read the hourly pay of all employees and create a new file showing what each employee will earn if they receive a 10% raise).

In a client/server environment, the employee data file can be located on a server and the various programs that operate on the file can be located on the same server. Client programs can then interact with the appropriate server programs as needed (Figure 6-1).

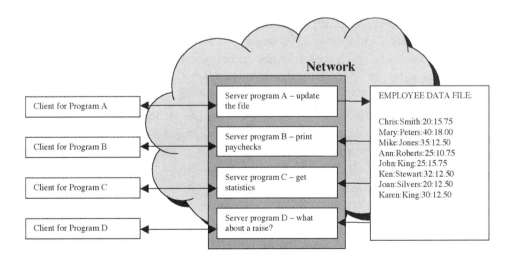

Figure 6-1: Accessing data in a client/server environment

Here are some of the advantages of a network-based design when working with stored data:

- The data file is stored in one secure, central location (the server) and can be easily backed up and maintained. Just imagine if each program or each user worked with their own copy of this file! What would happen if a new employee needed to be added, or other changes had to be made?
- The only programs with direct access to the data file are also stored on the server, so these programs can be easily modified without any need to change programs running on client computers. Similarly new programs can be added without any need to change existing programs, for example a new program could be added to compare the hourly wages of male and female employees.
- Client interfaces can be designed for specific users to allow access to appropriate programs on the server. For example a manager might need a client interface that provides access to Program C and Program D, while an administrative assistant may only have access to Program A.

Files and Databases

Files may be used to store data in many different formats. **Text files** contain data as one or more lines of plain text. Text files may be used to contain small and large data sets, from a few lines that contain, for example, the saved status of a computer game that can be retrieved when the player resumes the game, to thousands of lines that contain for example, hourly readings from weather stations all across the country. In either case, each line in the file is handled as a character string and can be processed by an application or viewed using a text editor.

While a data set can be as simple as a list of single data values, such as scores, it is often useful to store groups of related items together in the form of **records**. In our timesheet example, an employee's timesheet record consists of four data items: the employee's first name, last name, hours worked and hourly pay. In this case a data set might contain any number of these timesheet records, each for a different employee.

Text files may be used for storing records (usually one record on each line) but this approach is not very efficient when it comes to storing large amounts of data that must be processed quickly and efficiently. Any program that processes a file of records must provide all the instructions necessary to perform any required data operations such as inserting, updating, or adding records to the file, sorting the contents of the file, or searching the file for specific information. The use of text files is also not very secure since text files can be easily viewed by any person or program with access to the file.

Databases provide a much more sophisticated solution for storing data records. The most widely used type of database is a **relational database**, which allows an organization to store data in database **tables** consisting of rows (**records**) and columns (**fields**). Table 6-1 shows an example of a relational database table to store timesheet records with four fields in each record.

firstName	lastName	hoursWorked	hourlyWage
Chris	Smith	20	15.75
Mary	Peters	40	18.00
Mike	Jones	35	12.50
Ann	Roberts	25	10.75
John	King	25	15.75
Ken	Stewart	32	12.50
Joan	Silvers	20	12.50
Karen	King	30	12.50

Table 6-1: Example of a relational database table

Database tables can be related to one another to avoid duplication of information and simplify management. Databases incorporate many useful functions that facilitate table creation, data updates and deletions, data queries, and report creation. A **Relational Database Management System (RDBMS)** is software that provides a full range of management tools for working with databases. This greatly simplifies software development since other programs can call the functions provided by the RDBMS rather than providing their own functions. A RDBMS also implements sophisticated security so that access by people or programs to various tables and even individual fields can be controlled, based on ID's and passwords.

If you write programs that interact with databases, you will need to learn the language that the RDBMS uses to receive instructions. The most commonly used language for this purpose is **Structured Query Language** (SQL). There are various versions of SQL, used for working with different RDBMS systems.

Files and databases are both extremely important mechanisms for data storage, and the PHP language is designed to work effectively with both. In Chapter 14, we will learn how to use PHP to connect to a MySQL or MariaDB database. In this chapter, we will explore basic procedures associated with text file processing as an introduction to working with persistent data.

Working with a Text File

In order to work with a text file, a program must first **open** the file. There are basically three ways to open a text file:

Opening a File for Read Operations

This allows the program to **read** data **from** the file, in other words to use the file as a source of input. Assuming the file exists, this operation opens the file for **reading** and positions a **read pointer** at the beginning of the file. Once the file has been opened for read operations, the program may issue instructions to read data from the file one line at a time. After each read instruction, the read pointer advances so that the next read operation will access the next line in the file.

Opening a File for Write Operations

This allows the program to **write** data **to** the file, in other words to use the file for output. This operation always creates a new file even if a file with the same name already exists in the folder location. If a file with the same name already exists in the folder location, it is replaced by the new file so be very careful when using this operation!

Once the new file has been created it is opened for **writing** and the write marker is located at the beginning of the file. Each time data is added to the file, it is added to the location of the write marker and the write marker is advanced to the end of the data, ready for the next write operation.

You will open a file for **write** operations when you want to **replace** data in an existing file with new data. This is useful for example when saving the most recent status of a computer game (player name, score, position, etc.), or when you want to replace an old file backup with a more recent one. In these cases you want to replace a file containing older data with a file containing the current data. Any program or person that needs to read this data can open the file for reading, confident that the file contains the latest data.

Opening a File for Append Operations

This allows the program to **write** data **to the end of an existing file**. If the specified file does not already exist in the folder location, the file is created just as if the file had been opened for writing. The write marker is positioned at the end of any existing data ready for the next write operation.

You will open a file for **append** operations when you want to **add** data to an existing file. This is useful, for example, when adding a survey response to a file that contains a list of previous responses, or adding the latest hourly reading of weather data (temperature, precipitation, humidity, etc.) to a file that already has weather readings for the previous hours of the day. In these cases it's important to add, and not replace, data, so that **all** of the data that has previously been stored in the file remains available.

Closing a Text File

When a program that has opened a file completes its task, the file should be **closed**. The close operation places an **End-Of-File** (EOF) character at the end of the file and releases the file for access by other programs. This is very important. If the file is not closed properly, it may be corrupted and the contents lost.

As we have seen, a single file may serve multiple programs that need to access the file for different purposes or different users. Files should therefore be opened and closed as efficiently as possible, since an open file may not be accessible by other programs waiting to use it. Good programming practice is to: open a file only when the program is ready to work with it; close the file as soon as the program has finished using it. This is especially important in the case of network programming where hundreds or thousands of programs may need to access the same file within a short period of time (for example on a busy Web site).

Reading Data from a Text File

Let's start with an example where we open a text file, read data from the file, close the file, and then process the data. Consider a file named **scores.txt** that contains five scores on separate lines as follows:

```
89
77
92
69
87
```

Here is a program requirement to process the **scores.txt** file:

average-score requirement:

Read the five scores from the scores.txt file, then calculate and display the average score.

Here is a solution algorithm for **average-score.php**:

```
average-score.php algorithm:
  Open scores.txt as scoresFile for reading
  Read score1, score2, score3, score4, score5 from
  scoresFile
  Close scoresFile
  avgScore = (score1 + score2 + score3 + score4 + score5) / 5
  Display averageScore
END
```

Note that we are using some new words in our pseudocode.

Open

Use **Open** to indicate that the program must open a file and specify whether the file is to be opened for reading, writing or appending. We indicate that we are opening the **scores.txt** file as **scoresFile**, because programs use variables (in this case a variable named $scoresFile) to store the data connection to the file (sometime called the **file handle**). Once the file handle has been assigned to a variable, the variable is used to refer to the file in subsequent program statements. In the average-score algorithm, the remaining instructions that follow the "Open" instruction refer to the variable **scoresFile**, and not the actual file named **scores.txt**.

Read

Use **Read** to indicate that the program must read a value from a file into a variable. In this example, we read the values from five lines of the file into five program variables. The program then uses the values stored in these variables to calculate the average score.

Close

Use **Close** to indicate that the program must close a file. Note that our algorithm is designed to close the file as soon as the required data has been read from the file into program variables. The algorithm would be just as correct if the close operation was left until **after** the instructions to calculate and display the average score, but this would not be good programming practice. As mentioned previously, it is good practice to close a file as soon as the program no longer needs it.

PHP Functions to Read Data from a Text File

Here is the PHP code for the average-score algorithm (this program is available as **average-score.php** in the **samples** folder):

```
<html>
<head>
   <title>AVERAGE SCORE</title>
   <link rel="stylesheet" type="text/css" href="sample.css">
</head>
<body>
   <?php
      $scoresFile = fopen("scores.txt","r");

      $score1 = trim(fgets($scoresFile));
      $score2 = trim(fgets($scoresFile));
```

```
      $score3 = trim(fgets($scoresFile));
      $score4 = trim(fgets($scoresFile));
      $score5 = trim(fgets($scoresFile));

      fclose($scoresFile);

      $avgScore = ($score1 + $score2 + $score3 + $score4 +
        $score5) / 5;

      print ("<h1>AVERAGE SCORE</h1>");

      print("<p>The average score is $avgScore.</p>");

      print ("<p><a href=\"average-score.html\">Return to
        average-score form</a></p>");
  ?>
 </body>
 </html>
```

Code Example: average-score.php

Let's review this code line by line.

```
   $scoresFile = fopen("scores.txt","r");
```

This instruction uses the PHP **fopen**() function to open a file. The first parameter "**scores.txt**" indicates the name of the file to open. The second parameter "**r**" indicates how the file is to be opened. In this case the file is to be opened for reading ("**r**"), with the read pointer set to the beginning of the file.

The **fopen**() function provides a file reference (known as a **file handle**) that the program can use to refer to its connection with the file data in subsequent statements. This file handle is stored in the **$scoresFile** variable, and note that the **fgets**() and **fclose**() functions both refer to **$scoresFile**. Remember, once a file has been opened, any functions that you use to work with the file should refer to the variable that contains the file handle and not the actual name of the file.

```
   $score1 = trim(fgets($scoresFile));
```

The **fgets**() function is used to read the entire next line from the file as a character string. In this case the file handle is stored in **$scoresFile** so you can read the first line from the file into a variable named $score1 as follows:

```
   $score1 = fgets($scoresFile);
```

However if you try to do that you may get a warning notice when you run your program, something like "**non well formed numeric value encountered**", which refers to the line of code where $score1 is used in a calculation. What's going on?

The problem is that text files don't actually contain "lines" the way you see them displayed on your screen, one below the another; instead the text file contains special characters, often called **end-of-line** (or **eoln**) markers, that indicate where each new line should appear when the file is displayed. When the fgets() function reads the entire first line in the file, the line that is read **includes** this end-of-line character, which means that the value that is assigned to $score1 is not just "89", but "89" followed by the end-of-line character! That's why there is a warning when you use $score1 in a calculation, because it does not contain a "well formed numeric value".

Fortunately there is a simple solution for this, the PHP **trim()** function to the rescue! The trim() function is designed to remove any white space from the **beginning** and **end** of **any** character string (remember that "white space" refers to spaces, tabs, and also end of line characters), so you can use trim() to remove the end of line character from each line that fgets() reads from the file. To do this, change the statement **$score1 = fgets($scoreFile);** to **$score1 = trim(fgets($scoreFile));** Do you see how this works? The fgets() function still receives the entire line from the file as a character string, including the end-of-line character, but now you send the character string from fgets() directly to the trim() function, which removes any white space at the beginning and end of the line. The trim() function creates a new string that no longer includes the end-of-line character, which is then assigned to $score1. Note that you need **two** closing parentheses at the end of this statement: the first is for the fgets() function, the second is for the trim() function.

The reason that fgets() is designed to read the end-of-line character is that this will move the read pointer **after** the end-of-line character, so that the **next** time fgets() is used it will begin reading from the start of the next line. Now that we have read the first line we can use trim() and fgets() together to read the values from the remaining lines in the file as follows:

```
$score2 = trim(fgets($scoresFile));
$score3 = trim(fgets($scoresFile));
$score4 = trim(fgets($scoresFile));
$score5 = trim(fgets($scoresFile));
```

In each of these statements, the **fgets()** function reads and returns the content from the next line in the file, and this content is passed to the trim() function, which removes the white space; the result is then assigned to a variable. After each fgets() operation, the read marker is advanced to the next line. In this way the program processes the file, one line at a time.

```
fclose($scoresFile);
```

The **fclose()** function is used to close the file. It is good programming practice to close a file as soon as your program has finished using it. This ensures that the file is available for processing by other programs as soon as possible. Note that, just like fgets(), the fclose() function must also refer to the variable that contains the file handle (in this case $scoresFile).

```
$avgScore = ($score1+$score2+$score3+$score4+$score5) / 5;

print("<p>The average score is $avgScore. </p>");
```

This is more familiar code. The average is calculated and stored in **$avgScore**. The **print**() function outputs the average score in HTML format. Figure 6-2 shows how the program's output will appear as a Web page. The first screen shows **average-score.html** which is used to provide the user with a **submit** button to run **average-score.php** and the second screen shows the results after **average-score.php** has been processed.

You may have a number of questions at this time, for example "What if the file contains hundreds of line of data?", or "What if I don't know how many lines might be in the file when the program executes?" These are great questions. In this chapter we will learn basic operations on files. In later chapters we will learn how to use loop structures to process larger files and files of unknown length.

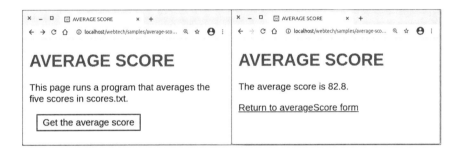

Figure 6-2: average-score.html and average-score.php screenshots

Writing Data to a Text File

Now consider the following requirement:

write-scores requirement:

Write a program that asks the user for five student scores. The program should receive the scores, write them to a file named my-scores.txt (each score on a separate line), and report back to the user.

For this requirement we will first create an HTML document (**write-scores.html**) that contains a form to receive the five scores. Then we will create a PHP file (**write-scores.php**) that will receive the scores, write the scores to the file, and report back to the user.

Here is the algorithm for **write-scores.html**:

```
write-scores.html algorithm:
Prompt the user for score1, score2, score3, score4, score5
Get score1, score2, score3, score4, score5
Submit score1, score2, score3, score4, score5, to write-
    scores.php
END
```

Here is the code for **write-scores.html**:

```html
<html>
<head>
<title>Save Your Scores</title>
<link rel="stylesheet" type="text/css" href="sample.css">
</head>
<body>
<h1>Save Your Scores</h1>
<form action="write-scores.php" method="post">
<label>Score #1: <input type="text" size="5"
  name="score1"></label>
<label>Score #2: <input type="text" size="5"
  name="score2"></label>
<label>Score #3: <input type="text" size="5"
  name="score3"></label>
<label>Score #4: <input type="text" size="5"
  name="score4"></label>
<label>Score #5: <input type="text" size="5"
  name="score5"></label>
<input class="submit" type="submit" value="Save the
  Scores">
</form>
</body>
</html>
```

Code Example: write-scores.html

Here is the algorithm for **write-scores.php**:

```
write-scores.php algorithm:
  Receive score1, score2, score3, score4, score5, from
    write-scores.html
  Open my-scores.txt as scoresFile for writing
  Write score1, score2, score3, score4, score5 to scoresFile
  Close scoresFile
  Display "File Created" message to user
END
```

Note that we use the word **Write** when we wish to indicate an instruction to write data to a file in pseudocode.

PHP Functions to Write Data to a Text File

The process of writing to files in PHP is similar to that of reading files. First we need to open the file for writing using the **fopen**() function, except that we now specify "**w**" instead of "**r**". If the file does not exist the file is created. If the file already exists it is replaced, so be careful how you use the "**w**" option!

Once the file has been opened for writing we can use the **fputs**() function as needed to write data to the file. When we are finished writing to the file, we close it using the **fclose**() function.

Here is the code for **write-scores.php**:

```
<html>
<head>
  <title>Save Your Scores</title>
  <link rel="stylesheet" type="text/css" href="sample.css">
</head>
<body>
  <?php
    $score1 = $_POST['score1'];
    $score2 = $_POST['score2'];
    $score3 = $_POST['score3'];
    $score4 = $_POST['score4'];
    $score5 = $_POST['score5'];

    $scoresFile = fopen("my-scores.txt","w");

    fputs($scoresFile, "$score1\n");
    fputs($scoresFile, "$score2\n");
    fputs($scoresFile, "$score3\n");
    fputs($scoresFile, "$score4\n");
    fputs($scoresFile, "$score5\n");

    fclose($scoresFile );

    print ("<h1>The following scores have been stored in
      my-scores.txt:</h1>");
    print("<p>$score1<br>$score2<br>$score3<br>
    $score4<b/>$score5</p>");
    print ("<p><a href=\"write-scores.html\">Return to
      write-scores form</a></p>");
  ?>
</body>
</html>
```

Code Example: write-scores.php

Let's review the PHP code carefully:

```
$score1 = $_POST['score1'];
$score2 = $_POST['score2'];
$score3 = $_POST['score3'];
$score4 = $_POST['score4'];
$score5 = $_POST['score5'];
```

These five statements extract the five scores that were input by the user from the PHP $_POST array.

```
$scoresFile = fopen("my-scores.txt","w");
```

This statement opens **my-scores.txt** for **write** operations. If the file already exists, it is automatically overwritten. If it does not exist, the file is created.

```
fputs($scoresFile, "$score1\n");
fputs($scoresFile, "$score2\n");
fputs($scoresFile, "$score3\n");
fputs($scoresFile, "$score4\n");
fputs($scoresFile, "$score5\n");
```

The **fputs**() function is used to **write** data to a file. The first argument is the variable that refers to the file (in this case the variable **$scoresFile**) and the second argument is a string containing the data that is to be written to the file.

Note that, in each case, the output consists of a variable (for example **$score1**) followed immediately by \n. The **fputs**() function does not automatically add a new line after writing data to the file, since you may wish to use subsequent fputs() statements to continue to add text to the same line. The \n **represents the new line** character and is included whenever you want a new line to be added to the file. The use of "\" with "n" is an example of an **escape character**. Escape characters are explained in more detail below. If you do **not** include new line characters in these statements, all five **fputs**() instructions will keep adding data to the same line (try it).

You can include multiple **new line** characters in a single **fputs**() statement, so instead of writing the five scores using five **fputs**() statements, you could actually write this using a single **fputs**() instruction:

```
fputs($scoresFile,"$score1\n$score2\n$score3\n$score4\n$score5\n");
```

Notice that the value from each variable is written to the file followed by a new line character, so the values will be displayed on five separate lines if viewed in a text editor. (If your text editor does **not** generate separate lines when you view your output, use "\r\n" instead of just "\n" when you include a new line in your fputs() statements. Originally a new line was generated by two characters (**return** and **new line**, like a type writer), and some editors still expect "\r\n" or "\r"; using both takes care of this problem.)

```
fclose($scoresFile);
```

The **fclose()** function closes the file. As always it is important to close a file once the program is done using it.

```
print(" <h1>The following scores have been stored in
    my-scores.txt</h1>");

print("<p>$score1<br>$score2<br>$score3<br>
    $score4<br>$score5</p>");

print(" <p><a href=\"write-scores.html\">Return to write-scores
    form</a></p> ");
```

This PHP code generates some HTML that informs the user that the file was created. Note the use of the break <br> tags to list the scores on separate lines.

Figure 6-3 shows a sample interaction.

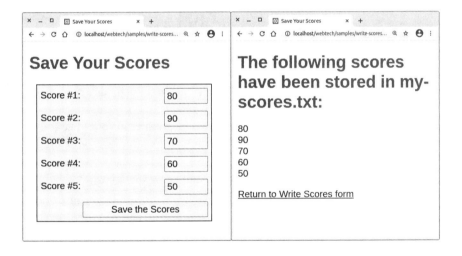

Figure 6-3: write-scores.html and write-scores.php screenshots

Here is the content of **myscores.txt** after this program has executed:

```
80
90
70
60
50
```

Try running this program a few times, using different scores each time. Check the content of **my-scores.txt** as you do this, and note that every time you submit new scores the previous copy of my-scores.txt is replaced by the new version and the previous scores are lost. Soon we will see how to preserve the previously submitted scores by **appending** to the file each time we submit new scores instead of overwriting it.

Why fgets() and fputs()?

In case you're wondering about the strange names, "fgets" stands for "file get string", and "fputs" stands for "file put string".

Using Escape Characters

As we just learned, when you are writing data to a text file, you sometimes need to specify when to begin a new line. We do this using the new line character **\n**. This is an example of an **escape character**. Escape characters are two-character sequences that represent characters that could not otherwise be included in output statements. Each escape sequence consists of a back slash \ followed by another keyboard character that indicates the actual character that is to be generated, for example **\n** which represents a new line character.

Another useful escape character is \" which represents a double quote. Why can't we just type the double quote directly when we need this character in our output? Since double quotes are used to indicate the beginning and end of the entire character string, we have to use an escape character if the text actually contains a double quote, otherwise the processor would assume that this double quote indicates the end of the character string.

Here are the most commonly used escape characters:

```
\t   generates a tab
\n   starts a new line
\"   generates a double quote "
\'   generates a single quote '
\\   generates a back slash \
```

Note that, since the back slash is used to indicate an escape character, we must use a **double** back slash if we wish to output the back slash character itself!

Here is an output example showing the use of a number of escape characters:

```
fputs($someFile, "He said \"That\'s fine,\"\n\tand then
    left.\n\nThe End.");
```

would store the following text in the file (note the quotes, new line and tab):

```
He said "That's fine,"
    and then left.

The End.
```

Note that to end a line and then generate a second blank line you will use two new line characters consecutively: **\n\n**.

Escape Characters and HTML Tags

Do not confuse the use of escape characters such as the \n new line character that is used to add new lines to text output with HTML tags such as the <br> or <p> tags. HTML tags are used to instruct the Web browser how to format text on a Web page. The new line character is used by a program to add new lines to strings of text. We have seen how a new line character can be used to add a new line to text that is written to a text file by the **fputs**() function. You can also include a new line character in a PHP **print** statement but this will **not** produce a line break in the Web page that the browser displays to the user; for this you must use the appropriate HTML tag.

Using PHP to Append Data to Files

Appending data to files is similar to writing data to files except that, with an append operation, if the file already exists the data will be **added** to the end of the existing file content. In other words existing files are not lost with append operations.

Append operations are useful whenever you need to add data to an existing file. This is a very common requirement. For example **log files** are files that keep track of some kind of activity. A print server application might append a message to a **print** log file each time a printer is used. A business owner might use an application that appends the mileage of each business trip to a **mileage** log file. A program that is processing a file of scores might append a message to an **error** log file each time a score is found that is out of range.

When data is appended to a file, any data already stored in the file is preserved. The file grows over time as new data is added.

Let's use the mileage log example to learn how to append data to a file. Many small business owners must keep track of the miles that they travel on each business-related trip for tax purposes. Consider the following requirement:

mileage-log requirement:

Write a program that allows a small business owner to submit travel mileage for a business trip. The program should receive the mileage and append this to a text file named mileage-log.txt, then inform the user that the data has been added.

The user can use the form to submit mileage as often as needed.

According to this requirement, when a user enters a mileage amount into the form and presses the Submit button, the input will be appended to the **mileage-log.txt** file.

Here is the pseudocode for the HTML document that will receive and submit the mileage:

```
mileage-log.html algorithm:
   Prompt for mileage
   Get mileage
   Submit mileage to mileage-log.php
END
```

Here is the code for **mileage-log.html**:

```
<html>
<head>
  <title>Mileage Log</title>
  <link rel="stylesheet" type="text/css" href="sample.css">
</head>
<body>
  <h1>Mileage Log</h1>

  <form action="mileage-log.php" method="post">
  <label>Enter your mileage:
    <input type="text" size="5" name="mileage"></label>
    <input class="submit" type="submit" value="Submit
      mileage">
  </form>
</body>
</html>
```

Code Example: mileage-log.html

Here is the pseudocode for the PHP program that will receive the user input and append the data to the **mileage-log.txt** file:

```
mileage-log.php algorithm:
  Receive mileage from mileage-log.html

  Open mileage-log.txt as logFile for appending
  Write mileage to logFile
  Close logFile

  Display "Mileage has been recorded" message to the user
END
```

PHP Functions to Append Data to a Text File

We use the same PHP functions to **append** to a file that we use to **write** to a file. The only difference is that we use "**a**" for append rather than "**w**" for write in our **fopen()** function. Here is the PHP code for **mileage-log.php**:

```
<html>
<head>
  <title>Mileage Log</title>
  <link rel="stylesheet" type="text/css" href="sample.css">
</head>
<body>
  <?php
    $mileage = $_POST['mileage'];

    $logFile = fopen("mileage-log.txt","a");
    fputs($logFile, "$mileage\n");
    fclose($logFile);

    print(" <h1>Your mileage submission ($mileage) has
        been recorded:</h1>");
    print(" <p><a href=\"mileage-log.html\">Submit
        another mileage</a></p>");
  ?>
</body>
</html>
```

Code Example: mileage-log.php

Let's review the PHP code line by line:

```
$mileage = $_POST['mileage'];
```

Here we extract the input from the PHP $_POST array and assign the value to a variable.

```
$logFile = fopen("mileage-log.txt","a");
```

This statement opens a file named **mileage-log.txt** for appending ("**a**"). If the file does not exist it is created. If the file does exist, the write marker is moved to the **end** of the existing data in the file.

```
fputs($logFile, "$mileage\n");
```

The **fputs**() function is used to write the mileage amount to the file. This function is used in exactly the same way whether a file is opened for write or append operations. Since the file was opened for appending, the data will be added to the end of any data that is already stored in the file.

It is important to include the **new line** character at the end of the output string so that the next time a mileage amount is added, it will appear on the next line of the file and not on the same line.

```
fclose($logFile );
```

The **fclose**() function closes the file. As always it is important to close a file once the program is done using it. The file can then be reopened when another mileage is submitted, or when it is time to process the mileages in the file.

Figure 6-4 shows a sample interaction.

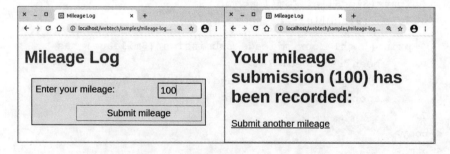

Figure 6-4: mileage-log.html and mileage-log.php screenshots

Open **mileage-log.html** yourself a few times and add new mileage amount each time. Each time you do this, check the contents of **mileage-log.txt** and observe that a new line is added to this file each time a new amount is submitted. For example here is how the content of **mileage-log.txt** might appear after submitting three mileage amounts:

```
100
45
234
```

Processing Files that Contain Complete Records on Each Line

Consider the following program requirement:

wage-report1 requirement:

Write a program that reads an employee timesheet record from a file named timesheet.txt. The file contains the employee's first name, last name, hours worked and hourly wage on a single line, for example:

Mike:Smith:20:12.55

The program should calculate and display the weekly wage.

What makes this requirement different from our previous file-processing examples?

Previously each line in our data files have contained only a single data value (for example a score or a mileage amount). As a result, each **fgets**() instruction retrieved a **single** value. Often, however, each line of a data file contains a **record** of some kind. Recall that a record is a grouping of related data items. A line that contains an entire record will include **multiple** data items. In this case, a single line in **timesheet.txt** contains a timesheet record with four values (first name, last name, hours worked and hourly wage).

Storing an entire record on a single line is a common practice since a single file can then easily contain any number of records, each record stored on a separate line. We introduce this topic by considering how to process a file that contains a single record.

Note that the four data values are separated by colons. When multiple values are stored on a single line, we need to some way to **separate** each value, otherwise a program that reads the data from the file will have no way to identify each value. Imagine for example if, instead of:

```
Mike:Smith:20:12.55
```

the line in the file looked like this:

```
MikeSmith2012.55
```

Can you see the problem? How can a program decide where each value ends and the next value begins?

To avoid this problem, standard practice is to add **separators** or **delimiters** between each value. The separator can be any character, as long as it will not appear in the values themselves. You may have heard the phrase "comma-delimited file" or "tab-delimited file". These phrases indicate a file where the values on each line are separated by commas or tabs respectively. Any program that is designed to read the data from the file must know what delimiter was used in order to know how to retrieve the separate values (we will learn how to do this shortly).

In our example we are using colons as delimiters.

PHP Functions to Parse a Delimited Character String

Recall that the PHP **fgets**() function reads an entire line from a text file. When we use **fgets**() to read a line containing a record with multiple values, the entire record is read from the file as a single character string. So if we use **fgets**() to read the line

---

```
Mike:Smith:20:12.55
```

---

and store this in a variable, the variable will contain a character string with the entire contents of the line, in other words: "Mike:Smith:20:12.55".

We need to extract the four values from this string in order to work with each value individually. The process of extracting values from a larger data string is known as **parsing**. We must parse the string "Mike:Smith:20:12.55" in order to extract the employee's first name, last name, hours worked this week, and hourly rate of pay. Once we have extracted the four values and stored these in separate variables, we can perform the required processing.

Here is the pseudocode for **wage-report1.php**:

```
wage-report1.php algorithm:
   Open timesheet.txt as timesheetFile for reading
   Read employeeRecord from timesheetFile
   Close timesheetFile

   Get firstName, lastName, hours, payRate from employeeRecord
   pay = hours * payRate
   Display lastName, firstName, pay
END
```

The algorithm instructs the program to open the timesheet file, read the first line from the file and store this in a variable named **employeeRecord**, and close the file. The algorithm then uses the word **Get** to indicate that the program must extract the four values from the character string stored in the **employeeRecord** variable, and store these values in the variables **firstName**, **lastName**, **hours** and **payRate,** respectively. Once the values have been stored in separate variables, the program then performs the required calculation and displays the results.

How do we convert this algorithm to PHP code? Remember that **fgets()** reads an entire line from a file, so we can easily obtain the employee record from the file as follows:

```
$timesheetFile = fopen("timesheet.txt","r");
$employeeRecord = trim(fgets($timesheetFile));
fclose($timesheetFile);
```

(Note the use of the trim() function with fgets() to remove the end-of-line character.) The $employeeRecord variable now contains the entire line of data from **timesheet.txt**. The question is: how can we parse the contents of this variable to get the values we need for $firstName, $lastName, $hours and $payRate?

PHP provides two useful functions that we can use in combination to parse our line of data. The PHP **explode()** function extracts data values from a character string based on a delimiter of some kind. To use the **explode()** function we must indicate the character that we are using as a delimiter (in this case the colon character), and we must specify the character string that is to be parsed (in this case the string that is stored in **$employeeRecord**):

```
explode(":", $employeeRecord)
```

The **explode()** function extracts the values between the colons. and provides these in a special data structure called an array (arrays are explained in Chapter 11). If **$employeeRecord** contains the character string "Mike:Smith:20:12.55", the array will contain the values "Mike", "Smith", "20", and "12.55".

The PHP **list()** function is designed to retrieve a list of values from an array and store these in separate variables. Here is a line of PHP code that shows how the **list()** function receives the values returned by the **explode()** function, and stores these values into four newly created variables:

```
list($firstName, $lastName, $hours, $payRate) = explode (":",
    $employeeRecord);
```

The four arguments supplied to the **list()** function are variables. Each variable will receive one of the values extracted from the character string by the **explode()** function. The extracted values will be assigned to these variables in order. If **$employeeRecord** contains the character string "Mike:Smith:20:12.55", the variable **$firstName** will contain "Mike", the variable **$lastName** will contain "Smith", the variable **$hours** will contain 20, and the variable **$payRate** will contain 12.55.

Once we have used the **explode**() and **list**() functions to extract the values from the line and store these in variables, we can then calculate and output the weekly wage. Here is the complete PHP code for **wage-report1.php**:

```
<html>
<head>
  <title>EMPLOYEE WEEKLY WAGE REPORT</title>
  <link rel="stylesheet" type="text/css" href="sample.css">
</head>
<body>
  <?php
    $timesheetFile = fopen("timesheet.txt","r");
    $employeeRecord = trim(fgets($timesheetFile));
    fclose($timesheetFile);

    list($firstName, $lastName, $hours, $payRate) =
      explode (":", $employeeRecord);
    $pay = $hours * $payRate;

    print ("<h1>EMPLOYEE WEEKLY WAGE REPORT </h1>");
    print("<p>$lastName, $firstName: $ $pay.</p>");

    print (" <p><a href=\"wage-report1.html\">Return to
      wage-report1 form</a></p> ");
  ?>
</body>
</html>
```

Code Example: wage-report1.php

Note that we closed the file before parsing the line of data. That's because we only need the file open to read the line from the file and store the content in a program variable. The process of parsing the line is performed on the variable and not on the file. It is always good practice to close a file as soon as you are finished using it.

The explode() and list() functions are used for a variety of purposes, not only to parse records from a file, and not always in combination with one another. The use of these two functions is explained more completely in chapter 11.

Processing a File with Multiple Records

Now let's look at a requirement to process a file that contains **multiple** records:

---

wage-report2 requirement:

Write a program that reads an employee timesheet from a file named timesheets.txt. The file contains three lines. Each line contains one employee's first name, last name, hours worked and hourly wage, for example:

Mike:Smith:20:12.55

Mary:King:40:17.50

Chris:Jones:35:9.50

The program should calculate and display the weekly wage for each employee and also calculate and display the total wages.

Each line in the **timesheets.txt** file contains a single employee record and each record contains four data fields: the employee's first name, last name, hours worked this week, and hourly rate of pay. The data fields are separated by colons. There are three records in the file.

This problem is not very different from the previous problem except that we need to process **three** lines instead of one, and we need to calculate and display the total pay in addition to the pay for each employee. Here is the algorithm:

```
wage-report2.php algorithm:

   Open timesheets.txt as timesheetFile for reading
   Read employeeRecord1 from timesheetFile
   Read employeeRecord2 from timesheetFile
   Read employeeRecord3 from timesheetFile
   Close timesheetFile

   Get firstName1, lastName1, hours1, payRate1 from employeeRecord1
   Get firstName2, lastName2, hours2, payRate2 from employeeRecord2
   Get firstName3, lastName3, hours3, payRate3 from employeeRecord3

   pay1 = hours1 * payRate1
   pay2 = hours2 * payRate2
   pay3 = hours3 * payRate3
   totalPay = pay1 + pay2 + pay3

   Display lastName1, firstName1, pay1
   Display lastName2, firstName2, pay2
   Display lastName3, firstName3, pay3
   Display totalPay
END
```

This looks complicated but if you look through this carefully you will see that the algorithm really breaks down into four groups of instructions. The first group of instructions open the file, read the three lines of data into variables and then close the file. The second group of instructions extract the first name, last name, hours worked and pay rate from the three variables. The next group of instructions performs the calculations. The last group of instructions generates the output. Here is the code for **wage-report2.php**:

```
<html>
<head>
  <title>EMPLOYEE WEEKLY WAGE REPORT</title>
  <link rel="stylesheet" type="text/css" href="sample.css">
</head>
<body>
  <?php
    $timesheetFile = fopen("timesheets.txt","r");
    $employeeRecord1 = trim(fgets($timesheetFile));
    $employeeRecord2 = trim(fgets($timesheetFile));
    $employeeRecord3 = trim(fgets($timesheetFile));
    fclose($timesheetFile);

    list($firstName1, $lastName1, $hours1, $payRate1) =
      explode(":",$employeeRecord1);
    list($firstName2, $lastName2, $hours2, $payRate2) =
      explode(":", $employeeRecord2);
    list($firstName3, $lastName3, $hours3, $payRate3) =
      explode(":", $employeeRecord3);

    $pay1 = $hours1 * $payRate1;
    $pay2 = $hours2 * $payRate2;
    $pay3 = $hours3 * $payRate3;
    $totalPay = $pay1 + $pay2 + $pay3;

    print("<h1>EMPLOYEE WEEKLY WAGE REPORT </h1>");
    print("<p>$lastName1, $firstName1: $ $pay1.");
    print("<br>$lastName2, $firstName2: $ $pay2.");
    print("<br>$lastName3, $firstName3: $ $pay3. </p>");
    print("<p><strong>TOTAL PAY: $ $totalPay.</strong></p>");
    print(" <p><a href=\"wage-report2.html\">Return to
      wage-report2 form</a></p>");
  ?>
</body>
</html>
```

Code Example: wage-report2.php

Figure 6-5 shows the output from **wage-report2.html** and **wage-report2.php**.

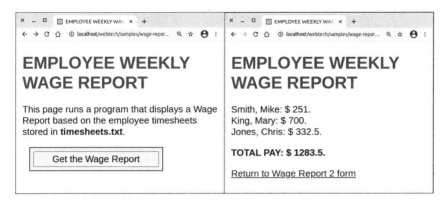

Figure 6-5: wage-report2.html and wage-report2.php screenshots

Perhaps you are wondering "This works fine for three records, but what if the file contains the records for 20, or 2,000 or 20,000 employees? What if you do not even know how many records will be stored in the file?" These problems are not as difficult as they sound. In fact they can be solved quite easily using program loops. In Chapter 10 we will see how we can process files with any number of records.

Appending Records to a File

We must often create programs that **write** or **append** lines that contain entire records. For example consider an online survey, where each submission constitutes a single survey response that must be appended to a file of survey responses. Here is such a requirement for our smoking survey:

---

smoking-survey requirement:

Write a program that prompts the user for their first and last name, the number of years they have smoked and daily average number of cigarettes they have smoked during this time. The program should receive the input and append this as a single line to a file named smoking-survey.txt, then inform the user that the data has been added.

Each value should be separated by colons.

According to this requirement, when a user completes the form and presses the Submit button, the input will be appended to the **smoking-survey.txt** file. This is a simple but powerful program. Many different people can submit a survey simply by accessing the form with their own Web browser. Each submitted survey will be added to the file which eventually may contain hundreds or thousands of surveys. Another program can be designed to read the **smoking-survey.txt** file, process the survey data, and report the results (we will develop this program in a later chapter).

Here is the pseudocode for the HTML document that we will use to receive the input from someone who wishes to submit a survey:

```
smoking-survey.html algorithm:
  Prompt for firstName
  Get firstName
  Prompt for lastName
  Get lastName
  Prompt for yearsSmoked
  Get yearsSmoked
  Prompt for smokedDaily
  Get smokedDaily

  Submit firstName, lastName, yearsSmoked, smokedDaily
    to smoking-survey.php
END
```

Here is the code for **smoking-survey.html**:

```
<html>
<head>
  <title>Smoking Survey</title>
  <link rel="stylesheet" type="text/css" href="sample.css">
</head>
<body>
  <h1>Smoking Survey</h1>

  <form action="smoking-survey.php" method="post">
    <label>First name?
    <input type="text" size="15" name="firstName"></label>

    <label>Last name?
    <input type="text" size="15" name="lastName"></label>

    <label>For how many years have you smoked?
    <input type="text" size="5" name="yearsSmoked"></label>

    <label>How many cigarettes have you smoked on average
    every day (roughly)?
    <select name="smokedDaily">
      <option>0</option>
      <option>1</option>
      <option>2</option>
      <option>5</option>
      <option>10</option>
      <option>20</option>
      <option>30</option>
```

```
      <option>40</option>
    </select></label>

    <p><input class="submit" type="submit" value="Submit
      survey data">
  </form>
  </body>
  </html>
```

Code Example: smoking-survey.html

Here is the pseudocode for the PHP program that will receive the user input and append the data to the **smoking-survey.txt** file:

```
smoking-survey.php algorithm:
  Receive firstName, lastName, yearsSmoked, smokedDaily from
    smoking-survey.html
  Open smoking-survey.txt as surveyFile for appending
  Write firstName, lastName, yearsSmoked, smokeDaily to surveyFile
  Close surveyFile
  Display "Data has been added" message to user
END
```

Here is the PHP code for **smoking-survey.php**:

```
<html>
<head>
  <title>Smoking Survey</title>
  <link rel="stylesheet" type="text/css" href="sample.css">
</head>
<body>

  <?php
    $yearsSmoked = $_POST['yearsSmoked'];
    $smokedDaily = $_POST['smokedDaily'];
    $firstName   = $_POST['firstName'];
    $lastName    = $_POST['lastName'];
    $surveyFile = fopen("smoking-survey.txt","a");

    fputs($surveyFile,
      "$firstName:$lastName:$yearsSmoked:$smokedDaily\n");

    fclose($surveyFile);

    print("<h1>Thank you for participating!</h1>");

    print("<p>Your data has been added to our survey.</p>");
```

```
        print ("<p><a href=\"smoking-survey.html\">Return to the
            Survey form </a></p>");
    ?>
</body>
</html>
```

<hr>

Code Example: smoking-survey.php

Let's review the PHP code line by line:

```
$yearsSmoked = $_POST['yearsSmoked'];
$smokedDaily = $_POST['smokedDaily'];
$firstName = $_POST['firstName'];
$lastName = $_POST['lastName'];
```

Here we extract the inputs from the PHP $_POST array and assign these to variables.

```
$surveyFile = fopen("smoking-survey.txt","a");
```

This statement opens a file named **smoking-survey.txt** for appending ("**a**"). If the file does not exist it is created.

```
fputs($surveyFile, "$firstName:$lastName:$yearsSmoked:
$smokedDaily\n");
```

The **fputs()** function is used to write a string of data to a file (the file referenced by the variable **$surveyFile**). Since the file was opened for appending, the data will be added to the end of any data that is already stored in the file.

In this example, we want our **fputs()** statement to add a single line to the file so that each line contains the data for an entire survey submission. We therefore include all four variables that contain input from the user **without** adding **new line** characters between each variable since we want all four values to be written to a **single** line. We provide a new line character at the **end** of the string so that the next survey that is submitted will be written to a new line in the file.

Notice also the colons between each of the variables. We are using the colons to separate the four values, so that they can be parsed easily by any program that reads the file. The colons will simply be written to the file along with the values of each variable, in the order indicated. If the four variables contained the values "John", "Smith", "2" and "20" our **fputs()** statement will append "John:Smith:2:20" to **smoking-survey.txt**.

```
fclose($scoresFile);
```

The **fclose()** function closes the file. As always it is important to close a file once the program is done using it.

Figure 6-6 shows a sample interaction. Open **smoking-survey.html** yourself a few times and add new survey data each time. Each time you do this, check the contents of **smoking-survey.txt** and observe that a new line is added to this file each time a new survey is submitted. Now imagine thousands of people submitting their own data. Every submission is processed by our PHP code and appended to the file.

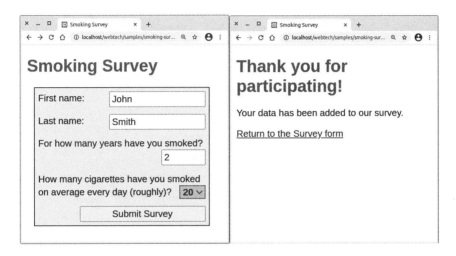

Figure 6-6: smoking-survey.html and smoking-survey.php screenshots

Working with Multiple Files

A program can open multiple files at the same time. Some files may be opened for reading, others for writing, others for appending, depending on the program requirements. As always each file should be opened when the program needs to use it and closed when the program is finished using it. It is easy to see why our file-related functions such as **fopen()**, **fgets()**, **fputs()** and **fclose()** all need an argument that references the file that they are intended to work with, for example **fclose($scoresFile)** will close the file referenced by the **$scoresFile** variable, while **fclose($surveyFile)** will close the file referenced by the **$surveyFile** variable. An example of a program that reads from one file and writes to another is included in the samples folder: **wage-report3.html** and **wage-report3.php**.

Additional Learning Materials

PHP provides a large number of standard functions for working with files. See **Chapter 16** for a more complete list.

The examples in this chapter always work with files in the same folder location. Data files are often located in different folders, requiring the fopen() function to specify a file path as well as the file name. See **Appendix B** to lean more about relative and absolute file addresses.

Appendix D will help you **debug** your exercises, listing a number of the most common errors that you are likely to encounter.

The **Chapter 6 Hints and Help** pages on the textbook Web site provide answers to FAQs from previous students as they worked through the end-of-chapter exercises.

Summary

Files and databases permit programs to work with **persistent** data—data with a life that extends beyond the time that a program is actually running.

Files must be **opened** and **closed** for use by a program. When a text file is opened it is necessary to specify whether the purpose is to **read**, **write** or **append** data.

If a file that does not already exist is opened for writing or appending, the file is created. If a file that already exists is opened for **writing**, the current file is **replaced** by the new file. If a file that already exists is opened for **appending**, any data that is written to the file is **added** to the end of the existing file content.

In PHP the function to open a file is fopen(). The value returned by the open operation provides a connection to the data associated with the file and is termed the **file handle**. The file handle should be assigned to a program variable—this variable is then used in subsequent program instructions to refer to the file.

The PHP function to read a line from the file is **fgets()**. The variable representing the file handle should be used as an argument. The function returns the content of the next line in the file. The trim() function should be used with fgets() to remove the end-of-line character that is included in the content read from the file. Once fgets() is executed, the **read pointer** is then advanced to the start of the next line.

The PHP function to write a line from the file is **fputs()**. This function takes two arguments: the variable that represents the file handle, and the character string to be written to the file. Once the string has been written to the file, the **write marker** is advanced to the position immediately following the last character in the file.

Escape characters are used to specify characters within character strings that could not otherwise be included. Escape characters consist of the \ character followed by a character that indicates the character to be included in the string. An example of an escape character is **\n** which indicates the new line character.

When writing to a file, the new line character must be indicated in the output string wherever you wish a new line to be added to the file.

Text files may include multiple values (data **records**) on each line. In such case, each value is usually separated by a special character, such as a comma, tab, or space. This character is termed the **separator** or **delimiter** and cannot occur within the values themselves.

In order to process lines that contain multiple values, the first step is to read the line. The contents of the line can then be parsed to extract the various values based on the delimiter. The PHP **explode**() function performs this task, and the PHP **list**() function can be used to receive the resulting list of values and store these values in individual variables.

The function to close a file is **fclose**(). File should always be closed when the program no longer needs access to the file. It is good practice to open, process and close files as quickly as possible so that the file has the greatest availability for other purposes.

A program can process multiple files at the same time.

Chapter 6 Review Questions

1. A program asks the user for their age and calculates and displays the numbers of years that they have until they retire. What type of data is this program working with?
   a. Transient data
   b. Persistent data
   c. A combination of transient and persistent data

2. A program asks the user for their ID and password, reads a file to determine their bonus, then displays the bonus to the screen. What type of data is this program working with?
   a. Transient data
   b. Persistent data
   c. A combination of transient and persistent data

3. How can a data file be accessed by a PHP program?
   a. Read data from the file
   b. Write data to the file
   c. Append data to the file
   d. Read or write as needed but not append
   e. Read, write or append as needed

4. Tables, records and fields are the basic elements of:
   a. Data files
   b. Relational Databases
   c. PHP programs
   d. Client/Server applications
   e. HTML documents

5. What happens if you open a text file for write operations and the file already exists?
   a. An error message is generated automatically
   b. The file is replaced by a new file and the content of the old file is lost
   c. The file is replaced by a new file and a backup is made of the old file
   d. The existing file is opened and any new output is added to the end of the current file content
   e. A new file is created so there are now two files with the same name in the same folder

6. What happens if you open a text file for append operations and the file already exists?
    a. An error message is generated automatically
    b. The file is replaced by a new file and the content of the old file is lost
    c. The file is replaced by a new file and a backup is made of the old file
    d. The existing file is opened and any new output is added to the end of the current file content
    e. A new file is created so there are now two files with the same name in the same folder

7. Which is the better programming practice?
    a. Open a file as soon as your program begins and close the file just before your program ends
    b. Open a file only when the program needs to work with it and close the file as soon as the program no longer needs it

8. What is wrong with this algorithm?

```
Open scores.txt as scoresFile for reading
Close scoresFile
Read score1, score2, score3, score4, score5 from scoresFile
```

    a. The file should have been opened for append operations
    b. The file should have been opened for write operations
    c. You must read the data from the file before opening the file
    d. You must read the data from the file before closing the file
    e. You can only read one value from a file

9. What is wrong with this code?

```
$scoresFile = fopen("scores.txt","w");
$score1 = trim(fgets($scoresFile));
$score2 = trim(fgets($scoresFile));
$score3 = trim(fgets($scoresFile));
fclose($scoresFile);
```

    a. The code is designed to read data but the program has been opened for write operations
    b. The code is designed to write data but the program has been opened for read operations
    c. In lines 2, 3 and 4, fgets($scoreFile) should be written fgets(scores.txt)
    d. The close($scoresFile) statement should be the second statement
    e. The close($scoresFile) statement should be close(scores.txt)

10. Consider the following code:

```
$someFile = fopen("somefile.txt","r");
$someValue = trim(fgets($someFile));
fclose($someFile);
```

Assume somefile.txt contains the following text on two lines:

```
2005
2004
```

What does $someValue contain after these statements are executed?
   a. 2005
   b. 2004
   c. 4009
   d. 20052004
   e. An error is generated since there is too much data in the file

11. Consider the following code:

```
$someFile = fopen("somefile.txt","r");
$someValue = trim(fgets($someFile));
fclose($someFile);
```

Assume somefile.txt contains the following text on two lines:

```
Chris:Smith:2005
Mary:Jones:2004
```

What does $someValue contain after these statements are executed?
   a. Chris
   b. Chris:Smith:2005
   c. Chris:Smith:2005:Mary:Jones:2004
   d. Mary:Jones:2004
   e. An error is generated since there is too much data in the file

12. Assume somefile.txt contains the following text on two lines:

```
Chris-Smith-2005
Mary-Jones-2004
```

What is being used as a delimiter in this file?
   a. firstName, lastName, and year
   b. The colon :
   c. The dash –
   d. The new line marker
   e. The year

13. Assume that a variable named $currentRecord has already been used to read a line of text from a file and contains the string "Chris:Smith:2005". Which of the following lines of code will correctly parse the string and store the three values into variables $firstName, $lastName, and $year?
   a. fgets($firstName, $lastName, $year) = explode(":", $currentRecord);
   b. list(":", $currentRecord) = explode($firstName, $lastName, $year);
   c. explode(":", $currentRecord) = list($firstName, $lastName, $year);
   d. list($firstName, $lastName, $year) = explode(":", $currentRecord);
   e. list($firstName, $lastName, $year) =trim(fgets(":", $currentRecord))

14. Which statement is true?
   a. A program can only open one file during the program's execution
   b. A program can open any number of files during the program's execution but only one file can be open at a time
   c. A program can open any number of files at the same time as long as they are all open for reading, or else all open for writing or else all open for appending
   d. A program can open any number of files at the same time for any operations as needed (reading, writing or appending)
   e. A program cannot open files

15. Which of the following instructions will write the message "This is a test" to a file referenced by the variable $someFile?
   a. fopen($someFile, "This is a test");
   b. trim(fgets($someFile, "This is a test"));
   c. fputs($someFile, "This is a test");
   d. list($someFile, "This is a test");
   e. explode($someFile, "This is a test");

16. How many lines will this statement store in the file referenced by the variable $someFile?

```
$fputs($someFile, "Testing..One\nTwo..Three\n");
```

a. 0
b. 1
c. 2
d. 3
e. 4

17. How many lines will this statement store in the file referenced by the variable $someFile?

```
$fputs($someFile, "Testing..\n\nOne\nTwo\nThree\n");
```

a. 1
b. 2
c. 3
d. 4
e. 5

18. Assume somefile.txt contains the following text on two lines:

```
Washington, USA
Paris, France
```

What will the file contain after the following instructions are executed?

```
$someFile = fopen("somefile.txt","a");
fputs($someFile, "London, England\n");
fputs($someFile, "Rome, Italy\n");
fclose($someFile);
```

a. Washington, USA
   Paris, France
   London, England
   Rome, Italy
b. London, England
   Rome, Italy
c. London, England
d. Rome, Italy
e. London, England

Rome, Italy
Washington, USA
Paris, France

19. Assume somefile.txt contains the following text on two lines:

Chris:Smith:2005
Mary:Jones:2004

What will the file contain after the following instructions are executed?

```
$someFile = fopen("somefile.txt","w");
fputs($someFile, "Mark:Jones:2003\n");
fputs($someFile, "Anne:Silvers:2004\n");
fclose($someFile);
```

   a. Chris:Smith:2005
      Mary:Jones:2004
      Mark:Jones:2003
      Anne:Silvers:2004
   b. Mark:Jones:2003
      Anne:Silvers:2004
   c. Anne:Silvers:2004
   d. Mark:Jones:2003
      Anne:Silvers:2004
      Chris:Smith:2005
      Mary:Jones:2004
   e. Chris:Smith:2005
      Mary:Jones:2004

20. Which operation might result in the loss of an existing file (assuming the file is opened and closed correctly)?
   a. Read operations only
   b. Write operations only
   c. Append operations only
   d. Write or append operations only
   e. Read, write or append operations

Chapter 6 Code Exercises

Your Chapter 6 code exercises can be found in your **chapter06** folder. This folder is included in your customized XAMPP installation at the following location:

>   htdocs\webtech\coursework\chapter06

Type your name and the date in the **Author** and **Date** sections of each file as you work on each exercise. **Remember** that the Students page on the textbook Web site includes **Hints and Help** pages for the exercises in this and every chapter.

Debugging Exercises

Your **chapter06** folder should contain a number of "fixit" files. Each of these files contains PHP code that has an error of some kind. The type of error is indicated in the comment section of each file. You will need to run each program in order to see the errors, and to debug and test the code to see if it works correctly. For example to run **fixit1.php**, first run the Web server, then use the URL:

>   http://localhost/webtech/coursework/chapter06/fixit1.php

Code Modification Exercises

Your **chapter06** folder contains a number of "modify" files. Each pair of files contains HTML and PHP code that needs to be modified to meet a requirement. The requirements are included in the comment section of each file. Modify the algorithms, being careful to make changes to the .html and .php files as directed. You will need to run each program in order to test your changes. For example to run **modify1.html**, first run the Web server, then use the URL:

>   http://localhost/webtech/coursework/chapter06/modify1.html

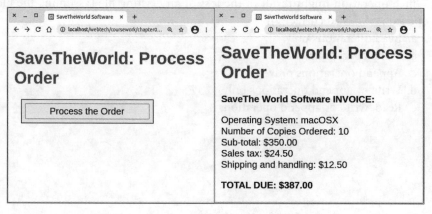

Figure 6-7: process-order.html and process-order.php screenshots

Code Completion Exercises

1. Your **chapter06** folder contains three files **paint-report.html, paint-report.php.** and **paint-contracts.txt.** You do not need to change **paint-report.html**—this simply contains a form with a Submit button to run **paint-report.php**. The **paint-contracts.txt file contains five numbers, each on a separate line, representing the income from this month's paint contracts.** Your job is to develop the code in **paint-report.php** in order to: open the **paint-contracts.txt** file; read the five lines from the file; close the file; calculate the total income. The print statement to display the five payments and the total has been provided. Note the variable names!

2. Your **chapter06** folder contains two files **submit-order.html** and **submit-order.php.** You will see that **submit-order.html** is exactly the same as **submit-order.html** that you developed in Chapter 5. The form is used to submit the operating system and number of copies. Your job is to provide the code in **submit-order.php** that will: open a file named **order.txt**; **write** the operating systems and number of copies received from the form to a single line in this file, separated by a colon; then close the file. For example if the user selected **macOS** and requested **10** copies, **submit-order.php** should create the file **order.txt** and write the following data to the file (followed by a new line character): **macOS:10.**

3. Your **chapter06** folder contains two files: **process-order.html** and **process-order.php.**

    You do not need to change **process-order.html**—this simply contains a form with a Submit button to run **process-order.php**. Your job is to develop the code in **process-order.php** to: open the **order.txt** file; read the line from the file; close the file; then parse the line to obtain the operating system and number of copies. The code to calculate and display the order cost has already been provided to save you time. Be sure to use the same variable names in your own code!

    Figure 6-7 shows sample screen shots if **order.txt** contains the line: **macOS:10**

4. Your **chapter06** folder contains two files: travel.html and travel.php.

    You do not need to change **travel.html**—this simply contains the same form that was used in the previous chapter to receive a travel submission from the user. Your job is to develop the code in **travel.php** to: open the **reservations.txt** file for **appending**; write the destination, number of travelers and number of nights to the file on a **single** line, separated by **colons**, and ending with a new line character; then close the file. The destination will always be "Rome", so if the user submits 3 travelers for 5 nights, your program should append the line: **Rome:3:5** to the file. Submit a few reservations to be sure that the program is appending each reservation to a new line in the file. You may want to delete the file a few times until you get the code working correctly.

5. Your **chapter06** folder contains a file named **restore-game.php, and a file named game-status.dat** (this is a simple text file — the **.dat** extension is often used instead of **.txt** to indicate that a file contains data). The **game-status.dat** file contains five lines of text: the first line contains the character's name; the second line contains the character's type; the third line contains the number of health tokens; the fourth line contains the number of experience tokens; and the fifth line contains the number of supply tokens.

    Your job is to develop the code in **restore-game.php** as follows: open the **game-status.dat** file for **reading**; read the five lines from the file; close the file. The code to display the information has been provided.

6. Copy **event.html** and **event.php** from your **chapter05** folder to your **chapter06** folder. This application processes ticket orders for a performance. Your chapter06 folder contains a file named **ticket-count.txt** which contains a single line containing the number of tickets that have already ordered for the performance. You are now going to modify your event.php program so that it will add the number of tickets that have just been ordered to the number already in the ticket-count.txt file. In other words the ticket-count.txt file will be updated every time a new ticket order is submitted, so that this file will always contain the count of ALL tickets purchased by ALL customers. Updating the number in the file requires a two-step procedure so read the following instructions carefully.

    In order to add the tickets just purchased, we must: (1) open the ticket-count.txt file for read operations, read the previous count of tickets sold from the file into a program variable, then close the file; (2) add the number of tickets that were just ordered (the number received from the form) to the previous count that was read from the file (this will provide the new count); and (3) open the ticket-count.txt file again, this time for write operations, write the new count to the file, and close the file.

    So for example if the user just requested 10 tickets, and ticket-count.txt previously contained 40, step (1) would read the 40 into a variable, step (2) would add 10 to this variable to make 50, and step (3) would write 50 back to the ticket-count.txt file (which would replace the 40 previously in the file). So the file will now contain 50.

    Test your program by using event.html to submit two or three orders. Use your text editor to open ticket-count.txt after each submission. You should see that the number in the file increases each time. We will make use of this file in future exercises.

7. For this exercise you will create a trip log that will keep track of your driving trips. Your **chapter06** folder includes a file named **trip-log.html**. This file contains a form that asks the user to submit the date and miles traveled, followed by four drop down lists to indicate whether or not the trip included breakfast, lunch, dinner, or a hotel (each of these allows the user to select **YES** or **NO**).

   Your folder also includes **trip-log.php** which must process the form. This program is partially completed. Add the code to APPEND the values received from the form to a file named **trip-log.txt**. The values should be appended as a single line of text, using colons to separate each value. Add a new line \n character at the end of the line. Here's how a line might appear in the file:

   3/15/2011:120:NO:YES:YES:YES

   Be sure your program is appending each entry to the file so that new entries are added to the next line and do not over-write previous entries. Run your program a few times, entering trip information for different dates. Use your text editor to open trip-log.txt and check that your program is working correctly.

Chapter 7

Programs that Choose — Introducing Selection Structures

Intended Learning Outcomes

After completing this chapter, you should be able to:

- Explain the purpose of a selection structure.
- Determine the result of a Boolean expression.
- Identify the relational operators.
- Evaluate a simple truth table.
- Distinguish between an IF and IF..ELSE structure.
- Choose an appropriate selection structure based on requirements.
- Design and code an application containing an IF structure.
- Design and code an application containing an IF..ELSE structure.
- Design and code an application that contains multiple, separate selection structures.
- Compare two strings without regard for case.
- Construct a string whose content is partially dependent on a selection structure.

Introduction

Until now all of our algorithms have consisted of a series of sequential instructions that are to be executed, one after the other, one instruction at a time. We are now ready to design applications that can perform tests while the program is running, and choose between different instructions based on the result of these tests. In other words, we are ready to write programs that make decisions.

We often make decisions based on tests in our own lives. For example, here are instructions for an attendant at a theater to check theater goers for tickets:

```
Ask the next party for their tickets
IF this party has valid tickets
   Direct them to their seats
ELSE
   Direct them to the ticket desk
```

In this case, the test is **this party has valid tickets**. The result of this test will always generate a **true** or **false** result. If the test is **true**, one set of instructions is performed (**Direct them to their seats**). If the test is **false**, a different set of instructions is performed (**Direct them to the ticket desk**).

This example demonstrates a **selection control structure,** also known as a **decision structure**. In programming, selection control structures allow us to design applications that can choose between different groups of program instructions by performing a test that will generate a **true** or **false** result. We can use selection control structures for many different purposes. Here are some common examples:

Selective Updates

Applications may need to selectively update data values based on some criterion. For example we might need to write a program that tests whether or not an employee's hourly wage is less than $8 an hour. If the test is true the hourly wage is updated to $8, otherwise the hourly wage is unchanged.

Selective Calculations

Applications may need to perform different calculations depending on some test condition. For example, a program designed to calculate bonuses might be required to test whether an employee has worked at least 35 hours. If the test is true, the program will assign and calculate a $50.00 bonus, otherwise the program will assign and calculate a $25.00 bonus.

Security

A common application requirement is to perform a process only if a valid ID/password combination is provided. The program would be designed to test an ID and password to see if these are valid. If the test is true, the program would fulfill the request, otherwise the program would issue some kind of error response.

Selective Response

Applications may need to be designed to respond to a user's input based on an evaluation of the input. For example, a user may be given a quiz question and the program must evaluate the answer and provide an appropriate response.

Input Validation

It is always important to ensure that all input is valid before performing any required processing. For example we might need to test that the user entered a positive number when asked for the hours that they have worked. If the test is true the program would go ahead and process the input according to the program requirements. If the test is false the program would generate an error message instead.

A program that finds an error in the data that it is processing may be programmed to terminate without further processing, or it may simply ignore any invalid input and continue to process valid input. For example a program designed to find the average of a list of scores in a file might test each score to ensure that it is valid (for example between 0 and 100). When the test is true, the score would be included in the average, when false, the score would be ignored (and perhaps a message would be appended to a log file for future reference).

Data Cleaning

Often data stored in files and databases contains errors, inconsistencies or omissions that need to be corrected before the data can be processed. As an example of correctable errors, consider a file containing misspelled city names. A program might be written to search through data and correct any name if it is misspelled. As an example of inconsistencies, consider a list of medical doctors. A program could be written to check that the title before each name is "Dr."; if it is different, for example, "Doc" or "Doctor" the title is changed to "Dr." for the sake of consistency. As an example of omissions, consider an address list where zip codes are missing from some addresses. A program could search the list and add the correct zip code to an address if it is missing.

The quality of stored data can be significantly improved by these kinds of **data cleaning** (or **data scrubbing**) operations, where a program reads, tests, and applies fixes to data (or ignores or deletes corrupted data). Data cleaning can be a career for some programmers.

Selective Reporting

Applications may need to perform statistics on data that requires selective reporting. For example, a program might be designed to read a file of scores and count the number of passing (scores that are 60 or higher) and failing scores (those less than 60). This program would need to read and test each score: every score of 60 or more would add 1 to the number of passing scores; every score below 60 would add 1 to the number of failing scores.

Selective Searching

Consider a requirement to search a file of employees and display the hourly pay of all employees with a job title of "manager". The program would need to read through all of the employee records in the file and test each one to see if the job title is "manager". If the test is true, the employee's hourly pay would be displayed, otherwise the program would not display anything for that record.

Sorting Data

A more advanced use of selection control structures is to sort data according to some sort criterion, for example, sort a list of employee records by last name. Sorting algorithms require repeated comparisons of data values in order to determine the required ordering.

In this chapter we will develop applications that use selection control structures to perform operations related to the first four of the examples listed here. In subsequent chapters we will learn how to develop algorithms that illustrate many of the other examples.

As you work through this chapter, take time to fully understand the logic. You are learning the fundamental structures of computer programming and it is important that you can apply these structures effectively when you develop your own applications.

Introducing IF and IF..ELSE Structures

In **Chapter 5** we created a simple wage processing application that required user input (**wage2.html** and **wage2.php** in your **samples** folder). In order to gain an understanding of selection structures, we will now develop three different versions of this application by adding selection structures to:

1. Update the wage of anyone earning less than 8.00 an hour
2. Assign a bonus based on the number of hours worked.
3. Obtain a password from the user and only process the wage if the password is correct.

We will develop our algorithms using two fundamental selection structures that are provided by every programming language: IF structures and IF..ELSE structures. The basic syntax of an IF structure written in pseudocode is:

```
IF (..a suitable test that might be true or false )
   Block of instructions to perform if the test is true
ENDIF
```

The basic syntax of an IF..ELSE structure written in pseudocode is:

```
IF (..a suitable test that might be true or false )
   Block of instructions to perform if the test is true
ELSE
   Block of instructions to perform if the test is false
ENDIF
```

Introducing Flow Charts

To more easily understand the way that selection structures work, we will make use of another useful design tool known as a **flow chart**. Programmers draw flow charts to better visualize the logical execution of their program instructions. Until now our programs instructions have simply executed in sequence, one instruction after another. Figure 7-1 provides a general illustration that shows how a simple sequence of instructions might appear in a flow chart.

Flow charts use different symbols to indicate the various statements and control structures that determine the logical execution of program code. Usually **rectangles with curved corners** are used to indicate the beginning and end of the code segment that is displayed in the flow chart, and **rectangles with square corners** are used to display each program statement. The arrows between the program statements indicate the flow of the program. The arrows in Figure 7-1 show us that each program statement is executed in order.

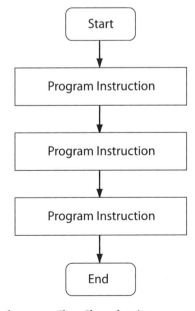

Figure 7-1 General-purpose Flow Chart showing a sequence of instructions

In this first example, the phrase "Program instruction" is used to indicate an instruction of some kind. As we shall see shortly, each rectangle will usually contain a more specific program instruction, such as "Print Welcome message" or "pay = wage * hoursWorked".

Now let's see how a flow chart can help us understand the logic of different selection control structures. Figure 7-2 provides an example of a generic flow chart that includes an **IF** structure. Note that this flow chart indicates some program instructions and then uses a **diamond** symbol to indicate a test. When the program performs this test it will "choose" between two paths depending on whether the test is true or false and the flow chart helps us to see this visually. In this case, we can see that if the test is **true**, the program will branch and execute a block of program instructions before moving on to the program instructions that appear in the next part of the program, but if the test is **false** the program will **skip** this block of instructions and just move on to the next instructions.

The diamond shape is a standard symbol in flow charts. It is used to indicate a decision point in the code, a test that will be true or false. Two arrows branch from a di-

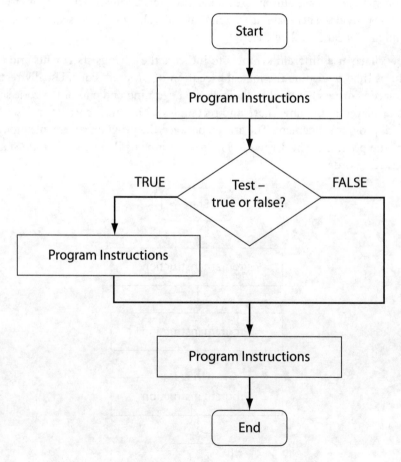

Figure 7-2 General-purpose Flow Chart showing an IF structure

amond symbol in order to display visually what happens if the test is true and what happens if the test is false.

Figure 7-3 provides an example of a flow chart for an **IF..ELSE** structure. This flow chart begins the same way as the **IF** structure example in Figure 7-2. However this time the chart shows us that the program will branch to one of two different blocks of instructions before moving on, depending on whether the test is true or false. So this is different from the IF structure where the program simply skipped to the next part of the program if the test was false.

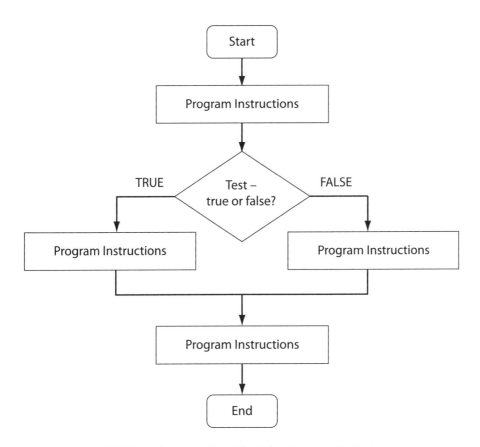

Figure 7-3 General-purpose Flow Chart showing an IF..ELSE structure

Compare these two flow charts to the pseudocode examples of IF and IF..ELSE structures that were listed earlier. Which is easier for you to understand? If you are a visual thinker, you may find it useful to draw your own flow charts as you work out the logic of your own programs.

Note that these examples are intended as an introduction only. We will use more specific examples of flow charts as we learn how to use selection structures to meet actual program requirements.

Boolean Expressions and Relational Operators

We have seen that IF and IF..ELSE structures are based on tests that have a **true** or **false** result. Before we can develop algorithms that include these structures we must first learn how to construct our tests. True/false tests are known as **Boolean expressions** (after the English mathematician George Boole) and the operators used to create Boolean expressions are known as relational operators. Table 7-1 shows how the standard **relational operators** are specified in the PHP language (and in most programming languages):

Relational Operation	Operator
Less than or equal to	<=
Less than	<
Equal to	==
Greater than	>
Greater than or equal to	>=
Not equal to	Either <> or !=

Table 7-1: The relational operators

Note that the **Equal to** operator is == and not = as you might expect. This is because most current programming languages use the = operator to assign values to variables. PHP allows the use of either <> or != to represent **Not equal to**. Most current languages use the != representation and we will use that in this book.

Assume that we are testing a variable named **$hourlyWage** that happens to contain the value 8.00. Here are the results of tests that use the various relational operators:

```
$hourlyWage < 8.00 is false   $hourlyWage <= 8.00 is true
$hourlyWage > 8.00 is false   $hourlyWage >= 8.00 is true
$hourlyWage == 8.00 is true   $hourlyWage != 8.00 is false
```

When you develop an algorithm you must determine which operator you need to use to create a test that will meet your program requirements correctly. Always consider your tests very carefully, because the wrong test will cause your program to produce incorrect results. For example, does your program requirement specify that (a) employees with wages **below** $8.00 an hour receive a wage increase or (b) employees with wages **not more than** $8.00 an hour receive a wage increase? If the answer is (a) then you would use the < operator in your test (for example **$hourlyWage** < **8.00**) but if the answer is (b) then you will need to use the <= operator (for example **$hourlyWage** <= **8.00**).

It is very easy to get confused between = and ==. A very common programming error is to write **if ($hourlyWage = 8.00)** instead of **if ($hourlyWage == 8.00)** which will cause an unwanted assignment operation and an incorrect test result. Remember that the = operator is an **assignment** operator, used to store a value in a variable. The expression **$hourlyWage = 8.00;** stores **8.00** in the variable **$hourlyWage**. The == operator is a **relational** operator and is used to compare two values and return a true or false result. The expression **($hourlyWage == 8.00)** will be **true** if $hourlyWage contains the value **8.00**, or **false** otherwise.

Selection Using the IF Structure

Consider the following requirement:

Wage3 requirement:

Write a program that asks the employee for an hourly wage and the number of hours worked.

If the hourly wage is below 8.00 it should be changed to 8.00. No change is needed if the hourly wage is already at least 8.00.

The program should then calculate and display the hourly wage, hours worked, and weekly wage.

To meet this requirement we need a selection structure to test if the hourly wage is less than 8.00, and, if the test is **true**, update the wage to 8.00. But what if the test is **false** (if the wage is already 8.00 or above)? In this case, our program does not need to do anything and the wage is left unchanged. When our requirement does not require any special action if a test is **false**, we can use an IF structure.

To meet these requirements, we first need to receive the hourly wage and hours worked from the user. Here is the algorithm for **wage3.html** (the HTML page that will use a form to receive the user input and submit the input to **wage3.php**):

```
wage3.html algorithm:
  Prompt for hourly wage
  Get hourlyWage
  Prompt for hours worked
  Get hoursWorked
  Submit hourlyWage and hoursWorked to wage3.php
END
```

Here is the HTML code for this document:

```
<html>
<head>
  <title>Wage Report</title>
  <link rel="stylesheet" type="text/css" href="sample.css">
</head>
<body>
  <h1>Wage Report</h1>
  <form action="wage3.php" method="post">
  <label>Hourly wage:
      <input type="text" size="10" name="hourlyWage"></label>
  <label>Hours worked:
      <input type="text" size="10" name="hoursWorked">
    </label>
    <input class="submit" type="submit" value="Get Your Wage
      Report Now">
  </form>
</body>
</html>
```

Code Example: wage3.html

Now let's develop the algorithm to process the input according to our requirement document. We will use an **IF** structure to update the hourly wage if the wage that was input by the user is less than 8.00. Here is the algorithm for **wage3.php:**

```
wage3.php algorithm:
  Receive hourlyWage, hoursWorked from wage3.html
  IF (hourlyWage < 8.00)
    hourlyWage =8.00
  ENDIF
  weeklyWage = hourlyWage * hoursWorked
  Display heading
  Display hourlyWage, hoursWorked, weeklyWage
END
```

After receiving the user input, the algorithm tests the value stored in the **hourlyWage** variable (the value received from the user). If this value is less than 8.00 then the test will be **true** so the statements inside the IF structure will be executed. In this case we only need a single statement in the IF structure which updates the value stored in **hourlyWage** to 8.00. If the test is **false** then the statements inside the IF structure will be skipped and the value stored in the **hourlyWage** variable will be left unchanged.

Next the program processes the statement **following** the IF structure. The value stored in **hourlyWage** (which may or may not have just been updated) is multiplied by the value stored in **hoursWorked** and the result is stored in **weeklyWage**. The program then displays a heading and the values of the three variables.

Figure 7-4 shows this algorithm as a flow chart, slightly simplified to focus on the selection structure. Examine this carefully so that you can see that the flowchart follows the same logic as the pseudocode but displays the logic visually. They say that a picture is worth a thousand words and perhaps you will agree that the algorithm is much easier to understand when it is presented this way.

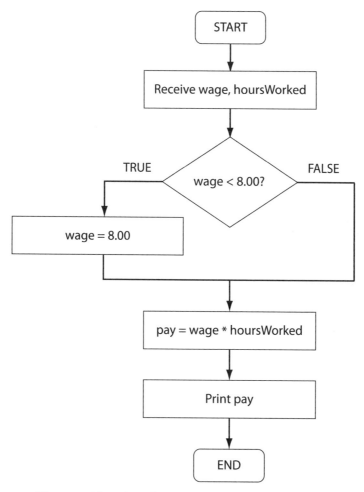

Figure 7-4: Flow Chart showing the algorithm for wage3.php

Here is the PHP code for **wage3.php** that implements this algorithm:

```
<html>
<head>
  <title>Wage Report</title>
  <link rel="stylesheet" type="text/css" href="sample.css">
</head>
<body>
  <?php
    $hourlyWage = $_POST['hourlyWage'];
    $hoursWorked = $_POST['hoursWorked'];

    if ($hourlyWage < 8.00)
    {
      $hourlyWage = 8.00;
    }
    $weeklyWage = $hourlyWage * $hoursWorked;

    print("<h1>Wage Report</h1>");
    print("<p>Your hourly wage is $$hourlyWage and you worked
        $hoursWorked hours.</p>");
    print("<p>Your wages are $$weeklyWage.</p>");

    print ("<a href=\"wage3.html\">Return to form</a>");
  ?>
</body>
</html>
```

Code Example: wage3.php

Notice that the IF structure is coded differently in PHP than in pseudocode. Here is the syntax for writing an IF structure in PHP:

```
if (test condition)
{
  // statements to perform if the test is true
}
```

The test in the heading of the IF structure should be enclosed in parentheses. Note the use of curly braces to enclose the block of statements that are to be executed if the test is **true** (there is no ENDIF instruction in PHP). Any statements **between** the curly braces will be executed only if the test is true. Any statements that **follow** the closing curly brace are not part of the IF structure, so these will be executed regardless of the test.

Never include a semi-colon directly following the test condition in the heading of the IF structure! A semi-colon indicates the end of a program instruction and the heading (first line) of a control structure is not considered to be a complete instruction. If you write **if ($hourlyWage > 0);** the processor will mistakenly assume that, if the test is true, the program should execute the instruction that comes before the semi-colon, which in this case is no instruction at all!

Testing Threshold Values

Since there are two paths through this code depending on the value of the hourly wage, you should test the application at least **twice**:

```
Test 1:    Enter an hourly wage less than 8.00
Test 2:    Enter an hourly wage 8.00 or above
```

When testing to ensure that a selection structure will work as expected, it is especially important to test the **threshold values**. These are the two values closest to your test condition that will generate a true and false result (if your test is correctly coded). Good threshold values in this case would be 7.99 and 8.00 since 7.99 is the value closest to the test that should generate a true result and 8.00 is the closest value to the test that should generate a false result.

Selection Using the IF..ELSE Structure

Take a look at the following program requirement:

Wage4 requirement:

Write a program that asks the employee for an hourly wage and the number of hours worked.

If the hours worked is at least 35, the program should assign a bonus of 50.00, otherwise the program should assign a bonus of 25.00.

The program should calculate and display the hourly wage, hours worked, bonus and weekly wage (including the bonus).

To meet this requirement we must design a program that will test the hours worked. Based on this test we want our program to either assign a 50.00 bonus or else assign a 25.00 bonus. In other words we want our program to choose between **two** different groups of statements depending on the result of the test. This requires the use of an IF..ELSE structure. Here is the algorithm for **wage4.php**:

```
wage4.php algorithm:
  Receive hourlyWage, hoursWorked from wage4.html
  IF (hoursWorked >= 35)
    bonus = 50.00
  ELSE
    bonus = 25.00
  ENDIF
  weeklyWage = hourlyWage * hoursWorked + bonus
  Display heading
  Display hourlyWage, hoursWorked, bonus, weeklyWage
END
```

This program will receive values for the **hourlyWage** and **hoursWorked** variables from the HTML form submitted by **wage4.html** (included in your **samples** folder). The program first performs a test: **IF (hoursWorked >= 35)**. This test will have a **true** or **false** result. If the test is **true**, then the statements between the IF and the ELSE are executed and the statements between the ELSE and ENDIF are skipped. If the test is **false**, then the statements between the IF and the ELSE are skipped and the statements between the ELSE and ENDIF are executed.

Figure 7-5 shows a slightly simplified version of this algorithm as a flow chart.

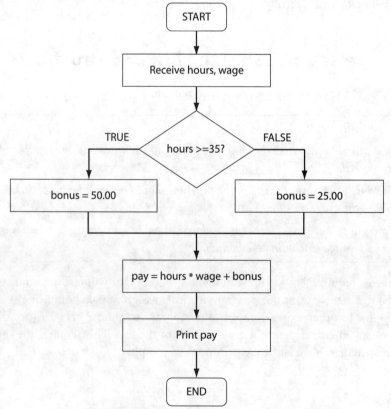

Figure 7-5: Flow Chart showing the algorithm for wage4.php

It is important to understand that each time this program runs, only one of these two blocks of statements will execute. In other words there are two possible paths through the program and only one path will be chosen each time the program runs.

Once the program has executed the IF..ELSE structure, it will have assigned either 50.00 or 25.00 to the **bonus** variable. The statements that **follow** the ENDIF are not part of the IF..ELSE structure. These statements will be executed whether the test was true or false. In this example, the next statement calculates the wage. This calculation includes the value stored in the **bonus** variable, which may be 50.00 or 25.00. The program then displays the values stored in the four variables.

Here is the PHP code for **wage4.php**:

```
<html>
<head>
  <title>Wage Report</title>
  <link rel="stylesheet" type="text/css" href="sample.css">
</head>
<body>
  <?php

    $hourlyWage = $_POST['hourlyWage'];
    $hoursWorked = $_POST['hoursWorked'];

    if ($hoursWorked >= 35)
    {
      $bonus = 50.00;
    }
    else
    {
      $bonus = 25.00;
    }

    $weeklyWage = $hourlyWage * $hoursWorked + $bonus;

    print("<h1>Wage Report</h1>");
    print("<p>Your hourly wage is $$hourlyWage and you
worked
      $hoursWorked hours.</p>");
    print("<p>Your bonus is $$bonus.</p>");
    print("<p>Your weekly wage is $$weeklyWage.</p>");
    print("<a href=\"wage4.html\">Return to form</a>");
  ?>
</body>
</html>
```

Code Example: wage4.php

Just as with **wage3.php**, notice the use of **curly braces** { and }. A pair of braces is used to enclose the block of statements that are to be executed if the test condition is **true** (the statements between the IF and the ELSE. A second pair of braces is used to enclose the block of statements that are to be executed if the test condition is **false** (following the ELSE). In this example, there is just one statement in each of these two blocks.

In PHP, **IF..ELSE** statements have the following general form:

```
if (test condition)
{
   // statements to perform if the test is true
}
else
{
   // statements to perform if the test is false
}
```

Always think carefully about which statements need to appear **before** the **IF..ELSE** structures, which statements need to be included between the { and } braces of the IF section, which statements need to be included between the { and } braces of the ELSE section, and which statements need to be **follow** the **IF..ELSE** section. If you place a statement in the wrong location, your program logic will be incorrect and your program will not work as intended.

Since there are two paths through this code depending on the value of the hours worked, you should test the application at least **twice**:

```
Test 1:    hours worked at least 35
Test 2:    hours worked less than 35
```

If we run the program using 35 for the hours worked and then a second time using 34 for the hours worked, this will ensure that these threshold values generate the expected results. Figure 7-6 shows the result if the user enters 35 when prompted for the hours worked.

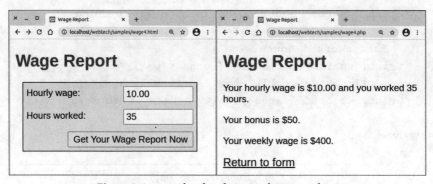

Figure 7-6: wage4.html and wage4.php screenshots

Figure 7-7 shows the result if the user enters 34.

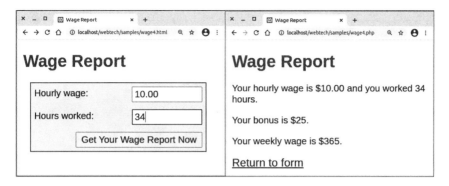

Figure 7-7: wage4.html and wage4.php screenshots

Indenting Code Inside Selection Structures

Take another look at the algorithms and code examples you have studied so far in this chapter. Notice the way they are written: the blocks of statements inside the IF and ELSE sections of the selection structures are always **indented**. The PHP processor ignores white space like this, so these indents are not required for the program to run successfully. Instead they are intended to provide you, the programmer, with a visual aid, showing more clearly which statements are be executed as part of the IF and ELSE sections. This can be very helpful if your program has errors, for example one or more missing curly braces. The indents can help you see where a brace needs to be added.

Programmers **always** indent statements inside control structures such as selection structures and you should follow this practice. You will see the value of indenting as you progress through this book and your code becomes more complex. Many text editors are "code-smart" and will recognize when you are writing code (for example if you save your file with a .php, .html, or other common programming language file extension). Automatic indentation is a common code-friendly feature: if you press the Return key after typing a left curly brace your editor may automatically indent the next line for you, and then go back one indent level when you type a closing curly brace. Similarly, if you use the Tab key to indent a line of code, the editor will start the next line at the same indent level each time you press Return (you can just use the Backspace key to go back one indent level when you are ready to do that).

When to Use Braces in IF..ELSE Statements

As previously mentioned, **braces** are used to tell the processor which statements in your code are part of the IF block and which statements are part of the ELSE block. Braces are actually only needed if there is more than one statement in the block. Here is a variation of the **wage4.php** code which is acceptable only because each of the sections contains a single statement:

```php
<?php

    $hourlyWage = $_POST['hourlyWage'];
    $hoursWorked = $_POST['hoursWorked'];

    if ($hoursWorked >= 35)
       $bonus = 50.00;
    else
       $bonus = 25.00;

    $weeklyWage = $hourlyWage * $hoursWorked + $bonus;

    print("<h1>Wage Report</h1>");
    print("<p>Your hourly wage is $$hourlyWage and you worked
       $hoursWorked hours.</p>");

    print("<p>Your bonus is $$bonus.</p>");
    print("<p>Your weekly wage is $$weeklyWage.</p>");

    print ("<a href=\"wage4.html\">Return to form</a>");

?>
```

Code Example: Alternative version of wage4.php

In this example no braces are used for either the IF section or the ELSE section because there is only a single statement to be executed in either case. You can still include braces if you prefer. The rule is that if you have more than one statement in either the IF section or in the ELSE section, then you **must** use braces for that section. To understand this better, take a look at the code in wage6.php, later in this chapter. In this example, the IF section contains three statements and the ELSE section contains two statements, so braces **must** be used in both sections. **Not including braces when they are needed is a very common programming error.**

Some programmers prefer to **always** use braces, even if there is only a single statement to execute in the IF or ELSE section. You might want to take this approach; using braces consistently means you are less likely to forget them when you need them (and if you find you need to add additional statements into the section, you have the braces already in place).

Creating a Program with Multiple but Independent Selection Structures

Real-world applications will use multiple selection structures in order to meet requirements. There are no restrictions on how many IF or IF..ELSE structures can be used, and these structures can be combined as needed. We will consider different ways to combine selection structures in Chapter 8; for now let's just consider an application that requires two separate selection structures. The following requirement combines the requirements from Wage3 and Wage4:

Wage5 requirement:

Write a program that asks the employee for an hourly wage and the number of hours worked.

If the hourly wage is below 8.00 it should be increased to 8.00. No increase is needed if the hourly wage is already at least 8.00.

The program should assign a bonus based on the hours worked. If the hours worked is at least 35, the program should assign a bonus of 50.00, otherwise the program should assign a bonus of 25.00.

The program should calculate and display the hourly wage, hours worked, bonus and weekly wage (including the bonus).

The algorithm that meets this requirement must include two separate selection structures. One selection structure is needed to update the hourly wage if necessary. The other will be used to calculate the bonus. Here is the algorithm for **wage5.php**:

```
wage5.php algorithm:

   Receive hourlyWage, hoursWorked from wage5.html

   IF (hourlyWage < 8.00)
     hourlyWage = 8.00
   ENDIF

   IF (hoursWorked >= 35)
     bonus = 50.00
   ELSE
     bonus = 25.00
   ENDIF

   weeklyWage = hourlyWage * hoursWorked + bonus
   Display heading
   Display hourlyWage, hoursWorked, bonus, weeklyWage
END
```

Look through this algorithm carefully. Notice that the hourly wage that was entered by the user may or may not be increased, but a bonus will **always** be calculated. This is because the first selection is an IF structure, with no action taken if the test is **false**, while the second structure is an IF..ELSE structure, which provides actions for either a **true** result or a **false** result. In this algorithm these two structures just happen to directly follow one another, but selection structures can be included anywhere in your algorithm as needed.

Consider the order of the statements in this algorithm. Since the two selection structures are unrelated to one another, they could be included in your algorithm in either order. In other words, the structure to assign a bonus could appear before the structure that determines whether or not to increase the hourly wage. This is not always the case — in the next chapter we will look at requirements where multiple selection structures **must** be ordered correctly or even **nested** inside one another.

The weeklyWage calculation uses the hourly wage and the bonus, so this calculation **must** appear after **both** selection structures, otherwise the calculation will be performed before a possible change to the hourly wage, and before a bonus has been assigned. Similarly the output statements must appear after all variables have been assigned values by the program. Always remember that a computer program cannot "look ahead", and that statements are processed in the order that they are listed.

Here is the PHP code for **wage5.php**:

```
<html>
<head>
  <title>Wage Report</title>
  <link rel="stylesheet" type="text/css" href="sample.css">
</head>
<body>
  <?php
    $hourlyWage = $_POST['hourlyWage'];
    $hoursWorked = $_POST['hoursWorked'];

    if ($hourlyWage < 8.00)
      $hourlyWage = 8.00;

    if ($hoursWorked >= 35)
      $bonus = 50.00;
    else
      $bonus = 25.00;

    $weeklyWage = $hourlyWage * $hoursWorked + $bonus;

    print("<h1>Wage Report</h1>");
    print("<p>Your hourly wage is $$hourlyWage and you worked
      $hoursWorked hours.</p>");
    print("<p>Your bonus is $$bonus.</p>");
    print("<p>Your weekly wage is $$weeklyWage.</p>");
    print ("<a href=\"wage5.html\">Return to form</a>");
  ?>
</body>
</html>
```

Code Example: wage5.php

How many tests are needed to test this code thoroughly? Note that there are **four** possible paths through this program: two paths through the **IF** structure, and two paths through the IF..ELSE structure. You should test for each possible path, as follows:

Test 1: A value for hourlyWage that is less than 8.00, and a value for hoursWorked that is 35 or above

Test 2: A value for hourlyWage that is less than 8.00, and a value for hoursWorked that is less than 35

Test 3: A value for hourlyWage that is 8.00 or higher, and a value for hoursWorked that is 35 or above

Test 4: A value for hourlyWage that is 8.00 or higher, and a value for hoursWorkedthat is less than 35

Do you see that all four tests are needed to be sure that all of the statements in the program are working correctly?

Comparing Strings — Testing for a Correct Password

Our examples so far have used selection structures to test **numeric** values. We can just as easily test character strings, for example a password that has been submitted by the user. Recall that a character string may contain any sequence of text characters. The following are all examples of character strings:

"John"	"123 Main Street"	"A123-HFC"
"123-45-6789"	"Enter your password:"	"Price: $10.75"

Consider the following requirement:

Wage6 requirement:

Write a program that asks the employee for an hourly wage, the number of hours worked, and a password.

If the password is correct, the program should calculate the weekly wage and display the hourly wage, hours worked, and weekly wage. Otherwise the program should display an error message.

For testing purposes, the correct password is "employee".

Of course in the real world, passwords are encrypted and stored in a database; the programmer will never know a user's actual password! But here we simply want to demonstrate how an IF..ELSE structure is used to handle a correct and incorrect password, so we'll just keep it simple and test the user's input against a "dummy" password named "employee".

To meet this requirement, we must design an algorithm for a program that will respond according to the user's input of a password. First, here is the algorithm that we will use to create a form for **wage6.html**:

```
wage6.html algorithm:

    Prompt for hourly wage
    Get hourlyWage
    Prompt for hours worked
    Get hoursWorked
    Prompt for password
    Get userPassword
    Submit hourlyWage, hoursWorked, password to wage6.php
END
```

Here is the HTML code for this document:

```
<html>
<head>
  <title>Wage Report</title>
  <link rel="stylesheet" type="text/css" href="sample.css">
</head>
<body>
  <h1>Wage Report</h1>
  <form action="wage6.php" method="post">
  <label>Hourly wage:
  <input type="text" size="10" name="hourlyWage"></label>
  <label>Hours worked:
  <input type="text" size="10" name="hoursWorked"></label>
  <label>Password:
  <input type="password" size="15"
    name="userPassword"></label>
  <input class="submit" type="submit" value="Get Your Wage
    Report Now">
</form>
</body>
</html>
```

Code Example: wage6.html

The form now includes a prompt and input box to receive a password. Usually we want passwords and other secure data entries to appear as **asterisks** when typed by the user. We achieve this by using an HTML **<input>** tag in our form with the type attribute set to be "**password**" instead of "**text**":

```
    <label>Password:
    <input type="password" size="15"
      name="userPassword"></label>
```

Here is the algorithm for **wage6.php**:

```
wage6.php algorithm:
   Receive hourlyWage, hoursWorked, password from wage6.html
   Display "Wage Report" heading
   IF (password == "employee")
     weeklyWage = hourlyWage * hoursWorked
     Display hourlyWage, hoursWorked, weeklyWage
   ELSE
     Display "Incorrect Password" message
     Display "Please try again"
   ENDIF
END
```

Note that the wage calculation is located **inside** the IF section. That's because it would be inefficient to perform this calculation if the password is false since there would be no need for it; the wage would not be displayed anyway. Here is the PHP code for **wage6.php**:

```
<html>
<head>
   <title>Wage Report</title>
   <link rel="stylesheet" type="text/css" href="sample.css">
</head>
<body>
   <?php
     $hourlyWage = $_POST['hourlyWage'];
     $hoursWorked = $_POST['hoursWorked'];
     $userPassword = $_POST['userPassword'];

     print("<h1>Wage Report</h1>");
     if ($userPassword == "employee")
     {
       $weeklyWage = $hourlyWage * $hoursWorked;

       print("<p>Your hourly wage is $$hourlyWage and you worked
         $hoursWorked hours.</p>");
       print("<p>Your wages are $$weeklyWage.</p>");
     }
     else
     {
       print("<p><strong>YOU ENTERED AN INVALID
         PASSWORD!</strong></p>");
       print("<p>Please try again</p>");
     }
     print ("<a href=\"wage6.html\">Return to form</a>");
   ?>
</body>
</html>
```

Code Example: wage6.php

First, note that the statements in both the IF and the ELSE sections must be enclosed in curly braces since there is more than one statement in each section.

Also note the use of the == operator to test whether the value stored in **$userPassword** is equal to **"employee"**. Be very careful not to use the = assignment operator by mistake, for example **if ($userPassword = "employee")**. If you make this mistake the processor will assume that you wish to store the value **"employee"** in the **$userPassword** variable, rather than test whether the variable contains this value.

For this algorithm, the **"Wage Report"** heading for the HTML must be displayed **before** the IF..ELSE structure. This will then be followed by either the output generated in the IF section or else the output generated inside the ELSE section. If the instruction to output the heading was located **inside** either the IF or the **ELSE** section, it would only be displayed if that section was executed. If the instruction was located **after** the entire IF..ELSE section, the heading would appear **following** the wage information or error message. An alternative would be to include the **print("<h1>Wage Report</h1>");** instruction in **both** the IF section **and** the ELSE section. This is considered bad programming practice since it requires code duplication. This increases the chance of typing errors, and also makes it harder to update code, for example if the heading needs to be changed a programmer might not realize that it needs to be changed in **two** places. **As a general rule, if you find that you have duplicated a line of code, you should probably rethink your program logic.**

Since there are two paths through this code depending on the value of the password, you should test the application at least **twice:**

```
Test 1:  enter "employee" as the password
Test 2:  enter an incorrect password
```

Try entering **"EMPLOYEE"** as the password. Does the program accept passwords that do not use the correct case? No because the code is specifically testing for **"employee"**, and this is probably appropriate in the case of passwords. But what if we want our application to test a character string but we don't care whether the string is upper or lower case, or any combination of these?

Ignoring the Case of a Character String

Our wage5 program will only accept "employee" as the correct password if the user enters this in lower-case characters. Sometimes when we test character strings we want to **ignore** any differences in case. For example let's say we asked the user to enter a country and we want to test if the country is "Canada". We may want to allow a true result whether the user types "Canada", "canada", "CANADA" or even "CaNaDa". Instead of testing for every possible combination it is much easier to first convert the user's input to all lower-case and then compare this with "canada", or to all upper-case and compare it to "CANADA".

Most programming languages, including PHP, provide a number of useful **string-processing** functions that make it easy to perform common operations on character strings. PHP provides the **strtolower()** and **strtoupper()** functions to convert a string to either lower or upper case. If we want our program to test a variable named **$country** without regard to case, we can convert it to all lower-case before the IF..ELSE section:

```
$country = strtolower($country);
```

This statement passes the string currently stored in **$country** to the **strtolower()** function. The function converts the string to all lower-case and returns the new version. This lower-case version of the country is then stored back in **$country**, replacing the original version. Now when the program compares $country with "canada" it will generate a true result even if the user originally submitted a country using a combination of upper- and lower-case letters.

In this example we actually changed the value stored in the **$country** to lower-case. That's not always a good idea; there may be reasons to keep the content of the variable in its original form, perhaps that will be necessary for subsequent processing. As an alternative we could leave the value of the variable unchanged and simply use the **strtolower()** function in the test itself:

```
if (strtolower($country) == "canada")
```

Here the string is converted to lower-case in order to perform the test but the converted string is not assigned to **$country** and so this variable still contains the original version of the string.

Note that the **strtolower()** and **strtoupper()** can be used to convert character strings that include non-alphabetical characters such as numbers or special characters. Non-alphabetical characters are unchanged.

Providing a Selective Response

Consider the following requirement:

Quiz1 requirement:

Write a program that provides the user with a quiz question using a drop down box with a list of possible answers. The program should display an appropriate response based on the user's input.

If the user provides the wrong answer the program should display the correct answer. For test purposes, ask the question: What is the name for expressions that evaluate to true or false? Provide these possible answers: Arithmetic, Boolean, and Relational.

In this case we want to provide a selective response based on the user's answer to a question. Here is the algorithm for the HTML document that will provide the input form (**quiz1.html**):

```
quiz1.html algorithm:
   Prompt for the answer to the quiz question
   Get userAnswer
   Submit userAnswer to quiz1.php
END
```

We can test user input from a drop down list just as easily as input from an input box, and in this case we want to restrict the user's input to some specific choices. Here is the code for **quiz1.html**:

```
<html>
<head>
  <title>QUIZ</title>
  <link rel="stylesheet" type="text/css" href="sample.css">
</head>
<body>
  <h1>QUIZ</h1>
  <form action="quiz1.php" method="post">
  <label>What is the name for expressions that evaluate to
    true or false?
  <select name="userAnswer">
  <option>Arithmetic</option>
  <option>Boolean</option>
  <option>Relational</option>
  </select></label>
  <input class="submit" type="submit" value="Submit your
    answer">
  </form>
</body>
</html>
```

Code Example: quiz1.html

Here is the algorithm for the PHP program that will process the input (**quiz1.php**):

```
quiz1.php algorithm:

   Receive userAnswer from quiz1.html
   Display "QUIZ" heading
   correctAnswer = "Boolean"
   IF (userAnswer == correctAnswer)
     Display "That is correct!"
   ELSE
     Display "That is incorrect!"
     Display correctAnswer
   ENDIF
END
```

Note once again the use of the = operator to assign a value to a variable (for example **correctAnswer** = "Boolean"), and the use of the == operator to compare two values, for example **userAnswer** == **correctAnswer**. In this case the value stored in the **userAnswer** variable is compared to the value stored in the **correctAnswer** variable.

Here is the code for **quiz1.php**:

```html
<html>
<head>
  <title>QUIZ</title>
  <link rel="stylesheet" type="text/css" href="sample.css">
</head>
<body>
  <?php

    $userAnswer = $_POST['userAnswer'];

    print("<h1>QUIZ</h1>");

    $correctAnswer = "Boolean";

    if ($userAnswer == $correctAnswer)
      print("<p>That is correct!</p>");
    else
    {
      print("<p>That is incorrect!</p>");
      print("<p>The correct answer is $correctAnswer</p>");
    }

  ?>
</body>
</html>
```

Code Example: quiz1.php

In this case, we are comparing the string that the user selected from the drop down list with the string stored in the **$correctAnswer** variable. Note that when processing input from a drop down list we never need to worry about the case, since we know exactly what text is listed inside each of the <**option**> </**option**>tags.

Note that the IF section contains only a **single** instruction and so curly braces are not needed. On the other hand the ELSE section contains **two** instructions and so these **must** be enclosed in braces.

Why did we assign the value "Boolean" to the variable **$correctAnswer** instead of referring to it directly in our code? This avoids duplication. If we were to change our quiz to handle a different question with a new correct answer, we would only have to change the instruction **$correctAnswer** = "Boolean"; to store the new correct answer in this variable. The rest of the code would then work correctly with no additional changes. Otherwise we would have to search through the code for every occurrence of the correct answer and change each one.

Using Selection to Construct a Line of Output

Often when a program generates output, some parts of the output will depend on the result of tests and must be included in selection structures, while other parts of the output will be the same regardless of any testing. These conditions may even apply to various parts of a sentence or paragraph. Consider the following requirement:

Grade1 requirement:

Write a program that asks the user to enter three exam scores. The program will calculate the average score and determine whether the average constitutes a passing or failing grade. A passing grade is 60 or higher.

The program should display the three scores followed by a line that begins "OVER-ALL GRADE:", followed by "Pass" or "Fail".

This requires us to create a line that begins the same no matter what the score (with the phrase "OVERALL GRADE: "), but ends with either "**Pass**" or "**Fail**" depending on the result of a test.

Here is the algorithm for the HTML document that will provide the input form (**grade1.html**):

```
grade1.html algorithm:
   Prompt for the score for Exam 1
   Get exam1
   Prompt for the score for Exam 2
   Get exam2
   Prompt for the score for Exam 3
   Get exam3
   Submit exam1, exam2, exam3 to grade1.php
END
```

Here is the HTML code for **grade1.html**:

```
<html>
<head>
  <title>EXAM GRADE</title>
  <link rel="stylesheet" type="text/css" href="sample.css">
</head>
<body>
  <h1>EXAM GRADE</h1>

  <form action="grade1.php" method="post">
  <label>Enter score for Exam 1:
    <input type="text" size="5" name="exam1"></label>
  <label>Enter score for Exam 2:
    <input type="text" size="5" name="exam2"></label>
  <label>Enter score for Exam 3:
    <input type="text" size="5" name="exam3"></label>
  <input class="submit" type="submit" value="Submit your
      scores">
</form>
</body>
</html>
```

Code Example: grade1.html

Here is the algorithm for the PHP program that will process the input (**grade1.php**):

```
grade1.php algorithm:
  Receive exam1, exam2, exam3 from grade1.html
  Display "EXAM GRADE"
  Display exam1, exam2, exam3
  Display "OVERALL GRADE: "
  averageScore = (exam1 + exam2 + exam3) /3

  IF (averageScore >= 60)
    Display "Pass"
  ELSE
    Display "Fail"
  ENDIF
END
```

Here is the PHP code for **grade1.php**:

```
<html>
<head>
  <title>EXAM GRADE</title>
  <link rel="stylesheet" type="text/css" href="sample.css">
</head>
<body>
  <?php
    $exam1 = $_POST['exam1'];
    $exam2 = $_POST['exam2'];
    $exam3 = $_POST['exam3'];

    print("<h1>EXAM GRADE</h1>");
    print("Exam 1 score: $exam1<br>");
    print("Exam 2 score: $exam2<br>");
    print("Exam 3 score: $exam3<br>");
    print("<p><strong>OVERALL GRADE: ");
    $averageScore = ($exam1 + $exam2 + $exam3) / 3;

    if ($averageScore >= 60)
      print("Pass</strong></p>");
    else
      print("Fail</strong></p>");

    print ("<p><a href=\"grade1.html\">Return to form</a></p>");
  ?>
</body>
</html>
```

Code Example: grade1.php

In order to display the word "**Pass**" or "**Fail**" on the same line as "**OVERALL GRADE** " we first used a print statement before the IF..ELSE structure to begin a paragraph with the words "**OVERALL GRADE:** ". We complete the paragraph in one of two different ways depending on the result of the test (**$averageScore** >= **60**).

It is possible to take another approach here and that is to progressively add (concatenate) all the output from the program to a single variable, and then simply print the contents of this variable in a single instruction once all required output has been added. Here is the relevant code from **grade2.php** which demonstrates this approach:

```php
<?php
  $exam1 = $_POST['exam1'];
  $exam2 = $_POST['exam2'];
  $exam3 = $_POST['exam3'];

  $report = "<h1>EXAM GRADE</h1>
       Exam 1 score: $exam1<br>
       Exam 2 score: $exam2<br>
       Exam 3 score: $exam3<br>
       <p><strong>OVERALL GRADE: ";

  $averageScore = ($exam1 + $exam2 + $exam3) / 3;

  if ($averageScore >= 60)
     $report = $report."Pass</strong></p>";
  else
     $report = $report."Fail</strong></p>";

  $report = $report."<p><a href=\"grade2.html\">
       Return to form</a></p>";
  print("$report");
?>
</body>
</html>
```

Here the variable **$report** is first assigned all of the output content that must appear **before** the output from the IF..ELSE structure. Then the appropriate string from the IF..ELSE structure is added to the previous content of the variable using the concatenation operator (this is a **period** in PHP). Following the IF..ELSE structure the last line of required output is added to the variable. Now that the **$report** variable contains all the required output, the program requires only a single **print()** statement.

This is an especially useful approach when the same text may need to be output to multiple locations, for example to a file and also to a Web page. As always, it is important for you as the program designer to consider carefully what you need to accomplish and assemble your logic in a way that meets the requirements correctly and efficiently. A good designer designs an application in a way that also anticipates **future** requirements.

Troubleshooting and Desk-Checking

As you start using selection structures you are likely to find yourself spending more time troubleshooting and debugging your code. Some problems will be **syntax errors** that prevent your code from executing; the most likely syntax errors associated with selection structures are:

- Missing opening or closing parentheses in the heading of an IF or IF..ELSE structure.

- A semi-colon at the end of the heading (remember, semi-colons should not be added to headings, although not technically a syntax error).

- Multiple statements in an IF or ELSE section that have not been enclosed in opening and closing curly braces.

- An opening curly brace at the start of a section without a closing curly brace at the end, or a closing brace with no opening brace.

- Missing semi-colons after one or more statements in the IF section or ELSE section. These statements are just like any other PHP statements and must end with semi-colons.

Note that the PHP processor will always report syntax errors but may mis-report the nature of the error, and may even give the wrong line number where the error occurred. That's because the processor cannot know what actually caused the error. For example, if your IF section has an opening curly brace but does not have a closing brace, the processor will not know there's a problem until it reaches the ELSE, at which point it will report the error as "Unexpected ELSE found on line xxx". When you get an error message, think about what may have caused it, and remember that the actual error might occur on one of the lines **before** the line where the error is reported.

Syntax errors may be frustrating but at least you will know there's a problem because the code won't execute. You are also likely to experience **logical errors**, and these can be more difficult to identify since, although the program will execute, it will deliver the wrong result. Sometimes this will be obvious, but other times an error may not be apparent unless you carefully test your results. For example, if a program assigns a different bonus depending on the hours an employee has worked, you can only tell if the results are always correct by testing with different values of the hours worked.

If you do discover a logical error, here are some things to look out for in your code:

- Check that you used == and not = when comparing two values to see if they are equal. If you use = you are ASSIGNING a value not comparing values, and since assignment is a valid operation you will not get an error message, which makes this problem hard to find since it's such an easy mistake to make when typing.

- Similarly be sure that you used = for assignment operations and not ==.

- Always consider the **order** of your instructions. For example what if your total cost for an order is supposed to include the tax but doesn't? Perhaps the statement that calculates the tax appears **after** the total is calculated, when it should of course appear **before**.

- Do you need to use curly braces in your IF or ELSE sections? Not including braces when you need to will not **always** generate a syntax error unless you have multiple statements in an IF section that is then followed by an ELSE; in other cases the processor will just assume that only the first statement is associated with the IF or ELSE, and that the remaining statements **follow** the selection structure but are not part of it. That will always cause hard-to-find logical errors.

- Consider carefully which statements need to located **inside** your IF and ELSE sections, and which statements should come **before** or **after** (or even in the other section).

Thorough testing is critical to catch logical errors, don't just run your programs once to decide if they work. Consider the different paths that the program might take through the code depending on the results of IF..ELSE tests and be sure to test for each of these.

Even when you find an unexpected result, it can be difficult to figure out what is causing the problem. It helps to "desk check" your code: walk through it one line at a time with a pencil and paper and note what should happen as each line executes. All programmers do this. List your variables and note the value of each one whenever a new value is assigned. Also make a note of the result of each test, and follow the logic to determine which code is executed in your IF/ELSE structures. Note any output that is generated. Do all this very methodically, one line at a time, and be sure that you're following the code as it is written, and that you are not assuming anything. Taking time do this will often reveal problems that you otherwise might miss. (There are lots of developer tools out there to help with desk-checking, often built into programming text editors, but it is a very good idea to start by using pencil and paper to get a feel for the process. It can help to make notes on a printout of your code as you work through it.)

Additional Learning Materials

Appendix D will help you **debug** your exercises, listing a number of the most common errors that you are likely to encounter.

The **Chapter 7 Hints and Help** pages on the textbook Web site provide answers to FAQs from previous students as they worked through the end-of-chapter exercises.

Summary

This chapter has introduced selection control structures which allow programs to make decisions. A decision is based on the result of a test that may be either **true** or **false**. Tests that have true or false results are known as Boolean expressions, and are based on comparisons using the relational operators (==, <, <=, >=, >, and !=).

The two most commonly used control structures are: IF structures, which provide a series of statements to be executed if the result of a test is **true**, and where no special action is needed if the result of the test is **false**; and IF..ELSE structures, which provide a series of statements to be executed if the result of a test is **true**, and an alternative series of statements to be executed if the result of the test is **false**.

General purpose algorithms generally use the words **IF** and **ENDIF** to indicate the beginning and end of an IF structure, and **IF**, **ELSE** and **ENDIF** to indicate the parts of an IF..ELSE structure.

In PHP curly braces { and } are used to surround the block of statements in the IF section of an IF or IF..ELSE structure, and to surround the block of statements in the ELSE section of an IF..ELSE structure. In either case, if there is just a single instruction to be performed, the braces can be left out.

The test that controls the selection structure should always be enclosed in parentheses.

A common programming error is to use = instead of == when comparing values for equality. Another common error is to include a semi-colon immediately following the test at the start of the IF structure.

Programs that include selection structures should be tested thoroughly with a test case for each possible path through the program. Programs with a single IF structure or a single IF..ELSE structure will require two tests, once where the test has a true result, and once where the test has a false result. Effective tests will use threshold values (values that are closest to the test condition). For example if the test is (**wage < 8.00**) the threshold values will be 7.99 and 8.00).

The **strtolower()** and **strtoupper()** functions allow you to convert the case of character strings. This is useful when you wish to test two strings without regard for case.

Syntax errors may be mis-reported by the processor; consider what might have caused the error and check the lines **before** the line where the error was reported.

Thorough testing and **desk-checking** (walking through the code step-by-step by hand) are the best ways to discover and fix **logical errors**.

Chapter 7 Review Questions

1. A test that evaluates to true or false is known as
   a. An arithmetic expression
   b. A Boolean expression
   c. A relational expression
   d. An assignment operation
   e. An algorithm

2. A selection control structure can contain
   a. An IF structure without an ELSE
   b. An IF structure with an ELSE
   c. An ELSE structure without an IF
   d. Either A or B but not C
   e. Either A or C but not B

3. What is wrong with the following piece of PHP code?

```
if ($answer = 4)
   print("<p>That's the correct answer!</p>");
```

   a. There must be an else section
   b. A semi-colon is missing at the end of the first line
   c. The = should be ==
   d. Curly braces must be included here
   e. There is nothing wrong with the code as written

4. What is wrong with the following piece of PHP code?

```
if ($carsSold <= 10);
   print("<p>If you sell more than 10 you get a bonus!</p>");
else
   print("<p>Good job - you sold more than 10 cars!</p>");
```

   a. The test should not be in parentheses
   b. There should not be a semi-colon at the end of the first line
   c. Curly braces must be included around the statement between the if
      and else
   d. Curly braces must be included around the statements after the else
   e. There is nothing wrong with the code as written

5. What is wrong with the following piece of PHP code?

```
if ($carsSold <= 10)
   print("<p>If you sell more than 10 you get a bonus!</p>");
else
   print("<p>Good job - you sold more than 10 cars!");
   print("You will receive a $500 bonus!</p>");
```

    a. The test should not be in parentheses
    b. There should be a semi-colon at the end of the first line
    c. Curly braces must be included around the statements between the if
       and else
    d. Curly braces must be included around the statements after the else
    e. There is nothing wrong with the code as written

6. Which of the following is NOT a relational operator
    a. =
    b. <
    c. <=
    d. !=
    e. >=

7. If a variable named $carsSold contains the value 10, what is the result of this test?

```
if ($carsSold <= 10)
```

    a. True
    b. False

8. If a variable named $carsSold contains the value 20, what is the result of this test?

```
if ($carsSold != 10)
```

    a. True
    b. False

9. What HTML output will be generated by the following PHP code?

```
$age = 55;
$retirementAge = 65;
$yearsToRetire = $retirementAge - $age ;
if ($yearsToRetire >= 10)
   print("<p> You have a long way to go yet..</p>");
else
   print("<p> You have $yearsToRetire years to retire..</p>");
print("<p>It will be here before you know it!</p>");
```

   a. <p> You have a long way to go yet..</p>
   b. <p> You have a long way to go yet..</p> <p>It will be here before you
       know it!</p>
   c. <p> You have 10 years to retire..</p>
   d. <p> You have 10 years to retire..</p> <p>It will be here before you
       know it!</p>
   e. <p> You have a long way to go yet..</p> <p> You have 10 years to re-
       tire..</p> <p>It will be here before you know it!</p>

10. Which of the following code segments shows the correct use of curly braces?
    a. if ($carsSold <= 10)

```
        print("<p>You did not sell many cars this month");
        print("<p>If you sell more than 10 you get a
           bonus!</p>")
     else
        print("<p>Good job - you sold more than 10 cars!");
```

    b. if ($carsSold <= 10)

```
     {
        print("<p>You did not sell many cars this month");
        print("<p>If you sell more than 10 you get a
           bonus!</p>")
     }
     else
        print("<p>Good job - you sold more than 10 cars!");
```

c. if ($carsSold <= 10)

```
    print("<p>You did not sell many cars this month");
    print("<p>If you sell more than 10 you get a
       bonus!</p>")
 else
 {
    print("<p>Good job - you sold more than 10 cars!");
 }
```

d. if ($carsSold <= 10)

```
 {
    print("<p>You did not sell many cars this month");
    print("<p>If you sell more than 10 you get a
       bonus!</p>")
 else
    print("<p>Good job - you sold more than 10 cars!");
 }
```

e. if ($carsSold <= 10)

```
    print("<p>You did not sell many cars this month");
    print("<p>If you sell more than 10 you get a
       bonus!</p>")
 {
 else
    print("<p>Good job - you sold more than 10 cars!");
 }
```

11. Which would be good **threshold** values to use as inputs to test a selection structure with the heading **if ($carsSold <= 10)**?
    a. 0 and 10
    b. 9 and 10
    c. 10 and 11
    d. 0 and 100
    e. 0 and -1

12. What is wrong with the following algorithm?

```
hourlyWage = 12.00
hoursWorked = 40
IF (totalWage < 200.00)
   bonus = 100.00
ELSE
   bonus = 50.00
ENDIF
totalWage = hourlyWage * hoursWorked
Display totalWage, bonus
```

   a. The IF..ELSE structure should be listed first
   b. Curly braces are missing
   c. The ENDIF should appear before the ELSE
   d. The calculation for totalWage should appear before the IF test
   e. The Display statement should appear before the IF test

13. What value will be stored in $cityName after the following statement is executed?

```
$cityName = strtoupper("New York City");
```

   a. New York City
   b. NEW YORK CITY
   c. newYorkCity
   d. new york city
   e. NEWYORKCITY

14. What value is stored in $result after these PHP instructions are executed?

```
$value1 = 10;
$value2 = 20;
if ($value1 > $value2)
   $value2 = 50;
$result = $value1 + $value2;
print("<p>The result is $result</p>");
```

   a. 0
   b. 30
   c. 50
   d. 70
   e. 80

15. What value is stored in $result after these PHP instructions are executed?

```
$value1 = 10;
$value2 = 20;
if ($value1 > $value2)
   $value2 = 50;
else
   $value1 = 30;
$result = $value1 + $value2;
print("<p>The result is $result</p>");
```

  a. 0
  b. 30
  c. 50
  d. 70
  e. 80

16. What value is stored in $result after these PHP instructions are executed?

```
$value1 = 10;
$value2 = 20;
if ($value1 > $value2)
   $value2 = 50;
$value1 = 50;
$result = $value1 + $value2;
print("<p>The result is $result</p>");
```

  a. 0
  b. 30
  c. 50
  d. 70
  e. 100

17. Which piece of code is correct to meet the following requirement:

Display "Good score" for scores above 85

  a. if ($score == 85)
      print ("<p>Good score</p>");
  b. if ($score <= 85)
      print ("<p>Good score</p>");
  c. if ($score < 85)
      print ("<p>Good score</p>");
  d. if ($score >= 85)
      print ("<p>Good score</p>");
  e. if ($score > 85)
      print ("<p>Good score</p>");

18. Which piece of code is correct to meet the following requirement:

Calculate and display the 7% sales tax if the purchase amount is positive,

otherwise display an error message

---

a. if ($purchaseAmount > 0)
```
        $salesTax = $purchaseAmount * 0.07;
        print ("<p>The sales tax is $salesTax</p>");
      print ("<p>Error: Purchase amount must be positive"</p>");
```

b. if ($purchaseAmount > 0)
```
        $salesTax = $purchaseAmount * 0.07;
        print ("<p>The sales tax is $salesTax</p>"); else
        print ("<p>Error: Purchase amount must be
          positive"</p>");
```

c. if ($purchaseAmount > 0)
```
      {
        $salesTax = $purchaseAmount * 0.07;
        print ("<p>The sales tax is $salesTax</p>");
      }
      else
        print ("<p>Error: Purchase amount must be
          positive"</p>");
```

d. if ($purchaseAmount <= 0)
```
      {
        $salesTax = $purchaseAmount * 0.07;
        print ("<p>The sales tax is $salesTax</p>");
      }
      else
      {
        print ("<p>Error: Purchase amount must be
          positive"</p>");
      }
```

e. if ($purchaseAmount == 0)
```
      {
        $salesTax = $purchaseAmount * 0.07;
        print ("<p>The sales tax is $salesTax</p>");
      }
      else
        print ("<p>Error: Purchase amount must be
          positive"</p>")
```

19. How many possible paths are there through a program that includes a single IF or IF..ELSE structure?
    a. 0
    b. 1
    c. 2
    d. 3
    e. 4

20. How many possible paths are there through a program that contains one IF structure followed by one (separate) IF..ELSE structure?
    a. 0
    b. 1
    c. 2
    d. 3
    e. 4

Chapter 7 Code Exercises

Your Chapter 7 code exercises can be found in your **chapter07** folder. This folder is included in your customized XAMPP installation at the following location:

htdocs\webtech\coursework\chapter07

Type your name and the date in the **Author** and **Date** sections of each file as you work on each exercise. **Remember** that the Students page on the textbook Web site includes **Hints and Help** pages for the exercises in this and every chapter.

Debugging Exercises

Your **chapter07** folder contains a number of "fixit" files. Each of these files contains PHP code that has an error of some kind. The type of error is indicated in the comment section of each file. You will need to run each program in order to see the errors, and to debug and test the code to see if it works correctly. For example to run **fixit1.php**, first run the Web server, then use the URL:

http://localhost/webtech/coursework/chapter07/fixit1.php

Code Modification Exercises

Your **chapter07** folder contains a numbr of "modify" files. Each pair of files contains HTML and PHP code that needs to be modified to meet a requirement. The requirements are included in the comment section of each file. Modify the algorithms, being careful to make changes to the .html and .php files as directed. You will need to run each program in order to test your changes. For example to run **modify1.html**, first run the Web server, then use the URL:

http://localhost/webtech/coursework/chapter07/modify1.html

Code Completion Exercises

1. Your **chapter07** folder contains modified versions of **paint-estimate.html** and **paint-estimate.php**. The code in **paint-estimate.html** does not need to be changed. The HTML form includes a drop down selection to ask the user if they are a first time customer. Note that the name for this input is **firstTime**, and the possible values are "**yes**" and "**no**". The PHP program should be modified to test the user's selection and, if the user chose "**yes**", should calculate a **10%** deduction to the **total** estimate and generate the following additional output: "<p>We want your service! Since you are a first time customer, we are offering a 10% deduction.</p><p>Your actual costs will be: $**xxx**</p>" where $**xxx** is their cost after the deduction. Make the changes to **paint-estimate.php** so that the program works as described. Should you use an IF or IF..ELSE structure when you modify **paint-estimate.php**?

Think carefully where your selection structure must appear in the code. Figure 7-8 shows examples of output where the user chose yes (first screen) and no (second screen). In both cases the user entered 10, 20 and 8 for the length, width and height.

Figure 7-8: Two different paint-estimate.php screenshots

2. Your **chapter07** folder contains versions of **software-order.html** and **software-order.php**. The code in **software-order.html** does not need to be changed. The PHP program should test the number of copies ordered. If there are **less than five copies** the shipping and handling charge is a standard **3.50** no matter how many copies, otherwise the shipping handling is **0.75** for each copy. Make the changes to **software-order.php** so that the program works as described. Should you use an IF or IF..ELSE structure when you modify **software-order.php**? Think carefully where your selection structure must appear in the code. Figure 7-9 shows output examples when either 4 or 5 is entered for the number of copies.

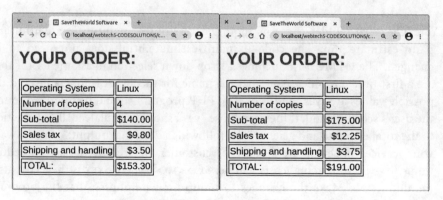

Figure 7-9: Two different software-order.php screenshots

3. Your **chapter07** folder contains modified versions of **travel.html** and **travel.php**. The code in **travel.html** does not need to be changed. This form now includes a choice of travel destinations. If the destination is Rome, the air fare is **$875** and the nightly hotel cost is **$110** (so for example a trip to Rome by two people for 5 nights would cost a total of $2850). If the destination is Tokyo, the air fare is **$1575** and the nightly hotel cost is **$240** (so for example a trip to Tokyo by two people for 5 nights would cost a total of $5550). Assume that each traveler has a separate room.

   Add the necessary selection structure. The PHP program already includes the code to perform the appropriate calculations and display the costs.

4. Your **chapter07** folder contains previous versions of **game-intro.html** and **game-intro.php**. Change **game-intro.html so that the user is also asked for a secret password in order to submit the character. The password is php123.** The PHP program should test the password and accept any combination of upper- or lower-case letters (for example PhP123 or pHP123 are both acceptable). If the password is accepted, the program calculates and displays the cost and other information, otherwise the program displays an error message: "<p>Sorry! That password is NOT correct! Please try again.</p>".

5. Copy **event.html** and **event.php** from your **chapter06** folder to your **chapter07** folder. Your **chapter07** folder already contains a file named **ticket-count.txt**. You are going to modify your event.php file so that, after receiving the form inputs, it will check the count of tickets sold (the number in ticket-count.txt) and then use an IF.. ELSE structure to either process the order or report that there are not enough seats available. Assume that the performance venue has seating for 100. You will need to think carefully about the order of your instructions and the placement of braces in your IF..ELSE structure.

   To check for available seats, after receiving the input from the form, your event.php program must: (1) open ticket-count.txt for read operations, read the count of tickets already sold, and close the file; (2) calculate the number of seats available (this will be 100 minus the count of seats already sold); and (3) use an IF..ELSE structure that tests whether the current order exceeds the number of available seats. If so, the program should simply notify the user that there are not enough tickets remaining to complete the order, otherwise the program should go ahead and process the order (this includes updating the ticket-count.txt file so that it contains the new count).

   Test your work to be sure that it works correctly in either situation. Does it work correctly if the number of seats being ordered is EXACTLY the number of available seats?

6. Copy **fuel-cost.html** and **fuel-cost.php** from your **chapter05** folder to your **chapter07** folder. Modify fuel-cost.html by adding a drop down list with a prompt that asks whether or not the trip is work-related. Name this input '**workRelated**' and allow the user to select YES or NO from the drop down list.

   Now modify fuel-cost.php to receive this input in addition to the other inputs. The program should calculate the fuel cost in the same way as before, but should then use an IF.. ELSE structure to test whether or not the trip is work related. If the trip IS work related, the program should calculate the amount that will be reimbursed to you by your employer, at the rate of 0.35 a mile (so for example, if the trip was 100 miles you would be reimbursed 0.35 x 100 or $35.00). If the trip is not work related, the amount to be reimbursed will be 0.

   Your program should then display the miles traveled, the fuel cost, whether or not the trip was work-related, and the amount to be reimbursed.

Chapter 8

Multiple Selection, Nesting, ANDs and ORs

Intended Learning Outcomes

After completing this chapter, you should be able to:

- Solve requirements that require multiple selection structures
- Recognize the syntax and use of the logical operators AND, OR, and NOT
- Nest selection structures to meet requirements
- Describe the importance of input validation
- Develop and implement basic validation rules
- Chain together multiple selection structures using ELSEIF
- Apply the trim() function to remove leading and trailing white space
- Apply the filter_var() function to remove HTML tags from input
- Apply top down design to solve more complex requirements
- Describe the challenge of software testing

Introduction

In the last chapter we learned to combine true/false tests (Boolean expressions) with IF and IF..ELSE selection structures which allow our applications to choose between different blocks of statements. Real world applications usually require the use of multiple IF and IF..ELSE selection structures, as well as more complex Boolean expressions, as follows:

- The **AND, OR,** and **NOT** logical operators can be used to construct **compound Boolean expressions** that will produce an overall single true/false result from a series of individual true/false tests.

- Applications can include any number of **independent** IF and IF..ELSE selection structures, each serving a distinct and separate purpose within the application.
- Selection structures may be **nested** inside other selection structures. In these cases, the inner selection structures will only be processed if the outer structure that contains them is executed.
- IF and IF..ELSE selection structures may also be **chained** together so that, instead of choosing between just two options, the application can choose between any number of options.

There is no limit to the ways in which multiple selection structures and compound expressions can be combined: large applications may contain hundreds or even thousands of selection structures. Hopefully this chapter will give you a taste of what is possible, and provide sufficient syntax to help you apply these structures to meet any set of application requirements.

Introducing the Logical Operators AND and OR

So far the true/false tests that we have used to control our IF and IF..ELSE structures have been based on just a single comparison, such as **hourlyWage** < **8.00**. However programming languages allow us to combine multiple comparisons into a compound test using the **logical operators AND** and **OR**. Expressions that combine multiple true/false tests are often referred to as **compound Boolean expressions**. To understand this, first consider the following algorithm that is designed to decide whether to accept a job offer or keep your current job:

```
IF the salary is better AND the prospects are good
   Accept the job offer
ELSE
   Keep your current job
ENDIF
```

This selection structure uses **two** tests, **each** of which may be **true** or **false**. The salary may or may not be better, and the prospects for advancement may or may not be good. The two tests are combined using the word AND, which indicates that **both** tests must be **true** in order to accept the job offer. If **either** or **both** tests are false, the decision is to keep your current job.

One way to understand the overall result of a compound expression is to construct a **truth table.** This is illustrated in Table 8-1.

Salary is better	Prospects are good	Overall result	Action
True	True	True	Accept job offer
True	False	False	Keep current job
False	True	False	Keep current job
False	False	False	Keep current job

Table 8-1: Truth table using the AND operator

As you can see, when two tests are combined using the AND operator, only **one** possible combination generates an overall true result, while **three** possible combinations generate an overall false result. Only if **both** tests are true will the overall result be true.

Now compare the previous algorithm to the following:

```
IF the salary is better OR the prospects are good
   Accept the job offer
ELSE
   Keep your current job
ENDIF
```

The only difference is that we have replaced the **AND** operator with the **OR** operator. Now the test instructs us to accept the job offer if the salary is better **OR** the prospects are good, or if **both** of these statements are true. Now we only keep our current job if **both** statements are **false**. Table 8-2 shows a truth table using the OR operator.

Salary is better	Prospects are good	Overall result	Action
True	True	True	Accept job offer
True	False	True	Accept job offer
False	True	True	Accept job offer
False	False	False	Keep current job

Table 8-2: Truth table using the OR operator

In this case, **three** possible combinations generate an overall true result, while only **one** possible combination generates an overall false result. Only if **both** tests are false will the overall result be false.

Now let's look at a programming example that uses the AND and OR operators by modifying our wage application. What if we wanted to assign a bonus based on the following requirement:

*If the hourly wage is less than 10.00 **and** the hours worked are 40 or higher, assign a 50.00 bonus, otherwise assign a 25.00 bonus.*

In other words a 50.00 bonus will only be given if the hourly wage is below 10.00 **and** the hours worked are at least 40; in all other cases the bonus is 25.00.

This requires our application to combine two tests into one compound expression:

```
IF hourlyWage < 10.00 AND hoursWorked >=40
   bonus = 50.00
ELSE
   bonus = 25.00
ENDIF
```

The PHP languages includes the words **AND** and **OR** so we can code this as follows:

```php
if ($hourlyWage < 10.00 and $hoursWorked >= 40)
   $bonus = 50.00;
else
   $bonus = 25.00;
```

Note the syntax in the IF heading: the entire expression is enclosed in parentheses; the expression consists of the first test followed by the **and** operator which is in turn followed by the second test.

PHP also allows us to use **&&** instead of **and** to represent the AND operator, for example **if ($hourlyWage < 10.00 && $hoursWorked >= 40**. The use of **&&** is actually more standard among programming languages since many do not include the word **and** as an option.

Now what if our requirements required the use of an OR operator as follows:

If the hourly wage is less than 10.00 or the hours worked are 40 or higher, assign a 50.00 bonus, otherwise assign a 25.00 bonus.

Now a 50.00 bonus will be given if the hourly wage is below 10.00 **or** the hours worked are at least 40; in other words everyone will get a 50.00 bonus except for those who earn 10.00 or higher **and who also** worked less than 40 hours. This will be coded:

```php
if ($hourlyWage < 10.00 or $hoursWorked >= 40)
   $bonus = 50.00;
else
   $bonus = 25.00;
```

PHP also allows us to use || instead of **or** to represent the OR operator, for example **if ($hourlyWage < 10.00 || $hoursWorked >= 40**. Just as with &&, the use of || is actually more standard among programming languages since many do not include the word **or** as an option.

Do you see how important it is to read the requirements very carefully to determine whether you need to use the AND operator or the OR operator? Just consider, if the requirement was for the AND operator and you used the OR operator, your application would award 50.00 bonuses to many employees who should have only received 25.00 bonuses. That will make many employees happy but definitely not your employer!

Another very important consideration: the test on either side of the **AND** or **OR** operator must be a complete true/false test. For example what if a 50.00 bonus is to be given to employees who worked at least 35 but not more than 40 hours? In English we might express this as "if the hours worked are at least 35 and not more than 40". and so it would seem reasonable to write something similar in code:

```
if ($hoursWorked >= 30 and <= 40)
   $bonus = 50.00;
else
   $bonus = 25.00;
```

This is an easy mistake for beginning programmer to make: this code will actually generate an error message because the syntax is incorrect. The problem is that there isn't a complete test after the **AND** operator. Although you and I can look at this and deduce that <= **40** is referring to **$hoursWorked**, the PHP processor has no way of interpreting this. It expects a complete true/false test on **both** sides of the AND operator. **Even if the same variable is being tested on both sides of the AND operator**, the variable must be specified in **both** tests as follows:

```
if ($hoursWorked >= 30 and $hoursWorked <= 40)
   $bonus = 50.00;
else
   $bonus = 25.00;
```

Introducing the NOT Operator

Programming languages provide a third logical operator, NOT, which reverses the value of a Boolean expression. The PHP language allows the ! character to represent the NOT operator. For example, if (**$hourlyWage** < 8) is **true** then (!(**$hourlyWage** < 8)) is **false**. You may wonder why would you ever need to use the NOT operator when you can simply rewrite your test. For example why not just use (**$hourlyWage** >= 8) instead of (!(**$hourlyWage** < 8)? Surely that is much easier to understand and achieves the same result. In this case that's quite correct but in some cases it's useful to use the NOT operator. For example, PHP includes a useful function named **is_numeric**() that tests whether or not a variable contains a number. If the variable **$hourlyWage** contains **8.00** then **is_numeric($hourlyWage)** will be **true**, but if the variable contains "**Ten Dollars**" then **is_numeric($hourlyWage)** will be **false**, since "**Ten Dollars**" is not a number. It's common to use this function to display an error message if a value submitted by the user is not numeric, and in these cases it can be simpler to use it with the NOT operator, for example:

```
if (!is_numeric($hourlyWage))
   print("<p>Error: the hourly wage must be a number</p>");
else
{
   // ..code to process the hourly wage..
}
```

The test in the IF heading is testing if the value in $hourlyWage is **not** numeric. We will use the NOT operator and the **is_numeric**() function later in this chapter in order to test the user's input to our Wage application.

Are you wondering about the two pairs of parentheses in the IF heading test? The outer parentheses indicate the beginning and end of the true/false test; these are needed in all IF headings. The inner pair of parentheses are part of the call to the is_numeric() function and contain the value that the function is to test, in this case $hourlyWage. All function names must be followed by a pair of parentheses, that's how PHP recognizes that the name is that of a function.

Validating User Input

All computer applications must work with data of some kind. Data might be input directly from the user, or from data files, databases or other sources. In order to ensure that the application will perform correctly, this data must first be tested to ensure it is **valid** (meets the application requirements), and **safe to use** (does not contain malicious content). This is not just important for correct processing: any data that the application **outputs**, to user interfaces, data files, and database systems, must also be valid and safe.

Throughout this book you are using HTML forms to submit user input to Web applications. Until now this input has not been tested, since testing generally requires familiarity with the selection structures that are being introduced in this chapter. In the following sections you will learn some useful procedures to validate form input, **Appendix** E provides a more complete overview of Web security and validation.

Validation Rules for the Wage Application

The previous wage examples allow the user to enter an hourly wage and hours worked, but this input has not been tested. **Figure 8-1** shows what happens if you submit -10 for an hourly wage and 0 for hours worked when using the wage5 application that was developed in Chapter 7.

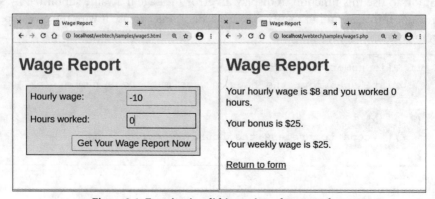

Figure 8-1: Entering invalid input into the wage5 form

Without any testing, the application processed this bad input as if it were valid, and even applied a $25 bonus based on incorrect values! Clearly some validation rules are needed to protect the application against these kind of errors. (As an exercise, work through the wage5.php code to see how the pay was determined, based on the user inputs that were submitted.)

A requirements document should always include **validation rules** for each data value that will be input to the application. Some rules will be fairly standard, such as ensuring that input fields are not empty, and that numeric input is, in fact, numeric, while other rules will be more specific, such as a rule that a number must be within a certain range, or that a product code must contain certain characters. These rules are usually listed in the order in which the tests should be applied, from more general to more specific. Here is a list of rules to validate our wage application:

hourly wage:

```
Must be submitted (input field not empty)

Must be a number

Must be at least 7.25 (minimum wage)
```

hours worked:

```
Must be submitted (input field not empty)

Must be a number

Must be in the range 0 to 60 (60 is maximum hours a week)
```

(It is often important to check that numbers are positive, if that is required, but in this case this is not necessary: one of the tests for the hourly wage already requires that its value will be at least 7.25; and one of the tests for hours worked requires that its value will be in a range between 0 and 60.)

Here is a revised requirement for our Wage program that includes a requirement for input validation:

Wage7 requirement:

Write a program that asks the employee for an hourly wage and the number of hours worked. The program should validate these inputs, according to the rules provided, and either generate appropriate error messages or process the inputs as follows:

If the hourly wage is below 8.00 it should be increased to 8.00. No increase is needed if the hourly wage is already at least 8.00.

The program should assign a bonus based on the hours worked. If the hours worked is at least 35, the program should assign a bonus of 50.00, otherwise the program should assign a bonus of 25.00.

The program should calculate and display the hourly wage, hours worked, bonus and weekly wage (including the bonus).

We will develop the validation tests in stages, to demonstrate different ways of combining IF..ELSE structures. Let's start by applying the first rule (that the hourly wage and hours worked must be submitted) and learn about **nested** selection structures.

Using A Nested Selection Structure to Validate Input

IF and IF..ELSE selection structures can be nested inside each other as needed to meet the requirements of an application. Let's look at an example where we nest selection structures in order to validate user input.

As a first step towards validating our form input, we want our wage7 program to calculate and display the weekly wage only if the user actually types a value into both the hourly wage and hours worked fields. If **either** or **both** of these fields are **empty** the program should simply output an error message. Here is an algorithm to achieve this input validation:

```
wage7.php algorithm:

   Receive hourlyWage, hoursWorked from wage7.html

   IF (hourlyWage is empty OR hoursWorked is empty)
      display an "empty field" error message
   ELSE
      process the weekly wage
   ENDIF
END
```

Notice that here we are using a "**high-level**" algorithm to work out the general logic of our program without getting into too much detail. The statement "process the weekly wage" actually represents quite a number of instructions. This high-level approach is helpful when we just want to plan our overall program structure before focusing on the details. Once we are satisfied with the general logic we can create a more detailed algorithm (see below). The general term used to describe working from a high-level to a detailed design is **top down design**.

In this algorithm we use the **OR** operator to combine two tests into one compound expression. As we have seen, when we use the word **OR** between two tests, we are testing whether **EITHER** or **BOTH** tests are **true**. The truth table in Table 8-3 shows each possible true or false outcome for this compound expression.

For example if the user submits nothing for **hourlyWage** and **20** for hoursWorked, we can see that the **hourlyWage is empty** test is **true** and the **hoursWorked is empty** test is **false**. Since we are using the OR operator to combine these tests, the overall result is **true**, and so the program will generate an error message. But if the user submits **10.00** for **hourlyWage** and **20** for **hoursWorked**, the **hourlyWage is empty** test is false and the **hoursWorked is empty** test is also **false** so the overall result is **false**, and the program will skip to the ELSE section and process the weekly wage. When the **OR** operator is used to combine two tests, the overall result will only be **false** if **both** tests generate a **false** result. In our algorithm, the program will only execute the ELSE section if hourlyWage contains a value and hoursWorked also contains a value.

hourlyWage is empty	hoursWorked is empty	Overall result	Action
True	True	True	Display error message
True	False	True	Display error message
False	True	True	Display error message
False	False	False	Process weekly pay

Table 8-3: Truth table using the OR operator to test for empty fields

Now here is the complete algorithm, including the statements to process the weekly wage.

```
wage7.php algorithm:

   Receive hourlyWage, hoursWorked from wage7.html

   Display "Wage Report" heading

   IF (hourlyWage is empty OR hoursWorked is empty)
      display an "empty field" error message
   ELSE
      IF (hourlyWage < 8.00)
         hourlyWage = 8.00
      ENDIF
      IF (hoursWorked >= 35)
         bonus = 50.00
      ELSE
         bonus = 25.00
      ENDIF
      weeklyWage = hourlyWage * hoursWorked + bonus
      Display hourlyWage, hoursWorked, bonus, weeklyWage
   ENDIF
END
```

Study this algorithm carefully. The first IF heading tests whether either hourlyWage or hoursWorked is empty. If either of these are empty, the program displays an error message and skips the ELSE section. This ELSE section contains **all of the remaining instructions in the algorithm!** In other words, if the first test is true, the program will display an error message and then end. But if hourlyWage and hoursWorked both contain values, then the first test will be false and the program will execute the first ELSE section, which contains all of the remaining code. The ELSE section of the first IF..ELSE structure includes two additional selection structures: **IF (hourlyWage < 8.00)** and **IF (hoursWorked >= 35)**. When a control structure is located inside another control structure we say that it is **nested**. So these two selection structures are **nested** inside the ELSE section of the first IF..ELSE structure; they will only be executed if the test of the first IF.. ELSE structure is false.

Note also that we have moved the instruction **Display "Wage Report" heading** so that it appears **before** the IF..ELSE structure. That is because we want to ensure that the heading will be displayed whether or not the program generates an error message or calculates the weekly pay. If we placed this instruction **inside** the first ELSE section it would be displayed if the wages were processed but not if the test produced an error message. As we add control structures we must be very careful to consider which statements should occur **before** the control structures, which should be contained **inside** the control structures, and which should appear **after** (or **between**) the control structures.

PHP provides a useful function to test whether or not a variable is empty. You guessed it, the function name is **empty()**! Here is the PHP code for this algorithm:

```
<html>
<head>
  <title>Wage Report</title>
  <link rel="stylesheet" type="text/css" href="sample.css">
</head>
<body>
  <?php
    $hourlyWage = $_POST['hourlyWage'];
    $hoursWorked = $_POST['hoursWorked'];

    print("<h1>Wage Report</h1>");

    if ( empty($hourlyWage) or empty($hoursWorked) )
      print("ERROR: Input is missing!");
    else
    {
      if ($hourlyWage < 8.00)
        $hourlyWage = 8.00;

      if ($hoursWorked >= 35)
```

```
      $bonus = 50.00;
   else
      $bonus = 25.00;

   $weeklyWage = $hourlyWage * $hoursWorked + $bonus;

   print("<p>Your hourly wage is $$hourlyWage and you
      worked $hoursWorked hours.</p>");
   print("<p>Your bonus is $$bonus.</p>");
   print("<p>Your weekly wage is $$weeklyWage.</p>");
   }

   print ("<a href=\"wage7.html\">Return to form</a>");
?>
</body>
</html>
```

Code Example: wage7.php

Designing Applications with Nested Selection Structures

When a selection structure is nested inside the IF section of another selection structure it will only be processed if the test for the outside selection structure is **true**. Similarly when a selection structure is nested inside the ELSE section of another selection structure it will only be processed if the test for the outside selection structure is **false**. Selection structures can be included inside the IF or ELSE sections of other selection structures just as any other program statements can be included in these sections. IF..ELSE structures can be nested inside other IF..ELSE structures that are nested inside other IF..ELSE structures and so on. Most applications of any kind of complexity will require multiple nested selection structures.

A flow chart can help us understand how nested structures are processed. Figure 8-2 shows a slightly simplified flow chart for this program. You can see that the visual nature of the flowchart makes it easier to understand the logic of this more complex structure. Take some time to compare this to the pseudocode version of the algorithm. Even a hand-drawn chart can help you design nested structures more easily.

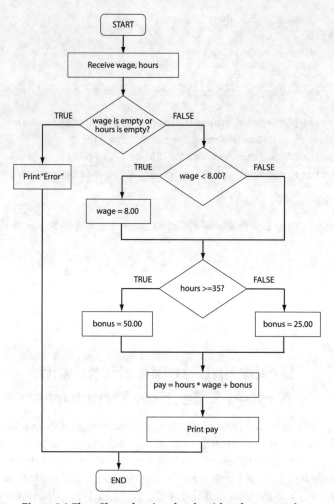

Figure 8.2 Flow Chart showing the algorithm for wage7.php

Use of Braces in Nested Selection Structures

Recall that the blocks of code inside IF and ELSE sections must be surrounded by opening and closing curly braces { and } unless the code consists of a single statement. Take another look at the wage7.php code and notice that all the code in the first ELSE section is enclosed in curly braces: this code includes an IF structure, an IF..ELSE structure, a calculation and two print statements. These braces are essential so that the processor will know that **all** of these statements are part of the first ELSE section and should only be executed if the test in the first IF..ELSE structure test is false. When you use nested selection structures, you will need to be very careful to ensure that you are using opening and closing braces appropriately. For example, can you see the problem with the following code snippet?

```
    if ( empty($hourlyWage) )
      print("ERROR: Input is missing!");
    else
    {
      if ($hourlyWage < 8.00)
      {
        $hourlyWage = 8.00;
        print("<p>Your hourly wage has been
increased.</p>");

        print("<p>Your hourly wage is $$hourlyWage</p>");
    }
```

A closing curly brace is missing between the two print statements. This missing brace indicates the end of the nested IF structure. The correct code looks like this:

```
    if ( empty($hourlyWage) )
      print("ERROR: Input is missing!");
    else
    {
      if ($hourlyWage < 8.00)
      {
        $hourlyWage = 8.00;
        print("<p>Your hourly wage has been
                increased.</p>");
      }
      print("<p>Your hourly wage is $$hourlyWage</p>");
    }
```

This is a common programming error, and this type of error can often be hard to find and correct. The processor will report the location of the error incorrectly, on a line that occurs later in the program code (perhaps even the last line of your program).

To understand this, take another look at the code that contains the error. The processor will find the first opening brace and proceed to treat the code that follows as part of the ELSE section of the first IF..ELSE structure. The processor then encounters the next opening brace and treats the code following that brace as part of the IF section of the nested IF structure. When the processor finds the closing brace after the second **print**() statement it assumes that this indicates the end of the IF section of the **nested** IF structure! The processor will continue to look for the closing brace of the ELSE component of the first selection structure, and will generate an error message only when it is clear that this brace cannot be found, which may not be before the last line of your program. If that's the case, the error message will indicate that the error was found in the last line!

This is just one situation where the processor reports the wrong line number when an error is found. This makes it hard to find errors such as those caused by missing braces. Since every opening brace must be paired with a closing brace, it can help to simply count the number of opening and closing braces in your code. This at least tells you whether or not a brace is missing. Finding the exact location of a missing brace requires careful review of your algorithm and program logic.

Indenting Nested Selection Structures

Chapter 7 highlighted the importance of indenting statements inside IF and ELSE code blocks. While this is not necessary for the code to execute successfully, correct indentation provides an important visual aid for you as a programmer, making it much easier to see which program statements "belong" to your IF and ELSE sections. They will also help you debug your program, for example to search for missing curly braces, or to check if a particular statement is located in the right block of code.

Indentation becomes even more important now you are nesting selection statements **inside** each other. Take another look at the last code example: the indentation clearly shows that the entire **second** IF structure, and the following print statement, are **both** located **inside** the ELSE block of the **first** IF..ELSE structure, and will only execute if the first test fails (if $hourlyWage is not empty). Note also that the statements of the **second** IF structure are indented again, to show that they "belong" to that structure and will only execute if the first ELSE section is executed, and then only if $hourlyWage is less than 8.00.

As you look at more examples in this chapter take note of the indentation, and do the same in your own code. It is standard practice and not only simplifies your own task when troubleshooting your code, but also helps other programmers who may need to review or modify code at some later date. The same rules of indentation also apply to other control structures; you will learn about these in upcoming chapters.

Chaining Related Selection Structures

In the last section we used an IF..ELSE structure to test that the user had submitted values in both fields. If either of the input fields was empty an error message was displayed, otherwise the weekly pay was processed. Now we want to apply the other validation rules: the hourly wage and hours worked must be **numeric** values; the hourly wage must be **at least 7.25**, and the hours worked must be **in the range 0 to 60**. We will need consider carefully how we are to connect these tests together to avoid incorrect results. Consider this algorithm:

```
IF (hourlyWage is empty OR hoursWorked is empty)

   display "empty" error msg

IF (hourlyWage is not numeric OR hoursWorked is not numeric)

   display "not a number" error msg

IF (hourlyWage < 7.25)

   display "below minimum" error msg
```

```
IF (hoursWorked < 0 or hoursWorked > 60)

  display "out of range" error msg

  ELSE

  IF (hourlyWage < 8.00)

    hourlyWage = 8.00

  ENDIF

  IF (hoursWorked >= 35)

    bonus = 50.00

  ELSE

    bonus = 25.00

  ENDIF

  weeklyWage = hourlyWage * hoursWorked + bonus

  Display hourlyWage, hoursWorked, bonus, weeklyWage

ENDIF
```

Does this look right to you? Actually this code has some serious problems. Let's see what happens in an interaction where the user input is not valid.

Let's say hourlyWage is **empty** and hoursWorked has a **valid** number. The first test is **true** so an "empty field" error message is displayed. The program then tests if either value is **not** numeric. Since hourlyWage does not contain a value it is not numeric so this test is also **true**, and a "not a number" message is displayed. The program moves to the next test, which is also **true** and a "below minimum wage" error message is printed. The program moves to the next test, which controls an IF..ELSE structure. This test is **false** (since hoursWorked is in range) so the program skips to the **ELSE** section and processes and displays the weekly wage! This is not what we want to happen. In fact, since the only error was an empty field, we would like the program to just display the "empty field" message and skip everything else.

Try a few test examples of your own with this algorithm and you will see that most tests that include input errors will lead to unacceptable results. In many cases, even if errors are found, the weekly pay will still be processed (incorrectly). That's because the test that controls the IF..ELSE statement is based solely on whether or not hoursWorked **is** in range: if hoursWorked is in range the pay is processed, even if the previous tests of hourlyWage found errors, because those earlier tests are not associated with the IF..ELSE statement.

The problem is that we want the program to choose only **one** out of the **five** possible actions: either **print one of the four error messages**, or **process the weekly pay**. Instead the program is taking multiple actions as it runs through the tests. How can we fix this?

The answer is to **connect** the four selection structures to one another so that the program will process these, in order, **only until it finds an error, or** (if there are no errors), **it processes the pay.** We can accomplish this by converting the first three **IF** statements into **IF..ELSE** statements, as follows:

```
IF (hourlyWage is empty OR hoursWorked is empty)
   display "empty" error msg
ELSE
   IF (hourlyWage is not numeric OR hoursWorked is not
      numeric) display "not a number" error msg
   ELSE
     IF (hourlyWage < 7.25)
       Display "below minimum" error msg
     ELSE
       IF (hoursWorked < 0 or hoursWorked > 60)
         display "out of range" error msg
       ELSE
         IF (hourlyWage < 8.00)
           hourlyWage = 8.00
         ENDIF
         IF (hoursWorked >= 35)
           bonus = 50.00
         ELSE
           bonus = 25.00
         ENDIF
         weeklyWage = hourlyWage * hoursWorked + bonus
         Display hourlyWage, hoursWorked,
                               bonus, weeklyWage
       ENDIF
     ENDIF
   ENDIF
ENDIF
```

Take some time to carefully analyze this structure. If the first test is **true** (an empty field is found), an "empty field" error message will be displayed and the ELSE section will be skipped. But this ELSE section contains **ALL** of the remaining IF..ELSE structures, so these will then be skipped, and no other tests will be made. The program simply displays the first error message and skips everything else.

If the **first** test is **false**, the program will skip to the first ELSE, which contains all the remaining statements. The first statement inside this ELSE is another (second) IF..ELSE structure which tests for non-numeric input. If **this** test is **true** the program will display a "not a number" error message and skip the ELSE. But this second ELSE contains **all** of the remaining statements, so these will then be skipped and no other tests will be made.

If this **second** test is **false**, the program will skip to the **second** ELSE structure, which contains all the remaining statements. The first statement inside this ELSE is another (third) IF..ELSE structure which tests if the hourly wage is below the minimum. If **this** test is **true** the program will display a "below minimum wage" error message and skip the ELSE. But this third ELSE contains **all** of the remaining statements, so these will then be skipped and no other tests will be made.

If this **third** test is **false**, the program will skip to the **third** ELSE structure, which contains all the remaining statements. The first statement inside this ELSE is another (fourth) IF..ELSE structure which tests if the hours worked is outside the range 0 to 60. If **this** test is true the program will display an "out of range" error message and skip the ELSE. This fourth ELSE contains all of the code to process the pay, so this code will then be skipped.

And if this **fourth** test is also **false**, the program will skip to the **fourth** ELSE structure, which contains the code to **process** the pay. The pay will now be processed correctly since the only way that the program reached this last ELSE was if all the previous tests were **false** and so no errors have been found. Note that the instructions to process the pay also include an IF statement and an IF..ELSE statement.

This is hard to follow and unfamiliar at first but take some time to work through the logic and see how it works. Basically you are looking at **four** IF..ELSE statements, in order, with each consecutive IF..ELSE nested **inside** the ELSE section of the **previous** IF..ELSE statement. As a result the program will only go to the **next** IF..ELSE statement if the previous test was **false**. And since each ELSE section contains all the remaining IF..ELSE statements, as soon as any test is **true**, all the remaining statements will be skipped.

This process of connecting multiple IF..ELSE structures to each other ensures that only **one** of the tests will result in an action. We often say the IF..ELSE structures are **chained** together. It's such a common use for IF..ELSE structures that some languages, like PHP, provide a special keyword **elseif** that can be used instead of **ELSE followed by IF**. Here is the PHP code for the algorithm, using elseif instead of else if:

```
print("<h1>Wage Report</h1>");


if (empty($hourlyWage) OR empty($hoursWorked))
   print("<p>ERROR: Input is missing,
                      please resubmit</p>");
elseif (!is_numeric($hourlyWage) OR !is_numeric($hour
   sWorked))
   print("<p>ERROR: Non-numeric input found,
                      please resubmit.</p>");
elseif ($hourlyWage < 7.25)
   print("<p>ERROR: Hourly wage is below minimum wage,
                      please resubmit.</p>");
```

```
elseif ($hoursWorked < 0 or $hoursWorked > 60 )
  print("<p>ERROR: Hours worked must be in range 0 .. 60,
                     please resubmit</p>");
else // no errors so process the pay
{
  if ($hourlyWage < 8.00)
    $hourlyWage = 8.00;
  if ($hourlyWage < 10.00 AND $hoursWorked >= 35)
    $bonus = 50.00;
  else
    $bonus = 25.00;

  $weeklyWage = $hourlyWage * $hoursWorked + $bonus;
  print("<p>Your hourly wage is $$hourlyWage and you
  worked $hoursWorked hours.</p>");
  print("<p>Your bonus is $$bonus.</p>");

  print("<p>Your weekly wage is $$weeklyWage.</p>");
}
```

Code Example: wage8.php

Figure 8-3 shows an example of valid input.

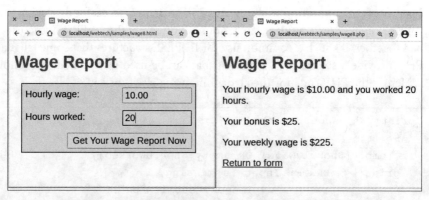

Figure 8-3: wage8.html and wage8.php screenshots (valid input)

Figure 8-4 shows an example of invalid input.

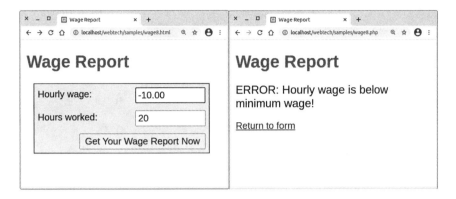

Figure 8-4: wage8.html and wage8.php screenshots (invalid input)

Run this program yourself and try various combinations of valid and invalid input to see that the different types of invalid input are handled correctly.

More About Chained Selection Structures

Chaining together selection structures is useful for input validation, but you will use different variations of this method for all kinds of purposes. Here is another common example, where a program must test a value and choose between more than two results. What if we want to assign one of **four** bonuses, based on the value of hours worked, as follows:

```
If the hours worked is greater than 40 assign $50

If the hours worked is greater than 30 assign $30

If the hours worked is greater than 20 assign $15

Otherwise assign $0 (no bonus)
```

Consider what would happen if we designed this as follows:

```
if ($hoursWorked > 40)

   $bonus = 50.00;

if ($hoursWorked > 30)

   $bonus = 30.00;

if ($hoursWorked > 20)

   $bonus = 15.00;

if ($hoursWorked <= 20)

   $bonus = 0;
```

This may look OK at first glance, but it is not correct. As always it is important to follow the program logic carefully.

Let's say that **$hoursWorked** contains **45**. The program encounters the **first** IF statement and performs the test, which is true (since $hoursWorked is greater than 40), so **$bonus** is (correctly) assigned **50.00**. The program then moves on to the **second** IF statement and performs the second test, which is **also true** (since $hoursWorked is greater than 30), so $bonus is now assigned **30.00**, and the previous value of 50.00 is replaced. The same things happens when the program moves on to the **third** IF statement, since this test is **also true** ($hoursWorked is greater than 20) and $bonus is now assigned **15.00**. The test for the last IF statement is **false**, so after all four IF statements have been processed **$bonus** contains the value **15.00**. Of course it should contain **50.00** if $hoursWorked contains **45**.

The solution is the same as the solution that we applied in the wage8 example: use **chained IF..ELSE** statements to ensure that, if a test generates a **true** result, the remaining IF..ELSE statements will be skipped, or if **no** tests are true, the ELSE section of the last IF..ELSE will be executed. Here is the correct algorithm, coded in PHP:

```
if ($hoursWorked > 40)

   $bonus = 50.00;

else

{

   if ($hoursWorked > 30)

      $bonus = 30.00;

   else

   {

      if ($hoursWorked > 20)
```

```
        $bonus = 15.00;
    else
        $bonus = 0.00;
  }
}
```

Braces are included in this code example to help you see which statements are included in each ELSE section. If the value of $hoursWorked contains **45**, the first test is **true** so $bonus is assigned **50.00**, and the **ELSE** section is skipped. Since this first ELSE section contains **all** of the remaining tests, these are all skipped and the program moves on with the correct bonus.

If $hoursWorked contains **35**, the first test is **false**, so the program skips to the **first** ELSE section, where it encounters the **second** IF..ELSE statement. This test is **true** so **30.00** is assigned to $bonus and the second ELSE section is skipped. Since this second ELSE section contains the third IF..ELSE statement, this statement is skipped.

If $hoursWorked contains **25**, the first and second tests are both **false**, so the program reaches the **third** IF..ELSE statement. This test is **true** so $bonus is assigned **15.00**.

And lastly if $hoursWorked contains **15**, the first and second tests are both **false**, so the program reaches the **third** IF.. ELSE statement. Since this test is also **false**, a $bonus of **0** is assigned.

The use of braces is helpful in this code example to see which statements are nested inside the different ELSE sections. Since each IF and ELSE section only contains a single statement, the braces are not actually required, so here is alternative PHP code, this time written without braces, and using **ifelse** instead of **if** and **else**:

```
if ($hoursWorked > 40)
   $bonus = 50.00;
elseif ($hoursWorked > 30)
   $bonus = 30.00;
elseif ($hoursWorked > 20)
   $bonus = 15.00;
else
   $bonus = 0.00;
```

Reducing Input Errors and Improving Security

In addition to applying validation rules and testing input, here are three steps to help **avoid** errors and security problems associated with user input:

1. Whenever possible, use **drop down lists**, **check boxes**, or **radio buttons** in your HTML forms. That way the user simply **selects** options rather than **typing** input at the keyboard (and possibly submitting errors). You have already learned to use drop down lists; **Chapter 17** explains how to use check boxes and radio buttons.

2. Use the PHP **trim**() function to remove leading and trailing white space (such as spaces, tabs or end-of-line characters) from all user input. These additional characters can become a problem when the input is processed (for example a password with an added space might be rejected even if the password itself is correct). Rather than testing for unwanted white space, it is usually simpler to just remove it. You have already used the PHP **trim**() function, in Chapter 6, to remove white space (especially end-of-line characters) from lines of text that have been read from text files, for example:

```
$nextLine = trim(fgets($someFile));
```

It is good practice to **always use** the **trim**() function to "clean" any kind of input before is tested and used. For example, the following statements will trim the content of $_POST["hourlyWage"] and $_POST["hoursWorked"] **before** these input values are assigned to the variables $hourlyWage and $hoursWorked:

```
$hourlyWage = trim($_POST["hourlyWage"]);
$hoursWorked = trim($_POST["hoursWorked"]);
```

Note that, if there is no leading or trailing white space, the trim() function simply returns the original value unchanged. The trim() function can be used as needed, to trim any value. For example to trim the content of a variable containing a last name:

```
$lastName = trim($lastName);
```

In this case the value stored in $lastName is trimmed, and the trimmed version is then assigned back to $lastName, replacing the untrimmed version.

3. **Use the PHP filter_var() function to remove HTML tags from user input before testing.**

User input can also present a **security vulnerability** since malicious scripts can be submitted via form text fields, as well as from other sources. Since executable scripts require the use of HTML tags, a simple preventative measure is to remove any tags that are found in input strings before the input is tested and used. The PHP **filter_var**() function provides a range of options to validate and "**sanitize**" input data; it will remove

HTML tags from a character string if used with the **FILTER_SANITIZE_STRING** option as a second argument (the first argument is the string to be sanitized). Here are two statements to remove any HTML tags from $_POST["hourlyWage"] and $_POST["hoursWorked"] **before** these input values are assigned to the variables $hourlyWage and $hoursWorked:

```
$hourlyWage = filter_var($_POST["hourlyWage"],
                    FILTER_SANITIZE_STRING);
$hoursWorked=filter_var($_POST["hoursWorked"],
                    FILTER_SANITIZE_STRING);
```

If the values do not contain any HTML tags, they are returned unchanged.

Since applications usually need to **both trim AND sanitize** user input, these two operations are often combined into a single statement (first trim, then sanitize the input) as follows:

```
$hourlyWage = filter_var(trim($_POST["hourlyWage"]),
                    FILTER_SANITIZE_STRING);
$hoursWorked=filter_var(trim($_POST["hoursWorked"]),
                    FILTER_SANITIZE_STRING);
```

More about Validation and Security

To avoid too much detail, and minimize code complexity, validation and security code is introduced in this chapter but will be **omitted** from future chapters and examples. You will not be expected to include this code in your chapter exercises unless explicitly requested to do so. This is, of course, an important topic: see **Appendix E** for a more extensive review, including code samples (this appendix will be especially important when you locate your applications on a "live" online Web server).

When to Use AND or OR?
Be Careful with Your Logic!

We have used the **OR** operator to combine two tests in order to validate user input, and we have used the **AND** operator to combine two tests for a requirement to assign a bonus. These are just examples and you can use either operator for any purpose when two or more true/false tests must be combined into a single compound expression.

Remember that two tests combined with the **AND** operator will **only** generate a **true** result if **both** tests are **true**. On the other hand, two tests combined with the **OR** operator will always generate a **true** result unless **both** tests are **false.** Consider very carefully whether you should use **AND** or **OR** in your solution algorithms to meet your program requirements. What happens in wage8.php if you mistakenly use **OR** instead of **AND** to calculate the bonus? Now employees who **either** earn less than 10.00 **or** work 35 hours or higher will get the 50.00 bonus! That will make a lot more employees happy but you are likely to be in trouble! What if your incorrect algorithm was used to generate pay checks for thousands of employees?

Read program requirements very carefully to be sure that you understand what is needed. Software designers quickly learn to focus on the **business rules** within a requirements document, such as the rules for assigning a bonus. Always ask for clarification if there is **any** uncertainty concerning these rules.

The Challenge of Software Testing

It is important to test a program thoroughly before releasing it for production, but this is not a trivial task. How many times do you need to test our **wage8.php** code to be sure that it works correctly under all conditions? The various selection structures means that there are many different paths through this code! Let's consider some of the tests that must be made to verify that our code will work as intended. These tests provide numerous combinations to test different paths through the four selection structures. Here are the various values that will need to be tested:

Test 01:	*hourly wage field is empty*
Test 02:	*hours worked field is empty*
Test 03:	*hourly wage field is non-numeric*
Test 04:	*hours worked field is non-numeric*
Test 05:	*hourly wage field < 7.25*
Test 06:	*hours worked field out of range*
Test 07:	*hourly wage field >= 7.25 and < 8.00*
Test 08:	*hourly wage field > 8.00*
Test 09:	*hourlyWage field >= 10.00 AND hoursWorked field < 35*
Test 10:	*hourlyWage field >= 10.00 AND hoursWorked field >= 35*
Test 11:	*hourlyWage field < 10.00 AND hoursWorked field < 35*
Test 12:	*hourlyWage field < 10.00 AND hoursWorked field >= 35*

Does this mean only 12 tests are required? Not at all! These tests must be made in all **combinations** to ensure that every possible combination of input values will generate the expected result. For example Test 01 should be combined with Test 02, but also with Test 04, Test 06, etc.

If you consider how many tests are needed for this relatively small piece of code that contains four selection structures, consider how much testing is required for applications with hundreds, thousands, or millions of lines of code. The testing has to be automated but even so there is a point that is reached quite quickly where it is literally impossible to test every possible path through a program and that is why there are so many bugs in software applications. Pseudocode can help programmers to develop and review their algorithms before writing actual code, which is much harder to debug. Other tools to reduce errors are:

- Take time in the design stage to develop clearly written algorithms, design documents, and testing procedures. Design documents should specify all required data validation rules, and application and data testing should be applied throughout the development process.
- Document your code with comments that clearly explain the purpose of each code section.
- Reuse existing code as much as possible, code that has already been tested and is well understood.
- Develop your code in modules, and test each module thoroughly before putting them together.
- Use version control software to track and manage your development process (see **Appendix G** for more about version control).
- Work in teams so that other programmers review and test algorithms and code modules throughout the development process.
- Create large sets of test data and write testing programs that run this data against your applications in order to automate the testing process as much as possible.

A Special Case: The Switch Statement

Sometimes we need to test a single variable multiple times in order to determine an appropriate action. As an example, we might want to test a variable that contains the **number** of a month (for example 3) in order to display the appropriate **name** of the month (for example "March"). We can accomplish this using chained IF..ELSE statements:

```
IF (month == 1)
   display "January"
ELSEIF (month == 2)
   display "February"
ELSEIF (month == 3)
   display "March"
ELSEIF (month == 4)
   display "April"
and so on..
```

However most languages provide a specialized selection structure, known as a **switch** (or **case**) structure, that can be used in these situations where a single variable must be tested multiple times for different values. The switch statement is described in Chapter 16, and the examples include the selection of a month name.

More Examples in the Samples Folder

For your interest and enjoyment a number of additional examples of applications that use selection structures are provided in the **samples** folder. These are intended to give you some ideas as you apply selection structures to your own applications. Here is a brief summary of these examples:

comparePets

The **comparePets.html** code uses two drop down lists that allow the user to rate dogs and cats as pets. The **comparePets.php** code uses an **if..elseif..else** structure to comment on the user's ratings.

mathProblem and mathSolution

It is common practice to use **.php** files instead of **.html** files to provide the HTML forms for user input. Sometimes this is necessary since the forms require some PHP processing. Here is an example where a PHP program is needed to generate the initial HTML form because the form includes two numbers that must be randomly generated using the PHP **rand()** function. The example also uses **hidden fields** in the form. (Hidden fields are used to send values that the user does not see to the receiving program. These values are sent in addition to the values that are provided by the user. In this case the two random numbers are sent as part of the form data so that the receiving program can compare the user's answer to the correct answer.) If you are interested in learning how to generate random numbers, take a look at this code.

quizProgram and quizResults

This example uses a PHP program (**quizProgram.php**) to generate the initial HTML form; PHP code is required here because the form contains three quiz questions that must be read from a file named **testbank.txt**. Each line of testbank.txt contains a question followed by three possible answers and the correct answer, all separated by colons. These values are read from the file and then added to a form containing drop down lists with the possible answers. The user's answers are sent to **quizResults.php** along with the correct answers (the correct answers are sent as **hidden** fields) and **quizResults.php** calculates and displays the score.

jokester

The **jokester.html** code uses a drop down list to allow the user to select a joke, and **jokester.php** uses an **if..elseif..else** structure to display the appropriate joke.

artGallery

The **artGallery.html** code uses a drop down list to allow the user to select an artist. The **artGallery.php** code tests the character string received from the form and displays a brief artist biography and a painting (using the HTML **<img>** tag).

Some Words of Encouragement

It is easy for anyone to feel overwhelmed or panicked when confronted with a requirement that needs to be converted to an algorithm and then into working code. One reason for this is that we assume that we should be able to understand and solve problems quickly and move on to the coding process. We feel that we are wasting time if we are not able to start coding immediately.

The truth is that very few people can look at a problem, immediately understand the requirements, and quickly develop an effective algorithm. It takes time to do this and the more time that is spent considering the problem carefully the better! Software designers allocate considerable time to review program requirements and develop an effective design.

It helps to stay away from the computer when you are working out your algorithm. Even if your programming problem is quite small, you should follow this practice. Use pencil and paper to make notes, decide your inputs and outputs and processes, and outline your algorithm. Take a divide-and-conquer approach—break the problem down into parts until you can clearly understand all of the steps and calculations that are needed. Desk-check your algorithm by walking through it using some test data. Only begin to code when you are reasonably satisfied that your algorithm should work, and be prepared to come back to the algorithm if you run into problems.

Software designers and programmers spend a great deal of time working together, away from the computer. They use sticky notes, white boards, and other tools to brainstorm, experiment and walk through the problem definition and solution algorithm. This approach may save you a lot of stress, and help you to produce a high quality and well-designed solution.

Additional Learning Materials

The **PHP SWITCH** statement is a useful alternative to chained **IF..ELSE** statements in cases where a single value is being tested for a range of possible actions. **Chapter 16** describes the switch statement, and provides examples that demonstrate different ways that it can be used.

Appendix D will help you **debug** your exercises, listing a number of the most common errors that you are likely to encounter.

Appendix E provides a more complete overview of security and data validation. This is a must-read for anyone developing code on a "live" online Web server.

The **Chapter 8 Hints and Help** pages on the textbook Web site provide answers to FAQs from previous students as they worked through the end-of-chapter exercises.

Summary

In this chapter we learned how to develop algorithms that include multiple selection structures and compound Boolean expressions. Multiple selection structures may be distinct from one another or may be **nested** inside one another in order to meet the program requirements. If necessary, IF..ELSE structures can also be **chained** together (as many as needed) to permit more than two possible outcomes to a business rule, for example to assign a bonus that may have more than two possible values. The resulting **IF..ELSE IF..ELSE** structure can also be written in the form **IF..ELSEIF..ELSE**.

The **AND** and **OR** operators can be used to combine two or more simple Boolean expressions to produce a compound Boolean expression. When two expressions are combined using the **AND** operator, both tests must generate a **true** result in order for the combined test to be **true**. When two expressions are combined using the **OR** operator, either or both tests can generate a **true** result in order for the combined test to be **true**.

In PHP the **AND** operator can be represented using **and** or **&&**.

In PHP the **OR** operator can be represented using **or** or ||.

The **NOT** operator is used to **reverse** the result of a true/false test.

In PHP the **NOT** operator can be represented using the ! character.

Input validation and data cleaning are important components of software design to ensure that a program does not attempt to process bad data. Explicit validation rules should be a part of every requirements document. Steps should also be applied to avoid input errors when possible, and prevent security vulnerabilities.

The PHP empty() function is used to test if a variable is empty (contains no value).

The PHP is_numeric() function is used to test if a variable contains a numeric value.

The PHP trim() function is used to trim leading and following white space from a character string. White space can include spaces, paragraph marks, or tabs.

The PHP filter_var() function is used to validate and sanitize data and can be used to remove HTML tags from character strings in order to prevent malicious scripts.

A **high-level design** (or **top down design**) approach is important when tackling more complex requirements. The designer develops the more general structure of the application before focusing on the details.

Programmers usually brainstorm **away** from the computer in order to work through requirements and develop effective algorithms.

Software testing is a complex and skilled task. Software can never be completely tested and this explains why there can often be so many bugs even after applications have been distributed.

Chapter 8 Review Questions

1. How many different paths are there through a program that contains one IF structure, followed by one (separate) IF..ELSE structure?
   a. 1
   b. 2
   c. 3
   d. 4
   e. 5

2. If $hourlyWage contains the value 10.00 and $hoursWorked contains the value 20, what value will $bonus contain after the following code is executed?

   ```
   if ($hourlyWage > 10 or $hoursWorked < 20)
      $bonus = $25.00;
   else
      $bonus = $50.00;
   ```

   a. 25.00
   b. 50.00

3. If $hourlyWage contains the value 10.00 and $hoursWorked contains the value 20, what value will $bonus contain after the following code is executed?

   ```
   if ($hourlyWage > 10 or $hoursWorked <= 20)
      $bonus = $25.00;
   else
      $bonus = $50.00;
   ```

   a. 25.00
   b. 50.00

4. If $hourlyWage contains the value 10.00 and $hoursWorked contains the value 20, what value will $bonus contain after the following code is executed?

   ```
   if ($hourlyWage > 10 and $hoursWorked < 20)
      $bonus = $25.00;
   else
      $bonus = $50.00;
   ```

   a. 25.00
   b. 50.00

5. If $hourlyWage contains the value 10.00 and $hoursWorked contains the value 20, what value will $bonus contain after the following code is executed?

```
if ($hourlyWage > 10 and $hoursWorked <= 20)
   $bonus = $25.00;
else
   $bonus = $50.00;
```

  a. 25.00
  b. 50.00

6. If $hourlyWage contains the value 10.00 and $hoursWorked contains the value 20, what value will $bonus contain after the following code is executed?

```
if ($hourlyWage >= 10 and $hoursWorked <= 20)
   $bonus = $25.00;
else
   $bonus = $50.00;
```

  a. 25.00
  b. 50.00

7. Given the following requirements which would be the appropriate test to use?

*A discount of 10% should be applied only when the following conditions **both** apply:*

  The customer has ordered at least 10 copies

  The item cost is above 25.00

  a. if ($numCopies > 10 and $itemCost > 25.00)
  b. if ($numCopies >= 10 and $itemCost >= 25.00)
  c. if ($numCopies >= 10 and $itemCost > 25.00)
  d. if ($numCopies >= 10 or $itemCost >= 25.00)
  e. if ($numCopies >= 10 or $itemCost > 25.00)

8. If a variable named $carsSold contains the value 8, what is stored in $bonus after this code is processed? (Are these structures separate or chained?)

```
if ($carsSold < 10)
   $bonus = 0.00;
elseif ($carsSold < 20)
   $bonus = 100.00;
else
   $bonus = 200.00;
```

    a. 0.00

    b. 100.00

    c. 200.00

9. If a variable named $carsSold contains the value 8 what is stored in $bonus after this code is processed? (Are these structures separate or chained?)

```
if ($carsSold < 10)
   $bonus = 0.00;
if ($carsSold < 20)
   $bonus = 100.00;
else
   $bonus = 200.00;
```

    a. 0.00

    b. 100.00

    c. 200.00

10. If a variable named $carsSold contains the value 8 and $yearsOnJob contains the value 2, what is stored in $bonus after this code is processed?

```
if ($carsSold < 10 and $yearsOnJob > 1)
   $bonus = 0.00;
elseif ($carsSold < 20)
   $bonus = 100.00;
else
   $bonus = 200.00;
```

    a. 0.00

    b. 100.00

    c. 200.00

11. Consider the following code? Which employees will get a 750.00 bonus?

```
if ($yearsWorked < 5)
{
   if ($salary < 18000.00)
      $bonus = 500.00;
   else
      $bonus = 400.00;
}
else
   $bonus = 750.00;
```

a. Employees who have worked at least 5 years, no matter what their salary is.
b. Employees who have worked at least 5 years, with a salary of at least 18000.00.
c. Employees who have worked at least 5 years, with a salary less than 18000.00.
d. Employees who have worked less than 5 years, no matter what their salary is.
e. Employees who have worked less than 5 years, with a salary of at least 18000.00.

12. Consider the following code. What bonus will be assigned for an employee who has worked 5 years and earns 18000.00?

```
if ($yearsWorked < 5)
{
   if ($salary < 18000.00)
      $bonus = 500.00;
   else
      $bonus = 400.00;
}
else
   $bonus = 750.00;
```

a. 500.00
b. 400.00
c. 750.00

13. If a variable named $ticketsOrdered contains the value 50, and $maximumOrder contains the value 25 what is stored in $totalCost after this code is processed?

```
if ($ticketsOrdered > $maximumOrder)
   $ticketsOrdered = $maximumOrder;
if ($ticketsOrdered >= 10 )
   $totalCost = $ticketsOrdered * 4.00;
else
   $totalCost = $ticketsOrdered * 5.00;
```

a. 0.00
b. 100.00
c. 125.00
d. 200.00
e. 250.00

14. How many different paths are there through the code segment in question 13?
    a. 1
    b. 2
    c. 3
    d. 4
    e. 8

15. If $result contains the value 4, what will be stored in $result after the following
    code is executed:

```
if ($rating >4)

  $result = "Must see";

if ($rating >3)

  $result = "Very good";

if ($score >2)

  $result = "Acceptable";

if $score <= 2

  $result = "Poor";
```
    a. "Must see"
    b. "Very good"
    c. "Acceptable"
    d. "Poor"
    e. $result has no value

16. In PHP, when the keyword else is immediately followed by the keyword if, you can
    substitute these two words with:
    a. else-if
    b. else_if
    c. elseif
    d. elseandif
    e. elseorif

17. What is the purpose of input validation?
    a. Check that the user's ID and password are valid
    b. Ensure that any data entered by the user is valid
    c. Process the user's data and display the results
    d. Test that any files needed by the program are actually on the disk
    e. Ensure that the file path of the PHP program is correct

18. The programmer made a mistake reading the requirements and used OR instead of AND in the following code! Will customers benefit or lose by this error?

```
if ($totalPurchases > 100.00 or $customerStatus ==
   "PREFERRED")
   $discount = 25.00;
else
   $discount = 0.00;
```

    a. The customers benefit—more customers will get a discount as a result of the error.
    b. The customers lose—less customers will get a discount as a result of the error.
    c. It makes no difference whether AND or OR is used here.

19. Dress shoes sell for 95.00, trail shoes sell for 75.00, and casual shoes sell for 55.00. Here's what a programmer wrote as a selection structure to display the price based on a user's style selection. The logic is incorrect since if the style is "Dress" two prices are displayed. What's wrong with the logic?

```
if ($style == "Dress")
   print ("<p>Price: $95.00</p>");
if ($style == "Trail")
   print ("<p>Price: $75.00</p>");
else
   print ("<p>Price: $55.00</p>");
```

    a. The second if should be an else.
    b. The else should be an elseif.
    c. The second if should be an elseif.
    d. Curly braces are needed around each print statement.
    e. The two == should each be =

20. Which statement is true?
    a. A program can include any number of if and if..else structures, which may be nested inside one another, chained together or entirely separate from one another, in any order, as required by the program logic.
    b. A program can include a maximum of two if structures and if..else structures.
    c. Multiple if..else structures must always be chained together.
    d. Multiple if..else structures must always be nested inside one another.
    e. If structures must always occur before if..else structures in a program.

Chapter 8 Code Exercises

Your Chapter 8 code exercises can be found in your **chapter08** folder. This folder is included in your customized XAMPP installation at the following location:

> htdocs\webtech\coursework\chapter08

Type your name and the date in the Author and Date sections of each file as you work on each exercise. **Remember** that the Students page on the textbook Web site includes **Hints and Help** pages for the exercises in this and every chapter.

Debugging Exercises

Your **chapter08** folder should contain a number of "fixit" files. Each of these files contains PHP code that has an error of some kind. The type of error is indicated in the comment section of each file. You will need to run each program in order to see the errors, and to debug and test the code to see if it works correctly. For example to run **fixit1.php**, first run the Web server, then use the URL:

> http://localhost/webtech/coursework/chapter08/fixit1.php

Code Modification Exercises

Your **chapter08** folder contains a number of "modify" files. Each pair of files contains HTML and PHP code that needs to be modified to meet a requirement. The requirements are included in the comment section of each file. Modify the algorithms, being careful to make changes to the .html and .php files as directed. You will need to run each program in order to test your changes. For example to run **modify1.html**, first run the Web server, then use the URL:

> http://localhost/webtech/coursework/chapter08/modify1.html

Code Completion Exercises

1. Read this exercise carefully and take your time to work out the logic. Your **chapter08** folder contains versions of **paint-estimate.html** and **paint-estimate.php**. The code in **paint-estimate.html** does not need to be changed. The HTML form includes a drop down selection to ask the user if they are a first time customer. The name for this input is **firstTime**, and the possible values are "**yes**" and "**no**". The HTML form also includes a drop down selection to ask the user what paint quality they want. The name for this input is **paint**, and the possible values are "**premium**" and "**regular**". Note that the first letter of each paint selection is lower-case.

    The PHP program already includes a calculation for the paint cost that assumes that the paint costs 17.00 for a gallon, however this is no longer correct. Replace this with a selection structure that will assign the paint cost as either **20.00** or **15.00** a gallon, depending on whether the user selected premium (**20.00**) or regular (**15.00**).

The program must **also** apply a new test to determine whether or not a customer should receive a discount. If the user is a first time customer and their total cost is at least 200.00, the program should calculate a 10% deduction to the total estimate, and, **instead** of displaying the total cost, should generate the following output: "<p>We want your service! Since you are a first time customer and your order is over $200.00, we are offering a 10% deduction.</p><p> Your actual costs will be: $**xxx**</p>" where $**xxx** is their cost after the deduction. **Otherwise** the program should display the total cost as provided in the existing code.

Make the changes to **paint-estimate.php** so that the program works as described. Think carefully where your two selection structures must appear in the code. Test your program carefully with various test input to be sure that your program is working correctly for first time and other customers, with initial total costs above and below 200.00, and choosing different choices of paint quality.

2. Read this exercise carefully and take your time to work out the logic. Your **chapter08** folder contains a previous version of **software-order.html** and **software-order.php**. You do not need to change **software-order.html**.

   The PHP program should now test the number of copies ordered. If the number of copies is less than 1, the program should display an error message and **should not calculate or display anything else** (the error message is already provided).

   The program **also** needs code to calculate the shipping and handling charge. If there are **less than five copies** the shipping and handling charge is a standard **3.50** no matter how many copies, otherwise if there are less than 10 copies, the shipping handling is **0.75** for each copy, otherwise the shipping handling is **0.85** for each copy.

   Make the changes to **software-order.php** so that the program works as described. Think carefully where your selection structures must appear in the code, and how they need be associated with one another. Test your code carefully with different inputs until you are satisfied that the selections structures are working as expected and delivering the correct results.

3. Read this exercise carefully and take your time to work out the logic. Your **chapter08** folder contains a modified version of **travel.html** and **travel.php**. You do not need to change **travel.html**. This form now allows the user to select among **five** travel destinations. The costs are as follows:

   Barcelona: the air fare is $875 and the hotel cost per night is $85
   Cairo: the air fare is $950 and the hotel cost per night is $98
   Rome: the air fare is $875 and the hotel cost per night is $110
   Santiago: the air fare is $820 and the hotel cost per night is $85
   Tokyo: the air fare is $1575 and the hotel cost per night is $240

You must add the code to assign appropriate airfare and hotel cost per night, depending on the selected destination. Use the same variables names that are provided in the existing code.

Also, if the destination is Tokyo, there is a special air fare discount of **$200 per traveler** if the party is staying at least 5 nights. You can use a nested IF structure to calculate this or you can use a compound Boolean expression.

To test your code, try entering 1 passenger for 1 night for each destination and compare your output with the values listed above. Then try entering 1 passenger for 5 nights to Tokyo (with the discount this should amount to $2575.00). Try one or two other tests to be sure your program is calculating correctly.

4. Read this exercise carefully and take your time to work out the logic. Your **chapter08** folder contains a modified version of **game-intro.html** and **game-intro.php**. You do not need to change **game-intro.html**.

   Do you remember that the player begins with 10 gold pieces? It is time to ensure that he or she did not overspend! If the total number of gold pieces spent is greater than 10, the program should only display an error message (this has been provided) and should not perform any additional processing or display any other output. Otherwise the program should assign bonus tokens to the character as follows:

   Wizards receive 2 extra experience tokens
   Humans and dwarfs receive 10 extra supply tokens
   Elves receive 5 extra health tokens

   The program should also calculate the number of gold pieces left so that this amount can be displayed as part of the output (all of the output statements have been provided—note the variable names).

   Be careful with the order of your statements and the location and organization of your selection structures. Test your code carefully. Be sure to test for overspending, and also test that the correct bonuses are assigned to each character type.

5. Your **chapter08** folder already contains **mileage-log.html**, **mileage-log.php**, and **mileage-log.txt**. You do not need to change **mileage-log.html**, which provides the user with a form to report their mileage for travel reimbursement. Modify **mileage-log.php** as follows:

   Modify the statement $mileage = $_POST['mileage']; to include the use of the **trim()** and **filter_var()** functions to remove leading and trailing white space and sanitize the mileage value in the $_POST array before the mileage value is assigned to $mileage.

Add code to **mileage-log.php** to apply the following validation rules:

The mileage field must not be empty
The mileage must be numeric
The mileage must be in the range 0 to 500

The first error found should generate a suitable error message, with no further testing. If no errors are found the program should process the four statements already provided (to open the .txt file, save the mileage to the file, close the file, and report that the mileage has been recorded). The link back to the submission form should be displayed whether an error was found or the mileage was recorded.

Hint: review the sections on input validation and chained IF..ELSE structures.

6. Your **chapter08** folder already contains **bus-travel.html** and **bus-travel.php**. You do not need to change bus-travel.html which provides the user with a form to submit business travel information for reimbursement. The form includes input fields for the date and miles traveled, followed by four YES/NO entries to indicate whether or not the travel included breakfast, lunch, dinner or hotel.

The bus-travel.php file already contains code to receive the form input and to display the results (note the variable names). Your job is to insert the code to process the form input and calculate the reimbursement for the trip. The basic reimbursement will be the miles traveled * 0.35. If breakfast was included add 6.00 to the reimbursement. If lunch was included, add 8.50 to the reimbursement. If dinner was included, add 17.50 to the reimbursement. If a hotel was included, add 110.00 to the reimbursement. So for example if the user submitted 120 for the mile traveled, "NO" for breakfast, and "YES" for lunch, dinner and hotel, the complete reimbursement will be 120*0.35 + 8.50 + 17.50 + 110.00, which is $178.00.

Be sure to test your program a few times so that you are sure it works correctly with different submissions. Try choosing "NO" for all of the drop down lists, then "YES" for all of the lists, then try different combinations of "YES" and "NO".

Chapter 9

Programs that Count — Harnessing the Power of Repetition

Intended Learning Outcomes

After completing this chapter, you should be able to:

- Describe the purpose of loop structures.
- Identify standard loop structures.
- Explain the purpose of each component of a FOR loop heading.
- Trace the processing of a simple FOR loop.
- Design and code a FOR loop.
- Use variables to control a FOR loop.
- Apply the loop counting variable to perform processing within a FOR loop.
- Use a FOR loop with an HTML table to generate output.
- Use a FOR loop to accumulate a total.
- Use a FOR loop to find high and low values in a series.
- Use a FOR loop to process a data file.
- Nest selection structures within a FOR loop.
- Nest a FOR loop within a FOR loop.

Introduction

We have learned how to write programs to process relatively small amounts of data such as calculating the weekly pay for a single employee, or converting a temperature from Centigrade to Fahrenheit, but what about programs that must handle much larger data sets? What if we need to write an application that calculates wages for a **thousand** employees? Or an application that converts to Fahrenheit all of the Centigrade temperatures between 0 and 100 degrees? Or that determines the average rainfall from data in a file that contains rainfall readings for an entire year?

These may appear to be more complicated problems that require extensive coding but in fact they are not very complicated at all. This is because computer programs can easily be designed to **repeat** a sequence of instructions as many times as needed in order to process very large amounts of data.

Loop, or **repetition,** structures provide one of the more powerful tools available to a programmer. Just as a selection structure allows a program to **choose between** two different blocks of statements based on a test condition, so a loop structure allows a program to **repeatedly execute** a block of statements, where the number of repetitions is based on a test condition. Programs can use loop structures to process larger data sets for any purpose, for example to convert data values, perform statistical operations, generate graphs or tables, search data, or sort data.

Loop structures and selection structures can be combined in any number of configurations to meet the requirements of any application. Together these structures provide the basic processing tools underlying all software design and development. Most current programming languages, including PHP, provide four different loop structures as follows:

FOR loops are most often used where a program can determine the required number of repetitions before the loop executes. FOR loops are often referred to as **count-controlled** loops since the loop is controlled by a counting variable.

For example a FOR loop could be used to process the monthly rainfall for each month of the year since the loop will need to repeat exactly 12 times (once for each month).

WHILE loops are most often used where the program cannot determine the required number of repetitions before the loop executes, for example when processing lines in a file of unknown length. WHILE loops are often referred to as **event-controlled** loops since they are designed to continue to repeat until a certain event occurs. WHILE loops will be introduced in Chapter 10.

DO..WHILE (or **REPEAT..UNTIL**) loops. These loops are similar to WHILE loops and may be used in situations where the loop must always repeat at least once (for example, when requesting a password and repeating if the password is invalid). These loops are described in Chapter 16.

FOREACH loops are a special type of counting loop, often used to simplify the processing of a list of values stored in a data structure known as an array. These loops will be introduced in chapters 11 and 12, which cover arrays.

In this chapter you will learn how to use FOR loops to repeat instructions using a counting variable, and how to include selection structures within a FOR loop to perform common processing operations.

Controlling a Loop by Counting

As a first example of a FOR loop, consider the following algorithm:

```
Testing1.php algorithm:
  Display "This is a test"
  FOR (counter = 1 to 3)
    Display "Testing ..."
  ENDFOR
  Display "End of test"

END
```

This algorithm first displays a heading, and then defines a FOR loop. Any instructions located between the FOR loop heading and ENDFOR will be repeated—in this example there is just one instruction: **Display "Testing ..."**. A FOR loop usually uses a counting variable to control the number of repetitions. In this algorithm a variable named **counter** is defined in the FOR loop heading to first receive the value 1, then the value 2, and then the value 3. For each value of the counter variable, the loop statements are executed, so this loop will run three times and the phrase "Testing ..." will display three times (see Figure 9-2). The counting variable is just a standard variable and can be given any name.

Figure 9-1 shows a flow chart for this algorithm. Notice how a flow chart can diagram the flow of a FOR loop structure. The test that controls the loop indicates that the loop control will be given successive values of 1, 2 and 3. Each time the loop repeats, the statements in the loop structure will be executed (in this case just one statement), and the program then returns to the loop test. When the loop test becomes false (after the third iteration), the program skips the loop structure and moves on to the next instruction following the loop.

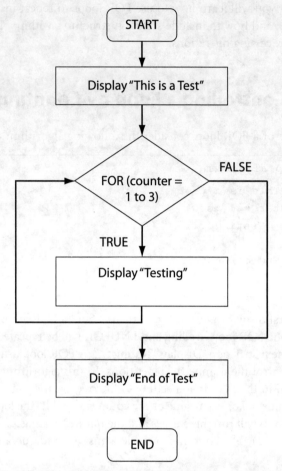

Figure 9.1 Flow Chart showing the algorithm for testing1.php

Coding a FOR Loop in PHP

The syntax of a FOR loop is similar in most programming languages. Here is the PHP code (testing1.php) that implements our algorithm:

```
<html>
<head>
  <title>Testing ... </title>
  <link rel="stylesheet" type="text/css" href="sample.css">
</head>
<body>
  <?php
    print("<h1>This is a test</h1>");

    for ($counter = 1; $counter <= 3; $counter = $counter + 1)
    {
       print("Testing ... <br>");
    }

    print("<h1>End of test</h1>");
  ?>
</body>
</html>
```

Code Example: testing1.php

The loop heading looks a little different from our pseudocode. Let's look at this heading carefully:

```
for ($counter=1; $counter<=3; $counter=$counter+1)
```

The heading of a FOR loop contains three sections, separated by two semi-colons:

- The **loop initialization section** appears before the first semi-colon and specifies the initial value for the variable that will be used to count the number of repetitions. In this example the variable is named **$counter** and the initialization statement is **$counter = 1**.
- The **loop condition section** appears after the first semi-colon and provides the test that determines whether or not the loop statements should continue to repeat. In this example the condition is **$counter <=3**.
- The **loop update section** appears after the second semi-colon and indicates how the value of the counting variable should be modified after each repetition of the loop statements. In this example the modification is **$counter = $counter + 1** which will add 1 to the value stored in **$counter** after each repetition.

The statements that are intended to execute repeatedly are listed below the loop heading and are enclosed within curly braces { and }. These statements are often referred to as the **body** of the loop. The braces are important since without these the processor will assume that only the first statement following the loop heading is to be repeated.

Let's look carefully at what happens when this loop is processed.

The first time that the program encounters the loop, the initialization statement is executed. In this case the **$counter** variable is created and assigned the value 1.

Next, the loop condition (**$counter** <= 3) is tested. Since **$counter** currently contains the value 1, the test is **true** and so the instructions inside the loop are executed. In this example the loop contains only a single statement: **print("Testing …
");**

Once the statements in the loop body have been executed, the loop update section is processed. In this example, the result of the update is that 1 is added to the value of **$counter** so this variable now contains 2.

Following the update, the loop condition is re-tested. Since **$counter** contains the value 2, the test is still **true** so the instructions inside the loop are executed. The loop update is again processed so the value of **$counter** is incremented to 3.

The loop condition is again tested. Since $counter contains the value 3, the test is **true** so the instructions inside the loop are executed again. The loop update is again processed so the value of $counter is incremented to 4.

The loop condition is again tested. Since the counter variable contains the value **4**, the test is **false**. A **false** result causes the program to stop processing the loop and skip past the loop to the next statement that follows the closing brace of the loop structure. In this case the next statement is **print("<h1>End of test</h1>");**.

The loop has therefore been designed to repeat three times, based on the initial value of the counting variable, the loop condition, and the loop update. Figure 9-2 shows the output from this program.

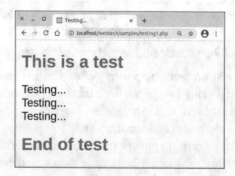

Figure 9-2: testing1.php screenshot

Run the program, and then modify it to get a feel how this works. Here are some suggested modifications:

1. Change $counter = 1; to $counter = 0; and run the program again. Why does the loop now repeat **4** times? Change the code back to its original form.
2. Change $counter = 1; to $counter = 10; and run the program again. Why does the loop now repeat **0** times? Change the code back to its original form.
3. Change $counter = $counter + 1; to $counter = $counter + 2; and run the program again. Why does the loop now repeat **2** times? Change the code back to its original form.
4. Change the loop test from ($counter <= 3) to ($counter < 3) and run the program again. Why does the loop now repeat **2** times? Change the code back to its original form.
5. Change the loop test from ($counter <= 3) to ($counter <= 100) and run the program again. Why does the loop now repeat **100** times? Change the code back to its original form.

General Syntax of a FOR Loop

You can use a FOR loop for many purposes, wherever you need a set of instructions to be repeated a predetermined number of times. In PHP (and most languages) the general syntax for writing a FOR loop is as follows:

```
for (loop initialization; loop condition; loop update)
{
    ... instructions to be repeated ...
}
```

Note that there is **no semi-colon** after the closing parenthesis at the end of the FOR loop heading! That's because headings of loop structures (just like headings of selection structures or any other structures) do not require semi-colons. This is very important—if you place a semi-colon at the end of the loop heading the statements in your loop structure will appear not to repeat! Since the semi-colon appears before the braces, the processor will assume that the loop consists of only a single statement, and that this statement is an instruction to do nothing each time the loop repeats!

Be sure that you understand how the different parts of the loop heading work together to control the loop. There is nothing magical about the way that a loop operates—the program simply processes the statements exactly as they are written. You have a lot of flexibility in how you decide to control a counting loop and this will depend on the details of your program requirement. You can specify any initial value for the loop counting variable, and you can increment the value of the variable by any amount each time through the loop.

Indenting Statements Inside a FOR Loop

Notice that the block of statements inside the FOR loop (between the opening and closing curly braces) are **indented**, just as statements are indented inside the IF and ELSE blocks of selection structures. This is standard practice for loop structures also, and for the same reason: the indentation makes it easier for anyone reading the code to identify which statements are part of the loop. It is important to follow this practice

Including the Counting Variable in Your Loop Statements

We have seen that the counting variable contains a different value each time that the loop is repeated. We can write statements within the loop structure that make use of this value. For example what if we want to display the value of the counter as a part of the output in our testing program? Take a look at Figure 9-3.

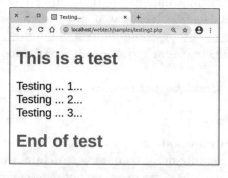

Figure 9-3: testing2.php screenshot

Here is the code for **testing2.php** which performs similarly to **testing1.php** except that it displays the value of the **$counter** variable each time that the loop statements are executed:

```
<html>
<head>
   <title>Testing ... </title>
   <link rel="stylesheet" type="text/css" href="sample.css">
</head>
<body>
   <?php
     print("<h1>This is a test</h1>");
     for ($counter = 1; $counter <= 3; $counter = $counter + 1)
     {
        print("Testing ... $counter ... <br>");
```

```
      }

      print("<h1>End of test</h1>");
    ?>
 </body>
 </html>
```

Code Example: testing2.php

The only difference is the line:

```
      print("Testing ... $counter ... <br>");
```

The value of $counter is included in the output. The first time through the loop, the value is 1, the second time the value is 2 and the last time the value is 3. You can use the value of the counting variable inside the loop structure for any purpose that you choose. We will see some other examples shortly.

Using a Variable to Control the Loop Condition

Our two examples have been coded to repeat a loop three times. We used a literal value (in this case 3) to achieve this but it is often useful to write a program that uses a **variable** to control the number of times that the loop will repeat.

Let's consider an example where the user is asked to specify how many times the loop should repeat. Here is code for **testing3.html** which includes a form that obtains this information from the user:

```
<html>
<head>
  <title>Testing..</title>
  <link rel="stylesheet" type="text/css" href="sample.css">
</head>
<body>
  <h1>Testing..</h1>
  <form action="testing3.php" method="post">

    <label>How many tests?
    <input type="text" size="5" name="numTimes"></label>
    <input class="submit" type="submit" value="Run the
      test!"></p>

</form>
</body>
</html>
```

Code Example: testing3.html

Here is **testing3.php** which receives the user's input in a variable named **$numTimes** and uses this to control the number of times that the loop repeats. Note the use of **$numTimes** in the loop condition section:

```
<html>
<head>
  <title>Testing ... </title>
  <link rel="stylesheet" type="text/css" href="sample.css">
</head>
<body>
  <?php

    $numTimes = $_POST['numTimes'];

    print("<h1>This is a test ($numTimes repetitions)</h1>");

    for($counter = 1;$counter <= $numTimes;$counter = $counter+1)
    {
      print("Testing ... $counter ... <br>");
    }

    print("<h1>End of test</h1>");

  ?>
</body>
</html>
```

Code Example: testing3.php

The loop condition now indicates **$counter** <= **$numTimes**, so the loop will repeat the number of times that the user requested. Note that the code **also** uses the value stored in **$numTimes** in the **print()** statement that generates a heading. Figure 9-4 shows some sample input/output for this program.

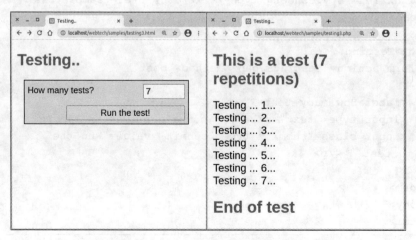

Figure 9-4: testing3.html and testing3.php screenshots

Converting from Celsius to Fahrenheit

Now let's see how we can use a FOR loop to generate a more useful table. Consider the following requirement:

temp-converter1 requirement:

*Create a program that converts all Celsius temperatures between 0° and 100° to Fahrenheit and displays these. The conversion formula is: (9 / 5) * C + 32.*

First take a moment to appreciate the difficulty of meeting this requirement without using a loop:

```
temp-converter1 algorithm (without a FOR loop):

  celsius = 0
  fahrenheit = (9 / 5) * celsius + 32
  Display celsius and fahrenheit
  celsius = 1
  fahrenheit = (9 / 5) * celsius + 32
  Display celsius and fahrenheit

  ... instructions here for all Celsius temperatures between 2
and 98! ...

  celsius = 99
  fahrenheit = (9 / 5) * celsius + 32
  Display celsius and fahrenheit
  celsius = 100
  fahrenheit = (9 / 5) * celsius + 32
  Display celsius and fahrenheit
END
```

This algorithm only shows the instructions to convert and display the first two and last two temperatures—the complete algorithm would actually need 300 instructions! It is easy to see that this is not practical. In fact this approach is impossible for some requirements. What if the program was required to convert all temperatures in a range where the starting and ending temperatures were to be input by the user? Since the programmer does not know in advance what the user will choose, there is no way to know how many statements to include.

Now look at how easily the same requirement can be handled using a FOR loop:

```
temp-converter1.php algorithm:


  FOR celsius = 0 to 100
    fahrenheit = (9 / 5) * celsius + 32
    Display celsius and fahrenheit
  ENDFOR
END
```

In this algorithm the variable named **celsius** is used as the loop counting variable. The loop statements will execute **101** times. The first time the loop is executed, **celsius** will have the value **0**, and the last time the loop is executed, celsius will have the value **100**. For each repetition, the loop statements will: convert the current value of **celsius** to Fahrenheit; assign the result of the conversion to the **fahrenheit** variable; and display the two temperatures.

Here is the PHP code for this algorithm:

```
<html>
<head>
  <title>Temperature Conversions</title>
  <link rel="stylesheet" type="text/css" href="sample.css">
</head>

<body>
  <?php
    print("<h1>Temperature Conversions</h1>");

    for ($celsius = 0; $celsius <= 100; $celsius = $celsius + 1)
    {
      $fahrenheit = (9 / 5) * $celsius + 32;
      print("$celsius degrees Celsius = $fahrenheit degrees
        Fahrenheit<br>");
    }
  ?>
</body>
</html>
```

Code Example: temp-converter1.php

Figure 9-5 shows the first few lines of the HTML document that this program creates.

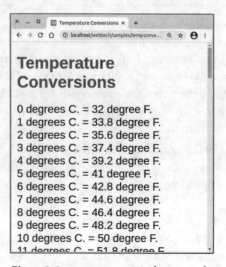

Figure 9-5: temp-converter1.php screenshot

Changing the Increment Value

Let's look at a modified requirement:

---

temp-converter2 requirement:

*Create a program that converts every 10th Celsius temperature (0° C., 10°C., 20°C., etc) between 0° and 100° to Fahrenheit and displays these. The conversion formula is: (9 / 5) * C + 32*

This is the same as the previous requirement except that the program should now only display every 10th conversion. We can do this easily by simply incrementing our counting variable by 10 instead of by 1. Here is a revised algorithm:

```
temp-converter2.php algorithm
   FOR celsius = 0 to 100 INCREMENT BY 10
      fahrenheit = (9 / 5) * celsius + 32
      Display celsius and fahrenheit
   ENDFOR
END
```

The INCREMENT BY 10 in the FOR loop heading indicates that the value of celsius is to be increased by 10 each time through the loop. We can code this in PHP as follows:

```
<html>
<head>
   <title>Temperature Conversions</title>
   <link rel="stylesheet" type="text/css" href="sample.css">
</head>
<body>
   <?php
      print("<h1>Temperature Conversions</h1>");

      for ($celsius = 0;$celsius <= 100;$celsius = $celsius + 10)
      {
         $fahrenheit = (9 / 5) * $celsius + 32;
         print("$celsius degrees Celsius = $fahrenheit degrees
            Fahrenheit<br>");
      }
   ?>
</body>
</html>
```

Code Example: temp-converter2.php

Just as in the algorithm, the only difference is the loop heading:

```
for ($celsius = 0; $celsius <= 100; $celsius = $celsius + 10 )
```

The loop counting variable ($celsius) is incremented by 10 each time the loop statements are executed. The first time through the loop, the value of $celsius is 0, the next time, 10, the next time, 20, and so on until the value of $celsius is incremented to 110 and the loop condition test is false. Figure 9-6 shows the output from this code.

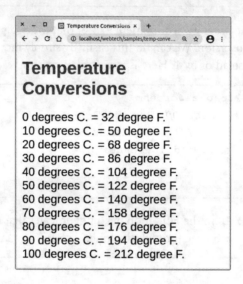

Figure 9-6: temp-converter2.php screenshot

Using Loops with HTML Tables

The output from our temperature conversion programs does not line up very nicely. You may be thinking that it would be much better to use an HTML table to display this output neatly in rows and columns. Loops can provide a very effective programming tool for creating HTML tables, since a new table row can be generated by each loop repetition.

Let's modify our temperature conversion program (**temp-converter3.php**) so that the output is formatted using table tags (Figure 9-7). Each row of the table contains two columns, one for the Celsius temperature and one for the Fahrenheit temperature. As you can see the appearance is much neater.

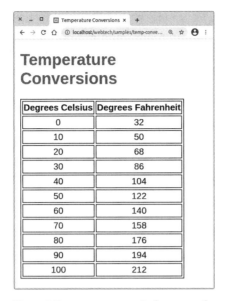

Figure 9-7: temp-converter3.php screenshot

Since we are using a loop to generate the table rows, coding this takes a little planning. Here is the PHP code for **temp-converter3.php**:

```
<html>
<head>
  <title>Temperature Conversions</title>
  <link rel="stylesheet" type="text/css" href="sample.css">
</head>
<body>
  <?php
    print("<h1>Temperature Conversions</h1>");

    print ("<table>");
    print ("<tr><td><strong>Degrees Celsius</strong></td>
      <td><strong>Degrees Fahrenheit</strong></td></tr>");

    for ($celsius = 0;$celsius <= 100;$celsius = $celsius + 10)
    {
      $fahrenheit = (9 / 5) * $celsius + 32;
      print("<tr><td class=\"center\">$celsius</td>
        <td class=\"center\">$fahrenheit</td></tr>");
    }

    print ("</table>");
  ?>
</body>
</html>
```

Code Example: temp-converter3.php

Take a good look at this PHP code. The print statements that generate the beginning <table> tag and the first <tr> row (the row that contains the row headings) are both located **before** the FOR loop structure. This is important, do you see why? The <table> tag and the row table headings should only occur **once**, at the start of the table. If these two print statements were located **inside** the loop, these elements would repeat every time the loop repeats! Similarly, the print statement that displays the closing </table> tag should only occur once, so this statement is located **after** the FOR loop structure.

The loop structure itself includes the statement to convert the current Celsius value to Fahrenheit, and a **print()** statement that generates a new table row containing the Celsius and Fahrenheit values. Each time the loop repeats, a new Celsius value will be converted to Fahrenheit, and a new row added to the table.

A critical design decision when you are coding any loop is to determine which statements must occur **before** the loop structure, which statements are to be repeated **inside** the loop structure, and which statements should **follow** the loop structure.

Allowing the User to Control the Loop

Now consider a more general purpose requirement where the **user** selects the range of temperatures to be converted:

---

temp-converter4 requirement:

Create a program that asks the user for a starting and ending temperature, and an increment value n. The program should then convert every nth temperature between the starting and ending temperature to Fahrenheit and display these. The conversion formula is: (9 / 5) * C + 32

Now our loop counter must be designed to count from an initial temperature value to an ending temperature value, both provided by the user. This value is to be incremented after each repetition by a value that is also provided by the user. Here is the algorithm for the HTML document designed to receive the user input:

temp-converter4.html algorithm:

```
Prompt user for startTemp
Get startTemp
Prompt user for endTemp
Get endTemp
Prompt user for increment
Get increment
Submit startTemp, endTemp, increment to TempConverter4.php
END
```

Here is the code for **temp-converter4.html**:

```
<html>
<head>
   <title>Temperature Conversions</title>
   <link rel="stylesheet" type="text/css" href="sample.css">
</head>
<body>

   <h1>Temperature Conversions</h1>
   <form action="temp-converter4.php" method="post">
     <label>Starting temp (C):
       <input type="text" size="5" name="startTemp"></label>
     <label>Ending temp (C):
       <input type="text" size="5" name="endTemp"></label>
     <label>Increment value:
       <input type="text" size="5" name="increment"></label>
     <input class="submit" type="submit" value="Display
         Table">
</form>
</body>
</html>
```

Code Example: temp-converter4.html

Here is the algorithm for **temp-converter4.php** that will receive the inputs from **temp-Converter4.html** and generate the conversion table:

```
temp-converter4.php algorithm:
   Receive startTemp, endTemp, increment from temp-converter4.html
   FOR celsius = startTemp to endTemp INCREMENT BY increment
     fahrenheit = (9 / 5) * celsius + 32
     Display celsius and fahrenheit
   ENDFOR
END
```

Note that this algorithm is essentially the same as before except that the loop variable is now controlled by the user's input. Here is the code for **temp-converter4.php**:

```
<html>
<head>
   <title>Temperature Conversions</title>
   <link rel="stylesheet" type="text/css" href="sample.css">
</head>
<body>
   <?php
     $startTemp = $_POST['startTemp'];
     $endTemp = $_POST['endTemp'];
```

```
$increment = $_POST['increment'];

print("<h1>Temperature Conversions</h1>");
print("<table>");
print("<tr><td><strong>Degrees Celsius</strong></td>
    <td><strong>Degrees Fahrenheit</strong></td></tr>");

for ($celsius = $startTemp; $celsius <= $endTemp;
    $celsius = $celsius + $increment )
{
  $fahrenheit = (9 / 5) * $celsius + 32;
  print("<tr><td class=\"center\">$celsius</td>
    <td class=\"center\">$fahrenheit</td></tr>");
}

print ("</table>");
?>
</body>
</html>
```

Code Example: temp-converter4.php

Look carefully at the FOR loop heading (the only line that has been modified). The initial value for $celsius is the value of $startTemp which was received from the user. The loop test uses $endTemp, also supplied by the user. And the value of $celsius is incremented each time by the value stored in $increment, which also came from the user. Figure 9-8 shows some sample input and output.

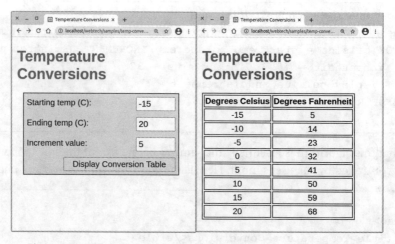

Figure 9-8: temp-converter4.html and temp-converter4.php screenshots

Improving Processing Efficiency

An experienced programmer is careful to design applications to minimize processing time wherever this can be achieved effectively. Since loop structures may repeat a series of processing instructions tens, hundreds, thousands or millions of times, it is always a good idea to examine the code within a loop structure to see if we can make it run more efficiently. For example our temperature conversion program contains a calculation to convert a Celsius temperature to Fahrenheit:

```
$fahrenheit = (9 / 5) * $celsius + 32;
```

This calculation must be processed every time that the program runs through the loop, using a different value stored in the $celsius variable. Is there anything that we can do to make this processing task more efficient?

The conversion formula includes the calculation (**9 / 5**). Every time the program loops with a new value of **$celsius**, the same division operation is repeated. What if we perform the **9 / 5** division **before** the loop and store the result in a variable? Now we can simply refer to the value stored in this variable every time a new temperature is calculated. In the example below we create a variable named **$conversionFactor** to store the result of **9 / 5** and then refer to this variable in the loop:

```
$conversionFactor = 9 / 5;
for ($celsius = $startTemp; $celsius <= $endTemp;
            $celsius = $celsius + $increment )
{
  $fahrenheit = $conversionFactor * $celsius + 32;
  print("<tr><td class=\"center\">$celsius</td>
    <td class=\"center\">$fahrenheit</td></tr>");
}
```

Do you see how this works? We have now improved our program's processing efficiency. For example if the program repeats the instructions in the FOR loop 100 times, we have just saved the processor **99** division operations since the **9/5** calculation is now performed only once, before the loop.

Performing 100 divisions is of course a trivial task on a modern high-speed computer, but software designers should always pay attention to processing efficiency. This is especially true with regard to client/server applications, where an application running on a server may be regularly executed by thousands of users worldwide. Under these conditions, small inefficiencies can add up quickly to slower performance for everyone.

Using Loops to "Crunch Numbers"

We often refer to the work of processing large sets of numeric data values as **number crunching**. Some common examples of number crunching are:

- Generating daily, weekly or annual weather statistics based on data readings.
- Calculating the average, high and low scores from a set of student scores.
- Reducing a large data set so that it can be rendered effectively into a visual format, such as a chart or graph.
- Processing a file of timesheet records in order to generate pay checks.

Loop structures are an important tool for number-crunching large sets of data values. Some standard algorithms are widely used to perform common operations on data sets, such as obtaining the sum or average, finding the highest and lowest values, etc. Once you understand how these algorithms work, you can apply them to process many different data sets.

Using a Loop to Accumulate a Total

A requirement to calculate the total of a series of values is very straightforward when only two or three values are involved. For example a requirement to calculate and display the total of the values stored in three variables can be handled as follows:

```
sum = number1 + number2 + number3
Display total
```

But what if your program needs to sum 10, 100, 1,000, or 1,000,000 values? If your instinct is "Hmmm, this sounds like a job for a loop structure" then you are thinking like a programmer.

To understand how to accumulate a total, let's forget about computer programs for a moment. Consider how YOU might calculate the sum of 100 numbers if someone asked you to do this. Your first reaction might be "I can't add 100 numbers!" but in fact you can handle this task quite easily.

Ask the person to read out the numbers, one by one. Let's say they begin with 8, 23, 19. In your head you start out with a total of 0. Each time a new number is provided, you add this to your total. So when you hear the first number 8, you add 8 to 0 and now you have a total of 8. the second number is 23 so you add 23 to 8 and now you have a total of 31. Then you add 19 to 31 to get a total of 50, and so on. To add 100 numbers you only need to deal with two numbers at a time — the total that you have already accumulated and the next number that needs to be added (this process is often referred to as "keeping a running total"). With a little care and patience, you can easily add thousands of numbers, of course it would quickly become tedious, much better to program a computer to do this for you!

Taking time to work out the steps to solve a problem yourself is often the best way to develop an algorithm for your code. Here is an algorithm to accumulate a total, using a FOR loop to read and add each number to the previous total:

```
total = 0
FOR count = 1 TO 100
   Read nextNumber
   total = total + nextNumber
END FOR
Display total
```

The variable named **total** is first assigned the value **0**. The loop is designed to repeat 100 times. Each time through the loop, the program reads the next number, adds this to the value currently stored in **total** and stores the result in **total**, replacing the previous value. By the time the loop has repeated 100 times, **total** will contain the sum of all of the values that have been read.

It's important to have a good understanding of this algorithm since variations of the basic structure will be extremely useful for many different data processing requirements. Let's walk through an example for a count of 1 to 5, assuming that the five values are 5, 15, 12, 3, and 15:

```
total = 0

count = 1:      total = 0 + 5      total is now 5
count = 2:      total = 5 + 15     total is now 20
count = 3:      total = 20 + 12    total is now 32
count = 4:      total = 32 + 3     total is now 35
count = 5:      total = 35 + 15    total is now 50
```

When the loop has repeated five times, the total contains the value 50 which is the sum of the five values.

The instruction **total = total + nextNumber** may look confusing at first, but remember that this is **not** a mathematical equation—it is an **assignment** operation. When this instruction is executed the expression on the **right** side of the assignment operator (**total + nextNumber**) is evaluated **first**, and the result is **then** assigned to the variable on the **left** (**total**), replacing the previous value stored in total. In this way the total of all the numbers is being accumulated, one number at a time, as the loop repeats. Take time to be sure you are comfortable with this procedure.

The first instruction sets the **total** variable to **0**. Why do we need this? Consider that when **total = total + nextNumber** is executed the very **first** time, the value of **nextNumber** must be added to a previous **total** so we assign **0** to **total before** the loop in order that this first calculation will work correctly.

Once again we must be careful to consider which statements should appear **before** the loop, **inside** the loop, and **after** the loop. It would be a mistake to assign 0 to total **inside** the loop, because then the total would be reset to 0 every time the loop repeats! Similarly if we were to **display** the total **inside** the loop instead of **after** the loop, the total would be displayed every time the loop repeats and a new number is added (100 times).

Note that this algorithm can be used to accumulate the total of **any** list of numbers as long as you know in advance how many numbers are to be processed. In this chapter you will also learn how to adapt the algorithm to accumulate totals of selected values from a list, and in Chapter 10 you will learn to use a similar algorithm when it is not known in advance how many numbers are to be processed.

Finding the Total and Average from a File of Numbers

Applications that use loops to perform more intensive processing of this kind will usually work with data that has been previously stored in files or databases. It is unlikely that we will want to ask the user to enter a long series of numbers in order to sum them or perform any other processing.

Consider the following requirement:

---

rainfall1 requirement:

Write a program that processes a file naed rainfall2007.txt. The file contains the year followed by 12 monthly rainfall amounts, each on a separate line. The program should display the year, total rainfall for the year and the average monthly rainfall.

Here's an example of the contents of the **rainfall2007.txt** file:

```
2007
3.21
3.61
2.84
1.06
0.16
0.04
0.02
0.11
0.45
0.52
2.03
2.20
```

In order to solve this problem we will need to first read the year from the first line of the file, then use a loop to read each of the 12 rainfall amounts from the file and accumulate these values in a total, just as we did in the previous algorithm. Once all the values have been read from the file and accumulated, the average can be calculated by dividing the final total by 12. Here is our algorithm:

```
rainfall1.php algorithm:

   Open rainfall2007.txt as rainfallData for reading
   read year from rainfallData
   totalRainfall = 0
   FOR count = 1 TO 12
     read nextRainfall from rainfallData
     totalRainfall = totalRainfall + nextRainfall
   ENDFOR
   Close rainfallData
   avgRainfall = totalRainfall / 12
   Display year, totalRainfall, avgRainfall
END
```

As always it is important to consider what instructions need to occur **before** the loop structure, which instructions are to be repeated **inside** the loop structure and which instructions should be executed **after** the loop structure. It is important to open the file, read the first line containing the year, and assign 0 to totalRainfall, **before** the loop because we do not want these instructions to repeat. On the other hand we need to read the next value from the file and add this to the total 12 times, so these instructions must be included **inside** the loop. The instructions to close the file, calculate the average and display the results should appear **after** the loop structure. (Beginning students often include the statement to calculate the average inside the loop, but you only need to calculate the average **once**, after the loop has completed and the program has calculated the final total.)

Here is the PHP code for **rainfall1.php**:

```
<html>
<head>
  <title>RAINFALL</title>
  <link rel="stylesheet" type="text/css" href="sample.css">
</head>
<body>
  <?php
    $rainDataFile = fopen("rainfall2007.txt","r");
    $year = trim(fgets($rainDataFile));
    $totalRainfall = 0;
    for ($count= 1; $count <= 12; $count = $count + 1)
    {
      $nextRainfall = trim(fgets($rainDataFile));
```

```
        $totalRainfall = $totalRainfall + $nextRainfall;
    }

    fclose($rainDataFile);

    $avgRainfall = $totalRainfall / 12;

    print("<h1>RAINFALL REPORT $year</h1>");
    print("<p>TOTAL RAINFALL: $totalRainfall.</p>");
    print("<p>AVERAGE MONTHLY RAINFALL: $avgRainfall.</p>");
    ?>
</body>
</html>
```

Code Example: rainfall1.php

Figure 9-9 shows the output from the program.

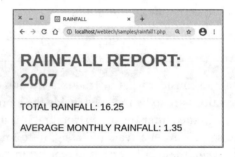

Figure 9-9: rainfall1.php screenshot

Using a Loop to Find the Total of Selected Values in a Series

Using a loop to accumulate the total of a series of numbers means adding the next number to a total each time the loop repeats. Often however we are required to find the total of **selected** numbers in a series. For example, what if your program is required to accumulate the total rainfall for just the months of **September, October**, and **November**? Since a text file is always opened with the read marker at the start of the file, the program will still need to read the year on the first line, and then use a loop to read through all the rainfall amounts, but this time it should only add the amounts to the total if the loop counter has a value of **9, 10**, or **11** (because these are the repetitions when the rainfall amounts for September, October, and November will be read from the file).

We can easily modify the PHP code in rainfall1.php to accomplish this, as follows:

```php
<?php
   $rainDataFile = fopen("rainfall2007.txt","r");
   $year = trim(fgets($rainDataFile));
   $totalRainfall = 0;
   for ($count= 1; $count <= 12; $count = $count + 1)
   {
      $nextRainfall = trim(fgets($rainDataFile));

      if ($count == 9 OR $count == 10 OR $count == 11)
      {
         $totalRainfall = $totalRainfall + $nextRainfall;
      }
   }

   fclose($rainDataFile);
   print("<h1>FALL RAINFALL FOR $year</h1>");
   print("<p>TOTAL RAINFALL FOR SEPTEMBER, OCTOBER, AND NOVEM-
BER:   $totalRainfall.</p>");
?>
```

Note that there is no **ELSE** section after the **IF** section: that's because no action is needed if the test is false: if the **$count** variable does not have a value of 9, 10, or 11, we don't want to do anything except move on to read the next rainfall amount.

You can easily modify this version to accumulate totals of different selected values just by changing the test. For example to find the total for the months of April to September you could use a different test:

```php
   if ($count >= 4 AND $count <= 9)
   {
      $totalRainfall = $totalRainfall + $nextRainfall;
   }
```

And if you wanted to find the total rainfall of all months with less than 1" of rain you could test the value of **$nextRainfall** instead of **$count** each time the loop repeats (since $nextRainfall contains the next rainfall amount that has been read from the file). To accomplish this just change the test as follows:

```
if ($nextRainfall < 1)
{
    $totalRainfall = $totalRainfall + $nextRainfall;
}
```

Take some time to work though these examples and be sure that you understand how they work. Try one of your own. You will find yourself developing variations of this basic algorithm to meet similar requirements for many different applications. Now let's consider a modified version that will **count**, instead of total, selected values.

Using a Loop to Count Selected Values in a Series

What if you were asked to develop the code to **count** the number of months with rainfall amounts above 2"?

```
rainfall2 requirement:

Write a program that processes a file named rainfall2007.txt.
The file contains the year followed by 12 monthly rainfall
amounts, each on a separate line. The program should count
the number of months with rainfall greater than 2".
```

In this case you would want to use the same basic algorithm that is designed to accumulate a total of selected values, but this time substitute a **counting** variable, that will initially be assigned an initial value of **0**, and that will have **1** added to its value every time the program reads a rainfall amount from the file that is greater than 2. Here is the algorithm for rainfall2:

```
rainfall2.php algorithm:

Open rainfall2007.txt as rainfallData for reading
read year from rainfallData
countMonths = 0
FOR count = 1 TO 12
    Read nextRainfallAmount from rainfallData
    IF nextRainfallAmount > 2
```

```
            countMonths = countMonths + 1

      ENDIF

ENDFOR

Close rainfallData

Display year, countMonths

END
```

Take time to understand how this algorithm works. After opening the file and reading the first line (which contains the year), the next instruction assigns **0** to **countMonths** (since no months have been counted yet). Then the loop runs 12 times. Each time, the next monthly rainfall amount is read from the file and stored in **nextRainfallAmount.** This value is then tested to determine if it is **greater than 2**; if it **is** then **1** is added to countMonths. This process continues until the loop has executed 12 times, when countMonths will have counted all monthly rainfall amounts greater than 2. No ELSE section is necessary since if nextRainfallAmount does **not** contain a number greater than 2 there is nothing to do except move on to read the next amount from the file.

Here is the code for rainfall2.php

```html
<html>
<head>
  <title>RAINFALL</title>
  <link rel="stylesheet" type="text/css" href="sample.css">
</head>
<body>
  <?php
    $rainDataFile = fopen("rainfall2007.txt","r");
    $year = trim(fgets($rainDataFile));
    $countMonths = 0;
    for ($count= 1; $count <= 12; $count = $count + 1)
    {
      $nextRainfall = trim(fgets($rainDataFile));
      if ($nextRainfall > 2)
      {
        $countMonths = $countMonths + 1;
      }
    }
    fclose($rainDataFile);
```

```
    print("<h1>RAINFALL SUMMARY FOR REPORT:$year</h1>");

    print("<p>NUMBER OF MONTHS ABOVE 2 INCHES:
        $countMonths.</p>");

  ?>

</body>

</html>
```

Code Example: rainfall2.php

Figure **9-10** shows sample output from rainfall2.php. You can easily adapt this basic structure to count selected values in any series, based on a suitable test.

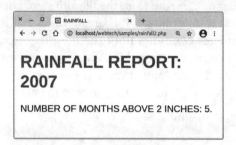

Figure 9-10: rainfall2.php screenshot

Just as with accumulating totals, counting selected values from a list is a very common programming task, and you are likely to develop many variations of this algorithm to meet actual requirements.

Finding the Highest and Lowest Values in a Series

Another common processing task is to find the highest and lowest values in a series. Once again, the easiest way to understand how to solve this problem is to consider how you would do it yourself. Let's first consider finding the highest value in a series of positive values.

Ask someone to read out a list of numbers. When the first number is read out, write this down as the highest number. Each time another number is read out, compare the new number with the number you have previously written down as the highest number. If the new number is higher, cross out your previous highest number and write the new number as the highest number. **Only do this if the new number is higher!** Repeat this procedure until all of the numbers have been read. At the end, you will have the highest value in the entire series.

Here is the algorithm for finding the highest number in a series of 100 positive numbers:

```
FOR count = 1 TO 100
  Read nextNumber
  IF count == 1 OR nextNumber > highestNumber
    highestNumber = nextNumber
  ENDIF
END FOR

Display highestNumber
```

This example shows a **selection** structure located **inside** a **loop** structure. Follow the logic carefully. Each time through the loop a new number is read into the **nextNumber** variable. The IF statement in the loop uses the OR operator to combine two tests. If this is the **first** number to be read (if the **count** variable contains **1**) then the value of **nextNumber** is assigned to the **highestNumber** variable. That's because the first time through the loop there is no previous value to compare so the first number must be the highest number at that point. The second test of the IF structure (**nextNumber** > **highestNumber**) compares the value of the number that has just been read with the value previously stored in **highestNumber**. If the new value is higher then the new value is assigned to highestNumber, replacing the previous value, and the loop repeats.

Since the IF structure contains no ELSE section, if the new value is **not** higher than the value already stored in the **highestValue** variable (and unless this is the first repetition), the loop simply repeats and the previous value of **highestNumber** is left unchanged. In this way the value of **highestNumber** will always contain the highest value that has been read so far.

A similar algorithm will find the **lowest** value in a series of numbers:

```
FOR count = 1 TO 100
  Read nextNumber
  IF count == 1 OR nextNumber < lowestNumber
    lowestNumber = nextNumber
  ENDIF
END FOR

Display lowestNumber
```

These examples demonstrate the use of an IF selection structure inside a loop structure. A loop structure might include any number of IF and IF..ELSE structures to meet the program requirements.

Performing Multiple Operations on a File of Numbers

Let's apply all of these algorithms to process our file of rainfall data, Here is a modified requirement:

---

rainfall3 requirement:

Write a program that processes a file named rainfall2007.txt. The file contains the year followed by 12 monthly rainfall amounts, each on a separate line. The program should display the year, total rainfall for the year, the average monthly rainfall, highest monthly rainfall amount and lowest monthly rainfall amount.

Here is the algorithm that includes the procedures to calculate the total and also obtain the highest and lowest values from the file of rainfall amounts:

```
rainfall3.php algorithm:
  Open rainfall2007.txt as rainfallData for reading
  read year from rainData
  totalRainfall = 0
  FOR count = 1 TO 12
    read nextRainfall from rainData
    totalRainfall = totalRainfall + nextRainfall
    IF count == 1 OR nextRainfall > highestRainfall
      highestRainfall = nextRainfall
    ENDIF
    IF count ==1 OR nextRainfall < lowestRainfall
      lowestRainfall = nextRainfall
    ENDIF
  ENDFOR
  Close rainData
  avgRainfall = totalRainfall / 12
  Display year, totalRainfall, avgRainfall, highestRainfall,
lowestRainfall
END
```

Here is the PHP code for **rainfall3.php**:

```
<html>
<head>
  <title>RAINFALL</title>
  <link rel="stylesheet" type="text/css" href="sample.css">
</head>
<body>
```

```php
<?php
   $rainDataFile = fopen("rainfall2007.txt","r");
   $year = trim(fgets($rainDataFile));

   $totalRainfall = 0;

   for ($count= 1; $count <= 12; $count = $count + 1)
   {
     $nextRainfall = trim(fgets($rainDataFile));
     $totalRainfall = $totalRainfall + $nextRainfall;

     if ($count == 1 OR $nextRainfall > $highestRainfall)
       $highestRainfall = $nextRainfall;

     if ($count == 1 OR $nextRainfall < $lowestRainfall)
       $lowestRainfall = $nextRainfall;
   }
   fclose($rainDataFile);

   $avgRainfall = $totalRainfall / 12;

   print("<h1>RAINFALL REPORT $year</h1>");
   print("<p>TOTAL RAINFALL: $totalRainfall.</p>");
   print("<p>AVERAGE MONTHLY RAINFALL: $avgRainfall.</p>");
   print("<p>HIGHEST MONTHLY RAINFALL:
           $highestRainfall.</p>");
   print("<p>LOWEST MONTHLY RAINFALL:
$lowestRainfall.</p>");
   ?>
</body>
</html>
```

Code Example: rainfall3.php

Figure 9-11 shows the Web page generated by this program.

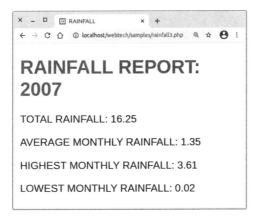

Figure 9-11: rainfall3.php screenshot

Nesting IF..ELSE Structures to Customize Output from a Loop

Consider the following requirement:

---

rainfall4 requirement:

*Write a program that processes a file named rainfall2007.txt. The file contains the year followed by 12 monthly rainfall amounts, each on a separate line. The program should display the year and then list the **name** of each month, followed by the rainfall amount for the month.*

It is simple enough to use a loop to read the file and display the value of each month:

```
rainfall4.php algorithm:
  Open rainfall2007.txt as rainfallData for reading
  read year from rainData
  FOR count = 1 TO 12
    read nextRainfall from rainData
    Display nextRainfall
  ENDFOR
  Close rainData
END
```

But how can we display the **name** of each month as well as the rainfall amount? To do this we must use a selection structure inside our loop to test the value of the count variable and display the appropriate month name for each repetition. Here is our revised algorithm:

```
rainfall4.php algorithm:
  Open rainfall2007.txt as rainfallData for reading
  read year from rainData
  FOR count = 1 TO 12
    read nextRainfall from rainData
    if (count == 1)
      Display January:
    elseif (count == 2)
      Display February:
    elseif (count == 3)
      Display March:
    elseif (count == 4)
      Display April:
    elseif (count == 5)
      Display May:
    elseif (count == 6)
      Display June:
    elseif (count == 7)
```

```
        Display July:
      elseif (count == 8)
        Display August:
      elseif (count == 9)
        Display September:
      elseif (count == 10)
        Display October:
      elseif (count == 11)
        Display November:
      else
        Display December:
      ENDIF
      Display nextRainfall
    ENDFOR
    Close rainData
  END
```

Each time the loop is processed:

1. The next value is read from the file and stored in the **nextRainfall** variable.
2. The program works through the nested IF..ELSEIF..ELSE structure, testing the value currently stored in the counting variable. When a **true** result is obtained, the appropriate month name is displayed.
3. The program then moves past any remaining tests in the selection structure and displays the value stored in the nextRainfall variable.

Let's convert this algorithm to PHP. In order to display the information neatly as an HTML document, we will use a table (see Figure 9-12).

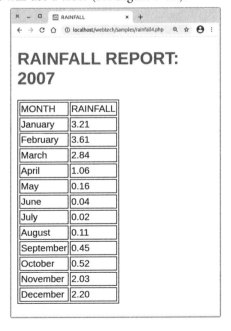

Figure 9-12: rainfall4.php screenshot

In order to produce this table correctly, the <**table**> tag and the row that contains the column headings must be generated **before** the loop. Inside the loop, the next rainfall amount is read from the file, then the opening <**tr**> tag for the next row is printed, followed by the IF statement which is used to print the first <**td**></**td**> tags that contain the appropriate month name. The IF structure is followed by another print statement that prints the second <**td**></**td**> tags that contain the monthly rainfall amount and also the closing </**tr**> tag to end the row. These instructions are repeated each time the loop repeats, adding a new row each time.

Once all of the rainfall amounts have been read from the file and printed in rows, the FOR loop ends and a print statement after the loop is used to print the closing </**table**> tag.

Here is the PHP code for **rainfall4.php**:

```
<html>
<head>
   <title>RAINFALL</title>
   <link rel="stylesheet" type="text/css" href="sample.css">
</head>
<body>
   <?php
      $rainDataFile = fopen("rainfall2007.txt","r");

      $year = trim(fgets($rainDataFile));
      print("<h1>RAINFALL REPORT $year</h1>");

      print("<table>");
      print("<tr><td>MONTH</td><td>RAINFALL</td></tr>");

      for ($count= 1; $count <= 12; $count = $count + 1)
      {
        $nextRainfall = trim(fgets($rainDataFile));
        print ("<tr>");
        if ($count == 1)
          print("<td>January</td>");
        elseif ($count == 2)
          print("<td>February</td>");
        elseif ($count == 3)
          print("<td>March</td>");
        elseif ($count == 4)
          print("<td>April</td>");
        elseif ($count == 5)
          print("<td>May</td>");
        elseif ($count == 6)
          print("<td>June</td>");
        elseif ($count == 7)
```

```
         print("<td>July</td>");
      elseif ($count == 8)
         print("<td>August</td>");
      elseif ($count == 9)
         print("<td>September</td>");
      elseif ($count == 10)
         print("<td>October</td>");
      elseif ($count == 11)
         print("<td>November</td>");
      else
         print("<td>December</td>");

      print("<td>$nextRainfall</td></tr>");

   }
   fclose($rainDataFile);
   print("</table>");
  ?>
</body>
</html>
```

Code Example: rainfall4.php

NOTE: The **switch** statement has already been mentioned in an earlier chapter. A switch statement provides an alternative to the use of chained IF..ELSE structures in situations where a single variable is to be tested for multiple values (as in this case, where the **$count** variable is tested for 12 possible values). Chapter 16 includes an example showing how a switch statement can be used to display the name of the month.

Loops within Loops—Creating a Bar Chart

Programmers are often required to develop code that displays numeric information **visually**. Charts and images are often much easier to understand than lists of numbers. Here is a revised requirement to display the monthly rainfall data in a **bar graph**:

---

rainfall5 requirement:

Write a program that processes a file named rainfall2007.txt. The file contains the year followed by 12 monthly rainfall amounts, each on a separate line. The program should display the year and list the name of each month, followed by a colored bar that represents the rainfall amount for the month.

One way to create a colored bar that indicates the rainfall amount for each month is to display a series of colored squares. If the rainfall amount is 1 or less, we display just one square (■). If the amount is greater than 1 but less than 2, we display two squares (■ ■), and so on. We can easily create an image of a colored square using any graphics package. We will use an image of a red square stored as **inch-of-rain.jpg** (this file is in your **samples** folder).

To determine how many squares to display for each month, we must first round **up** the current rainfall amount to the nearest whole number using the PHP **ceil**() function. We can then use our rounded number with a FOR loop to display our image the required number of times. For example, if the January rainfall amount is 3.21, this value rounds up to 4, so we will want our loop to display the image four times (■■■■).

Note that we round **up** rather than down so that rainfall amounts below 1 will be displayed as a single square rather than as 0 squares. Here is the algorithm:

```
chartLength = ceil(nextRainfall)
FOR numInches = 1 TO chartLength
   Display inch-of-rain.jpg
ENDFOR
```

Figure 9-13 shows a table that includes bar charts for every month of the year.

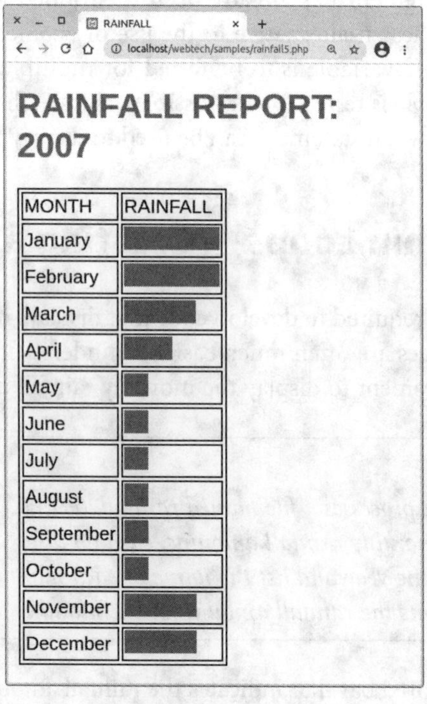

Figure 9-13: rainfall5.html and rainfall5.php screenshots

In order to display each rainfall amount as a bar chart, we must include the FOR loop that generates the series of squares for each bar **inside** the FOR loop that counts through the months. Here is the algorithm for rainfall5.php:

```
Rainfall5.php algorithm:
  Open rainfall2007.txt as rainfallData for reading
  read year from rainData
  FOR count = 1 TO 12
    read nextRainfall from rainData
    if (count == 1)
      Display January:
    elseif (count == 2)
      Display February:
    elseif (count == 3)
      Display March:
    elseif (count == 4)
      Display April:
    elseif (count == 5)
      Display May:
    elseif (count == 6)
      Display June:
    elseif (count == 7)
      Display July:
    elseif (count == 8)
      Display August:
    elseif (count == 9)
      Display September:
    elseif (count == 10)
      Display October:
    elseif (count == 11)
      Display November:
    else
      Display December:
    ENDIF
    chartLength = ceil(nextRainfall)
    FOR numInches = 1 TO chartLength
      Display inch-of-rain.jpg
    ENDFOR
  ENDFOR
  Close rainData
END
```

It is important to understand that the loop that creates a new bar chart for each month must be **nested inside** the FOR loop that counts from 1 to 12. This ensures that the FOR loop that generates a bar chart will run **completely every time that the outer loop processes once.**

Here is the PHP code for **rainfall5.php**; look over this carefully:

```php
<html>
<head>
  <title>RAINFALL</title>
  <link rel="stylesheet" type="text/css" href="sample.css">
</head>
<body>
  <?php
    $rainDataFile = fopen("rainfall2007.txt","r");
    $year = trim(fgets($rainDataFile));

    print ("<h1>RAINFALL REPORT $year</h1>");
    print("<table>");
    print ("<tr><td>MONTH</td><td>RAINFALL</td></tr>");
    for ($count= 1; $count <= 12; $count = $count + 1)
    {
      $nextRainfall = trim(fgets($rainDataFile));
      print ("<tr>");
      if ($count == 1)
        print("<td>January</td>");
      elseif ($count == 2)
        print("<td>February</td>");
      elseif ($count == 3)
        print("<td>March</td>");
      elseif ($count == 4)
        print("<td>April</td>");
      elseif ($count == 5)
        print("<td>May</td>");
      elseif ($count == 6)
        print("<td>June</td>");
      elseif ($count == 7)
        print("<td>July</td>");
      elseif ($count == 8)
        print("<td>August</td>");
      elseif ($count == 9)
        print("<td>September</td>");
      elseif ($count == 10)
        print("<td>October</td>");
      elseif ($count == 11)
        print("<td>November</td>");
      else
        print("<td>December</td>");

      print ("<td>");
```

```php
      $chartLength = ceil($nextRainfall);

      for ($numInches = 1; $numInches <= $chartLength;
                        $numInches = $numInches + 1)
      {
        print("<img src=\"inch-of-rain.jpg\">");
      }
      print("</td></tr>");
    }
    fclose($rainDataFile);
    print("</table>");
  ?>
</body>
</html>
```

Code Example: rainfall5.php

The **print**() statement inside the inner FOR loop generates an HTML <**img**> tag to display a single square (the image stored in **inch-of-rain.jpg**). Since this statement is inside the loop, the image will be displayed multiple times, based on the value of **chartLength**, which controls the loop and is based on the current month's rainfall amount.

Each time the outer FOR loop repeats, the month name and the bar showing the rainfall amount will be added as a new row in an HTML table. To achieve this, we first print the <**table**> tag and the first row (containing the table headings) **before** the loop (we don't want these to be repeated!).

For each loop repetition, we print the opening <**tr**> to start a new row, then print <**td**></**td**> tags containing the month name so that this appears in the first column. To print the bar in the second column, we first print the opening <**td**> tag, then provide the code (including our new loop) to display the bar, and then print the closing </**td**> tag and end the row with the </**tr**> tag.

Once the outer loop has completed, we print the closing </**table**> tag.

Selecting from a List of Data Files

Our rainfall applications have all operated on data stored in a single data file named **rainfall2007.txt**. It would be useful to apply these programs to process **any** file that contains a year followed by 12 lines of rainfall amounts.

A simple way to achieve this is to create an HTML document that allows the user to select any file that contains rainfall data. Since the user could easily mistype a filename, we can design our input form to provide a drop down list that contains the names of the available data files. The user can simply select the file that they wish to view and press Submit.

Here is the code for **rainfall6.html** which provides the user with a form:

```
<html>
<head>
  <title>RAINFALL</title>
  <link rel="stylesheet" type="text/css" href="sample.css">
</head>
<body>
  <h1>RAINFALL REPORTS</h1>

  <form action="rainfall6.php" method="post">
    <label>Choose a year:
    <select name="rainFile">
    <option>rainfall2003.txt</option>
    <option>rainfall2004.txt</option>
    <option>rainfall2005.txt</option>
    <option>rainfall2006.txt</option>
    <option>rainfall2007.txt</option>
    </select></label>
    <input class="submit" type="submit" value="SUBMIT">
  </form>
</body>
</html>
```

Code Example: rainfall6.html

Now we must adapt our PHP application to receive the user's selection and open the appropriate file. This is very simple. First we add a statement to receive the file name selected by the user and store this in a variable:

```
$rainFile = $_POST['rainFile'];
```

We then refer to **$rainFile** in our fopen() statement in order to open the correct file. To accomplish this we replace:

```
$rainDataFile = fopen("rainfall2007.txt","r");
```

with:

```
$rainDataFile = fopen($rainFile,"r");
```

Figure 9-14 shows a sample user interaction.

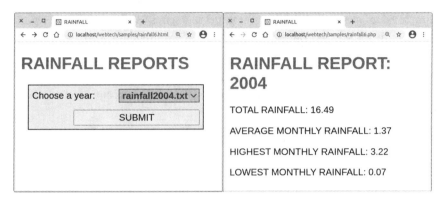

Figure 9-14: rainfall6.html and rainfall6.php screenshots

Additional Learning Materials

Appendix D will help you **debug** your exercises, listing a number of the most common errors that you are likely to encounter.

The **Chapter 9 Hints and Help** pages on the textbook Web site provide answers to FAQs from previous students as they worked through the end-of-chapter exercises.

Summary

This chapter is more complicated than the previous chapters because it is more difficult to follow and apply the logic of repetition structures.

A FOR loop is used to control a loop by counting.

A FOR loop consists of a loop **heading** that is used to control the loop, and a loop **body** that contains the statements that are to be repeatedly executed.

The FOR loop heading contains three sections, separated by semi-colons: the loop **initialization** is used to assign an initial value to the counting variable; the loop **condition** provides a Boolean expression that is tested each time the loop begins in order to determine whether or not the loop body should be processed; the loop **update** increments or decrements the value stored in the counting variable following each repetition.

The counting variable can be assigned any starting value. The counting variable can also be incremented (or decremented) by any value. These may be literal numeric values or values stored in variables.

An important application of loop structures is to process data sets in order to produce useful information. Some common processing tasks are to find the sum, average, highest, and lowest values in a series, and to count values in a series. Variations of these algorithms are used to process selected values to meet different requirements. Loop structures make it easy to process data sets of any size.

Loop structures can include selection structures, as well as other loops. If one loop is nested inside another loop, the inner loop will run through its entire set of repetitions every time the outer loop repeats once.

Chapter 9 Review Questions

1. Which of the following describes the purpose of a repetition structure?
   a. Choose between two or more blocks of statements based on a test condition
   b. Loop through a block of statements until a test condition changes
   c. Perform a sequence of statements in order

2. Which of the following is NOT an example of a repetition structure?
   a. for
   b. while
   c. do..while
   d. foreach
   e. if..else

3. How many times will the following loop repeat?

```
for ($count = 1; $count <= 5; $count = $count + 1)
{
   print ("<p>Hello!</p>");
}
```

   a. 1
   b. 3
   c. 4
   d. 5
   e. This is an infinite loop

4. How many times will the following loop repeat?

```
for ($count = 1; $count < 5; $count = $count + 1)
{
   print ("<p>Hello!</p>");
}
```

   a. 1
   b. 3
   c. 4
   d. 5
   e. This is an infinite loop

5. How many times will the following loop repeat?

```
for ($count = 1; $count <= 5; $count = $count + 2)
{
   print ("<p>Hello!</p>");
}
```

   a. 1
   b. 3
   c. 4
   d. 5
   e. This is an infinite loop

6. How many times will the following loop repeat?

```
for ($count = 1; $count <= 5; $count = $count + 5)
{
   print ("<p>Hello!</p>");
}
```

   a. 1
   b. 3
   c. 4
   d. 5
   e. This is an infinite loop

7. How many times will the following loop repeat?

```
for ($count = 0; $count <=6; $count = $count + 1)
{
   print ("<p>Hello!</p>");
}
```

   a. 0
   b. 4
   c. 5
   d. 6
   e. 7

8. Which of the following FOR loop headings will cause the loop to repeat the number of times stored in the variable $numTimes?
    a. for ($count = $numTimes; $count <= 5; $count = $count + 1)
    b. for ($count = 1; $count <= $numTimes; $count = $count + 1)
    c. for ($count = 1; $count <= 5; $count = $count + $numTimes)
    d. for ($numTimes = 1; $numTimes <= 5; $numTimes = $numTimes + 1)
    e. for ($numTimes = 1; $count <= $numTimes; $count = $count + 1)

9. The following code processes a file containing five positive numbers. What will the variable $result contain after the code is executed?

```
$result = 0;
$someFile = fopen("some-file.txt", "r");
for ($count = 1; $count <= 5; $count = $count + 1)
{
   $nextNum = trim(fgets($someFile));
   if ($nextNum > $result)
      $result = $nextNum;
}
fclose ($someFile);
print ("<p>The result is $result</p>");
```

    a. The sum of the five numbers in the file
    b. The highest of the five numbers in the file
    c. The lowest of the five numbers in the file
    d. The value of the first number in the file
    e. The value of the last number in the file

10. The following code processes a file containing five positive numbers. What will the variable $result contain after the code is executed?

```
$result = 0;
$someFile = fopen("some-file.txt", "r");
for ($count = 1; $count <= 5; $count = $count + 1)
{
   $nextNum = trim(fgets($someFile));
   $result = $result + $nextNum;
}
fclose ($someFile);
print ("<p>The result is $result</p>");
```

    a. The sum of the five numbers in the file
    b. The highest of the five numbers in the file
    c. The lowest of the five numbers in the file
    d. The value of the first number in the file
    e. The value of the last number in the file

11. The following code processes a file containing five positive numbers. What will the variable $result contain after the code is executed?

```
$result = 0;
$someFile = fopen("some-file.txt", "r");
for ($count = 1; $count <= 5; $count = $count + 1)
{
   $nextNum = trim(fgets($someFile));
   $result = $nextNum;
}
fclose ($someFile);
print ("<p>The result is $result</p>");
```

   a. The sum of the five numbers in the file
   b. The highest of the five numbers in the file
   c. The lowest of the five numbers in the file
   d. The value of the first number in the file
   e. The value of the last number in the file

12. What is displayed after the following code is executed?

```
print ("<p>");
for ($count = 1; $count <= 3; $count = $count + 1)
{
   print("*****");
}
print ("</p>");
```

   a. A single paragraph containing 5 asterisks
   b. A single paragraph containing 15 asterisks
   c. Three paragraphs containing 5 asterisks in each line
   d. Three paragraphs containing 15 asterisks in each line
   e. Fifteen paragraphs containing 1 asterisk in each line

13. If a loop is used to generate an HTML table which table tags and data should be generated each time that the loop repeats?
   a. The tags and data for the **next** table row and the columns within this row
   b. The tags and data for **all** of the table rows and columns
   c. **All** of the table tags and data including the <table> and </table> tags
   d. The tags and data for the **next** column
   e. The tags and data for **all** the table columns

14. What output does the following code generate?

```
for ($count = 1; $count <= 3; $count = $count + 1)
{
    print ("$count and..");
}
```

    a. One and..Two and..Three and..
    b. One and..Two and..Three
    c. 1 and..2 and..3 and..
    d. 1 and..2 and..3
    e. 1, 2, 3, and..

15. The following code displays the values between 1 and 25. What would you change to display only the **odd** numbers from 1 to 25?

```
for ($count = 1; $count <= 25; $count = $count + 1)
{
    print ("<p>$count</p>");
}
```

    a. Change $count = 1; to $count = 0;
    b. Change $count = 1; to $count = 2;
    c. Change $count <= 25; to $count < 25;
    d. Change $count = $count + 1; to $count = $count + 2;
    e. Change $count = $count + 1; to $count = $count + 3;

16. What is wrong with the following code which is designed to read and output five numbers stored in a file?

```
for ($count = 1; $count <= 5; $count = $count + 1)
{
    $someFile = fopen("some-file.txt", "r");
    $nextNum = trim(fgets($someFile));
    print("$nextNum<br>");
}
fclose ($someFile);
```

    a. A semi-colon is missing at the end of the first line
    b. The file should be opened before the FOR loop begins
    c. The file should be closed inside the FOR loop
    d. The print statement should appear after the FOR loop ends
    e. There is nothing wrong with the code

17. What does "number crunching" mean?
    a. Breaking a number down into individual digits
    b. Processing a set of data values to obtain useful results
    c. Parsing a string of characters to see if it contains a number
    d. Creating a conversion table of some kind
    e. Reading a file of numeric values

18. Which statement is false?
    a. In PHP, the heading of a FOR loop must end with a semi-colon
    b. Loop structures can include selection structures
    c. Loop structures can include other loop structures
    d. In PHP, the counting variable that controls a for loop does not have to be named $count
    e. In PHP, multiple statements inside a loop structure must be enclosed in curly braces

19. How many columns will be displayed in this table?

```
print ("<table>");
for ($count = 5; $count <=25; $count = $count + 5)
{
   $result = $count * $count * pi();
   print("<tr><td>$count</td><td>$result</td></tr>");
}
print ("</table");
```

    a. 1
    b. 2
    c. 3
    d. 5
    e. 20

20. How many rows will be displayed in this table?

```
print ("<table>");
for ($count = 5; $count <= 25; $count = $count + 5)
{
   $result = $count * $count * pi();
   print("<tr><td>$count</td><td>$result</td></tr>");
}
print ("</table");
```

    a. 1
    b. 2
    c. 3
    d. 5
    e. 20

Chapter 9 Code Exercises

Your Chapter 9 code exercises can be found in your **chapter09** folder. This folder is included in your customized XAMPP installation at the following location:

htdocs\webtech\coursework\chapter09

Type your name and the date in the **Author** and **Date** sections of each file as you work on each exercise. **Remember** that the Students page on the textbook Web site includes **Hints and Help** pages for the exercises in this and every chapter.

Debugging Exercises

Your **chapter09** folder should contain a number of "fixit" files. Each of these files contains PHP code that has an error of some kind. The type of error is indicated in the comment section of each file. You will need to run each program in order to see the errors, and to debug and test the code to see if it works correctly. For example to run **fixit1.php**, first run the Web server, then use the URL:

http://localhost/webtech/coursework/chapter09/fixit1.php

Code Modification Exercises

Your **chapter09** folder contains a number of "modify" files. Each pair of files contains HTML and PHP code that needs to be modified to meet a requirement. The requirements are included in the comment section of each file. Modify the algorithms, being careful to make changes to the .html and .php files as directed. You will need to run each program in order to test your changes. For example to run **modify1.html**, first run the Web server, then use the URL:

http://localhost/webtech/coursework/chapter09/modify1.html

Code Completion Exercises

1. Read this exercise carefully and take your time to work out the logic. Your **chapter09** folder contains versions of **squares1.html** and **squares1.php**. The code in **squares1.html** does not need to be changed—it just provides a form with a Submit button to run **squares1.php**. Provide a loop in **square1.php** to display the numbers 1 through 10, along with their squares. The <hr> tags already included in **squares1.php** simply displays a line (hard rule) across the page. Figure 9-15 shows how the output should appear.

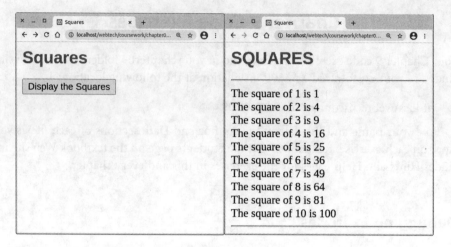

Figure 9-15: squares1.html and squares1.php screenshots

2. Read this exercise carefully and take your time to work out the logic. Your **chapter09** folder contains versions of **squares2.html** and **squares2.php**. The code in **squares2.html** does not need to be changed—it provides a form with inputs for a starting number, ending number and an increment. Provide a loop in **squares2.php** to display a list of numbers and their squares from the starting number to the ending number in increments according to the increment provided by the user. Review the **temp-converter4** example if you need help. Figure 9-16 shows some sample output.

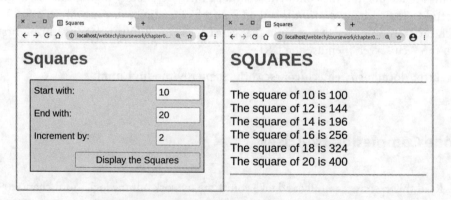

Figure 9-16: squares2.html and squares2.php screenshots

3. Read this exercise carefully and take your time to work out the logic. Your **chapter09** folder contains versions of **weekly-report1.html**, **weekly-report1.php** and **weekly-data.txt**. The code in **weekly-report1.html** does not need to be changed—it just provides a form with a Submit button to run **weekly-report1.php**. The file **weekly-data.txt** contains a list of daily income from completed paint jobs over a one week (7 day) period. Each line contains the total income amount for a single day. Use a FOR loop to read the 7 lines from the file and include the necessary processing to calculate the total income, the average income, and the number of days with no income. The output code is already provided—note the variable names. If your loop statements are correct the total will be $906.00, the average will be $129.43, and the number of "no income" days will be 2.

   HINT: Review the first two rainfall examples in the chapter. The first shows how to accumulate a total and calculate the average, and the second shows how to count selected values (which in this exercise will be a count of the days with 0 income). You can combine these two procedures into a single loop.

4. This program is similar to the previous exercise. Your **chapter09** folder contains versions of **weekly-report2.html**, **weekly-report2.php** and **weekly-data.txt**. The code in **weekly-report2.html** does not need to be changed—it just provides a form with a Submit button to run **weekly-report2.php**. The file **weekly-data.txt** contains a list of daily income from completed paint jobs over a one week (7 day) period. Each line contains the total income amount for a single day. Use a FOR loop to read the 7 lines from the file. Assume that the first number represents the income for Monday, the second day for Tuesday, and so on, with the last number in the file representing the income for Sunday. For each line that the program reads from the file, display the day of the week, followed by the income for that day.

   HINT: One of the rainfall examples in the chapter is very similar.

5. Read this exercise carefully and take your time to work out the logic. Your **chapter09** folder contains versions of **currency.html** and **currency.php**. The code in **currency.html** does not need to be changed — it just provides a submit button to execute **currency.php**. Modify **currency.php**, using a FOR loop to display a table with two columns, where the rows in the first column show different US dollar amounts from $100 to $1000, in increments of $100 (so ten rows in total), and the second column shows the equivalent amounts in each row, converted to Canadian dollars (this will be US dollar amount multiplied by the conversion rate). The headings for the two columns should be "**USA $**" and "**CAN $**". The code already includes a variable named **$conversionRate** and an introductory paragraph. The conversion rate was accurate at the time of writing and you might like to change this to the current rate.

6. Your **chapter09** folder contains **ticker-printer.html**, **ticker-printer.php**, and **ticket-count.txt**. The code in **ticker-printer.html** does not need to be changed. The **ticket-count.txt** file contains the count of tickets that have been sold. Your **ticker-printer.php** file already contains code to read the number from **ticket-count.txt** into a program variable.

    Your job is to add a **FOR** loop to **ticket-printer.php** that will "print" all the tickets. Instead of actually printing, you will use a print statement so that each ticket will display on the Web page as "ADMIT 1:" followed by the name of the performance (Rolling Stones, or any name you want), followed by "TICKET #" followed by the ticket number. The first ticket will be numbered 1 and so on, up to the number that was read from **ticket-count.txt**. For example, if the performance was "Rolling Stones", and if **ticket-count.txt** contained the number 50, the first ticket would display as "ADMIT 1: Rolling Stones TICKET #1", and the last ticket would display as "ADMIT 1: Rolling Stones TICKET #50". In your loop, print each ticket between <p> and </p> tags and then include a second paragraph that just prints a line of dashes. This will ensure that a line of dashes will appear between each ticket. Be sure that your FOR loop will work for any number that is stored in **ticket-count.txt**.

7. For this exercise you will create a program that helps the user understand his or her fuel costs. Your **chapter09** folder contains **fuel-costs.html** and **fuel-costs.php**. The code in **fuel-costs.html** includes a form that allows the user to enter the make and model of their car, the average fuel consumption (mpg), and the average fuel cost per gallon. Your **fuel-costs.php** file receives this input.

    Your job is to provide a FOR loop in **fuel-costs.php** that displays a table showing the fuel costs for journeys of different lengths between 100 and 1000 miles, in 100 mile increments (so the first row will show the cost for 100 miles of travel, the second row will show the cost for 200 miles, and so on, until the last row shows the costs for 1000 miles). To calculate the fuel costs, divide the **journey length** by the **mpg** (to obtain the number of gallons) and multiply the result by the **cost per gallon**. Use a table with a column for the journey length and a column for the fuel cost. Think carefully about the opening and closing <table>, <tr> and <td> tags. Which tags should appear **before** the loop, **inside** the loop and **after** the loop?

    HINT: use your loop counter to loop through the required journey lengths and use this variable in your fuel cost calculations.

8. For this exercise create a new version of the rainfall examples in this chapter. Your **chapter09** folder contains **rainfall-report.php** and **rainfall2007.txt**. This new version should use a loop to read the monthly rainfall from the **rainfall2007.txt** file, accumulate the total rainfall for the first 3 and last 3 months of the year (6 months altogether), and also display the name of the month and monthly rainfall for each of

these 6 months. You don't need to use a table although you can if you'd like to. The result should be something like this:

```
JAN:  3.21
FEB:  3.61
MAR:  2.84
OCT:  0.52
NOV:  2.03
DEC:  2.20


Total Rainfall for these months: 14.41 inches
```

HINT: Review the first four rainfall examples in the chapter. You may find it useful to copy some of the code in these files (in your **samples** folder) into **rainfall-report.php**. Of course you will need to modify the code to meet these new requirements. Each time the loop repeats a new rainfall amount is read from the file. Consider carefully what you need to do inside the loop, remember that you must print the name of each month and the amount, and also accumulate the total, but only for the first 3 and last 3 months.

Chapter 10

"While NOT End-Of-File" — Introducing Event-Controlled Loops

Intended Learning Outcomes

After completing this chapter, you should be able to:

- Summarize the characteristics of event-controlled loops.
- Trace the processing of a simple WHILE loop.
- Design and code a WHILE loop.
- Identify and apply the standard algorithm to process a file of unknown length.
- Use a WHILE loop to process a simple data file.
- Include selection structures within a WHILE loop.
- Use a WHILE loop to process a file of records.
- Use a WHILE loop to process selected records in a file of records.
- Use a WHILE loop to process selected fields in a file of records.

Introduction

We have learned how to develop loop structures where the number of repetitions is controlled by a counting variable. However we often have to design solutions where the number of repetitions cannot be determined in advance. Under these circumstances a counter-controlled loop will not work for us. Instead of repeatedly incrementing and testing a counting variable we must design a loop that uses some other test to decide when the loop should stop repeating.

Event-controlled loops are loops that will repeat 0 or more times until a specific event occurs. In this chapter we will learn how to design and develop applications that include event-controlled loops using the WHILE loop structure. Specifically, we will learn how to use WHILE loops to process text files of unknown length containing data of some kind. We also will learn how to include selection structures in these loops to extract useful information for many different purposes. Although we will work with text files, many of the concepts and processes covered here will also apply when you move on to work with database tables and records.

Characteristics of WHILE Loops

Loops that are not controlled by counters are controlled by **events**. Consider the following instructions to inflate a tire to the recommended air pressure:

```
TireInflation:

   remove the valve cap
   check the air pressure in the tire
   WHILE airPressure < recommendedAirPressure
     add a small amount of air
     check the air pressure in the tire
   ENDWHILE
   replace the valve cap
END
```

The first two instructions direct you to remove the valve cap and check the air pressure of the tire. The next instruction is the heading of a WHILE loop which contains a condition that may be **true** or **false**. In this example the loop condition is **airPressure < recommendedAirPressure.** If this test is **true**, the instructions inside the loop are executed, then we return to the loop heading and test the loop condition again to decide whether or not to repeat the instructions in the loop. If the test is **false** that means that the tire is at the recommended pressure so we skip the instructions inside the loop and move on to the next instruction following the loop structure (in this case the next instruction is to replace the valve cap).

Figure 10-1 shows a flow chart of the same algorithm. Read the last paragraph again, this time referring to the flow chart.

Take time to study the pseudocode and flow chart versions of this algorithm carefully. Pay attention to the logical structure of the loop. Don't just look at the algorithm briefly and decide "Oh I understand—we're adding air to the tire until it's correctly inflated". That is quite correct but it's important to understand exactly how the algorithm is accomplishing this step by step so that you can apply this structure to other problems. Beginning programmers often have a lot of trouble understanding how to apply WHILE loops correctly in their own algorithms.

It helps to walk through the algorithm using some test values and following the instructions exactly. As a first example, let's assume that the recommended air pressure for a tire is 32 pounds per square inch (32 psi). You remove the valve cap and test the tire pressure, which turns out to be 28 psi. You then come to the WHILE loop heading

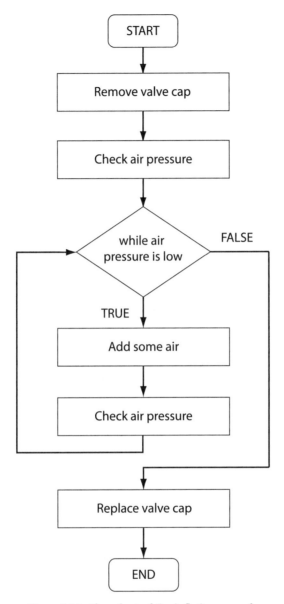

Figure 10-1: Flow chart of tire inflation example

and test the loop condition. Since the actual air pressure is less than the recommended air pressure, the loop condition it **true** so you perform the instructions inside the loop, adding some air and then checking the air pressure again. Let's say that the air pressure is now 30 psi. You return to the start of the loop and test the loop condition again. The test is once again **true** so you repeat the instructions in the loop, adding some air and testing the air pressure again. Let's say that the air pressure is now 32 psi. You return to the start of the loop and test the loop condition again. The test is now **false** since the actual pressure is no longer less than the recommended air pressure, so you skip the loop instructions and move on to the next instruction, which is to replace the valve cap.

Suppose the first time that you test the pressure, the actual pressure is 32 psi. That means that the first time that you test the loop condition the test is **false**, so you immediately skip past the loop and replace the valve cap. In this case, the loop instructions are **never** executed.

There are three important things to notice about this WHILE loop example. First, it is not possible to determine in advance how many times the loop will repeat. The loop is not controlled by a counting variable—instead the loop is controlled by an **event**. The event in this case is the air pressure in the tire reaching the recommended air pressure.

The second thing to notice is that the loop might execute 0 times. The algorithm includes an instruction to check the air pressure **before** the loop structure. If the air pressure is already at the recommended pressure the loop condition will be immediately **false** and the loop instructions will never be executed.

The third thing to notice is that the instruction to check the tire's air pressure appears **twice**. This instruction must appear **before** the WHILE loop in order to test the loop condition the first time, and this instruction must **also** be included **inside** the loop, **after** the instruction to add more air so that the air pressure will be tested again each time the loop repeats. If this instruction was not included **inside** the loop then the loop would execute forever since it would continue to refer to the results of the initial air pressure check even after more air was added. Also, if the instruction appeared **before** the instruction to add more air, the next test would be inaccurate since more air would be added **after** re-testing the air pressure. These are important logical considerations when designing an event-controlled loop.

You may be wondering "But what if there is too **much** air in the tire?" A more accurate algorithm would be:

```
TireInflation:

   remove the valve cap
   check the air pressure in the tire
   WHILE airPressure is not equal to the recommendedAirPressure
      if airPressure is less than the recommendedAirPressure
         add a small amount of air
      else
         release a small amount of air
      check the air pressure in the tire
   ENDWHILE
   replace the valve cap
END
```

If you review this carefully you will see that it handles tires that are under-inflated, over-inflated or correctly inflated. Can you draw a flow chart for this revised tire inflation algorithm?

The Structure of WHILE Loops

A WHILE loop will execute a number of statements 0 or more times, until the loop condition generates a false result. The general structure of a while loop written in pseudocode is as follows:

```
WHILE ( loop test )
   loop instructions
ENDWHILE
```

where (**loop test**) is any Boolean expression that will generate a **true** or **false** result, for example:

```
Prompt for password
Get userInput
WHILE ( userInput != correctPassword )
   Display "That is not the correct password - please try again"
   Prompt for password
   Get userInput
ENDWHILE
```

In this case the Boolean expression is **userInput != correctPassword**, which tests whether the value stored in the **userInput** variable is not equal to the value stored in **correctPassword**. The Boolean expression in a WHILE loop heading can use any relational operators (==, <=, <, >, >=, !=) and can combine expressions using any logical operators (**AND**, **OR**, or **NOT**).

An Algorithm to Process Files of Unknown Length

An important use of WHILE loops is to read data from a file when it is not certain at the time the program is written how much data the file will actually contain. A data file may contain a few lines of data or thousands of lines. The file may even be empty.

Consider a program that must process a file which contains the weekly timesheets of hourly employees (one timesheet on each line in the file). The program will need a loop to repeatedly read each line in the file in order to calculate each employee's pay, but how many times should this loop repeat? The length of the file may vary from week to week as employees leave or start work.

As another example, recall our **smoking-survey.html** and **smoking-survey.php** application that appended a new line of data to a file (**smoking-survey.txt**) every time a new smoking survey was submitted by a user. What if we are required to write a program that will process all the submitted surveys in **smoking-survey.txt** and produce a report? Since we may not know how many surveys were submitted, this program must be written in a manner that can handle any number of surveys in the file.

In order to process files of unknown length, we use a loop that repeatedly reads and processes lines from the file until the **end-of-file (EOF) marker** is found. The EOF marker is a special character that follows the last data value stored in a file. We can use a WHILE loop for this purpose by controlling the loop with the heading WHILE NOT EOF.

Programmers use a very standard, general-purpose algorithm to process files of unknown length. This is one of the more important and widely used algorithms for data processing so it is well worth taking the time to understand how it works:

```
STANDARD ALGORITHM TO PROCESS A FILE OF RECORDS:

  Open the file for reading

  Read nextLine from file
  While NOT EOF
    Process the data stored in nextLine
    Read nextLine from file
  ENDWHILE

  Close the file
```

Figure 10-2 shows a flow chart for the standard file processing algorithm.

This algorithm can be customized for your specific requirements by replacing the statement **Process the data stored in nextLine** with the specific instructions that your program needs to process each line in the file. Can you see how similar this algorithm is to the algorithm to achieve the correct air pressure in a car tire?

The key to understanding this file-processing algorithm is to pay careful attention to which instructions occur **before** the loop structure, which instructions are located **inside** the loop structure and which instructions **follow** the loop structure.

There are two instructions **before** the loop structure. The first instruction opens the file for reading. The second instruction reads the first line of data from the file and stores this data in a variable (here the variable is named **nextLine** but this could be any variable name). If the file is empty, this first **Read** instruction will find the **EOF** marker.

The loop structure appears next. The loop is controlled by the loop condition WHILE NOT EOF. Since this condition cannot be tested unless the program has already attempted to read a line from the file, the first **Read** instruction must appear **before** the WHILE loop, as shown here. The first **Read** instruction is often referred to as the **priming read**.

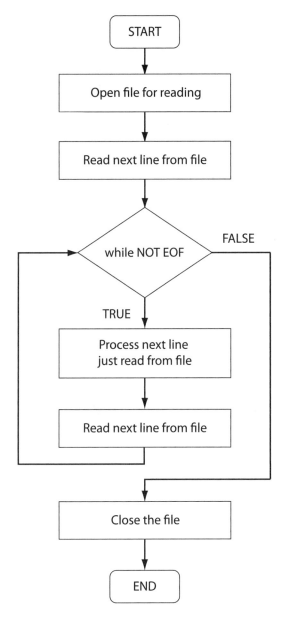

Figure 10-2: Flow chart illustrating the algorithm to process a file of records

If the loop test is **true** (the end of the file has **not** been found), the program enters the loop structure and executes the statements inside the loop. These statements should include the instructions required to process the line of data currently stored in the **nextLine** variable, followed by an instruction to read the **next** line from the file into the **nextLine** variable. The program then returns to the start of the loop to test whether or not the **EOF** marker was found during this last Read operation. If the EOF marker was **not** found , the loop repeats, processing the data stored in the **nextLine** variable and then reading the next line from the file. If the EOF marker **was** found, the loop is skipped and the program moves on to close the file.

Note that the last instruction inside the loop structure reads the next line from the file into the **nextLine** variable, replacing the previous value stored in that variable. For this reason it is important that the program performs all necessary processing to the line of data currently stored in the variable **before** the next line is read from the file. The actual processing will vary according to the needs of your application and we will consider a number of examples in this chapter.

Once the EOF marker has been found, and the file has been closed, the program may need to perform additional steps to meet the application requirements. For example the program may need to display a total or average or other summary statistics.

The purpose of the priming read should now be clear: this allows the program to correctly handle an empty file. If the EOF marker is found when reading the first line, the loop structure is skipped entirely and the file is closed. The instruction to **Read nextLine from file** must therefore appear **twice** in this algorithm. It is written **once before** the loop to perform the priming read, and it must be written **again** as the **last** statement **inside** the loop to read the next record from the file after the previously read line has been processed. If you forget to include this statement inside the loop the program will repeatedly process the content of the first line in the file.

Using a WHILE Loop to Process a File of Scores

Consider the following requirement:

---

process-scores1 requirement:

Create an application that opens a file of scores selected by the user, reads each score from the file, and displays the scores.

For testing purposes, allow the user to choose between four different files: scores1.txt, scores2.txt, scores3.txt, and scores4.txt. Each of these files contains a different number of scores.

This requirement allows the user to choose between a number of different data files (all located in the **samples** folder). This will allow us to test our programs on a number of files of different lengths and containing various combinations of valid and invalid data. The **scores1.txt** file contains **five** scores, as follows:

```
89
77
92
69
87
```

The scores2.txt file is **empty**.

The scores3.txt file contains **ten scores, two of which are invalid (these scores are out of the range 0 and 100):**

```
89
77
92
69
87
101
-2
80
100
50
```

The **scores4.txt file contains four scores, all invalid (these scores are out of the range 0 and 100):**

```
-2
101
-1
102
```

Here is the algorithm for the HTML form that allows the user to select any scores file:

```
process-scores1.html algorithm:
   Prompt the user for a file name
   Get fileName
   Submit fileName to process-scores1.php
END
```

Here is the HTML document (**process-scores1.html**) that uses a drop-down list to implement this algorithm:

```
<html>
<head>
  <title>STUDENT SCORES</title>
  <link rel="stylesheet" type="text/css" href="sample.css">
</head>
<body>
  <h1> STUDENT SCORES </h1>

  <form action="process-scores1.php" method="post">

    <p>Choose a scores file:</p>

    <label><select name="fileName">
      <option>scores1.txt</option>
      <option>scores2.txt</option>
      <option>scores3.txt</option>
      <option>scores4.txt</option>
    </select></label>
    <input class="submit" type="submit" value="Display the
      scores">
  </form>
</body>
</html>
```

Code Example: process-scores1.html

Here is the algorithm for the PHP code that will open, process, and close the selected data file:

```
process-scores1.php algorithm:

   Receive fileName from process-scores1.html
   Open fileName as scoreFile for reading

   Read nextScore from scoreFile
   WHILE NOT EOF (scoreFile)
     Display nextScore
     Read nextScore from scoreFile
   ENDWHILE

   Close scoreFile
END
```

Note that this algorithm is based on the general-purpose algorithm that was shown previously. This requirement is simply to display each score so the instruction to process each line from the file is simply: **Display nextScore**.

Here is the PHP code for this algorithm (**process-scores1.php**):

```
<html>
<head>
  <title>STUDENT SCORES</title>
  <link rel="stylesheet" type="text/css" href="sample.css">
</head>
<body>
  <h1> STUDENT SCORES </h1>
<?php
  $fileName = $_POST['fileName'];

  $scoreFile = fopen("$fileName","r");
  $score = trim(fgets($scoreFile));

  while (!feof($scoreFile))
  {
    print ("$score <br>");
    $score = trim(fgets($scoreFile));
  }
  fclose($scoreFile);

  print("<p>END OF FILE REACHED</p>");
?>
</body>
</html>
```

Code Example: process-scores1.php

This program receives the file name selected by the user and assigns this value to the variable **$fileName**. The file is opened for reading using the value stored in this variable:

```
$scoreFile = fopen("$fileName","r");
```

Now the program reads the first line from the file (the priming read) and stores the content of the line in the variable **$score**:

```
$score = trim(fgets($scoreFile));
```

If the file contains data the first line of data is now stored in **$score**. If the file is empty, then this read operation finds the EOF marker.

Next the program encounters the heading of the while loop and tests the loop condition the first time:

```
while ( !feof ($scoreFile) )
```

The WHILE NOT EOF test is written in PHP using a PHP function named **feof()**. This functions tests whether the EOF marker has been found. Notice the use of the NOT operator which is expressed in PHP using an exclamation mark (!). By associating this operator with **feof()** we are testing for NOT EOF. In other words, if the EOF marker has **not** been found yet, the test will be **true**, whereas if the EOF marker **has** been found, the test will be **false**.

Each time that the loop repeats, the program executes two instructions:

```
{
    print ("$score <br>");
    $score = trim(fgets($scoreFile));
}
```

First the score that was previously read from the file and stored in the **$score** variable is displayed, followed by a line break. Second, the score from the next line in the file is retrieved and stored in the **$score** variable (replacing the previous score).

Note that curly braces are required to indicate which statements are included in the loop structure.

Each time the program reaches the end of the loop statements it returns to the start of the loop to test again if the line that was just read contains the EOF marker. This cycle repeats until the EOF marker has been read from the file. The loop test then generates a **false** result and the program moves on to the instructions that follow the loop structure:

```
fclose($scoreFile);
print("<p>END OF FILE REACHED</p>");
```

Figure 10-3 shows an example of input/output if the user selects **scores1.txt** from the form.

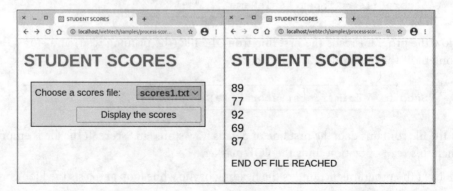

Figure 10-3: process-scores1.html and process-scores1.php screenshots

Figure 10-4 shows output from two other executions of **processScores1.php**. The first screen shows the output generated if the user selects **scores2.txt** which contains 0 scores (recall that this file is empty). The second screen shows the output generated if the user selects **scores3.txt** which contains 10 scores.

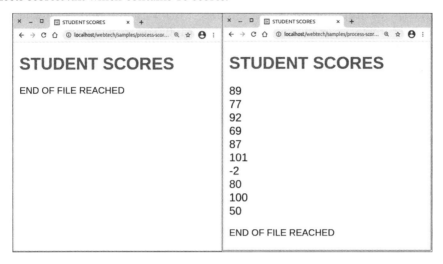

Figure 10-4: Two different process-scores1.php screenshots

Including Selection Structures Inside a WHILE Loop

As you can see, the **scores3.txt** file contains two incorrect scores (scores that are either below 0 or above 100). Here is a revised requirement to handle this problem:

---

process-scores2 requirement:

Create an application that opens a file of scores selected by the user, reads each score from the file, and displays only the scores that are within the range 0..100. Out of range scores should be ignored.

For testing purposes, allow the user to choose between four different files: scores1.txt, scores2.txt, scores3.txt, and scores4.txt. Each of these files contains a different number of scores.

Let's modify our algorithm to ignore any invalid scores as follows:

```
process-scores2.php algorithm:
   Receive fileName from process-scores2.html
   Open fileName as scoreFile for reading
   Read nextScore from scoreFile
   WHILE NOT EOF (scoreFile)
     IF nextScore >= 0 AND nextScore <= 100 THEN
       Display nextScore
     Read nextScore from scoreFile
   ENDWHILE
   Close scoreFile
END
```

Just as in the previous example, this algorithm uses a WHILE loop to read and process each line from the file until the EOF marker is found. However in this case an **IF** struc-ture is included inside the loop to test if the score that was just read from the file con-tains a value that is at least 0 and not more than 100. The score is only displayed if it is within range.

Note that the instruction to read the next score from the file is part of the WHILE loop structure but is **not** part of the IF structure. That's because we need to read the next score in the file **whether or not** the previous score was in range. The code for **process-scores2.html** and **process-scores2.php** can be found in the **samples** folder. Here is the code for **process-scores2.php**:

```
<html>
<head>
  <title>STUDENT SCORES</title>
  <link rel="stylesheet" type="text/css" href="sample.css">
</head>
<body>
  <h1> STUDENT SCORES </h1>
  <?php
    $fileName = $_POST['fileName'];
    $scoreFile = fopen("$fileName","r");
    $score = trim(fgets($scoreFile));

    while (!feof($scoreFile))
    {
      if ($score >= 0 and $score <= 100)
      {
        print("$score <br>");
      }
      $score = trim(fgets($scoreFile));
    }

    fclose($scoreFile);
    print("<p>END OF FILE REACHED</p>");
  ?>
</body>
</html>
```

Code Example: process-scores2.php

The braces are not necessary for the IF structure since this structure contains only a single statement, but you can see these braces make it easier to follow the logic. Note once again that the instruction **$score = trim(fgets($scoreFile));** is a part of the loop body but is **not** part of the IF structure.

Figure 10-5 shows the output that is generated if scores3.txt is selected by the user for processing. Note that the data in this file includes two out of range scores which are not displayed.

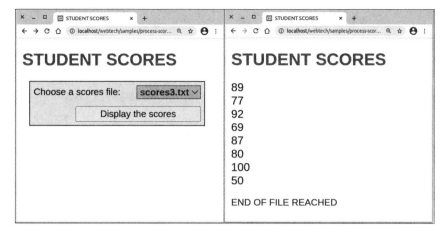

Figure 10-5: process-scores2.html and process-scores2.php screenshots

Try running the program on the other three text files to see the results.

Using a WHILE Loop to Count, Sum and Average Data

Now let's look at a requirement to read a file of scores and perform some statistics:

---

process-scores3 requirement:

Create an application that opens a file of scores selected by the user, reads each score from the file, and calculates and displays the number of valid scores in the file (within the range 0..100), the number of invalid scores in the file, and the average of the valid scores.

For testing purposes, allow the user to choose between four different files: scores1.txt, scores2.txt, scores3.txt, and scores4.txt. Each of these files contains a different number of scores.

This requires us to process the data in these files quite differently. In order to calculate the **average** score in the file we need to **count** the number of valid scores and accumulate the **sum** of the valid scores as we read each score from the file. We must also **count** the number of invalid scores. Also, before our program attempts to divide the sum by the count to obtain the average we must ensure that the count of valid scores is greater than 0! There is always a possibility that the file contains no valid scores and an attempt to divide by 0 will crash our program. Here is the solution algorithm:

```
process-scores3.php algorithm:
  Receive fileName from process-scores3.html

  sum = 0
  validCount = 0
  invalidCount = 0

  Open fileName as scoreFile for reading

  Read nextScore from scoreFile
  WHILE NOT EOF (scoreFile)
    IF nextScore >= 0 AND nextScore <= 100 THEN
      sum = sum + nextScore
      validCount = validCount + 1
    ELSE
      invalidCount = invalidCount + 1
    ENDIF
    Read nextScore from scoreFile
  ENDWHILE

  Close scoreFile

  Display validCount, invalidCount

  IF validCount > 0 THEN
    average = sum / validCount
    Display average
  ENDIF
END
```

The algorithm uses a variable to sum the valid scores, a variable to count the number of valid scores, and a variable to count the number of invalid scores. All three variables must be initialized to 0 **before** any of the scores are processed. The program opens the file, reads the first score from the file, then tests the WHILE loop condition. If the EOF marker was found during the first read operation, the loop test is **false** and the program will skip past the loop structure with the **sum**, **validCount** and **invalidCount** variables all still containing 0. If the EOF marker was **not** found, the loop test is **true** so the program enters the loop. If the current score is within range, the value of the score is added to the **sum** variable and 1 is added to the **validCount** variable. If the score is out of range, 1 is added to the **invalidCount** variable and the **sum** is left unchanged. The program then reads the next score and returns to the start of the loop to test whether the EOF marker was found during the last read operation.

This cycle repeats until the program finds the EOF marker and drops out of the loop. The sum variable will have accumulated the total of all of the valid scores, and the two counting variables will contain the number of valid and invalid scores in the file.

Following the WHILE loop structure, the program closes the file, then displays the valid and invalid score counts. If there is at least one valid score, the average of the valid scores is also calculated and displayed. The use of a selection structure here avoids a division-by-zero error if there are no valid scores in the file.

Walk through this algorithm carefully until you understand how it works. Here is the PHP code (**process-scores3.php**):

```
<html>
<head>
  <title>STUDENT SCORES</title>
  <link rel="stylesheet" type="text/css" href="sample.css">
</head>
<body>
  <h1> STUDENT SCORES </h1>
  <?php
    $fileName = $_POST['fileName'];

    $sum = 0;
    $validCount = 0;
    $invalidCount = 0;

    $scoreFile = fopen("$fileName","r");

    $score = trim(fgets($scoreFile));

    while ( !feof($scoreFile) )
    {
      if ($score >= 0 AND $score <= 100)
      {
        $sum = $sum + $score;
        $validCount = $validCount + 1;
      }
      else
        $invalidCount = $invalidCount + 1;

      $score = trim(fgets($scoreFile));
    }

    fclose($scoreFile);

    print("<p>Number of valid scores: $validCount</p>");
    print("<p>Number of invalid scores: $invalidCount</p>");
    if ($validCount > 0)
    {
      $average = $sum / $validCount;
      print("<p>Average of valid scores: $average</p>");
    }
  ?>
</body>
</html>
```

Code Example: process-scores3.php

Take some time to study this code — it incorporates most of the programming logic that we have covered so far. Run the program on each of the four scores files (**scores1.txt, scores2.txt, scores3.txt** and **scores4.txt**). The **scores4.txt** file contains only invalid scores so this will test the IF statement at the end of the program, which is designed to avoid a division by zero. Figure 10-6 shows the output when the program processes **scores3.txt** and **scores4.txt**.

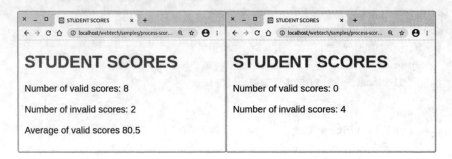

Figure 10-6: process-scores3.php — two sample screenshots

Using a WHILE Loop to Process a File of Records

The previous examples in this chapter have processed files that contain a single data **value** (a score) on each line in the file. Now we will consider a requirement to process a file that contains a complete data **record** on each line:

---

process-wages1 requirement:

Create an application that opens a file that contains a list of employee timesheets, each timesheet record on a separate line. Each timesheet record contains an employee's first name, last name, hours worked and hourly wage, with each data item separated by a colon. For example:

Mike:Smith:20:12.55

The application should read all of the records from the selected file and display them as an HTML document. For testing purposes, allow the user to choose between three different files: timesheets1.txt, timesheets2.txt and timesheets3.txt. Each of these files contains a different number of timesheets.

The three timesheet files are included in the **samples** folder. The **timeshects1**.txt file contains **three records**, as follows:

```
Mike:Smith:20:12.55
Mary:King:40:17.50
Chris:Jones:35:9.50
```

The **timesheets2.txt** file is **empty.**

The **timesheets3.txt** file contains **ten records:**

```
Mike:Smith:20:10.55
Mary:King:40:17.50
Chris:Jones:35:10.55
John:Anderson:50:10.55
Anne:Frame:10:10.55
Catherine:Olson:35:10.55
Steve:Jones:35:17.50
Joseph:Canton:50:8.50
Beth:Jones:35:25.25
Peter:Anderson:16:17.50
```

The code for **process-wages1.html** allows the user to select any of the three files for processing. Since this is similar to **process-scores1.html**, the algorithm and code is not shown here (the file is included in the **samples** folder).

Earlier, we learned how to parse a line containing a record with multiple data items (you will recall that we achieve this in PHP using a combination of the **explode()** and **list()** functions). We can now apply these tools to process a file of records of unknown length. Here is the algorithm to meet the requirement for process-wages1:

```
process-wages1.php algorithm:
   Receive fileName from process-wages1.html
   Open fileName as timesheetFile for reading

   Read empRecord from timesheetFile
   WHILE NOT EOF (timesheetFile)
     Get firstName, lastName, hrsWorked, hrlyWage from empRecord
     Display firstName, lastName, hrsWorked, hourlyWage
     Read empRecord from timesheetFile
   ENDWHILE

   Close timesheetFile
END
```

Here is the PHP code (**process-wages1.php**) which uses the **explode()** and **list()** functions to obtain the first name, last name, hours worked and hourly wage from each line that is read from the file, and displays this information using an HTML table:

```
<html>
<head>
  <title>WEEKLY WAGE REPORT</title>
  <link rel="stylesheet" type="text/css" href="sample.css">
</head>
<body>
  <h1> WEEKLY WAGE REPORT </h1>
  <?php
    $fileName = $_POST['fileName'];

    print ("<table>");
    print ("<tr><td>NAME</td><td>HOURS</td><td>HRLY
      WAGE</td></tr>");

    $timesheetFile = fopen("$fileName","r");
    $empRecord = trim(fgets($timesheetFile));

    while ( !feof($timesheetFile) )
    {
      list($firstName, $lastName, $hours, $payRate) =
        explode(":", $empRecord);

      print ("<tr><td> $firstName $lastName </td>");
      print ("<td> $hours </td>");
      print ("<td> $payRate </td></tr>");

      $empRecord = fgets($timesheetFile);
    }
    fclose($timesheetFile);

    print("</table>");
    print("<p>END OF FILE REACHED</p>");
  ?>
</body>
</html>
```

Code Example: process-wages1.php

Note that the <table> tag and the first table row containing the headings are printed
before the file is processed. Each time the loop structure repeats, a table row is created
that displays the information that is parsed from the current line using the **explode()**
and **list()** functions. Once the loop has completed, the ending </table> tag is printed.
Figure 10-7 shows the output that is displayed if the program reads **timesheets1.txt**.

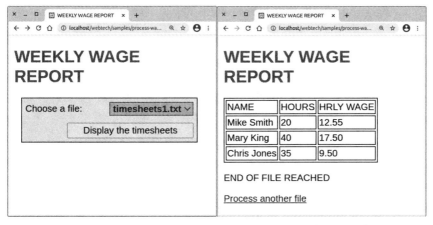

Figure 10-7: process-wages1.html and process-wages1.php screenshots

Processing Weekly Wages from a File of Timesheet Records

Here is a requirement to process the timesheet files and calculate and display the weekly wages of each employee:

---

process-wages2 requirement:

Create an application that opens a file that contains a list of employee timesheets, one timesheet record on a separate line. Each timesheet record contains an employee's first name, last name, hours worked and hourly wage, with each data item separated by a colon. For example:

Mike:Smith:20:12.55

The application should read all of the records from the selected file and calculate and display the employee's first name, last name and weekly wage in a check format.

For testing purposes, allow the user to choose between three different files: timesheets1.txt, timesheets2.txt and timesheets3.txt. Each of these files contains a different number of timesheets.

There is little difference between this and the previous algorithm except that here we are adding a calculation and displaying the employee's first and last name and weekly wage in the form of a pay check. We do not display the hours worked or hourly wage.

Here is an algorithm that meets this requirement:

```
process-wages2.php algorithm:

    Receive fileName from process-wages2.html
    Open fileName as timesheetFile for reading
    Read empRecord from timesheetFile
    WHILE NOT EOF (timesheetFile)
      Get firstName,lastName,hrsWorked,hrlyWage from empRecord
      weeklyWage = hrsWorked * hrlyWage

      Display"PAY TO firstName lastName
            THE SUM OF $ weeklyWage"
      Read the next empRecord from timesheetFile
    ENDWHILE

    Close timesheetFile
END
```

Here is the code for this algorithm (**process-wages2.php**) which uses the PHP **number_format**() function to display the wages to two decimal places:

```
<html>
<head>
  <title>WEEKLY WAGE REPORT</title>
  <link rel="stylesheet" type="text/css" href="sample.css">
</head>
<body>
  <h1> WEEKLY WAGE REPORT </h1>
  <?php
    $fileName = $_POST['fileName'];

    $timesheetFile = fopen("$fileName","r");

    $empRecord = trim(fgets($timesheetFile));

    while ( !feof($timesheetFile) )
    {
      list($firstName, $lastName, $hours, $payRate) = explode(":",
          $empRecord);
      $weeklyWage = $hours * $payRate;

      print ("PAY TO $firstName $lastName SUM
        OF $".number_format($weeklyWage, 2)."<br>");

      $empRecord = trim(fgets($timesheetFile));
    }
```

```
        fclose($timesheetFile);
        print("<p>END OF FILE REACHED</p>");
    ?>
</body>
</html>
```

Code Example: process-wages2.php

Figure 10-8 shows the output if the program reads **timesheets1.txt**.

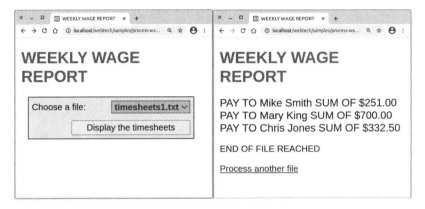

Figure 10-8: process-wages2.html and process-wages2.php screenshots

Processing Selected Records from a File of Timesheet Records

Often when we process a file of records, we are only interested in processing specific records. Consider the following requirement:

---

process-wages3 requirement:

Create an application that allows the user to input an employee's first name and last name, and the name of a timesheet file. The application should read all of the records from the selected file and display the first name, last name and hours worked of any employees whose first and last names match the user input.

For testing purposes, allow the user to choose between three different files: timesheets1.txt, timesheets2.txt and timesheets3.txt. Each of these files contains a different number of timesheets.

In order to meet this requirement we must develop an algorithm for an HTML form that will obtain the required user input, and an algorithm for the PHP program that will read the records in the file, test each record to see if the first and last names match those entered by the user, and display the hours worked of an employee if a match is found. There may be 0 or more records that match. Here is the algorithm for the HTML form (**process-wages3.html**):

```
process-wages3.html algorithm:

   Prompt for file name
   Get fileName
   Prompt for first name to search for
   Get searchFName
   Prompt for last name to search for
   Get searchLName
   Submit filename, searchFName, searchLName to process-wages3.php
END
```

Here is the code for the form (**process-wages3.html**):

```
<html>
<head>
  <title>WEEKLY WAGE REPORT</title>
  <link rel="stylesheet" type="text/css" href="sample.css">
</head>
<body>
  <h1> WEEKLY WAGE REPORT </h1>
  <form action="process-wages3.php" method="post">
    <p>Choose a file:</p>

    <label><select name="fileName">
      <option>timesheets1.txt</option>
      <option>timesheets2.txt</option>
      <option>timesheets3.txt</option>
    </select></label>

    <label>First Name:
    <input type="text" size="15" name="searchFName"></label>

    <label>Last Name:
    <input type="text" size="15" name="searchLName"></label>
    <input class="submit" type="submit" value="Display Hours
      Worked">
</form>
</body>
</html>
```

Code Example: process-wages3.html

Here is the algorithm for **process-wages3.php**:

```
process-wages3.php algorithm:

   Receive filename, searchFName, searchLName from
process-wages3.html
   Open fileName as timesheetFile for reading

   Read empRecord from timesheetFile
   WHILE NOT EOF (timesheetFile)
     Get firstName,lastName,hrsWorked,hrlyWage from empRecord

     IF firstName == searchFName AND lastName == searchLName THEN
       Display "firstName lastName HOURS WORKED: hrsWorked"
     ENDIF

     Read the next empRecord from timesheetFile
   ENDWHILE

   Close timesheetFile
END
```

And here is the PHP code for **process-wages3.php**:

```php
<?php
   $fileName = $_POST['fileName'];
   $searchFName = $_POST['searchFName'];
   $searchLName = $_POST['searchLName'];

   $timesheetFile = fopen("$fileName","r");

   $empRecord = trim(fgets($timesheetFile));

   while ( !feof($timesheetFile) )
   {
     list($firstName, $lastName, $hours, $payRate) =
       explode(":", $empRecord);

     if ($firstName == $searchFName AND
         $lastName == $searchLName)
     {
       print ("$firstName $lastName HOURS WORKED:
         $hours<br>");
     }

     $empRecord = trim(fgets($timesheetFile));
   }
```

```
        fclose($timesheetFile);

        print("<p>END OF FILE REACHED</p>");

    ?>
```

Code Example: process-wages3.php

Note the use of the AND operator to combine the tests for first name AND last name. Figure 10-9 shows sample input and output.

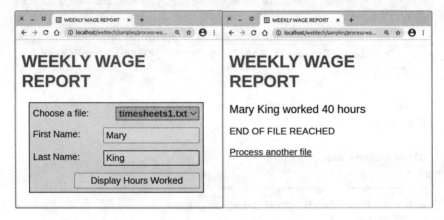

Figure 10-9: process-wages3.html and process-wages3.php screenshots

Processing Selected Fields from a File of Records

The last example demonstrated how to work with selected **records** in a file. Now let's see an example where we work with selected **fields** from each record.

process-wages4 requirement:

Create an application that reads all of the records from a file of timesheets and calculates and displays the average hours worked by the employees.

For testing purposes, allow the user to choose between three different files: timesheets1.txt, timesheets2.txt and timesheets3.txt. Each of these files contains a different number of timesheets.

In order to fulfill this requirement, our program is only concerned with the hours worked by each employee. We need to sum and count these values to calculate the average hours worked by all employees. However in order to obtain this data, the program must still read all of the data from each line in the file, and parse the data from each line to obtain the hours worked. We can then accumulate the total of the hours worked and count the number of lines in the file (since this will tell us the number of employees). Before calculating the average we must also test the count in case the file contains 0 records. Once again we must be careful to consider which statements occur **before** the loop structure, which statements should be located **inside** the loop structure and which statements **follow** the loop structure. Here is the algorithm:

```
process-wages4.php algorithm:
  Receive fileName from process-wages4.html
  Set sum = 0
  Set count = 0

  Open fileName as timesheetFile for reading

  Read empRecord from timesheetFile
  WHILE NOT EOF (timesheetFile)
    Get firstName, lastName, hrsWorked, hrlyWage from empRecord
    sum = sum + hrsWorked
    count = count + 1
    Read the next empRecord from timesheetFile
  ENDWHILE

  Close timesheetFile

  IF count > 0 THEN
    averageHours = sum /count
    Display averageHours
  ELSE
    Display "FILE IS EMPTY"
  ENDIF
END
```

Here is the PHP code (**process-wages4.php**):

```
<html>
<head>
  <title>WEEKLY WAGE REPORT</title>
  <link rel="stylesheet" type="text/css" href="sample.css">
</head>
<body>
  <h1> WEEKLY WAGE REPORT </h1>
  <?php
    $fileName = $_POST['fileName'];

    $sum = 0;
    $count = 0;

    $timesheetFile = fopen("$fileName","r");
    $empRecord = trim(fgets($timesheetFile));

    while ( !feof($timesheetFile) )
    {
      list($firstName, $lastName, $hours, $payRate) =
```

```
        explode(":", $empRecord);
    $sum = $sum + $hours;
    $count = $count + 1;
    $empRecord = trim(fgets($timesheetFile));
    }

    fclose($timesheetFile);

    if ($count > 0)
    {
        $averageHours = $sum / $count;
        print("<p>AVERAGE HOURS WORKED: $averageHours</p>");
    }
    else
        print("<p>NO RECORDS FOUND</p>");
    ?>
</body>
</html>
```

Code Example: process-wages4.php

Figure 10-10 shows the output if this program processes **timesheets3.txt**.

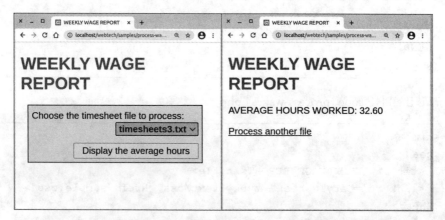

Figure 10-10: process-wages4.html and process-wages4.php screenshots

Processing Selected Records from a File of Records

Let's modify the last example so that, instead of finding the average number of hours worked by **all** employees, we are asked to find the average hours worked by **only those employees who earn less than $12.00 an hour**:

process-wages5 requirement:
Create an application that reads all of the records from a file
of timesheets and calculates and displays the average hours
worked by the employees whose hourly pay rate is less than $12.

In order to fulfill this requirement, our program needs to begin by setting the total number of hours worked and also the count of employees earning less than 12.00 hourly to 0. The program should then read the employee records from the file. For each record the program must: extract the employee's first name, last name, hours worked and the pay rate; determine if the employee's pay rate is less than 12.00 and, if so, add the number of hours worked to the total, and add 1 to the count of employees earning less than 12.00. These steps will ensure that, after all the records have been read from the file, the total will contain the total number of hours worked by all employees earning less than 12.00 hourly, and the count will contain the number of these employees. The program can then calculate the average hours worked by these employee by dividing the total by the count. Before calculating the average we must also test the count to avoid division by 0 (if there were no employees earning less than 12.00). Here is the algorithm:

```
process-wages5.php algorithm:
   Receive fileName from process-wages4.html
   Set sum = 0
   Set count = 0

   Open fileName as timesheetFile for reading

   Read empRecord from timesheetFile

   WHILE NOT EOF (timesheetFile)
     Get firstName, lastName, hrsWorked, hrlyWage from
       empRecord
     IF hrlyWage < 12.00
       sum = sum + hrsWorked
       count = count + 1
   ENDIF
   Read the next empRecord from timesheetFile
ENDWHILE

Close timesheetFile

IF count > 0 THEN
   averageHours = sum /count
   Display averageHours
ELSE
   Display "NO EMPLOYEES EARN LESS THAN $12.00"
ENDIF
END
```

Here is the PHP code for **process-wages5.php**:

```
<html>
<head>
  <title>WEEKLY WAGE REPORT</title>
  <link rel="stylesheet" type="text/css" href="sample.css">
</head>
<body>
  <h1> WEEKLY WAGE REPORT </h1>
  <?php
    $fileName = $_POST['fileName'];

    $sum = 0;
    $count = 0;

    $timesheetFile = fopen("$fileName","r");
    $empRecord = trim(fgets($timesheetFile));

    while ( !feof($timesheetFile) )
    {
      list($firstName, $lastName, $hours, $payRate) =
        explode(":", $empRecord);
      if ($payRate < 12.00)
      {
        $sum = $sum + $hours;
        $count = $count + 1;
      }
    $empRecord = trim(fgets($timesheetFile));
    }
    fclose($timesheetFile);

    if ($count > 0)
    {
      $averageHours = $sum / $count;
      print("<p>AVERAGE HOURS WORKED BY EMPLOYEES
        EARNING LESS THAN $12.00: "
        .number_format($averageHours, 2)."</p>");
}
else
    print("<p>NO EMPLOYEES EARN LESS THAN $12.00</p>");
?>
</body>
</html>
```

Code Example: process-wages5.php

Processing a File of Survey Data

Let's consider one more file-processing example to demonstrate how much information can be extracted from a relatively simple data set. Earlier, we developed an application to receive smoking surveys submitted via an HTML form and append each survey to a file named **smoking-survey.txt**. Here is a requirement to process this file and generate a report:

---

process-survey requirement:

Create an application that reads all of the records from a file that contains records of smoking surveys (each survey on a separate line in the file). Each record consists of a first name, last name, years smoked, and number of cigarettes smoked daily. The four data items in each record are separated by colons, for example:

John:Smith:2:20

The program should display: The number of surveys collected, the number and percentage of survey takers who have never smoked, the number and percentage of survey takers who have smoked, the number of survey takers who are heavy smokers (smoke 20 or more cigarettes a day for at least 5 years), the average number of cigarettes smoked daily by survey takers who smoke, and the average number of years that survey takers who smoke have smoked.

This requires us to plan carefully! We will need a number of variables to count and accumulate as we process each record from the data file. We will need variables to keep track of the number of smokers and non-smokers. We will need a variable to count the number of heavy smokers. And we will need variables to accumulate the total number of years that the smokers have smoked, and the total number of cigarettes that the smokers have smoked—we will use these to calculate the required averages. All of these counting and accumulating variables will need to be initialized to 0 before our program begins to process the file.

Each time the program processes a line from the file, we will need to test whether the survey taker entered 0 for the number smoked daily. If this is the case, we will count the survey taker as a non-smoker, otherwise we will count the survey taker as a smoker. If the survey taker is a smoker, we must add the years he or she has smoked and number of cigarettes smoked daily to our two totals. And we must test if the years smoked is at least 5 and the number of cigarettes smoked is at least 20 to determine whether or not to count this person as a heavy smoker.

We must also remember to read the next line from the file after we process each record.

Once the program reaches the end of the file it must calculate the various statistics that are required. We can calculate the total number of survey takers by adding the count of smokers to the count of non-smokers. We can calculate the percentage of smokers and non-smokers by dividing each of the counts of smokers and non-smokers by the total number of survey takers. We can calculate the average number of years that smokers have smoked and average number of cigarettes that smokers have smoked daily by dividing the appropriate totals by the count of smokers.

Here is the algorithm that meets these requirements:

```
process-survey.php algorithm:


Receive fileName from process-survey.html

countHeavySmokers = 0;
countSmokers = 0;
countNonSmokers = 0;
totalSmokedDaily = 0;
totalYearsSmoked = 0;


Open fileName as surveyFile for reading
Read nextSurvey from surveyFile
WHILE NOT EOF (surveyFile)
  Get firstName, lastName, yearsSmoked, smokedDaily from
    nextSurvey
  IF (smokedDaily == 0)
    countNonSmokers = countNonSmokers + 1
  ELSE
    countSmokers = countSmokers + 1
    totalSmokedDaily = totalSmokedDaily + smokedDaily
    totalYearsSmoked = totalYearsSmoked + yearsSmoked
    IF (smokedDaily >= 20 AND yearsSmoked >= 5)
      countHeavySmokers = countHeavySmokers + 1
    ENDIF
  ENDIF
  Read nextSurvey from surveyFile
ENDWHILE


Close surveyFile

totalSurveys = countSmokers + countNonSmokers
percentNonSmokers = 100 * countNonSmokers / totalSurveys
percentSmokers = 100 * countSmokers / totalSurveys
avgSmokedDaily = totalSmokedDaily / countSmokers
avgYearsSmoked = totalYearsSmoked / countSmokers

Display Survey heading
Display totalSurveys, countSmokers, countNonSmokers,
  percentSmokers, percentNonSmokers, countHeavySmokers,
  avgSmokedDaily, avgYearsSmoked.
END
```

This algorithm includes selection structures within the loop structure. The first selection structure is used to determine whether to count the survey taker as a smoker or non-smoker. Non-smokers are simply counted but smokers require a number of processing steps; these include a second selection structure that is nested inside the ELSE section of the outer selection structure and used to count heavy smokers.

The PHP code (**process-survey.php**) uses a table with no border to display the survey results. Note the use of an internal stylesheet in the head section to remove any table border: this ensures that the table is not visible to the viewer but lines up the output nicely.

```
<html>
<head>
<title>SMOKING SURVEY REPORT</title>
<link rel="stylesheet" type="text/css" href="sample.css">
<!-- example of an internal style sheet, used here to over-
ride the border setting for tables in sample.css so no bor-
der is displayed -->
<style>table, th, td {border:none;}</style>
</head>
<body>
  <?php
    $fileName = $_POST['fileName'];

    $countHeavySmokers = 0;
    $countSmokers = 0;
    $countNonSmokers = 0;
    $totalSmokedDaily = 0;
    $totalYearsSmoked = 0;

    $surveyFile = fopen("$fileName","r");
    $nextSurvey = trim(fgets($surveyFile));

    while ( !feof($surveyFile) )
    {
      list($firstName, $lastName, $yearsSmoked, $smokedDaily) =
        explode(":", $nextSurvey);

      if ($smokedDaily == 0)
      {
        $countNonSmokers = $countNonSmokers + 1;
      }
      else
      {
        $countSmokers = $countSmokers + 1;
        $totalSmokedDaily =
```

```
        $totalSmokedDaily + $smokedDaily;
      $totalYearsSmoked =
        $totalYearsSmoked + $yearsSmoked;

      if ($smokedDaily >= 20 AND $yearsSmoked >= 5)
      {
        $countHeavySmokers =
        $countHeavySmokers + 1;
      }
    }

    $nextSurvey = trim(fgets($surveyFile));
  }

  fclose($surveyFile);

  $totalSurveys = $countSmokers + $countNonSmokers;
  $percentNonSmokers = 100 * $countNonSmokers / $totalSurveys;
  $percentSmokers = 100 * $countSmokers / $totalSurveys;
  $avgSmokedDaily = $totalSmokedDaily / $countSmokers;
  $avgYearsSmoked = $totalYearsSmoked / $countSmokers;

  print ("<h1>SMOKING SURVEY REPORT</h1>");
  print("<p>(Report generated from data file:
    <strong>$fileName </strong>)</p>");
  print ("<table>");
  print ("<tr><td>Total number of people
    surveyed:</td><td>$totalSurveys</td></tr>");
  print ("<tr><td>Number of
    smokers:</td><td>$countSmokers</td></tr>");
  print ("<tr><td>Number of non-smokers:</td>
    <td>$countNonSmokers </td></tr>");
  print ("<tr><td>Percentage of smokers:</td>
    <td>$percentSmokers %</td></tr>");
  print ("<tr><td>Percentage of non-smokers:</td>
    <td>$percentNonSmokers %</td></tr>");
  print ("<tr><td>Heavy smokers (20+ a day for at least 5
    years):</td><td>$countHeavySmokers</td></tr>");
  print ("<tr><td>Average cigarettes smoked daily by
    smokers:</td><td>$avgSmokedDaily</td></tr>");
  print ("<tr><td>Average years that smokers have
    smoked:</td><td>$avgYearsSmoked</td></tr>");
  print ("</table>");

  ?>
</body>
</html>
```

Code Example: process-survey.php

This is a more complex piece of code and it is worth taking some time to read through it until you understand all of the components. Figure 10-11 shows the results of processing a file of survey data named **sample-survey.txt** (in the **samples** folder).

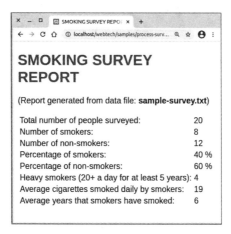

Figure 10-11: process-survey screenshot

Additional Learning Materials

Almost all programming languages provide another type of event-controlled loop, where the loop test appears at the **end** of the loop structure rather than the beginning. This structure is implemented as either a DO..WHILE loop or REPEAT..UNTIL loop, depending on the programming language. **Chapter 16 includes a description of the PHP DO..WHILE loop, including a code example.**

Appendix D will help you **debug** your exercises, listing a number of the most common errors that you are likely to encounter.

The **Chapter 10 Hints and Help** pages on the textbook Web site provide answers to FAQs from previous students as they worked through the end-of-chapter exercises.

Summary

Event-controlled loops allow us to repeat a series of instructions without the need to know in advance how many times the loop is to repeat. We achieve this by using a loop condition that allows the loop to repeat until some event occurs.

One example of an event-controlled loop is a loop that repeatedly reads and processes lines from a file until the **end-of-file (EOF) marker** is read. In this case the event is reading the end of file marker.

Just as a **FOR** loop is the usual choice for count-controlled loops, the most commonly used structure for event-controlled loops is a WHILE loop. The general syntax of a WHILE loop is:

```
while ( loop test )
   loop instructions
ENDWHILE
```

A WHILE loop can be used to process a file of unknown length. The standard algorithm to achieve this is as follows:

```
Open the file for reading
Read nextLine from file
While NOT EOF
   Process data stored in nextLine
   Read nextLine from file
ENDWHILE
Close the file
```

The statement **process nextLine** may include any number of instructions, including selection structures and even other loop structures. Processing may include counting, accumulating, testing, performing calculations or displaying information as required. Since the algorithm uses a loop to process one record at a time, it is important that any processing applied to each record must be performed inside the loop **before** the next record is read from the file.

When designing event-controlled loops, it is important to determine what instructions must be performed **before** the loop structure, which statements should be repeated **inside** the loop structure, and which statements should be performed **following** the loop structure.

Another type of event-controlled loop is a DO..WHILE or REPEAT..UNTIL loop, where the loop test occurs at the **end** of the loop structure.

Chapter 10 Review Questions

1. Consider a loop that repeatedly reads lines from a file of unknown length until the end of the file is reached. What term is commonly used to describe this kind of loop?
    a. A selection loop
    b. A sequential loop
    c. A count-controlled loop
    d. An event-controlled loop
    e. A for loop

2. Study the following algorithm. How many times will the user be allowed to attempt to enter a password until a correct password is submitted?

```
Prompt for password
Get userInput
WHILE (userInput != correctPassword )
  Display "That is not the correct password - try again"
  Prompt for password
  Get userInput
ENDWHILE
Display "Welcome!" message
```

    a. Once
    b. Twice
    c. Three times
    d. Four times
    e. Any number of times

3. What is the LEAST number of times this loop might repeat?

```
Prompt for password
Get userInput
WHILE (userInput != correctPassword )
  Display "That is not the correct password - try again"
  Prompt for password
  Get userInput
ENDWHILE
Display "Welcome!" message
```

a. 0
b. 1
c. 2
d. This cannot be determined in advance.
e. This is an infinite loop.

4. Consider the following instructions for a bank teller. What event controls this loop?

```
WHILE there are more customers waiting in line
   Call the next customer
   IF the customer needs a loan
     Refer them to the Loan Officer
   ELSE
     Handle the customer's transaction
   ENDIF
ENDWHILE
```

a. There are more customers waiting in line
b. Call the next customer
c. The customer needs a loan
d. Refer them to the Loan Officer
e. Handle the customer's transaction

5. How do we usually process a file of unknown length?
a. Read the first line from the file, then use a loop to process the line that has just been read and read the next line, until the EOF marker is read
b. Use a loop to read the next line from the file and process it, until the EOF marker is read

6. Which PHP function is used to test whether the End Of File marker has been read from a file?
a. The eof() function
b. The EOF function
c. The feof() function
d. The fclose() function
e. The endOfFile() function

7. Which statement is **false**?
a. WHILE loop structures can include selection structures.
b. WHILE loop structures can include other loop structures.
c. A WHILE loop can repeat 0 or more times.
d. WHILE loops can be used to process files of unknown length.
e. In PHP, the heading of a WHILE loop must end with a semi-colon.

8. How many scores will the following loop process?

```php
$scoreFile = fopen("scores.txt","r");
$score = trim(fgets($scoreFile));
while (!feof($scoreFile))
{
   print ("$score <br>");
   $score = trim(fgets($scoreFile));
}
fclose($scoreFile);
```

   a. 0 scores
   b. 0 or more scores, depending on the content of scores.txt
   c. 1 or more scores, depending on the content of scores.txt
   d. 2 scores
   e. 2 or more scores, depending on the content of scores.txt

9. What does this loop actually do?

```php
$number = 0;
$scoreFile = fopen("scores.txt","r");
$score = trim(fgets($scoreFile));
while (!feof($scoreFile))
{
   $number = $number + 1;
   $score = trim(fgets($scoreFile));
}
fclose($scoreFile);
print ("<p>$number </p>");
```

   a. Displays the scores in scores.txt
   b. Counts the scores in scores.txt
   c. Sums the scores in scores.txt
   d. Averages the scores in scores.txt
   e. Adds 1 to each score in scores.txt

10. What does this loop actually do?

```
$number = 0;
$scoreFile = fopen("scores.txt","r");
$score = trim(fgets($scoreFile));
while (!feof($scoreFile))
{
  $number = $number + $score;
  $score = trim(fgets($scoreFile));
}
fclose($scoreFile);
print ("<p>$number </p>");
```

   a. Displays the scores in scores.txt
   b. Counts the scores in scores.txt
   c. Sums the scores in scores.txt
   d. Averages the scores in scores.txt
   e. Sets each score to 0 in scores.txt

11. What does this loop actually do?

```
$number = 0;
$ageFile = fopen("ages.txt","r");
$age = trim(fgets($ageFile));
while (!feof($ageFile))
{
  if ($age > 65)
    $number = $number + 1;
  $age = trim(fgets($ageFile));
}
fclose($ageFile);
```

   a. Displays all the ages
   b. Counts all the ages
   c. Counts all the ages above 65
   d. Sums all the ages
   e. Sums all the ages above 65

12. What is wrong with this code?

```
$ageFile = fopen("ages.txt","r");
$age = trim(fgets($ageFile));
while (!feof($ageFile));
{
  print("$age <br>");
  $age = trim(fgets($ageFile));
}
fclose($ageFile);
```

    a. The first age in the file will not be displayed because two statement are in the wrong order

    b. The last age in the file will not be displayed because two statement are in the wrong order

    c. A semi-colon needs to be removed, otherwise the loop will not perform correctly

    d. The file should be opened inside the loop

    e. The file should be closed inside the loop

13. What is wrong with this code?

```
$ageFile = fopen("ages.txt","r");
$age = trim(fgets($ageFile));
while (!feof($ageFile))
{
   $age = trim(fgets($ageFile));
   print("$age <br>");
}
fclose($ageFile);
```

    a. The first age in the file will not be displayed because two statement are in the wrong order

    b. The last age in the file will not be displayed because two statement are in the wrong order

    c. A semi-colon needs to be removed, otherwise the loop will not perform correctly

    d. The file should be opened inside the loop

    e. The file should be closed inside the loop

14. The following code is designed to process one of the following files. Which one?

```
$value = 0;
$someFile = fopen("someData.txt","r");
$nextItem = trim(fgets($someFile));
while (!feof($someFile))
{
   $value = $value + $nextItem;
   $nextItem = trim(fgets($someFile));
}
fclose($someFile);
print ("<p>$value </p>");
```

a. A file containing exactly two lines of data
b. A file containing a list of numbers, one number on each line
c. A file containing a list of numbers, all on the same line, separated by colons
d. A file containing a name, colon, and number on each line
e. A file containing a name on the first line, a colon on the second line, and a number on the third line

15. The following code designed to process one of the following files. Which one?

```
$someFile = fopen("someData.txt","r");
$nextItem = trim(fgets($someFile));
while (!feof($someFile))
{
   list($value1, $value2) = explode(":", $nextItem);
   print ("<p>$value1 $value2</p>");
   $nextItem = trim(fgets($someFile));
}
fclose($someFile);
print ("<p>$value </p>");
```

a. A file containing exactly one line of data
b. A file containing exactly two lines of data
c. A file containing a list of numbers, one number on each line
d. A file containing a name, colon, and number on each line
e. A file containing a name on the first line, a colon on the second line, and a number on the third line

16. What length of file can be processed using a WHILE loop
a. Only files that contain no data (empty file)
b. Files that contain exactly one line of data
c. Files that contain exactly two lines of data
d. Files that contain 0 or more lines of data
e. Files that contain 1 or more lines of data

17. What does this code actually do?

```
$value = 0;
$someFile = fopen("someData.txt","r");
$nextItem = trim(fgets($someFile));
while (!feof($someFile))
{
   list($item1, $item2) = explode(":", $nextItem);
   $value = $value + $item2;
   $nextItem = trim(fgets($someFile));
```

```
    }
    fclose($someFile);
    print ("<p>$value </p>");
```

a. Reads a file containing a list of values, one on each line, and sums them
b. Reads a file containing two values on each line and sums all of the values in the file
c. Reads a file containing two values on each line and sums the first values on each line
d. Reads a file containing two values on each line and sums the second values on each line
e. Reads a file containing two lines and sums the values on these lines

18. What does this code actually do?

```
    $value = 0;
    $someFile = fopen("someData.txt","r");
    $nextItem = trim(fgets($someFile));
    while (!feof($someFile))
    {
        list($item1, $item2) = explode(":", $nextItem);
        if ($item1 == "Smith")
            $value = $value + $item2;
        $nextItem = trim(fgets($someFile));
    }
    fclose($someFile);
    print ("<p>$value</p>");
```

a. Reads a file containing two values on each line and counts the lines where the first value is "Smith"
b. Reads a file containing two values on each line and sums the second values of the lines where the first value is "Smith"
c. Reads a file containing two values on each line and sums the first values of the lines where the second value is "Smith"
d. Reads a file containing two values on each line and sets the second value to 0 if the first value is "Smith"
e. Reads a file containing two lines and doubles the value of the second line if the value of the first line is "Smith"

19. The textbook provides a smoking-survey example. How are the total number of surveys calculated in the algorithm for this program?
   a. By using a counter to count each survey that is read from the survey file
   b. By using counters to count the number of smokers and non-smokers in the survey file, then adding these after the file has been processed
   c. By adding the total smoked daily by all survey takers and dividing this by the number of smokers
   d. By using a form that asks the user for the number of surveys in the file
   e. The total number of surveys is not calculated in this program

20. When using a WHILE loop to read records from a file of unknown length, why is it important to read the first record BEFORE the loop test?
   a. In order to determine how many records are in the file
   b. In order to determine what type of records are in the file
   c. In case the file contains duplicate records
   d. In case the EOF marker is on the first line (the loop will then be skipped)
   e. The program should NOT read the first record BEFORE the loop test!

Chapter 10 Code Exercises

Your Chapter 10 code exerecises can be found in your **chapter10** folder. This folder is included in your customized XAMPP installation at the following location:

htdocs\webtech\coursework\chapter10

Type your name and the date in the **Author** and **Date** sections of each file as you work on each exercise. **Remember** that the Students page on the textbook Web site includes **Hints and Help** pages for the exercises in this and every chapter.

Debugging Exercises

Your **chapter10** folder should contain a number of "fixit" files. Each of these files contains PHP code that has an error of some kind. The type of error is indicated in the comment section of each file. You will need to run each program in order to see the errors, and to debug and test the code to see if it works correctly. For example to run **fixit1.php**, first run the Web server, then use the URL:

http://localhost/webtech/coursework/chapter10/fixit1.php

Code Modification Exercises

Your **chapter10** folder contains a number of "modify" files. Each pair of files contains HTML and PHP code that needs to be modified to meet a requirement. The requirements are included in the comment section of each file. Modify the algorithms, being careful to make changes to the .html and .php files as directed. You will need to run each program in order to test your changes. For example to run **modify1.html**, first run the Web server, then use the URL:

http://localhost/webtech/coursework/chapter10/modify1.html

Code Completion Exercises

1. Read this exercise carefully and take your time to work out the logic. Your **chapter10** folder contains versions of **software1.html** and **software1.php** as well as a text file named **orders.txt** which contains a list of software orders. Each line in the file contains the name of an operating system (**Linux, Windows,** or **macOS**) followed by a colon, followed by the number of copies ordered, for example:

   macOS:2

   Add the necessary code to **software1.php** to process the data in **orders.txt** using a WHILE loop to calculate the total number of copies that have been ordered and to count the number of separate orders. For testing purposes, the correct total is **52** and the correct number of orders is **20** (but your code should still work correctly if you change the data in the file). Be sure to use a priming read and remember that you will need to parse each line to obtain the operating systems and number of copies for each order. The output and some other statements have been provided to save time.

Not sure what to do? Use your text editor to open orders.txt. Now take a piece of paper and pencil, and read the lines in the file to calculate the total and the count. Think about the procedure you are following when you do this; each time you read a line from the file and identify the operating system and number of copies, what do you add to your total and what do you add to your count? Now consider how to follow the same procedure in your code. Note that you need to extract both the operating system and the number from each line, even though you only need the number. **HINT:** Review the **process-wages4** example in the chapter, which also accumulate a total and a count; consider how you might modify this algorithm to meet the requirements of this exercise.

2. Read this exercise carefully and take your time to work out the logic. Your **chapter10** folder contains versions of **software2.html** and **software2.php** as well as a text file named **orders.txt** which contains a list of software orders. Each line in the file contains the name of an operating system (**Linux, Windows,** or **macOS**) followed by a colon, followed by the number of copies ordered, for example:

   macOS:2

   This exercise also processes **orders.txt** but this time you are asked to develop a WHILE loop that contains **selection structures**. Add the necessary code to **software2.php** to process the data in **orders.txt** and count the number of orders that request more than one copy, the number of copies of **Linux** software ordered, the number of copies of **macOS** software ordered, and the number of copies of **Windows** software ordered. The correct counts are **8** orders with multiple copies, **13** copies of Linux, **23** copies of macOS , and **16** copies of Windows (but your code should still work correctly if you change the data in the file). The output and some other statements have been provided to save time.

   Not sure what to do? Use your text editor to open **orders.txt**. Now take a piece of paper and pencil, and solve the problem as if you are the software2.php program. Each time you read a line from the file and identify the operating system and number of copies, what test should you use to decide whether or not to increment the variable that is counting the number of orders with more than one copy? Should you increment this count by 1 or by the number of copies? And then, what tests will you need to decide which operating system this order is for, and what value should you add to the total number of copies for that operating system? **HINT:** Review the **process-wages5** example in the chapter, but note that you will need **multiple** tests to count the number of orders with more than one copy, and to decide whether to add the number of copies to your Window, macOS, or Linux totals.

3. Read this exercise carefully and take your time to work out the logic. Your **chapter10** folder contains versions of **rome-report.html** and **rome-report.php** as well as a text file named **travel.dat** which contains a list of travel reservations. Each line in the travel.dat file contains a single reservation: the name of a destination, number of people traveling, and number of nights staying, for example:

    Rome:2:12
    Tokyo:3:15

    The program should read the file and report the number of reservations in the file for **Rome**, and the total number of people traveling to **Rome**. For testing purposes, the correct number of reservations for Rome is **7** and the correct number of people traveling to Rome is **18** (but your code should still work correctly if you change the data in the file). Note that the data file is named travel.**dat** and not travel.**txt**.

    Not sure what to do? Use your text editor to open travel.dat. Now take a piece of paper and pencil, and solve the problem as if you are the rome-report.php program. Each time you read a line from the file and identify the destination, number of people traveling, and number of nights staying, how are you deciding whether or not to increase the count of Rome reservations, and the total of the number of people traveling to Rome, and what amount are you adding to the count of Rome reservations and the total number of Rome travelers? Now consider how to follow the same procedure in your code. HINT: Review the process-wages5 example in the chapter. Although that code is designed to calculate a average you will see that it uses a similar procedure to the one you will need to develop for this exercise.

4. Read this exercise carefully and take your time to work out the logic. Your **chapter10** folder contains versions of **find-character.html** and **find-character.php** as well as a text file named **characters.txt** which contains a list of records with character information. Each line in the **characters.txt** file contains the name of a character, the character type, the number of health tokens, number of experience tokens, and number of supply tokens. Note that these are separated by **commas** (not colons) for example:

    Mozart,Elf,10,2,25

    The form in **find-character.html** asks the user for a character name to search for (this file does not need to be changed). The **find-character.php** program receives this name and must use a WHILE loop to read the file and display the information for the character if the name is found.

    Note that the program includes a variable **$notFound** which is assigned an initial value of **true**. If this variable still contains a value of **true** after the loop has been process, a message is displayed indicating that the character was not found, so be sure that your file-processing code includes a statement to set this variable to **false** if the character is found in the file. All required output statements are already provided, along with some other statements to save you some time.

Be sure to test your program with a character name that is in the file and a name that is not in the file. For testing purposes, the following names can be found in the file: Mozart, Leamus, Pete, Tara, Petal, Drake, Sert, Brian, Siren, and May.

Not sure what to do? Use your text editor to open characters.txt. Now take a piece of paper and pencil, and solve the problem as if you are the find-character.php program. Each time you read a line from the file and identify the name, type, and different token counts, what are you doing to decide whether or not this is the character you are looking for, and if it is, to display the character's information? **HINT**: Review **process-wages3.php** to see how to compare a name provided in an HTML form with a name in a file. Now consider how to follow the same procedure in your code.

5. Your **chapter10** folder contains **events.html**, **events.php**, and **events.txt**. The code in events.html does not need to be changed. The events.txt file contains a list of dates and performers, separated by colons, for example **1/15/2011:Rolling Stones**. Each event appears on a separate line. Open this file in your text editor and add 5 more lines with dates and performers (feel free to also change the events already listed).

Add the necessary code to events.php to display a list of dates and performers, where each date appears as an <h2> heading and each performer appears below the date as an <h1> heading. You will need a WHILE loop to read the entries from the file and each time you read a line you will need to extract the date and performer and then print this information. Be sure to test your work.

6. Your **chapter10** folder already contains **bus-travel.html**, **bus-travel.php**, and **bus-travel.txt**. You do not need to change **bus-travel.html** or **bus-travel.txt**. Your **bus-travel.txt** file is a trip log that contains information about business trips, each on a separate line. Each line contains a date and miles traveled, followed by four YES/NO entries to indicate whether or not the travel for that date included breakfast, lunch, dinner or hotel. Here are examples of the first two lines in the file:

```
3/15/2011:120:NO:YES:YES:YES:
3/16/2011:100:YES:YES:NO:NO:
```

Your job is to provide the code in **bus-travel.php** to process this file and calculate the reimbursement for these business trips. Open the file for reading, then use a WHILE loop to read each line from the file until the end of the file is reached. Each time a line is read from the file the six values must be extracted from the line and the reimbursement must be calculated as follows: The basic reimbursement will be the miles traveled x 0.35. If breakfast was included add 6.00 to the reimbursement. If lunch was included, add 8.50 to the reimbursement. If dinner was included, add 17.50 to the reimbursement. If a hotel was included, add 110.00 to the reimbursement. So for example the cost of the first line will be 120*0.35 + 8.50 + 17.50 + 110.00, which is $178.00.

(Note that these are the same calculations that you used in the corresponding Chapter 8 exercise. The only difference is that now the program should add the total reimbursement for each trip to a running total so that after the loop has completed, the total reimbursement can also be displayed.)

After the loop, the program should close the file and display the total reimbursement. If your code is correct this should amount to $884.60.

NOTE: For a more challenging and professional exercise, instead of just displaying the total reimbursement, display a table with rows for each trip, with columns that display the trip and reimbursement amounts for car use, breakfast, lunch, dinner, and hotel.

Chapter 11

Structured Data — Working with Arrays

Intended Learning Outcomes

After completing this chapter, you should be able to:

- Summarize key characteristics of arrays.
- Create an array using index value.
- Create an array using the array() function.
- Assign values to array elements.
- Access array elements in expressions.
- Create and work with arrays of strings.
- Use a variable to reference an array index.
- Use the sizeof() function to control a FOR loop.
- Use a WHILE loop to read data from a file into an array.
- Use a FOR loop to process an array.

Introduction

Computer programs use variables to store data temporarily while the application is executing. Until now, we have created a separate variable for each value that our program needs to store. Each of these variables may only contain a single value at any time.

The use of separate variables to store various data values works well for many purposes, but there are limitations. Consider a program that uses variables to store three scores—we can create three separate variables named $score1, $score2 and $score3. To sum these values we would write $score1 + $score2 + $score3. This a little tedious with just three variables but what if we needed to write a program to sum and display 20 scores, or 100 scores, or 1,000 scores? Using separate variables for each score is now not only tedious but unfeasible. And just imagine if you wrote this code and are then told to modify your code to work with a different number of scores!

Fortunately programming languages provide more complex data structures that allow us to work with large or small groups of data values much more efficiently. One of the most widely used data structures is an **array**, which can be used to store any number of data values and refer to these using a single variable name. In this chapter we will learn how to create array variables, how to store values in arrays, and how to access and process these values.

What Is an Array?

An array is a data structure that contains multiple data values, where each individual value is referenced using an **index** of some kind. The simplest type of array is indexed using integer values, beginning with an index value of **0**. Let's start with an example. Suppose that we have to write a program that needs to work with 5 scores. We could create 5 separate variables, and store our scores in each variable:

```
$score1 = 90;
$score2 = 87;
$score3 = 74;
$score4 = 80;
$score5 = 94;
```

But a better solution is to create a single **$scores** variable that will reference an array to store all 5 scores. Each of the five scores will be stored in an indexed location in the **$scores** array (we often refer to each indexed location as an array **element**). Here is one way to create an array of five scores in PHP:

```
$scores[0] = 90;
$scores[1] = 87;
$scores[2] = 74;
$scores[3] = 80;
$scores[4] = 94;
```

We now have a single array variable, **$scores**, which contains 5 values (90, 87, 74, 80, and 94). We can reference any of these values using the appropriate index position within the array, for example $scores [2] refers to the **third** element which contains the value **74**. Note that the five elements are indexed from 0 to 4 and not from 1 to 5 as you might expect. The reason for this is explained later in the chapter. Also note that the index value is indicated inside **square brackets** []. Be sure to use square brackets when working with array index values—do not use curly braces or parentheses.

You can also create an array of values in PHP by calling the **array**() function and sending all of the values to be assigned to the array as a list of arguments:

```
$scores = array (90, 87, 74, 80, 94);
```

This statement achieves the same result as the previous five statements combined. Instead of assigning values to each array element separately, we use the **array()** function to create the entire array in a single statement. In this example, the **array()** function creates an array with five index values ($scores[0], $scores[1], $scores[2], $scores[3], and $scores[4]), and assigns the values 90, 87, 74, 80 and 94 to these indexed locations. The function returns the complete array which is then assigned to the $scores variable.

The **array()** function can be used most effectively when the values that are to be assigned to the array are known at the time the array is created. As we shall see, that is not always the case.

Working with Array Elements

You can store, change, and access values in any element of an array variable just as with any other variable; the only difference is that you need to include the index position to identify which element is to be referenced.

You can **assign** a value to any position in an array. Just as with any variable, if an array element already contains a value, the previous value is replaced.

Here are three examples:

```
$scores[2] = 85;
$scores[3] = $exam1 * 0.85;
$scores[4] = $scores[2] + 5;
```

You can use an array element as part of an **expression**. Here are three examples:

```
$revisedScore = $scores[0] + 10;

$averageScore = ($scores[0] + $scores[1] + $scores[2] +
        $scores[3] + $scores[4]) / 5;

if ($scores[1] >= 60)
  print("PASS!");
else
  print("FAIL!");
```

(NOTE: if the array variable is referenced on the right side of an assignment, be sure that it has already received a value. For example the first example above adds 10 to the value already stored in **$scores[0]**, so **$scores[0]** should have been assigned a value before this statement is executed.)

You can **update** a value that was previously assigned to an array element. The following two examples both add a number to the value currently stored in an array element, and store the result back into the same element (replacing the previous value):

```
$scores[4] = $scores[4] + 5;
$scores[2] = $scores[2] + 1;
```

Extending an Array

Unlike most programming languages, PHP allows you to add a new element to an array at any time. For example, you can add a sixth and seventh element to the **$scores** array simply by creating these elements:

```
$scores[5] = 75;
$scores[6] = 65;
```

PHP also allows you to add new elements to the end of an array without specifying the index position:

```
$scores[] = 80;
$scores[] = 55;
```

When elements are added in this way, the new elements are given index positions that follow on from the previous highest index values. In this case, if our **$scores** array already has seven elements, indexed from 0 to 6, two new elements are created at index positions 7 and 8. These new elements (**$scores[7]** and **$scores[8]**) contain the values 80 and 55 respectively. This feature can be very useful where new elements are added to an existing array since your application does not have to determine the next index value.

PHP provides a large number of functions for working with arrays. See Chapter 16 for additional information concerning these functions.

Displaying Array Values

You can display array values in PHP **print()** statements just as any other variables. For example to display a value from the **$scores** array:

```
print("<p> SCORE 1: $scores[0]</p>");
```

When referring to an array variable directly in a print statement, be sure that there are no spaces between the array name and the square brackets containing the index.

The following example shows how you might print a **$scores** array containing five scores in an HTML table:

```
print("<h1>SCORES</h1>
   <table>
   <tr><td>SCORE 1</td><td>$scores[0]</td></tr>
   <tr><td>SCORE 2</td><td>$scores[1]</td></tr>
   <tr><td>SCORE 3</td><td>$scores[2]</td></tr>
   <tr><td>SCORE 4</td><td>$scores[3]</td></tr>
   <tr><td>SCORE 5</td><td>$scores[4]</td></tr>
   </table>");
```

If you're wondering how you would achieve this with an array containing many more values, we will explain that shortly.

Receiving Scores into an Array from an HTML Form

The following requirement will demonstrate various ways of working with array elements:

arrays1 requirement:

*Create an application that provides a form for the user to submit five scores. The first three scores are **exam** scores, the fourth score is an **essay** score and the fifth score is a **project** score.*

*The applications should receive the five scores and calculate the average of the three **exam** scores. If this average is 90 or above, a 5 point **bonus** should be added to the **project** score, but the project score should not exceed 100.*

*The application should display the five scores, the **total** of the five scores, the **average** of the three exam scores, and an **explanatory message** concerning the project score.*

Here is the HTML code for **arrays1.html**:

```html
<html>
<head>
  <title>Scores Entry Form </title>
  <link rel="stylesheet" type="text/css" href="sample.css">
</head>
<body>
  <h1>Score Entry Form</h1>
  <form action="arrays1.php" method="post">
  <label>Score for Exam 1:
  <input type="text" size="5" name="exam1"></label>
  <label>Score for Exam 2:
  <input type="text" size="5" name="exam2"></label>
  <label>Score for Exam 3:
      <input type="text" size="5" name="exam3"></label>
  <label>Essay score
  <input type="text" size="5" name="essay"></label>
  <label>Project score:
  <input type="text" size="5" name="project"></label>
  <input class="submit" type="submit" value="Submit the
      Scores">
  </form>
</body>
</html>
```

Code Example: arrays1.html

Our PHP program (**arrays1.php**) will receive the five values from the form, assign each of these values to an element of the **$scores** array, and then process the array as indicated by the application requirements. Here is the code for **arrays1.php**:

```html
<html>
<head>
  <title> Scores Report</title>
  <link rel="stylesheet" type="text/css" href="sample.css">
</head>
<body>
```

```php
<h1>Scores report </h1>

<?php
  $scores[0] = $_POST['exam1'];
  $scores[1] = $_POST['exam2'];
  $scores[2] = $_POST['exam3'];
  $scores[3] = $_POST['essay'];
  $scores[4] = $_POST['project'];

  $averageExamScore = ($scores[0]+$scores[1]+$scores[2]) / 3;

  If ($averageExamScore >= 90)
  {
    if ($scores[4] > 95)
      $scores[4] = 100;
    else
      $scores[4] = $scores[4] + 5 ;
  }

  $totalScore = $scores[0] + $scores[1] + $scores[2] +
        $scores[3] + $scores[4];

  print ("Exam 1: $scores[0]<br>");
  print ("Exam 2: $scores[1]<br>");
  print ("Exam 3: $scores[2]<br>");
  print ("Essay : $scores[3]<br>");
  print ("Project: $scores[4]<br>");
  print ("<p>Your total score is: <strong>$totalScore </strong>
    out of a possible 500 points.</p>");

  print ("<p>Your average for the three exams is: <strong>
    $averageExamScore</strong>. If this average is 90 or
    above, 5 points has been added to your project score
    (up to a maximum project score of 100 points).</p>");
?>
</body>
</html>
```

Code Example: arrays1.php

When receiving values from a form, most of our examples so far have used PHP variables with the same name as the **name** attribute in the form. This is not required and here we simply assign the five values received from the form to indexed elements of the $scores array:

```
$scores[0] = $_POST['exam1'];
$scores[1] = $_POST['exam2'];
$scores[2] = $_POST['exam3'];
$scores[3] = $_POST['essay'];
$scores[4] = $_POST['project'];
```

These statements could have been written as follows:

```
$scores[] = $_POST['exam1'];
$scores[] = $_POST['exam2'];
$scores[] = $_POST['exam3'];
$scores[] = $_POST['essay'];
$scores[] = $_POST['project'];
```

since PHP will automatically create another array element each time a value is assigned to $scores[].

The $scores array could also have been created using the **array()** function:

```
$scores = array ($_POST['exam1'], $_POST['exam2'],
        $_POST['exam3'], $_POST['essay'], $_POST['project']);
```

In this case, we are using the **array()** function to create the array and assign all five values as a list enclosed in parentheses. However, as you can see, this makes the code harder to read.

The next instruction calculates the **average** of the three exam scores, which are stored in $scores[0], $scores[1], and $scores[3]. These three values are added, and the result is divided by 3:

```
$averageExamScore = ($scores[0]+$scores[1]+$scores[2]) / 3;
```

The requirements indicate that the project score should be increased by 5 points (up to a maximum of 100) if this average is above 90. The next code section achieves this by **nesting** an IF..ELSE structure inside an IF structure. The IF structure tests if $averageExamScore is above 90, and, **only** if it is, the **IF..ELSE** structure is executed and either **assigns 100 to $scores[4]** (if $scores[4] is already greater than 95), or **else adds 5** to $scores[4]:

```
if ($averageExamScore >= 90)

{

   if ($scores[4] > 95)

      $scores[4] = 100;

   else

      $scores[4] = $scores[4] + 5 ;

}
```

This provides a useful example of **nested selection statements**. Note that, since the **IF..ELSE** statement is located inside the outer **IF** statement, it will only execute if the test for the outer **IF** statement is **true**, if the test is **false** the **IF..ELSE** statement will be skipped entirely. Note also that there are **three possible paths** through this code, and each one should be tested to be sure the program works as expected: an average exam score of **89 or less** would test that the IF statement is skipped, with no changes to the project score; an average exam score of **90 or above** and a project score **above 95** would test that the project is assigned **100**; and an average exam score of **90 or above** and a project score of **95 or less** would test that the project score is increased by 5 points.

The next instruction calculates the **total score** by adding the values of all five array elements:

```
$totalScore = $scores[0] + $scores[1] + $scores[2] +

$scores[3] + $scores[4];
```

The remaining print statements display and explain the results. Figure 11-1 shows a sample interaction.

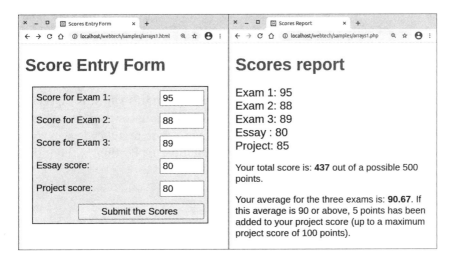

Figure 11-1: arrays1.html and arrays1.php screenshots

Arrays of Strings

Arrays can be used to store any type of data, and it is often useful to create arrays that contain character strings. For example, applications must often include statements to display various error messages. Instead of including these messages directly in your **print**() statements, it can be useful to store all the error messages in an array and then refer to them as needed. Here is how we might construct an array of standard error messages:

```
$errorMessage[0] = "ERROR: You submitted a form with empty
   fields";
$errorMessage[1] = "ERROR: You submitted non-numeric data";
$errorMessage[2] = "ERROR: The value is out of range";
$errorMessage[3] = "ERROR: Incorrect User ID";
$errorMessage[4] = "ERROR: Incorrect Password";
```

Now your program can print any error message by referencing the appropriate array element. Here are three examples:

```
if (empty ($hoursWorked) OR empty ($hourlyWage))
   print ("<p>$errorMessage[0] </p>");
if ($score[0] < 0 OR $score[0] > 100)
   print ("<p>$errorMessage[2] </p>");
if ($password != $correctPassword)
   print ("<p>$errorMessage[4] </p>");
```

This may not seem very useful, after all why not simply include the appropriate error message directly in your **print**() statements? However there are a number of advantages to this approach. First it simply helps us organize our messages and makes them easy to find if we wish to change them. Second, if we need to use the same message in more than one location in our application we can avoid duplicating the message. And third, we can share this entire array of standard error messages among multiple Web applications! That means that we can use the same array in different applications without having to duplicate all that code. This approach also promotes a common look and feel between our programs which is especially important when we are developing a number of applications for the same company or Web site. In the next chapter we will learn how to store useful code such as arrays in separate files and then include this code in multiple applications without the need to copy the code.

Using a Variable as an Array Index

Let's consider another example of an array of strings in order to demonstrate how a variable can be used as an array index. Consider the following requirements, designed to help book-keeping students decide which course module to start with:

---

book-keeping requirement:

Write a program that asks the user to provide their current book-keeping skill level (between 0 and 5), and responds with the appropriate course to begin their training, as follows: a level of 0 indicates "BKG 101: Getting Started"; 1 indicates "BKG 115: Book-Keeping Fundamentals"; 2 indicates "BKG 120: Working with Spreadsheets"; 3 indicates "BKG 130: Business Processes 1"; 4 indicates "BKG 230: Business Processes 2"; and 5 indicates "BKG 240: Final Project, Starting a Business".

The **book-keeping.html** page will include a drop down list in a Web form to obtain the user's estimated experience:

```
<form action = "book-keeping.php" method = "post" >
<label>Rate your experience
  <select name = "experience">
    <option>0</option>
    <option>1</option>
    <option>2</option>
    <option>3</option>
    <option>4</option>
    <option>5</option>
  </select></label>
<input class="submit" type = "submit" value = "Submit">
</form>
```

The **book-keeping.php** page will define an array that contains 6 different module descriptions, as follows:

```
$module[0]  = "BKG 101: Getting Started";

$module[1]  = "BKG 115: Book-Keeping Fundamentals";

$module[2]  = "BKG 120: Working with Spreadsheets";

$module[3]  = "BKG 130: Business Processes 1";

$module[4]  = "BKG 230: Business Processes 2";

$module[5]  = "BKG 240: Final Project, Starting a Business";
```

The program will receive the user's experience level as **$_POST["experience"]**, save this value to a variable named **$experience**, and then use **$experience** to select a course from the **$module** array:

```
$experience  = $_POST['experience'];


print ("<p>Based on your experience, we suggest that you
begin
with:</p><p><strong>".$module[$experience]."</strong></p>");
```

Figure 11-2 shows a sample interaction.

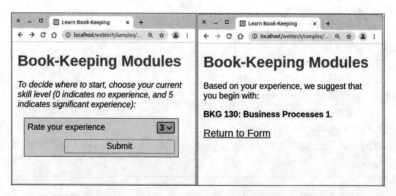

Figure 11-2: book-keeping.html and book-keeping.php screenshots

Do you see how this works? The user's experience (a value between 0 and 5) is stored in **$experience**. The program can then use **$module[$experience]** to choose a string from the **$module** array. Using a variable to store the index of an array element can be useful for a wide range of requirements; next you will learn how a **FOR** loop can use the loop control variable to work with a different array element each time the loop repeats.

How Large Is the Array?

As we will see, it is often useful to determine the number of elements that an array contains (often termed the **length** of an array). You can always obtain the length of an array using the **sizeof**() function, for example **sizeof**($scores) would return 5 if there are 5 elements in the $scores array. Note that the **sizeof**() function returns the **total** number of elements in the array and not the **index position** of the last element (in the case of 5 elements the last index position would be 4 since the first element is in index position 0).

The sizeof() function is especially useful when using a FOR loop to process an array. This topic will be covered later in the chapter.

Why Do Array Indices Begin with 0 and Not 1?

You may be wondering why array index positions begin with 0 and not 1. Recall that all variables are names for memory locations. Since an array uses a single name to refer to an area of memory that will be used to store multiple values, it must be able to keep track of the location of each value. The index position indicates the number of elements that each element is **offset** from the **first** memory location of the array. So $scores[2] is stored in a location that begins 2 elements from the array's starting memory location. The reason that the first index position is 0 is that the first element in the array is stored in a location that is 0 elements from the array's starting memory location (in other words, at the start of the memory location of the array).

Using FOR Loops with Arrays

Often we need to write instructions that process all of the values stored in an array. For example here is the **print**() statement that we used earlier to display the five values in the $scores array as a table:

```
print("<h1>SCORES</h1>
<table>
<tr><td>SCORE 1</td><td>$scores[0]</td></tr>
<tr><td>SCORE 2</td><td>$scores[1]</td></tr>
<tr><td>SCORE 3</td><td>$scores[2]</td></tr>
<tr><td>SCORE 4</td><td>$scores[3]</td></tr>
<tr><td>SCORE 5</td><td>$scores[4]</td></tr>
</table>");
```

The following statement finds the sum of the five values in the **$scores** array:

```
$totalScore = $scores[0] + $scores[1] + $scores[2] +
              $scores[3] + $scores[4];
```

It is tedious to write out statements that must reference every element in an array! Consider what these two examples would look like if the array contained 100 elements or 1,000 elements! In fact statements like this are often unfeasible since it is not always known in advance how many elements might be stored in an array.

FOR loops provide us with a very efficient way to process all the elements of an array for any purpose. Remember that we use a counting variable to control the number of times that a FOR loop repeats. What if we create a FOR loop with a counting variable that increments from 0 to the last index position in an array? Now we can use the counting variable inside the loop to refer to a different array index position each time that the loop repeats.

Here is a simple FOR loop that uses the loop counting variable to display the values in the **$scores** array:

```
print("<h1>SCORES</h1>");
for ($i = 0; $i < 5; $i = $i + 1)
{
    print("<p>$scores[$i]</p>");
}
```

The FOR loop is designed with a counting variable named **$i**, and the loop will repeat five times. The variable **$i** is also used **inside** the loop as the array **index**. The first time the loop executes, **$i** will have the value 0, and so **$scores[0]** will be printed. The second time the loop executes, **$i** will have the value 1, and so **$scores[1]** will be printed, and so on. It is important that the initial value of **$i** is 0, and that the loop condition is **$i** < 5 and not **$i** <= 5 since the array indices are 0, 1, 2, 3, 4.

The decision to name the counting variable **$i** may surprise you since we have talked about the importance of meaningful variables names. It is traditional (but not required) to use the names **$i**, **$j**, and **$k** to represent array indexing variables in loop structures.

If the **$scores** array contained 100 elements, we would simply change **$i** < 5 in the loop heading to **$i** < 100.

Using the sizeof() Function to Control a FOR Loop

This loop becomes even more useful if we use the **sizeof()** function to control the number of times that the loop repeats:

```
print("<h1>SCORES</h1>");
for ($i = 0; $i < sizeof($scores); $i = $i + 1)
{
    print("<p>$scores[$i]</p>");
}
```

Now instead of $i < 5, we use $i < sizeof($scores) to control the number of repetitions. This ensures that the loop will process the entire array no matter how many elements are in the array! If we change the number of scores that are stored in the array we no longer have to change the loop since the sizeof() function will always provide the correct length. Do you see how efficient this is? Not only does this loop process a $scores array containing 5 scores, but the same loop would work with no change if the $scores array contained 100 scores, or 1,000 scores!Again, note that the loop test must be $i < sizeof($scores) and not $i <= sizeof($scores). That's because the last index position is one **less** than the size of the array (remember that the array index positions begin with 0).

Summing and Averaging the Values in an Array

Let's see how we can use a FOR loop to find the **sum** and **average** of the values stored in our **$scores** array:

```
$sum = 0;
  for ($i = 0; $i < sizeof($scores); $i = $i + 1)
  {
    $sum = $sum + $scores[$i];
  }
$average = $sum / sizeof($scores);
```

Before we begin the FOR loop we create a **$sum** variable and initialize this to 0. Once again the loop is controlled by a counting variable (**$i**) which will be used inside the loop to refer to each index position in the array. Each time the loop repeats, the value of the next array element is added to the value stored in the **$sum** variable. The result is assigned to **$sum**, replacing the previous value. By the time the loop has completed, the **$sum** variable contains the sum of all the values in the array.

Once the loop has completed, we also use the **sizeof()** function to calculate the average by dividing the value stored in the **$sum** variable by the length of array. Since we use the **sizeof()** function to control the loop **and** to calculate the average, this code will work no matter how many values are stored in the **$scores** array.

NOTE: as always, when you are working with loops like this, think carefully about the statements that should appear **before** the loop, the statements that are **part of** the loop, and the statements that should **follow** the loop. For example you would not want to include the statement **$sum = 0;** inside the loop structure since that would reset the **$sum** variable to 0 each time the loop repeated!

Counting Selected Values in an Array

Our array-handling loops can include any statements necessary to perform the required processing. Here is a FOR loop that includes an IF structure to count the number of **passing** scores in our **$scores** array (assuming that a passing score is 60 or above):

```
$numPassingScores = 0;

for ($i = 0; $i < sizeof($scores); $i = $i + 1)
{
   if ($scores[$i] >= 60)
      $numPassingScores = $numPassingScores + 1;
}
```

In this example, each time through the loop, the program tests whether the score at the current index position is at least 60. If it is, then 1 is added the count of passing scores.

Multiple Operations on an Array

Let's put together the previous examples, and write a program that: creates an array of 10 scores; displays the scores in a table; calculates the sum and average; counts the number of passing and failing scores; and displays the results. The program uses a single FOR loop to perform all of the necessary operations on the array. Here is the code for **arrays2.php**:

```
<html>
<head>
   <title>SCORES REPORT</title>
   <link rel="stylesheet" type="text/css" href="sample.css">
</head>
<body>
   <?php
      $scores = array(80, 55, 75, 97, 88, 82, 59, 60, 96, 78);
      $sum = 0;
      $numPassingScores = 0;
```

```
    print("<h1>SCORES REPORT</h1>");
    print("<table>");

    for($i = 0; $i < sizeof($scores); $i = $i + 1)
    {
      $scoreNum = $i + 1;
      print("<tr><td>SCORE $scoreNum</td>
             <td>$scores[$i]</td></tr>");

      $sum = $sum + $scores[$i];

      if ($scores[$i] >= 60)
        $numPassingScores = $numPassingScores + 1;
    }
    print("</table>");

    $numFailingScores = sizeof($scores) - $numPassingScores;
    $average = $sum / sizeof($scores);

    print("<p>AVERAGE SCORE: $average <br>");
    print("NUMBER OF PASSING SCORES: $numPassingScores
<br>");
    print("NUMBER OF FAILING SCORES: $numFailingScores
</p>");
    ?>
</body>
</html>
```

Code Example: arrays2.php

In this example, the **array**() function is used to assign 10 scores to the **$scores** array.

The FOR loop counting variable is used to reference a new array element each time the loop repeats. The loop includes statements to: display the value of the current element in a table row; add this score to the sum of the scores; add 1 to the number of passing scores if the score is 60 or above.

Following the FOR loop, the number of failing scores is calculated by subtracting the number of passing scores from the total number of scores in the array. The average of the ten scores is also calculated. The **sizeof**() function is used in both calculations in order to determine the total number of scores in the array. If you look through this code carefully you will see that you can change the number of scores initially assigned to the scores array with no other changes to the code required. This code will work correctly with any number of scores.

Figure 11-2 shows the output from **arrays2.php**. Note that the scores are numbered from 1 to 10, even though the array is indexed from 0 to 9. In order to accomplish this, the code includes a variable named **$scoreNum** which is assigned a value 1 greater than the current index position each time that the loop repeats.

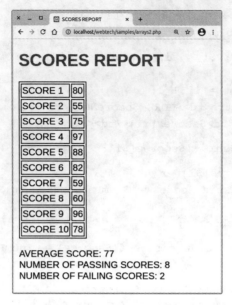

Figure 11-2: arrays2.php screenshot

Reading Data from a File into an Array

We can also read data from a file (or database) into an array. We can open the file, use a loop to read each line from the file into an array and then close the file. After closing the file, we can process the data stored in the array instead of processing this data while the file remains open.

This is actually quite an important design decision: whether to (a) **process** the lines of a file in the same loop that reads these lines **from** the file (as you learned in chapters 9 and 10), or (b) first read **all** the lines from the file into an array, close the file, and then process the array.

The advantage of processing the lines in the file directly is that your program does not need to set aside additional memory to copy the entire contents of the file into an array. Instead each line is read and processed without being stored for further reference. This is often a good approach when processing very large files where memory usage is a significant issue.

However the disadvantage of this approach is that the file must be left open for a longer period while all the lines are processed. The advantage of first reading the contents of the file into an array and then processing the array is that the file can be opened and closed much more quickly, making it available for other applications that may need to access the file.

Another advantage of first reading the data into an array is that this separates the code that **obtains** the data from the code that **processes** the data. As long as the code that reads the file stores the data in an array, the processing code will still work. This is useful, for example, if the data source changes, or if you want to use the same data-processing code for different applications.

Let's look at an example. The following requirements may seem familiar:

Arrays3 requirement:

Write a program that processes a file named rainfall2007.txt. The file contains the year followed by 12 monthly rainfall amounts, each on a separate line. The program should display the year, total rainfall for the year, the average monthly rainfall, highest monthly rainfall amount and lowest monthly rainfall amount.

We worked with the same requirements to develop **rainfall2.php** in Chapter 9. Here we will meet these requirements by first using an array to read the 12 rainfall values from the file, then processing the array to obtain the required results.

```
arrays3.php algorithm:

  Open rainfall2007.txt as rainfallData for reading

  Read year from rainData
  FOR count = 0 TO 11
    read rainfall[count] from rainData
  ENDFOR

  Close rainData

  totalRainfall = 0
  FOR count = 0 TO 11
    totalRainfall = totalRainfall + rainfall[count]
    IF count == 0 OR rainfall[count] > highestRainfall
      highestRainfall = rainfall[count]
    ENDIF
    IF count == 0 OR rainfall[count] < lowestRainfall
      lowestRainfall = rainfall[count]
    ENDIF
  ENDFOR

  avgRainfall = totalRainfall / 12

  Display year, totalRainfall, avgRainfall, highestRainfall,
    lowestRainfall
END
```

We open the data file, read the year, then use a FOR loop to read the 12 rainfall amounts into an array (named **rainfall**), then close the file. With this approach we have opened the file only long enough to obtain the year and rainfall amounts, and then closed it. The rainfall values are now stored in an array and we use a second FOR loop to process these values by accessing each element of the array in turn.

Here is the PHP code for arrays3.php:

```
<html>
<head>
  <title>RAINFALL</title>
  <link rel="stylesheet" type="text/css" href="sample.css">
</head>
<body>
  <?php
    $rainDataFile = fopen("rainfall2007.txt","r");
    $year = trim(fgets($rainDataFile));

    for ($i = 0; $i < 12; $i = $i + 1)
    {
      $rainfall[$i] = trim(fgets($rainDataFile));
    }
    fclose($rainDataFile);

    $totalRainfall = 0;
    for ($i = 0; $i < sizeof($rainfall); $i = $i + 1)
    {
      $totalRainfall = $totalRainfall + $rainfall[$i];

      if ($i == 0 OR $rainfall[$i] > $highestRainfall)
        $highestRainfall = $rainfall[$i] ;

      if ($i == 0 OR $rainfall[$i] < $lowestRainfall)
        $lowestRainfall = $rainfall[$i];
    }

    $avgRainfall = $totalRainfall / sizeof($rainfall);

    print("<h1>RAINFALL SUMMARY FOR $year</h1>");
    print("<p>TOTAL RAINFALL: $totalRainfall.</p>");
    print("<p>AVERAGE MONTHLY RAINFALL: $avgRainfall.</p>");
    print("<p>HIGHEST MONTHLY RAINFALL:
          $highestRainfall.</p>");
    print("<p>LOWEST MONTHLY RAINFALL: $lowestRainfall.</p>");
  ?>
</body>
</html>
```

Code Example: arrays3.php

As you can see, we now use two FOR loops, one to read the contents of the file into the array, and the second to process the array. Our new version requires the use of additional memory to store the array, however the file is opened and closed much faster.

By using an array, we have also separated two operations: **obtaining** the data and **processing** the data. This turns out to be very useful. If we need to obtain our rainfall data from some other source, we can replace the first loop with new code. As long as the new code stores the rainfall data in the **$rainfall** array, the second FOR loop will process the data correctly with no changes required.

Note that the first FOR loop cannot be controlled by the **sizeof()** function but must be explicitly directed to run **12** times. That's because the array size will not become 12 until **after** this loop has completed since the loop is adding a new element to the array with each repetition.

Reading Data into an Array from a File of Unknown Length

We were able to use a FOR loop in the last example because we were told that the file contained exactly 12 rainfall amounts. Often however we want to read values into an array from a file that of unknown length. In these cases we can use a WHILE loop and test for the end of file marker to decide when to stop reading more lines from the file.

In **arrays2.php** we assigned 10 scores to an array of scores and then processed the scores. Let's modify that program to read scores from a file named **scores1.txt**.

The replacement code will need to open the file, use a WHILE loop to read scores from the file until the EOF marker is found, and close the file, as follows:

```
$scoreFile = fopen("scores1.txt", "r");
$i = 0;
$score = trim(fgets($scoreFile));

while (!feof($scoreFile))
{
  $scores[$i] = $score;
  $score = trim(fgets($scoreFile));
  $i = $i + 1;
}
fclose($scoreFile);
```

Since a WHILE loop does not normally use a counting variable, we have created a variable **$i** to reference the next index position in the **$scores** array as the loop repeats. Before the loop begins, **$i** is assigned the value 0. The first line of the file is read. If this line does not contain the end of file marker, the line is processed inside the loop. The score is assigned to the next element of **$scores**, the next line is then read from the file, and the value of **$i** is incremented by 1 so that the next value read from the file will be assigned to the next index location in the array.

This sequence repeats until the end of file marker is found. If you trace through this carefully using some sample data you will see that the code correctly reads all scores from the file and assigns each score to the next element in the **$scores** array, using **$i** to indicate the appropriate index value. The code will work no matter how many scores are stored in the file (this example assumes that each score is stored on a separate line).

Take time to understand this code. Pay special attention to the need to initialize **$i** to **0** before the loop begins, and to add 1 to the value of **$i** each time the loop repeats. The complete program is provided in your samples folder as **arrays4.php**. Consider the importance of the **sizeof()** function in this code. We must use this function to determine the length of the array since we do not know the actual number of elements that will be stored in the **$scores** array until the program actually executes.

Note that this code example uses a variable named **$score** and another variable named $scores. Be careful not to confuse these two variables, or to use one where the other should be used. The **$score** variable is a simple variable used to store the next score that is read from the file. The **$scores** variable is an array variable, used to store all the scores. To avoid confusion you might prefer to change the name of **$score** to $nextScore. You could also eliminate the need for the **$score** variable entirely by reading the values directly from the file into the array, for example:

```
$scoreFile = fopen("scores1.txt", "r");
$i = 0;
$scores[$i] = trim(fgets($scoreFile));
while (!feof($scoreFile))
{
   $scores[$i] = trim(fgets($scoreFile));
   $i = $i + 1;
}
fclose($scoreFile);
```

Using [] with no Index Value

You may recall that PHP has a special feature that allows you to add new elements to an array without specifying the index position. We could take advantage of this feature as follows:

```
$scoreFile = fopen("scores1.txt", "r");
$score = trim(fgets($scoreFile));
while (!feof($scoreFile))
{
   $scores[] = $score;
   $score = trim(fgets($scoreFile));
}
fclose($scoreFile);
```

And here is the same code reading the values from the file directly into the array variable:

```
$scoreFile = fopen("scores1.txt", "r");
$scores[] = trim(fgets($scoreFile));

while (!feof($scoreFile))
{
        $scores[] = trim(fgets($scoreFile));
}
fclose($scoreFile);
```

Although this is a very handy feature in PHP, we have demonstrated how an index variable can be used with a WHILE loop since this can be useful for other purposes (and most programming languages require the use of an indexing variable).

Reading Selected Data from a File into an Array

In our last example, we read all the scores from the scores1.txt file into an array. What if, for our purposes, we only need an array that contains the passing scores (scores of 60 or above)? In that case we can simply test each score that we read from the file and decide whether or not to add it to the array, based on the score value:

```
$scoreFile = fopen("scores1.txt", "r");
$i = 0;
$nextScore = trim(fgets($scoreFile));

while (!feof($scoreFile))
{
  if ($nextScore >= 60)
  {
    $passingScores[$i] = $nextScore;
    $i = $i + 1;
  }
  $nextScore = trim(fgets($scoreFile));
}
fclose($scoreFile);

print("<p>There are ".sizeof($passingScores)." passing scores in
  the file.</p>");
```

Since the array only contains scores that are 60 or above, we can use the sizeof() function to obtain the number of passing scores that were in the file.

It is important to understand which code should be located within the braces of the IF structure, and which should not. The statements:

```
$passingScores[$i] = $nextScore;
$i = $i + 1;
```

are located inside the braces since these two statements should only execute if the next score is to be added to the array. And it is essential that the statement:

```
$nextScore = trim(fgets($scoreFile));
```

is not inside the braces, since we want the program to read the next line from the file whether or not the current score is a passing score.

Reading Data from a File into Multiple Arrays

We might also want to read the scores from the file into two arrays, where one array will store the passing scores and one will store the failing scores. We can do this with some careful modifications:

```
$scoreFile = fopen("scores1.txt", "r");
$i = 0;
$j = 0;
$nextScore = trim(fgets($scoreFile));
while (!feof($scoreFile))
{
   if ($nextScore >= 60)
   {
      $passingScores[$i] = $nextScore;
      $i = $i + 1;
   }
   else
   {
      $failingScores[$j] = $nextScore;
      $j = $j + 1;
   }
   $nextScore = trim(fgets($scoreFile));
}

fclose($scoreFile);

print("<p>There are ".sizeof($passingScores)." passing scores in
   the file.</p>");
print("<p>There are ".sizeof($failingScores)." failing scores in
   the file.</p>");
```

We have added an ELSE section to our IF structure, and we are now using a $failingScores array to store any failing scores. But note also that we now need two indexing variables, one for each array. We use $i to keep track of the index of the $passingScores array, and $j to keep track of the index position of the $failingScores array. And once again, note that the fgets() statement is not included in either the IF or ELSE section, since we want to read the next score no matter whether the current score is a passing or failing score.

Reading Selected Data from a File of Records into an Array

We may sometimes need to read values from a file that contains records on each line. For example, scores5.txt contains the gender of each student as well as the score, in the following format:

```
m:70
f:85
f:69
```

In other words, each line contains a gender ("m" or "f") followed by a colon followed by a score.

If we just wanted to read all the scores from this file into an array, we can do this using the explode() and list() functions to extract the two values from each line, and then simply ignoring the gender:

```
$scoreFile = fopen("scores5.txt", "r");
$i = 0;
$nextRecord = trim(fgets($scoreFile));

while (!feof($scoreFile))
{
    list($gender, $score) = explode(":", $nextRecord);
    $scores[$i] = $score;
    $i = $i + 1;
    $nextRecord = trim(fgets($scoreFile));
}

fclose($scoreFile);
```

But what if we need to store the scores of male and female students in two separate arrays? We can test the gender on each line to decide which array the score belongs to:

```
$scoreFile = fopen("scores5.txt", "r");
$i = 0;
$j = 0;
$nextRecord = trim(fgets($scoreFile));
while (!feof($scoreFile))
{
  list($gender, $score) = explode(":", $nextRecord);
  if ($gender == "f")
  {
    $femaleScores[$i] = $score;
    $i = $i + 1;
  }
  else
  {
    $maleScores[$j] = $score;
    $j = $j + 1;
  }

  $nextRecord = trim(fgets($scoreFile));
}
fclose($scoreFile);

print("<p>There are ".sizeof($femaleScores)." female scores in
  the file.</p>");
print("<p>There are ".sizeof($maleScores)." male scores in the
  file.</p>");
```

This example is provided in the arrays.6.php file in your samples folder. It would of course be easy to add additional code to process these two arrays and generate useful statistics regarding the performance of male and female students.

More About the explode() and list() Functions

Throughout this book we have used the explode() and list() functions to parse records that have been read from a text file. Now that we know something about arrays we can investigate the way these functions actually work, and learn how to use them for other purposes.

Let's assume that a variable named **$appointment** contains the character string **"Dentist:10:15:AM"** that has been previously read from a file. This character string contains four values separated by colons: the type of appointment ("Dentist"), the hour

("10"), the minutes ("15"), and the time of day ("AM"). As we have already seen we can extract these four values into separate variables using the explode()and list() functions as follows:

```
list($appointmentType, $hour, $minutes, $timeOfDay) =
    explode(":", $appointment);
```

After this statement has executed, $appointmentType will contain "Dentist", $hour contains "10", $minutes contains "15", and $timeOfDay contains "AM".

Let's look more closely at what is happening here. The explode() function receives a separator value (":") and a string to be parsed ("Dentist:10:15:AM"). The function parses the string based on the separator and **returns an array that contains the extracted values**. In this case the function returns an array of four elements where the element [0] contains "Dentist", element [1] contains "10", element [2] contains "15", and element [3] contains "AM".

The list() function is a function that receives any array of values, extracts each value from the array, and assigns these values to the variables that are listed as arguments. So in this example the value stored in position [0] of the array ("Dentist") is assigned to the variable $appointmentType, the value stored in position [1] of the array ("10") is assigned to the variable $hour, the value stored in position [2] of the array ("15") is assigned to the variable $minutes, and the value stored in position [3] of the array ("AM") is assigned to the variable $timeOfDay.

We have been using the explode() and list() functions together, however this is not required. For example we might just want to store the values that have been extracted by the explode() function into an array:

```
$myAppointment = explode(":", $appointment);
```

The $myAppointment variable now contains an array with four values, for example $myAppointment[0] contains "Dentist", and so on. This variable can then be used just like any other array variable.

Similarly the list() function can be used with any array, not just an array that has been created by the explode() function. For example, perhaps your program includes an array named $regionalSales that has been assigned four regional sales figures:

```
$regionalSales = array(3245, 4674, 1674, 5878);
```

If you need to assign these four values into separate variables, you can achieve this using the list() function:

```
list($northRegion, $southRegion, $westRegion, $eastRegion) =
    $regionalSales;
```

In this case, the list() function assigns the elements of the $regionalSales array to each of the four variables, so that $northRegion now contains "3245", $southRegion contains "4674", and so on.

In summary, we can use the explode() function to parse any string that includes multiple values separated by a delimiter of some kind. The function returns an array of indexed elements, where each element contains one of the parsed values. Similarly, the list() function can be used to extract values from any array and store these values in separate variables.

A Special Loop for Processing Arrays — FOREACH

It is an extremely common requirement to process every element in an array, one element at a time, and many current programming languages provide a special simplified loop for exactly this purpose, usually known as a FOREACH loop. The syntax of a FOREACH loop varies between languages. In PHP the syntax is as follows:

```
foreach ($arrayName as $variable)
{
   loop instructions here
}
```

where $arrayName is the name of the array that is to be processed by the loop, and $variable is the name of a variable that will be used inside the loop and will contain the value of the **first** element in the array on the **first** loop iteration, the value of the **second** element on the **second** iteration, and so on. The loop will repeat for each array element.

To use a FOREACH loop to sum the values in the **$scores** array:

```
$total = 0;
foreach ($scores as $nextScore)
{
   $total = $total + $nextScore;
}
```

In this example the FOREACH loop processes the **$scores** array, one element at a time. Each time the loop repeats, the value of the next element in the array is stored in **$nextScore**, so this variable contains a different value from the array on each repetition.

As you can see, a FOREACH loop is simpler to construct than a FOR loop but can only be used when the entire array is to be processed, and when the loop code does not need to perform any complicated processing of the array elements (such as referring to multiple elements in a single repetition).

Multi-Dimensional Arrays

All of the array examples in this chapter are "1-dimensional" in the sense that each array consists of a set of indexed elements that each store a single value. But each array element can be assigned **another array**, so that, instead of an array of single values, we have an **array of arrays**, in other words, a "2-dimensional" array. These arrays can also contain arrays, so that we can create "multi-dimensional" arrays of any number of dimensions. Multi-dimensional arrays are an extremely important data structure that can be used to store information such as topological data, weather data, flight trajectories and paths through 3-dimensional space, mathematical models, game environments, and so on. Chapter 16 provides some simple examples and demonstrates some common procedures for accessing and processing elements in multi-dimensional arrays.

Additional Learning Materials

Chapter 16 includes a description and examples of **multi-dimensional arrays** and **ragged arrays**.

PHP provides a large number of standard **array-processing functions**. **Chapter 16** includes a list of these functions.

Appendix D will help you **debug** your exercises, listing a number of the most common errors that you are likely to encounter.

The **Chapter 11 Hints and Help** pages on the textbook Web site provide answers to FAQs from previous students as they worked through the end-of-chapter exercises.

Summary

An array is a data structure that contains multiple data values. Each value in the array is known as an array **element** and is referenced using a unique **index** location.

A simple array uses integer values to index the array elements, starting with index position 0. The index position refers to the number of elements the current element is offset from the beginning of the array (the initial memory location).

Values can be assigned to individual array elements by referring to the array name and the appropriate index position, for example **$someArray[0] = 100;**

In PHP, values can be assigned to an entire array in a single statement using the **array()** function, for example **$someArray = array (100, 50, 25, 0);** will store 100, 50, 25 and 0, in array locations **$someArray[0]**, **$someArray[1]**, **$someArray[2]**, and **$someArray[3]**.

Also in PHP the square brackets can be used with **no** index location. In this case an element will be added to the end of the array with an appropriate index, for example if **$someArray** already contains four elements, **$someArray**[] = **75;** will store 75 in **$someArray**[4] (the fifth element).

Each element of array can be used just as any other variable in programming statements.

An array element can be assigned any type of value, for example a character string can be stored in an array element.

In PHP, the number of elements in an array can be ascertained using the **sizeof**() function. Other languages provide a similar function.

Arrays are often processed with FOR loops since a FOR loop can be constructed with a counting variable that increments from 0 (the first array index location) to 1 less than the size of the array (the ending array index location). Each time the loop repeats, the current value of the counting variable can be used inside the loop to reference the next array element.

When using a FOR loop to process an entire array, the **sizeof**() function should be used to control the number of repetitions. That way the loop will work even if the size of the array is changed.

It is often useful to read data from a file into an array before processing the data. The advantage is that the file is open for the minimum time. The disadvantage is that additional memory is required to store the array.

When processing a file of unknown length, a WHILE loop can be used to store the lines from the file in an array. In that case, a counting variable will need to be explicitly created and initialized to 0 **before** the loop, and incremented each time the loop repeats. This variable will be used to add the next line in the file to the next index position in the array.

The **explode**() function returns an array where each element is one of the values that was parsed by the function.

The **list**() function receives an array and assigns the values for the array to each of the variables listed as the function arguments.

The explode() and list() functions can be used independently as needed by the application requirements.

A FOREACH loop provides an efficient way of processing an entire array where the next element in the array is to be processed each time the loop repeats.

Array elements can store other arrays, allowing a programmer to create multi-dimensional arrays. In addition to general data processing, multi-dimensional arrays are important for modeling and simulation applications.

Chapter 11 Review Questions

1. What type of data structure is used to store multiple values using a single variable name, where each value is referenced by an index value?
   a. A selection structure
   b. A loop structure
   c. An array
   d. A numeric variable
   e. A session

2. What PHP function can be used to determine the number of elements in an array?
   a. The sizeof() function
   b. The numElements() function
   c. The length() function
   d. The array_size() function
   e. There is no such function

3. Which of the following would refer to the value stored in the **fourth** element of an array named $sales?
   a. $sales [0]
   b. $sales [1]
   c. $sales [2]
   d. $sales [3]
   e. $sales [4]

4. What value is stored in $sales[2] after the following statement is processed?

   ```
   $sales = array (200, 300, 400, 500, 600);
   ```

   a. 200
   b. 300
   c. 400
   d. 500
   e. 600

5. What value is stored in $sales[2] after the following statements are **all** processed in order?

```
$sales [0] = 200;
$sales [1] = $sales [0] + 200;
$sales [2] = $sales [1];
$sales [2] = $sales [2] + $sales [0];
$sales [0] = 400;
```

a. 200
b. 400
c. 600
d. 800
e. 1000

6. What value is stored in $sum after the following statements are processed?

```
$sales = array(100, 200, 300, 400, 500);
$sum = 0;
for ($i = 0; $i < sizeof($sales); $i = $i + 1)
   $sum = $sum + $sales[$i];
```

a. 0
b. 500
c. 1000
d. 1400
e. 1500

7. What value is stored in $sum after the following statements are processed?

```
$sales = array(100, 200, 300, 400, 500);
$sum = 0;
for ($i = 1; $i < 3; $i = $i + 1)
   $sum = $sum + $sales[$i];
```

a. 0
b. 500
c. 1000
d. 1400
e. 1500

8. Which is the equivalent FOREACH loop to the following FOR LOOP?

```
$sum = 0;
for ($i = 0; $i < sizeof($sales); $i = $i + 1)
    $sum = $sum + $sales[$i];
```

a. foreach ($sales as $nextSale)
    $sum = $sum + $nextSale;
b. foreach ($sales as $nextSale)
    $sum = $sum + $sales[i];
c. foreach ($sales[i] as $nextSale)
    $sum = $sum + $nextSale;
d. foreach ($nextSale as $sales)
    $sum = $sum + $nextSale;
e. foreach ($nextSale as $sales)
    $sum = $sum + $sales[i];

9. What, if anything, is wrong with this FOR loop?

```
for ($index = 0; $index <= sizeof($sales); $index = $index + 1)
    print("<p>NEXT SALE: $sales[$index]</p>");
```

a. The loop variable should begin with the value 1 not 0
b. The loop variable should be named $i not $index
c. The loop test should be $index < sizeof($sales), not $index <= sizeof($sales)
d. The array element cannot be displayed inside a character string
e. There is nothing wrong with this FOR loop

10. What is the last index position of $sales after these two statements are processed?

```
$sales = array(100, 200, 300, 400, 500);
$sales[] = 600;
```

a. 4
b. 5
c. 6
d. 7
e. There is an error—the second statement is missing an index value between the brackets

11. What value is stored in $result after the following statements are processed?

```
$sales = array(100, 200, 300, 400, 500);
$result = $sales[0];

for ($i = 1; $i < sizeof($sales); $i = $i + 1)
{
  if ($sales[$i] > $result)
    $result = $sales[$i];
}
```

   a. The sum of the values stored in the $sales array
   b. The number of values in the $sales array greater than the first value
   c. The lowest number stored in the $sales array
   d. The highest number stored in the $sales array
   e. The first number stored in the $sales array

12. What value is stored in $result after the following statements are processed?

```
$sales = array(100, 200, 300, 400, 500);

for ($i = 0; $i < sizeof($sales); $i = $i + 1)
{
  $result = $sales[$i];
}
```

   a. The sum of the values stored in the $sales array
   b. The number of values in the $sales array greater than the first value
   c. The lowest number stored in the $sales array
   d. The highest number stored in the $sales array
   e. The last number stored in the $sales array

13. What value is stored in $result after the following statements are processed?

```
$sales = array(100, 200, 300, 400, 500);
$result = 0;

for ($i = 0; $i < sizeof($sales); $i = $i + 1)
{
  if ($sales[$i] > $sales[0])
    $result = $result + 1;
}
```

   a. The sum of the values stored in the $sales array
   b. The number of values in the $sales array greater than the first value
   c. The lowest number stored in the $sales array
   d. The highest number stored in the $sales array
   e. The last number stored in the $sales array

14. If an array named $scores is indexed from 0 to 7, what value would sizeof($scores) return?
    a. 0
    b. 7
    c. 8
    d. The sum of the scores in the array

15. Which approach uses less memory when working with large data files?
    a. Process the data while reading it from the file and close the file when done.
    b. Read the data from the file into an array, then close the file and process the data in the array.

16. Which statement is true?
    a. The list() and explode() functions must always be used together.
    b. The list() and explode() functions can be used together or independently.

17. What does the explode() function return?
    a. A list of variables, each containing one of the values extracted from the string that was passed to the function for parsing.
    b. An array containing the values extracted from the string that was passed to the function for parsing.
    c. A count of the values extracted from the string that was passed to the function for parsing.
    d. A string containing the values extracted from the string that was passed to the function for parsing, separated by a colon.

18. What does the list() function do?
    a. Sums the values that are listed as arguments.
    b. Converts the values that are listed as arguments into a single character string.
    c. Takes an array of values and assigns each value to one of the variables in the function's list of arguments.
    d. Takes an array of values and extracts these based on a delimiter.

19. An array containing a set of indexed elements that each store a **single** value is an example of:
    a. A 1-dimensional array
    b. A 2-dimensional array
    c. A multi-dimensional array

20. True or False? An array can contain other arrays as array elements
    a. True
    b. False

Chapter 11 Code Exercises

Your Chapter 11 code exercises can be found in your **chapter11** folder. This folder is included in your customized XAMPP installation at the following location:

> htdocs\webtech\coursework\chapter11

Type your name and the date in the **Author** and **Date** sections of each file as you work on each exercise. **Remember** that the Students page on the textbook Web site includes **Hints and Help** pages for the exercises in this and every chapter.

Debugging Exercises

Your **chapter11** folder should contain a number of "fixit" files. Each of these files contains PHP code that has an error of some kind. The type of error is indicated in the comment section of each file. You will need to run each program in order to see the errors, and to debug and test the code to see if it works correctly. For example to run **fixit1.php**, first run the Web server, then use the URL:

> http://localhost/webtech/coursework/chapter11/fixit1.php

Code Modification Exercises

Your **chapter11** folder contains a number of "modify" files. Each pair of files contains HTML and PHP code that needs to be modified to meet a requirement. The requirements are included in the comment section of each file. Modify the algorithms, being careful to make changes to the .html and .php files as directed. You will need to run each program in order to test your changes. For example to run modify1.html, first run the Web server, then use the URL:

> http://localhost/webtech/coursework/chapter11/modify1.html

Code Completion Exercises

1. Read this exercise carefully and take your time to work out the logic. Your **chapter11** folder contains versions of **weekly-report.html, weekly-report.php**. The code in **weekly-report1.html** does not need to be changed—it just provides a form with a Submit button to run **weekly-report.php**. Open **weekly-report.php** and create an array named **$weeklyContracts** that contains seven elements. Each element contains the daily income from completed paint jobs, as follows: 236.00, 284.00, 148.00, 128.00, 0.00, 110.00, 0.00. Use a FOR loop to process the array and calculate the total income, the average income, and the number of days with 0 income. The output code is already provided—note the variable names. If your loop statements are correct the total will be $906.00, the average will be $129.43, and the number of "0 income" days will be 2.

2. Read this exercise carefully and take your time to work out the logic. Your **chapter11** folder contains versions of **inventory.html** and **inventory.php**. This application allows the user to select a paint color from a drop down list. The inventory.php program already includes an array named **$paintInventory** where each array element contains the number of cans of paint that are available for each color. The values are stored in the following order: **white**, cream, beige, yellow, green, red, maroon, blue, teal, gray, so for example **$paintInventory**[0] contains the number of cans of white paint, and **$paintInventory**[5] contains the number of cans of red paint.

   The inventory.html file provides an HTML form that asks the user to select a color. Your job is to add code to inventory.php to test the color submitted by the user and display the number of cans available for that color. You will need a selection structure to determine which array element to display. For example, if the submitted color is "white", the program should indicate that 65 cans are available since that is the value stored in $paintInventory[0].

3. Read this exercise carefully and take your time to work out the logic. Your **chapter11** folder contains versions of **orders.html** and **orders.php**. This application allows the user to obtain a report concerning orders for blueberry bushes. Create an $orders array with the following 10 values: 2, 17, 4, 6, 1, 3, 1, 15, 1, 6. You can use any approach to create the array.

   Now write the code to display the orders in a table with two columns. The heading for the first column is Order #, and the heading for the second column is Quantity. These are provided. Use a FOR loop to display rows containing the orders stored in the array. For each row, the order number will be 1 added to the index of the current array element (so the orders will be numbered 1, 2, 3, etc), and the quantity will be the value stored in the current element. Use the **sizeof**() function to control the loop.

   Now add a second FOR loop to obtain the sum of all the bushes in these orders, and also count the number of orders that are for more than one bush. Use the **sizeof**() function to control the loop. The sum should be **56** and the count should be **7**. Add a print statement to display the count of orders for more than one bush.

4. Read this exercise carefully and take your time to work out the logic. Your **chapter11** folder contains versions of **parking.html** and **parking.php**. This application allows a parking attendant to select a parking space number from a drop down list (there are 20 parking spaces numbered from 0 to 19). The parking.php program already includes an array named **$parkingPermits** where each array element contains the license number of the car that has a permit for the parking space with the same value as the array index. So for example the license that has been registered for parking space 0 is **"LYD EW25"** and this is stored in **$parkingPermits**[0].

Add a single print statement to display the correct license plate number from the $parkingPermits array based on the user's form submission. The paragraph should display the permit number as well as the license number, for example:

"The license plate number for parking space 0 is LYD EW25."

HINT: The HTML form in parking.html will send the parking space number. The $parkingPermits array contains the license number for each parking space, and the index for each of these is the same as the parking space number; remember that you can use a variable to reference an array index, for example $somearray[$someIndex].

5. Read this exercise carefully and take your time to work out the logic. Your **chapter11** folder contains versions of **city-survey.html** and **city-survey.php**. Your **city-survey.php** application includes an array named **$citySurvey** that contains the results of a survey where 20 people indicated which city they would most like to visit ("London", "Paris", or "Rome"). Add a FOR loop to process this array and count the number of people who chose each of these cities. When your program has completed the loop, display the results in a table that prints the city names in the first column and the count for each city in the second column.

6. For this exercises you will create a Seating Maintenance Report for a small concert hall. Your **chapter11** folder contains **seating.html** and **seating.php**. The code in seating.html does not need to be changed. You will see that your seating.php file already includes an array named **$seating** that stores the condition of each of the 100 seats in the concert hall. The seats are numbered 1 to 100, so $seating[0] contains the condition of seat 1, and $seating[99] will contain the condition of seat 100. Each array element contains either the value "OK" or "REPAIR" (note that these are upper-case).

Provide a FOR loop to process the array and print the numbers of every seat that need to be repaired. You will need an IF structure in the loop that uses the loop index variable to test the next element in the array each time the loop repeats. Remember that the array index begins with 0 and not 1 when you print the seat numbers. The loop should ALSO count the seats that need to be repaired and report the total count of seats in need of repair at the end of the list.

7. Read this exercise carefully and take your time to work out the logic. Your **chapter11** folder contains the files **sales.html** and **sales.php**, and also a data file named **sales-data.txt**. The sales-data.txt file contains the value of each sale made by two sales people named **Smith** and **Jones**. Each line in the file contains a sale person's name

followed by a colon, followed by the value of a single sale. For example the first line contains **Smith:345.50** which means that Smith made a sale worth 345.50.

Add code to sales.php to: open the file; read each line and extract the name of the sales person and value of the sale; and add the value as a new element in either the **$smithSales** or **$jonesSales** array. Remember to close the file when you are done. When the loop has completed the $smithSales array should contain the values of all of Smith's sales, and the $jonesSales array should contain the values of all of Jones's sales.

Now use a FOR loop to calculate the total value of all the sales in the $smithSales array, and another FOR loop to calculate the total value of all the sales in the $jonesSales array. Calculate the average value for each salesperson using the totals that you just calculated, and the **sizeof()** function to obtain the size of each array. Display the total sales value for each sales person, the number of sales by each sales person, and the average sale of each sales person, as follows:

```
Smith achieved 6 sales with a total value of $2,469.15, and
an average sale value of $411.53.
Jones achieved 4 sales with a total value of $2,411.15, and
an average sale value of $602.79.
```

Chapter 12

Associative Arrays and Web Sessions

Intended Learning Outcomes

After completing this chapter, you should be able to:

- Summarize key characteristics of associative arrays.
- Create an associative array.
- Identify useful applications for associative arrays.
- Use a literal key value to access a value in an associative array.
- Use a variable that contains a key value to access a value in an associative array.
- Describe the structure of the PHP $_POST array.
- Summarize the basic characteristics of a Web session.
- Create and destroy a Web session.
- Use the $_SESSION array to share variables between pages in a Web session.
- Recognize other superglobal arrays.
- Combine a Web form with the code to process the form in a single page.

Introduction

Chapter 11 demonstrated the structure and use of arrays that are indexed with numerical values. Many languages, including PHP, also permit the use of **associative arrays**. An associative array is indexed with **character strings** that describe the content of each element. For example here is an associative array that contains scores for three exams, an essay and a project:

445

```
$scores['Exam 1'] = 90;
$scores['Exam 2'] = 93;
$scores['Exam 3'] = 87;
$scores['Essay'] = 78;
$scores['Project'] = 80;
```

Notice that the elements are now indexed with the character strings "Exam 1", "Exam 2", "Exam 3", "Essay", and "Project", instead of 0, 1, 2, 3, and 4. The character strings used to name each array index are known as **keys**, so for example 'Exam 1' is the key for the first element in the $scores array. Any array element can now be accessed by referring to the key used as an index, for example **$scores**['Essay'] uses the key **'Essay'** to indicate the location of the value of the essay score. This score is stored as the fourth array element but **$scores**['Essay'] is obviously more meaningful than **$scores**[3].

Associative arrays are very useful where an array contains a relatively small number of values, and where meaningful key names can be provided for each array element.

In this chapter we will learn how and when to use associative arrays. We will also learn that the $_POST array is an example of a standard associative array, and we will learn how to start and stop and make use of Web sessions using another standard associative array, the $_SESSION array.

Using a Variable to Reference the Key of an Associative Array

Here is an associative array that contains user ID's as the keys, and user passwords as the values:

```
$userList['mike75'] = "abc123";
$userList['mary2'] = "xyz999";
$userList['chris17'] = "abc999";
$userList['chris84'] = "xyz123";
```

In this example, 'mike75' and 'mary2' are different user ID's and "abc123" and "xyz999" are their respective passwords. We can obtain the password for the person with user ID "chris17" by using this ID as the index to look up the password for this user. For example we might use this in a print statement:

```
print("<p>Your user ID is chris17 and your password is
    $userList['chris17']</p>");
```

But note that we don't have to use the **literal** key as the index value. Instead we can use a **variable** that **contains** the literal key. So for example if the variable **$id** already stores the value "chris17" we can obtain the password for that ID using **$userList[$id]**.

This is very useful since it allows us to write code that looks up an item in an associative array dynamically, for example, based on user input. What if our program is designed to process a form that asks the user for an ID and password and then check the submitted ID and password against an array of ID's and passwords to see if the password is correct? Our program would first obtain the ID and password from the $_POST array, for example:

```
$id = $_POST['id'];
$password = $_POST['password'];
```

Assuming our program has already defined the $userList array (see above), the password that the user submitted can now be tested against the ID as follows:

```
if ($userList[$id] == $password)
  print("<p>WELCOME $id! You are now logged in!</p>");
else
  print("<p>LOGIN FAILED</p>");
```

Do you see how this works? The program is using the **$id** variable that contains the ID entered by the user as the key to look up a password in the **$userList** array. If the password stored in the array at the location indicated by **$id** contains the same password that the user entered then the login is valid. For example if **$id** contains "mary2" and **$password** contains "xyz999" then the test would be:

```
if ($userList['mary2'] == "xyz999")
```

which would generate a **true** result since the value "xyz999" is stored in that location.

However if **$id** contains "mary2" and **$password** contains "xyz123" then the test would be:

```
if ($userList['mary2'] == "xyz123")
```

which would generate a **false** result.

Using Associative Arrays as Lookups

In the previous example the $userList array contained a list of user passwords that are referenced by the user ID. Associative arrays are extremely useful to store all kinds of useful lookups for any number of purposes. For example we could use an associative array to store useful information about our company:

```
$companyInfo['name'] = "Most Excellent Web Design, Inc.";
$companyInfo['street'] = "123 Main Street";
$companyInfo['city'] = "Sometown";
$companyInfo['state'] = "SomeState";
$companyInfo['zip'] = "12345";
$companyInfo['email'] = "excellent@mewd.com";
$companyInfo['phone'] = "(123) 456-7890";
$companyInfo['fax'] = "(098) 765-4321";
```

This array can now be used by any application that needs to refer to information about this company. For example, a program could display the company's e-mail address using $CompanyInfo ['email'].

Here is an associative array that lists capital cities, indexed by country names:

```
$capitals['FRANCE'] = "PARIS";
$capitals['ENGLAND'] = "LONDON";
$capitals['AFGHANISTAN'] = "KABUL";
$capitals['ANGOLA'] = "LUANDA";
$capitals['BOLIVIA'] = "SUCRE";
```

A program could find the capital of, for example, Angola, by referring to $capitals['ANGOLA'].

Even better, we can look up a capital using a variable that stores the key. Consider a program that allows the user to choose a country from a drop down list in an HTML form, using the name 'country'. The receiving program can receive the selected country and store this in a variable, for example:

```
$country = $_POST['country'];
```

The program can now use this variable as the key for the $capitals array to display the capital for whichever country the user requested:

```
print("<p>The capital of $country is $capitals[$country]</p>");
```

Consider how efficient it can be to develop associative arrays that contain useful lookups that can then be shared by different applications and programmers. Consider for example an array of state names using the state abbreviations as keys, or an array that stores explanations of different payroll codes using the payroll codes as the keys. Or an array that stores course descriptions that are indexed by the course ID's, or that stores scene descriptions for a game with the scene titles as the keys? And what if another programmer provides you with a useful associative array of this kind that saves you many hours of work? You can easily copy and paste useful associative arrays directly into your application code, and in the next chapter we will learn how to store useful associative arrays in a separate file and then simply refer to that file when we wish to include an array in an application.

Using the array() Function to Create Associative Arrays

The PHP **array**() function can also be used to create associative arrays using the => operator to associate keys and values. For example here's how we would use the **array**() function to create our **$capitals** array:

```
$capitals = array ('FRANCE' => "PARIS", 'ENGLAND' => "LONDON",
   'AFGHANISTAN' => "KABUL", 'ANGOLA' => "LUANDA",
   'BOLIVIA' => "SUCRE");
```

This is equivalent to the method that we discussed earlier:

```
$capitals['FRANCE'] = "PARIS";
$capitals['ENGLAND'] = "LONDON";
$capitals['AFGHANISTAN'] = "KABUL";
$capitals['ANGOLA'] = "LUANDA";
$capitals['BOLIVIA'] = "SUCRE";
```

Associative Arrays and the FOREACH Loop

Sometimes we need to process every element in an associative array; for example, we might need to sum all the elements of our $scores array to get the total score. But how can we use a FOR loop to count through the array index if the array is indexed with character strings instead of numbers? A FOR loop won't work with our $scores array now that it is not indexed numerically:

```
$scores['Exam 1'] = 90;
$scores['Exam 2'] = 93;
$scores['Exam 3'] = 87;
$scores['Essay'] = 78;
$scores['Project'] = 80;
```

Earlier we learned how to use a FOREACH loop to process a numerically indexed array, but a **FOREACH** loop is especially useful for processing an associative array. The heading of the FOREACH loop defines a variable that is used to store the value of a single element of the array: each time the loop repeats, the next value in the array is automatically assigned to this variable. We can include statements in the loop that refer to this variable knowing that it will contain the value of the next array element each time the loop repeats.

The same FOREACH loop that we reviewed with a numerically indexed array will work just as well with an associative array:

```
$total = 0;
foreach ($scores as $nextScore)
{
   $total = $total + $nextScore;
}
```

Just as before, the FOREACH loop processes the **$scores** array, one element at a time. Each time the loop repeats, the value of the next element in the array is stored in $nextScore, so this variable contains a different value from the array on each repetition.

Let's explore how we can use a FOREACH loop with our array of capital cities. We can use the same syntax to print a list of all the capital stored in the $capitals array:

```
foreach ($capitals as $nextCapital)
{
   print("The capital is $nextCapital");
}
```

But you may be thinking, that's great but what if I wanted to print the **name** of the country as well as the capital? In other words what if we want to use the key of each element as well as (or even instead of) the value of each element? This is a common requirement and the FOREACH loop allows us to access the key as well as the value using a special syntax:

```
foreach ($capitals as $nextCountry => $nextCapital)
{
   print("The capital of $nextCountry is $nextCapital");
}
```

The use of **$nextCountry => $nextCapital** in the FOREACH loop heading means that, each time the loop repeats, the **key** of the next element in the **$capitals** array will be stored in the variable **$nextCountry**, and the **value** of the same element will be stored in **$nextCapital**. This is a terrific tool and you will find it useful in many applications. Note that, when using a FOREACH loop, the first variable in the heading must be the name of the array you wish to process. You can use any variable names for the key and value variables. The operator => is required between the two variables if you include a variable for the key.

More about the $_POST Array

You have learned how to create your own associative arrays but PHP also defines a number of "**superglobal**" associative arrays that you can use in any of your applications (superglobal variables are standard PHP variables that can be accessed directly from any PHP script). These superglobal arrays provide very useful services and are readily identified by the $_ that begins the array name (this naming convention helps to ensure that you don't create an array with the same name as a standard array).

In fact you have been using a superglobal associative array throughout this book: the $_POST array. When a user submits a form that uses the **method = "post"** attribute, the submitted values are received into the $_POST array. The **keys** of the $_POST array are the **names** associated with each input field in the form, and the **values** in the $_POST array are the **values** submitted by the user in these fields.

Here again is the code for **wage2.html** (our very first HTML form example):

```
<html>
<head>
  <title>Wage Report</title>
  <link rel="stylesheet" type="text/css" href="sample.css">
</head>
<body>
  <h1>Wage Report</h1>
  <form action="wage2.php" method="post">
    <label>Hourly wage:
    <input type="text" size="10" name="hourlyWage"></label>
    <label>Hours Worked:
    <input type="text" size="10" name="hoursWorked"></label>
    <input class="submit" type="submit" value="Get Your Wage
        Report Now">
  </form>
</body>
</html>
```

Code Example: wage2.html

The **action** and **method** attributes of the <**form**> tag indicate that **wage2.php** should be used to process the form input, and that the submitted names and values should be passed to the $_POST array. When the form is submitted, the values for hourly wage and hours worked are assigned to the $_POST array and indexed with the names "hourlyWage" and "hoursWorked" (since these were the names provided on the form), so the $_POST array contains two elements:

$_POST ['**hourlyWage**'] contains the value submitted by the user
   in the field named "hourlyWage".

$_POST ['**hoursWorked**'] contains the value submitted by the user in the field named "hoursWorked".

We have been writing statements in our program examples to retrieve these values from the **$_POST** array and store them in program variables, for example:

```
$hourlyWage = $_POST['hourlyWage'];
$hoursWorked = $_POST['hoursWorked'];
```

In this textbook we have always copied the values from the **$_POST** array into separate variables and then used these variables in subsequent instructions. Actually it is perfectly acceptable to use the elements of the **$_POST** array directly without any need for additional variables. Values stored in the **$_POST** array can be used and modified throughout your code just as any other variables. The practice of copying **$_POST** array values into separate variables is quite common since it makes the code more readable. We have taken that approach here to help us to keep the focus on basic concepts.

PHP provides two other associative arrays to receive values from an HTML form. The **$_GET** array is used when the **method** attribute of the <form> tag is assigned the value **"get"** instead of **"post"**. The **"get"** method is less secure since the values are submitted as part of the URL, and therefore visible. The **"get"** method also limits the number of characters that can be submitted, so **"post"** is more commonly used, and this is the method we have used here.

The **$_REQUEST** array can be used to receive values from forms whether the <form> attribute has the value **"get"** or **"post"**. We could use **$_REQUEST** in all our form-processing code instead of **$_POST**. The **$_REQUEST** array is a good choice, for example, when a single program may need to handle from input from multiple sources, and where it may not be known whether the input is submitted using the **"get"** or **"post"** method.

Other Superglobal Variables

Another useful superglobal array is named **$_SERVER**, and this can be used to access all kinds of useful information associated with the server and current activity. Here are just a few examples:

$_SERVER['PHP_SELF'] returns the filename of the currently executing script.

$_SERVER['SERVER_NAME'] returns the name of the server.

$_SERVER['REQUEST_METHOD'] indicates the request method used to access the page (such as "POST").

$_SERVER['REMOTE_ADDR'] returns the user's IP address.

PHP provides a number of other superglobal variables that you will want to research, including **$_SESSION**, **$_COOKIE**, **$_FILES**, and **$_GLOBALS**. The **$_SESSION** array will be covered in more detail later in this chapter.

Using the $_SERVER Array to Combine Web Form and Form Processing Code in a Single Page

You can use $_SERVER['REQUEST_METHOD'] to test if the $_POST array has actually received values from a form, for example:

```
if ($_SERVER["REQUEST_METHOD"] == "POST")
```

This is a very useful test. If the test is **true**, it indicates that the current file is being executed because a form was submitted. If the test is **false**, then it indicates that the current file has been requested for another reason, for example because a user typed the URL. You can use this test to develop a single PHP page that contains both the Web form **AND** the code that processes the form. Here's the basic algorithm for the page:

```
if the test is true
{
  // this means a form has been submitted, so
  //execute statements to process the form values
}
else
{
  // this means a form has not been submitted, so
  // display the form for the user to submit
}
```

In other words, the page has two components, the code to display the form, and the code to process the form.

Confused? Let's look at a complete example. Your samples folder contains a file named add-two-numbers.html which contains a form that asks the user for two numbers and submits these for processing by a program named add-two-numbers.php. The add-two-numbers.php application receives the two numbers from the $_POST array, adds them, and displays the results. This is the approach we've been using throughout this textbook: an .html file that provides the input form, and a .php file that contains the code that processes the form data.

But the code in these two files can be combined into a single file, by testing **$_SERVER["REQUEST_METHOD"]** to decide whether to **display** the form or **process** input that has been submitted **from** the form. Your samples folder also contains a file named **add-two-improved.php**. Examine the IF structure used in this code:

```php
<?php
if ($_SERVER["REQUEST_METHOD"] == "POST")
{
  $number1 = $_POST['number1'];
  $number2 = $_POST['number2'];
  $result = $number1 + $number2;
  print("<h1>RESULTS</h1>");
  print("<p>$number1 + $number2 = $result.</p>");
  print("<p><a href=\"add-two-improved.php\">Return to the
    Input Form</a></p>");
}
else
{
?>
<h1>ADD TWO NUMBERS</h1>
<form action = "add-two-improved.php" method = "post">

<label>1st number:
  <input type = "text" size = "5" name = "number1"></label>
<label>2nd number:
  <input type = "text" size = "5" name = "number2"></label>

<input class = "submit" type = "submit" value = "Tell me the
sum" name = "submit">
</form>
<?php

}
?>
```

You can see that the IF structure is used to determine whether to **process** the form or **display** the form, depending on whether or not form input was received into the $_POST array. If form input WAS received, this indicates that the application is being executed because a form was submitted, so the form data can be processed. If this was **not** received, this indicates that a form has **not** been submitted, so the application displays the form for the user. Note that the **action** attribute of the form now calls the same file that contains the form (**add-two-improved.php**).

The combination of a Web form with the code to process the form into a single file is a widely used design approach since it allows for more compact and modular application development.

NOTE: did you notice that this code sample included **two** PHP sections? The **first** PHP section ends after the opening brace that marks the beginning of the ELSE block. This is followed by 10 lines of HTML code that display the form, and then a **second** PHP section simply provides the closing brace of the ELSE block. The ten lines of HTML could have been included in PHP print statements, but all of those double quotes would have needed to be written as escape characters (\") so it was much easier to simply switch from PHP to HTML to provide the form. The PHP processor can handle any number of PHP and HTML code sections, as long as the HTML sections do not contain any PHP, and as long as the PHP sections use PHP **print** (or **echo**) statements to provide any content that is to be added to the Web page. For simplicity, the PHP files in this book have mostly consisted of an HTML section followed by a single PHP section, followed by an HTML section, but this is not a requirement.

Web Sessions and the $_SESSION Array

We use program variables to store and modify values while a PHP page is being processed but the contents of these variables are lost when the processing is completed. That has not been a problem so far since our applications have all consisted of a single PHP page. But a Web application might include multiple PHP pages that need to share information. Consider an online store, where the customer browses through many pages, adding items to his or her shopping cart. How does the application keep track of the customer's name and the items that the customer has selected as the customer moves from one page to the next? What about a game application that contains multiple PHP pages, each handling a different game scene: how does each page pass on the information such as the player's name and score to the page that handles the next game scene? To put it another way, if your application consists of multiple PHP pages (as most real-world applications do), how can you create variables that are **available** for use **throughout** the application, that can be used or modified by **any** of the pages that comprise the application?

To understand this better, let's consider a simple application that handles prizes for a raffle. The application contains three files. The first file is named **raffle.html** and presents a form to the user that allows them to enter their first name, their city, and their raffle ticket number. This form is submitted to a PHP program named **raffle.php** which receives the first name, city and raffle ticket number, and checks to see if the raffle number is the winning number (for our example let's just say the winning number is 45678). If the user submits the winning number, the application presents **another** form to the user, this time allowing them to choose from a list of prizes. This form is submitted to another PHP program named **choose-prize.php** which receives the user's selection and tells them how to pick up their prize. Figures 12-1 and 12-2 provide screen shots of this application.

Figure 12-1: raffle.html provides the first form

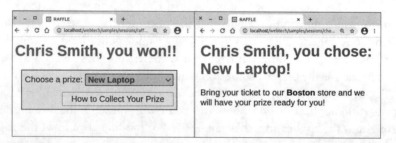

Figure 12-2: raffle.php (with the second form) and choose-prize.php

That all seems straightforward—we know how to create and process Web forms like this. The problem is that **choose-prize.php** needs to display a message that includes the user's name and city. These two values were received by **raffle.php** from the form provided in **raffle.html** but how does **raffle.php** share these values with **choose-prize.php**? It's true that **choose-prize.php** also contains a form but this form is used only to submit the user's choice of a prize. It would make no sense to use this form to ask the user for their name and city again! So how can **raffle.php** share the user's name and city with **choose-prize.php**?

There are in fact a number of solutions, but here we will use this problem to explain the use of Web **sessions**. A Web session allows us to track a user's activity from the time the session is initiated to the time the session is ended (closing the Web browser will also end the Web session). Data values that need to be used throughout the session are stored in **session variables**, which are stored independently of each page that participates in the session. These values are stored in a **$_SESSION** array, which is another standard associative array, similar to the $_POST array. All pages that participate in the session can work with the $_SESSION array, referencing or changing the values of variables that are already stored in the array, or adding new variables to the array. Session variables are available to any pages that use the session from the time the session variable is added to the $_SESSION array until the session ends. Before we learn how to write code that uses the $_SESSION array, let's get a better understanding of how a session actually works.

When a user opens a Web page that initiates a session, a unique identification (UID) number is created on the Web server for that user (the user never actually sees this UID and you and your application do not need to know what it is either). Note that many users may be accessing the same Web application at the same time (for example on a shopping site or in a Web-based interactive game), and each user is assigned their own unique UID. The Web server associates a $_SESSION array with each UID, and this allows the application to use the $_SESSION array to store and modify values that can be shared by any pages that participate in the session. You don't have to worry about the fact that multiple users might be using your pages at the same time—the data for each user is automatically maintained in a separate $_SESSION array associated with the user's UID. This is important—you would not want your online purchases to be confused with those of **another** user!

Adding Code to Manage a Web Session

In PHP, a session is started using the **session_start**() function, and the session can be ended using the **session_destroy**() function. A session also ends if the user closes his or her browser (but note that the browser must be shut down, it is not enough to only close the page that is using the Web session and leave other pages open).

Every page that is intended to participate in a Web session **must** include a call to the **session_start**() function, and not just the page that you intend to be starting page. This function call **must** appear in a PHP section **before** any HTML tags that appear in the file, for example:

```
<php
   session_start();
?>

<html>
 . . . HTML and additional PHP code here..
</html>
```

Each page that includes the call to the **session_start**() function can make use of the $_SESSION array to store, access or modify values that are to be shared with other pages that are also participating in the session.

Any page that executes the **session_destroy**() function will end the session. Once a session is ended, no pages will have access to the $_SESSION array that was created for the session and values stored in this array will be lost.

Creating, Initializing and Modifying Session Variables

Once you have included a **session_start**() call in a page that will be a part of your session, you can include code on that page to add elements to the $_SESSION array. To add a new element, simply define a new $_SESSION array key, just as with any associative array. You can then assign a value to this new element.

For example in our raffle.php program we will receive the user's first name and city from the form in raffle.html:

```
$firstName = $_POST['firstName'];
$city = $_POST['city'];
```

In order to share these values with other pages (here we want to share them with choose-prize.php), we can create two elements with key names 'firstName' and 'city' in our $_SESSION array and copy the values that were received from the form into these elements:

```
$_SESSION['firstName'] = $firstName;
$_SESSION['city'] = $city;
```

Actually you can copy these values directly from the $_POST array to the $_SESSION array:

```
$_SESSION['firstName'] = $_POST['firstName'];
$_SESSION['city'] = $_POST['city'];
```

Now the user's first name and city are stored in elements of the $_SESSION array and these can be accessed by any PHP program that is participating in the session (remember that these programs must include the call to the session_start() function). For example here's how a participating page might display the user's first name:

```
print ("<p>Hi, ".$_SESSION['firstName']."!</p>");
```

In our examples we are using the same key names for variables in our $_POST array and our $_SESSION array. This is not required—your $_SESSION variables can be given any key names.

Here is the code for the three pages in our raffle application. This code is provided in your **samples/sessions** folder. Note the use of the **session_start**() function in **raffle.php** and **choose-prize.php**, the use of the **$_SESSION** array in these programs, and the use of the **session_destroy**() function in **choose-prize.php**. Note also that the ticket number in raffle.php and the selected prize in choose-prize.php are stored in ordinary variables. That's because these variables are only needed in a single page so there is no need to share them with other pages in the $_SESSION array.

```
<html>
<head>
   <title>RAFFLE</title>
   <link rel="stylesheet" type="text/css" href="sample.css">
</head>
<body>
   <h1>Raffle Results</h1>

   <form action="raffle.php" method="post">
   <label>Your full name?
   <input type="text" size="15" name="fullName"></label>

   <label>Your city:
   <input type="text" size="15" name="city"></label>

   <label>Ticket number?
   <input type="text" size="15" name="ticketNum"></label>

   <input class="submit type="submit" value="Let's see if you
      won!">
</form>
</body>
</html>
```

Code Example: raffle.html

```php
<?php
  session_start();
?>
<html>
<head>
  <title>RAFFLE</title>
  <link rel="stylesheet" type="text/css" href="sample.css">
</head>
<body>
<?php
  $_SESSION['fullName'] = $_POST['fullName'];
  $_SESSION['city'] = $_POST['city'];

  $ticketNum = $_POST['ticketNum'];

  if ($ticketNum == "45678")
  {
    print("<h1>".$_SESSION'fullName'].", you won !!!</h1>");

    print("<form action=\"choose-prize.php\" method=\"post\">
        <label>Now choose a prize:
        <select name=\"prize\">
        <option>A New TV</option>
        <option>A New Laptop</option>
        <option>Used Pair of Socks</option>
        </select></label>
      <input class=\"submit\" type=\"submit\" value=\"Click
    Here to Learn How to Obtain Your Prize\">
  </form>");
  }
  else
  print("<h1>Sorry ".$_SESSION['fullName'].", you didn't win
      anything - better luck next time..</h1>");
?>
</body>
</html>
```

Code Example: raffle.php

```php
<?php
  session_start();
?>
<html>
<head>
  <title>RAFFLE</title>
  <link rel="stylesheet" type="text/css" href="sample.css">
</head>
<body>
<?php
  if (isset($_POST['prize']) and
isset($_SESSION['fullName']))
  {
    $prize = $_POST['prize'];

    print("<h1>".$_SESSION['fullName'].", you chose
      $prize!</h1>");

    print("<p>Bring your ticket to our <strong>"
      .$_SESSION['city']."</strong> store and we will have your
      prize ready for you!</p>");
  }

  session_destroy();
?>
</body>
</html>
```

Code Example: choose-prize.php

Validating $_SESSION and $_POST Arrays

You have to take some care to manage any page that make use of $_SESSION variables. One question you must ask is: what happens if a user links to a page "out of sequence." For example in our raffle application, what would happen if a user directly typed the URL for choose-prize.php without submitting the forms in raffle.html and raffle.php? In that case the message displayed by choose-prize.php would be missing the user's first name and city since these $_SESSION elements were not created by raffle.php. The page would also be missing the prize selection since this was not submitted by the form in raffle.php to the $_POST array.

In this case, the problem is caused by the user typing the wrong URL. This may be very unlikely since most users will have been directed to use raffle.html and will not know that choose-prize.php exists. But it is often important to handle this situation by including code to test the page and display an error message if the $_SESSION variables or $_POST variables do not contain values.

The PHP **isset**() function receives a variable name and tests whether or not the variable has already been created. This function can be used with any variable including variables that are elements of associative arrays. For example, **isset($_SESSION ['fullName]')** will return **true** if **$_SESSION['fullName']** already exists, **false** otherwise.

So we can use an IF..ELSE structure to decide what actions should be performed when a player visits a page that uses a session, for example:

```
if (isset($_SESSION['fullName']) )
{
  // Statements to execute if the element exists
}
else
{
  // Error message or nothing at all if you simply wish to
  // present a blank page
}
```

Now the page will only process normally if $_SESSION ['fullName'] has already received a value from another page.

The isset() function can also be used with the $_POST array, for example:

```
if (isset($_POST['prize']) )
```

This ensures that the user came to this page by submitting a form containing an input field named 'prize'. And of course these tests can be combined to ensure that the user submitted a form to arrive at this page, and also that the required $_SESSION variables have already been created:

```
if (isset($_POST['prize']) and isset($_SESSION['fullName']) )
```

Another useful function when working with $_SESSION and $_POST array variables is the **empty**() function. In this case we can test not whether the element was created, but if it contains a value, for example we could use this in raffle.php to ensure that the user submitted a name:

```
if (empty($_POST['fullName']) )
{
  print("<p>ERROR, a name is required!</p>");
  print("<p><a href=\"raffle.html\">Return to the form</a></p>");
}
else
{
  // process the form
}
```

This section is only intended as an introduction to the general procedure for managing and validating Web sessions. You will want to study further and advance your skills before producing Web sessions that are fully secure and robust. The next section shows to manage a page that a user might visit multiple times during a single session.

Revisiting the Same Page in a Web Session

Well-designed Web applications often require the user to return to the same page multiple times. For example a game player might need to return to the same scene page, and an online shopper might return to the same product page. Your programs must be able to handle this type of activity. For example, perhaps your first game scene sets a variable named $_SESSION['score'] to 0. If the player is allowed to return to this game scene more than once while playing, it's important that his or her score is not reset to 0 each time the player visits the page. We can use our isset() and empty() functions to handle these situations.

Let's consider a simple, one page online quiz that tests a child's addition skills. The page (**math-quiz.php** in the **samples/sessions** folder) displays either a welcome message (the first time) or the result of the previous addition (if the child has already played), followed by the current score, followed by a form that displays two random numbers between 1 and 20 and asks the player to submit the sum. This form calls the **same page** (math-quiz.php) to receive the sum submitted by the player, check whether or not the answer is correct, display the result, update the count and score, and display the form again with two new numbers. The player can continue to play for as long as they wish. To quit the player clicks the **"Ready to Quit"** link which links to **math-quit.php**. Figures 12-3 and 12-4 provides sample screenshots.

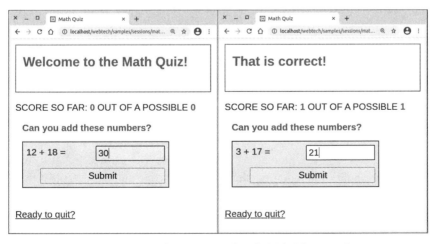

Figure 12-3: math-quiz screenshot (initial visit to page)

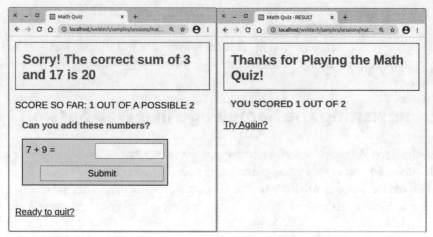

Figure 12-4: math-quiz screenshot (subsequent visit to page)

Play the game yourself so that you are familiar with how it behaves. Note that the application is located in the **samples/sessions** folder so the URL is:

```
http://localhost/webtech/samples/sessions/math-quiz.php
```

(This program uses a slightly modified version of sample.css, named **quiz.css**.)

Before looking at the code for this application, it's important to understand why the form on the page must be designed to call the same page. It would be impractical to create multiple pages, one page for each time the player needs a form to submit another addition. Apart from the duplication of code, there is simply no way to predict how many pages the player might need!

But to use a single page requires some careful planning. Even though the player is returning to the same page each time the form is submitted, the page will be executed again for each visit. So the page will need to use $_SESSION variables to keep track of the player's score and the count of the player's attempts. The first time the player comes to the page (the start of the session) these two variables should be set to 0. These variables should not reset to 0 each time the player returns to the page. Instead, each time the player tries another addition, the count should increment by 1, while the score should increment by 1 only if the player submitted the correct answer.

The next consideration is that the page should not try to process the $_POST array the first time the page is displayed since the player has not submitted anything yet so there is nothing to process.

And last, the application requires a link to a second page that will execute if the player chooses to quit. This page will display the score and count and then destroy the session so that the next time the player returns to the first page (math-quiz.php), the game will reset to a score and count of 0 and will display the initial Welcome message again.

Look over the code for **math-quiz.php** and **math-quit.php** (these are located in your **samples/sessions** folder). Consider how this code works to allow the player to begin playing, and attempt as many additions as he or she wishes until choosing to quit. Note that, when the player quits, the **math-quit.php** program **destroys** the session. This is important to ensure that, if the player wishes to play again, the test (**!isset($_SES-SION**['score'])) will be **true**, so math-quit.php will display the Welcome page and set the **$_SESSION**['score'] and **$_SESSION**['count'] variables to **0**.

(When you look over this code you will notice two unfamiliar statements **print** ("**<div class='heading'>**"); and **print** ("**</div>**"); These are used to define styles for the heading area at the top of the quiz pages: a **<div>** is an HTML "container" that is used to set CSS styles for the container itself and for any HTML elements (in this case the headings) that are located inside the container. The use of the **<div>** tag is explained in more detail in Chapter 17.)

```php
<?php
  session_start();
?>
<html>
<head>
  <title>Math Quiz</title>
  <link rel="stylesheet" type="text/css" href="quiz.css">
</head>
<body>
<?php
print ("<div class='heading'>");
  if (!isset($_SESSION['score']))
  {
    $_SESSION['score'] = 0;
    $_SESSION['count'] = 0;
    print ("<h1>Welcome to the Math Quiz!</h1>");
  }

  if (isset($_POST['userAnswer']))
  {
    $_SESSION['count'] = $_SESSION['count'] + 1;
    $userAnswer = $_POST['userAnswer'];
    $correctAnswer = $_SESSION['num1'] + $_SESSION['num2'];
    if ($correctAnswer == $userAnswer)
    {
      $_SESSION['score'] = $_SESSION['score'] + 1;
      print ("<h1>That is correct!</h1>");
    }
    else
      print ("<h1>Sorry! The correct sum of ".$_SESSION['num1'].
        " and ".$_SESSION['num2']." is $correctAnswer</h1>");
  }

  print ("</div>");

  print("<p>CURRENT SCORE: ".$_SESSION['score']." OUT OF A
```

```
            POSSIBLE ".$_SESSION['count']."</p>");
    print("<h2>Can you add these numbers?</h2>");
    print("<form action=\"math-quiz.php\" method=\"post\">");
    $_SESSION['num1'] = rand(1, 20);
    $_SESSION['num2'] = rand(1, 20);
    print("<label>".$_SESSION['num1']." + ".$_SESSION['num2']."
        = ");
    print("<input type=\"text\" size=\"10\" name=\"userAnswer\">
        </label>");
    print("<input class = \"submit\" type = \"submit\" value =
        \"Submit\" ></form>");
    print("<p><a href=\"math-quit.php\">Ready to quit?</a></p>");
?>
</body>
</html>
```

Code Example: math-quiz.php

```
<?php
  session_start();
?>
<html>
<head>
  <title>Math Quiz - RESULT</title>
  <link rel="stylesheet" type="text/css" href="quiz.css">
</head>
<body>
<?php
    print ("<div class='heading'>");
    print("<h1>Thanks for Playing! </h1>");
    print ("</div>");
    print("<h2>YOU SCORED ".$_SESSION['score'].
      " OUT OF ".$_SESSION['count']."</h2>");
    session_destroy();
    print("<p><a href = \"math-quiz.php\">Try Again?</a></p>");
?>
</body>
</html>
```

Code Example: math-quit.php

This is an important example for anyone wishing to develop Web applications. The code has been kept simple to focus on the general design—a real world application would include additional validation and features. For example, additional information about the player could be requested, and upon quitting the player's information and score could be maintained in a file or database so that the application could keep track of progress.

The **gold-hunter** application in the **samples/sessions** folder provides one more example of a page that calls itself, this time to provide a simple game.

Additional Learning Materials

Chapter 16 includes a description and examples of **multi-dimensional associative arrays that contain numerically-indexed arrays.**

PHP provides a large number of standard **array-processing functions.** Chapter 16 includes a list of these functions.

Appendix D will help you **debug** your exercises, listing a number of the most common errors that you are likely to encounter.

The **Chapter 12 Hints and Help** pages on the textbook Web site provide answers to FAQs from previous students as they worked through the end-of-chapter exercises.

Summary

An **associative** array uses character strings to index each element. Each index of an associative array is known as a **key**. The value of each element in an associative array is referenced using the appropriate key.

A common use of an associative array is to provide **lookups**.

The standard PHP **$_POST** array is an associative array. A $_POST array is automatically created for any PHP program that receives values from an HTML form that specifies the "**post**" method. Each value submitted from the form is assigned to an element of the **$_POST** array. Each element is identified by a key using the same character string that was assigned to the corresponding **name** attribute in the HTML form.

Similarly the standard PHP **$_GET** array is created for a program that receives values from an HTML form that specifies the "**get**" method. The standard PHP **$_REQUEST** array is created for a program that receives values from an HTML form that specifies either the "**get**" **or** "**post**" method. The $_REQUEST array can therefore be used instead of the **$_POST** or **$_GET** arrays.

The **isset**() function can be used to test whether or not a $_POST array element has been created. This allows us to combine the code to display a Web form with the code to process the form in a single file.

A Web session allows multiple pages to share data. The data values are maintained in the standard PHP **$_SESSION** associative array. Each value is created using a descriptive key, and these values can be accessed or modified by any page that participates in the session. To participate in a session, each page must include a PHP section that includes a call to the **sesson_start**() function. This call must appear **before** any HTML code in the file.

A user's session can be explicitly destroyed by calling the **session_destroy**() function. When this function is called the contents of the **$_SESSION** array for that user are lost.

Since a user can enter a session from any page, and can return to any page (including a page that contains code to initialize the session variables), care must be taken to ensure that session data is handled correctly each time a specific page is visited. The **isset**() function is used to test whether or not a variable has already been created and this can be used to determine whether or not **$_SESSSION** or **$_POST** array elements have been created in order to construct various responses for a user. The **empty**() function is also useful to ensure that input was actually received into a **$_SESSSION** or **$_POST** array.

Chapter 12 Review Questions

1. What type of array uses character strings as the index of each array element?
    a. Associative array
    b. Named Array
    c. Character Array
    d. String Array

2. What type of data structure is this?

```
$menu['coffee'] = 1.75;
$menu['tea'] = 1.25;
$menu['cake'] = 2.25;
```

    a. An array indexed by numbers
    b. An associative array
    c. A single variable containing a character string
    d. A single variable containing a number
    e. A data file

3. Which assertion is true concerning the following statement?

```
$menu['tea'] = 1.25;
```

    a. 'tea' is a key and 1.25 is a value
    b. 'tea' is a value and 1.25 is a key
    c. $menu is a key and 'tea' is a value
    d. $menu is a key and 9.75 is a value
    e. $menu is a value and 'tea' is a key

4. What will be displayed?

```
$menu['tea'] = 1.25;
print("<p>Tea is ".$menu['tea']."</p>");
```

    a. Tea is tea
    b. Tea is 1.25
    c. Tea is $menu['tea']
    d. Tea is $menu
    e. Tea is menu

5. A $_POST array receives values from an HTML form. Which statement is correct?
    a. The $_POST array is also called a $_GET array
    b. The values stored in a $_POST array must be assigned to variables with the same name as the keys of the $_POST array.
    c. The $_POST array must be created by the programmer.
    d. The $_POST array is used to maintain session data
    e. The keys of a $_POST array are the same as the names given to the input elements submitted from the form.

6. When should the session _start() function be used?
    a. Only in page that the user opens to start the session
    b. On every page that is part of the session

7. When should you create a session?
    a. Whenever the user will access multiple pages on your Web site
    b. Only if the user must login to your Web site
    c. Whenever data must be shared across multiple pages on your Web site
    d. Whenever data must be shared between multiple users of your Web site
    e. Whenever associative arrays are used on your Web site

8. What is the general purpose of the isset() function?
    a. Tests whether the $_POST array has been created
    b. Tests whether the $_SESSION array has been created
    c. Tests whether a particular value was submitted from a form
    d. Tests whether any variable has been created
    e. Tests whether the session has been started

9. True or False? A single PHP file can contain the code to display a Web form and the code to process the form.
    a. True
    b. False

10. Which of the following is **not** an example of a standard associative array?
    a. $_POST
    b. $_SESSION
    c. $_GET
    d. isset()

Chapter 12 Code Exercises

Your Chapter 12 code exercises can be found in your **chapter12** folder. This folder is included in your customized XAMPP installation at the following location:

   htdocs\webtech\coursework\chapter12

Type your name and the date in the **Author** and **Date** sections of each file as you work on each exercise. **Remember** that the Students page on the textbook Web site includes **Hints and Help** pages for the exercises in this and every chapter.

Debugging Exercises

Your **chapter12** folder should contain a number of "fixit" files. Each of these files contains PHP code that has an error of some kind. The type of error is indicated in the comment section of each file. You will need to run each program in order to see the errors, and to debug and test the code to see if it works correctly. For example to run **fixit1.php**, first run the Web server, then use the URL:

   http://localhost/webtech/coursework/chapter12/fixit1.php

Code Modification Exercises

Your **chapter12** folder contains a number of "modify" files. Each pair of files contains HTML and PHP code that needs to be modified to meet a requirement. The requirements are included in the comment section of each file. Modify the algorithms, being careful to make changes to the .html and .php files as directed. You will need to run each program in order to test your changes. For example to run modify1.html, first run the Web server, then use the URL:

   http://localhost/webtech/coursework/chapter12/modify1.html

Code Completion Exercises

1. Your **chapter12** folder contains two files named **my-info.html** and **my-info.php**. The my-info.html file does not need to be changed. Open **my-info.php** and add an associative array named **$myInfo**. The array should contain 8 elements that store your first name, last name, street address, city, state, zip (or postal code), email address, and phone number. Use descriptive names for each element, for example $myInfo['first name']. You can add more elements if your address requires them. Now add code that obtains the necessary values from the $myInfo array to display your name and address as it might appear on an envelope, for example:

```
Chris Jones,
100 King Street,
Chicago, Illinois 60604
```

2. Read this exercise carefully and take your time to work out the logic. Your **chapter12** folder contains versions of **inventory.html** and **inventory.php.** This application allows the user to select a paint color from a drop down list. The **inventory.php** program already includes an associative array that indicates the number of cans of paint that are available for each color. Your job is simply to complete a single line of code that will look up the color selected by the user in order to find the number of cans available in that color. The result is stored in a variable which is then displayed (the necessary print statements are provided). For example, if the user selects white, the program will indicate that **65** cans are available, and if the user selects maroon, the program will indicate that **0** cans are available.

3. Your **chapter12** folder contains two files named **employees.html** and **employees.php.** The employees.html file contains an HTML form that asks the user for an employee ID, using a drop down list. The employees.php file receives the ID and also defines two arrays. The $salaries array contains salaries, indexed by employee ID. The **$employees** array contains employee names, also indexed by ID. Add code to display the employee's name and salary by using the ID submitted by the user to look up these values in the two arrays. For example if the employee's ID is 12345 your page should display the following:

```
Employee 12345 is Mary Smith, with a salary of $54,555.00
```
---

4. Read this exercise carefully and take your time to work out the logic. Your **chapter12** folder contains versions of **travel-costs.html** and **travel-costs.php.** This application allows the user to select a destination in order to find out the air fare and nightly hotel cost. Create **two** associative arrays named **$airFare** and **$hotel.** The $airFare array should contain the five destinations as **keys** (Barcelona, Cairo, Rome, Santiago, and Tokyo), and the fares for these destinations as **values** (875.00, 950.00, 875.00, 820.00, 1575.00). The **$hotel** array should contain the same five destinations as **keys**, and the nightly rates for these destinations as **values** (85.00, 98.00, 110.00, 85.00, 240.00).

    Use the variable that contains the destination submitted by the user to look up the appropriate air fare and the hotel rate from these two arrays, so that these will be displayed. The print statements have been provided.

5. Read this exercise carefully and take your time to work out the logic. Your **chapter12** folder contains versions of **scenes.html** and **scenes.php.** This application allows the user to select a direction in order to find out what happens.

    You do not need to change scenes.html. The scenes.php program already includes an associative array that describes different scenes using directions as keys. Your job is simply to add a single print statement to the end of the code in order to display the correct scene from the array, based on the destination selected by the user.

6. Your **chapter12** folder contains two files named **date-converter.html** and **date-converter.php**. The **date-converter.html** file contains an HTML form that asks the user for a day, month name, and year. The **date-converter.php** file receives these three values and also defines an array named **$months** that contains the month numbers using the month names as indices, for example **$months['January']** contains 1, and **$months['February']** contains 2. Add code that uses the month name provided by the user to look up the month number and displays the date as three numbers separated by /'s. For example if the user submitted 2, June and 2013, the program would display:

```
The date is 2/6/2013.
```

7. Your **chapter12** folder contains **city-trips.html** and **city-trips.php**. The code in **city-trips.html** does not need to be changed—it contains a form that allows the user to choose any of five cities from a drop down list in order to obtain the mileage and fuel costs to the city from NYC. Add an associative array to your **city-trips.php** file that uses city names as keys to store distances to the following five cities from NYC:

```
Atlanta 880
Boston 225
Chicago 788
Detroit 614
Miami 1275
```

   Now add code that: receives the city, fuel cost (per gallon), and car mileage (mpg) submitted by the user; looks up the distance to that city; calculates the fuel cost (distance / mpg * fuel cost per gallon); and then displays the city, distance and fuel cost.

8. Review the chapter material that explains the purpose and construction of applications that use Web sessions. Study the code examples carefully. Now develop a small application of your own that uses a Web session to track one or more data values between multiple Web pages (for example the user's name and a score, or a selection that the user has made on a previous page). Keep it simple and don't use more than three or four pages. As you become more comfortable using Web sessions you will be able to develop more complex applications, such as small Web-based games.

Chapter 13

Program Modularity — Working with Functions

Intended Learning Outcomes

After completing this chapter, you should be able to:

- Summarize the importance of modular approaches to software design.
- Describe key characteristics of functions.
- Explain the purpose of arguments and parameter lists.
- Write code that calls a function based on the function name and required arguments.
- Write code that receives a value returned by a function call.
- Find and use common pre-defined PHP functions.
- Use the PHP die() or exit() function to end an application's execution.
- Create a new function and use this in a PHP application.
- Determine whether the code inside a function should be separated into multiple functions.
- Write function code that includes calls to other functions.
- Create and save a library of useful functions for use with multiple applications.
- Create and use include files to avoid duplication of HTML and PHP code.
- Incorporate include statements in an application.

Introduction

Since the first computers appeared in the 1940s, computer technology has evolved rapidly. The first desktop computer appeared in 1982. The World Wide Web emerged in 1994. Throughout this period we have seen dramatic advances in operating systems, microprocessors, network systems, and also in programming languages. New languages are constantly being developed, not only to take advantage of new hardware and network capabilities, but also to reflect our increasing understanding of effective **software design**.

Perhaps more than anything else, modern software design is concerned with **code modularity**: development of code in separate, functional components in order to maximize **reusability** and minimize **duplication**. With the development of computer networks, the application of code modularity has extended beyond the design of individual applications to facilitate access to common code and inter-communications between applications world-wide (**interoperability**). This in turn has led to greater cooperation between software companies and developers to achieve **common standards**.

The development and delivery of common modules remains a work in progress, and many programmers continue to develop new code that simply duplicates code already written and tested. To take some simple examples, consider how many times code might have been written to perform standard tax computations on employee wages, convert temperatures, sort a list of names alphabetically, or sum a list of numbers.

Good programmers quickly learn to first research the availability of pre-existing code modules that can be used in their applications. When existing code is not available, good software design calls for new code to be developed in many small modules that each perform well-defined tasks. These modules can then be "glued" together as needed into working applications to meet specific requirements.

For example, consider the advantage of developing distinct code modules that carry out tax-related calculations, perform standard temperature conversions, or process various banking transactions? If you think about it, it makes sense to always try to develop code in small reusable modules. You can liken this approach to the way that we design and build houses. The contractor constructs a house to meet the specific requirements of the home-owner but, instead of building the entire structure from scratch, he or she makes use of pre-assembled components (doors, windows, plumbing fixtures, drywall panels, etc.). These components are designed to meet common standards so that they can be used interchangeably. Old components can be easily replaced with new and improved versions.

Just as there are entire companies whose business is to design and develop standard housing components such as windows and plumbing fixtures, so many software companies design and develop standard software components that are then sold to other developers for inclusion in working applications.

Individual code modules are called **functions, methods, sub-programs , sub-routines , or procedures , depending on the programming language.** We will use the term **function** here since this is the term used in PHP. Each function is identified by a **function name** and contains the necessary code to perform a specific, well-defined task. Functions are easy to identify in most languages—the function name is always followed by a pair of parentheses.

You have been using many pre-defined PHP functions already. For example you have used the **pow()**, **pi()**, **round()**, **ceil()**, **floor()**, and **random()** functions to perform various mathematical operations, the **fopen()**, **fclose()**, **feof()**, **fputs()** and **fgets()** functions to process text files, and the **list()**, **explode()**, **trim()**, **strtoupper()**, **strtolower()**, and **number_format()** functions to work with character strings.

In this chapter you will learn more about using pre-defined functions, and you will also learn how to create and use your own functions, and how to store these in **include** files for use by any number of applications.

Using Functions

As a general rule, programmers should strive to avoid writing duplicate code. Duplicate code, whether within a single application or in different applications, is not only unnecessarily repetitive, but can also lead to problems if the code needs to be updated at a later date. The more you program, the more you will hesitate whenever you find yourself rewriting the same code in different parts of your application.

One important way to minimize code duplication is to break your code down into distinct modules (known as **functions** in PHP and many other languages). Once developed, a function can be "called" as many times as needed by your application. If you design your functions carefully, it is quite likely that they can be used by many different applications. The secret to **reusability** is to develop each function to perform a single, very precise task. For example, don't design a single function to both calculate the surface area of a floor **and** the cost to carpet it. If you do, the function could not be used by an application that only needed to determine the surface area of the floor, or only needed to know the cost to carpet a floor. Instead design one function to calculate the surface area, and another function to calculate the cost to carpet a floor. That way your applications can call either function as needed, and if an application needs to determine the area of a floor **and** the cost to carpet that floor, it can simply call **both** functions.

As mentioned earlier, you have been using functions all along. Functions are easily recognized in PHP and most languages, because each call to a function requires you to specify the function **name** followed by a pair of parentheses, that may or may not contain a list of **arguments**, for example **pow(7, 3)**. Like most programming languages, PHP supplies many useful pre-defined functions that you can use in your programs as needed.

When you think about it, a function works in your program the way an employee or contractor performs in the workplace: you call up the function whenever you need a specific task performed, and give it the information it needs, and trust that it will take care of the task for you, just as you (hopefully!) trust an employee or contractor to have the skills needed to perform their job. In either case, you do not need to know how the work is actually done.

In order to **use** a function you only need to know **four** things:

1. What is the name of the function?
2. What **task** does the function perform?
3. What input does the function need in order to perform its task (in other words, what **arguments**, if any, must you send to the function)?
4. What **output** does the function generate (in other words, what type of value, if any, does the function **return** to your program when it completes its task)?

Consider the **pow()** function. You know that the function name is **pow()**, that the function's purpose is to multiply a value by itself the number of times indicated by an exponent, that the required arguments are the base value and the exponent, and that the return value is the result of this operation. This is all you need to know in order to use the pow() function in your programs. You don't need to know the code that the pow() function uses to perform the required calculation.

Once you know these four things about any function, you can write code to call the function, send it any values that it needs, and receive the result (if any) that the function returns. Let's look more closely at how we do this.

Understanding Function Arguments

Many functions need to receive some values in order to perform their task. For example, the **pow()** function needs to receive a base value and an exponent in order to perform a calculation: if your code executes **pow(7, 3)**, the pow() function will receive the values 7 and 3 and return the value of 7 cubed. The values that we send to a function are called **arguments**. Arguments must be listed between the parentheses that follow the function name. The pow() function needs **two** arguments: the first is the base value (in this case 7), the second is the exponent (in this case 3). We don't have to send literal values as arguments, we can also send variables: for example if we need to raise the value stored in the variable **$someNumber** to the power of **5**, we can use **pow($someNumber, 5)**, or if a variable **$exponent** contains the value of the exponent that we want, we could use **pow($someNumber, $exponent)**.

Arguments **must** be listed in the correct order! When we use the **pow()** function, the first argument must be the base number and the second argument must be the exponent. If we supplied these values in the wrong order, the **pow()** function would still work, but would generate an unintended result, for example pow(3,7) would return the value of 3 raised to the power 7.

Different functions require different numbers of arguments. The **pi()** function does not require **any** arguments since it simply returns the value of PI (but notice that, since this is a function, you must still supply the parentheses). The **strtoupper()** function requires a single argument, for example **strtoupper("London")**: Here the argument is the **character string** "London" and the function will return "LONDON".

The **feof()** function also takes a single argument, for example **feof($someFile)**. In this case the argument is the **file handle** that the function will refer to in order to determine whether or not the EOF marker for the file has been read. The **fopen**() function uses **two** arguments: the **name** of the file to be opened and the **mode** (indicating whether the file is to be opened for read, write or append operations, or some combination of these), for example **fopen("textfile.txt", "r")**.

Some functions are designed so that they can be used with **different** numbers of arguments. In actuality a different version of the function is executed depending on the number of arguments that are sent. An example of this is the **round**() function. Sometimes we want to just round off to whole numbers and we call the function using just one argument, for example **round (14.626)** will return **15**. But other times we may want to round a value to a specific number of decimal places. In that case we can call a version of the **round**() function that accepts **two** arguments, for example **round (14.626, 2)**; now the **round**() function returns **14.63**, the value rounded off to two places, as specified in the second argument.

By the way, the **fgets**() function is another example of a function that can be used with one or two arguments. We have used the single argument version but a two-argument version allows you to specify the number of bytes that are to be returned by the read operation.

Receiving Values from a Function

As we have seen, many functions are designed to **return** a value once they have completed their task. If a function returns a value, the program that calls the function will usually want to use this value in some way.

A program may assign the value that is returned by a function to a variable for use in subsequent statements. For example in the statement **$result = pow(7, 3)**; the value returned by **pow(7, 3)**; is stored in the variable **$result**. Similarly in the statement **$nextLine = fgets($someFile)**; the value returned by **fgets($someFile)** is stored in the variable **$nextLine**.

A program may also use the value returned by a function directly in an expression of some kind. For example in the statement **while (!feof($someFile))** the **true** or **false** value returned from the **feof**() function is not stored in a variable. Instead it is used directly to decide whether or not to repeat the statements inside the while loop.

Similarly, the value that is returned by a function can be used directly in **print**() statements. However note that a call to a function cannot be included inside a character string that is enclosed in double quotes. That's because the PHP processor will assume that a statement such as:

```
print("<p>The square of 3 is pow(3, 2)</p>");
```

is intended to generate the string exactly as written, so this statement will produce: "<p>The square of 3 is pow(3, 2)</p>". As described in Chapter 5, in order to call a function within a **print**() statement we need to separate the function call from any character strings and **concatenate** the function call to these strings using periods (the period is the PHP concatenation operator). Here is the correct version of the previous statement:

```
print("<p>The square of 3 is ".pow(3, 2)."</p>";
```

Note that the call to the **pow**() function is now separated from the character string "<p>The square of 3 is " and the character string "</p>". The result of pow(3,2) is calculated and returned, and this value is concatenated (joined) to the other strings to create "<p>The square of 3 is 9</p>".

Researching Available Functions

An important skill for any programmer is to research the availability of existing functions and other code modules in order to reduce the need to develop and test new code.

PHP provides a large number of pre-defined, or standard, functions. At the time of publishing, you can view a list of these at **https://www.php.net/manual/en/funcref.php**, otherwise Google "standard PHP functions." These are functions that the PHP processor will recognize. Don't be intimidated by all the different function categories and number of available functions! Programmers tend to learn functions on an as-needed basis. As a programmer you will become increasingly skilled at using functions most relevant to your own work, and to quickly find and make use of new functions when you need them.

The best way to get a feel for the more commonly used function is to look them up by general category, for example functions associated with dates, math operations, string processing, file handling, or arrays. Lists of functions by category are widely available on the Web; you can also find a list of these functions in Chapter 16.

Apart from the **standard** PHP functions, many other useful functions have been developed by other programmers. Useful functions can be found by searching the Web, looking through programming books, requesting help from other programmers, etc. A great deal of code is freely shared but be careful to ensure that any functions that you find are intended for general use and not copyrighted.

Often collections (or **libraries**) of related functions are developed for specific purposes. Some function libraries are freely available, while others are distributed as a commercial product. If you go to work as a programmer, you may be provided with function libraries that have been developed internally to support your company's specific business applications.

Reasons to Use Pre-Defined Functions

It is often far more efficient and practical to make use of existing functions than to write new code for the same purpose, for a number of reasons:

Rapid development: Use of code that already exists reduces the time needed to develop new applications.

Improved code: Code that has already been shared has usually been evaluated by many programmers and can usually (not always!) be assumed to be accurate and efficient.

Reduced testing: Code that has been previously developed has usually already been rigorously tested, whereas any new code that you create must be tested carefully for errors.

Ease of maintenance: Code can be maintained and improved separately by different programmers or development teams.

Duplication of effort: Why write code that has already been written when your efforts are better spent developing something new?

Self-documenting code: Programmers must often maintain applications that have been developed by others. It is easier to read and understand the purpose of code that makes use of standard or commonly-used functions.

Increased standardization: The greater the standardization of code between applications, the more easily applications can work together. This is increasingly important in a global, inter-connected software environment.

Using die() or exit() to Terminate an Application

Some **standard** functions are particularly important to be aware of, since they handle tasks that could not otherwise be easily coded. An example is the **die**() function. Sometimes applications must be designed to end immediately in the event an error occurs. For example in Chapter 6 we saw how to work with text files. The fopen() function is used to open a file and provide a handle to the connection which is usually assigned to a variable, like this:

```
$someFile = fopen("some-file.txt", "r");
```

But what happens here if a problem occurs when the application tries to open the file? For example, what if the file does not exist? In cases such as this, the fopen() function simply returns FALSE. In our sample code, therefore, FALSE would be stored in the variable $someFile. Clearly if the file cannot be opened, the application should not be allowed to go ahead and use fgets() or the fclose() functions to process the file. Doing so would cause the application to abruptly terminate with a PHP error message. We can avoid this by testing $someFile and, if the variable contains FALSE, we can simply force the program to end with a suitable error message of our own design. The die()

function will do this for us. Here is a general template for closing a program if an attempt to open a file fails:

```
$someFile = fopen("some-file.txt", "r");

if (!$someFile)
    die("<h1>File I/O Error</h1><p>Sorry, this file could not be
    opened. The application is now closing.</p>");
```

The die() function takes any message that you want to provide as an argument, and this message will be displayed before the application closes.

You may be wondering why the IF structure does not include an ELSE section to contain the code that will process the file if the fopen() operation is successful. The ELSE section is not needed here because the die() function will immediately end the application so no following code will be executed if this function is called. If the test is false, the call to the die() function will be skipped and any following code will be executed.

PHP also provides an **exit**() function which is functionally the same as the die() function. These two functions can therefore be used interchangeably.

The die() and exit() functions can be used in any situation where you wish the application to exit immediately under some circumstance without "crashing" with a system error message. In the next chapter we will see how we can use these functions when trying and failing to connect to a database.

Creating Your Own Functions

Despite the availability of a wide range of functions designed to handle many different operations, you will still often need to develop functions of your own. When you do, you may then want to share these with other programmers.

You can create your own functions quite easily. It is useful to develop functions in groups that are related by some general purpose. We will begin by developing some functions for use with our temperature conversion applications. Many weather-related applications might need to convert temperatures between Celsius and Fahrenheit, so it makes sense to provide a library of functions for this purpose that can then be called up by any applications as needed.

Let's start with a function to convert Celsius to Fahrenheit. This function must receive a single argument (a Celsius temperature), and must return a Fahrenheit temperature. We'll call the function **toFahrenheit**() Here's how we construct the function in PHP:

```
function toFahrenheit($celsius)
{
    $fahrenheit = (9 / 5) * $celsius + 32;
    return $fahrenheit;
}
```

The function definition begins with a heading: **function toFahrenheit ($celsius)**. This heading includes the word **function** followed by the name that we wish to give the function (**toFahrenheit**), followed by a pair of parentheses that must contain a list of variables that the function will use to receive the actual arguments that are sent to it each time the function is called by a program. These "receiving variables" are known as the function's **parameters**. Each parameter must receive a value when the function is called and the parameters can be referenced as needed in the function's internal code.

In this case the **toFahrenheit()** function has one parameter, a variable named **$celsius**. Whenever we call this function, we must supply a single argument. The function will receive whatever value is sent as an argument in the **$celsius** parameter. The **$celsius** variable can then be used within the function as needed.

For example, if we want to use this function in a program that needs to convert 20° Celsius to Fahrenheit and store the result in a variable named $fTemp, we could include the following statement:

```
$fTemp = toFahrenheit(20);
```

The **toFahrenheit()** function will be executed and the argument **20** would be received by the function and stored in the parameter variable **$celsius**. Any reference to the **$celsius** variable inside the function would obtain the value 20, so the statement:

```
$fahrenheit = (9 / 5) * $celsius + 32;
```

would be processed as:

```
$fahrenheit = (9 / 5) * 20 + 32;
```

which will store 68 in $fahrenheit. The second statement in this function is:

```
return $fahrenheit;
```

and this will return the value 68 to the calling program.

We could also call the function using a variable as an argument, for example:

```
$fTemp = toFahrenheit($someTemperature);
```

Here the value stored in the argument **$someTemperature** would be passed to the parameter **$celsius**.

So a function definition consists of the function **heading** and the function **body**. The function **body** contains the code that the function needs to perform its task. The code is provided between a pair of {} braces, and can contain any programming structures (sequential, selection or loop statements, or even calls to other functions). A function can contain any number of instructions but remember that good program design calls for each function to only perform a single task—this ensures that programmers have the greatest flexibility in the ways they can use the function in their own applications.

Our **toFahrenheit()** function contains two statements. The first statement uses the value received by the parameter **$celsius** to calculate the Fahrenheit and assign the result to the variable **$fahrenheit**. The second statement in the function is a return statement. The value that follows **return** (in this case the value stored in **$fahrenheit**) is returned to the program that called the function. If you do not include a return statement, the function will not return a value.

Do you see how this works? The function is designed independently of any program that calls it. The program that calls the function can send any numeric value, either a literal value such as **34.25**, or the value stored in a variable, such as a variable named **$someTemperature** or even a value stored in a variable that happens to be named **$celsius** (the same name as the function's parameter). The programmer who is **writing** the function simply provides a variable in the parameter list to receive the value that is sent as an argument. The programmer who is developing the program that **calls** this function does not need to know that the parameter is named **$celsius**, only that the function must be sent a number as an argument.

Here is the code for a second function, **toCelsius()** that receives a Fahrenheit temperature, converts this to Celsius, and returns the result:

```
function toCelsius($fahrenheit)
{
    $celsius = ($fahrenheit - 32) / (9 / 5);
    return $celsius;
}
```

Now we have **two** useful functions that could be used in any applications that need to convert temperatures. The mark of a good programmer is to think beyond any specific application and develop libraries of related functions that can then be used as needed to minimize duplication of code. What else might we add to our group of temperature-related functions?

Perhaps it would be useful to include functions that return the actual **conversion formulas** that are used to perform these conversions. An application can call these functions if it simply needs to display the formulas themselves. Here is the code for two functions named **strFahrenheitFormula()** and **strCelsiusFormula()** that return character strings containing the actual formulas:

```
function strFahrenheitFormula()
{
    return "Fahrenheit = (9 / 5) * Celsius + 32";
}

function strCelsiusFormula()
{
    return "Celsius = (Fahrenheit - 32) / (9 / 5)";
}
```

These two functions do not include any parameters. That's because these functions do not require any arguments. They each simply return the character string that describes the appropriate formula. Note that a function with no parameters **must** still include the parentheses in the function heading even though there is nothing between them.

Now let's add a function name **getWindChill**() to calculate the wind chill temperature. There are different ways to calculate windchill; this function uses the wind chill formula developed by the US National Weather Service in 2001:

```
function getWindchill($fahrenheit, $windSpeedMPH)
{
   $windchill = 35.74 + (0.6215 * $fahrenheit) -
      (35.75 * pow($windSpeedMPH, 0.16)) +
      (0.4275 * $fahrenheit * pow($windSpeedMPH, 0.16));
   return $windchill;
}
```

Now here's a great example of why it is so useful to create a function to perform a common task! How many times would you want to see that code repeated in different programs? What would be the likelihood of errors? In fact this is a good example of a function that should be written once and then made available to programmers everywhere!

Also notice that this function requires **two** parameters. The first parameter receives the temperature in Fahrenheit and the second parameter receives the wind speed in miles per hour. In PHP multiple parameters are separated by **commas**. If you call a function with more than one parameter, be sure that the arguments that you send to the function are in the same order as the parameters in the function heading! For example if you wanted the wind chill for a temperature of 30 and a wind speed of 15, you must call the function using getWindchill(30, 15) since that is the order of the parameters. If you called the function with getWindchill(15, 30), the function would receive 15 into the $fahrenheit parameter and 30 into the $windSpeedMPH parameter so the result would be incorrect. This would result in a significant error that might be very difficult to discover. It's the kind of error that can have very serious real-world consequences: sometimes an error like this may not be caught until some time after the application has been in production. This is why careful testing is such an important part of all software development.

Where Do I Put My Functions?

Functions can be included directly in a program simply by typing the function definition in your code **before** the function is actually called. Look at the code for **temp-converter5.php** which shows how our **toFahrenheit**() function can be included directly in an application. This is a revised version of **temp-converter3.php** which used a FOR loop to display the Celsius and Fahrenheit temperatures from 0 to 100 in increments of 10. The new version defines the **toFahrenheit**() function and then calls this function each time the loop repeats in order to obtain the next conversion value.

```
<html>
<head>
  <title>Temperature Conversions</title>
  <link rel="stylesheet" type="text/css" href="sample.css">
</head>
<body>
  <?php
    function toFahrenheit($celsius)
    {
      $fahrenheit = (9 / 5) * $celsius + 32;
      return $fahrenheit;
    }

    print("<h1>Temperature Conversions</h1>");

    print ("<table>");
    print ("<tr><td><strong>Degrees Celsius</strong></td>
        <td><strong>Degrees Fahrenheit</strong></td></tr>");

    for($celsius = 0; $celsius <= 100; $celsius = $celsius + 10)
    {
      $fahrenheit = toFahrenheit($celsius);
      print("<tr><td class=\"center\">$celsius</td>
        <td class\"center\">$fahrenheit</td></tr>");
    }
    print ("</table>");
  ?>
</body>
</html>
```

Code Example: temp-converter5.php

You can include any number of functions in your code, as long as each function is listed before it is called. However this approach means that the function will only be available to a single application. If you wanted to use the toFahrenheit() function in other applications you would need to copy the function definition to each application file.

In order to share functions among any number of applications it is far more useful to store your functions in a separate file so that any application can reference them. A good approach is to create a number of different function files so that each file contains a group of related functions. This helps to keep functions organized and easier to locate and manage. Files of related functions are often known as function **libraries**.

Creating a Library of Functions

We have created five functions. Since they are all related to temperatures, we will create a library of temperature functions by storing them in a file named **inc-temp-functions.php** as follows:

```php
<?php
  function toFahrenheit($celsius)
  {
    $fahrenheit = (9 / 5) * $celsius + 32;
    return $fahrenheit;
  }
  function toCelsius($fahrenheit)
  {
    $celsius = ($fahrenheit - 32) / (9 / 5);
    return $celsius;
  }
  function strFahrenheitFormula()
  {
    return "Fahrenheit = (9 / 5) * Celsius + 32";
  }
  function strCelsiusFormula()
  {
    return "Celsius = (Fahrenheit - 32) / (9 / 5)";
  }
  function getWindchill($fahrenheit, $windSpeedMPH)
  {
    $windchill = 35.74 + (0.6215 * $fahrenheit) -
      (35.75 * pow($windSpeedMPH, 0.16)) +
      (0.4275 * $fahrenheit * pow($windSpeedMPH, 0.16));
    return $windchill;
  }
?>
```

Code Example: inc-temp-functions.php

Note that this file simply contains a group of PHP functions. The file is not intended to generate a Web page and contains no HTML code and no PHP other than the code used to create the functions. It is simply a "utility" file for use by other applications. Note also that beginning and ending PHP tags are required to surround this code.

So now we have a file that contains a group of useful temperature-related functions. How do we **reference** these functions in our applications?

Including Functions from External Files

In PHP, we can tell the processor to include code from external files before processing the PHP instructions in our applications. One way to do this is by issuing an **include**() statement. For example if we wish to include the code in the **inc-temp-functions.php** file in an application, we can use the statement:

```
include("inc-temp-functions.php");
```

This statement **must** appear **before** any code that references the code contained in the included file. When a file is included in another file, the content of the included file is added to the existing code at the location of the **include**() statement. The code in the included files can therefore be referenced by any statements that follow this location.

Notice that we named our file of functions **inc-temp-functions.php**. We can use any name for files that are to be included in other files. But using "**inc**" as the first part of the file name helps us to recognize the purpose of these files: they are not in themselves working applications but instead contain code that can be included in our applications.

Look at the code for **temp-converter6.php**. This is a revised version of **temp-converter5.php**. The new version uses the **toFahrenheit**() function from the **inc-temp-functions.php** file to convert the temperature, and also calls the **strFahrenheitFormula**() function from the same file to display the formula.

```
<html>
<head>
   <title>Temperature Conversions</title>
   <link rel="stylesheet" type="text/css" href="sample.css">
</head>
<body>
   <?php
     include("inc-temp-functions.php");
     print("<h1>Temperature Conversions</h1>");
     print("<p>NOTE: These conversions use the formula:
        <br>".strFahrenheitFormula()."</p>");
     print("<table>");
     print("<tr><td><strong>Degrees Celsius</strong></td>
        <td><strong>Degrees Fahrenheit</strong></td></tr>");
     for ($celsius = 0;$celsius <= 100; $celsius = $celsius + 10)
     {
        $fahrenheit = toFahrenheit($celsius);
        print("<tr><td class=\"center\">$celsius</td>
           <td class=\"center\">$fahrenheit</td></tr>");
     }
     print("</table>");
   ?>
</body>
</html>
```

Code Example: temp-converter6.php

The first PHP statement is an **include** statement which will add the code in the file **inc-temp-functions.php** to the code in temp-converter6.php.

The second **print**() statement calls the **strFahrenheitFormula**() function which returns the formula so that this can be displayed. The processor recognizes this function because it is listed in the **inc-temp-functions.php**, which has previously been included. The character string returned by **strFahrenheitFormula**() is added to the output of the **print**() statement (note the use of the periods to concatenate the function call with the two character strings).

The FOR loop repeats 11 times to produce the required table rows. Each row contains a temperature conversion from Celsius to Fahrenheit. The counting variable is named **$celsius** and this variable is incremented by 10 for each repetition, with values from 0 to 100. The two statements in the loop body perform the following operations:

- The current value of **$celsius** is sent as an argument to the toFahrenheit() function. The function calculates and returns the equivalent Fahrenheit temperature which is stored in the $fahrenheit variable.
- The print statement uses the values stored in the $celsius and $fahrenheit variables to generate a new table row containing the Celsius and Fahrenheit temperatures.

Using the Same Functions in Different Programs

The value of developing a group of related functions and then storing them in a separate file is that we can use these functions for different purposes in different programs. Consider the following requirement for another temperature-related application:

---

calc-windchill requirements:

Write an application that asks the user for the current temperature (in degrees Celsius) and the wind speed (mile per hour). The program should then display the wind chill for these conditions (also in degrees Celsius).

To meet these requirements, we need a form to receive the required input from the user. Here is the pseudocode for **calc-windchill.html**:

```
calc-windchill.html algorithm:

    Prompt the user for the temperature in Celsius
    Get celsius
    Prompt the user for the windspeed
    Get windspeed
    Submit celsius, windspeed to calc-windchill.php
END
```

Here is the code for calc-windchill.html:

```html
<html>
<head>
  <title>WIND CHILL CALCULATOR</title>
  <link rel="stylesheet" type="text/css" href="sample.css">
</head>
<body>
  <h1>WIND CHILL CALCULATOR</h1>

    <form action="calc-windchill.php" method="post">
    <label>Temp in degrees Celsius:
    <input type="text" size="5" name="celsius"></label>
    <label>Wind speed in miles per hour:
    <input type="text" size="5" name="windspeed"></label>
    <input class="submit" type="submit" value="Display the Wind
      chill temperature">
</form>
</body>
</html>
```

Code Example: calc-windchill.html

Next we need to design a program to process the user input. We can use our previously developed **getWindchill**() function, but the requirements tell us to obtain the temperature in degrees Celsius, and also display the results in Celsius. Since our **getWindchill**() function is designed to receive the temperature in degrees Fahrenheit and return the wind chill in degrees Fahrenheit we will need to use the **toFahrenheit**() function to convert the Celsius input to Fahrenheit before calling the **getWindchill**() function, then use the **toCelsius**() function to convert the windchill temperature from Fahrenheit back to Celsius **after** calling the **toCelsius**() function.

Here is the pseudocode for calc-windchill.php:

```
calc-windchill.php:

  receive celsius, windspeed from calc-windchill.html
  fahrenheit = toFahrenheit(celsius)
  windchillF = getWindchill(fahrenheit, windspeed )
  windchillC = toCelsius(windchillF)
  Display celsius, windspeed, windchillC
END
```

Here is the code for calc-windchill.php:

```
<html>
<head>
   <title>WIND CHILL CALCULATOR</title>
   <link rel="stylesheet" type="text/css" href="sample.css">
</head>
<body>
   <h1>WIND CHILL CALCULATOR</h1>

<?php
     include("incTempFunctions.php");

     $celsius = $_POST['celsius'];
     $windspeed = $_POST['windspeed'];
     $fahrenheit = toFahrenheit($celsius);
     $windchillF = getWindchill($fahrenheit, $windspeed);
     $windchillC = toCelsius($windchillF);

     print("Temperature (Celsius): $celsius<br>);
     print("WindSpeed (miles per hour): $windspeed<br>);
     print("Windchill (Celsius): ".number_format($windchillC, 2)
        ."<br>");
?>
</body>
</html>
```

Code Example: calc-windchill.php

Figure 13-1 shows a sample interaction.

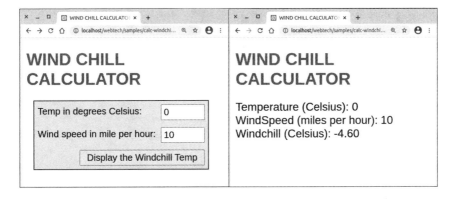

Figure 13-1: calc-windchill.html and calc-windchill.php screenshots

This example should give you a feel for the importance and value of developing libraries of useful functions. Some programmers may spend most of their time developing general purpose code libraries of this kind, while other programmers develop applications that make use of these function libraries to meet specific requirements. There is an important difference in approach. An application programmer is focused on developing a custom solution for a specific set of requirements. But a programmer who is developing general purpose code is not thinking about any specific application. Instead he or she is considering the most generally useful way to develop code functions for maximum reusability.

Functions Calling Functions

You can code a function in the same way as you code your main application. You can include selection structures, loop structures; you can even include calls to other functions. Calling one function from another can help you avoid the trap of writing code inside a function that could be separated out and used to define a separate useful function. This is central to the idea of creating functions that each perform a single useful task. As an example, let's say that you often need to calculate the number of days in a month, based on the name of the month and the year. Why do we need to know the year as well as the month? Because if the month is "February", the number of days will depend on whether or not the year is a leap year. We often think of a leap year as any year that is divisible by 4, but actually it's a bit more complicated: a year is a leap year if it is divisible by 4 **and either** the year is not divisible by 100 **or** the year IS divisible by 400. In other words, leap years come every 4 years, except not on the turn of the century years, unless it's a 4th century year. How's that for complicated!

It would be useful to create a function that receives any month and year and returns the number of days in the month based on these two values. This could be useful in many different applications. Let's code a function named **daysInMonth**() that receive two arguments, the name of a month and the year. It's simple enough to include code that handles months that have 31 or 30 days:

```
function daysInMonth ($month, $year)
{
if ($month == "January" or $month == "March" or $month == "May"
or
   $month == "July" or $month == "August" or
   $month == "October" or $month == "December")
{
   return 31;
}
else if ($month == "April" or $month == "June" or
   $month == "September" or $month == "November")
   {
      return 30;
   }
   // still need to test for "February"
}
```

Now we need to add another ELSE to handle the one remaining month, "February", which will either contain 28 days or 29 days. To make this determination, we need to test if the year is divisible by 4 **and either** the year is not divisible by 100 **or** the year IS divisible by 400. If this test is true, then the year is a leap year and February has 29 days, otherwise February has 28 days. How do we test is a number is divisible by another number with no remainder? Recall that the **modulus** (%) operator calculates the **remainder** of a division. If we use this operator to divide a number by another and get a 0 remainder, we know that the first number is divisible by the second. So if a year is stored in a variable named **$year**, the test **$year % 4 == 0** will be true only if the year is divisible by 4, false otherwise. Similarly the test **$year % 100 != 0** will be true only if the year is **not** divisible by 100. And the test **$year % 400 == 0** will be true only if the year is divisible by 400, false otherwise. We can put these three tests together to create a leap year test as follows:

```
( ($year % 4 == 0) and (($year % 100 != 0) or ($year %400 == 0))
)
```

Take some time to understand the placement of the parentheses in this expression, to ensure that the three tests are evaluated in the correct order.

Here is the complete code solution for daysInMonth() that includes the leap year test:

```
function daysInMonth ($month, $year)
{
   if ($month == "January" or $month == "March" or
      $month == "May" or $month == "July" or
      $month == "August" or $month == "October" or
      $month == "December")
   {
      return 31;
   }
   else if ($month == "April" or $month == "June" or
      $month == "September" or $month == "November")
   {
      return 30;
   }
   else if (($year % 4 == 0) and
       (($year % 100 != 0) or ($year %400 == 0)))
   {
      return 29;
   }
   else
   {
      return 28;
   }
}
```

The function will return 31, 30, 29, or 28 depending on the month and year that are sent as arguments.

However, while this is a very useful function, it does not meet the ideal that we strive for with regard to code modularity. We want our functions to each perform a single useful task so that we can use them as effectively as possible. As written, this function contains the code for **two** useful services: it determines whether or not a year is a leap year, and it **also** determines the number of days in a month. What if we just needed to know if a year is a leap year? The function calculates this but does not return this answer. It would be more useful if the code to determine a leap year was developed in a **separate** function, for example named **isLeapYear()**. That way the daysInMonth() function can call the isLeapYear() function to perform that test, but we can **also** call the isLeapYear() function directly in our code if we just want to check if a year is a leap year.

Here is the code for a function isLeapYear(). Note that this function just needs to receive the year as an argument, and will return **true** or **false**, depending on the result of the test that the function performs:

```
function isLeapYear($year)
{
  return ($year % 4 == 0) and (($year % 100 != 0) or ($year % 400
== 0));

}
```

And now here is a revised code for a daysInMonth() function that calls the isLeapYear() to test if the year is a leap year:

```
function daysInMonth ($month, $year)
{
  if ($month == "January" or $month == "March" or
    $month == "May" or $month == "July" or
    $month == "August" or $month == "October" or
    $month == "December")
  {
    return 31;
  }
  else if ($month == "April" or $month == "June" or
    $month == "September" or $month == "November")
  {
    return 30;
  }
  else if (isLeapYear($year))
  {
    return 29;
  }
  else
  {
    return 28;
  }
}
```

There a few things to notice here. First is that isLeapYear() returns the result of a test, which will be either true or false, Second, isLeapYear() only needs one parameter since it just needs the year to determine if it is a leap year. Third is that, although daysInMonth() no longer contains the code to test if the year is a leap year, it still needs to receive the year; it needs it so that it can pass it on to isLeapYear(). The daysInMonth() function only calls isLeapYear() if the month is February: if isLeapYear() returns **true** then daysInMonth() returns 29; if isLeapYear() returns **false** then daysInMonth() returns 28.

Using these two functions, any application could call daysInMonth() with code such as

```
$days = daysInMonth("September", 2017);
$days = daysInMonth("February", 2016);
$days = daysInMonth($birthMonth, $birthYear);
```

An application could also call the isLeapYear() function directly if it only needed to know whether or not a year is a leap year. For example:

```
if (isLeapYear($year))
   print("<h1>Happy New Leap Year!!!</h1>");
else
   print("<h1>Happy New Year!!!</h1>");
```

As a general rule, whenever you are developing a function, consider whether the function code is actually performing multiple tasks that could be broken down into separate functions, for improved modularity.

Learning to Think Beyond Specific Applications

As we have seen, modular programming changes the way that we think about software design. Instead of designing and developing code for a specific set of requirements, we start to think on a larger scale. Let's look at one more example of a function library.

We have already developed code to process a file of numbers containing rainfall data and then perform various operations on this data: display the numbers, calculate the total, calculate the average, find the highest rainfall, and find the lowest rainfall. These applications worked with rainfall data, but we might ask "Don't we often need to perform similar operations on all kinds of files that contain numeric values, for example files of scores, or files of payroll amounts?"

What if we simply develop a set of functions that we could use to process **any** file that contains a list of numbers? We could include a function to simply display the values in the file, and functions to obtain the total, count, average, highest and lowest values? Then we could use these functions as needed in any program required to process a file of numbers, whether the file contained rainfall, student scores, wages, ages, sales figures, or anything else. The functions would have to receive the appropriate file name as an argument in order to know which file to open, and the file would need to simply contain a list of numbers since that is what these functions will be designed to handle.

Your **samples** folder includes a file named inc-numeric-file-functions.php. This file contains a number of functions that are designed to work with any file that contains a list of numbers, where each number appears on a separate line in the file. Each function uses a parameter to receive a file name, then opens the file and processes it in some way:

The **printData()** function opens the file with the filename that is sent as an argument, outputs the numbers contained in the file, then closes the file.

The **getTotal()** function opens the file with the filename that is sent as an argument, calculates the total of the numbers contained in the file, closes the file, and returns the total.

The **getCount()** function opens the file with the filename that is sent as an argument, counts the numbers contained in the file, closes the file, and returns the count.

The **getAverage()** function opens the file with the filename that is sent as an argument, calculates the average of the numbers contained in the file, closes the file, and returns the average.

The **getHighest()** function opens the file with the filename that is sent as an argument, finds the highest value of the numbers contained in the file, closes the file, and returns the highest value.

The **getLowest()** function opens the file with the filename that is sent as an argument, finds the lowest value of the numbers contained in the file, closes the file, and returns the lowest value.

Here is the code for **inc-numeric-file-functions.php:**

```php
<?php

    function printData($fileName)
    {
        $dataFile = fopen("$fileName","r");
        $nextValue = trim(fgets($dataFile));
        while (!feof($dataFile) )
        {
            print("$nextValue <br>");
            $nextValue = trim(fgets($dataFile));
        }
        fclose($dataFile);
    }


    function getTotal($fileName)
    {
        $total = 0;
        $dataFile = fopen("$fileName","r");
        $nextValue = trim(fgets($dataFile));
        while (!feof($dataFile) )
        {
            $total = $total + $nextValue;
            $nextValue = trim(fgets($dataFile));
        }
        fclose($dataFile);
        return $total;
    }

    function getCount($fileName)
    {
        $count = 0;
        $dataFile = fopen("$fileName","r");
        $nextValue = trim(fgets($dataFile));
        while (!feof($dataFile) )
        {
            $count = $count + 1;
            $nextValue = trim(fgets($dataFile));
        }
        fclose($dataFile);
        if ($count > 0)
            return $count;
        else
            return -1;
    }
```

```php
function getAverage($fileName)
{
  $count = getCount($fileName);
  $total = getTotal($fileName);
  if ($count > 0)
    return $total / $count;
  else
    return -1;
}
function getHighest($fileName)
{
  $dataFile = fopen("$fileName","r");
  $nextValue = trim(fgets($dataFile));
  $highest = $nextValue;
  while (!feof($dataFile) )
  {
    if ($nextValue > $highest)
      $highest = $nextValue;
    $nextValue = trim(fgets($dataFile));
  }
  fclose($dataFile);
  return $highest;
}

function getLowest($fileName)
{
  $dataFile = fopen("$fileName","r");
  $nextValue = trim(fgets($dataFile));
  $lowest = $nextValue;
  while (!feof($dataFile) )
  {
    if ($nextValue < $lowest)
      $lowest = $nextValue;
    $nextValue = trim(fgets($dataFile));
  }
  fclose($dataFile);
  return $lowest;
}
?>
```

Code Example: inc-numeric-file-functions.php

This library of functions can be included and used by any application that needs to process a file that contains a list of numbers, where each number is stored on a separate line in the file.

The **process-scores4.php** program shows how we can use our new function library to display a list of student scores from a file named **scores1.txt**, and also display the count and average of these scores. Here is the code:

```
<body>
   <h1> STUDENT SCORES </h1>
<?php
     include("incNumericFileFunctions.php");

     $fileName = $_POST['fileName'];

     printData($fileName);

     $avgScore = getAverage($fileName);
     $numScores = getCount($fileName);

     print("Number of Scores: $numScores <br />");
     print("Average Score: $avgScore <br />");
?>
</body>
</html>
```

Code Example: process-scores4.php

As you can see by the reduced amount of code, our use of pre-written functions **greatly** simplifies the work of the application programmer!

As a professional programmer, you will probably find that your work focuses on a specific subject area. For example if you work in an educational setting you may work mostly with student records. Or you may work as an independent contractor developing Web sites for small companies. If you take care to build useful function libraries that are directly related to your work you will find that these will help you (and your programming team) create new applications quickly and easily.

More about Include Files

Do not think that PHP include files are only for use with libraries of functions. Include files can be used to include **any** code in a PHP file. When you include a file, the contents of the file are simply added to the content of the current file at the location of the include statement, so you can think of this as a simple "paste" operation. Let's explore some other uses of include files.

In our chapter on arrays, we mentioned the usefulness of associative arrays to contain lookups of various kinds, for example a list of standard error messages, or a lookup of company information (address, phone, e-mail, etc.). Arrays of this kind can be developed and stored in include files (for example **inc-error-messages.php** or **inc-company-info.php**) that can then be included in any programs that need to reference these arrays. This promotes standards and consistency in the manner in which this information is displayed by different applications and avoids duplicating the same information in multiple applications.

As another important example, many pages on a Web site often contain the same HTML code, for example the information in the <head> section may be the same for each page, or the pages may have the same menus or footers. Instead of duplicating this material in each file, the HTML code can be saved in an include file. Note that an include file that contains only HTML code should not have opening and closing PHP tags since the file does not contain PHP code.

Your samples folder contains two examples that demonstrate more extensive use of include files. The file **include-demo.php** uses a number of include files to: (1) add the head and foot sections to the page (**inc-head.php** and **inc-foot.php**); (2) make use of an associative array that contains company information (**inc-company-info.php**) and (3) make use of an associative array that contains a list of error messages (**inc-error-messages.php**). This program opens a file of sales data and generates a report. The file **include-demo2.php** goes one step further and also includes **inc-numeric-file-functions.php** in order to use these functions to process the data file. Look at these programs carefully to understand the value and efficiency of include files in your code.

IMPORTANT NOTE: Since the include statement is a PHP statement, **any** file that contains this statement must have a .php extension. This is true even if you only want to include HTML code in this file. And each include statement must be located in a PHP section at the location where you want the content of the include file to be pasted, even if the PHP section contains nothing more than the include statement. Actually it is quite standard for **all** files in a Web application to use .php extensions even if the file contains only HTML code. We have used files with .html extensions in this textbook only so that we can use the same file names for pairs of pages where the first .html page displays an HTML form and the second .php page contains the code to process the form.

As a Web developer, you will quickly learn to develop a library of small include files that each display individual components for your Web pages. You can then include each file as needed to assemble each page. Just as important, if you need to change a standard feature on your pages, you can make the change in the appropriate include file and all of your pages will reflect the change.

Additional Learning Materials

Chapter 16 lists a wide range of standard PHP functions for different purposes.

Often you will want to reference **include** files that are located in a different folder. **Appendix B** provides help with **relative** and **absolute** file addresses.

Appendix D will help you **debug** your exercises, listing a number of the most common errors that you are likely to encounter.

The **Chapter 13 Hints and Help** pages on the textbook Web site provide answers to FAQs from previous students as they worked through the end-of-chapter exercises.

Summary

Code modularity is an important feature of effective software design that minimizes duplication of code, reduces testing requirements, simplifies maintenance, permits rapid development, facilitates code documentation, and promotes standardization.

Small code modules that perform single tasks may be referred to as **functions, methods, sub-programs, sub-routines,** or **procedures,** depending on the language. In PHP, code modules are referred to as **functions**.

Functions permit code to be written once and then used by multiple applications. With this in mind, functions should be designed to be as generally useful as possible. Each function should be designed to perform a single task only. Libraries of functions are files that contain a number of functions that are related in purpose.

Standard functions are provided as a standard part of a programming language. The **pow**() function is an example of a standard PHP function.

In order to use a function, a programmer must know the name of the function, the purpose of the function, the number of **arguments** that the function requires when it is called, and the type of value (if any) that the function **returns** when it has completed its task. For example the **pow**() function requires two arguments, a base value and an exponent, and returns the value of the base raised to the power of the exponent.

Different functions require different numbers of arguments. Some may require **no** arguments. Some functions can accept different numbers of arguments. For example the PHP **round**() function can be used with one or two arguments.

If a function returns a value, the program that calls the function will usually want to use the value that is returned. This value can be assigned to a program variable for subsequent use, or used directly in an expression.

The die() or exit() functions can be used when you need the application to exit immediately, with an appropriate message for the user.

Functions can be created easily in PHP. Each function definition consists of the word function, followed by the name of the function, followed by a list of **parameters** enclosed inside a pair of parentheses. Each parameter is a variable that is used to receive a value sent as an argument by the calling program. These parameter variables can then be used inside the function. The body of the function is enclosed in braces {} and contains any code needed to perform the function's task. If the function returns a value, the code will include a **return** statement, consisting of the word **return** followed by the value that is to be returned.

In PHP, files containing useful functions can be incorporated into an application using an **include** statement, for example **include("inc-temp-functions.php")**; This statement tells the processor to include the code from the file that is referenced, at the current location in the application code. The include statement must occur before any program statements that call functions from the included file.

Placing libraries of functions in separate files means that these functions can be used in multiple programs for different purposes.

A key consideration for effective software design is to think beyond any particular application requirements and ask how code might be broken down into small modules that can serve multiple applications.

Chapter 13 Review Questions

1. Which term refers to small code modules that each perform a single task in PHP?
    a. functions
    b. methods
    c. sub-programs
    d. sub-routines
    e. procedures

2. Look at the following statement:

```
$result = doSomething(5);
```

How many arguments does the doSomething() function require?
    a. 0
    b. 1
    c. 2
    d. 3
    e. 4

3. Consider the following function definition:

```
function doIt($num1, $num2)
{
    $answer = $num1 + $num2;
    return $answer;
}
```

How many parameters does this function have?
    a. 0
    b. 1
    c. 2
    d. 3
    e. 4

4. Consider the following function definition:

```
function doIt($num1, $num2)
{
    $answer = $num1 + $num2;
    return $answer;
}
```

Which of the following is an acceptable way to call this function?
  a. $result = doIt(3, 4);
  b. $result = $doIt(3, 4);
  c. $result = doIt(3);
  d. $result = doIt(4);
  e. $result = doIt();

5. Consider the following function definition:

```
function doThis()
{
    return "This is a test";
}
```

How many parameters does this function have?
  a. 0
  b. 1
  c. 2
  d. 3
  e. 4

6. Consider the following function definition:

```
function doThis()
{
    return "This is a test";
}
```

Which of the following is an acceptable way to call this function?
  a. $result = doThis("Testing");
  b. $result = doThis(3, 4);
  c. $result = doThis(3);
  d. $result = doThis(4);
  e. $result = doThis();

7. What value will the following call return?

```
round(13.3478, 3)
```

  a. 13
  b. 14
  c. 13.35
  d. 13.348
  e. 13.3478

8. Which of the following is a correct definition for a function named circleArea()
   that receives a radius and returns an area?

   a.

   ```
   function circleArea($pi, $pow, $radius, $area)
   {
      return pi() * pow($radius, 2);
   }
   ```

   b.

   ```
   function circleArea($pi, $radius, $area)
   {
      return pi() * pow($radius, 2);
   }
   ```

   c.

   ```
   function circleArea($radius, $area)
   {
      return pi() * pow($radius, 2);
   }
   ```

   d.

   ```
   function circleArea($radius)
   {
      return pi() * pow($radius, 2);
   }
   ```

   e.

   ```
   function circleArea()
   {
      return pi() * pow($radius, 2);
   }
   ```

9. You want to use a function named doIt() which is located in a file named inc-stuff.php. Which statement is needed before you can use the doIt() function in your PHP program?
   a. include("doIt()");
   b. include("doIt.php");
   c. include("inc-stuff()");
   d. include("inc-stuff.php");
   e. include("inc-stuff.php->doIt()");

10. How many parameters does the pow() function have?
   a. 0
   b. 1
   c. 2
   d. 3
   e. 4

11. Which of the following is **not** an important reason to use functions in your programs?
   a. Increased standardization by using common code
   b. Increased processing power
   c. Rapid development
   d. Avoids duplication
   e. More efficient testing

12. If you use an include statement to include a file containing a group of functions, which statement is correct?
   a. You can only use a single function from the file of functions.
   b. You must use every function in the file of functions.
   c. You can use any function as needed, as often as you need.

13. How would you use the getHighest() function from the inc-numeric-file-functions.php file to find the highest value in a file of numbers named numbers.txt?
   a. include("numbers.txt");
      $highNum = getHighest();
   b. include("numbers.txt");
      $highNum = getHighest("numbers.txt");
   c. include("inc-numeric-file-functions.php");
      $highNum = getHighest("numbers.txt");
   d. include("inc-numeric-file-functions.php");
      $highNum = getHighest();
   e. include("numbers.txt");
      $highNum = getHighest("inc-numeric-file-functions.php");

14. True or False: The code inside one function can include a call to another function.
    a. True
    b. False

15. Which PHP function is used to end a program immediately, with a suitable message?
    a. terminate()
    b. end()
    c. close()
    d. die()

16. What is wrong with this function?

```
function getWeeklyWage($hourlyRate, $hoursWorked)
{
   $weeklyPay = $hourlyRate * $hoursWorked;
}
```

    a. $WeeklyPay should be a parameter
    b. The word function should not be there
    c. The heading should end with a semi-colon
    d. The return statement is missing
    e. The parameters should not have $ signs since they are not variables

17. What is wrong with this function?

```
function getBonus(wage)
{
   if ($wage > 200)
      $bonus = 75.00;
   else
      $bonus = 50.00;
   return $bonus;
}
```

    a. $bonus should be a parameter
    b. The return statement should appear before the selection structure
    c. The heading should end with a semi-colon
    d. You cannot use selection structures in a function
    e. The wage parameter should have a $ sign since it is a variable

18. When you create your own functions, how many different tasks should each function be designed to perform?
    a. 0
    b. 1
    c. 2
    d. one or more
    e. 0 or more

19. What kind of code can be included in a function?
    a. sequence statements
    b. selection structures
    c. loop structures
    d. calls to other functions
    e. any combination of these can be included

20. A function must always be designed to return a value:
    a. True
    b. False

Chapter 13 Code Exercises

Your Chapter 13 code exercises can be found in your **chapter13** folder. This folder is included in your customized XAMPP installation at the following location:

htdocs\webtech\coursework\chapter13

Type your name and the date in the **Author** and **Date** sections of each file as you work on each exercise. **Remember** that the Students page on the textbook Web site includes **Hints and Help** pages for the exercises in this and every chapter.

Debugging Exercises

Your **chapter13** folder should contain a number of "fixit" files. Each of these files contains PHP code that has an error of some kind. The type of error is indicated in the comment section of each file. You will need to run each program in order to see the errors, and to debug and test the code to see if it works correctly. For example to run **fixit1.php**, first run the Web server, then use the URL:

http://localhost/webtech/coursework/chapter13/fixit1.php

Code Modification Exercises

Your **chapter 13** folder contains a number of pairs of "modify" files. Each pair of files contains HTML and PHP code that needs to be modified to meet a requirement. The requirements are included in the comment section of each file. Modify the algorithms, being careful to make changes to the .html and .php files as directed. You will need to run each program in order to test your changes. For example to run **modify1.html**, first run the Web server, then use the URL:

http://localhost/webtech/coursework/chapter13/modify1.html

Code Completion Exercises

1. Read this exercise carefully and take your time to work out the logic. Your **chapter 13** folder contains versions of **paint-estimate.html** and **paint-estimate.php** as well as a file of PHP functions named **inc-paint-functions.php** which contains a list of functions.

   The **paint-estimate.php** program already includes the code to receive the inputs from **paint-estimate.html** and to display the results. Your job is to include **inc-paint-functions** in **paint-estimate.php**, and use the functions appropriately to calculate the wall area, ceiling area, total area, paint cost and labor cost. Be sure to include the file, and use the correct variables ($wallArea, $ceilingArea, $totalArea, $paintCost, and $laborCost) to send values to, and receive values returned by, each function.

2. Read this exercise carefully and take your time to work out the logic. Your **chapter13** folder contains versions of **software-order.html** and **software-order.php** as well as a file named **inc-software-order.php**. The code in **software-order.php** includes calls to a number of functions. Your job is to add the functions to the **inc-software-order.php** file so that the program works correctly:

   The **getSubtotal()** function should receive the number of copies being ordered, multiply this by **35.75** (the cost of each copy), and return the result.

   The **getSalesTax()** function should receive a sub-total, calculate the sales tax by multiplying this by **0.07**, and return the result.

   The **getShippingHandling()** function should receive the number of copies. The function should return **3.50** if the number of copies is less than **five**, otherwise the function should multiply the number of copies by **0.75** and return the result of this calculation.

   Your functions should use the **round()** function to round off the calculations to two places before returning the results (see examples in **inc-wage-functions.php** which is included with these exercises).

3. Read this exercise carefully and take your time to work out the logic. Your **chapter13** folder contains versions of **give-away.html** and **give-away.php**. Create a function named **freeTrip()** and add it to the beginning of the PHP section in give-away.php.

   The freeTrip() function does not need any parameters. The function should generate a random number between 1 and 5 and then use this number to return one of five possible locations: Aruba, Cairo, London, Rome, or Tokyo. So for example if the number is 1 the function would return "Aruba", if it is 4 the function would return "Rome". You can generate a random number between 1 and 5 and store the number in a variable named **$trip** using this statement: **$trip = rand(1, 5);**

   Add a statement in the code to call this function and display the destination to the lucky winner.

4. Read this exercise carefully and take your time to work out the logic. Your **chapter13** folder contains versions of **travel.html** and **travel.php** and a function library named **inc-travel.php**. Look through these files carefully. The code in travel.php must be completed so that this program will use the functions supplied in inc-travel.php to obtain the air fare, nightly hotel rate, cost of the tickets, and cost of the hotel, based on the user's inputs. In other words you must complete the following statements:

```php
$airFare = ;
$hotelRate = ;

$ticketCost = ;
$hotelCost = ;
```

The statements to receive the user's input and generate the output have been provided. Don't forget that you must also include the **inc-travel.php** file in your **travel.php** code!

5. Read this exercise carefully and take your time to work out the logic. Your **chapter13** folder contains versions of airFare.html and airFare.php and a function library named **inc-travel.php**. This exercise is similar to the last one, except that here you have to first add another function named **getAirline()** to **inc-travel.php** that will return an airline based on a destination, as follows:

Barcelona	Web Airlines
Cairo	PHP Air
Rome	Air Java
Santiago	SQL Air
Tokyo	Object-Oriented Airlines

Add code to airfare.php to include the inc-travel.php functions, and call the appropriate functions to obtain the air fare and airlines based on the destination selected by the user. The statements to receive the user's input and generate the output have been provided (be sure to use the same variable names).

6. Your **chapter13** folder contains **lookup.html** and **lookup.php**. The code in lookup.html contains a form that allows the user to look up a performer. Look over this code — it does not need to be changed. The code in lookup.php includes a function named **getPerformanceDate()**. You do not need to change this function.

   Modify the code in this file so that the program will use the getPerformanceDate() function to look up the date for whichever performer the user submitted.

7. Your **chapter13** folder contains **bus-travel.html** and **bus-travel.php** and also **inc-travel-allowances.php**. The bus-travel.html and bus-travel.php files process trip information submitted by the user in order to determine reimbursement costs. This is identical to the related exercise in Chapter 8 except that now the code in bus-travel.php calls functions in the inc-travel-allowances.php file.

   Your job is to open inc-travel-allowances.php and complete the code for these functions, then ensure that the program works correctly. Note that this is a simple exercise: these functions do not need any parameters and simply return the appropriate value. But this is a common programming task — the advantage of placing these in an include file is that they can be used by any program, and the allowances can be changed as needed in this single file.

Chapter 14

Connecting to a Database — Working with MySQL

Intended Learning Outcomes

After completing this chapter, you should be able to:

- Describe the basic structure of a relational database.
- Identify records and fields in a sample database table.
- Identify key characteristics of a Database Management System (DBMS).
- Explain the general purpose of Structured Query Language (SQL).
- Write PHP code to open and close a connection to a MySQL database.
- Identify the purpose and result of MySQL SELECT queries, that may include FROM, WHERE, and ORDER BY clauses, and relational and logical operators.
- Design, code and submit syntactically correct SELECT queries in PHP applications.
- Write PHP code to receive and process the result sets that are returned by MySQL SELECT queries.
- Identify the purpose and result of MySQL INSERT, UPDATE, and DELETE queries.
- Design, code and submit syntactically correct INSERT, UPDATE, and DELETE queries in PHP applications.
- Apply a basic error-handling template to PHP code that interacts with a MySQL database.
- Use a PHP include statement to maintain MySQL connection values more efficiently and securely.

Introduction

Chapter 6 introduced ways to work with data that must be preserved beyond the lifetime of the application (persistent data). That chapter focused on the use of **text files**. We learned how to open and close text files in PHP, how to read lines from text files, and how to write and append data to text files. In subsequent chapters we learned how to process data in text files using selection and loop structures.

We are now ready to look at a more sophisticated approach to data storage and retrieval, using relational databases. We will learn about the basic structure of **relational databases** and explore the procedures and syntax required to interact with a widely used relational database system called **MySQL**. This chapter does not provide comprehensive coverage of MySQL but it will provide a solid introduction. You are encouraged to build on what you learn here through further reading, experimentation, and coursework.

What Is a Relational Database?

As you may recall from Chapter 6, a **relational database** allows us to store data in one or more related **tables**. Each table in a database contains **records** of some kind, and each record contains a set of specific data values, stored in **fields**. Relational database tables can be visualized, rather like a spreadsheet, as a set of rows and columns. Each row contains a record, and each column contains a field of the record. For example, Table 14-1 provides a visualization of a simple table of employee records, stored in a table named **personnel**.

As you can see, there are currently 10 records in the personnel table, presented here as 10 rows. Each record contains five fields, presented here as five columns, and each field contains a data value associated with the employee. These fields are named empID (the employee's unique ID), firstName, lastName, jobTitle, and hourlyWage.

The Relational Database Management System (RDBMS)

A single database may include any number of related tables, and a single database system may contain any number of databases. A **Relational Database Management System (RDBMS)** provides a full range of management tools for storing, managing, and using relational databases. For example, an RDBMS incorporates many useful functions that facilitate common operations such as: creating, modifying and removing databases and tables; adding, modifying, and deleting records; searching (querying) tables; generating reports; assigning user accounts. An RDBMS implements sophisticated security controls: each user is assigned a specific level of access to each database, table, and even to

empID	firstName	lastName	jobTitle	hourlyWage
12345	Chris	Smith	sales	12.55
12347	Mary	Peters	sales	12.55
12348	Mike	Jones	manager	24.15
12353	Anne	Humphries	accountant	25.45
12356	Ann	Jones	sales	13.75
12357	John	Jackson	reception	8.75
12358	John	King	cleaner	7.75
12360	Ken	Stewart	accountant	28.55
12361	Joan	Smith	cleaner	8.25
12363	Jesse	Andrews	sales	10.75

Table 14-1: Example of a relational database table (the personnel table in the test database on your server)

individual fields, to ensure appropriate use of the data. Communications with the RDBMS are written using the RDBMS's **Structured Query Language** (SQL).

The effective design of an RDBMS to deliver databases and tables that are easy to maintain and search, and that do not include any unnecessary duplication of data, is the responsibility of a **database administrator**. A database administrator has a range of responsibilities: the overall security, maintenance, backup and performance of the RDBMS; design, creation, and maintenance of databases and tables; creation and removal of user accounts and related access permissions that specify what each user can or cannot do; oversight of procedures and related functions that deliver useful services to programmer and end-users. Database administration is a highly skilled profession that is also in high demand. Most companies and institutions require at least one database administrator to manage their data systems.

Structured Query Language — MySQL

You have already learned how to work with text files. You have used loops to read lines from a file, one line at a time, and to extract the different values on each line based on a delimiter. You have also developed code to process these values, for example to display the contents of the file, search for specific values, perform counts and other calculations, accumulate totals, or determine highest or lowest values. All of this has required you to write your own custom code to meet the requirements of each application. This is because text files are just that, simple files of text.

Unlike text files, the databases and tables in an RDBMS are not directly accessible to your programs. Instead you must submit requests that are written in the Structured Query Language that the RDBMS provides. The RDBMS processes each request (called a **query**) and returns a result. The query language is very powerful and allows you to request a wide range of operations that relieve you from having to write so much custom code. This not only simplifies the work of the application programmer but also helps to ensure efficient data processing, simplified data management, and enhanced data security.

Each RDBMS provides its own version of SQL. For many years by far the most popular open source SQL, widely used for Web applications, was **MySQL**. MySQL was acquired by Oracle in 2010 and at that time an independent version (a "fork") of MySQL was developed under the new name **MariaDB**. MariaDB is intended to remain freely available, and is included in your XAMMP installation, pre-configured for your use to include the **test** database with the **personnel** table that was shown in Table 14-1. Although we are using MariaDB, at this time MariaDB remains compatible with MySQL; to keep things simple and remain consistent with the names of the PHP function calls, the rest of the chapter will refer to MySQL.

Starting Your MySQL Server

Before you can work with the MySQL RDBMS you must first start your MySQL server. You can do this in the XAMPP control panel in the same way that you start your Web server (always remember to return to the control panel to stop your servers when you have finished working). Note that Linux users who use the "lampp start" and "lampp stop" commands to run the Web server do not need to do anything else since these commands also start and stop MySQL.

Be sure your MySQL server is running before you continue. If you have any problems, check the textbook Web site for the latest instructions on configuring and starting your MySQL server.

Configuring MySQL for Use with This Textbook

In order to use MySQL with the textbook examples and exercises, you must first add the required tables and user account. You only need to follow these instructions once, but you can also repeat this step if you ever mess up and need to recreate the original tables. Start your Web server and MySQL server if you have not already done so. Now open a Web browser and type **http://localhost** to connect to the Web server, then click the **samples** folder and run the application named **mysql-setup.html** (the complete URL is **http://localhost/samples/mysql-setup.html**). This program will create a MySQL user named **wbip** with a password **wbip123**, and will also create two tables in the **test** database, named **personnel** and **timesheet** (in case you're wondering, **wbip** is just the acronym for Web-Based Introduction to Programming).

Three Ways to Work with MySQL

Once your MySQL server is running, you have three options to issue queries to the RDBMS: from the **command line**; through a **graphical interface**; or from a custom application that has been developed in a programming language such as PHP.

Since this book is focused on Web-based programming, in this chapter we will learn how to submit and process MySQL queries from custom PHP applications. The textbook Web site includes some guidelines and references that explain how to access MySQL from the command line, or from a powerful and easy to use Web-based graphical interface named **phpMyAdmin** (phpMyAdmin is included in your Web server installation). Appendix E also provides a useful introduction to phpMyAdmin.

Working with PHP and MySQL

You will recall from Chapter 6 that in order to interact with an external device, a PHP program must (1) open a connection; (2) perform the required operations; and (3) close the connection. We learned to interact with text files using the fopen(), fgets(), fputs(), and fclose() functions, and later we also learned to use the feof() function. Now we will learn to use some of PHP's MySQL functions that allow our programs to open a connection to a MySQL server, interact with a database, and close the connection. We will take this step by step until we have all the code needed to develop a working application.

Using PHP to Open and Close a Connection to a MySQL Server

Before we can submit queries to a MySQL database, we must first connect to the MySQL server and select the database that we wish to use. We can do this in PHP by calling the **mysqli_connect**() function, and providing four arguments: the URL of the MySQL RDBMS, a user ID that has been registered with the system, the user password, and the name of the specific database we wish to work with.

The URL for our MySQL system is **"localhost"**. A user named **"wbip"** (short for Web-based Introduction to Programming) has already been created for this system, with all privileges to create, remove, and modify databases, tables, records and fields. The "wbip" user has been assigned the password **"wbip123"**. And we will work with a database named "test".

Here is a PHP statement that uses the mysqli_connect() function to connect to the MySQL server using these arguments:

```
$connect = mysqli_connect('localhost','wbip','wbip123','test');
```

Note that there is nothing special about the variable name **$connect**; this variable can have any name. The mysqli_connect() function returns a reference to the connection which is assigned to $connect. This variable is then used in subsequent instructions when it is necessary to refer to the connection. For example, when we are finished using this database, we call the **mysqli_close**() function, using $connect as an argument:

```
mysqli_close($connect);
```

In our mysqli_connect() example, we provided literal values for the four connection values that were passed to the function as arguments. Actually, it is good practice to first assign these connection values to variables and then use the variables as arguments:

```
$server = "localhost";
$user = "wbip";
$pw = "wbip123";
$db = "test";
$connect = mysqli_connect($server, $user, $pw, $db);
```

The mysqli_connect() function will return **false** if the connection fails for any reason (for example if the user ID or password is not accepted, or if the URL is incorrect, or the database does not exist). This means that we can test our $connect variable to be sure that it doesn't contain the value **false**. Here is a general code template that ensures that we don't try to work with the database if the connection attempt fails:

```
<?php
$server = "localhost";
$user = "wbip";
$pw = "wbip123";
$db = "test";
$connect = mysqli_connect($server, $user, $pw, $db);
if(!$connect)
{
   die("ERROR: Cannot connect to database $db on server
      $server using user name $user (".mysqli_connect_errno().
      ", ".mysqli_connect_error().")");
}
// place the code here to work with the database
mysqli_close($connect); // close the connection

?>
```

The test **if(!$connect)** will be true if $connect contains **false**, and in this case the program will exit with an error message. You will recall from Chapter 13 that the **die**() or **exit**() function can be used to terminate a PHP script with an optional error message. In this case we use this function to terminate the script if a database connection cannot be achieved. The error message includes a call to the PHP **mysqli_connect_errno**() function in order to display the error number that was generated, and also calls the **mysqli_connect_error**() function which provides a description of the error that occurred (for example if the user name or password was incorrect, this function will return an "Access denied" message).

Using the MySQL SELECT Query

Now that we know how to connect to a MySQL database, we can learn how to submit and process queries. But before we can learn how to do this in PHP we must first learn the necessary MySQL syntax.

We are going to work with the **personnel** table that is included in your test database. Take a few minutes to review Table 14-1 which shows this table. The table contains ten employee records, and each record contains data stored in five fields named **empID**, **firstName**, **lastName**, **jobTitle**, and **hourlyWage**.

Remember that we cannot actually access the information in our MySQL tables directly. Instead we must issue commands (queries) using the keywords and syntax of the MySQL language. You have already learned some of the syntax of HTML, CSS, and PHP; you will now learn some MySQL. As you are discovering, a single Web-based application requires the use of a number of different languages, each with its own grammar and syntax.

First we will learn how to use the MySQL **SELECT** query to retrieve values in the fields and records of MySQL tables that match your search criteria. Here is a simple query using SELECT to search for all the fields in all the records in the personnel table:

```
SELECT * FROM personnel
```

That looks straightforward. The asterisk * between SELECT and FROM means "all fields". The word **FROM** allows a clause to be added to the SELECT query that specifies which table in the database should be searched. So this query is asking the RDBMS to send the data stored in **all** fields in all the records in the **personnel** table. The results that are returned by the query are known as the **result set**, so in this case the result set will will contain the values from the empID, firstName, lastName, jobTitle, and hoursWorked fields from each of the 10 records in this table.

What if we don't actually need the data from **all** of the fields in each record? Instead of using the asterisk to indicate **all** fields, we can specify the fields we're interested in. Here's another SELECT query:

```
SELECT lastName FROM personnel
```

This query will search the personnel table but in this case the result set will only contain the last name from each of the 10 records. We can also request data from multiple fields, separated by commas, for example:

```
SELECT firstName, lastName FROM personnel
```

This query will return the first and last names in each of the records. We can request data from any number of fields in this way, or we can use the asterisk to obtain the values from all the fields.

Selecting Specific Records

We have seen how to obtain values from specific **fields** in all of the records in the table, but how can we obtain values from just some of the records? For example, what if we're only interested in the personnel records where the job title is 'accountant'?

If we want our SELECT query to match specific records we must add another clause to our SELECT query, a **WHERE** clause. For example here's how we can find all the accountants in our table:

```
SELECT * FROM personnel WHERE jobTitle='accountant'
```

Now the result set will only contain those records that meet the criteria specified in the WHERE clause, in this case where the job title is 'accountant'. Note the use of single quotes to enclose the data value.

Note that the result set may contain 0 or more records, depending on whether or not any records in the personnel table contain this job title.

What if we wanted to look up information about a single employee? You might consider a search based on the last name field, but more than one employee might have the same last name. However each employee will always have a unique employee ID, so we can use this to search for a specific person, for example:

```
SELECT * FROM personnel WHERE empID='12347'
```

In this case note that the result set might contain 0 or 1 records, depending whether or not there is an employee record with the ID that is requested.

We can still restrict our result set to values from specific fields when we include a WHERE clause. For example, the following query will produce a result set containing the the ID, first name, and last name of all our accountants:

```
SELECT empID, firstName, lastName FROM personnel
   WHERE jobTitle='accountant'
```

Relational Operators in MySQL

Did something surprise you about the last examples? In your PHP code you have been using == to test whether or not two values are equal. But in MySQL queries we use a single = for the same purpose. Each language has its own syntax so we must be careful to apply the correct syntax depending on the language we are using.

Our WHERE clause can use other relational operators. For example to obtain the first and last names of employees who earn less than 15.00 an hour:

```
SELECT firstName, lastName FROM personnel
  WHERE hourlyWage < '15.00'
```

Similarly we can use the operators <=, >, >= and !=.

MySQL provides many other special operators that can be useful in our SELECT queries. For example:

```
SELECT firstName, lastName FROM personnel
  WHERE hourlyWage BETWEEN '10.00' AND '15.00'
```

The **BETWEEN** operator finds values **between** the two values that are provided, so this test will find all records where the hourlyWage is **greater than** or **equal to** 10.00 and **less than** or **equal to** 15.00.

We can also use the **LIKE** operator for **pattern matching**. This operator will match character strings that include **wildcard** (undefined) characters. Here's a search for all employees whose first name begins with 'Ann':

```
SELECT firstName, lastName FROM personnel
  WHERE firstName LIKE 'Ann%'
```

The LIKE operator looks for values that match the search string. If the search string contains the '%' "wildcard" character, this indicates that there may be **0 or more** unknown characters in this position, so 'Ann%' will find 'Ann', 'Anne', 'Annie', Annette', etc.

You can also use the '_' wildcard character to indicate exactly **one** unknown character in a specific location in the string. And you can combine these wildcards in any combination, for example:

```
SELECT firstName, lastName FROM personnel
  WHERE lastName LIKE '%m_t%'
```

This search will find last names that include any number of unknown characters followed by 'm' followed by exactly one unknown character, followed by 't', followed by any number of unknown characters. So this search will find a match with 'Smith' or 'Lamotte' or 'Mitchell' but will not for example find 'Smart' or 'Stormont' (because the single underscore in the search string indicates that only one unknown character can occur between the 'm' and 't').

The Logical Operators AND and OR

We can also use the AND and OR operators to combine tests, similar to PHP, for example:

```
SELECT firstName, lastName FROM personnel
   WHERE jobTitle='accountant' OR jobTitle='sales'
```

Here we are searching for the first and last names of all employees who are either accountants or sales people. Now consider:

```
SELECT firstName, lastName FROM personnel
   WHERE jobTitle='accountant' AND hourlyWage < '25.00'
```

In this case we are searching for the first and last names of all accountants who earn less than 25.00 an hour.

As always be careful when to use AND and OR in your WHERE clauses. For example if you wrote a query that included:

```
WHERE jobTitle='accountant' AND jobTitle='sales'
```

then **no** records would be returned! That's because no records contain a jobTitle that contains **both** 'accountant' **and** 'sales'. So we need to use OR to find every record with a jobTitle field that contains either 'accountant' OR 'sales'.

Notice that, just as in PHP, you must provide a complete test on either side of these operators. For example, although in English you might say:

```
WHERE jobTitle='accountant' OR 'sales'
```

in MySQL this must be written as follows:

```
WHERE jobTitle='accountant' OR jobTitle='sales'
```

Ordering Your Query Results

Unless you specify otherwise, the results of your SELECT query will be returned in the order of the records in the table. Often we want to order these some other way, for example by last name. We can do this by adding an **ORDER BY** clause to our query. Consider the following:

```
SELECT * FROM personnel ORDER BY lastName
```

This query will produce a listing of all the records in the personnel table, ordered by last name. Similarly:

```
SELECT firstName, lastName FROM personnel
  WHERE jobTitle ='accountant'
  ORDER BY lastName
```

This query will produce a listing of all the accountants ordered by last name. Note that the field that you use to order the list does not need to be included in the list, so if you wanted to obtain a list of first and last names, ordered by job title, you can do that:

```
SELECT firstName, lastName FROM personnel ORDER BY jobTitle
```

And if you want to order by **two** fields, for example first by last name, and then (if a number of employees have the same last name) by first name, we can provide a list of fields in the ORDER BY clause, separated by commas:

```
SELECT firstName, lastName FROM personnel
  ORDER BY lastName, firstName
```

If you want to order by more than one field, note that the result set will be ordered, first by the first field, and then by the second field, and so on.

If you want to the results to be generated in descending order, add the **DESC** keyword after the field name(s), for example:

```
SELECT firstName, lastName FROM personnel
  ORDER BY jobTitle DESC
```

You can also specify **ASC** for ascending order, however since the default ordering is ascending this is often left out.

Viewing Your Query Results

You have just learned how to issue **SELECT** queries modified using the **FROM**, **WHERE** and **ORDER BY** clauses. But how do you submit these queries and how do you receive and view the results in PHP?

MySQL queries are submitted using the **mysqli_query**() function. This function returns the result of the query so you will want to provide a variable to receive this. Here is an example:

```
$result = mysqli_query($connect, "SELECT firstName, lastName
  FROM personnel");
```

The mysqli_query() function sends the SELECT query to the MySQL RDBMS which processes it. The result is returned and assigned to the **$result** variable ($result is a PHP variable and can have any name).

Note that you cannot use mysqli_query() to submit a query unless you have already opened a connection using mysqli_connect(). The first argument to the mysqli_query() function is the variable that references the database connection (in this case a variable named **$connect**, which we used in our previous examples).

The second argument to the mysqli_query() function is the query itself. In this example we included the query directly as the second argument but a better approach is to first store the query in a variable, and then use this variable as the second argument, for example:

```
$userQuery = "SELECT firstName, lastName FROM personnel";
$result = mysqli_query($connect, $userQuery);
```

If your query is successfully processed, the mysqli_query() function returns the result set that contains the requested fields of all the records that met the requirements of your query. Note that the query is successfully processed even if no records actually met the requirements. However if the query **cannot** be processed (for example if there was no connection to the database, or if the query contained a syntax error), then the mysqli_query() function returns **false**.

Since the variable $result contains the result that was returned by the mysqli_query() function, we should now test this variable to be sure that the query was processed successfully. If $result contains the value **false**, a simple option is to exit with an error message that includes a call to the **mysqli_error**() function to explain the error:

```
if (!$result)
{
  die("Could not successfully run query ($userQuery) from
    $db: " . mysqli_error($connect) );
}
```

The mysqli_error() function will return a MySQL error message associated with the error that occurred. Note that this function requires the $connect variable as a parameter.

What if the query was successful but no records met the requirements? We might want to print a message to report this to the user. One way to do this is by obtaining a count of the number of records that were returned by the query and testing to see if this count is 0. We can do this using the **mysqli_num_rows()** function, for example:

```
if (mysqli_num_rows($result) == 0)
{
   print("No records were found with query $userQuery");
}
else
{
   // process the result set
}
```

If our query did not generate any errors, and did not generate a result set with 0 records, we can process $result. Since the result set will usually contain one or more records, we usually use a loop that extracts each record from the result set until no more records are found. The records can be extracted in different ways. An efficient approach is to extract each record from $result into an associative array, where each of the array elements contains a value from one of the record fields, and the keys for these elements are the names of these fields. This allows us to work with these values as needed by referring to each value stored in the array using the appropriate field name.

Here's the code to process the results of our "SELECT firstName, lastName FROM personnel" query:

```
print("<h1>LIST OF EMPLOYEES</h1>");
while ($row = mysqli_fetch_assoc($result))
{
   print ("<p>".$row['firstName']." ".$row['lastName']."</p>");
}
```

The **mysqli_fetch_assoc()** function extracts the next record from $result into an associative array or returns **false** if there are no more records to extract. So each time the loop repeats, the loop heading is designed to extract the next record from the result set as an associative array into **$row**. The loop continues to do this until **the mysqli_fetch_assoc()** array returns **false**, indicating there are no more records.

Inside the loop we can provide whatever code you need to process each record according to your application requirements. In this case, we just want to display the results. Since $row contains an associative array with the values of the record indexed by the field names, we can reference, for example, the value of the firstName field using $row['firstName']. Each time the loop repeats the first and last names of the next record that was returned by the query will be processed.

Note that the query in this example is "SELECT firstName, lastName FROM personnel". That means the result set will **only** contain the firstName and lastName values from each of the records that were matched by the SELECT query. So your query must request all the fields that your program needs to work with. For example what if you 475

```
print ("<p>".$row['empID'].": ".
    $row['firstName']." ".$row['lastName']."</p>");
```

Now your query must request these three fields:

```
"SELECT empID, firstName, lastName FROM personnel"
```

Using an HTML Table to Display the Query Results

In this example we listed the names using HTML paragraph tags. It would of course be more elegant to display these in an HTML table:

```
print("<h1>LIST OF EMPLOYEES</h1>");
print("<table>");
print("<tr><th>First Name</th><th>Last Name</th></tr>");

while ($row = mysqli_fetch_assoc($result))
{
   print ("<tr><td>".$row['firstName'].
     "</td><td>".$row['lastName']."</td></tr>");
}

print("</table");
```

Putting It All Together

We have walked through the code to connect to a MySQL database, submit a query, and receive and process the query results. Figure 14.1 shows the complete code for this application.

```php
<?php
$server = "localhost";
$user = "wbip";
$pw = "wbip123";
$db = "test";
$connect = mysqli_connect($server, $user, $pw, $db);

if(!$connect)
{
  die("ERROR: Cannot connect to database $db on server
    $server using user name $user (".mysqli_connect_errno().
    ", ".mysqli_connect_error().")");
}

$userQuery = "SELECT firstName, lastName FROM personnel";
$result = mysqli_query($connect, $userQuery);

if (!$result)
{
  die("Could not successfully run query ($userQuery) from
    $db: ". mysqli_error($connect) );
}

if (mysqli_num_rows($result) == 0)
{
  print("No records found with query $userQuery");
}
else
{
  print("<h1>LIST OF EMPLOYEES</h1>");
  print("<table>");
  print("<tr><th>First Name</th><th>Last Name</th></tr>");
  while ($row = mysqli_fetch_assoc($result))
  {
    print ("<tr><td>".$row['firstName'].
      "</td><td>".$row['lastName']."</td></tr>");
  }
  print("</table");
}

mysqli_close($connect); // close the connection

?>
```

Figure 14.1 Code for mysql1.php

Run this program to see that it works. Now run the **mysql2.php** example which contains the "SELECT * FROM personnel" query. Note that this query returns **ALL** records and **ALL** fields from each record. If you look at the code for mysql2.php, you will see just two changes from mysql1.php. First, of course, the query itself has been changed. In addition the print statements that display the table heading and table rows have also been changed. That's because this query will return values from all five fields for each record and not just the firstName and lastName fields:

```
print("<tr><th>EMP ID</th><th>First Name</th>
    <th>Last Name</th><th>Job Title</th>
    <th>Hourly Wage</th></tr>");
while ($row = mysqli_fetch_assoc($result))
{
    print("<tr><td>".$row['empID']."</td><td>"
        .$row['firstName']."</td><td>"
        .$row['lastName']."</td><td>"
        .$row['jobTitle']."</td><td>"
        .numberformat($row['hourlyWage'], 2).
        "</td></tr>");
}
```

Now take some time to try some of the other SELECT queries that were described in this chapter. To do this, open **mysql3.php** in your text editor. This file contains the same code as mysql2.php. Modify mysql3.php as needed to try different queries and remember to modify your table each time so that only the fields included in the query are displayed. This will help you become comfortable with the process of coding MySQL queries.

Using Input from an HTML Form to Construct a Query

Instead of writing values directly into our query we can construct the query with data that has been previously assigned to variables, for example data that has been submitted from an HTML form. The form in **mysql4.html** asks the user for a last name to search for, and **mysql4.php** is coded to receive the user input into a variable named **$search-Name** which is then used in the MySQL SELECT query:

```
$searchName = $_POST['searchName'];
$userQuery = "SELECT * FROM personnel
    WHERE lastName='$searchName'";
```

This query will return all fields of all records where the lastName field in the record contains the same name as the search name that the user requested.

Processing Queries with a Single Result

As we have seen, some queries will produce just one result. For example since each employee has a unique employee ID, we could look up the job title and hourly wage of a particular employee by his or her ID. This example assumes that the user has submitted an ID from an HTML form:

```
$searchID = $_POST['searchID'];
$userQuery = "SELECT jobTitle, hourlyWage FROM personnel
   WHERE empId='$searchID'";
```

Since we know that the query will not return more than one record, we can extract this from the result set without using a WHILE loop:

```
$row = mysqli_fetch_assoc($result);
print("<p>ID: ".$searchID."<br>
    Job title: ".$row['jobTitle']."<br>
    HourlyWage: $".number_format($row['hourlyWage'], 2).
    "</p>");
```

This example is demonstrated in **mysql5.html** and **mysql5.php**.

Performing Calculations with the Result Set

Note that, once we have extracted our values from the result set into an associative array, we can use the array values in calculations just like values stored in any other variable. For example if the wages of all cleaners are based on a 35 hour work week, we can construct a query to obtain the first names, last names, and hourly wage of all cleaners:

```
$userQuery = "SELECT firstName, lastName, hourlyWage
   FROM personnel
   WHERE jobTitle='cleaner'";
```

Then our WHILE loop can loop through the result set to calculate and display the weekly pay for each cleaner:

```
print("<h1>PAY CHECKS</h1>");
while ($row = mysqli_fetch_assoc($result))
{
  $weeklyPay = $row['hourlyWage'] * 35;
  print ("<p>PAY TO: ".$row['firstName'].
    " ".$row['lastName']." THE SUM OF $".
    number_format($weeklyPay,2)."</p>");
}
```

The complete code for this example is provided in **mysql6.php**.

Performing Aggregate Operations on MySQL Queries

We have mentioned that an RDBMS provides many useful functions that reduce the need for custom programming. As an example, MySQL provides a number of **aggregation functions**, for example to find the **count, sum, average, minimum,** or **maximum** of the values in a specified field based on the records that meet the query criteria. No need for you to write your own code to process the records and calculate these values!

These MySQL functions are named COUNT(), SUM(), AVG(), MIN(), and MAX() and should not be confused with PHP functions. MySQL functions are used in your SELECT queries. For example, here is a query to find the average hourly wage of all employees in the personnel table:

```
$userQuery = "SELECT AVG(hourlyWage) FROM personnel";
```

If we use the mysqli_fetch_assoc() function to obtain the result set, we can obtain the result returned by the AVG function in this example by referring to **$row['AVG(hourlyWage)']**, for example:

```
$row = mysqli_fetch_assoc($result);
print("<p>Average hourly wage:
  $".number_format($row['AVG(hourlyWage)'], 2)."</p>");
```

This example is provided in **mysql7.php**.

What if we wanted to know the average hourly wage of our sales staff? We simply restrict our query as follows:

```
$userQuery = "SELECT AVG(hourlyWage) FROM personnel
  WHERE jobTitle='sales'";
```

Similarly we can find the **highest** wage paid to accountants:

```
$userQuery = "SELECT MAX(hourlyWage) FROM personnel
  WHERE jobTitle='accountant'";
```

Note that we must now refer to MAX(hourlyWage) in our print statement:

```
print("<p>Highest wage for accountants:
  $".number_format($row[MAX(hourlyWage)'], 2)."</p>");
```

Or we can count the number of cleaners:

```
$userQuery = "COUNT(empID) FROM personnel
  WHERE jobTitle='cleaner'";
```

In this case the print statement becomes:

```
print("<p>Number of cleaners: ".$row['COUNT(empID)']."</p>");
```

You are invited to play around with mysql7.php to try these and other queries that perform aggregate operations on the result set.

The aggregation functions are much more powerful than the examples shown here and can also be used to generate results by sub-groups of the result set. This is beyond the scope of this textbook, but you can research these functions to learn more of their capabilities.

Performing JOIN Operations on Multiple Tables

So far our SELECT queries have all been performed on a **single** table, the **personnel** table. An important characteristic of an RDBMS is the ability to relate records in **multiple tables**, based on some kind of relationship between the tables. This allows us to submit queries that will produce a result set that includes values from fields taken from more than one table. To demonstrate, your **test** database includes a second table named **timesheet**. Table 14-2 provides a visualization of the timesheet table, which provides a sample weekly employee **timesheet**:

empID	hoursWorked
12345	30
12347	35
12348	40
12353	35
12356	20
12357	40
12358	32
12360	20
12361	32
12363	35

Table 14-2: Example of a relational database table (the timesheet table in the test database)

Like personnel, the timesheet table currently contains 10 records, one for each employee. Each record consists of just two fields: the employee's unique ID, and the hours that the employee worked this week.

Notice that the personnel and timesheet table both include an **empID** field. This allows us to **relate** the two tables based on the employee's ID. For example we can associate the hours worked by an employee record in the timesheet table with the same employee's firstName, lastName, and hourlyWage in the personnel table by looking for records with the same empID in each table. Here is an example of this query:

```
$userQuery = "SELECT personnel.firstName, personnel.lastName,
   personnel.hourlyWage, timesheet.hoursWorked
   FROM personnel, timesheet
   WHERE personnel.empID = timesheet.empID";
```

Each field name that is used in the **SELECT** statement is now preceded by the appropriate table name, to indicate which table contains the required field. A period is used to separate the table name and the field name, for example **personnel.firstName**. The **FROM** clause lists **both** tables, separated by commas. The **WHERE** clause indicates that the results set should only include the firstName, lastName, hourlyWage and hoursWorked of an employee where a record in the timesheet table matches the empID of a record in the personnel table.

Since the result set of this query contains each employee's first name, last name and hourly wage from the personnel table and the hours worked from the timesheet table, we can use this to calculate the weekly pay checks:

```
print("<h1>PAY CHECKS</h1>");
while ($row = mysqli_fetch_assoc($result))
{
   $weeklyPay = $row['hourlyWage'] * $row['hoursWorked'];
   print ("<p>PAY TO: ".$row['firstName']." ".
   $row['lastName']." THE SUM OF $".
   number_format($weeklyPay,2)."</p>");
}
```

The complete code for this example is provided in **mysql8.php**.

This is intended as an introductory example of a MySQL **JOIN** operation, where values from multiple tables are obtained by relating the tables in some way. JOIN operations can become very complex and you will want to conduct additional research or take a database course if you are planning to apply these operations in a production application.

Using INSERT to Add Records to a Table

So far we have looked at the use of the MySQL SELECT query to search and retrieve records from an existing MySQL table. What if we want to **add** a record to our table?

To add records to a table we must use the MySQL **INSERT** query. Here's a query that will add a new record to our personnel table:

```
$userQuery = "INSERT INTO personnel
   (empID, firstName, lastName, jobTitle, hourlyWage)
   VALUES ('23456', 'James', 'Joyce', 'sales', '10.75') ";
```

The INSERT command allows you to specify a list of the fields in the new record that are to receive values, followed by a VALUES clause which lists the values themselves. The values are stored in the fields in the order that the fields are listed. You can omit the list of fields, for example:

```
$userQuery = "INSERT INTO personnel VALUES
   ('23456', 'James', 'Joyce','sales', '10.75')";
```

In this case the values are always added in the same order that the fields are listed in the table.

Here's another example where an HTML form has been used to receive the values for the new record. In this case the variables that contain these values are used to construct the INSERT query:

```
$empID = $_POST['empID'];
$firstName = $_POST['firstName'];
$lastName = $_POST['lastName'];
$jobTitle = $_POST['jobTitle'];
$hourlyWage = $_POST['hourlyWage'];
$userQuery = "INSERT INTO personnel (empID, firstName,
   lastName, jobTitle, hourlyWage) VALUES ($empID, $firstName,
   $lastName, $jobTitle $hourlyWage)";
```

The **mysql9.html** and **mysql9.php** files in your samples folder include the complete code for this example. Note that this code does not need statements to process the result set since this is not a SELECT query.

Using UPDATE to Modify a Record

We can also modify existing records using the MySQL **UPDATE** query. For example, here's a query to modify Chris Smith's job title from 'sales' to 'manager':

```
$userQuery = "UPDATE personnel SET jobTitle='manager'
  WHERE empID='12345'";
```

Here we use a **WHERE** clause to specify which record is to be updated. Note that we use the employee's empID rather than first and last names in the WHERE clause. That's because the empID uniquely identifies each employee, whereas it's possible that two or more employees might have the same first and last names. We want to make sure that the right Chris Smith is promoted to manager!

The **SET** clause is used to update the **jobTitle** field of this record to 'manager'. We can update multiple fields in this record by including a **list** of updates in the SET clause, separated by commas. For example to change Chris Smith's job title to 'manager' and **also** update his or her hourly wage to '20.00':

```
$userQuery = "UPDATE personnel SET jobTitle='manager',
  hourlyWage='20.00' WHERE empID='12345'";
```

We can also code our WHERE clause to update **multiple** records. For example here's a query that updates the hourly wage of **all** employees who earn less than 8.00:

```
$userQuery = "UPDATE personnel SET hourlyWage='8.00'
  WHERE hourlyWage < '8.00'";
```

We can add an AND operator to this query if we only want to increase the hourly wage of **cleaners** who earn less than 8.00:

```
$userQuery = "UPDATE personnel SET hourlyWage='8.00'
  WHERE jobTitle='cleaner' AND hourlyWage < '8.00'";
```

This example is provided in **mysql10.php**. Once again, note that this code does not need statements to process the result set since this is not a SELECT query.

Removing a Record

We can **delete** records from a table using the MySQL **DELETE** query. Here's a query to delete the record of employee with the ID '12345':

```
$userQuery = "DELETE FROM personnel WHERE empID='12345'";
```

And here's a DELETE query that uses the WHERE clause to delete **all** employees with the job title of 'cleaner':

```
$userQuery = "DELETE FROM personnel
  WHERE jobTitle='cleaner'";
```

Be very careful when using the DELETE query! After all, you do not want to delete records that you may need at a later date. For example we might need to look up a former employee for some reason. It is often preferable to make records 'inactive' rather than deleting them entirely. We can achieve this by adding some kind of 'status' field to the table structure. This field can store a value that indicates whether or not each record is currently active. We can then include an additional test in the WHERE clause of all our SELECT queries if we only want to search for active records. Here are two examples that assume that the personnel records contain a field named **status**, and that this field contains the value 'active' or 'inactive':

```
SELECT * FROM personnel WHERE status='active'
SELECT empID, firstName, lastName FROM personnel
   WHERE status='inactive' AND jobTitle='accountant'
```

Of course these queries could only be used if the personnel table includes the status field.

Storing MySQL Connection Data in an Include File

So far our examples have included the MySQL connection data (hostname, user ID, user password, and database name) directly in our PHP application code. This means that we would have to update **every** application whenever the connection data changes, for example if the password is changed, or the database is moved to a different host. It also means that this very sensitive data is visible to anyone viewing the application code, for example on a printed copy.

A simple solution is to move the statements that assign the four connection values to variables to a separate file. Your samples folder contains a file named **incConnect-MySQL.php** that contains the following lines:

```
<?php
$server = "localhost";
$user = "wbip";
$pw = "wbip123";
$db = "test";
?>
```

The **mysql11.php** file in your samples folder contains the same code as mysql1.php except that these four statements have been removed and replaced by a PHP **include** statement:

```
include("incConnectMySQL.php");
```

This ensures that the four statements will be added to the code when the file is actually processed. This is much better practice: if any of the connection data changes we only have to update the incConnectMySQL.php file and all the applications that include this file will use the new connection values. This also improves security since the values are maintained in a separate file.

Creating, Dropping, and Altering Databases and Tables

In a real-world database environment, the accounts and privileges provided to programmers usually restrict them to work with specific databases and tables, and to only use queries such as SELECT, UPDATE and INSERT. Usually only the database administrator has full privileges, that will include the ability to **CREATE**, **DROP** (remove), or **ALTER** the structure of databases and tables, or to add, remove, or modify user accounts and privileges. Programmers may sometimes function as their own database administrators, for example when working on small scale applications or Web sites.

The design and management of database systems is an extremely serious business, and great care must always be taken to prevent inappropriate use, security breaches, inefficient processing, or data corruption. This topic is beyond the scope of this textbook, but the textbook Web site includes some material to introduce the MySQL commands to create, drop, and alter databases and tables.

Additional Learning Materials

In this chapter you learned how to use PHP functions to submit MySQL queries. This approach is necessary when coding Web applications that require MySQL services, but you will also want to work **directly** with your MySQL system, for example to perform administrative tasks, submit your own queries, and manage user accounts. Many **GUI interfaces** are available for this purpose, and you can also work with MySQL from the **command line** (you can even use your **MS Access** or **Libre Office Base** interfaces to query MySQL databases).

Your **xampp** installation includes a widely used MySQL interface known as **phpMyAdmin**, which is the standard interface provided by Web hosting services. **phpMyAdmin** (which is written in PHP) allows you to administer your MySql server over the Web. **Appendix H** provides a short tutorial that demonstrates how to use phpMyAdmin to connect to your server and perform common management tasks and queries. You can use phpMyAdmin to test and experiment with MySQL queries without having to code them in PHP.

Chapter 16 references a list of standard PHP msqli functions.

Appendix D will help you debug your exercises, listing a number of the most common errors that you are likely to encounter.

The **Chapter 14 Hints and Help** pages on the textbook Web site provide answers to FAQs from previous students as they worked through the end-of-chapter exercises.

Summary

A **relational database** is composed of 1 or more related tables of data. Each table is composed of columns (fields) and rows (records).

A **Relational Database Management System (RDBMS)** provides a full range of management tools for storing, managing, and using relational databases.

Communications with the RDBMS are written using the RDBMS's **Structured Query Language (SQL)**. MySQL is a widely used, SQL-based RDBMS.

The effective design and management of an RDBMS is the responsibility of a **database administrator**.

There are three ways to interact with the MYSQL RDBMS: from the **command line**; through a **graphical interface** such as **phpMyAdmin**; or from a **custom application** that has been developed in a programming language such as PHP.

The PHP **mysqli_connect**() and **mysqli_close**() functions are used to open and close connections to a MySQL server and database.

The MySQL **SELECT** query is used to retrieve values in the fields and records of MySQL tables that match specified search criteria. The values that are returned by a SELECT query are referred to as the **result** set.

A SELECT query can be defined to just return values from specific fields from each of the records that match the query.

A SELECT query can include a **WHERE** clause to match specific records.

A WHERE clause can include the use of relational operators, as well as logical operators such as **AND** and **OR**. MySQL provides a number of other operators such as **BETWEEN .. AND**, and **LIKE** (used for pattern-matching).

The LIKE operator can include the **wildcard** characters % (to indicate 0 or more characters in this position) and _ (exactly one character in this position).

A SELECT query can include an **ORDER BY** clause to define the ordering of the result set. The records returned by the result set are ordered by a specific field. If you want to order by more than one field, the result set will be ordered, first by the first field, and then by the second field, and so on.

The ORDER BY clause can include the **ASC** or **DESC** keyword after the field name(s) to indicate the result set should be ordered in ascending or descending order (the default as ascending).

PHP variables can be used in MySQL queries so, for example, input from a HTML form can be included in the construction of a query.

The PHP **mysqli_query()** function is used to submit MySQL queries. If the query cannot be submitted successfully this function returns **false**, otherwise it returns the query result.

The PHP **mysqli_error()** function will return a MySQL error message associated with a query error. This function is often used to inform the user of a problem when a call to the mysqli_query() function returns **false**.

The PHP **mysqli_num_rows()** function returns the number of records in the result set of a MySQL SELECT query.

The PHP **mysqli_fetch_assoc()** function is used to extract the next record from the result set of a MySQL SELECT query into an associative array or returns false if there are no more records to extract. This function is often used to control a WHILE loop when the results might contain 0 or more records. In that case the next record is extracted from the result set into an associative array each time the loop repeats until all the records in the result set have been processed.

The values that are returned in the result set of a MySQL SELECT query can be used in calculations. MySQL also provides a large number of functions to perform calculations that are returned as part of the result set. This removes the need for special coding by the applications. Examples of MySQL functions are **SUM()**, **AVG()**, **COUNT()**, **MAX()**, and **MIN()**.

MySQL **JOIN** operations are used to relate data between multiple tables.

The MySQL **INSERT** query is used to add records to a MySQL table. The INSERT command allows you to specify a list of the fields in the new record that are to receive values, followed by a VALUES clause which lists the values themselves.

The MySQL **UPDATE** query is used to modify existing records in a MySQL table. The WHERE clause is used to match the record(s) that are to be updated. The SET clause specifies the fields that are to be modified and the new values that are to be assigned.

The MySQL **DELETE** query is used to remove existing records in a MySQL table. The WHERE clause is used to match the record(s) that are to be deleted.

It is a best practice to maintain your MySQL connection values in a separate file, and then **include** this file in your application code. This reduces duplication and improves security.

Usually only the database administrator has full privileges to manage an RDBMS. These privileges include the ability to **CREATE**, **DROP** (remove), or **ALTER** the structure of databases and tables, or to add , remove, or modify user accounts. Programmers may sometimes function as their own database administrators, for example when working on small scale applications or Web sites.

Chapter 14 Review Questions

1. Which is correct?
    a. A database contains tables and a table contains records and fields
    b. A table contains databases and a database contains records and fields
    c. A record contains tables and a table contains databases and fields
    d. A database contains records and a record contains tables and fields

2. In a visual representation of a table, a record is shown as a
    a. Field
    b. Column
    c. Row
    d. Database

3. Which of the following best describes a RDBMS?
    a. A test database that is included with MySQL
    b. A database used to store personnel data
    c. A language used to submit queries
    d. A system to store, manage and use relational databases

4. Which of the following best describes SQL?
    a. A test database that is included with MySQL
    b. A database used to store personnel data
    c. A language used to submit queries to an RDBMS
    d. A system to store, manage and use relational databases

5. Which of the following is true?
    a. MySQL is a version of SQL
    b. SQL is a version of MySQL

6. What value will $connect have after the following statement is executed if the connection fails?

```
$connect=mysqli($host, 'wbip', 'wbip123', 'test');
```

    a. false
    b. true
    c. no value
    d. "Connection could not be completed"

7. Look at the following statement. What is the user password?

```
$connect=mysqli('localhost', 'this', 'that', 'other');
```

   a. localhost
   b. this
   c. that
   d. other

8. Which MySQL command is used to search a table for specific fields and records?
   a. SEARCH
   b. QUERY
   c. SELECT
   d. UPDATE

9. Which fields will have values included in the result set of this query?

```
SELECT empID, jobTitle FROM personnel
   WHERE hourlyWage < 10.00 ORDER BY lastName
```

   a. empID and jobTitle
   b. hourlyWage only
   c. astName only
   d. empID, jobTitle, hourlyWage, and lastName

10. What is wrong with this query?

```
SELECT title, hourlyWage FROM personnel
   WHERE lastName=='Jones'
```

   a. You must always include an ORDER BY clause in a SELECT statement
   b. WHERE lastName=='Jones' should be IF(lastName=='Jones')
   c. WHERE lastName=='Jones' should be WHILE(lastName=='Jones')
   d. WHERE lastName=='Jones' should be WHERE lastName='Jones'

11. Which query will return the title and hourly wage of all employees whose hourly wage is at least 10.00 but not more than 20.00?
   a. SELECT title, hourlyWage FROM personnel
         WHERE hourlyWage >= 10.00 AND <= 20.00
   b. SELECT title, hourlyWage FROM personnel
         WHERE hourlyWage >= 10.00 AND hourlyWage <= 20.00
   c. SELECT title, hourlyWage FROM personnel
         WHERE hourlyWage BETWEEN 10.00 AND 20.00
   d. SELECT title, hourlyWage FROM personnel
         WHERE hourlyWage BETWEEN 10.00 AND <= 20.00

12. Which query will return the title and hourly wage of all employees whose hourly wage is greater than 10.00 and less than 20.00?
    a. SELECT title, hourlyWage FROM personnel
       WHERE hourlyWage > 10.00 AND < 20.00
    b. SELECT title, hourlyWage FROM personnel
       WHERE hourlyWage >= 10.00 AND hourlyWage <= 20.00
    c. SELECT title, hourlyWage FROM personnel
       WHERE hourlyWage BETWEEN 10.00 AND 20.00
    d. SELECT title, hourlyWage FROM personnel
       WHERE hourlyWage BETWEEN 10.00 AND < 20.00

13. Which of the last names will be matched by the WHERE clause in the following query?

```
SELECT empID from personnel WHERE lastName LIKE 'Jo%s'
```

    a. Jons will be matched but Johns and Johnson will not be matched
    b. Jons and Johns will be matched but Johnson will not be matched
    c. Jons, Johns and Johnson will all be matched
    d. None of these three last names will be matched

14. Which of the last names will be matched by the WHERE clause in the following query?

```
SELECT empID from personnel WHERE lastName LIKE 'Jo_s'
```

    a. 'Jons' will be matched but 'Johns' and 'Johnson' will not be matched
    b. 'Jons' and 'Johns' will be matched but 'Johnson' will not be matched
    c. 'Jons', 'Johns' and 'Johnson' will all be matched
    d. None of these three last names will be matched

15. Assume that the personnel table contains three records of employees with these first and last names:

```
Peter  Jones
Mary   Jones
Robert Johnson
```

How would these three records be ordered in the result set of the following query?

```
SELECT firstName, lastName from personnel
  ORDER BY lastName, firstName
```

    a. Mary Jones, then Peter Jones, then Robert Johnson
    b. Mary Jones, then Robert Johnson, then Peter Jones
    c. Peter Jones, then Mary Jones, then Robert Johnson
    d. Robert Johnson, then Mary Jones, then Peter Jones

16. What is the correct MySQL command to add a new record to a table?
    a. ALTER
    b. UPDATE
    c. ADD
    d. INSERT

17. What is the correct MySQL command to modify the values stored in a record?
    a. ALTER
    b. UPDATE
    c. ADD
    d. INSERT

18. Assume an application uses the following query:

```
$userQuery = "SELECT jobTitle FROM personnel
              WHERE hourlyWage > 15.00";
$result = mysqli_query($connect, $userQuery);
```

and then uses the following heading for the loop that will process the result set:

```
while($row = mysqli_fetch_assoc($result))
```

Which statement below should appear inside the loop to process the values in the result set?
    a. print ("<p>$jobTitle</p>");
    b. print ("<p>$row['jobTitle']</p>");
    c. print ("<p>$result['jobTitle']</p>");
    d. print ("<p>$userQuery['jobTitle']</p>");

19. Which statement will generate the lowest hourly wage in the personnel table?
    a. SELECT MIN(hourlyWage) FROM personnel
    b. SELECT * FROM personnel WHERE MIN(hourlyWage)
    c. SELECT hourlyWage FROM personnel WHERE hourlyWage < lowest
    d. SELECT hourlyWage FROM personnel ORDER BY hourlyWage DESC

20. What value will be stored in the lastName field of this record after this query is executed? (be careful)

```
INSERT INTO personnel (empID, lastName, firstName, jobTitle,
hourlyWage) VALUES (67890, 'Michael', 'Peter', 'cleaner',
12.50)
```

    a. 67890
    b. Michael
    c. Peter
    d. cleaner
    e. 12.50

Chapter 14 Code Exercises

Your Chapter 14 code exercises can be found in your **chapter14** folder. This folder is included in your customized XAMPP installation at the following location:

htdocs\webtech\coursework\chapter14

Type your name and the date in the **Author** and **Date** sections of each file as you work on each exercise. **Remember** that the Students page on the textbook Web site includes **Hints and Help** pages for the exercises in this and every chapter.

Debugging Exercises

Your **chapter14** folder should contain a number of "fixit" files. Each of these files contains PHP code that has an error of some kind. Open the file in a text editor and read the comment section in the file to see what to do to fix them. You will need to run each program in order to see the errors, and to test that your fixes have worked correctly. For example to run **fixit1.php**, first run the Web server, then use the URL:

http://localhost/webtech/coursework/chapter14/fixit1.php

Code Modification Exercises

Your **chapter14** folder contains a number of "modify" files. These contain HTML and PHP code that needs to be modified to meet a requirement. The requirements are included in the comment section of each file. Modify the algorithms, being careful to make changes to the .html and .php files as directed. You will need to run each program in order to test your changes. For example to run **modify1.html**, first run the Web server, then use the URL:

http://localhost/webtech/coursework/chapter14/modify1.html

Code Completion Exercises

1. Complete the code in **staff-report1.php** so that the program provides a table that shows the empID and job title of all employees.

2. Complete the code in **staff-report2.php** so that the program provides a table that shows the empID, first name, last name, job title and hourly wage of all managers and accountants. Use the * to indicate all fields in your SELECT statement.

3. Complete the code in **staff-report3.php** so that the program provides a table that shows the first names, last names and job titles of managers and sales people ordered by job title then last name.

4. Complete the code in **cleaners.php** so that the program displays the lowest hourly wage of the cleaners. HINT: use a MySQL function to accomplish this.

5. The **job-titles1.html** file includes a form that asks the user for an employee ID. Complete the code in **job-titles1.php** so that this program displays the employee's ID, job title and hourly wage.

6. The **job-titles2.html** file includes a form that asks the user for a job title. Complete the code in **job-titles2.php** so that this program displays the first and last names of all employees with this job title.

7. Complete the code in **raises.php** so that the program finds the empID for all employees who earn less than 10.00, and displays the message "Employee XXX needs a raise!", for each of these employees, where XXX is the empID of the employee.

8. Anne Humphries needs to change her last name and she has also received a promotion! Complete the code in **name-change.php** so that the last name of the employee with ID 12353 is changed to 'Jackson' and the job title is changed to 'manager'. You can run **name-change-test.php** to check that the record was changed correctly.

9. The **wage-report.html** file includes a form that asks the user for an hourly wage and a job title. Complete the code in **wage-report.php** to find the empID of all employees with this job title who earn this hourly wage or higher. Note that in some cases this will return 0 records.

10. The **add-sales-person.html** file includes a form for entering a record for a new sales person. The form asks the user for the new sales person's empID, first name, and last name. Complete the code in **add-sales-person.php** so that this program adds this employee to the personnel table with the job title 'sales' and an hourly wage of **14.25**. You can run the **employees.php** program (provided) to confirm that the new employee was added to the table. NOTE: If you make a mistake and need to delete a record, you can use the **delete-employee.php** file (if you do this, you will first need to modify the value assigned to the $empID variable in delete-employee.php in order to delete the correct record).

Chapter 15

Introduction to Object-Oriented Programming

Intended Learning Outcomes

After completing this chapter, you should be able to:

- Explain the significance of Object-Oriented Programming (OOP).
- Summarize the general structure and purpose of an object.
- Interpret a class definition for a simple object that includes private class variables and public get and set methods.
- Create instances of a class using the new operator with the class constructor.
- Use an object's public methods to work with class instances.
- Create a class definition for a simple object that includes private class variables, and public get and set methods.
- Use the $this variable to refer to class variables inside methods, to distinguish these from local variables.
- Add a custom constructor method to a class.
- Distinguish between the private, protected, and public access modifiers.
- Explain the meaning and value of class inheritance.
- Create a child class that extends (inherits from) a parent class.
- Explain the meaning and purpose of the abstract keyword.
- Label a class as abstract to ensure that it cannot be instantiated.
- Define abstract methods to ensure that these methods appear in child classes.
- Explain the meaning and purpose of encapsulation, instantiation, inheritance, method overloading, method over-riding, and poly-morphism.
- Recognize the important relationships between object-oriented design, user interfaces, and data sources.

Introduction

As we have seen, programming is essentially concerned with performing useful work on data. We have also learned from our work with data files and databases that our applications usually work with groups of related data values, for example: data related to an **employee** might consist of the employee's ID, social security number, first name, last name, job title, starting date, and hourly wage; a **game character** might consist of a name, current score, health rating, and various skill ratings; a **bank account** might contain an account ID and a current balance; a **weather station reading** might consist of a temperature, wind speed, wind direction, precipitation amount, humidity level, and cloud conditions; an **item for sale** might consist of a stock number, a sale price, a description, and other details such as size, color, and weight; an **email message** might consist of message headers (to, from, cc, and bcc fields), a subject, and the email message; even a **rectangle** on the computer screen must be described by a group of individual data items such as height, width, x and y coordinates (position), and fill color.

It is helpful to consider any group of related data values as a single entity. Consider an employee: instead of working with many separate variables such as the employee's ID, first and last names, job title, hourly wage, etc., it would be far more efficient if we could simply work with an employee as a complete item, referenced by a single variable. This employee entity could then "contain" all of the different data values, or **attributes**, that describe the employee, and the attributes could also be associated with a set of functions that process the employee data in useful ways. For example we could call an employee-related function to change the last name of an employee, or call another employee-related function to calculate an employee's weekly pay.

This approach, combining a group of related data with the functions that operate on the data, is the basis of **Object-Oriented Programming (OOP)**. **OOP** provides a powerful modular approach to the way that we work with groups of related data. In the language of OOP, an entity such as an employee is termed an **object**. An object consists of a set of data values (attributes) combined with a set of operations (methods) that allow us to work with the object's data in any way needed to meet our requirements.

OOP brings enormous benefits. We have already discussed the value of code modularity in modern software design. Objects can be designed and developed independently of any application, and application programmers can simply make use of these pre-defined objects in their code without reinventing the wheel. An employee object can be passed between modules very easily , as a single item. And the attributes and methods that make up an object can be maintained, modified and tested independently of the applications that use the object.

It would take far too much space to examine OOP in great detail in this introductory textbook, and PHP is not the most suitable language to develop object-oriented code (Java and Python are examples of fully object-oriented languages). But every programmer should be aware of the general concepts and application of OOP. In this chapter we will introduce you to the design and use of objects, explain some common OOP terminology, and provide some simple working examples in PHP that will get you started and prepare you for further study in subsequent courses or personal research.

What is an Object?

Simply stated, an **object** combines a group of related data values (usually known as the object's **attributes, fields** or **class variables**) with a set of functions (usually known as the object's **methods**) that perform useful operations on these fields. The code structure that defines an object is known as a **class.** For example a simplified **Employee class** might contain the following class variables that, taken together, define an employee:

```
empID                    // the employee's ID
firstName                // the employee's first name
lastName                 // the employee's last name
jobTitle                 // the employee's job title
hourlyWage               // the employee's hourly wage
```

The Employee class might also provide the following methods that would allow a programmer to perform useful operations on these five variables:

```
getID()                       // retrieve the employee's ID
setID($id)                    // modify the employee's ID
getFirstName()                // retrieve the employee's first name
setFirstName($firstName)      // modify the employee's first name
getLastName()                 // retrieve the employee's last name
setLastName($lastName)        // modify the employee's last name
getJobTitle()                 // retrieve the employee's job title
setJobTitle($jobTitle)        // modify the employee's job title
getHourlyWage()               // retrieve the employee's hourly wage
setHourlyWage($hourlyWage)    // modify the employee's hourly wage
getWeeklyPay ()               // calculate the employee's weekly pay
findEmployee($id)             // search the employee data source
                              // (file or database) for a record
                              // that matches the ID, and assign
                              // this employee's data to the
                              // class variables
addEmployee()                 // add the employee to the employee
                              // data system (file or database)
```

As you work through this chapter you will learn how to code this class, and to develop applications that make use of the class. Of course a real Employee class would have many more data values and allow many more operations. Once an Employee class has been defined, your applications can generate copies of the class as needed, one copy for each employee that the application needs to work with. In Object-Oriented jargon each individual copy (each employee) is called an **instance** of the Employee class, and each instance has its own class variables, separate from any other instances. For example a copy of the Employee class used for an employee named "Chris Smith" would be one

Employee instance, and a copy of the Employee object used for an employee named "Mary King" would be another, separate, Employee instance. Once an instance has been created, your application can use the object's methods to: assign values to the class fields for that instance; retrieve these values; and perform other useful operations. For example, the application might use the setFirstName() method to set an instance's first name field to "Chris", and the setLastName() method to set the same instance's last name field to "Smith".

Creating and Using Instances of a Class

In order to work with an instance of an Employee in your application, you must first create, or **instantiate**, the instance. Every object class includes a special method called a **constructor method**, which always has the same name as the class name, and this is used with a special operator, the **new** operator to create a new instance. The instance can then be assigned to a variable for use in your application. The constructor method of the **Employee** class will be automatically named **Employee()**; here's how to create an instance of Employee and assign this instance to a variable named **$emp1**:

```
$emp1 = new Employee();
```

And here's how to create a second instance and assign it to a variable named **$emp2**:

```
$emp2 = new Employee();
```

We now have two instances (or copies) of the Employee class, and the methods that are a part of the Employee class can now be used to work with each instance's class variables as needed. Here's how you can use the Employee methods that we listed above to assign values to each of the class variables of the $emp1 instance:

```
$emp1->setID("012345");
$emp1->setFirstName("Chris");
$emp1->setLastName("Smith");
$emp1->setJobTitle("Manager");
$emp1->setHourlyWage(36.50);
```

As you can see, there is a special syntax that must be used when we want to work with an instance of a class; we use the name of the variable that refers to the instance (in this case **$emp1**), followed by the -> characters (no spaces between these), followed by the name of the class method that we wish to use, for example **setID()**. You can use the same class methods to assign values to the **$emp2** instance:

```
$emp2->setID("345678");
$emp2->setFirstName("Mary");
$emp2->setLastName("King");
$emp2->setJobTitle("Accountant");
$emp2->setHourlyWage(35.75);
```

If you wanted to print the ID and job title of the employee stored in the $emp1 instance, you can do this using the getID() and getJobTitle() methods of the Employee class:

```
print ("<p>The job title of employee #".$emp1->getID().
    " is ".$emp1->getJobTitle().".</p>");
```

The list of Employee class methods also included a method called getWeeklyPay() that will calculate the pay. You could obtain the weekly pay of $emp1 and store it in a variable named **$emp1Pay** as follows:

```
$emp1Pay = $emp1->getWeeklyPay();
```

And to obtain the weekly pay for $emp2 and store it in a variable named **$emp2Pay** :

```
$emp2Pay = $emp2->getWeeklyPay();
```

Note that, as an application programmer, you no longer need to code the weekly pay calculations, or even know how these calculations are performed. You only need to call the object's getWeeklyPay() method which will return the pay to your application. To do this you just need to know what class methods and variables are provided by the Employee class.

Using Employee Objects in an Application

Review the list of methods that are contained in the Employee class, and the purpose of each method. Let's look at two simple applications that each use instances of Employee to work with employee data in different ways. First, consider the following requirement:

*Requirement: develop a Web application named **new-employee** that provides the user with a form to obtain the ID, first name, last name, job title, and hourly wage of a new employee. Use an Employee instance to add this data to the company's data source. The code that defines the Employee class is provided for you in a file named inc-employee-object.php so this file must be included in your code. Note that you don't need to know anything about the data source (which may be a file or database) since this is handled by the addEmployee() method which is part of the Employee class.*

The Web form is simple, and can be coded as follows:

```
<h1>Add New Employee Form</h1>
<form action="new-employee.php" method="post">
  <label>ID:
  <input type="text" size = "15" name="id"></label>
  <label>First Name:
  <input type="text" size = "15" name="firstName"></label>
  <label>Last Name:
  <input type="text" size = "15" name="lastName"></label>
  <label>Job Title:
  <input type="text" size = "15" name="jobTitle"></label>
  <label>Hourly Wage:</td>
  <input type="text" size = "15" name="wage"></label>

  <input class = "submit" type = "submit" value = "Add
    Employee">
</form>
```

Code Example: new-employee.html

The PHP code that processes this form must:

Include the code that provides the Employee class definition
Retrieve the employee's attributes from the form data
Create an Employee instance
Call appropriate Employee methods to assign the employee's attributes to the instance
Call the appropriate Employee method to add the employee to the data source

Here is the code for new-employee.php:

```php
<?php
include("inc-employee-object.php");

$id = $_POST["id"];
$firstName = $_POST["firstName"];
$lastName = $_POST["lastName"];
$title = $_POST["jobTitle"];
$hourlyWage = $_POST["wage"];

$emp = new Employee();

$emp->setID($id);
$emp->setFirstName($firstName);
$emp->setLastName($lastName);
$emp->setJobTitle($title);
$emp->setHourlyWage($hourlyWage);

$emp->addEmployee();

print("<p>The new employee ($id) has been added to the employee
file.</p>");
?>
```

Code Example: new-employee.php

This code first includes the code (**inc-employee-object.php**) that defines the Employee class (we will examine this code later in the chapter), then retrieves the five values from the form submitted by the user (the new employee's ID, first name, last name, job title and hourly wage). The next statement creates a new Employee instance and assigns this to a variable named **$emp**. This is followed by five statements that call the setID(), set-FirstName(), setLastName(), setJobTitle(), and setHourlyWage() methods of the Employee class to assign the values from the form to the five fields in the **$emp** instance. These values are now stored in the instance but they have not yet been added to the data system. To do this we must use the addEmployee() method which has been coded to add the values of the class fields as a new record in the employee data source, which will be described later in the chapter. Note that the application programmer doesn't need to know the names of the class fields in the Employee class, or the connection to, or structure of, the data sources that contains the employee data, or even whether the data is being stored in a file or database; he or she only needs to know the names and purpose of each of the methods that will perform the different tasks.

Now let's look at another application that calculates the weekly pay for two employees as follows:

> *Requirement: develop a Web application named employee-pay that provides the*
> *user with a form to obtain the ID for an employee. Use an Employee instance to*
> *find the employee in the data source, then displays the employee's first name, last*
> *name and weekly pay. The code that defines the Employee class is provided for you*
> *in a file named inc-employee-object.php so this file must be included in your code.*

In this case the Web form only needs to obtain the employee's ID and hours worked
from the user:

```
<h1>Weekly Pay Calculator</h1>
<form action="employee-pay.php" method="post">
<label>Employee ID<input type="text" name="id"></label>
<input class = "submit" type = "submit" value = "Calculate
Weekly      Pay">
</form>
```

Code Example: employee-pay.html

The PHP code that processes this form must:

Include the code that provides the Employee class definition
Retrieve the employee's ID from the form data
Create an Employee instance
Call the appropriate Employee method to find the employee with the requested
    ID
Call the appropriate Employee methods to print the first names, last names, and
weekly pay of the employee.

Here is the code for employee-pay.php:

```
<?php
include("inc-employee-object.php");

$id = $_POST["id"];
$emp1 = new Employee();
$emp1->findEmployee($id);

print ("<p>Weekly Pay for ".$emp1->getFirstName().
    " ". $emp1->getLastName().": $".
    $emp1->getWeeklyPay()."</p>");
?>
```

Code Example: employee-pay.php

This code first includes the code that defines the Employee object (we will examine
this code later in the chapter), then retrieves the form data submitted by the user (the
employee's ID). The next statement creates an Employee instance. The next statement

uses the object's **findEmployee**() method to retrieve the data for the employee from the data system and store this data in the instance's class variables. The application then calls the **getFirstName**(), **getLastName**(), and **getWeeklyPay**() methods to display the employee's first name, last name, and weekly pay.

Once again note how elegant our application code has become; the application programmer only needs to know the names and purpose of the object's methods to work with an Employee instance. Do you see from these examples how greatly this simplifies the work of the application programmer, and how the Employee objects can be used in different ways to meet the requirements of different applications? Can you think of other ways that Employee objects might be used by an application?

Defining an Object

We have seen two examples showing how our application might **use** an Employee object. But we still don't know how the Employee class is actually coded, what it actually looks like. In fact, many application programmers use object classes without actually seeing the class code. They simply work from the class documentation to create instances and use the class methods for the purposes of their application. Other programmers design, code, and documents object classes for use by application programmers. Let's look at the code of the Employee class so we can get a better understanding of how object classes are designed and coded. The class fields of our simplified Employee class are as follows:

```
empID                    // the employee's ID
firstName                // the employee's first name
lastName                 // the employee's last name
jobTitle                 // the employee's job title
hourlyWage               // the employee's hourly wage
```

The functions (methods) that will allow a programmer to work with these fields are as follows:

```
findEmployee(id)         // read an employee from the data source
addEmployee()            // add the employee to the data source
getID()                  // to obtain the employee's ID
setID(id)                // to modify the employee's ID
getFirstName()           // to obtain the employee's first name
setFirstName(firstName)  // to modify the employee's first name
getLastName()            // to obtain the employee's last name
setLastName(lastName)    // to modify the employee's last name
getJobTitle()            // to obtain the employee's job title
setJobTitle(jobTitle)    // to modify the employee's job title
getHourlyWage()          // to obtain the employee's hourly wage
setHourlyWage(hourlyWage) // to modify the employee's hourly wage
getWeeklyPay ()          // to calculate the employee's weekly pay
```

Each of these methods perform a very specific and often quite simple task, so that programmers who need to work with objects of this class can easily perform any operation that is required. The idea is that a program that needs to work with employee data for one or more employees can create an **instance** of Employee for each employee and then use the object's methods to work with any employee's data (class variables) as needed. Of course this is a simplified example. In a real world application we would include all kinds of additional data, as well as functions designed to handle tasks related to health insurance, retirement contributions, tax exemptions and tax calculations.

Coding the Object Class

Here is how an Employee object class might actually be defined in PHP (this definition is provided in the **inc-employee-object.php** file in your **samples** folder). You will see that object class definitions incorporate some operators and other features that we have not seen before:

```php
<?php
class Employee
{
    private $empID;
    private $firstName;
    private $lastName;
    private $jobTitle;
    private $hourlyWage;

    public function getID()
    {
        return $this->empID;
    }

    public function setID($empID)
    {
        $this->empID = $empID;
    }

    public function getFirstName()
    {
        return $this->firstName;
    }
    public function setFirstName($fName)
    {
        $this->firstName = $fName;
    }
```

```php
public function getLastName()
{
  return $this->lastName;
}

public function setLastName($lName)
{
  $this->lastName = $lName;
}

public function getJobTitle()
{
  return $this->jobTitle;
}

public function setJobTitle($title)
{
  $this->jobTitle = $title;
}

public function getHourlyWage()
{
  return $this->hourlyWage;
}

public function setHourlyWage($hourlyWage)
{
  $this->hourlyWage = $hourlyWage;
}

public function getWeeklyPay()
{
  return number_format ($this->hourlyWage * 40, 2);
}

public function addEmployee()
{
  $empRecord = $this->empID.", ".$this->firstName.
    ", ".$this->lastName.", ".$this->jobTitle.
    ", ".$this->hourlyWage."\n";

  $empFile = fopen("employees.txt", "a");
  fputs($empFile, $empRecord);
  fclose($empFile);
```

```
      } // end of addEmployee method

      public function findEmployee($id)
      {
        $empFile = fopen("employees.txt", "r");
        $empRecord = trim(fgets($empFile));
        $notFound = true;
        while (!feof($empFile) and $notFound)
        {
          list ($empID, $fName, $lName, $title, $wage) =
                      explode(",", $empRecord);
          if ($id == $empID)
          {
            $this->empID = $empID;
            $this->firstName = $fName;
            $this->lastName = $lName;
            $this->jobTitle = $title;
            $this->hourlyWage = $wage;
            $notFound = false;
          }
          $empRecord = trim(fgets($empFile));
        }
        fclose($empFile);
      } // end of findEmployee method

    } // end of class definition
    ?>
```

Code Example: inc-employee-object.php

The entire class definition for the Employee object begins with a class heading that consists of the keyword **class** followed by the name of the class. The entire body of the class definition is enclosed in { } braces. The variables that will store the data values of the object are known as **class variables** (also known as class fields or attributes). The class variables are listed separately from (and usually above) the class methods. The class variables are used to store the object's data values. Note that the definitions of each of the class variables of the Employee class are preceded by the keyword **private**, which is an **access modifier**. This means that these variables can only be accessed or modified by the methods that are part of this class; they cannot be accessed or modified directly by other classes or by applications that use the class. Defining these variables as private ensures that the only way to work with them is by using the class methods that are provided. We say that the private class variables are **encapsulated** by the class methods. If for some reason you wanted to allow applications to directly access or modify any of these variables you could declare them as **public**, but usually we want to avoid this: encapsulation is a key feature of object-oriented programming: by forcing applications to use the methods that have been provided, we reduce the chance of badly written application code using the data incorrectly. There are actually three different access modifiers, the third is **protected**. The **protected** access modifier is similar to **private**, but **protected** class variables may also be accessed and modified by methods in other classes that **inherit** this class; we will discuss inheritance and the use of the **protected** modifier later in the chapter.

The **class methods** are listed below the class variables. As you can see the methods are defined as functions, just like any other functions in PHP. The methods are generally defined as **public**, which means they can be used by other classes or applications. The public class methods therefore provide a **programming interface** between the class variables and any application that uses instances of the class; the only way to work with private class variables is to use the public class methods. If for any reason you wanted to restrict access to some methods so that they can only be called by other methods within this class, you could define them as **private** (or **protected**), just like the class variables.

Most class methods are designed to perform a simple operation of some kind that usually involves accessing or modifying one or more class variables. Some methods include parameters since they must be sent values when they are called, other do not need parameters. For example the **getHourlyWage()** method simply **returns** the value stored in the **$hourlyWage** class variable, so this method does not require any parameters. On the other hand, the **setHourlyWage()** method receives a value from an application and **stores** this in the **$hourlyWage** class variable, so this method includes a parameter to receive the hourly wage.

It is standard practice to use the words **get** or **set** followed by the name of a class variable when naming methods that return or update the values of class variables. This approach ensures that the method names clearly indicate their purpose as well as which class variable they are working with. These types of method are often referred to as **getter** and **setter** methods.

You will notice that the code inside the class methods uses an unfamiliar syntax to refer to the class variables. For example, rather than referring to $hourlyWage, the **getHourlyWage()** method refers to the variable as **$this->hourlyWage**. Remember that a function can be considered a small independent program. Without the use of the special identifier **$this**, the method would assume that **$hourlyWage** is a variable for use only within the function. The use of **$this->hourlyWage** refers to **this** instance's **class** variable **$hourlyWage**; this ensures that the class-level variables are not confused with any variables defined inside the functions that may have the same name.

You can see the importance of this if you look at the **setHourlyWage()** method. This method contains a parameter named **$hourlyWage**. The method is designed to assign the value received in the $hourlyWage parameter to the class variable **$hourlyWage**. But the parameter has the same name as the class variable. The statement **$this->hourlyWage = $hourlyWage** avoids any ambiguity by using **$this->hourlyWage** to specify that the value received in the method's **parameter** variable **$hourlyWage** is to be assigned to the **class** variable **$hourlyWage**. The use of the **$this** identifer ensures that these two variables are not confused although both have the same name.

As you can see, get and set methods are provided for each class variable. This ensures that any application that works with Employee instances can access and modify any of these variables as needed. There are also three other methods in the Employee class. The **getWeeklyPay**() method is designed to multiply the employee's hourly wage by 40, and return this as the weekly pay, formatted to two places (of course in a real world application the calculation would depend on the actual hours worked, but here we'll keep it simple). The **findEmployee**() method receives an employee ID and uses this to search through a data source to locate that employee's attributes (first name, last name, job title, and hourly wage). If it finds the employee, the method then assigns these values to the instance's class variables so the instance now contains information concerning a specific employee. Note that the method is actually coded to search through a text file named **employees.txt** in which individual data values are separated by commas, but this could be changed to search through a different data source (usually of course, employee data would be stored in a database table and not a text file; a text file is used here simply to keep the focus on object design, and to serve readers who might have skipped the MySQL chapter). The application programmer who uses the findEmployee() method doesn't need to know anything about where the employee data is stored; he or she just calls this method to obtain an employee's data. The other method **addEmployee**() simply takes the values stored in the instance's class variables and adds these as a new record in the data source. In this case, they are appended to the employees.txt file, but, once again, this code could be changed if the employee data was relocated to a different file or database.

Rather than thinking about the requirements for a specific application, the designer of an object class such as the Employee class considers all the different ways that programmers might need to work with the Employee data for different applications, and develops methods to allow for all these different uses. Often class variables and methods are added or modified as new requirements are identified.

Creating and Using Instances of an Object Class

In order to use a class, a programmer needs to know the name of the class and also what methods are available to work with the data that the class provides. Now that the Employee class has been defined, we can write applications that create and use **instances** of this class as needed, one instance for each employee that our application needs to process. Each instance will contain its own set of class variables, and the class methods can be used as needed to work with these values. We have already looked at two examples of applications that work with instances of the Employee class.

The Class Constructor Method

We have seen that each new instance of an Employee object is created by using the **new** operator to call a special **constructor** method, which has the same name as the class. In this case the constructor method is named **Employee()**. The constructor method automatically creates a new **copy** (instance) of the object for use by the program. The constructor method is only used to create new instances. Once the instance has been created, the other functions (methods) in the Employee class can be used to work with the class variables.

A default version of the class constructor method is provided automatically as a part of the class definition, so you don't have to create it in your code. However if you want to ensure that certain tasks are always performed whenever a new instance of a class is created, you can add your own constructor method to the class and add any code that you want. If you do this, your customized constructor will replace the default constructor, and will be used whenever a new instance of the class is created. You can also include parameters if you want arguments to be passed to the constructor method. Constructor methods in PHP must use the following format (note the two underscores):

```
public function __construct()
{
   // code that you want to execute whenever a new instance is
   created
}
```

Note that there are **two** underlines in the standard method name for constructors: **__construct()**. When would you want to write your own constructor method? One example might be if you always wanted to obtain values from a file or database in order to initialize the class variables whenever a new instance is created. This would ensure that your instance contains values before any other methods are used. In this case you could add a parameter to receive an employee ID, and include a call to the findEmployee() method in the body of your constructor to look up the ID in a file or database and assign the employee's data values to the instance's data fields:

```
public function __construct($id)
{
   $this->findEmployee($id);
   }
```

New instances of Employee will now be created using your customized constructor, so any application that needs to create a new Employee instance will need to send an ID to the constructor, for example:

```
$emp = new Employee("012345");
```

Alternatively, you could specify **five** parameters for the constructor (in the case of the Employee class) and code statements in the constructor to assign these to the instance's five class variables:

```
public function __construct($id, $firstName, $lastName, $title,
$wage)
{
   $this->empID = $id;
   $this->firstName = $firstName;
   $this->lastName = $lastName;
   $this->jobTitle = $title;
   $this->hourlyWage = $wage;
}
```

Now any programmer that needs to create a new Employee instance will always need to send five values to the constructor, for example:

```
$emp = new Employee("555666", "Jane", "Doe", "Sales", 17.50);
```

Method Overloading

You might be thinking that all three of the constructors listed above might be useful at different times. Sometimes you might want to use the constructor with no arguments, to create an instance without assigning any values to the class variables. Sometimes you might want to use a constructor that receives an employee ID as an argument, and uses this to retrieve the employee data from a file or database. And sometimes you might want to use a constructor that you can send five arguments (an employee's ID, first name, last name, job title and hourly wage), so the constructor can assign these values to the class variables when the instance is created. If you were coding this class using a fully object-oriented language like Java, you can provide multiple constructors in this way, each with a different parameter list. The compiler will determine which constructor method is intended based on the number and type of arguments sent to the constructor. The term for using multiple methods with the same name but different parameters is **method overloading**. Unfortunately, PHP does not allow method overloading since it is not a compiled language. As a result only one constructor is allowed, and although there are workarounds these can be quite complicated.

Why do Objects Matter?

There are many reasons to follow the Object-Oriented approach. First, just consider the number of variables that the application would need just to work with a single employee. In our example we just use five data values for each employee but in the real world, there would be many more, for example: employee ID, first name, middle name, last name, job title, department, office phone, office location, email address, hourly wage or salary, tax exemptions, accumulated vacation, accumulated sick leave, type of health insurance, etc. Imagine creating and dealing with all these variables, not just for one employee but for many employees! It is much easier to just assign an Employee object to a single variable such as **$emp**, knowing that **all** of these data values are now associated with this single variable, and that all the class methods associated with these data values are available for your use.

The Employee object can be used by any number of applications. If additional fields are needed they can be added to the object so and these applications can be updated to use the latest version. Also the methods in the Employee object can be updated without having to change the code in the applications that use the object; for example the getWeeklyPay() might be updated to meet new policy requirements. And new methods can be added if needed.

Furthermore, the use of a standard Employee object ensures that all application programmers are working with the same methods and procedures and not writing their own custom code. The Employee class might even be shared between different institutions or offices, making it easier for Employee objects to be shared more easily between organizations and allowing operations in Human Resources offices to be more streamlined as applications become standardized and more easily maintained.

The object-oriented approach is fundamental to most modern application design and development; application programmers are often required to familiarize themselves with object classes that have been provided for their use: they must read the class documentation and learn the names and characteristics of each class's attributes and methods. For example graphics programmers frequently need to work with all kinds of standard graphics objects, such as points, lines, rectangles, and circles. Rather than code these themselves, these programmers simply learn to make use of pre-written classes of common graphics objects. Here's how a graphic artist might display a moon, first creating a $moon instance of a Circle class, and then applying various Circle methods:

```
$moon = new Circle();
$moon->setRadius (40);
$moon->fillColor (white);
$moon->setPosition (20, 40);
$moon->draw();
```

And here's another example, where a game programmer makes use of a GameCharacter class to develop a game character named "Hercules":

```
$hercules = new GameCharacter();
$hercules->setName ("Hercules");
$hercules->setPosition (20, 40);
$hercules->setPoints (0);
$hercules->setHealth (10);
$hercules->fight();
```

These are both simplified and made-up examples to demonstrate how different kinds of objects are used for a wide range of purposes. In both examples the application programmer makes use of pre-written classes to develop his or her application. The OOP approach allows a high degree of standardization and reusability that greatly simplifies and speeds up application development. It allows data to be exchanged easily between applications and organizations. As a result, OOP has quickly become the standard approach for most modern application development, including development of mobile apps, data driven Web sites, scientific and health-related applications, games, and much more.

Object Design and Inheritance

Another key concept of OOP is an **object hierarchy**, where the class variables and functions of one object class are **inherited** by another object class, which then **extends** these with additional variables and methods for a more specific purpose. Inheritance plays a critical role in object-oriented design, since it ensures that different but related classes can be developed without duplication, and also that new classes follow certain design requirements. To understand the general principle of inheritance, let's take another look at our Employee class. Our earlier version of this class used five class variables: $empID, $firstName, $lastName, $jobTitle, and $hourlyWage. Four of these ($empID, $firstName, $lastName, and $jobTitle), are valid for **all** employees, but **$hourlyWage** might not always be appropriate. For example some employees might receive an an annual **salary** instead of an hourly wage.

One solution to this problem would be to forget about the Employee class altogether and just create two separate classes: a SalariedEmployee class and an HourlyEmployee class. These two classes would each contain the same class variables and methods that we used in the Employee class, except that the SalariedEmployee class would contain a $salary class variable, and getSalary() and setSalary() methods, while the HourlyWage class would contain an $hourlyWage class variable, along with getHourlyWage() and setHourlyWage() methods. In addition the two classes would need different code inside their getWeeklyPay() methods: the getWeeklyPay() method in the SalariedEmployee class would divide the annual salary by 52 to calculate the weekly pay, whereas the getWeeklyPay() method in the HourlyEmployee class would multiply the hourly wage by 40 to calculate the weekly pay. They would also need slightly different addEmployee() and findEmployee() methods since these would would need to refer either the $salary or $hourlyWage variables. Once we have created these two classes, we can just create instances of each class as needed, depending on whether an employee is salaried or hourly.

The problem with this approach is that much of the code in these two classes is duplicated. Four of the class variables are the same, as well as the get and set methods related to these four variables. This can create serious problems in terms of maintenance and updates to the code. Whenever changes are needed to the class variables and methods that are common to both classes, these must now be updated in **both** classes. This not only means more work but increases the possibility of an error: a programmer up-dating one class may not realize that the same code must also be updated in the other class.

The solution is to **keep** our original Employee class, but modify it so that it only contains the class variables and methods that are common to both salaried **and** hourly employees. Then create new SalariedEmployee and HourlyEmployee classes that **inherit** the variables and methods of the Employee class, and also add the class variables and methods that are specific to their own type of employee. We say that these classes **extend** the Employee class. In other words the Employee class will be the same as before except that it will no longer include the $hourlyWage class variable or the getHourly-Wage() and setHourlyWage() methods. The SalariedEmployee class will **extend** the Em-ployee class by providing the $salary class variable and the getSalary() and setSalary() methods, while the HourlyEmployee class will **extend** the Employee class by providing the $hourlyWage class variable, and getHourlyWage() and setHourlyWage() methods. And each of these classes will also provide their own getWeeklyPay(), addEmployee(), and findEmployee() methods, since these methods will require different code depend-ing on whether the employee is salaried or hourly. When one class extends another, the extending class inherits all of the class variables and methods of the class that is being extended. We often say that an extending class is a **child** class of the extended class, and the extended class is the **parent** class of the extending class.

It is very simple to create a class that extends another: for example, to create a SalariedEmployee class that extends the Employee class we simply add **extends Em-ployee** to the header of the SalariedEmployee class:

```
class SalariedEmployee extends Employee
{
   // class variables and methods here
   }
```

Similarly, to create an HourlyEmployee class that extends the Employee class:

```
class HourlyEmployee extends Employee
{
   // class variables and methods here
   }
```

Since the methods of the two extending classes must be able to work with the class vari-ables of the Employee class ($empID, $firstName, $lastName, and $jobTitle), the access modifier that was specified in the Employee class for these variables must be changed from **private** to **protected**. That's because the **private** modifier only allows methods in the **same** class to access these variables, whereas the **protected** modifier allows methods in the same class **and also** classes that **extend** the class to access the variables.

In order to separate this inheritance version from the previous Employee example, your **samples** folder includes a sub-folder named **oo-inheritance**. The **inc-employee-**

object.php file in this sub-folder contains the complete code for **all three** classes, the revised Employee class as well as the SalariedEmployee and HourlyEmployee classes (these classes could also have been stored in three separate include files).

Here is the code for the revised Employee class, followed by the code for the SalariedEmployee and HourlyEmployee classes. For the moment don't worry about the use of a new keyword **abstract** that appears in the heading and three method headings in the Employee class; this will be explained later in the chapter.

```php
<?php
abstract class Employee
{
    protected $empID;
    protected $firstName;
    protected $lastName;
    protected $jobTitle;

    public function getID()
    {
        return $this->empID;
    }

    public function setID($empID)
    {
        $this->empID = $empID;
    }

    public function getFirstName()
    {
        return $this->firstName;
    }

    public function setFirstName($fName)
    {
        $this->firstName = $fName;
    }

    public function getLastName()
    {
        return $this->lastName;
    }

    public function setLastName($lName)
    {
        $this->lastName = $lName;
```

```
   }

   public function getJobTitle()
   {
     return $this->jobTitle;
   }

   public function setJobTitle($title)
   {
     $this->jobTitle = $title;
   }

   abstract public function getWeeklyPay();
   abstract public function addEmployee();
   abstract public function findEmployee($id);
} // end of Employee class definition

class SalariedEmployee extends Employee
{
   private $salary;

   public function addEmployee()
   {
     $empRecord = $this->empID.", ".$this->firstName.",
       ".$this->lastName.", ".$this->jobTitle.",
       ".$this->salary."\n";
     $empFile = fopen("employees.txt", "a");
     fputs($empFile, $empRecord);
     fclose($empFile);
   }

   public function findEmployee($id)
   {
     $empFile = fopen("employees.txt", "r");
     $empRecord = trim(fgets($empFile));
     $notFound = true;
     while (!feof($empFile) or $notFound)
     {
       list ($empID, $fName, $lName, $title,
         $salary) = explode(",", $empRecord);
       if ($id == $empID)
       {
         $this->empID = $empID;
         $this->firstName = $fName;
```

```
              $this->lastName = $lName;
              $this->jobTitle = $title;
              $this->salary = $salary;
              $notFound = false;
            }
          $empRecord = trim(fgets($empFile));
        }
      fclose($empFile);

    }

    public function getSalary()
    {
      return $this->salary;
    }

    public function setSalary($salary)
    {
      $this->salary = $salary;
    }

    public function getWeeklyPay()
    {
      return number_format ($this->salary/52, 2);
    }

} // end of SalariedEmployee class definition

class HourlyEmployee extends Employee
{
  private $hourlyWage;

  public function addEmployee()
  {
    $empRecord = $this->empID.", ".$this->firstName.",
      ".$this->lastName.", ".$this->jobTitle.",
      ".$this->hourlyWage."\n";
    $empFile = fopen("employees.txt", "a");
    fputs($empFile, $empRecord);
    fclose($empFile);
  }
```

```php
   public function findEmployee($id)
   {
     $empFile = fopen("employees.txt", "r");
     $empRecord = trim(fgets($empFile));
     $notFound = true;
     while (!feof($empFile) or $notFound)
     {
       list ($empID, $fName, $lName, $title, $wage) =
           explode(",", $empRecord);
       if ($id == $empID)
       {
         $this->empID = $empID;
         $this->firstName = $fName;
         $this->lastName = $lName;
         $this->jobTitle = $title;
         $this->hourlyWage = $wage;
         $notFound = false;
       }
       $empRecord = trim(fgets($empFile));
     }
     fclose($empFile);

   }
   public function getHourlyWage()
   {
     return $this->hourlyWage;
   }

   public function setHourlyWage($hourlyWage)
   {
     $this->hourlyWage = $hourlyWage;
   }

   public function getWeeklyPay()
   {
     return number_format ($this->hourlyWage * 40, 2);
   }
} // end of HourlyEmployee class definition

?>
```

Code Example: inheritance version of inc-employee-object.php

Review the code of each class carefully. Notice how the class variables and methods are distributed between the three classes: the Employee class provides the class variables that are common to all employees ($empID, $firstName, $lastName, and $jobTitle) along with the get and set methods used with these variables, and these class variables are now declared to be **protected** so that they are accessible to methods in any class that extends Employee; the SalariedEmployee class **extends** Employee (so it has access to the class variables and methods of the Employee class), and adds just one class variable, $salary, along with **getSalary()** and **setSalary()** methods; the HourlyEmployee class also extends Employee and adds one class variable $hourlyWage, along with **getHourlyWage()** and **setHourlyWage()** methods. SalariedEmployee and HourlyEmployee each contains its own version of the **getWeeklyPay()**, **addEmployee()**, and **findEmployee()** methods; for example, the getWeeklyPay() method in SalariedEmployee calculates the pay by dividing the salary by 52, while the getWeeklyPay() method in HourlyEmployee calculates the pay by multiplying the hourly wage by 40.

The **oo-inheritance** sub-folder also includes two applications that demonstrate how these new classes might be used: a modified version of the **employee-pay** application asks the user for an employee ID and employee type (salaried or hourly), then creates an instance of either SalariedEmployee or HourlyEmployee, as appropriate, and displays the employee's weekly pay; a modified version of the **new-employee** application, obtains the data values for a new employee, as well as the employee type (salaried or hourly) then creates an instance of either SalariedEmployee or HourlyEmployee, as appropriate, assigns the data values to the instance, then calls the addEmployee() method to update the employee file.

Here is the revised form for **employee-pay.html**:

```
<body>
  <h1>Weekly Pay Calculator</h1>
  <form action="employee-pay.php" method="post">
      <label>Employee ID
        <input type="text" name="id"></label>
      <label>Employee Type
        <select name = "empType">
        <option>Salaried</option>
        <option>Hourly</option>
        </select></label>
    <input class = "submit" type = "submit" value = "Calculate
    Weekly Pay">
  </form>
</body>
```

Code Example: inheritance version of employee-pay.html

And here is the revised code for employee-pay.php, that works with an instance of either SalariedEmployee or HourlyEmployee depending on the form input:

```
<body>
<?php
    include("inc-employee-object.php");

    $id = $_POST["id"];
    $empType = $_POST["empType"];

    if ($empType=="Salaried")
        $emp1 = new SalariedEmployee();
    else
        $emp1 = new HourlyEmployee();

    $emp1->findEmployee($id);

    print ("<p>Weekly Pay for ".$emp1->getFirstName().
      " ". $emp1->getLastName().": $".
      $emp1->getWeeklyPay()."</p>");
?>
</body>
```

Code Example: inheritance version of employee-pay.php

A selection structure determines whether the employee instance **$emp1** is declared as a SalariedEmployee or HourlyEmployee instance. The $emp1 instance then calls the findEmployee(), getFirstName(), getLastName(), and getWeeklyPay() methods. Since $emp1 can be an instance of either of two different classes, these calls are only possible if the methods in both of these classes have been given the same names. An important feature of OOP allows us to require that **all** classes that extend another class **must** include certain methods with a pre-defined name and parameter list. We do this using the **abstract** keyword.

Abstract Classes and Methods

A review of the revised Employee class reveals that the class heading is preceded by the keyword **abstract**:

```
abstract class Employee
{
    // class variables and methods here
}
```

When a class is defined to be abstract, it is not possible for any application to create instances of the class. This is important: we want programmers to be able to create instances of SalariedEmployee and HourlyEmployee, which both inherit the Employee class, but we don't want programmers to be able to create instances of the Employee class because the Employee class does not include any wage or salary class variables or methods. The Employee class is only being used to provide shared class variables and methods to the classes that extend it, and so we define this class as abstract.

You will also notice that, although the Employee class includes the **headings** for methods named getWeeklyPay(), addEmployee(), and findEmployee(), each of these methods is also declared to be abstract and does not contain a body with the method's code; instead each method's heading simply ends with a semi-colon:

```
abstract public function getWeeklyPay();
abstract public function addEmployee();
abstract public function findEmployee($id);
```

You may wonder why these methods are included in the Employee class at all. After all they are not used in the Employee class; different versions of these methods are fully defined in the SalariedEmployee class and HourlyEmployee class. It is quite true that these three statements could be removed from the Employee class and the two child classes would function just as well.

However the inclusion of an **abstract method definition** in the Employee class ensures that all classes that extend this class **must** provide a method with the same name and parameter list as the abstract method defined in the parent class. This valuable OOP feature enforces a **design requirement** on any programmer who wants to extend the Employee class. The getWeeklyPay(), addEmployee(), and findEmployee() methods in any extending class can be coded in any manner that is appropriate for a particular type of employee, but no matter how they are coded, these three methods **must** be provided. This requirement ensures that application programmers who use instances of any class that extends Employee can do so knowing that these methods are available to them.

Any class that defines at least one abstract method **must** also be defined to be an abstract class. This makes sense when you consider that a class that contains at least one abstract method cannot be instantiated since the abstract method contains no code and cannot be used.

There is no restriction on the number of levels that classes can inherit from one another: classes that extend other classes and methods can also be extended. Similarly classes that extend abstract classes can also be abstract and can include, or pass on, abstract methods.

Method Over-riding

Sometimes a class that extends (inherits) another class needs to replace a method from the parent class with a new method of the same name. This is done simply by coding the new method in the extending class. If the method has the same name and parameter list as a method in the parent class, it will **over-ride** the method of the parent class.

Including a method in a child class that replaces an abstract method in the parent class is an example of method over-riding.

Polymorphism

Another important feature of OOP is **polymorphism**, which is beyond the scope of this book. In general usage, the term polymorphic means "many shaped"; in OOP, polymorphism allows applications to determine the specific type of object within an object hierarchy that it is to be processed at the time the application is running. For example an application might not "know" until it is actually executing whether to treat an employee as a salaried or hourly employee. This type of dynamic selection provides great flexibility for software designers, and once again reduces code duplication.

OOP and Databases

Our Employee class includes two methods that connect our object to an external data source, in this case a text file containing employee records. Of course in a real world application, employee data would almost certainly be stored in a database, not a text file; these methods connect to a text file only to allow flexibility for readers who wish to skip the database chapter. If you have studied Chapter 14, you will see that it would be a simple matter to modify this code to work with a database.

OOP and databases are very good neighbors: object classes are frequently developed to give application programmers a programming interface to databases. This is of such critical importance to modern application design that it's worth discussing the reasons here:

Ease of use: with an object interface between application and data source, the application developer does not need to design and write custom code to access the database directly, and does not need to know the syntax of the database language. Instead he or she simply instantiates an object that provides all the database operations he or she needs, and then uses the object's methods as needed. The object therefore provides an application programming interface (API) to the database; once developed, this interface can be used by any number of applications, which dramatically reduces the time for coding, testing and maintenance.

Protecting the data source: since application programmers have no direct access to the data source but only to the classes that provide a programming interface, they can only modify the data source in the ways permitted by the class methods. This protects the data source from accidental or intentional misuse, and from possible security breaches that may occur when connection information must be widely shared.

Separation of the user interface from the data source: the use of an object to interface between the application and its data sources enables a complete separation between these two components. This is extremely important. As a result of this separation, the data source can be changed in any way without requiring changes to the application: field names can be changed, tables can be redesigned and modified, the location and connection may change, the data source itself may transition from one database product to another. Since the application is not interacting directly with the data source, but instead calling pre-written methods in an object, the application code does not to be changed; only the code in the object's methods needs to be updated. The findEmployee() and addEmployee() methods in our Employee class provide a simple example of this. In their current form, these two methods connect to a text file containing a list of records comprised of five data values each, separated by commas. This file might need to be updated: additional data values might be added to each record, or the data values might be re-ordered, or the separators might be changed from a comma to a colon. Or the text file might be replaced by a MySQL or some other database, and then the database might itself be modified over time. Consider the nightmare if the code inside every application that worked with the employee data had to be changed every time the data source changed! Instead the applications use instances of an Employee class to call Employee methods that contain all the code to interact with the data source; when the data source changes, only the code in the Employee methods needs to be changed; the application code will continue to work in its original form.

OOP Development

After reading the database and OOP chapters, it is easy to see that there are quite different components of software design and development, and these are often quite independent of one another. Application (interface) programmers develop the "front end" interfaces between users and the data that they need to work with. Database programmers design, develop, protect, and maintain data sources that may serve any number of applications, and different types of user. Object programmers, design and develop objects that serve the needs and reduce the coding requirements of application developers, and often provide an interface between applications and their data sources. Object programmers think beyond the needs of specific applications and instead focus on encapsulating data within an object which provides methods to enable and control access to the data.

OOP Languages

Fully Object-Oriented languages, such as **Java**, are designed so that **all** application development is derived from objects. OOP languages provide large numbers of standard object classes that programmers can use to develop applications quickly and easily. For example, Java provides a rich set of standard object classes for developing graphical user interfaces and graphics quickly and easily. Java is an excellent language to develop a complete understanding of object-oriented design and programming.

Additional Learning Materials

While this chapter introduces the topic, OOP design and coding is a fundamental skill expected of any professional programmer. Look for opportunities to learn an OO language such as Java, and to design and develop OO code in any language that you are using.

Appendix D will help you **debug** your exercises, listing a number of the most common errors that you are likely to encounter.

The **Chapter 15 Hints and Help** pages on the textbook Web site provide answers to FAQs from previous students as they worked through the end-of-chapter exercises.

Summary

Object-Oriented Programming (OOP) is a very important approach to code modularity. The combination of a specific set of data with all of the functions needed to operate on this data constitutes an **object**, and an object is defined as a **class**. In OOP terminology, the variables that contain the object's data values are generally referred to as **fields** or **class variables** or **attributes**, while the object's functions are usually referred to as the class **methods**. The class variables and methods together constitute the **members** of the class. In object-oriented design, programmers who wish to work with the data associated with an object are expected to use the methods that are provided for this purpose. This is usually enforced by making the class variables **private** (or **protected**) and the methods **public**. The methods therefore provide a **programming interface** to the data, and we say that the data is **encapsulated**.

Once a class has been developed, any number of **instances** of the class can be created for use by any application that has access to the class code. Each class contains a special **constructor** method that has the same name as the class and is executed only when an instance is created. The **new** operator is used to create an instance and call the constructor method.

The class variables and functions of one class can be **inherited** by another class, which then **extends** these with additional variables and functions for a more specific purpose. This constitutes an **object hierarchy**; the extended class is often referred to as the **parent** class, while an extending class is referred to as a **child** class. For example, an **Employee** class may consist of class variables and functions common to **all** employees, while a **SalariedEmployee** class might inherit these variables and methods and provide additional variables and methods that are appropriate only for **salaried** employees. Similarly, an **HourlyEmployee** class might **also** inherit the data and methods of the **Employee** class but would add data and methods that are appropriate only for **hourly** employees. Inheritance provides a powerful design structure for OOP and minimizes code duplication. For example by inheriting the data and methods of **Employee** class, the **SalariedEmployee** and **HourlyEmployee** classes do not need to duplicate the class variables and methods that are common to all employees; they share these while adding other variables and methods that are unique to themselves.

Classes that are defined to be **abstract** can be extended but cannot be instantiated. Methods that are defined to be abstract in one class **must** be included in any class that extends that class. The presence of an abstract method therefore creates a design requirement for programmers who are coding child classes. A class that contains at least one abstract method must also be defined to be abstract.

Another important feature of OOP is **polymorphism**, which allows applications to dynamically determine the specific type of object within an object hierarchy that it is to be processed at the time the application is running.

OOP allows different methods to share the same name if they have different parameter lists, as long as the compiler can determine which method is intended based on the arguments that are sent. This feature is termed **method overloading**. Constructor methods can be overloaded, allowing new instances of a class to be instantiated in different ways by calling different constructors. Method overloading is not available in PHP.

Sometimes an extending class needs to replace a method in the parent class with a different method. This is achieved by coding a new method with the same name and parameter list in the extending class. This is termed **method over-riding**.

Object-Oriented Programming is strongly associated with access to databases by user applications. Objects are developed to provide an interface between applications and data sources. This interface: eliminates the need for application programmers to write code to directly query the data source; protects the data source from unintentional or intentional misuse; provides a complete separation between the user application (interface) and the data source, so that changes to the data source do not require changes to the application, but only to the object.

Java is a fully object-oriented programming language.

Chapter 15 Review Questions

1. Which term refers to a structure that defines an object's attributes and methods?
   a. polymorphism
   b. class variables
   c. class
   d. instance
   e. hierarchy

2. What keyword is used to create new instances of a class?
   a. new
   b. instantiate
   c. $this
   d. public
   e. class

3. What is the purpose of the constructor method?
   a. create a class variable
   b. create an instance of a class
   c. create a class method
   d. extend a class
   e. overload a class method

4. Consider the following line of code:

```
$catWoman = new GameCharacter();
```

   Which one of the following is NOT true?
   a. GameCharacter() is a constructor of the GameCharacter class
   b. $catWoman is a constructor of the GameCharacter class
   c. $catWoman contains an instance of the GameCharacter class
   d. GameCharacter is a class
   e. The new operator is used to create new instances of a class

5. Assume you are working with a class named Account. Which of the following statements correctly creates an instance of the Account class?
   a. $acct = Account;
   b. $acct = new Account;
   c. $acct = Account();
   d. $acct = new Account();
   e. $acct = $this->Account

6. Assume that an instance of the Account class has been assigned to a variable named $acct. Assume also that the Account class includes a method named getBalance(). Which of the following statements correctly uses $acct to obtain the account balance for that instance?

   a. $acct = Account($balance)
   b. $acct = $this->getBalance()
   c. $acct->getBalance()
   d. getBalance($acct)
   e. $acct.getBalance()

7. Assume that you are developing an Account class and must define a method named getBalance() that returns the value of a class variable named $balance. Which of the following statements should you use in the body of the getBalance() method?

   a. return $balance;
   b. return this->$balance;
   c. return $this->balance;
   d. return new Balance;
   e. return getBalance();

8. What term is used to describe the use of multiple methods with the same name but different parameter lists?

   a. Overriding
   b. Overloading
   c. Instantiation
   d. Polymorphism
   e. Extension

9. What keyword is used to indicate that a class inherits the class variables and methods of another class?

   a. overrides
   b. overloads
   c. instantiates
   d. extends
   e. attributes

10. What is the purpose of the "private" modifier?

   a. Prevents a class variable or method from being changed
   b. Ensures that a class variable or method can only be accessed by methods that are part of the same class
   c. Prevents a class from being extended
   d. Ensures that new instances of a class cannot be created
   e. Prevents a class from being included in another application

11. Which modifier allows a class variable to be accessed by methods in a class that extends the class that contains the variable?
    a. public
    b. private
    c. protected

12. If a class named Queen extends a class named Chesspiece, which statement is true?
    a. Queen is the parent class of Chesspiece
    b. Chesspiece is the parent class of Queen

13. What does it mean if a class is defined to be abstract?
    a. The class does not have a constructor method
    b. The class can be extended but cannot be instantiated
    c. The class can be instantiated but cannot be extended
    d. The class is the child of another class
    e. The class must contain abstract methods

14. What does it mean if a method is defined to be abstract?
    a. A method with the same name and parameters must be defined in any class that extends the class that contains the abstract method
    b. The method must be defined as protected
    c. The method must return a value
    d. The method must modify a class variable
    e. The method is a constructor method

15. Which of the following is true?
    a. You must always include a customized constructor method in your class definition.
    b. A default constructor method is automatically provided and cannot be replaced with a customized constructor.
    c. A default constructor method is automatically provided but you can replace this with a customized constructor.

Chapter 15 Code Exercises

Your Chapter 15 code exercises can be found in your **chapter15** folder. This folder is included in your customized XAMPP installation at the following location:

   htdocs\webtech\coursework\ chapter15

Type your name and the date in the **Author** and **Date** sections of each file as you work on each exercise. **Remember** that the Students page on the textbook Web site includes **Hints and Help** pages for the exercises in this and every chapter.

Debugging Exercises

Your **chapter15** folder should contain a number of "fixit" files. Each of these files contains PHP code that has an error of some kind. The type of error is indicated in the comment section of each file. You will need to run each program in order to see the errors, and to debug and test the code to see if it works correctly. For example to run **fixit1.php**, first run the Web server, then use the URL:

   http://localhost/webtech/coursework/chapter15/fixit1.php

Code Modification Exercises

Your **chapter15** folder contains a number of "modify" files. Each pair of files contains HTML and PHP code that needs to be modified to meet a requirement. The requirements are included in the comment section of each file. Modify the algorithms, being careful to make changes to the .html and .php files as directed. You will need to run each program in order to test your changes. For example to run **modify1.html**, first run the Web server, then use the URL:

   http://localhost/webtech/coursework/chapter13/modify1.html

Code Completion Exercises

1. Read this exercise carefully and take your time to work out the logic. Your **chapter15** folder contains versions of **paint-estimate.html** and **paint-estimate.php** as well as a file named **inc-rectangle-object.php** which contains code that defines a class named Rectangle. Review the Rectangle class carefully: it contains two class variables, $x and $y, that store the height and width of a rectangle, and five methods, to get and set the height and width, and get the area of the rectangle.

    The form provided in **paint-estimate.html** asks the user to submit the height, length, and width of a room. The **paint-estimate.php** program already includes the code to receive the form inputs from **paint-estimate.html**. Add code to: include the inc-rectangle-object.php file; create two Rectangles instances named $longWall and $shortWall; call the Rectangle class's setX() and setY() methods to assign values for each of the two instances (for example, if the height, width and length of the room are 90 and 180, and 120 then the x and y values of the $longWall rectangle will be 90 and 180, and the x and y values of the $shortWall rectangle will be 90 and 120); call the getArea() method of the Rectangle class for each of the two instances; calculate the total area for all four walls by adding the areas together (remember there are two long walls and two short walls); display the total area.

2. Read this exercise carefully and take your time to work out the logic. Your **chapter15** folder contains versions of **software-order.html** and **software-order.php** as well as a file named **inc-order-object.php**, which contains the code that defines an Order class. Review the Order class carefully: it contains two class variables, $itemCost and $numItems, that stores the cost of an item, and the number of items ordered, and eight methods, four of which are used to get and set the item cost and the number of items, the remaining methods work as follows:

The **getSubtotal**() method returns the item cost multiplied by the number of items.
The **getSalesTax**() method returns the sales tax.
The **getShippingHandling**() method returns the shipping and handling cost.
The **getTotal**() method returns the total cost.

Your software-order.html file already contains a form to request the item cost and number of items being ordered. Your software-order.php already contains the code to receive the form input. Add code to: include the **inc-order-object.php** file; create an Order instance named **$order**; call the Order class's **setItemCost**() and **setNumItems**() methods to assign the values received from the form to the class variables of the $order instance; call each of the four methods described above and use the values that are returned to display the sub-total, sales tax, shipping and handling, and total of the order.

3. Create a class of your own named **GameCharacter** that contains two class variables, $playerName and $score. Add get and set methods to work with each class variable. Save this in your Chapter15 folder in a file named **inc-game-character-object.php**. Now create a PHP application that includes the class, creates two instances (two different game characters), assigns names and scores to each instance, and displays these. Add code to the application (not the class) that compares the two scores and displays the winning character.

4. Your **chapter15** folder contains a file named **inc-rectangle-object.php** which contains code that defines a class named Rectangle. Review the Rectangle class carefully: it contains two class variables, $x and $y, that store the height and width of a rectangle, and five methods, to get and set the height and width, and get the area of the rectangle. Now create a class named **Cube** that **extends** the Rectangle class and save this in your Chapter15 folder in a file named **inc-cube-object.php**. Add a class variable named **$z** to the Cube class which will be used to store the height of a cube. Add get and set methods to work with the $z class variable. Note that the Cube class

inherits the class variables and methods of the Rectangle class, so it will contain the attributes and methods to work with all three dimensions ($x, $y, and $z) of a cube. Now add a method to the Cube class named getArea() that calculates and returns the total area of the six sides of the cube. The total area will be 2 multiplied by the value of $x multiplied by the value of $y plus 2 multiplied by the value of $x multipled by the value of $z plus 2 multiplied by the value of $y multipled by the value of $z. Add another method to the Cube class named getVolume() that calculates and returns the **volume** of the cube, which will be the value of $x multiplied by the value of $y multiplied by the valiue of $z.

Important: since the getArea() and getVolume() methods in the Cube class need to acccess the $x and $y class variables in the Rectangle class, you will need to change the access modifiers that are used with these two variables in the Rectangle class.

An application named **test-cube.php** has been provided in your Chapter15 folder which tests your Cube class using three Cube instances. You don't have to change this application, just run it. If you have coded your Cube class correctly and modified the access modifiers in the Rectangle class, the three areas should be displayed as 104, 150, and 136, and the three volumes should be 60, 125, and 80.

5. Create a simple class of your own using what you have learned in this chapter, and develop two simple applications that use the class in different ways. Keep it simple, you don't have to extend the class; the main purpose here is to get some practice developing and using objects. If you're stuck for ideas, consider a simplified version of one of the examples in the introduction to this chapter.

Chapter 16

More About PHP

Intended Learning Outcomes

After completing this chapter, you should be able to:

- Access textbook and global PHP help resources.
- Distinguish between conventions used in this textbook and PHP requirements and best practices.
- Choose between the PHP print and echo statements.
- Choose between single and double quotes when enclosing strings.
- Use the PHP shortcut operators when incrementing, decrementing, or accumulating values.
- Recognize when the PHP concatenation operator must be used in strings.
- Use the PHP SWITCH statement instead of chained IF..ELSE statements where this is an option.
- Utilize the PHP DO..WHILE statement instead of a WHILE statement when an event-driven loop is required to iterate at least once.
- Create and process numerically indexed multi-dimensional arrays.
- Create and process ragged multi-dimensional arrays.
- Create and process an associative array that contains any number of numerically indexed arrays.
- Describe the basic data types and convert values to different data types using the cast operator.
- Use some common PHP date and time functions.
- Utilize a broad range of standard PHP functions.

Introduction

Congratulations! By now you should have a good grasp of basic program logic and design, as well as some understanding of HTML, CSS, MySQL, and PHP. The purpose of this chapter is twofold: first to identify some of the conventions used throughout the book that should not be confused with actual requirements of the PHP language; and second, to extend your knowledge of PHP by describing additional shortcut operators and control structures, date and time functions, PHP tools for data validation and sanitizing, and PHP data types. The chapter ends with an extensive (but by no means complete) list of standard PHP functions.

Visit the textbook Web site for the latest version of the appendices, for corrections, and for additional learning materials:

```
https://www.mikeokane.com/textbooks/wbip/
```

You will also want a standard reference to PHP syntax and functions. For a complete PHP reference consult the PHP home page:

```
https://www.php.net/
```

There are also many excellent forums, books, and online references available. For a very good online PHP tutorial and easy-to-use reference, try:

```
https://www.w3schools.com/php/default.asp
```

Textbook Conventions

A major challenge writing this textbook has been to keep the focus on the fundamentals of program logic and design, while at the same time providing the valuable practical experience that comes with hands-on coding and learning a specific language. In order to balance these goals in a manner suitable for beginning programmers, decisions were made concerning the level and type of detail to include. In some cases, some procedures were neglected to avoid introducing too much syntactical detail, or too many options at once, that might distract from achieving key learning outcomes and fundamental concepts. The danger of this approach is that the reader might easily confuse the author's strategic design decisions with actual requirements of the PHP language. With this in mind, the initial sections in this chapter identify some of the practices that were followed in this textbook, that are **not** required PHP procedures and do **not** necessarily represent best practices when developing PHP applications.

Code Comments

The textbook examples include comment sections at the top of each file, but for the most part do not include line by line comments. This was to make it easier to read the examples in the book but is not a good approach in practice. It is more standard to provide a small comment at the beginning of each code section to explain the purpose, or a longer comment when needed to describe a specific methodology, explain an approach, or indicate a section that needs testing or review. This is an important and expected procedure: it encourages a thoughtful approach to the coding process itself; provides a guide to another programmer who might be reviewing or testing (or even inheriting) your code. Well commented code also serves your own needs: code that you are familiar with today might not look at all familiar when you return to it at a later date.

(Remember that PHP Permits two type of comments: **Multi-line comments** begin with /* and end with */, while **line comments** begin with // and extend to the end of the current line.)

Location of Curly Braces

Curly braces { and } are used to indicate which statements belong to a particular block of code, for example to indicate the block of statements in the IF or ELSE sections of a selection structure, or the block of statements in a loop structure. When curly braces appear in the code examples in this textbook, the left and right braces are both aligned below the headings of the structure, and the statements enclosed in each block are indented, for example:

```php
if ($hoursWorked > 40)
{
   $bonus = 50;
   print ("<p>You receive a $50.00 bonus this week.</p>");
}
else
{
   $bonus = 0;
   print ("<p>No bonus this week.<p>");
}
```

While this layout is used by many programmers, a more common approach is to type the beginning { curly brace on the same line as the heading, as follows:

```
if ($hoursWorked > 40) {
  $bonus = 50;
  print ("<p>You receive a $50.00 bonus this week.</p>");
}
else {
  $bonus = 0;
  print ("<p>No bonus this week.</p>");
}
```

Since the processor ignores white-space, either approach is acceptable. The decision was made to use the less common convention simply because aligning the { and } braces at the same indent level, below the block heading, seemed to provide beginning students with a clearer picture of the overall structure. It is important to be familiar with both conventions since the second approach will be seen more often when looking at code examples, not just in PHP but most languages.

HTML and PHP Files

Most of the applications in the samples and coursework folders were developed using pairs of .html files (to contain HTML forms) and .php files (to process the form input using a mix of HTML and PHP code). This was just a useful convention, used to more easily identify the names of related files in these folders, and to reduce any file-name ambiguity when completing exercises. There is no need for files that work together to be related by name, furthermore a file that contains only HTML code can be named with a .php extension, and many PHP coders follow this approach.

A single Web page may contain multiple forms, and each of these may reference a different .php file to process the form input (the .php file that is actually executed will depend on which form is submitted by the user). Furthermore, the use of two separate files to display and process a form is not a best practice for PHP coding. A better approach is to combine the code to display the form and the code to process the form in a single .php file. You can find a detailed explanation of this procedure in the "Web Sessions" section of Chapter 12.

Most real world PHP applications will consist of code that is assembled from any number of files with significant sections of code provided by include files (see Chapter 13). This reduces duplication of code since the code in include files can be included in any number of different PHP applications.

Multiple PHP Sections

The textbook PHP code examples almost all follow a format where a .php file contains an initial HTML section, followed by a PHP section, followed by a final HTML section. In fact, a PHP file can include any combination of HTML and PHP sections in any order. A PHP file may consist entirely of PHP code, and may even consist entirely of HTML code (no PHP code at all).

Usually a working program contains many small sections of PHP code interspersed with HTML code. This minimizes the need for the escape characters needed to display quotes and other special characters when the HTML code is generated by PHP print or echo statements. The only HTML text that must be generated inside PHP sections is text that includes values derived from PHP variables, functions, or expressions.

Program Variables and the $_POST Array

The textbook examples also followed a convention of creating a variable with the same name as an HTML form input box or other input element, if the variable was used to receive the value from the form element, for example: $hourlyWage = $_POST['hourlyWage'];

This was just a textbook convention, to make it easier to see the relationship between the variable and the user's form input; there is no PHP requirement to use the same name, for example, $wage = $_POST['hourlyWage']; is perfectly acceptable.

Furthermore it is not necessary to always assign the value from the $_POST array to a new variable. After all $_POST['hourlyWage'] is itself a variable (it is an element of the $_POST associative array). However it is fairly standard to assign $_POST array values to individual variables in order improve readability.

Naming Files, Variables, and Constants

When naming files for use with this textbook, the author has used all lower-case letters combined with numbers, and hyphens are used to represent spaces between English words.

The book uses camel case, or camelback, notation to name variables (for example $hourlyWage). This is the convention followed by programmers working in most current languages. Some PHP programmers prefer to use underscores instead of camelback notation when naming variables (for example $hourly_wage).

The usual convention when naming constant values is to use all upper-case letters, with underscores to represent spaces between English words.

Choosing Between print and echo

The textbook uses the PHP print statement throughout to generate HTML output. The PHP echo statement can be used just as well for this purpose. The two are almost identical in operation, and most programmers simply choose one over the other. For example:

```
print("Hello, ". $firstName." how are you today?");
```

could be written:

```
echo "Hello, ".$firstName." how are you today?";
```

Either **print** or **echo** statements can be used with or without parentheses. Users of the **echo** statement usually leave out the opening and closing parentheses since parentheses do not work when concatenation is included in an echo statement. Although parentheses are also not required when using the **print** statement, the textbook examples have followed this convention in order to more closely reflect the use of functions in most other languages to deliver output (functions always require parentheses).

Unlike print statements, the echo statement also allows a list of arguments (like a function), separated by commas, which means that a series of strings can be published in sequence, but this is not very different from using the concatenation operator to join strings and then publish them (there can some improved efficiency in cases of very large numbers of iterations).

Single or Double Quotes in PHP

Throughout this textbook, character strings are surrounded in **double quotes**. PHP allows either **double** or **single** quotes to be used around strings, as long as the same quote is used to indicate the start and end of each string, in other words "test" and 'test' are both acceptable but "test' is not. It can be useful to choose one of the other to avoid escaping quotes within a string, for example **"She's coding right now."**, or '**<p>He said "I like to code".</p>**'.

There are some significant differences to be aware of when choosing between single and double quotes. For example if a **variable** is included in a string enclosed in **double** quotes, the **value** of the variable will be used in the string. However if a variable is included in a string enclosed in **single** quotes, the variable **name** will be used in the string. Another difference applies when escape characters are included within a string: only the \' and \\ **escape characters** can be used in strings enclosed in single quotes, whereas **any** escape characters can be included in strings enclosed in double quotes. Here's an example to show the difference (assuming $age contains the value **24**):

```
print ("<p>He said \"yes, I'm $age years old\".</p>");
```
The use of **double** quotes generates <p>He said "yes, I'm 24 years old".</p>

```
print ('<p>He said \"yes, I'm $age years old\".</p>');
```
The use of **single** quotes generates <p>He said "yes, I'm $age years old".</p>

Beware of "Smart" Quotes!

Note that, typographically, quotes can be "simple" (or "straight") quotes, where opening and closing quotes are the same (as used "here"), or "smart" quotes (as used "here"), where the opening and closing quotes are different from one another. **Text editors** use **straight** quotes but **word processors** by default usually use **smart** quotes, This is important because the PHP processor only recognizes **straight** quotes, so you will have problems if your code includes smart quotes. This can happen, for example, if you **paste** text that contains smart quotes from a word-processing document or some other source into your text editor.

The PHP Concatenation Operator

Unlike most programming languages, PHP requires the $ symbol as the first character of each variable name. This allows some unusual practices that would not work in other languages. For example, a PHP programmer can include direct references to variables inside character strings, using statements such as: **"You are $age years old.".**

The reference to $age within the character string is possible because the $ symbol indicates that $age is a variable that contains a value, and not simply the word "age". Other languages **always** require concatenation when a value stored in a variable is to be included in a character string. Concatenation of a simple variable is optional in PHP, but required when the string includes PHP expressions, function calls, and objects. For example **"You have 65 - $age years until retirement."** will not work, and should be written using the concatenation operator. **"You have ".(65 - $age)." years until retirement."** Similarly **print("<p>Your wages are number_format($wage, 2)</p>");** will not work and should be written as **print("<p>Your wages are ".number_format($wage, 2)."</p>");**

Some programmers prefer to **always** use the concatenation operator to combine variable values with strings since it makes code easier to understand and follows a similar syntax to other languages. For example, **"You are ".$age." years old."** or **"Your pay is $".$weeklyPay[$id]."."**

(Note that although concatenation is a standard feature of most languages, the period is not always used as the concatenation operator. Some languages use the + character as the concatenation operator, so the same string in, for example, a Java statement would be written as **"You are " + age + " years old."** Notice also that variables do not begin with a $ character in Java.)

PHP Shortcut Operators

In addition to the standard arithmetic operators, most programming languages provide **shortcut operators.** The operators are very efficient and commonly used when an operation is intended to increment, decrement, add to, subtract from, multiply, or divide the numeric value currently stored in a variable, with the result replacing the previous value in the variable. Chapter 5 introduced the increment and decrement operators, here is the complete list:

Instead of:	Use the shortcut operator:
`$count = $count + 1;`	`$count++;`
`$count = $count - 1;`	`$count-;`
`$value = $value + $number;`	`$value += $number;`
`$value = $value - $number;`	`$value -= $number;`
`$value = $value * $number;`	`$value *= $number;`
`$value = $value / $number;`	`$value /= $number;`
`$value = $value % $number;`	`$value %= $number;`

The PHP SWITCH Statement

Most languages provide a SWITCH statement that can be used as an alternative selection structure to chained IF..ELSE statements in cases where the possible actions are all based upon the value of a single variable.

For example a SWITCH structure could be used instead of multiple chained IF..ELSE structures to determine which month name to display based on the numeric value stored in the variable $month:

```
switch ($month)
{
   case 1: print("January"); break;
   case 2: print("February"); break;
   case 3: print("March"); break;
   case 4: print("April"); break;
   case 5: print("May"); break;
   case 6: print("June"); break;
   case 7: print("July"); break;
   case 8: print("August"); break;
   case 9: print("September"); break;
```

```
   case 10: print("October"); break;
   case 11: print("November"); break;
   case 12: print("December"); break;
   default: print("ERROR!"); break;
}
```

The variable to be tested (**$month**) appears in the switch statement heading, enclosed in parentheses. Each possible value of this variable is handled by a case statement inside the SWITCH structure. The processor tests the value in each **case** against the value stored in the variable. When a match is found, the statements following the relevant **case** are executed.

Each case may include any number of program statements and a **break** statement is added to break out of the switch statement and move on to the next code statement. If the **break** statement is **not** included at the end of a case, the statements in subsequent case statements will also be processed until a **break** statement is found. This feature allows multiple cases to use the same statements, for example:

```
switch ($month)
{
   case 2: print("This month has 28 or 29 days"); break;
   case 4:
   case 6:
   case 9:
   case 11: print("This month has 30 days"); break;
   case 1:
   case 3:
   case 5:
   case 7:
   case 8:
   case 10:
   case 12: print("This month has 31 days"); break;
   default: print("ERROR!"); break;
}
```

In this case, if **$month** has the value 2, only the **first** case is executed. If **$month** has the value 4, 6, 9, or 11, the **fifth** case is executed. If **$month** has the value 1, 3, 5, 7, 8, 10, or 12, the **twelfth** case is executed. If **$month** has any other value the **thirteenth** case is executed.

Another useful characteristic of omitting break statements from some cases is that this can allow a **cascade** of case actions to be executed since the statements in every case below the case that contained the correct value will be executed until a break is encountered. Here's an example where the cases are based on a movie rating between 5 and 1:

```
switch ($movieRating)
{
  case 5: print("TOP RATING!");
  case 4:
  case 3: print("Worth seeing!"); break;
  case 2:
  case 1: print("Don't bother!"); break;
}
```

Note that the first two cases do **not** include break statements. If the rating is 5, **"TOP RATING!"** will be printed, followed by **"Worth Seeing!"** since the first break occurs at the end of case 3. If the rating is 4 or 3,**"Worth Seeing!"** will be printed. If the rating is 2 or 1,**"Don't bother!"** will be printed. Note that in this example the **default** option is not included. This option is not needed if it is known that the variable being tested does not contain any value others than those listed.

In the previous examples, each case only required a **single** statement to be executed. In fact each case can include any number of statements and even other control structures. Here is another example where a switch statement is used to determine discounts and shipping costs as part of a customer billing calculation:

```
$unitCode = "12345";
$unitCost = 4.75;
$numItems = 10;
$subtotal = $numItems * $unitCost;

switch ($numItems)
{
case 1: $discountRate = 0;
  $shipping = 1.50;
  break;
case 2: $discountRate = 0;
  $shipping = 2.50;
  break;
case 3:
case 4: $discountRate = 0.05;
  $shipping = 3.50;
  break;
default: $discount = 0.1;
  if ($subTotal > 100)
    shipping = 0;
  else
    shipping = 3.50 + numItems - 4 * 0.50;
}
```

```
$discount = $subTotal * $discountRate;
$total = $subTotal - $discount + $shipping;
```

The PHP DO..WHILE Loop

Most languages provide an additional loop structure that was not described in the two loop chapters. This is the DO..WHILE or REPEAT—UNTIL loop (the specific structure depends on the programming language).

Do..WHILE and REPEAT..UNTIL loops are event-controlled loops, just like the WHILE loop. However the test that controls a WHILE loop appears at the **start** of the loop structure, and so a WHILE loop may execute 0 times. The test for DO..WHILE and REPEAT..UNTIL loops appears at the **end** of the loop structure, and so the instructions in these loops will always execute at least once.

Here is a real world example of a DO..WHILE loop:

```
DO
   Instruct your dog to "sit"
WHILE the dog refuses to sit
Give the dog a treat
```

Here the test is "the dog refuses to sit" and the loop repeats as long as this test is true. Since the test is at the end of the loop, the loop instruction will always be executed at least once. In this case you want to instruct the dog to sit at least once, so this is an more appropriate loop than a WHILE loop.

Here is the same example using a REPEAT..UNTIL loop:

```
REPEAT
   Instruct your dog to "sit"
UNTIL the dog sits
Give the dog a treat
```

The REPEAT..UNTIL structure is basically the same as the DO..WHILE except that the logic of the test is reversed. Instead of repeating **while** a condition is true, the loop repeats **until** a condition becomes true.

PHP uses the DO..WHILE statement structure rather than the REPEAT..UNTIL structure. Here is a PHP example of a DO..WHILE loop used to display the value of 2 raised to exponents between 0 and 5:

```
$exponent = 0;
$value = 2;
do
   $result = pow($value, $exponent);
   print("$value to the power of $exponent is $result<br>");
   $exponent = $exponent + 1;
while ($exponent <= 5);
```

Note that the test of this loop statement must be followed by a semi-colon, to indicate the end of the structure.

Note also that braces are **not** required between the **do** and the **while** since these two words are sufficient to tell the processor where the loop instructions begin and end.

Multi-Dimensional Arrays

Chapter 11 focused on the use of **one-dimensional** numerically-indexed arrays. Arrays can include any number of dimensions. For example, a **two-dimensional** array could store 3 scores for each of 5 students:

```
$scores[0] = array(90, 80, 92);
$scores[1] = array(82, 81, 83);
$scores[2] = array(87, 90, 84);
$scores[3] = array(78, 69, 73);
$scores[4] = array(89, 91, 92);
```

Here, the $scores array is an array that contains five elements indexed from 0 to 4. Each of these elements of the $scores array is **also** an array, each containing three **elements**, indexed from 0 to 2. To obtain the **second** score of the **third** student we must reference element 1 of the $scores[2] array as follows: $scores[2][1].

If you wish to use a **FOR** loop to find the average score of the fifth student, you can simply refer to the array named $scores[4] in your loop, and use the loop variable to reference the index of each element of this array:

```
$totalScore = 0;
for ($i = 0; $i < sizeof($scores[4]); $i = $i + 1)
{
   $totalScore = $totalScore + $scores[4][$i];
}
```

This loop will repeat for index positions 0 through 2 to add the values of each element of the array named $scores[4].

If you wish to use a FOR loop to find the average score for each of the five students, you can use a FOR loop nested inside **another** FOR loop:

```
for ($i = 0; $i < sizeof($scores); $i = $i + 1)
{
   $totalScore = 0;
   for ($j = 0; $j < sizeof($scores[$i]); $j = $j + 1)
   {
      $totalScore = $totalScore + $scores[$j][$i];
   }
   $averageScore = $totalScore / sizeof($scores[$i]);
   print("Average score for student $i is $averageScore");
}
```

Consider this code carefully. First note that the two loops must use different variables to count through the array indexes so that there is no conflict when the loops are processed. Here the outer loop uses **$i** as a counting variable, and the inner loop uses **$j**.

Next note that the outer loop is controlled by **$i** < **sizeof($scores)**. That's because we want this loop to repeat for each of the five elements of the $scores array.

Since the inner loop is located inside the outer loop, the inner loop will be processed **entirely** for every repetition of the outer loop. The inner loop is controlled by **$j** < **sizeof($scores[$i])**. That's because we want this loop to repeat for each of the three elements in the array stored in $scores[$i]. Does that make sense?

Inside the inner loop, the **$totalScore** variable accumulates the values from each element of $scores[$i] and the average score for that student is calculated and displayed. Note that the $totalScore must be reset to **0** for each student each time the outer loop repeats, otherwise it would add the next student's scores to the previous total. Similarly, the average score must be calculated and displayed for each student before the outer loop moves on the next student. If you instead wanted to obtain the **overall** average of **all** the scores of **all** the students, you would initialise $totalScores to 0 **before** the outer loop, and only calculate and display the average **after** the outer loop has completed (the total would need to be divided by the total number of elements in all the arrays).

Ragged Arrays

Each element of a multi-dimensional array such as $scores contains an array. These inner arrays can actually contain different numbers of elements. These are then known as **ragged** arrays. For example consider a 2-dimensional array that contains donations that have been received by five different participants in a fund-raiser:

```
$donations[0] = array(25.00, 35.00, 25.00, 15.00);
$donations[1] = array(45.00, 55.00, 75.00, 25.00, 25.00,
35,00, 50.00);
$donations[2] = array(25.00, 45.00);
$donations[3] = array(15.00);
$donations[4] = array(65.00, 35.00, 35.00, 20.00, 30.00);
```

Here is another example that demonstrates the usefulness of the **sizeof**() function, since this will tell us the number of elements in any array. If you needed to find the total of all donations, you can use the same pair of nested loops as in the previous example:

```
$total = 0;
for ($i = 0; $i < sizeof($donations); $i = $i + 1)
{
  for ($j = 0; $j < sizeof($donations[$i]); $j = $j + 1)
  {
    $total = $total + $donations[$j][$i];
  }
}
```

The outer loop will repeat 5 times since that is the number of elements in the $donations array. However the inner loop will repeat a different number of times for each repetition of the outer loop. That's because the inner loop is controlled by sizeof($donations[$i]), and this value will be different for each element of $donations.

Multi-Dimensional Associative Arrays

Associative arrays can also be multi-dimensional, and we can even create multi-dimensional arrays that combine associative arrays with numerically-indexed arrays. For example a 2-dimensional array could be used to store the number of cars sold by an auto sales business every quarter for 3 years:

```
$carSales["2005"] = array (121, 174, 165, 112);
$carSales["2006"] = array (134, 143, 146, 121);
$carSales["2007"] = array (101, 203, 149, 101);
```

Here, the **$carSales** array is an associative array that contains three elements ("2005", "2006", and "2007"). Each of these elements contains a numerically-indexed array of four numbers. To obtain the number of cars sold in the 3rd quarter of 2006 we can reference the $carSales["2006"] array as follows: **$carSales["2006"][2]**.

If you wish to use a FOR loop to find the total sales for 2007, you can simply refer to that array in your loop:

```
$total2007 = 0;
for ($i = 0; $i < sizeof($carSales["2007"]); $i = $i + 1)
{
   $total2007 = $total2007 + $carSales["2007"][$i];
}
```

If you wish to use a FOR loop to find the total sales for ALL THREE years, you can use a FOR loop nested inside a FOREACH loop (the use of FOREACH loops with associative arrays is covered in Chapter 12):

```
$total = 0;
foreach ($carSales as $nextYear)
{
   for ($i = 0; $i < sizeof($nextYear); $i = $i + 1)
   {
     $total = $total + $nextYear[$i];
   }
}
```

In this case, each time the FOREACH loop repeats, the next element of $carSales is assigned to $nextYear. Each of these elements is an array, so the nested FOR loop processes the array of the $carSales element that is currently stored in $nextYear, adding every value to the total. When the FOR loop completes, control returns to the FOREACH loop which assigns the next element to $nextYear, and so on.

PHP Data Types

Variables may be used to store data of various **data types**. Each data type is stored in a different manner and allows specific operations. PHP supports the following data types:

Integer: A whole number (**int** data type), such as -100, -1, 0, 1, 25, or 7388. Note that integers can be expressed in **decimal** (base 10), **octal** (base 8), **hexadecimal** (base 16), or **binary** (base (2).

Floating point number: A decimal number (**float** data type), such as 5.24 or 123.456789. Float values can also be expressed as **exponents**, for example 1.4e27.

Boolean: A TRUE or FALSE value.

String: A sequence of 0 or more characters (**string** data type), such as "Joe Smith", or "What is your name?" or "123 Main Street" or "<p>This is a paragraph.</p>".

Object: An object data type is an instance of an OO class.

Array: An array is a variable that contains multiple values, referenced by an index.

Null: a simple data type with only one value (NULL), which is no value. It can be used to de-value a variable of any data type, or to test if a variable of any data type has been has not been assigned a value.

Resource: this special data type acts as a reference to an external source of data such as a file or database. For example **fopen**() returns a Resource data type that references the file stream. Similarly **mysqli_connect**() returns a Resource data type that references the link to the SQL database. In both cases the reference that is returned is assigned to a variable that is then included in subsequent function calls that are intended to work with the data source, for example fgets() and mysqli_query().

Unlike most languages, PHP allows you to use variables without first defining their data type. PHP evaluates each expression by **context**, and determines which data type is appropriate at the time a value is assigned, and again when a value is used in an expression.

To ensure that a value is being handled as a specific data type you can **type cast** the variable. For example you can use the **int** cast operator to cast a string or float value as an integer (note that if a float value is converted to an integer it will be truncated, so any decimal part will be lost). Here is a simple example, where we cast the value stored in $someValue to an integer value and store this in **$intValue:**

```
$intValue = (int) $someValue;
```

You need to be careful to choose between typecasting a single value or the value of an expression. For example compare these two statements:

```php
$result = (int) ($num1 * $num2);
$result = (int) $num1 * (int) num2;
```

In the first case the result of the entire expression is cast as an integer, so if **$num1** contains 2.5 and **$num2** contains 4.5, these two values are multiplied to obtain **11.25**, and then this value is cast as an integer to obtain **11**, which is stored in **$result**.

In the second case, the values of **$num1** and **$num2** are both cast as integers **before** the expression is evaluated, so if $num1 contains 2.5 and $num2 contains 4.5, the value of $num1 is cast as an integer to obtain **2**, then the value of $num2 is cast as an integer to obtain **4**, and then these values are multiplied to obtain **8**, which is stored in **$result**.

In some circumstance you may need to ensure that a variable that contains a string version of a number will treat it as a numeric value, for example if an hourly wage of 15.75 was read from a file and stored as "15.75", you can ensure that it will stored as a float value as follows:

```php
$hourlyWage = (float) $hourlyWage;
```

And to convert a float value to a string:

```php
$wageString = (string) $hourlyWage;
```

You can use the **gettype()** function to determine the data type of a variable. For example **gettype($hoursWorked)** would return "integer".

PHP allows the following casts: (**integer**) or (**int**), (**boolean**) or (**bool**), (**float**) or (**double**), (**string**), (**array**), (**object**), or (**unset**), which casts to NULL.

PHP Tools to Validate and Sanitize Data

Data sanitizing and validation are critical components of any real world application that must work with data, whether directly received from the user or from files, databases, or other sources. **Sanitizing** refers to the process of **changing** data (removing or rendering harmless) in order to protect against corrupt or malicious content, while **validation** refers to **testing** data, to be sure that input meets requirements. All input data should be sanitized and validated, in that order.

Appendix E provides an important introduction to security and validation, and is a **must-read** if you are planning to develop your applications online. The appendix describes the use of a number of PHP functions that will help to keep your applications secure, and to validate your application input. This appendix also includes a brief introduction to regular expressions (**regex**).

PHP Date and Time Functions

The need to process or display dates and times is an important requirement for many applications. Your computer stores dates and times in a special **timestamp** format, which defines a specific time as the number of seconds since midnight Greenwich Mean Time on January 1, 1970 (known as the beginning of the Unix epoch). Fortunately PHP provides objects and functions that make it easy to work with timestamps, using our usual measuring system (years, months, days, hours, minutes, and seconds). This short introduction will provide a few examples just to get you started.

The PHP **date**() function will return a date and time string, derived from any timestamp, formatted to your specific requirements. The function has two parameters: the first is **required** and consists of a character string that combines different character codes to define the required date format; the second is an **optional** timestamp that specifies a specific time (if a timestamp is not included, the date() function will use the timestamp of the current moment). To start with an example, **date("Y:m:d")** contains the format string **"Y:m:d"**, which uses three format codes: 'Y' indicates the **year**, expressed as 4 digits, 'm' indicates a 2-digit **month** number, and 'd' a 2-digit **day** number. The two **colons** are also to be included in the formatted date string. Since there is no second parameter, the current time stamp is assumed. If today's date is **April 14, 2021**, **date("Y:m:d")** would return **"2021:04:14"**.

The format string can be constructed with any combination of format codes, in any order, to construct the desired output, and can also include any of the following separators: ';', ':', '/', ',', '-', '(', ')', as well as simple **spaces** ' '):

d - Day of the month as 2 digits (01, 02,)
j - Day of the month as 1 or 2 digits (1, 2, .., 10, 11, ..)
D – Three-letter abbreviation of the day ("SUN", "MON", ..)
S - The English suffix ("st", "nd", "rd", or "thv). This can used after j, for
        example to create "1st" or "14th")
l (lowercase 'L') the full day name ("Sunday", "Monday"..)
F – The full month name ("January", "February", ..)
m – The 2-digit month number (01, 02, ..)
n – The 1-digit month number (1, 2, .., 10, 11, ..)
M - Three-letter abbreviation of the month ("JAN", "FEB",)
L – returns 1 if it is a leap year, 0 if it is not
Y – The year as 4 digits (2021, 2022, ..)
y - The year as 2 digits (21, 22, ..)
a - Lowercase am or pm
A - Uppercase AM or PM
g or h - 12-hour format of an hour (1, .., 12)
G or H - 24-hour format of an hour (0, .., 23)
i – 2 digit minutes (00, 01, ..)
s – 2-digit seconds (00, 01, ..)

The following examples demonstrate just a few ways in which these codes can be combined for different purposes. Your **samples** folder includes **date-time.php**, which includes these and other examples.

To display the time of day (hour and minutes) in 12-hour format followed by "am" or "pm" (for example "**The time is 7:45am**"):

```
print("<p>The time is ".date("g:ia")."</p>");
```

To display the day of the week (for example "**Today is Wednesday**"):

```
print("<p>Today is ".date("l")."</p>");
```

To provide a morning wake up message consisting of the time, day of the week, name of the month, followed by the day and a suitable suffix ("st", "rd", or "th"), and the year (for example "**Good morning! It's 7:45am, Wednesday April 14th, 2021**"):

```
print("<p>Good morning! It's ". date("g:ia, l F jS,
   Y")."</p>");
```

A **copyright** notice is often a necessary feature on a Web page. A string returned by the date() function can be concatenated with other text to ensure that the notice always displays the current year, for example "**Copyright © 2021**". In the example below the "**©**" part of the string is an HTML **entity** that will display the copyright symbol, entities are explained in chapter 17.

print("<p>Copyright © ".date("Y")."</p>");

Here's another interesting use of a date string. It is often useful to include a date as part of the name of a data file (such as those rainfall files you worked with in Chapter 6). This is useful for reference, and a "**year-month-day**" format will also ensure that similarly named files will be listed in date order when sorted by name. Here is a statement that creates a file name by concatenating a formatted date with a filename that begins "**rainfall-**" and ends with the extension "**.txt**", for example "**rainfall-2021-04-21.txt**":

```
$fileName = "rainfall-".date("Y-m-d").".txt";
print("<p>The filename is $fileName</p>");
```

One way to create any timestamp is to use the PHP **mktime()** function, which takes 6 parameters (hour, minute, second, month, day, year). To create a timestamp for **April 14, 2021**:

```
mktime (0,0,0,4,14,2021);
```

You could use this for example to check the **day** of your birthday:

```
$birthday = mktime (0,0,0,4,14,2021);
print("<p>My birthday will be on a ".date("l",
    $birthday)."</p>");
```

You can easily improve this code so it will continue to work over time, for any year, by first using the **date**() function to obtain the current year, then including this as the year parameter in the call to **mktime**():

```
$year = date("Y");
$birthday = mktime (0,0,0,4,14,$year);
print("<p>My birthday will be on a ".date("l",
$birthday)."</p>");
```

You will want to extend your familiarity with PHP date and time functions, and also calendar functions. The **w3schools** site provides a useful introduction and code samples.

Standard PHP Functions

PHP provides many useful functions for a wide range of common programming tasks. We have used a few of these in this book. For an exhaustive list of PHP functions see: **https://php.net/manual/en/funcref.php**.

This list is quite overwhelming! It is often more useful to see a list of functions, organized by category (for example math functions, string functions, array functions, etc). A list of this kind can be found at the **w3schools** site (see the additional reference section at the end of this chapter).

To get you started, on the following pages you will find lists of the more commonly used PHP functions, by category. These include the functions that have been introduced in this book as well as many more, with short descriptions. You are encouraged to go online and research the use of any of these functions that interest you or that meet your requirements.

First, here are a few general-purpose functions that may be especially useful as you build on what you have learned in this book:

empty()   checks whether a variable is empty, useful for validating form input

is_numeric() checks whether a variable contains a number

file_exists()   checks whether a file exists before trying to open a file

define()   defines a constant variable (a variable that cannot be changed)

phpinfo()   displays in-depth information about your PHP installation

isset()   checks whether a variable contains a value

unset()   destroys a variable

Standard PHP Array Functions

Here are some commonly used array-processing functions:

array()   creates a new array

array_fill()   fills an array with values

array_key_exists()   checks if a certain key exists in the array

array_keys() returns the key values of an array

array_merge() merges one or more arrays into a single array

array_pop() removes the last element from an array

array_push() adds one or more elements to the end of an array

array_reverse() returns an array with the values in reverse order

array_search() searches an array for a value and returns the key

array_shift() removes the first element from an array, and returns the value of the removed element

array_slice() returns specific parts of an array

array_sum() returns the sum of the values in an array

array_unique() removes duplicate values from an array

array_unshift() adds one or more elements to the beginning of an array

arsort() sorts an associative array in descending order, based on the values

asort() sorts an associative array in ascending order, based on the values

count() returns the number of elements in an array, same as sizeof()

krsort() sorts an associative array in descending order, based on the key values

ksort()   sorts an associative array in ascending order, based on the key values

list()   assigns values to variables from an array

rsort()   sorts values in an indexed array in descending order

sizeof()   returns the number of elements in an array, same as count()

sort()   sorts values in an indexed array in ascending order

Standard PHP File Functions

Be careful how you use these file functions. Some have the ability to overwrite or delete files or folders!

basename()	returns the filename from a complete path name
copy()	copies a file
dirname()	returns the folder name from a complete path name
disk_free_space()	returns the available space
disk_total_space()	returns the total size
fclose()	closes a file
feof()	tests for end-of-file (EOF)
fflush()	flushes buffered output to an open file
fgets()	returns a string containing the text from the next line in a file
file_exists()	checks whether or not a file or folder exists
file_get_content()	reads an entire file into a string
file_put_contents	writes a string to a file
fopen()	opens a file or url
fputs()	writes a string to a file, same as fwrite()
fwrite()	writes a string to a file, same as fputs()
is_executabl()	checks if a file is executable
mkdir()	creates a new folder
rename()	renames a file or folder
rmdir()	removes an folder (if it is empty)
stat()	returns information about a file
umask()	changes file permissions
unlink()	deletes a file

Standard PHP Math Functions

abs()	returns the absolute value of a number
acos()	returns the arccosine of a number
asin()	returns the arcsine of a number
atan()	returns the arctangent of a number
bindec()	converts a binary number to a decimal number

ceil()	returns the value of a number rounded upwards to the nearest integer
cos()	returns the cosine of a number
decbin()	converts a decimal number to a binary number
dechex()	converts a decimal number to a hexadecimal number
decoct()	converts a decimal number to an octal number
deg2rad()	converts a degree to a radian number
floor()	returns the value of a number rounded downwards to the nearest integer
hexdec()	converts a hexadecimal number to a decimal number
hypot()	returns the length of the hypotenuse of a right-angle triangle
is_finite()	returns true if a value is a finite number
is_infinite()	returns true if a value is an infinite number
is_nan()	returns true if a value is not a number
log()	returns the natural logarithm (base e) of a number
log10()	returns the base-10 logarithm of a number
max()	returns the number with the highest value of two specified numbers
min()	returns the number with the lowest value of two specified numbers
octdec()	converts an octal number to a decimal number
pi()	returns the value of pi
pow()	returns the value of x to the power of y
rad2deg()	converts a radian number to a degree
rand()	returns a random integer
round()	rounds a number to the nearest integer
sin()	returns the sine of a number
sinh()	returns the hyperbolic sine of a number
sqrt()	returns the square root of a number
tan()	returns the tangent of an angle

Standard PHP String Functions

bin2hex()	converts a string of ascii characters to hexadecimal values
chr()	returns a character from a specified ascii value
count_chars()	counts the number of times an ascii character occurs within a string
echo()	outputs strings

explode()   parses a string into an array of substrings

fprintf()   writes a formatted string to an output stream

html_entity_decode() converts html entities to characters

htmlentities() converts characters to html entities

htmlspecialchars_decode()   converts specific html entities to characters

htmlspecialchars()   converts specific characters to html entities

ltrim()   removes whitespace from the left side of a string

money_format()   returns a string formatted as currency

number_format()   formats a number according to a format specification

ord()   returns the ascii value of the first character in a string

print()   outputs a string

printf()   outputs a formatted string

rtrim()   removes whitespace from the right side of a string

str_word_count()   counts the words in a string

strcasecmp() compares two strings (case-insensitive)

strcmp()   compares two strings (case-sensitive)

strlen()   returns the length of a string

strrev()   reverses a string

substr()   returns a part of a string

substr_count()   counts the number of times a substring occurs in a string

substr_replace()   replaces part of a string with another string

trim()   removes whitespace from both sides of a string

wordwrap()   wraps a string to a specified number of characters

A lengthy list of standard PHP mysql functions can be found at

```
https://www.w3schools.com/php/php_ref_mysqli.asp
```

A list of standard PHP date and time functions and constants can be found at:

```
https://www.w3schools.com/php/php_ref_date.asp
```

Chapter 17

More about HTML and CSS

Intended Learning Outcomes

After completing this chapter, you should be able to:
- Incorporate additional elements into your HTML forms (hidden fields, radio buttons, single and multiple checkboxes, text areas, and reset buttons).
- Distinguish between data validation and data sanitizing.
- Recognize and implement ordered, unordered (bulleted), and definition lists.
- Add horizontal rules of varying lengths and heights to a Web page.
- Utilize the HTML <blockquote> and <cite> elements.
- Apply background images to your Web pages.
- Use clickable images to provide links to other Web pages.
- Use <div> and <span> containers to apply styles to specific sections of a Web page.
- Include HTML entities in your page content to render special characters.

HTML and CSS were introduced in Chapter 4, with the goal of providing sufficient coverage of these languages to support the overall purpose of the book (to teach fundamental programming algorithms, syntax and control structures). Chapter 17 is designed to supplement Chapter 4 by introducing other HTML elements: additional form elements (**hidden fields, radio buttons, check boxes, text areas**, and **reset buttons**); different kinds of lists (**ordered, unordered**, and **definition** lists); **horizontal rules**; the <**block-quote**> and <**cite**> elements (used to identify quotes from other sources, and titles of creative works); the <**div**> and <**span**> elements (used to assign CSS styles to specific sections of a Web page), and **html entities** (used to render special characters). In your **samples** folder you will find a **more-html** folder which contains the examples that are used in this chapter.

The chapter ends with a brief discussion of deprecated HTML tags, and a list of useful references

More About HTML Forms

In Chapter 4 you learned to create forms that contained **input text boxes**, **drop down lists**, and **submit buttons**. HTML forms can also include **hidden fields**, **radio buttons**, **check boxes**, **text areas**, and **reset buttons**. These are explained here, and the **more-html** folder (under your **samples** folder) includes an example that demonstrates the use of these elements in an application (**pizza-order.php** and **confirm-order.php**).

Hidden Fields

You have learned that drop down lists and input text boxes should include a **name** attribute. When the form is submitted to Web server each **value** is assigned to the **$_POST** array to an element indexed with the same **name**. Consider this code in an HTML form:

```
<label>Your first name:
<input type="text" name="custName" size = "10"></label>
```

The PHP program that processes the form can receive the value submitted from this input box as follows:

```
$customerName = $_POST["custName"];
```

In addition to input provided by the user, it is often useful to code a form to also submit other values that might be needed to process the form input. For example, a form designed to allow a user to order a pizza for pickup might also need to submit the **price** of the pizza when the form is submitted, which is not a value that the user should provide!

Forms can include **hidden fields**. These fields are defined with names and values that will be included when the form data is submitted to the $_POST array, although the values were not provided by the user. Hidden fields are created using an **<input>** tag, but with the **type** attribute set to **"hidden"**, and the **value** attribute set to the required value, for example:

```
<input type="hidden" name="price" value="12.75">
```

Although the user does not see this field, the **name** and **value** from the field is included when the form is submitted. In this example, the value **12.75** is stored in the

$_POST["price"] element, and can be retrieved in the same way as any other form input, for example:

```
$pizzaPrice = $_POST["price"];
```

This example shows a **literal** value (**12.75**) being sent in a hidden field. A value stored in a **variable** can also be sent. For example it is probably important to send the **time** that the order was submitted. Chapter 16 demonstrated how to use the PHP **date**() function to obtain the current time in any format; the following assignment will assign the current time to a variable named **$time**, in the format "**2:30pm**" (or whatever the time is):

```
$time = date("g:ia");
```

The form could include a hidden field that submits the value stored in **$time** as follows:

```
<input type="hidden" name="timeOfOrder" value=$time>
```

And once again this value can be retrieved from the $_POST array as follows:

```
$timeOfOrder = $_POST["timeOfOrder"];
```

Note that the **value** stored in $time was sent to the $_POST array, associated with the name "**timeOfOrder**"; the actual variable **$time** is **not** sent.

A single HTML form can combine any number of hidden fields, along with fields designed to receive input from the user.

Radio Buttons

Radio buttons provide the user with a list of options, only one of which can be chosen. If the user clicks a button it is **selected**, and any previously selected button is **deselected**. The form in our pizza order example asks the user to choose a **crust** from three options (**thin**, **thick**, or **stuffed**). These could be displayed as a drop down list, but radio buttons are more visually intuitive. Radio buttons are created using an <**input**> element with the type set to "**radio**". Radio buttons are associated with one another by using the **same name for each button** (this is important because you may have more than one group of radio buttons in your form: each group of radio buttons would use a different name). Although each button has the same name, they must each have a different **value**: the value of the button that is selected by the user will be sent to the Web server along with the name. Here is the example from **pizza-order.php**:

```
<p>Which type of crust would you like?</p>

<label>Thin Crust
    <input type="radio" name="crust" value="thin"></label>
<label>Thick Crust
    <input type="radio" name="crust" value="thick"></label>
<label>Stuffed Crust
    <input type="radio" name="crust" value="stuffed"></label>
```

Each button's **label** text describes each option to the user, and the **value** attribute indicates the actual **value** that is to be sent to the **$_POST** array, with the **name** "crust" (if that button is selected). The program that receives the form input (in this case **confirm-order.php**) will retrieve the user's selection as follows:

```
$crust= $_POST["crust"];
```

In this example, **$_POST**["**crust2**"] will contain either "thin", or "thick", or "stuffed".

Single and Multiple Check Boxes

Just like radio buttons, **check boxes also** provide the user with a list of options, but in this case with the option to select as many options as he or she wants, just by clicking boxes on and off. In the pizza example, an excellent use of check boxes will be to allow the user to choose any number of pizza toppings (is this making you hungry?). Sometimes a form component only requires a single check box, usually to obtain a **yes** or **no** response. For example our pizza form may also ask the user to check a single box to indicate that he or she has a coupon to get a free topping.

Check boxes are created using an **<input>** element with the type set to **"checkbox"**. If just a **single** check box is needed for a form component, then the element should have a **unique name**, and the **value** attribute can be used to send a value to the $_POST array if the check box is checked. It is important to note that **no** value will be sent if the check box is **not** checked. Here is the pizza order example, where the check box name is "**freeTopping**", and the value "**yes**" is sent if the box is checked:

```
<label>Do you have a "Free Topping" Coupon?
    <input type="checkbox" name="freeTopping"
      value="yes"></label>
```

However the $_POST array will **only** include a "freeTopping" element if the freeTopping checkbox was **checked**. If **confirm-order.php** attempts to retrieve a value from **$_POST** ["**freeTopping**"], the processor may issue a warning if **$_POST** ["**freeTopping**"] doesn't exist. One way to avoid this is to use the **isset**() function to test if this array element has been set, and assign the result (**true** or **false**) of this test to a variable, for example:

```
   if (isset($_POST["freeTopping"]))
   {
      // code if freeTopping was set (the box was checked)
   }
   else
   {
      // code if freeTopping was not set (the box was NOT
checked)
   }
```

You may be wondering, if we are using the **isset**() function to test if **$_POST["freeTopping"]** exists, why do we need to send a value at all? After all, if isset() returns **true** that in itself indicates that the check box **was** checked, and, if **false** then the checkbox was **not** checked. While there may be some instances where, when working with a single checkbox, it is useful to send a value, in most cases it is not really needed, so the input element could be coded with no **value** attribute:

```
   <label>Do you have a "Free Topping" Coupon?
      <input type="checkbox" name="freeTopping" </label>
```

Now let's look at a form requirement that requires a **group** of check boxes. The pizza order form must allow the user to select any number of pizza toppings. In this case, the check box for each topping must contain a unique value that will be passed to the $_POST array if that box is checked (for example "mushroom", or "olives"). Since the user can check any number of these boxes, how can you code this so that a list of the names of the selected toppings will be sent to the $_POST array? The answer is to submit an **array** of the checked toppings: the check boxes share the same name (just as with radio buttons), but the name now includes square brackets to indicate that the value of the check box will be sent as one element in an array:

```
   <label> Extra Cheese Topping
      <input type="checkbox" name="toppings[]"
value="cheese"></label>
   <label> Green Pepper Topping
      <input type="checkbox" name="toppings[]"
value="pepper"></label>
   <label> Mushroom Topping
      <input type="checkbox" name="toppings[]"
value="mushroom"></label>
   <label> Onion Topping
      <input type="checkbox" name="toppings[]"
value="onion"></label>
   <label> Olive Topping
      <input type="checkbox" name="toppings[]"
value="olives"></label>
```

In the example the five **toppings** check boxes all use the same name: **"toppings[]"**. The inclusion of square brackets means that a numerically indexed array containing the values of every checked check box will be sent to the $_POST array with the name **"toppings"**. However if **no** check boxes are checked the $_POST array will not receive this array, so once again you should use the **isset()** function to test that the array exists as an element in the $_POST array:

```
if (isset($_POST["toppings"]))
{
   $toppings = $_POST["toppings"]; //assign array to $toppings
   // code to execute if there are toppings
}
else
{
   // code to execute if there are no toppings
}
```

In this example, if $_POST["toppings"] is set, the array is assigned to a variable named **$toppings**, and this variable can then used to refer to the array. While it not required to copy **$_POST["toppings"]** to **$toppings**, it is less cumbersome, and more readable, to use **$toppings**, rather than **$_POST["toppings"]**, in every program statement that works with the array.

If an array of toppings has been received, you can determine how many items are in the array using either the **count()** or **sizeof()** function (these two functions are the same), for example **count($toppings)**. You can also reference a specific array element using its index position (for example $toppings[2]), would refer to the **third** element of the array), but this would be dangerous since the array may only contain 1 or 2 elements (if the user only chose 1 or 2 toppings. A better approach to work with individual toppings is to use the **in_array()** function, which takes **two** arguments, a **search** value, and the **array** to be searched. So for example, if the user checked **"mushroom"** but not **"olives"**, **in_array("mushroom", $toppings)** would return true, but in_array("olives", $toppings) would return false.

In many cases, you will be more interested in using a loop to work with **all** the values in the array. A **FOR** loop can be used for this purpose (using **count($toppings)** to control the number of repetitions), but a **FOREACH** loop is designed for this purpose. The **confirm-pizza.php** program uses a **FOREACH** loop to simply display a list of the toppings that were ordered. Here is a simplified version of this code (the complete version will be shown shortly):

```
        print ("<p>You ordered ");
        foreach ($toppings as $topping) {
            print ("$topping and ");
        }
            print ("hey that sounds truly delicious!</p>");
```

This code segment first begins a paragraph with the words "You ordered", and then, each time the loop repeats, the program prints the next topping in the **$toppings** array, followed the word "and". Once the loop has completed, the paragraph ends with the phrase "hey that sounds truly delicious!". If the user had only checked olives this would produce "**<p>You ordered olives and hey that sounds truly delicious!</p>**". If the user had selected cheese, mushroom, and olives, this would produce "**<p>You ordered cheese and mushroom and olives and hey that sounds truly delicious!</p>**".

Text Areas

Unlike the HTML **input text box** that displays as single line, a **text area** displays as a box containing multiple rows, and can be used to invite the user to enter a message of some kind, for example feedback, or a comment, or instructions. The pizza program will use a text area to allow the user to provide delivery instructions:

```
<label>Special delivery instructions?
  <textarea name="delivery" rows="2" cols="38"
    maxlength = "80"></textarea></label>
```

As always the **name** attribute is used to associate a name with the user input. The **rows** and **cols** attributes are used to set the displayed size of the text area (the size of the text area can also be defined in CSS). Note that the user can expand or diminish the size (also the text that the user types in the text area can be scrolled up and down). The number of characters that can be typed can be controlled with the optional **maxlength** attribute. The program that receives the form input (in this case **confirm-order.php**) will retrieve the user's message as follows:

```
$instructions= $_POST["delivery"];
```

Processing the Form

Let's see how all of these different form elements can work together in a simple pizza order application. Open **pizza-order.php** and try submitting some orders. **Figure 17-1** shows a sample interaction.

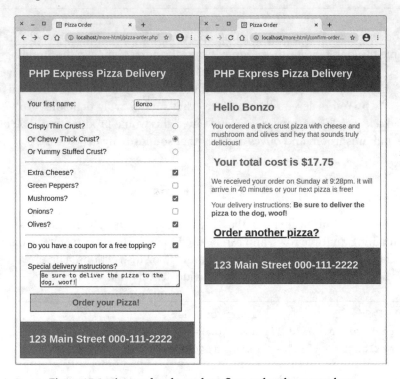

Figure 17-1: pizza-order.php and confirm-order.php screenshots

Here is **pizza-order.php** which displays the order form:

```
<form action= "confirm-order.php" method = "post">
<?php
  $time = date("l")." at ".date("g:ia");
  print ("<input type=\"hidden\"
    name=\"timeOfOrder\" value=\"$time\">");
 ?>


<input class="hidden" type="hidden" name="pizzaCost"
value="12.75">
<input class="hidden" type="hidden" name="toppingCost"
value="2.50">


<label>Your first name:
  <input type="text" name="custName" size = "10"></label>
```

```
<hr>
<label>Crispy Thin Crust?
  <input type="radio" name="crust" value="thin"></label>
<label>Or Chewy Thick Crust?
  <input type="radio" name="crust" value="thick"></label>
<label>Or Yummy Stuffed Crust?
  <input type="radio" name="crust" value="stuffed"></label>
<hr>
<label>Extra Cheese?
  <input type="checkbox" name="toppings[]"
value="cheese"></label>
<label> Green Peppers?
  <input type="checkbox" name="toppings[]"
value="pepper"></label>
<label>Mushrooms?
  <input type="checkbox" name="toppings[]"
value="mushroom"></label>
<label>Onions?
  <input type="checkbox" name="toppings[]" value="onion"></label>
<label>Olives?
  <input type="checkbox" name="toppings[]"
value="olives"></label>
<hr>
<label>Do you have a coupon for a free topping?
  <input type="checkbox" name="freeTopping"></label>
<hr>
<label>Special delivery instructions?
  <textarea name="delivery" rows="2" cols="38"
  maxlength = "80"></textarea></label>
<input type="submit" class="submit" value="Order your Pizza!" />
</form>
```

Look through this code and identify the various form elements that have been discussed above. The code for pizza-order.php also includes <hr> (hard rule) tags, which generate a line across the page, and <div> tags (not shown here) which are used to assign different styles to different code sections. These and other HTML elements will be discussed later in this chapter.

The **confirm-pizza.php** program receives and processes the form input from this form. The $_POST array will contain: the user's name (text input box) , the time of the order (hidden field), the pizza cost (hidden field), the toppings cost (hidden field), the type of crust (radio button input), the list of toppings (array of checked check box values, but only if at least one topping was checked), the user's response when asked if he or she has a coupon (single check box input, but only if this box was checked), and special delivery instructions, if any (text area). The program then displays a Web page in response to the user's order that calculate and displays the cost of the pizza, which is

based on the number of toppings (allowing for no toppings) and includes a deduction
if the user had a coupon. The program also tells the user what time the order was received, guarantees the pizza will be ready within 40 minutes of that time, and confirms
the delivery instructions if any were provided.

Here is the code for confirm-pizza.php:

```php
$timeOfOrder = $_POST["timeOfOrder"];
$pizzaCost = $_POST["pizzaCost"];
$toppingCost = $_POST["toppingCost"];
$customerName = $_POST["custName"];
$crust= $_POST["crust"];
$instructions = $_POST["delivery"];

print ("<h2>Hello ".$customerName."</h2>");
print ("<p>You ordered a $crust crust pizza with ");

if (isset($_POST["toppings"]))
{
  $toppings = $_POST["toppings"];

  foreach ($toppings as $topping) {
    print ("$topping and ");
  }
  print ("hey that sounds truly delicious!</p>");
  if (isset($_POST["freeTopping"]))
    $totalToppingCost = (count($toppings)- 1) *$toppingCost;
  else
    $totalToppingCost = count($toppings) *$toppingCost;
}
else
{
  print ("no toppings</p>");
  $totalToppingCost = 0;
}

$totalCost = $pizzaCost + $totalToppingCost;

print ("<h2>Your total cost is <strong>$".number_format($total-
Cost, 2)."</strong></h2>");

print ("<p>We received your order on ".$timeOfOrder.". It will
arrive in 40 minutes or your next pizza is free!</p>");
```

```
if (!empty($instructions))
  print ("<p>Your delivery instructions: <strong>".
    $instructions."</strong></p>");


print ("<h2><a href=\"pizza-order.php\">Order another
pizza?</a></h2>");
```

Run the program a few times, using different inputs, while you examine the logic in this code.

HTML Form Reset Buttons

Web forms can also include **reset** buttons, which can be provided in addition to a **submit** button. A reset button is useful in the case of longer forms, or forms with extensive text entry: if the user clicks the reset button the form is reset to its original state, and any previous user input is cleared. A reset button is coded just like a submit button except the type is changed to "reset", for example:

```
<input type="reset" value="Clear the form">
```

Validating and Sanitizing Form Input

As you can see, a number of HTML form elements allow the user to type text directly from the keyboard (for example, text input boxes, text areas, and password input boxes). This input data should **always** be thoroughly **validated** and **sanitized** before it is "cleared for use" by your application. "Validation" refers to procedures that **test** procedures that ensure that the submitted data corresponds to a required format (for example numeric values, dates, zip codes, email addresses). "Sanitizing" refers to procedures that **remove** content that might contain malicious code (for example certain characters, such as '<' and '>', that might indicate the presence of a script).

The pizza order example does not include any validation of the user name, choice of crust, or delivery instructions in order to keep the focus on the handling the various form elements. Before you move your applications to a "live" online server, where they will be vulnerable to misuse, it is critical that you make them secure. **Appendix E** covers this topic in more detail, including explicit steps to accomplish this.

HTML List Elements

Web pages often need to display **lists** of different kinds. HTML distinguishes between **three** types of list: **ordered** lists, **bulleted** (unordered) lists, and **definition** lists. Let's consider these in turn.

Ordered Lists

Ordered lists use **numbers** or **letters** to display an ordered sequence of list items. An entire ordered list is enclosed inside <**ol**> and </**ol**> tags. Nested inside these tags, each **list item** is enclosed inside <**li**> and </**li**> tags. The **type** attribute can be used in the <**ol**> tag to specify a preferred ordering system. For example **type** = "1" indicates a **numerically** ordered list (1, 2, 3, ..), whereas **type** = "a" or **type** = "A" indicates a list ordered by **letters** (a, b, c, ..) or (A, B, C, ..), and **type** = "i" indicates a list ordered by **Roman numerals** (i, ii, iii, ..). If no type attribute is included the list will be ordered numerically (1, 2, 3, ..). Here is an example using Roman numerals to explain why programming is a good career choice:

```
<ol type = "i">
<li>Coding is fun</li>
<li>There are many different careers</li>
<li>Employment outlook is good</li>
</ol>
```

Bulleted Lists

Bulleted lists are lists that use **bullets** to identify each list item. An entire bulleted list is enclosed inside <**ul**> and </**ul**> (unordered list) tags. Nested inside these tags, each **list item** is enclosed inside <**li**> and </**li**> tags. The **type** attribute can be used to specify the type of bullet. For example **"disc"** indicates the use of filled circle bullets, **"square"** indicates square bullets, and **"circle"** indicates unfilled circles. If no type attribute is included the list will be use discs. For example, here is a list using square bullets:

```
<ul type = "square">
<li>Coding is fun</li>
<li>There are many different careers</li>
<li>Employment outlook is good</li>
</ul>
```

Definition Lists

Definition lists contain terms followed by indented definitions of these terms. An entire definition list is enclosed inside <**dl**> and </**dl**> tags. Nested inside these tags, each definition term is enclosed enclosed inside <**dt**> and </**dt**> tags, and each data definition is enclosed enclosed inside <**dd**> and </**dd**> tags. For example:

```
<dl>
  <dt>VCS</dt>
  <dd>Stands for Version Control System.</dd>
  <dt>git</dt>
  <dd>A freely available open source version control
  software,available for Windows, macOS, and Linux.</dd>
  <dt>GitHub</dt>
  <dd>A cloud-based repository, founded on git, that facilitates
  distribution, collaboration, and project development.</dd>
</dl>
```

Terms and definitions can be mixed as needed, for example a single term might be followed by multiple definitions. Note that you will need to style the **dt** selector in CSS if you want the terms to appear differently from the definitions (for example you may want your terms to display as bold).

The **lists.php** file, in the **more-html** folder, generates and displays examples of ordered, unordered, and definition lists, and **Figure 17-2** provides a screen shot.

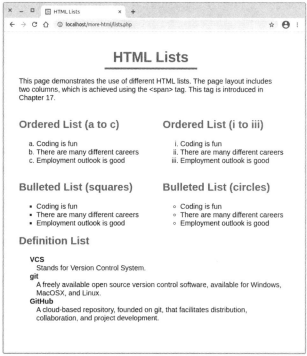

Figure 17-2: lists.php screenshot

Horizontal Rules

The horizontal rule (<**hr**>) element simply draws a line across the page, and is used to visually separate content on a page. A horizontal rule can be defined to cross the entire page, or just a percentage of the page width, or a specified distance. Other settings include height (thickness) and color. The screenshot in **Figure 17-1** shows how **pizza-order.php** uses green horizontal rules to separate different components of the order form. **Figure 17-2** shows a rule below the page heading in **lists.php** that is centered across **35%** of the page, **3 pixels** high, with a color and background color of **red** (note that the color property will apply to the **border** of a rule and the background-color will apply to the area **within** the border). Here is the CSS that was used in lists.php:

```
hr {   margin:auto; width:35%; height:3px;
    color:red; background-color:red }
```

Background Images for Web Pages

Use your style sheet ir you want to apply a background image to your Web page: add a **background** property to the body selector, with a **url** value that specifies the address of the image. By default the image will **repeat**. If you don't want it to repeat, add a **background-repeat** property with the value **no-repeat**. For example here is the CSS to apply a **repeating** image stored in a file named "**test.jpg**" to your entire page:

```
body { background:url(test.jpg);}
```

To apply the same image as a **non-repeating** image:

```
body {background:url(test.jpg); background-repeat:no-repeat;}
```

Creating a Clickable Image

You already know how to create a text-based link to a Web page, for example:

```
<a href="example.html">Click here for an example</a>
```

In this case the page displays a link text ("Click here for an example") that the user can click to open the **example.html** page. Instead of link text, you can provide an **image** that the user can click to go to the linked page: simply locate an image element **inside** your anchor <a> element instead of text:

```
<a href="example.html"><img src="SomeImage.jpg"></a>
```

Block Quotes and Citations

HTML provides a <**blockquote**> element to use when you need to indicate a quote from another source, and also a <**cite**> element to identify a title of a creative work of some kind. These can be used independently of one another, but here is a simple example using them together:

```
<blockquote>"It was the best of times, it was the worst of
times, it was the age of wisdom, it was the age of foolishness,
it was the epoch of belief, it was the epoch of incredulity, it
was the season of Light, it was the season of Darkness, it was
the spring of hope, it was the winter of despair."</blockquote>
<cite>A Tale of Two Cities</cite>
```

DIV and SPAN Containers

The HTML <**div**> and <**span**> tags are used as "containers", to mark the beginning and end of sections of your Web page content, in order to apply specific styles to different sections. The <**div**> tag is a **block-level** container, meaning that the content within a <div> section will begin on a new line and extend across the entire page. The <**span**> tag is an **inline** container, meaning that the content within this section will **continue** across the page from the previous content without beginning a new line (unless the previous content ended with a closing block element, such as a </div> or </p>), and content **after** this section will continue across the page without starting on a new line (unless the closing </span> is followed by an opening block element, such as a <div> or <p>).

These tags are used extensively to layout and design Web pages, allowing custom CSS to be applied to different areas of the page. The three code examples in the **more_html** folder all provide simple applications of these tags.

Both pages of the pizza order application (**pizza-order.php** and **confirm-order.php** use <**div**> tags to provide a header and footer for each page. Here is the HTML code for the header section:

```
<div style ="height:80px; background:green;">
<h1>PHP Express Pizza Delivery</h1>
</div>
```

and here is the HTML code for the footer section:

```
<div style ="height:80px; background:red;">
<h1>123 Main Street 000-111-2222</h1>
</div>
```

In both cases, inline styles are applied to create a container that is **80px** high, with a different background color as the rest of the page (the header has a **green** background and the footer has a **red** background, to replicate the colors of the Italian flag). Each section only contains a single <**h1**> element (the color for the **h1** selector was specified to be **white** in **pizza.css**).

Open **pizza-order.php** in your Web browser (to see the page in color), or review the screenshot in **Figure 17-1, earlier in this chapter.**

The **lists.php** page demonstrates the use of different lists. This page uses four <**span**> containers to locate the four list examples. The first and third of these spans are identified with the class name "**leftCol**":

```
<span class="leftCol">
```

and the second and fourth spans are identified with class name "**rightCol**":

```
<span class="leftCol">
```

The only CSS property applied to these two classes is **float**, which is assigned the value **left** in the **leftCol** class and **right** in the **rightCol** class:

```
span.leftCol {float:left; }
span.rightCol {float:right;}
```

Each span element contains a heading and an ordered or unordered (bulleted) list. The first and third containers are floated to the left of the page, while the second and fourth are floated to the right, in effect creating two columns and two rows of lists. Open **lists.php** in your Web browser (to see the page in color), or review the screenshot in **Figure 17-2**, earlier in this chapter.

The **containers.php** page provides a more complete example, including both <**div**> and <**span**> containers, and applying a number of styles to each container. **Figure 17-3** provides a screen shot of this page but you will probably want to open the page in a Web browser to see the colors.

The page is divided into **three** sections, using class names ("**header**", "**main**", and "**footer**") to identify each <**div**> container. The **header** section contains a heading and a sub-heading; the **main** section contains a heading and a paragraph; and the **footer** section also contains a heading and a paragraph. Within the paragraph in the main section, two <**span**> containers are used to mark text that will receive special styling. The first <**span**> has the class name "**red**" and the second has the class name "**green**". The internal style sheet specifies the CSS for these five classes.

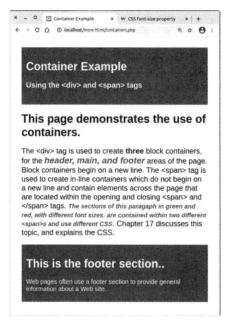

Figure 17-3: containers.php screenshot

Here is the code for **containers.php**:

```
<html>
<head>
<title>Container Example</title>
<style>
   body {width:400px;padding:15px;
      font-family: Arial,Helvetica,Sans-serif;}
   h1 {font-size:18pt}
   h2 {font-size:12pt}
   div.heading {height:100px; padding:10px;
      background: red; color:white;}
      div.main {background:white; color:black;font-size:12pt}
   div.footer {height:100px; padding:10px; background:green;
      font-size:10pt; color:white }
   span.green {font-weight:bold; color:green;
      font-style:italic; font-size:10pt}
   span.red {font-weight:bold; color:red;
      font-style:italic; font-size:14pt}
</style>
</head>

<body>
```

```
<div class="heading">
<h1>Container Example</h1>
<h2>Using the &lt;div&gt; and &lt;span&gt; tags
</div>

<div class="main">
<h1>This page demonstrates the use of containers.</h1>
<p>The &lt;div&gt; tag is used to create <strong>three</strong>
block containers, for the <span class="red">header, main, and
footer</span> areas of the page. Block containers begin on a new
line. The &lt;span&gt; tag is used to create in-line containers
which do not begin
on a new line and contain elements across the page that are lo-
cated within the opening and closing &lt;span&gt; and
&lt;/span&gt; tags. <span class="green">The sections of this
paragraph in green and red, with different font sizes. are con-
tained within two different &lt;span&gt;s and use different
CSS</span>. Chapter 17 discusses this topic, and explains the
CSS.</p>

<div class="footer">
<h1 style="color:white">This is the footer section..</h1>
<p>Web pages often use a footer section to provide general in-
formation about a Web site.</p>
</div>
</body>
</html>
```

Refer to the internal CSS in the <head> section to see what styles are applied to the content of each container. This example demonstrates the difference between **block-level** <**div**> elements that begin and end on a new line and extend across the page, and **inline** <**span**> elements, that are rendered within the current line.

HTML Entities

You may have noticed some unusual code in **containers.php**, for example

```
<h2>Using the &lt;div&gt; and &lt;span&gt; tags </h2>
```

and

```
<p>The &lt;div&gt; tag is used ..
```

Since the Web browser treats the '<' (less than) and '>' (greater than) characters as indicators of HTML tags, how do you include these characters in the actual text of your Web page?

HTML includes **entities**: special characters that can be specified in text using a special code to reference each character, surrounded by the & (ampersand) and ; (semicolon) characters. For example the '<' (**less than**) character can be included in your text using < and the '>' (**greater than**) character can be specified using >. In containers.php, the text <div> will display as "<div>", and <span> will display as "<span>".

A large number of entities are available, including special symbols such as the copyright and trademark symbols, some currency symbols, mathematical symbols, Greek characters, and much more. Here are just a few examples: © (copyright), ® (registered trademark), ¥ and € (Japanese Yen and Euro currency symbols), ° (degree symbol), Δ and δ (upper and lower case versions of the Greek delta character).

Another HTML entity, the non-breaking space character ( ), can be very useful when formatting text. Use this character to tell the browser not to break two words across a line (for example, with normal spaces, "**20 mph**" might end up with "**20**" at the end of one line and "**mph**" at the start of the next, whereas "**20 mph**" will ensure that the entire text "**20 mph**" will be moved to the start of the next line). This entity can also be used to ensure that the browser will correctly render multiple adjacent spaces in a text string, since usually the browser will collapse multiple spaces into a single space. For example, the text string "**Testing   1, 2, 3**" will display five spaces after the word "Testing".

For a comprehensive list Google "HTML entities", or see:

```
https://dev.w3.org/html5/html-author/charref
```

Deprecated HTML Tags

The specifications for HTML have evolved steadily. Many tags and attributes that were developed early on have since been **deprecated**, which means they have been replaced by more efficient solutions. As you explore HTML you will often find references to tags that have been deprecated. Although the most widely used browsers all continue to recognize deprecated tags, at some point in the future, deprecated tags may no longer be recognized, so you should avoid using these tags. Examples of deprecated tags are <u> (underline), <center>, and <font>. Examples of deprecated attributes are **align**, **bgcolor**, and **width**.

Useful References

For complete information about HTML and CSS you will want to refer to the World Wide Web Consortium's (WC3's) current standards:

>   https://www.w3.org/standards/
>   https://www.w3.org/Style/CSS/

Here are two **excellent** online resources to teach you more about HTML and CSS, including tutorials and best practices:

>   https://developer.mozilla.org/en-US/docs/Learn
>   https://www.w3schools.com/

For a good reference to color names that are recognized by most browsers, go to:

>   https://www.w3schools.com/colors/colors_names.asp

To learn more about using **Web fonts**, delivered from a Web server, as an alternative to desktop fonts:

>   https://developer.mozilla.org/en-US/docs/Learn/CSS/Styling_text/Web_fonts

Chapter 18

Where to Go from Here ...

Introduction

Congratulations! By now you should have a good grasp of basic program logic and design. This last chapter suggests ten steps that you will want to consider as you move forwards.

1. Read Chapters 16 and 17

This book is designed to help beginners to learn key programming concepts and procedures. To achieve this a number of decisions were made to avoid too much complexity that might undermine confidence when starting. Chapter 16 attempts to provide a more complete picture by: providing a more complete list of available PHP functions; introducing additional procedures, structures and operators that were not included in previous chapters, reviewing the use of the print and echo statements, and the inclusion of variables in strings; working with dates and times, and more. The chapter also clarifies where the author made use of conventions to simplify the learning process. You will find this material a valuable way to move forward with a more complete grasp of PHP essentials.

Similarly Chapter 17 provides additional coverage of HTML elements to the HTML that you learned in Chapter 4, with special attention to Web forms, quotes and citations, lists, images, HTML entities, and use of <DIV> and <SPAN> containers.

2. Take Your Work Online

When you feel ready, consider getting a **Web hosting account** and **domain name**, so that you can start working online. If you intend to continue working with languages you have learned in his book you will want to ensure that your hosting services includes a current version of PHP and MySQL/MariaDB.

Before you do, however, be sure to learn more about **security** and **validation** since your applications will now be exposed. You will need to take steps to always thoroughly **sanitize** and **validate** all **input** into your applications (from forms, files, databases, etc), and all **output** to your data sources . This is critically important: see **Appendix E** to learn about key validation procedures, and some specific security measures that must always be applied.

You will also want to become familiar with online development tools such as **FTP**, **Version Control with Git and GitHub**, and **phpMyAdmin**. These tools are all introduced in the textbook appendices, and the latest versions of the tutorials are provided on the textbook Website.

3. Review/Download the Support Tutorials

This textbook has now been used by students and instructors for a number of years. During this time requests have been made to provide additional materials to introduce related topics and procedures. To accommodate these requests a number of support tutorials have been developed and are available on the textbook Web site. The advantage of this approach is that students and instructors can download and use these as separate handouts, and avoids "mission creep" in the textbook itself. Each tutorial is short and specific, designed to introduce an important tool that you will want to become familiar with as you continue your learning, whether in other courses, at home, or in the workplace. These support tutorials include the following:

Working From the Command Line. This tutorial explains how to use the command line, lists some common commands (primarily associated with file and folder management), and includes a review of relative and absolute addresses. The tutorial is also available as Appendix C in the book, but the textbook Web site provides the latest version.

Security and Validation. This tutorial offers a basic template to protect your applications from malicious input (from forms, files, database, and other data sources), and how to validate input data according to your application requirements. The tutorial also offers useful strategies to help protect your databases against Cross Site Scripting (XSS) attacks. See Appendix E for an introduction to this material.

An Introduction to File Transfer Protocol (FTP). This tutorial allows you to transfer files between local and remote sites and is a key tool when developing a Web site located on a Web hosting service. The tutorial explains the basic steps to install an FTP client, connect to an FTP server and exchange files. Since your xampp installation includes an FTP server you can get used to the process even without access to remote hosting service. This tutorial is also available as Appendix F in the book, but the textbook Web site provides the latest version.

An Introduction to Version Control Using Git and GitHub. Version control is critical for all software development, allowing you to maintain a coherent record of ongoing modifications and release versions, develop and merge application components, collaborate with others, revert to previous versions, distribute your work, and much more. This tutorial introduces key features of Version Control Systems (VCS), and provides two hands-on tutorials to begin working with a widely used VCS known as **Git**, and to develop and distribute your Git projects using a closely related online repository, **GitHub**. You will find these tools extremely valuable in your work and studies, furthermore familiarity with Git and GitHub are increasingly expected in the workplace. See Appendix G for an introduction to this material.

An Introduction to phpMyAdmin. Chapter 14 demonstrated how to develop PHP code work with Mysql/MariaDB databases. While a coding approach is necessary when developing user applications it is not efficient when managing your databases. phpMyAdmin is a Web-based (GUI) interface to your databases. You can use phpMyAdmin to: create, drop and configure databases and tables; manage user accounts and privileges; submit SQL queries; manage your data (for example edit, insert, and delete records and fields); perform imports and exports; create views; and much more. phpMyAdmin is included in your xampp installation and is a standard tool provided by Web hosting services. This tutorial shows you how to run phpMyAdmin and takes you on a short tour to get you started. The tutorial is also available as Appendix H in the book, but the textbook Web site provides the latest version.

Selected Textbook Chapters. Chapters **14** (MySQL), **15** (Object Oriented Programming), **16** (More About PHP), and **17** (More About HTML) are also provided as handouts since these may be especially useful as "standalone" materials for subsequent work.

Additional Tutorials. Other tutorials may be added as time allows.

These tutorials can be accessed at **https://mikeokane.com/textbooks/ wbip/ support.php**, and also on GitHub at **https://github.com/mickokane.**

4. Learn to use Git and GitHub for Version Control

A **Version Control System (VCS)** is an essential tool for any software development and will allow you to: track and synchronize changes made to multiple files (code, stylesheets, media, documents, data, etc); compare and retrieve different versions (even line by line) as needed; maintain a complete, documented, version history of a project; develop different requirements independently (merging these with the main development only when the work on each requirement is completed); collaborate with others at each stage (design, coding, testing, review, maintenance, etc).

Git is a widely used, open source, and freely available VCS that runs on MS Windows, macOS, and Linux platforms. **Git** tracks changes across your entire application development, taking a "snapshot" whenever directed to do so, and can recreate any version by referring to this record. Once Git has been installed, you can define any work folder to function as a Git **repository** or **repo**, which allows you to apply Git commands to the files in the folder.

While Git functions very well as a standalone tool for local development, it is often used in conjunction with a cloud-based hosting and version control service called **GitHub**. GitHub is founded on Git tools, and facilitates code sharing, project planning and management, version-based documentation, collaborative development, remote storage, and product distribution. It is very common practice to use Git and GitHub together; a standard approach is to maintain your application's "home" repository in GitHub while downloading (**cloning**) a version to your local git repository to work on. This practice ensures that your modifications are developed separately from the "production" version (which may be private or publicly available) in GitHub. Your local work can be uploaded (**pushed**) to GitHub at any stage, as often as needed, and, once in GitHub, may optionally be shared, reviewed and tested by others before being merged to be incorporated into the production version of the application. Similarly, you can download (**pull**) components, or complete versions, to your local repository from GitHub as needed.

There is an initial learning curve to become familiar with the terminology and features of Git and GitHub but the effort is well worth it. Familiarity with these tools not only adds a key resource to your work process, but also increases your professional value. See **Appendix G** for more about these tools. The textbook Web site includes a hands on, step-by-step tutorial to get you started.

5. Investigate IDEs, Frameworks, and Patterns

Programmers now have access to powerful design tools to develop their applications. **Integrated Development Environments** (IDE's) are available that simplify and standardize the process of designing interfaces, objects, and application modules quickly and easily. IDE's include design templates, color-coded editors, compilers, debuggers, and trouble-shooting tools. As a programmer, you will very likely be expected to use an IDE and other development tools that are standard in your workplace. Some employment opportunities will depend on familiarity on a specific IDE.

Frameworks provide another important tool for application developers. A framework delivers previously developed and tested units of code that can be assembled and modified as needed for a specific application. Frameworks are based on common and well-defined **design patterns** such as the **Model View Controller** (MVC) pattern that separates the user interface of an application from its processing logic and data management services. Some widely used frameworks at the time of writing are: Angular, Django, Laravel, Rails, React, Spring, and Vue.

Design patterns are basically templates or development guidelines, tthat can be customized to solve commonly encountered problems when designing applications. Design patterns are evolved from practical experience and are continually refined; they can save you a great deal of time and resource.

Agile is an widely used approach to software design and development based on frameworks, collaboration and teamwork, shared methodologies, and best practices.

6. Learn more about OOP

This textbook provides only a brief introduction to **Object-Oriented Programming (OOP)**. OOP is fundamental to most application development. Many modern languages are founded on OOP, and strong relationships exist between OOP methodologies and data sources. If you plan a career as a professional applications programmer you will want to develop your Object-Oriented programming skills by learning a fully object-oriented language such as Java.

7. Learn Javascript

This textbook has focused on the use of PHP to handle all of the processing functions required by a Web application. That means that all input validation and other processing tasks must be performed on the server following submissions by the user.

This is not always very efficient. For example a great deal of input validation can be performed **before** a form is submitted to the server for processing. This requires the use of a **client-side** application and in most cases that means **Javascript**.

Javascript should not be confused with Java which is a quite separate language. Support for Javascript is already provided by your Web browser and so you can include Javascript code in your HTML code (using the <script> tag). Javascript is used with the **Document Object Model (DOM)** interface to dynamically modify and process elements of an HTML page without interaction with a server. In addition to form validation, Javascript provides a range of functions that allow you to build a more interactive Web interface without the need for server-side processing. Most Web sites make extensive use of Javascript to achieve visually exciting, dynamic, and user-friendly interfaces.

Ajax (Asynchronous JavaScript And XML) is a component of Javascript that also makes it possible to update individual page components from remote sources without the need to update an entire page. This can result in greater efficiency, faster processing times, and less page-reloading than has been possible with more traditional client/server interactions.

Note that Javascript is **not** an **alternative** to PHP (or any server-side language). The two languages are often used together. Javascript is used to minimize the use of server-side processing, and provide a higher quality interface, while PHP manages processes that must be handled on the server.

Also note that, although the Javascript code **executes** on the client computer, the **code** is still **delivered** from the server, included in the HTML code for a Web page. So Javascript code is still **maintained** in files on the server, with the usual benefits of maintenance and ease of modification.

8. Explore other Languages

As a developer, you will find you need to learn a number of different programming languages, in order to accomplish different tasks, meet your workplace standards, or adapt to emerging technologies. Some examples of widely used languages are Javascript, Java, C++, C#, C, R, and Python. Mobile applications are developed for use on hand-held devices. These applications access **the cloud** for updates and to obtain the data need to deliver useful on-demand services to the user, often associated with location. The term "cloud" simply refers to resources delivered by a networked service, usually over the Internet. **Mobile applications** are developed for specific operating systems, such as **Android** and **iOS**, using a programming language designed for the operating system.

Much of what you have learned in this book will prepare you for learning other languages: most languages make use of the same basic selection and loop structures, arithmetic and logical operators, file and database operations, complex data types such as strings, arrays and objects, etc. While much of the syntax of PHP is quite similar to that of other current programming languages, there are also many differences. Here are two significant differences that might otherwise surprise you when you learn another language.

Variable Naming Rules

Each language has its own rules for naming variables. PHP uses the $ symbol as the first character of each variable name. This is unusual and, in some situations, permits practices that will not work in most languages. For example, a PHP programmer can include direct references to variables inside character strings, using statements such as: "Your pay is $ $pay this week.". The reference to $pay within the character string is feasible only because the $ symbol indicates that $pay is a variable and not simply the word "pay" that should be displayed as written. Other languages do not use the $ symbol as the first character of variable names and so these languages require concatenation when the values stored in variables are to be added to character strings. This is optional in PHP where it is achieved using the period as the concatenation operator, for example "Your pay is $". $pay."this week.".

(Although concatenation is a standard feature of most languages, the period is not always used as the concatenation operator. Some languages use the + character as the concatenation operator, so the same string in, for example, a Java statement would be written as "Your pay is " + pay + " this week.".)

Variable Declarations and Data Types

Unlike PHP, most languages require that: (a) variables must always be **declared** before they can be used, and (b) the variable declaration statement must indicate not only the variable name but also the type of data that the variable will contain. This requirement has many advantages. For example, since the variable **name** must be declared **before** the variable can be used, the compiler or interpreter can detect misspelled variables. And the data type declaration for each variable determines: (a) the amount of memory that is to be set aside for the variable; (b) the range and type of values that can be assigned to the variable; and (c) the type of operations that can be performed with the variable. This prevents many errors related to inappropriate use of variables, and also provides much greater control and efficient use of memory. Languages that exert significant control over variable declarations and data types are referred to as strongly typed languages. Java and C++ are examples of **strongly typed** languages.

Basic data types usually fall into four basic categories. **Integer** data types allow storage of whole numbers and permit integer operations (arithmetic operations involving whole numbers that generate an integer result). Integers are also used to store the memory locations of arrays, objects, and other data structures. **Floating point** data types allow storage of numbers with decimal places and permit floating point operations (arithmetic operations involving decimal values that generate a decimal result). The **character** data type allows storage of single characters. The **boolean** data type permits only two values: false and true, and permits boolean operations (comparisons that generate a true or false result).

Different languages will provide additional granularity in the choice of data types. For example the Java language provides eight basic data types (known as **primitive** data types). Four of these data types permit storage of different sizes of integer values and are termed **byte**, **short**, **int**, and **long**. Two data types permit storage of different sizes of floating point values (**float** and **double**). The other two primitive types are **char** (to store single characters) and **boolean**.

In addition to these basic types, programming languages support the construction of **complex** data types. Complex data types allow storage of multiple values that can be referenced and processed using a single variable name. Examples of complex data types are character strings (which contain multiple characters), arrays, records, and objects. In a fully object-oriented language such as Java, all complex data types (including character strings and arrays) are treated as objects.

9. Join Online Communities, Forums and Projects

One of the easiest ways to learn new things is to interact more with people. It is understandable to be reluctant to ask others for help, but you will find a rich and supportive professional community out there, and one day will have the satisfaction of helping someone else.

Talk to your friends, and get connected to various programming related forums, such as **Stack Overflow**, **Reddit**, **SitePoint** and **Google Groups**. There also forums focused on a specific language (for example the PHP Forum at **https://www.php-forum.com/phpforum/**). Get a **GitHub** account (see the tutorial on the textbook Web site), and consider getting helping out on an open project. You will almost certainly be asked to share your experience of engaging with online communities in any interview situation.

10. Consider your Professional Direction

Digital Media: Digital media refers to content that has been encoded (compressed) and includes: music and other audio content, movies and other videos, animations, and images. Media content is usually developed by digital media professionals and other artists and is often quite independent of specific software applications or Web sites, although it is often integrated with these applications for delivery purposes (either streamed or downloaded). Digital media artists work with specialized hardware, software, and programming languages that have been designed for use with specific types of media. **Processing** is a significant new language that is increasingly popular for creative and media-related work (Processing is based on the Java language).

Graphical User Interfaces and Interface Design: The design and development of effective graphical user interfaces is a field of its own within software design. Interfaces connect users to the services provided by a software application and the success of an application will depend on the ease of use, and efficiency of the interface. Usability testing is a key phase of software development that provides vital feedback to the application designer that can result in significant changes to requirements. Interface designers often combine programming expertise with backgrounds in art, design, sociology or anthropology, English, digital media, technical communications, or psychology.

Web Design and Content Management: Increasingly Web design and content services are handled by Content Management Systems (CMS's) such as **WordPress, Wix, Joomla!** and **Drupal.** A CMS makes it easy to develop and maintain Web sites and other digital content services, and works well for sites of all sizes. While there remains a lot of demand for custom made Web sites, these are far more costly to maintain and extend. Many CMS's allow extensive customization and modification using HTML, PHP and MySQL. For these reasons, many institutions and online services maintain professional staff to manage their CMS; these staff members can include programmers, trainers, technical writers, and content developers. Individuals and small business owners may use a CMS for their own Web sites or to publish blogs.

Database Programming and SQL: Many applications are data-driven. The language most commonly used to communicate with relational databases is Structured Query Language (SQL). SQL comes in various flavors, customized for use with specific database vendors. PHP is commonly used with **MySql** and most PHP distributions include MySql, or its open source fork, **MariaDB**, which is included in your xampp installation.

If you are planning to work as a programmer or Web developer, you will want to familiarize yourself with at least one version of SQL in order to develop applications that interact with databases. In the process, you may find yourself more deeply interested in this subject. In that case, be sure to research the fields of database programming and database administration.

Another important development, associated with mobile applications and cloud computing, is the increasing use of non-relational databases, often termed NoSQL databases. NoSQL databases are not always based on relational tables: they sacrifice some of the security and integrity of relational database design for the sake of faster processing, especially with regard to very large data sets.

And Step 11 ... Have Fun and Follow your Heart!

Hopefully this short overview is useful as you consider where to go next. There are many opportunities in this vast field, and it is well worth taking the time to think about your own personality, your own way of working, and your personal interests. Do you like to work with other people or do you prefer to work alone? Do you prefer **coding** applications or **designing** applications? Are you happiest when you are writing queries and reports that obtain data from databases? Are you interested in the way that different applications combine to manage the flow of information and business processes throughout an organization? Do you like testing software and resolving errors? Do you enjoy writing manuals and training people to use software? Or are you most interested in creating animations, graphics, or effective user interfaces?

Often when we begin to program, we may be surprised to find that our interests evolve as we learn more about our own aptitudes and interests. As you take next steps to develop your programming skills, keep an open mind to what is possible, work hard, have fun, keep exploring, and remember to **follow your own heart!**

Appendix A

Data Representation and Formats

This Appendix provides an introduction to data representation, explaining how bits and bytes can be used to represent any kind of data once a data representation scheme has been defined.

Introduction

Moment by moment, each one of us is constantly processing **data** in order to obtain and use **information**. We may sniff an appetizing aroma and identify the smell of apple pie, look at a tall shape above us and recognize a tree, listen to a sequence of sounds and hear music, read a series of symbols and translate these into words and sentences, or see a small red circle ahead of us and brake for a traffic light. Our **information environment** includes the natural world, other people, traffic signals, clocks and calendars, books and magazines, TV and movies, e-mail, social media, and the Web.

An increasing amount of our information environment is **digital**. Digital information is stored and transmitted in some physical form that we treat as a sequence of 0s and 1s using electronics, optics or other technologies. Data that is represented in patterns of 0s and 1s is known as **binary data.**

We can represent all kinds of information as binary data. It is just a matter of agreeing on **standard data representation schemes**, usually referred to as **data formats**. For example we use a wide range of standard data formats to represent plain text, formatted text, numbers, images, audio, videos, even program instructions. Let's get a feel for how some of these formats work.

Storing Data in Bits and Bytes

All binary data formats are based on patterns of 0s and 1s. The smallest unit of binary data is known as a **bit**, which can store a single 0 or 1 value. How many possible patterns can be stored in one bit? The answer is two, either a 0 or a 1. If one bit can store one of two possible values, how many possible patterns can **two** bits store? The answer is **four**. The first bit can store either a 0 or a 1, and the second bit can also store a 0 or 1, so two bits together could store any of the following patterns: 00, 01, 10, or 11.

Similarly **three** bits can be used to store any of **eight** patterns of 0s and 1s (000, 001, 010, 011, 100, 101, 110, or 111). **Four** bits can be used to store any of **sixteen** possible patterns (0000, 0001, 0010, 0011, 0100, 0101, 0110, 0111, 1000, 1001, 1010, 1011, 1100, 1101, 1110, or 1111), and **five bits can be used to store any of thirty two** different patterns of 0s and 1s (00000, 00001, 00010, 00011, 00100, 00101, 00110, 00111, 01000, 01001, 01010, 01011, 01100, 01101, 01110, 01111, 10000, 10001, 10010, 10011, 10100, 10101, 10110, 10111, 11000, 11001, 11010, 11011, 11100, 11101, 11110, or 11111). Do you get the general idea?

A **byte** is simply a sequence of **eight** bits, so how many different patterns of 0s and 1s can be stored in a byte? Or in two bytes (sixteen bits)? Or in **n** bytes, where **n** is any number of bytes you can think of? If you consider the examples above you will notice that the number of possible patterns doubles each time another bit is added. The number of possible combinations that **n** bits can store is 2^n. So a single bit can contain 2^1 or 2 different patterns of 0s and 1s, two bits can store 2^2 or 4 different patterns of 0s and 1s, a byte (eight bits) can store any of 2^8 or 256 different patterns of 0s and 1s. And two bytes (sixteen bits) can store 2^{16} or **65,536** different patterns of 0s and 1s.

How Multimedia Data Is Represented in Binary

It may be interesting to learn how many possible patterns of 0s and 1s can be stored in a specific number of bits or bytes but what does all this have to with data representation? Let's start with how we might use sequences of binary data to represent multimedia. Figure A-1 shows a black and white drawing of an arrow.

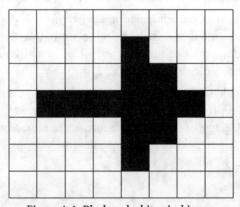

Figure A-1: Black and white pixel image

Each square in this image is a **picture element**, or **pixel**, so the drawing contains 56 pixels, some rendered in white, others in black. Since a single bit can store either a 0 or 1, we can use a single bit to store the value for each pixel. A bit that contains 0 will represent a white pixel and a bit that contains 1 will represent a black pixel. Using this scheme, here is a sequence of bits that represents the drawing:

00000000 00001000 00001100 01111110 00001100 00001000 00000000

The sequence is shown in groups of eight bits to make the pattern easier to read. Each group of eight bits represents one line of the drawing. The entire drawing can be represented and stored in 56 bits. Since there are eights bits in a byte, that means the drawing can be stored in seven bytes. Do you see how this works?

Each pixel in the black and white image could be represented by a single bit since there are only two possible values (black or white). But what if we wish to store a color image? The amount of bits needed to represent each pixel depends on how many possible colors that the pixel might contain. Let's say we want to represent an image of the same size as the one shown above, but this time each pixel can be any of 256 different colors? It takes eight bits (or one byte) to store 256 different patterns of 0'1 and 1s. If each of these 256 patterns is used to represent a different color, we will need a byte to store the color for each pixel. Fifty six bytes would therefore be needed to store the colors of all of the pixels in this image since it contains 56 pixels.

The most common method to represent colors accurately on a computer is **24-bit graphics**, which requires three bytes to represent the color of each pixel. You may recall from your physics classes that all colors are a combination of red, green and blue light. Using the 24 bit scheme, the first of the three bytes indicates the density of red light, the second byte indicates the density of green light, and the third byte indicates the density of blue light. Together the three bytes specify the overall color. This scheme allows us to specify any of 2^{24} (16,777,216) possible colors for each pixel! A typical computer screen usually displays 1024 x 768 pixels, for a total of 786,432 pixels. If three bytes are used to represent the color of each pixel on the screen then 2,359,296 bytes are needed to represent the entire display.

In general, this method of using bit patterns to store each pixel of an image is referred to as **bitmapping**, and images stored this way are called **bitmapped** (or **.bmp**) images. As you can see bitmap images take a lot of storage space! For this reason, a number of more efficient ways have been developed to store images, using various **compression schemes** (for example **.GIF**, **.JPG**, **.PNG** and **.TIF**), or quite different schemes for representing graphical data, such as **vector graphics**. Although these methods all use different representation schemes, they all store images in patterns of 0s and 1s.

Similar binary representation schemes are used to store other multimedia formats as sequences of 0s and 1s. Examples of representation schemes for audio formats are **.AU**, **.WAV**, **.RA** and **.MP4**. Examples of schemes for video formats are **.AVI**, **.MOV**, **MP4**, and **.MPG**.

How Numeric Values Are Represented in Binary

We have learned that multimedia can be stored in binary formats. What about numeric data? Numeric values must be stored on a computer so that we can maintain records, perform arithmetic calculations, and compare data values. In binary representation a number is represented by a pattern of 0s and 1s, just like images or other types of data. For example, since a byte can contain 256 different possible patterns of 0s and 1s we can use a byte to represent any numeric value between 0 and 255. Recall that there are eight bits in a byte. In order to store a numeric value, the rightmost bit is used to represent the decimal value 1, the next bit to the left represents 2, the next represents 4, the next represents 8, the next represents 16, the next represents 32, the next represents 64, and the leftmost bit represents 128. If the bit at any of these eight positions is set to 1, the value that the bit represents is **included** in the overall value of the number. If the bit at any position is set to 0 then the value that it represents is **not included** in the overall value of the number. Table A-1 shows how the decimal values 65, 32, 48 and 137 can be represented by a byte pattern using this scheme:

	2^7	2^6	2^5	2^4	2^3	2^2	2^1	2^0
	128	64	32	16	8	4	2	1
65 =	0	1	0	0	0	0	0	1
32 =	0	0	1	0	0	0	0	0
48 =	0	0	1	1	0	0	0	0
137 =	1	0	0	0	1	0	0	1

Table A-1: Binary representation of decimal values

The decimal value 65 is stored as 01000001. This binary sequence contains a 1 in the **64** column and a 1 in the **1** column, and 0s in all other columns. This pattern represents the value 65 since that is the sum of 64 and 1.

Similarly the decimal value 137 is stored as 10001001. This binary sequence contains a 1 in the **128** column, 1 in the **8** column, and 1 in the **1** column, and the sum of these three values is 137.

Do you see how this works? The decimal value 11 would be stored in binary as 00001011. The decimal value 0 would be stored as 00000000. How would you store the decimal value 40? The decimal value 104? What decimal value does 10101010 represent?

A single byte can only be used to store positive values in the range 0 (represented as 00000000) through 255 (represented as 11111111). We usually need to handle numbers in a much larger range than this so in fact more bytes are used to present numeric values. This scheme is also slightly modified in reality so that computer programs can handle positive or negative numbers and floating point numbers.

How Plain Text Is Represented in Binary

We also store **plain text** as binary data. Text is a collection of individual characters organized into **character strings**, for example:

| "John" | "123 Main Street" | "A123-HFC" |
| "123-45-6789" | "Enter your password: " | "Price: $10.75" |

These are examples of very small character strings. A character string could be an entire e-mail message or even an entire book! A **text file** is basically a character string stored on a disk that includes end-of line characters to mark the end of each line.

Initially the standard representation scheme for text was **ASCII** (**American Standard Code for Information Interchange**). The ASCII system uses a single byte to store each character of a character string—each character is represented by a different pattern of 0s and 1s. Since a byte can store any of 256 different patterns, the ASCII scheme can only include 256 different characters. This works just fine to represent all of the upper- and lower-case characters of the English alphabet, as well the ten numeric digits and some other commonly used symbols that you typically find on a computer keyboard. However a single byte does not provide nearly enough different patterns to represent the character sets of all of the world's major alphabets.

For this reason the standard representation for text is now **Unicode**, which uses **two** bytes to represent a single character. Since two bytes can store any of 65,536 possible patterns of 0s and 1s, Unicode can represent any of the characters of all of the world's major alphabets (and most minor alphabets). As an example of Unicode representation, the upper-case letter 'A' is stored as 01000001 (which has the numeric value 65), the lower-case 'a' is stored as 01100001 (the numeric value 97), the space character is stored as 00100000 (which has the numeric value 32), the copyright character (c) is stored as 10101001 (which has the numeric value 169) and so on. The good news is that the ASCII values that were defined to represent the characters of the English alphabet have the same values in Unicode.

How Source Code and Markup Code Is Represented in Binary

Program source code (such as PHP code) and markup code (such as HTML code) is stored as plain text, so this code is treated just the same as any other text. Source code simply uses the syntax and key words of a programming language so that the instructions can be recognized and processed correctly buy the language interpreter or compiler. Markup code uses the < and > characters to enclose tags so that the markup instructions can be recognized and processed by the browser or other software that is processing the markup file. The < and > characters are of course text characters themselves (their Unicode/ASCII values are 60 and 62 respectively).

Since source code and markup code are written in plain text, this code can be developed and read using any text editor.

How Program Instructions Are Represented in Binary

Computer programs are basically a sequence of instructions to be performed by the computer's microprocessor. The microprocessor contains an **instruction set** which defines all of the basic instructions that the microprocessor can perform. The microprocessor's instruction set is the basis of the computer's **machine language** and the available instructions defines the tasks that the computer can actually perform. For example instruction sets include **add** instructions that allows the computer to add numbers, and **move** instructions that allow the computer to copy data between registers and other locations. These instructions are called **opcodes**. Each opcode is represented by a specific numeric value that the microprocessor uses to identify the instruction to be performed.

We have seen that numbers can be represented in binary. When the microprocessor treats a binary value as a number representing an opcode, a program instruction is executed.

How Memory Addresses Are Represented in Binary

A computer uses memory to temporarily store programs and data that are currently in use. Each byte of memory is identified by a unique **memory address**. Memory addresses are used to track where programs and data are stored while the computer is running.

Memory addresses are simply numeric values stored as a pattern of 0s and 1s. When the microprocessor treats a binary value as a number representing a memory address, data can be retrieved from, or stored in, memory.

Data Formats and File Types

Different data formats continue to be developed and standardized to meet a broad range of requirements. Every file that you work with contains data that has been saved in a specific format, appropriate for its intended use, for example as plain text, a word processing or other office-related document, an executable program (compiled code), or a multimedia format. The name of each usually includes a **file type** extension that indicates the format that the file contains. Table A-1 shows just a few examples of common file types and file extensions that you may have encountered (some will be very familiar after working through this book):

File Type	File Extension	Description
Text	.txt	Plain text file
HTML	.html, .htm	Text file containing HTML document
CSS	.css	Text file containing Cascading Style Sheet
PHP source code	.php	Text file containing PHP source code
XML	.xml	Text file containing XML document
Java	.java	Text file containing Java source code
Java byte code	.class	Java byte code
Bitmap	.bmp	Bitmap file (uncompressed image file)
JPEG	.jpeg, .jpg	JPG format compressed image file
GIF	.gif	GIF format compressed image file
PING	.png	PING format compressed image file
MOV	.mov	Quick Time Movie
MP3	.mp3	MP3 Format Sound File
ODF Text Document	.odt	Open Document Format word processing
ODF Spreadsheet	.ods	Open Document Format spreadsheet

Table A-1: Examples of Common File Formats and File Extensions

In order to open a file you must have a program that can handle the format that the file contains. For example Libre Office Writer can open an .odt file, while any text editor can handle any file that contains plain text (for example .txt, .php, .html. .css. .java, or .xml files). Some applications can recognize and handle multiple data formats, for example most image processing software can open .bmp, .png, .gif and .jpg files.

Your operating system is usually pre-configured to choose a default application to open files with a specific file extension. You can of course open a file using any application designed to handle it; "default" simply indicates which application the operating system will choose to open a file if you click the file in your File Manager, or in some cases if the file is downloaded to your device. So for example, the default software to open **.html** files in Windows 10 is the **Microsoft Edge** Web browser, while in macOS it is the **Safari** browser. Similarly **Notepad** is the default **text editor** for Windows 10, and **Textedit** is the default for macOS. (Since there are any number of different Linux distributions, the default applications will vary.)

You can change any of these defaults to your preferred application for a certain format. For example you might want to change the default application to open your .txt, .php, and .css files to **Notepad++** on Windows, or to **BBEdit** on macOS. (Note that you could also specify a text editor to serve as the default application to open **.html** files; if you do this the .html file will be opened for **editing** rather than being displayed by a **Web browser.**)

If no program has been associated with a specific file extension, the operating system will ask you to choose a program every time you attempt to open a file of that type. You can of course specify default applications for other file types.

What Else Can Be Represented in Binary?

By now you should have the general idea that binary data (patterns of 0s and 1s) can be used for any kind of data representation. It is mostly a matter of agreeing on a standard of some kind (such as Unicode for text representation, or a standard 24-bit representation for colors). Some formats can be very targeted, for example a text-based format for defining weaving patterns would allow patterns saved in this format to be interpreted by different weaving design applications.

In fact you can easily invent your own representation system but, unless you can get others to accept your new standard, your representation scheme will only work for you!

Appendix B

File Storage, File Types, and File Addresses (Absolute and Relative)

Files and Folders

Everything you save to a disk drive is saved as a file of some kind. Since there may be thousands of files on a single disk, computer operating systems provide a file management system that uses folders and sub-folders to organize your files. Chapter 2 includes an introduction to the default organization of user files on Windows, macOS and Linux. You have a great deal of control over how you organize and manage your files and folders in a manner that works for you. This includes: creating, copying, moving, renaming, and deleting files and folders; setting permissions that determine the extent to which individual users can view, modify, or delete specific files and folders; searching for specific files or folders, or file content; and backing up your file system to reduce the risk of data loss. You will usually use your File Manager's graphical interface to conduct these operations, but as a developer you will need to learn how to conduct at least some of these operations from the command line, and also to indicate file names and file addresses in your code. This Appendix will explain more about file addresses, while Appendix C will introduce the command line.

File Storage Locations

Most computing devices usually provide multiple storage options for your files. These options usually include at least one non-removable "fixed" drive with a large storage capacity and fast access times. In addition your device may allow you to attach portable storage, such as USB drives and SD cards. Your device may also be directly connected to other computers via a Local Area Network (LAN), in which case you will probably have access to a centralized file server, designed for shared data storage and file access between users of the same network.

And of course if your device has an Internet connection, you will be able to copy files to and from Internet-based file servers. Internet-based storage is usually referred to as "cloud storage" and cloud storage providers make use of an Internet protocol known as **File Transfer Protocol** (**FTP**) to transfer and manage files and folders. You can use FTP directly if you have an account on an FTP server, for example with a Web hosting service. In fact an FTP server is included in your xampp installation, see Appendix F for more about using FTP to transfer files to and from remote servers.

Wherever a file is stored, its location can be identified by the file's name and its file path, or file address.

Naming Files

A file is identified by a file name followed by a period followed by a file type. While different operating systems may have slightly different rules for naming files, keep in mind that the file may at some point need to be copied to a different file system, and may also need to be referenced in your code, which may be running on a different file system than the system you are developing on. With that in mind, as a developer, it's a good idea to follow naming conventions that are likely to be acceptable to other operating systems, and to simplify file management:

- Don't start or end your filename with a non-alphanumeric character, space, period, hyphen, or (usually) underscore.

- Only use lowercase letters. Since most operating systems are case-sensitive this practice helps to avoid names being mis-spelled.

- Keep your filenames to a reasonable length, for example less than 30 characters. (At the same time ensure the name is long enough to reasonably identify the file's content and purpose.)

- Don't use spaces or (in most cases) underscores, instead use hyphens to separate English words in your file names. Spaces require additional steps to ensure a name will be considered as a whole, while underscores may be misread by users as a space (which is why Google for example recommends using hyphens over underscores when naming files). Hyphens are also preferred over the use of camel case in file names, to avoid the use of uppercase letters.

- When including dates in file names, consider using the convention **year-month-day** (4 digits, 2 digits, 2 digits), for example, **tax-report-2021-12-31.ods**, or **tax-report-20211231.ods**). Consistent use of this convention means that a directory listing will sort files with the same name but different dates in date order.

File Addresses

As a developer you will frequently need to be able to reference files in your code, by providing their address, or **file path**. Throughout this book you have referenced files in this way, for example:

- You have used the **action** attribute of the HTML <**form**> tag to specify the name and location of the file that should process the form data when the form is submitted.

- You have used the **src** attribute of the HTML <**img**> tag to specify the name and location of an image that you want to display on your Web page.

- You have used the **href** attribute of the HTML <**a**> (anchor) tag to specify the name and location of a file that you want your Web page to provide a link to.

- You have used the **href** attribute of the HTML <**link**> tag to specify the name and location of an external CSS style sheet.

- You have included an argument in your **fopen**() function calls to indicate the name and location of files that you wish to open for read, write, or append operations.

- You have included an argument in your **include**() function calls to indicate the name and location of files when you wish to add the contents of these files to the content of the current file.

In most (but not all) of these cases, you provided the file name only, for example when you created **circle.html** in Chapter 2, you referenced **circle.php** in a Web form as follows:

```
<form action="circle.php" method="post">
```

The reason that you could reference "circle.php" without indicating its exact folder location is because this file is (hopefully) in the same folder as circle.html. This is an example of a **relative** file address, where the address of a file is indicated **relative to the folder location of the current file**. By contrast **absolute** file addresses provide the complete path to a file. On the Internet absolute addresses are specified as a **Uniform Resource Locator**, or URL, for example, the absolute address for circle.php is:

```
http://localhost/webtech/coursework/chapter02/circle.html
```

You could have used this complete URL with your form tag. This raises the question: when should you use a relative address or an absolute address in your code? Before we consider this, let's first learn a little more about relative addresses.

Relative Addresses

Relative addresses refer to a file's folder location based on the location of the file that is providing the address. The simplest relative address consists of just a file name, which indicates that the file is in the same folder, but relative addresses can reference a file in any location within the same domain as the file making the reference. This is achieved by specifying a file path from the current file location; this file path can include the use of a "**parent folder**" indicator, which consists of 2 periods (..) to indicate the folder in which the current folder is located. The parent folder indicator can be used as many times as needed in a file path, combined with actual folder names, to provide a navigation to the file being referenced. The best way to understand this is to look at some examples; here are paths from the current file location to possible folder locations of a file named **my-image.jpg** to show how this works (note the use of the backslash / as the separator between folder names):

- **my-image.jpg**: the file is in the current folder.
- **images/my-image.jpg**: the file is in the **images** folder which is located inside the **current** folder.
- **media/images\my-image.jpg**: the file is located inside the **images** folder, which is inside the **media** folder, which is inside the **current** folder.
- **../my-image.jpg**: the file is located inside the **parent** folder of the current folder (so for example if the current folder is located inside a folder named **about**, this would mean that **my-image.jpg** is located inside the **about** folder).
- **../../my-image.jpg**: the file is located inside the **parent** folder of the **parent** folder of the current folder (so for example if the current folder is located inside a folder named **about**, and **about** is located inside a folder named **htdocs**, this would mean that **my-image.jpg** is located inside the **htdocs** folder).
- **../images/my-image.jpg**: the file is located in the **images** folder, which is inside the **same parent** folder as the **current** folder (so for example if the current folder is located inside a folder named **about**, this would mean that **my-image.jpg** is located inside the **about/images** folder).
- **../../media/images/my-image.jpg**: the file is located inside the **images** folder which is inside the **media** folder which is inside the **parent** folder of the **parent** folder of the **current** folder (so for example if the current folder is located inside a folder named **about**, and **about** is located inside a folder named **htdocs**, this would mean that **my-image.jpg** is located inside the **htdocs/media/images** folder).

This may look a bit bewildering at first, but it's quite straightforward once you see that, for every ../ in the path you move up one level through the folder system, and come down one level for every folder name in the path, from left to right. This simple addressing scheme, allows you to refer to any file under your domain (usually the root folder of a domain is htdocs) relative to the location of the file that includes the reference. Here are a few examples showing how relative addresses might appear in HTML tags and PHP function calls:

```
<a href="../../about/contact-info.html">Contact Info</a>


<a href="purchasing/order-form.html">Order Form</a>


<link rel="stylesheet" type="text/css" href="../../css/sam-
ple.css"


<form action="testarea/my-first.php" action="post">


<form action="../data/reports/process-report.php"
action="post">


<img src="../../../images/logo.jpg" />


include ("../../common-header.php");


fopen ("../data/wages/weekly-hours.txt");
```

Absolute Addresses

Note that relative addresses are **only** unique within a specific domain, so a file on your Web site might have the same name and relative address as a file on another Web site. There is no ambiguity in this case since relative addresses are always relative to a location within the same domain; if you use a relative address it cannot refer to a file located in a different domain.

An **absolute** file address, on the other hand, provides the complete URL, which is unique across the Internet, and so absolute addresses can refer to a file located in any domain worldwide. We could have written the form tag in circle.php using the absolute address as follows:

```
<form action="http://localhost/webtech/coursework/chapter02/
    circle.html" method="post">
```

(Looking at this you might first wonder: why use a URL and not the file path on the computer where the file is located? It is important to distinguish between the address of a file that is only accessible on a local file system, and the address of a file that is accessible on the Internet. A file address on your local file system needs only to be unique within that system, but a file that is referenced on a Web page must have an address that is unique across the Web, just as your home address must be unique. A URL, is composed of an Internet domain name followed by a file path within that domain, and this ensures that every file across the entire World Wide Web, has a unique address. Since we are coding Web-based applications we need to use complete URL's to indicate a file's absolute address.)

Absolute URL's are **always** necessary whenever a file is located under a **different** domain than the domain under which the application is running. So if you are including an <**href**> link to a page on someone else's Web site, you will need to provide the complete URL. There are also times when you might need to reference a file on a different domain from your <form>, <link>, or <img> tags, or your include() or fopen() statements, and in these and similar cases a complete URL is always necessary. Note that, just as with any links to different domains, any link to a file on another domain that is not under your control runs the risk of that file being changed, modified or deleted (an example would be if one of your <img> tags referenced the URL of a remote image, located on a different Web site).

When to Use Absolute or Relative Addresses

The choice between using an absolute or relative address becomes less clear when the file that is being referenced is located under the same domain name as the file making the reference. Complete URLs could have been used in all of the examples in the "**Relative Addresses**" section above. For example if these files were all located in various folders under **mikeokane.com**, the first two and the last examples could have been written as follows:

```
<a href = "https//www.mikeokane.com/about/contact-
info.html">Contact Info</a>


<a href = "https//www.mikeokane.com/instruct/examples/pur-
chasing/order-form.html">Order Form</a>

fopen ("https//www.mikeokane.com/instruct/data/wages/weekly-
hours.txt");
```

The choice between using relative and absolute addresses will depend on the nature of the Web site, and workplace policies. Two advantages of using relative addresses are:

Ease of coding: it's a **lot** faster to just code file names and relative file paths than to code an entire URL every time a file is referenced. It's also somewhat easier for another programmer reading your code to identify relative links and see where different files are located on the server.

Ease of transfer between domains: for example if you are developing your code locally, with URL's based on the localhost domain, you will have to edit all these when the application is moved to the live Web server, to reflect the true Web site domain. If you used relative addresses, this would not be necessary since the file paths would remain the same relative to one another.

Now here are two reasons to consider using absolute addresses:

SEO: The main advantage of using absolute addresses is associated with **Search Engine Optimization** (SEO) and will usually apply on larger, or busier, busy Web sites. This is more technical but the general issue is that, if a complete URL is not provided, Google may not be able to associate URL's to the same page that begin with **http://** and **htpps://**, or that may or may not include **www**. This can lead to penalties for duplicate content, and to unscanned pages.

Security: Another possible consideration is that using complete URLs helps to protect your Web site from being copied (especially in the case of larger sites). If all the local addresses are relative, it is quite easy to copy the entire site and run it under a different domain, this becomes a little harder when all the addresses include the domain, not a lot harder but that extra effort can act as a deterrent.

As long as you are working on a relatively small Web site, it is not a major effort to make one decision for now and change your mind later. If you are working for a software company you will probably be told which approach to follow.

Using File Addresses at the Command Line

You will also need a good understanding of file addresses, and relative and absolute addresses, in order to work from your computer's **command line**, accessible through a **Terminal** window. **Appendix C** introduces the command line and you will find it useful to review that material now that you have read Appendix B.

Appendix C

Working from the Command Line

Operating systems (Windows, Linux, macOS, etc) include graphical File Managers that allow you to easily manage a range of operations associated with your file system, for example: **move**, **copy**, **delete**, **rename**, **compress** files and folders; **assign** or **remove permissions**; **install** and **execute programs**; conduct **searches**. Your operating system also provides a **text-based command line** interface that can be used to conduct not only these operations (often with additional functionality), but **any** operating system commands. An extensive overview of these commands is beyond the scope of this book but this appendix will demonstrate how to work from the command line to issue some common file management commands, which will give you some familiarity with the interface and encourage further research. Appendix G introduces two tutorials to introduce version control systems, and these tutorials make extensive of the command line.

The Terminal Window

In order to work from the command line, you must first open a **Terminal window** which provides a **command prompt** from which to issue instructions. This is straightforward but since the method varies between operating systems and versions, check how to do this on your computer.

Go ahead and open a Terminal window on your computer. You will see a **command prompt**, waiting for your next command. The prompt itself includes the file path of your current folder location within the file system, initially this is most likely your home directory (if the location includes the ~ **tilde** character this always refers to your home directory). Any commands that you issue from the prompt will be executed with reference to your current location (you can easily change your location as you will see). Each time you type a command and press the Enter key, the operating system will execute the command and may display some kind of result, or error message, before returning to the command prompt, ready for your next command.

The following list of examples will demonstrate some ways in which you can navigate your file system and manage files and folders from the command line. Note that Windows commands derive from the **Microsoft Disk Operating System** (MS DOS), while macOS and Linux commands derive from Unix so the examples will show both versions when these differ. Note also that some commands are relatively harmless and do not make changes, for example displaying the contents of a directory. Other commands do make changes, for example, renaming or deleting files or folders. Be careful that you understand its purpose before issuing any command.

(The terms folder and directory are used interchangably.)

To View the Operating System Version

Windows: type **ver** at the command prompt and press **Enter**

macOS: type **sw_vers** at the command prompt and press Enter

Linux: type **cat /etc/os-release** at the command prompt and press **Enter** (this runs the **cat** (short for **concatenate**) utility which, among other useful things, can be used to display the content of a file, in this case a file named **os-release**, which is located in the **/etc** folder).

To Clear the Screen

Sometimes it is helpful to clear the screen, for example to view a long directory all at once. Type **cls** (Windows) or **Ctrl L** (Linux or macOS).

To View the Content of the Current Folder

Windows: type **dir** and press **Enter**. A list of the files and folders in this directory will be displayed, including some additional information such as the creation date and time, **DIR** if the item is a folder, and the size of the file. If the list is too long to be seen on a single screen you can use **dir /p** which will pause the listing so that you can view it one screen at a time (just press **Enter** to continue the listing). To view only the file and folder names **across** the screen, type **dir /w** (wide).

macOS, Linux: type **ls** and press **Enter**. You will see a list of files and folders across the screen, with different colors to indicate files and folders. For a more detailed listing type ls -l (lower-case L) which will list each item on a separate line. Each listing will include a d at the start if the item is a directory, followed by: the permissions assigned to different user categories; the number of hard links; the owner and the group associated with the item; size; last modification date; and name. Type **ls -a** if you want the listing to include **hidden** files.

The use of **/p** or **/w** with the **dir** command, or **-l** or **-a** with the **ls** command are examples of the options that can be used with different commands. The large number of these options permit far more specificity and functionality than you can achieve using your operating system's graphical file manager.

To View the Contents of a Different Folder

You can view the content of another folder without changing your current folder location: simply use a **relative address** or **absolute address** (complete address from the root folder) to identify the location of the other folder. If you read Appendix B you will be familiar with the use of relative and absolute addresses to locate files on a Web server and you can use the same syntax when working with your local file system (refer to Appendix B for some help with relative addresses). Here are some examples using the **dir** or **ls** command (note that Windows uses the **back slash** \ character to separate items in a path, where macOS and Linux use the **forward slash** / character).

Windows:

dir images will display all files and folders in the **images** folder, located inside the current folder.

dir media\images will display all files and folders in the **images** folder which is located in a folder named **media** which is located inside the current folder.

dir ..** will display all files and folders in the parent folder (the folder that **contains the current folder).

dir ..\images to display all files and folders in the folder named **images** which is in the same parent folder that **contains** the current folder.

dir ..\..\media\images to display all files and folders in the folder named **images**, which is in a folder named **media**, which is in the folder that **contains** the folder that **contains** the current folder.

dir \Users\sarah\documents\images to display all files and folders in the **images** folder, using an absolute address starting from the root folder (the root folder is indicated by the initial back slash \).

macOS/Linux:

ls images will display all files and folders in the **images** folder, located inside the current folder.

ls media/images will display all files and folders in the **images** folder which is located in a folder named **media** which is located inside the current folder.

ls ../ will display all files and folders in the parent folder (the folder that **contains** the current folder).

ls ../images to display all files and folders in the folder named **images** which is in the same parent folder that **contains** the current folder.

ls ../../media\images to display all files and folders in the folder named images, which is in a folder named media, which is in the folder that contains the folder that contains the current folder.

ls /Users/sarah/documents/images (macOS) or ls /home/sarah/documents/images (Linux) to display all files and folders in the **images** folder, using an absolute address starting from the root folder (the root folder is indicated by the initial forward slash /).

Using wildcards

You can construct **search patterns** by including any number of asterisks * and question marks ? in your file names in order to restrict listings to elements that match these patterns. An asterisk in a pattern indicates any number of unidentified characters at that location within a name (including **no** characters), whereas a question mark indicates exactly one single unidentified character at that location within a name. Here some examples:

Windows:

dir *.jpg will display **all** files in the current folder with any name that ends with the **.jpg** extension.

dir m* will display all items that begin with **m**, followed by any sequence of characters, including any extensions, that are located in the current folder.

dir m*.jpg will display all items that begin with **m** followed by any sequence of characters, followed by a **.jpg** extension, that are located in the current folder.

dir m*t?.jpg will display all items that begin with **m** followed by any sequence of characters, followed by t followed by exactly one character, followed by a **.jpg** extension, that are located in the current folder.

dir ..\..\media\images*.jpg will display all .jpg files in the folder named **images** which is in a folder named **media**, which is in the folder that contains the folder that contains the current folder.

macOS/Linux:

ls *.jpg will display **all** files in the current folder with any names that ends with the **.jpg** extension.

ls m* will display all items that begin with **m**, followed by any sequence of characters, including any extensions, that are located in the current folder.

ls m*.jpg will display all items that begin with **m** followed by any sequence of characters, followed by a **.jpg** extension, that are located in the current folder.

ls m*t?.jpg will display all items that begin with **m** followed by any sequence of characters, followed by t followed by exactly one character, followed by a **.jpg** extension, that are located in the current folder.

ls ../../media\images/*.jpg will display all .jpg files in the folder named **images** which is in a folder named **media**, which is in the folder that contains the folder that contains the current folder.

To Change to Another Folder Location

Use the **cd** (**change directory**) command to change from your current location to a different folder. The cd command is the same on Windows, macOS and Linux. In the following examples **xxx**, **yyy** and **zzz** represent the names of folders on your disk (note that the forward slash / is used in these examples, for Windows be sure to substitute the back slash character \).

cd / will change your location to the **root** folder.

cd /xxx will change your location to a folder named **xxx** that is located in the root folder.

cd /xxx/yyy will change your location to a folder named **yyy** that is located inside a folder named **xxx** which is located in the root folder.

cd .. will change your location to the parent folder of the current folder (the folder that contains the current folder).

cd ../xxx will change your location to a folder named **xxx** which is located in the same parent folder as the current folder.

To Copy Files

Use the copy (Windows) or cp (macOS/Linux) to copy files. The copy command can include relative addresses and wildcards.

Windows:

copy ex1.txt ex2.txt will copy a file named **ex1.txt** to a file named **ex2.txt** that will be created in the current folder

copy ex1.txt xxx\ex2.txt will copy a file named **ex1.txt** from the current folder to a file named **ex2.txt** in a folder named **xxx** that is located inside the current folder.

copy ex1.txt ..\yyy\ex1.txt will copy a file named **ex1.txt** from the current folder to a file also named **ex1.txt** that will be created in a folder named **yyy** that is located inside the same parent folders as the current folder. Note that, since the new file is to have the same name, copy **ex1.txt ..\yyy** would achieve the same result.

copy *.txt ..\yyy will copy all files with a .txt extension from the current folder to a folder named yyy that is located inside the same parent folder as the current folder.

copy xxx\ex1.txt ..\yyy\ex2.txt will copy a file named **ex1.txt** from the **xxx** folder in the current folder to a file named **ex2.txt** that will be created in a folder named **yyy** that is located inside the same parent folder as the current folder.

macOS/Linux:

cp ex1.txt ex2.txt will copy a file named ex1.txt to a file named ex2.txt that will be created in the current folder

cp ex1.txt xxx/ex2.txt will copy a file named **ex1.txt** from the current folder to a file named **ex2.txt** in a folder named **xxx** that is located inside the current folder.

cp ex1.txt ../yyy/ex1.txt will copy a file named **ex1.txt** from the current folder to a file also named **ex1.txt** that will be created in a folder named **yyy** that is located inside the same parent folders as the current folder. Note that, since the new file is to have the same name, **copy ex1.txt ../yyy** would achieve the same result.

cp *.txt ../yyy will copy all files with a .txt extension from the current folder to a folder named yyy that is located inside the same parent folders as the current folder.

copy xxx/ex1.txt ../yyy/ex2.txt will copy a file named **ex1.txt** from the **xxx** folder in the current folder to a file named **ex2.txt** that will be created in a folder named **yyy** that is located inside the same parent folder as the current folder.

To Rename or Move a File

Use the **ren** command (Windows) or **mv** (macOS/Linux) to rename a file. For example in Windows, **ren ex1.php ex2.php** will rename a file from **ex1.php** to **ex2.php**, whereas under macOS or Linux, the same operation is achieved using **mv ex1.php ex2.php**.

The **mov** command is used in Windows to move a file to another location, while macOS and Linux use the same **mv** command that is used to rename a file (since a move operation applied to a file without indicating a new folder location is equivalent to renaming the file). For example, in Windows **mov * ..** will move all the files in the current folder to the parent folder of the current folder, while **mv * ../** will perform the same operation under MacSOX or Linux.

Deleting Files

Files can be deleted using the **del** command in Windows or the **rm** command under macOS or Linux. Just as with previous commands these can include the use of relative addresses to apply to files in other folders, and use of wildcards to operate on multiple files that match a search pattern.

Creating and Removing Folders

Windows, macOS, and Linux all use the **mkdir** command to create a new folder and the **rmdir** command to remove a folder. As a precaution, a folder must first be empty before **rmdir** can be successfully applied.

Running Programs from the Command Line

Many programs are designed to run from the command line, some are included with your operating system, while others can be installed, and some will even perform installations. For a harmless example a version of the **more** program is available on Windows, macOS and Linux; this program can be used to display the contents of a file in the Terminal window one screen page at a time (just press the space bar for the next page). For example to use more to view the contents of a file named **test.php** in the current folder you would simply type **more test.php**.

Running git Commands at the Command Line

The tutorials referenced in Appendix G provide instructions to install and run a version control program named **git**, and demonstrate how to work with this program from the command line.

Recalling Previous Commands

It can be tedious to retype the same commands time after time, especially when these commands include lengthy file paths, or when you forget the exact syntax of the command. Your operating system maintains a lengthy **history** of your previous commands, extending beyond the current session to previous sessions. You can use the **Up** and **Down** cursor keys in the Terminal window to scroll through a history of previous commands, with each command sequentially listed at the current prompt as you scroll. This makes it easy to recall and re-execute a previous command, and you can even modify a previous command to suit your current purpose.

Creating Batch or Bash Files

A **batch** (Windows) or **bash** (macOS and Linux) file is a text file that contains a list of one or more operating system commands. Once created you can "run" the file, so that the commands listed in the file will execute in sequence. This is useful if you have to issue the same set of commands regularly (for example to process some code you are working on, start or exit a number of programs, copy a set of files to another local or remote folder location, or to perform deletions and other cleanup operations at the end of a work session).

In Windows batch files usually end with a **.bat** extension and simply contain a list of one or more commands in the correct sequence. Under macOS and Linux executable bash files usually end with an **.sh** extension (although no extension is required) and must include a specific first line that tells the location of the program (**bash**) that will execute the remaining lines. Here are examples of simple batch and bash files and how to run them:

Windows: Use any text editor to create a new text file that contains the three lines listed below, then save the file to your home (or any other) directory with the name **test.bat** (or any name with a .bat extension). Here are the three lines to add to the file:

```
@echo off
dir
echo Hello world
```

Each line is a separate command (the **@echo off** command ensures that the output will be displayed on a clean line in the Terminal window, without a prompt). To run this batch file simply go to your Terminal window and change directory to the folder where **test.bat** is located. Now type **test.bat** and press **Enter**. The commands in the file will be executed and you should see a directory listing, followed by the message "Hello World".

macOS and Linux: Use any text editor to create a new text file that contains the three lines listed below, then save the file to your home (or any other) directory with the name **test.sh** (or any name). Here are the three lines to add to the file:

```
#!/bin/bash
  ls
echo Hello world
```

Note that the line **#!/bin/bash** (often referred to as the **shebang**) must **always** appear on the very **first** line in the file. To run the commands in this file simply go to your Terminal window and change directory to the folder where **test.sh** is located. In order to treat this as an executable file you must first allow the file to be executable (files are not executable by default). You can use the **chmod** command to set the appropriate file permissions: just type **chmod 755 test.sh** (this allows you, as the owner, to **write** and **modify** the file, while anyone can **execute** it). Now type **bash test.sh** at the command line and press **Enter**. The commands will be executed and you should see a directory listing, followed by the message "Hello World".

These are, of course, simple and harmless examples. As a programmer you will find many, often very powerful, uses for batch or bash files to serve your purposes. Go carefully at first and build and test your executable files one line at a time.

Conclusion

As you can see, you can conduct any file management operations at the command line, including operations that you more usually conduct using your GUI File Manager. Once you become accustomed to the command line, and to batch processing, you are likely to find that some operations can be performed much more efficiently at the commend line, while other operations can **only** be performed at the command line.

Appendix D

Debugging Your Code

This appendix will help you find errors in your HTML and PHP code. Also be sure to check the chapter-by-chapter **Hints and Help** pages on the textbook Web site: these provide answers to FAQ's associated with the specific chapter exercises.

Problems Viewing Your HTML or PHP Programs

This section relates to problems that occur when you attempt to open your HTML and PHP files in a Web browser. Check here if you can't seem to access your files, if you see PHP code instead of the program output, or if the browser displays previous versions of your work.

> **Problem: I start my Web server and then open a Web browser and type any URL beginning with http://localhost. When I do this, I get a message telling me that there is a problem accessing the page.**

First try just typing http://localhost and if that generates an error it means that your Web server is not actually running. Check that you started your Web server. If your server is not starting refer to the installation document on the textbook Web site for help.

If your server is running and you can access other pages on the server, refer to the next solution for help.

> **Problem: I created an HTML file or PHP program but when I try to view it in my Web browser, I get a message that the file cannot be found.**

First try typing **http://localhost/webtech/samples/add-two-numbers.html** in your browser address box. If this program displays and runs correctly then your Web server is running just fine so the problem is probably one of the following:

  a. You typed the URL for your file incorrectly. Check the URL carefully in case you mistyped anything.
  b. Perhaps you saved your file to the wrong location. Your files must be saved in an appropriate folder under the **htdocs** folder. If your file is not located

somewhere under the **htdocs** folder the Web server will not be able to find it. For example if you are saving a file named **paint-estimate.html** for **chapter05** then this file work would be saved in the location **htdocs/webtech/coursework/chapter05**. In order to view the file in your Web browser you must first start your Web server and then use the URL:

http://localhost/webtech/coursework/chapter05/paint-estimate.html

c. Perhaps you have multiple installations of the Web server on your computer (for example one version on your hard drive and another on a portable drive). Be sure to run the version that contains the folders and files that you wish to view.

Problem: I modified an HTML file or PHP program but when I try to view it I see the previous version in my Web browser. My changes don't show up!

First check that you saved your changes!

Next, if the file is an HTML file be sure to refresh your Web browser window, otherwise the previous version of the file may be displayed.

If neither of these works, perhaps your modified file was not saved to the location that you are viewing (for example, if you have multiple installations of the server — check the previous solution for more help with this).

The last possibility is that the Web browser is in fact showing your file but your changes contain errors. To test this, try making an obvious and simple change (for example add XXX to a heading) and see if this appears when you view the file in your browser window. If it does, you are seeing the latest version but there are bugs in your code to figure out.

Problem: I submitted my HTML form but the results appeared to come from the wrong PHP program!

Check the **action** attribute in your <form> tag. You probably pasted an incorrect PHP file name here, or else mistyped the file name.

Problem: I modified a PHP program but when I try to view it I see the code instead of the results!

That means that you are accessing your HTML and PHP files using a local file path instead of a URL. Look in your browser's address window. The address should begin **http://localhost/** which connects to your Web server. The address should NOT begin with file://!

For example to open **modify1.html** located in your **Chapter05** folder, the URL would be:

http://localhost/webtech/coursework/chapter05/modify1.html

The **modify1.html** page displays a form for user input. If you complete the form and submit it, the Web server will run the PHP program **modify1.php**. Since you are correctly using a URL the application will be processed by the Web server. The program would not run correctly if you opened the application by just clicking the file in your File Manager since the pages would not then be processed by your Web server.

Similarly, to run **fixit1.php** from the same folder:

> http://localhost/webtech/coursework/chapter05/fixit1.php

If your server is running and this does not work, then carefully check your file name and file path. Try the URL: **http://localhost/webtech/**

If you see the **coursework** and **samples** folders, your server is working just fine. You can then click through the appropriate folders in your browser window until you locate the file you want (in this case, click on **chapter05**, and then click **fixit1.php**).

NOTE: If you receive PHP error messages, that means that you are accessing the server correctly but there are errors in your PHP code (see below).

In summary, here's what **not** to do when you wish to connect to your Web server in order to view files in your Web browser. Do **not** use your local File Manager to navigate to your samples or coursework folders and then double click the files to open them. This works to view **.html** files but you are not connecting to the Web server and so any attempt to access **.php** files will simply display the source code, or a blank page. Always check your browser's address window—it should display a URL that begins **http://localhost** and not a file path that begins **file://**.

Problems with HTML Layout

Sometimes your HTML layout will not appear as expected. Here are some common errors:

- You mistyped a tag name.
- You accidentally typed additional < or > characters when adding tags. This may be the problem if these characters appear unexpectedly on your Web page.
- You forgot a closing tag or mistyped the name of the closing tag. If nothing appears, check that you included a closing comment tag --> at the end of your initial comment section.
- You forgot the closing </table> tag in a table. This can generate some very unexpected results so always check this if parts of your page do not display, or display in expected locations.
- You forgot to include the <form> tags around the components of your form. Remember that **all** elements of a form must be included inside the opening and closing <form> tags.
- You forgot to use double quotes around the value supplied to your attributes, for example <input type = text..> instead of <input type = "text"..>.

- You forgot to include the style sheet in your folder, or you typed the wrong style sheet file name when specifying the style sheet in your <head> section.

Locating PHP Syntax Errors

The PHP processor will generate either **parse** errors or **fatal** error messages when it cannot understand the syntax of your code. Bear in mind that the error messages are the processor's best attempt to guess the problem. The error messages indicate the line number where an error was discovered, so it helps to have line numbering switched on in your text editor if your editor provides this option.

Unfortunately, the line number that is reported is not always the line where the error actually occurs. For example, if you leave out a semi-colon at the end of a statement, and the next line begins with the name of a variable, PHP will not find a problem until it reaches the variable and you will get the message:

UNEXPECTED T_VARIABLE on line XXX

(where **XXX** is the line number that the processor is reporting).

(**T_VARIABLE** simply refers to a program variable, just as **T_STRING** refers to a character string. The "T" stands for "Token" since all components of a PHP program are considered to be tokens.)

When you are debugging an error message, always look at the line **before** the line where the error was reported **as well as** the line **indicated** in the error message.

Keep in mind also that the error may be **many** lines previous to the line that is reported. For example you may forget to add an ending double quote to a character string. In that case the processor can only assume that all the code that follows the missing quote is still part of the character string until it reaches the **next** double quote in your code. The processor will assume that this quote must be the closing quote that you left out, when in fact it is probably an opening quote for another character string in your code, so the error message may indicate the character that follows **this** quote. If there are not more quotes in your code, the error may be reported on the last line in the file!

Look at your error message carefully. Let's say you see an error message such as:

Parse error: syntax error, unexpected '>' in
/opt/lampp/htdocs/samples/add-two-numbers.php on line 23

Look at the character that appears on this line **before** the unexpected character (in this case the unexpected character is >). If the preceding character is a quote, there is probably a quote missing somewhere in your code before this line.

Common PHP Syntax Errors

Here are some examples of common parse errors to help you debug your code. You can save some time by looking over your code for these errors before you try running the program:

Semi-colon is missing at the end of a statement.

This will generate an error message at the start of the next line.

An opening or closing quote for a character string is missing.

These are hard to track down. The error may be located many lines previous to the line that is reported.

You forgot to use \" instead of " when you wish to include a double quote within a character string.

Remember that the double quotes indicate the start and end of a string. If the string must **include** a double quote you must indicate this using \" otherwise the processor will assume the quote indicates the end of the string and will have a problem trying to process the next word in the string. A common example is when your print statement includes an HTML tag that requires an attribute. Since the attribute values are enclosed in quotes, these quotes must be escaped using \" rather than simply using ".

A function name is misspelled so the processor cannot find the function.

For example, you may have typed **ciel($number)** instead of **ceil($number)**.

An opening or closing parenthesis is missing in a function call.

For example, you may have typed **print "Hi!");** instead of **print("Hi!");**

An opening or closing parenthesis is missing in a statement that requires multiple parentheses.

These can be tough to find. For example **while** (!feof($someFile) should be (!feof($someFile)). It helps to count the number of opening and closing parentheses in an expression to determine if a parenthesis is missing. Be careful to add the missing parenthesis in the correct location!

An opening or closing curly brace is missing.

This problem can also be hard to find, and the error might not be reported until the last line of your code. Count your opening and closing braces to figure out what is missing. Be careful to place any missing braces in the correct location! If you are indenting your code nicely, this will help to make a visual check. Trace through your code. Each IF section, ELSE section, and loop structure should have opening and closing braces unless they consist of a single statement.

Common Logical Errors

Logical errors will not be reported by the PHP processor. Instead the program will run but will not perform as expected. Logical errors can be caused in many ways and it is important to test your code to help locate these errors. Test with different values and try to keep these values simple so that you check the results more easily.

A useful trick when you are trying to figure out where a logical error is occurring is to add print statements to your PHP code to print out the values of each variable (along with the name of the variable) at each step. You can use some special indicator to distinguish these from your normal output, for example a sequence of asterisks. For example:

```
print("*** hoursWorked = $hoursWorked ***<br>").
```

Now you can run your program and look through your output for the *** lines and see if the variables have the values that you expect them to have. When you find incorrect values, you have a better idea where to look in your code to find the problem. When your program is running as expected you will want to remove these lines from your code (or else comment them out if you think you might need them again).

Here are some common logical errors to watch out for ...

You run your program after making corrections but the corrections do not appear to have any effect.

Perhaps you forgot to save the latest version so the processor is still running the previous version. Or you may have saved your new version to the wrong location. Remember that the **localhost** domain refers to the **htdocs** folder under your **xampp** folder, and the **coursework** files are located in this folder under **webtech/coursework**. So if, for example, you are working on **modify1.php** for **chapter05**, this file must be saved under your **xampp** folder in **htdocs/webtech/coursework/chapter05**

If you are running the program using an HTML form, check that the form is specifying the **correct** PHP program in the form's **action** attribute. Also refresh the browser window to open the latest version of your form.

Your selection structure or loop structure is not working correctly.

There are a number of things to check in this situation:

Perhaps you added a semi-colon to the end of the heading. Remember that the headings of selection and loop structures should not be followed by semi-colons. Semi-colons are required at the end of **statements**, and the heading of a control structure is not considered a statement.

You may have used = instead of == in the test that controls your selection or loop structure. Remember that = assigns a value to a variable, whereas == compares whether or not two values are the same.

You may have forgotten to include { and } braces to surround the code in your selection or loop structure. Remember that if you do not use { and } PHP will assume that the structure only includes a single statement. In that case, any additional statements will be treated as program statements that **follow** (and are not part of) the control structure.

Be careful to **initialize** all required variables before your loop begins.

Be careful not to include statements in your selection structure or loop structures that should not be part of these structures.

Your file processing code is not working correctly.

File processing may generate many errors. If you are reading or appending to a file, be sure that the correct version of the file exists and is in the correct location (for the chapter exercises this will be the same folder as your program). Be sure that you understand the basic logic of file operations, such as the use of the priming read, how to count records, and methods of accumulating totals, determining high or low values, etc.

The best way to debug file-processing loops is to step through them carefully and be sure that each statement performs as expected. Print out the values of variables within your loop in order to satisfy yourself that these variables are performing correctly. Here are a few common file-related errors to lookout for.

When using **fopen**() be careful not to specify the wrong file name or indicate a file that is not in the current folder or has a different file path.

When using WHILE loops to read data from a file, remember that you need an **fgets**() call **before** the loop to read the first line (priming read), and you need a second **fgets**() call inside the loop, usually as the last statement. Otherwise the program will continue to read the first line each time the loop repeats.

Be careful not to test for **feof**() instead of **!feof**() in your WHILE loop heading. Remember that we are testing **while NOT EOF**.

Don't forget the **fclose**() statement and don't include this **inside** the loop!

Your output displays 0s or nothing at all where you expected your variables to display results.

There are a number of things to check in this situation:

You may have forgotten to include a $ symbol in front of a variable name.

You may have mistyped a variable name. Remember that variable names are case sensitive. Copying and pasting variable names is a good way to ensure that you are not mistyping.

You may have left out a statement that assigns a value to a variable.

If the program needs to receive data from a form, be sure to first use the form to enter the data and then press Submit. If you run the PHP program directly without using the form, the variables intended to receive values from the form will instead be assigned 0's or empty character strings.

Also check your form to be sure that your input boxes and drop down lists are listed **between** the <form> and </form> tags. If these inputs are not located within a form, the values will not be submitted.

You may have mistyped the name of a form's input field in your $_POST array reference. For example if you defined a text box with **name="hours"** in your form, the statement **$hoursWorked = $_POST['hoursWorked'];** would assign 0 to **$hoursWorked** since there is no form input with the name **"hoursWorked"**.

Appendix E

Security and Validation

These topics were introduced in Chapter 8 in the context of learning the design and application of selection structures. Security protects against malicious attempts to inject scripts that will compromise users, while validation is concerned with ensuring that all input data meets the application requirements. These are both critical concerns for all application development. Once you start to develop your applications online, you must ensure that your code **always** contains the necessary safeguards and tests to protect your users, data sources, and requirements, from malicious attacks and invalid data. This appendix will describe some important safeguards (for Web input and output, and MySQL databases), introduce some important PHP security and validation functions, and demonstrate the use of regular expressions to validate specific string formats.

Security and Cross Site Scripting (XSS)

Cross Site Scripting (XSS) is an attack where a client can interact with a Web server in order to compromise other clients. It is important to protect your applications against XSS attacks. To understand the high degree of risk, let's begin with a harmless example where an XSS attack is carried out on an unprotected application (like those in your samples folder). The **city-weather** application in the **xss** folder under your **samples** folder allows you to either submit a city and today's weather, or view the weather of cities already submitted.

Open **city-weather.html** and click the link to view the cities. Now submit a city, and view the list again. When you submit the form, your input (the city and its weather) is sent to the **$_POST** array, and **city-weather.php** processes the form, sends back a confirmation page, and saves the city and weather to a file named **weather.txt**. If you click the **Weather Report** link, **weather-report.php** is opened, which reads the cities from the file and displays them on a Web page. As you can see this is a very simple application with no purpose other than to demonstrate how an insecure application can experience an XSS attack.

Open **city-weather.html** and this time paste the following script into the **City** input box (the **city-weather.html** page includes this text for your use, so you can just copy and paste it into the form):

```
<script>alert("XSS")</script>:Sunny
```

This time when you press the submit button an alert message will display on your screen with the message **"You have been hacked!!"**. What happened? In this case, when the form was submitted to **city-weather.php**, the "city" field contained a malicious program script, written in Javascript. The **$_POST** array received the script, which was then assigned to a variable named **$city**. The program then (assuming the script was a name of a city) appended the script and the weather to **weather.txt**, and sent a new page to your Web browser to confirm you that the city and weather had been recorded. However the city that was sent back to your browser was actually the script, which your browser automatically executed. The script delivered a "You are hacked!!" alert message but could have been coded to do something worse. This is an example of XSS **reflection**, where a program inadvertently **reflects** a malicious script back to a Web client by confirming the content that had been submitted from the form.

But note that the script was not **only** reflected back to the same client, it was also **stored**, in **weather.txt**. The **weather-report.php** program is designed to read the list of cities and weather from this file and send these as a Web page to any Web browser that requests it. One of the "cities" in weather.txt is now a malicious script, and when any Web browser renders the Web page that weather-report delivers, it will inadvertently execute the script. This is even more dangerous than the first example, because every user who opens **weather-report.php** will receive the script. This is an example of a **stored** XSS, where the script is stored on the Web server (in a file or database or other data source), and then inadvertently sent to any browser that requests a page that includes this data.

In this case the script simply generated a harmless message, but among other things, the script could have been designed to access the user's session information, or cookies, which can be used to compromise the user. As a Web developer you have a responsibility to ensure that XSS attacks do not succeed.

How can you protect against XSS attacks? The simplest option is to **entirely remove** any HTML that has been inserted into your program input, **before** the input is processed. This will remove any script tags; it also often a good idea to remove quotes and some other special characters that might be manipulated to modify strings.

The process of removing or modifying characters to protect against scripts or other attacks is known as **sanitizing**. The PHP's **filter_var()** function is a powerful multi-use function that will allow you to conduct a number of different sanitizing or validation operations depending on the parameter that you provide. Using this function is similar to using the trim() function, which you have already used to remove leading and training white space from an input string, for example:

```
$city = trim($_POST["city"]);
```

You can use the **filter_var()** function in a similar way. Here is a statement to **remove ALL** HTML tags (including script tags) from a $_POST array element, and return the sanitized string:

```
$city = filter_var($_POST["city"], FILTER_SANITIZE_STRING);
```

In this example, **two** arguments are sent to **filter_var()**: the first argument is the **string** that you want to be sanitized (in this case $_POST["city"]), the second is a code that specifies what type of operation is to be performed. The code **FILTER_SANITIZE_STRING** specifies removal of all HTML tags, and by default will also convert quotes to HTML entities (see Chapter 17 for more about entities). In fact, the function will treat any character sequence as a tag if it begins with a < symbol, and will remove this symbol and the characters that follow, until a closing > is found. If the closing > is not found all remaining characters in the string will be removed.

In general you can sanitize most of your program input by applying **filter_var()** with the **FILTER_SANITIZE_STRING** filter to each input value (for example to all elements in the $_POST array). Since it is also a good idea to remove any leading or trailing white space from all input values, you can combine the use of **filter_var()** with your use of the trim() function. For example to trim **and** sanitize **$_POST["city"]**:

```
$city = filter_var(trim($_POST["city"]), FILTER_SANITIZE_
    STRING);
```

This should be your standard approach to sanitize most program input from untrusted sources.

However there are cases where your sanitizing procedure must be adapted to meet your application requirements. For example, by default, the filter **FILTER_SANITIZE_ STRING** will not only cause all HTML tags to be removed from a string, as mentioned above, it will **also convert single and double quotes** to HTML entities. For example my last name **O'Kane** contains a single quote and would be converted to **O'Kane**. If this was then displayed on a Web page the browser would correctly convert ' back to a single quote, but if the value was stored in a file or database, it would be stored as **O'Kane**. A flag can be added to **FILTER_SANITIZE_STRING** to specify that quotes should be left unchanged:

```
$city = filter_var($_POST["city"],
    FILTER_SANITIZE_STRING,FILTER_FLAG_NO_ENCODE_QUOTES);
```

Other flags can be applied to make other adjustments. However before altering the default behavior of this operation, do your own research and be sure that the modifications you are making will still satisfy your security and application requirements.

Furthermore, it is not **always** possible to use the filter **FILTER_SANITIZE_STRING** to remove all HTML from an input string: what if your application requirements **allow** the user to enter HTML (for example to submit a blog entry, or update a profile). In these cases, there are other ways to use filter_var(), to **convert** dangerous characters, such as the '<' and '>' symbols, to HTML entities, for example by using the **FILTER_SANITIZE_SPECIAL_CHARS** filter:

```
$city = filter_var($_POST["city"], FILTER_SANITIZE_
    SPECIAL_CHARS);
```

The **filter_var**() function also provides other sanitizing options. In all cases do careful research before deciding on your best course of action. If you are not sure what you are doing, follow the basic procedure described above, or ask for help.

Here is a list of filters that can be applied when using filter_var():

```
https://www.php.net/manual/en/filter.filters.sanitize.php
```

Protecting MySQL Databases

Stripping input of HTML tags provides protection against XSS, but a different approach must be taken to protect your MySQL databases against injections. If data from a Web form (or any untrusted source) is to be included in a MySQL query, the best protection will be to use MySQL **prepared statements**. A prepared statement separates the structure of a query from the data that is to be included, which makes it impossible for an attacker to inject malicious SQL. Prepared statements are easy to create and are also the best approach for coding queries since they are very efficient. The **w3schools** site provides a good introduction to SQL injection and prepared statements, with code examples to get you started:

```
https://www.w3schools.com/sql/sql_injection.asp
https://www.w3schools.com/php/php_mysql_prepared_statements.asp
```

Validating Input

You now know how to **sanitize** your program input, the next step is to **validate** the input. Validation rules are an important part of every application's requirements document and should specify what tests and associated actions should be applied to each input. Some of these rules will apply to most, or all, inputs and applications, for example: any **required fields** must have in fact been submitted and contain a value; **numeric** fields must contain a valid number; special-purpose strings such as **email addresses, phone numbers, social security numbers, state abbreviations, zip codes, and URLs** must conform to the correct formats. Other validation rules will be specific to a particular input, for example: a numeric input, such as an age, must be within a certain **range; a** sales code or date must conform to a prescribed **format**; or an input value description must be of, or below, a certain **length**.

PHP provides a number of standard functions designed to handle common validation needs but you must also develop your own code to handle more specific tests. While you have done some validation as you worked through this book, validation tests on a working application must be thorough and complete, and every input value must be tested in all ways necessary to ensure that the application will work correctly. Any validation errors will usually need to be reported, either directly to the user, or in an error log of some kind.

Here is a sequence of tests that you are likely to need in order to validate each input value:

> If the input is **required** (not optional), the PHP **isset**() function will test if a variable has been set, for example **if (isset($_POST["city"])**. If the variable has either not been declared or has been assigned **NULL** this function will return **false**, otherwise **true**. The PHP **empty**() method should then be used to test whether or not a variable contains a value, for example **if (!empty($_POST["city"])**.

> The PHP **is_numeric**() function will test if a value is numeric, for example if (**is_numeric($_POST["age"])**).

> You have already seen how the PHP **filter_var**() function can be used to **sanitize** data; it can also be used to **validate** certain types of data, for example **filter_var($email, FILTER_VALIDATE_EMAIL)** will test if a variable named $email contains a **valid email** address. The **filter_var**() function will also validate URLs, integer values, floating point values and more. For a complete list see:

```
https://www.php.net/manual/en/filter.filters.validate.php
```

Beyond these more standard tests, using available PHP functions, you will also need to develop code of your own to perform customized validation that are more specific to your application requirements, such as checking that a number is within a certain range, or that a character sequence contains one of a number of allowed codes. In some of these cases, **regular expressions** can provide another useful validation tool.

Regular Expressions

Your application may work with input that must conform to a special format of some kind. For example: dates might be required to be in a certain format, such as "year-month-day"; passwords might be restricted to letters and numbers and a few special characters, and might also be required to not exceed a maximum length; employee IDs might be all numeric digits and 8 characters long; similarly product codes might be constructed of 3 upper-case letters, followed by 6 numbers followed by an optional lower-case letter. In all these cases, **regular expressions** can be applied to ensure that the input value meets the requirements. A regular expression (**or regex**) is constructed using a formal language to define a **search pattern** that can then be applied to any character string. Regular expressions are utilized for a wide range of search operations, including input validation.

As a simple example, here is a regex search pattern that will accept product codes that meet the requirement listed above and reject any strings that fail to fit the pattern:

```
[A-Z]{3}[0-9]{6}[a-z]?
```

This pattern is defined as follows: exactly 3 upper-case letters, followed by exactly 6 numeric digits, followed 0 or 1 lower-case letters.

The PHP **preg_match**() function can be used to apply a regular expression to a value and will return 1 if the value meets the requirements of the search patter, 0 otherwise. For example:

```
$pattern = "#[A-Z]{3}[0-9]{6}[a-z]?#";

$value1 = "TEC672452w"
$value2 = "TEC672452"
$value3 = "TEC67w452"
$value4 = "TEC67w"

preg_match($pattern, $value1) will return 1
preg_match($pattern, $value2) will return 1
preg_match($pattern, $value3) will return 0
preg_match($pattern, $value4) will return 0
```

Note that the expression stored in **$pattern** begins and ends with '#'. PHP uses "Perl-Compatible Regular Expressions" (**PCRE**) syntax, which requires a delimiter at the start and end of the expression. A delimiter can be any non-alphanumeric, non-backslash, non-whitespace character. Commonly used delimiters are forward slashes (/), hash signs (#) and tildes (~).

This is just a simple example; regular expressions are very sophisticated and skilled. Many excellent tutorials and reference are available online.

Useful Code Samples

The w3schools site provides a very helpful walk through of a basic Web form validation process:

```
https://www.w3schools.com/php/php_form_validation.asp
```

The validation code for this example will provide a useful template for your own form-processing code: find it under the "Try It" link, or go to (the complete URL should be a single line):

```
https://tryphp.w3schools.com/showphp.php?filename=demo_form
     _validation_complete
```

*NOTE: PHP also provides two other functions that perform similarly to certain configurations of **filter_var()** to **sanitize** data: the **htmlspecialchars()** function will take any string as an argument and, by default, will return the same string, except that any occurrences of the following characters will have been replaced with their HTML entity equivalents: double quotes (**"**), the "less than" symbol '<' (**<**), the "greater than" '>' symbol (**>**), and the ampersand '&' character (**&**); a companion function, **htmlentities()**, will convert ALL characters that have equivalent HTML entities to their entity designations.*

Appendix F

Working with FTP

(NOTE: check the textbook Web site for the latest version of this tutorial.)

The **File Transfer Protocol** (**FTP**) is a standard Internet protocol designed to facilitate file transfer and file management operations between computers over the Internet. For example the FTP protocol allows you to copy files from one computer to another, and to **create**, **rename**, **copy**, or **delete** files or folders remotely.

You do not need to use FTP as long as you are developing your Web applications on a **locally-installed** standalone server. In this case you can just save your files to folders located under the **xampp/htdocs** folder on your local disk drive.

Sooner or later however you will want to make your Web pages and programs available on the Web and at that time you will need to connect to a "live" Web server (usually provided by a Web hosting service), and will then need to familiarize yourself with FTP in order to transfer files to and from the server. Even before you take that step you can learn to use FTP: your **xammp** installation actually includes an FTP server (currently a product named **Filezilla** if you installed xampp on **Windows**, or **ProFTPD** if you installed on **macOS** or **Linux**). This means that you can explore FTP and become familiar with the interface on your local computer, just as you have been doing with the standalone Web server. The following instructions will help you get started, just remember that the procedures you are learning here are the same as if you were connecting to, and exchanging files with, a remote FTP server provided by a Web hosting service.

Starting your FTP Server

You can start your FTP server at the same time that you start your Apache Web server: just follow your usual procedure when you start your Web server and be sure to also start the FTP server.

FTP Server Accounts

Although your FTP server is running you will need a user account in order to be able to log in (the log in process will be explained below). FTP user accounts are granted specific access privileges to files and folders located under the **htdocs** folder of your

Web server. An account can be granted **full** privileges to **all** folders under the **htdocs** folder, or may be restricted to specific sub-folders and/or actions.

If you installed xampp under **macOS** or **Linux**, your FTP server is already configured with a default user account with full privileges, so you can use this account. The default username should be **daemon** with password **xampp** (if this doesn't work, try username **nobody** with password **xampp**).

If you are using **Windows**, you will need to create a user account yourself. Instructions to do this are provided in the next section (macOS and Linux users can skip the next section).

NOTE: These instructions are correct at the time of publishing; be sure to check the textbook Web site for the latest updates and instructions if you run into any problems or would like to know more about setting up additional user accounts on any operating system.

Setting up your local FTP server in Windows (Filezilla)

(macOS and Linux should skip this section and continue to **Installing an FTP Client**.)

If you are running Windows the FTP server that comes with xampp is called Filezilla. To start your FTP server running, start the **XAMPP Control Panel** and click **Start** for the Filezilla module. To manage your FTP server, click **Admin** (also for the Filezilla module). You will first be asked to create an **admin** password: use any password you wish (**but be very careful to type this correctly and be sure to record it!**).

Next you will want to create a **user account** (which you can use to connect to the FTP server), and assign **permissions** to this user:

Click the **Edit** menu and choose **Users**.

Click **Add** under **Users**. Type a username, which can be any name you want, and click OK. With the user highlighted in the User window, click the **Password** checkbox and type a password for this user. Be sure to remember the username and password you have chosen.

You can now define which directories and permissions this user can access on your Web server. This is important since you can restrict different users to only have ftp access to specific folders or actions.

Click the **Shared** folder page, then click **Add** under **Shared** folders.

To get started just choose **htdocs** to allow this user to have ftp access to all your Web server's folders and files (if you wanted to restrict privileges for this user you might for example choose the **htdocs/webtech/coursework** folder to restrict access to this folder, and its sub-folders).

Now set the type of access you are providing to this user: check the **Read**, **Write**, **Delete**, and **Append** boxes so that this user has a full range of permissions. Also check boxes to allow the user to **create**, **delete**, **view (list)** directories.

If you click **Set as home dir** then the selected folder (for example **htdocs**) will be the one that is first displayed when this user connects to the FTP server.

Note that in cases where you wanted to restrict a user's access to certain folders you can add multiple folders and set the access levels to each of these to completely customize access privileges.

When you are done click the **OK** button.

Installing an FTP Client

(Remember you will be connecting to the FTP server as if it is running remotely and not on your local computer, for this reason we will refer to the FTP server as a **remote** server). Now that your FTP server is running and you have a user account, you are ready to connect to the server. To do this you need an **FTP client** program, just as you need a Web browser (which is a Web client) to communicate with your Web server. There are many FTP clients available; we will use the **Filezilla** client which is available for Windows, macOS, and Linux, and which will communicate with any FTP server, including **Filezilla** and **ProFTPD**. If you prefer not to use a client with a graphical user interface, you can also issue your FTP commands directly from the command line (Google "FTP command line" for a list of common commands).

Go to **https://filezilla-project.org/** to download and install the Filezilla FTP client; be sure to download the correct version for your own operating system.

Using Your FTP Client to Connect to Your FTP Server

When you run your FTP client you will see that most of the interface is composed of two file system windows. The left window shows you the contents of a default folder on your local file system (probably the **root** folder of your local user account). The right window is empty; it will show your Web server's files and folders once you make a connection.

At the top of the page, below the menu, you will see **"Quick Connect"** input boxes for **Host**, **Username**, **Password**, and **Port**. Filezilla needs this information to connect to an FTP server:

Host: this is the domain name of the FTP server. If you were connecting to a remote server the FTP host name would have been provided to you by your Web hosting service. In our case we are connecting to our local server, so the name is just **localhost** (or **127.0.0.1**).

Username: macOS and Linux users, use **daemon**. Windows users, use the username for the FTP account that you created.

Password: macOS and Linux users, use **xampp**. Windows users, use the password for the FTP account that you created.

Port: the port number is **21**, unless you changed this.

Once your FTP client has connected to the FTP server the window on the right will display files and folders from the remote site. Usually the root folder will have been defined by your hosting provider, however since we are connecting to our local server, the root will be the **xampp/htdocs** folder.

Getting to Know Your FTP Client Interface

You are now looking at local files and folders on the left and "remote" files and folders on the right. You can click through folders on either side to navigate to specific folders on either system. Because your "remote" server is actually local, you could actually navigate to the xampp/htocs folder in the left panel and see the same files and folders that are displayed in the right panel! Just keep in mind that the right panel will usually show the contents of a server in a different location, while the left panel shows your local file system.

Here are a few exercises to get used to using the Filezilla FTP client interface.

Navigate through the folders in the **left** panel to find your **Documents** folder. When the contents of your Documents folder are displayed, right click in this window and choose **Create Directory**. Create a folder with the name **testarea**. When you do this you will see a new folder named **testarea** appear in the list of folders under **Documents** (if you don't see it, go to the **View** menu in FileZilla and click **Refresh**). Now click on **testarea** so that you are looking inside this folder; it will be empty except for a small folder icon followed by two periods, which symbolizes the previous folder, you can click this to return to the **Documents** folder. If you try this, return again to the **testarea** folder.

Now navigate through the folders in the **right** panel to find your **coursework** and **samples** folders (inside the **webtech** folder). Drag and drop a few files from these folders into the testarea folder in your **left** panel. Don't worry about which ones, you are **copying** these files not **moving** them and this is just to get used to the interface.

In the **right** panel, navigate to the root folder (the **htdocs**) folder. In your left panel, go back to the Documents folder. Now drag the **testarea** folder over to the right panel. The **testarea** folder and its contents will be copied to your "remote" server. Note that you now have **two** copies of this folder, the first copy is located under your local Documents folder, the new copy is located under your Web server. If your Web server is running you can view the files under your Web server using a URL, just like any other files inside your htdocs folder, for example if you have a file in **testarea** called **welcome.html** you can view it using the URL: **http://localhost/testarea/welcome.html**.

Now use your text editor to open one of the files in your **Documents/testarea** folder (left panel). Make some changes to this file and save it in the same location with the same name. Back in Filezilla, drag and drop the modified file to the **testarea** folder on your Web server. Since there is already a file with this name you will be asked it you want to replace it. Go ahead and replace the file. If you view this file in your Web browser you will see the changes that you made.

Back in the left panel right-click the same file and select **Rename** from the drop down. Change the name of the file. Now drag the renamed file over to the **testarea** folder of your Web server. This time the file will be copied without a warning since it is not replacing an existing file.

This is a typical work process: you work on files on your local computer, and when you are ready (usually when they have been thoroughly tested), you move the files to the live Web server where they will be publicly visible.

Experiment a little to get a feel for using the interface but be careful only to make changes inside the **testarea** folders in either location, you don't want to make changes to your coursework or samples folders! As you do this consider the power of FTP: although you are working locally for now, usually these operations involve moving and managing file and folders between remote computer systems anywhere in the world.

Closing Your FTP Connection

When you are have finished working with the FTP server, you may wish to delete the **testarea** folders under your **Documents** folder (left window) and **htdocs** folder (right window), or you may want to keep these folders for further experimentation at a later date.

To disconnect your FTP client from the FTP server, click the **Server** menu in your Filezilla client application and choose **Disconnect**. You can then quit the application by choosing **Exit** from the **File** menu.

Note that these steps disconnected your FTP **client** but the FTP **server** is still running. Be sure to stop the FTP server, you will do this in the same way that you stop your Web server.

Summary

FTP provides a powerful file management resource when working between two file systems that are remote from one another. Web developers often use FTP to transfer files and folders between a local computer and a remote Web server. Here are some some standard operations you can perform with FTP:

- File and folders can be copied from one system to another.
- Files and folders can be created, copied, deleted, and renamed on either system.
- When a folder is copied, the copy operation includes all files and sub-folders inside the folder. This means that an entire Web site can be easily copied by drag-

ging the root folder to the local or remote system. This makes it easy to create a **backup** or **mirror** of a Web site.

- Operations on files and folder in the local or remote system do not change anything on the other system. You must explicitly transfer files and folders for changes made in one location to apply to the other system.

This is just a brief introduction to FTP. Check the version of the tutorial on the textbook Web site for the latest new information related to setting up and using your standalone FTP server.

Appendix G

Tracking Your Changes: Version Control Using Git And GitHub

(Note: While not required to complete this book, learning to use Git and GitHub is well worth the effort. At first you may use these tools only to backup and keep track of your work; over time you will learn to use and appreciate all of the functionally that these provide, and that will serve you both as a student and in the workplace. The material provided here, and in the companion tutorials on the textbook Web site, can be studied at any stage. Some students may prefer to defer this topic until after completing the course, while others may wish to take advantage of this software while working through the chapter exercises.)

Introduction

Perhaps the best way to introduce version control is to consider how you work on the exercises in this book. You may have quickly learned to save your code a number of times, using a slightly different file name each time, so you could retrieve a previous version if you got stuck. For example if you were working on an exercise file named **software-order.php**, you might have saved your first modifications as **software-order-1.php**, your second as **software-order-2.php**, and so on. You may have also learned to make a note in the comment section of each file to remind yourself of the changes that you made since the previous version. Once you completed the exercise, you might have then saved or renamed the final "production" version as **software-order.php**, and either deleted the previous versions or kept them as a history of your work.

This is a basic version control system: beginning with an initial version; developing, documenting, and saving different versions whenever you make significant changes, or complete different requirements, or simply stop for the day; and eventually integrating these changes into a final working version. Each version captures your work at a particular stage of development, so that you can refer back to it if needed, or even revert to a previous version if your current work is going nowhere.

Saving files with different names is better than nothing but is not a very efficient version control system. There is the problem of managing an increasingly large number of files, with similar names and often containing much of the same code. There is also the challenge of tracking and documenting your changes clearly. There is the difficulty of synchronizing changes made to multiple files (for example **include** files, **.css** files, image files, etc). You may have already experienced how confusing and overwhelming it can be to keep track of everything, even when developing small applications.

What is a Version Control System?

A **Version Control System** (VCS) will allow you to : track and synchronize changes made to multiple files (code, stylesheets, media, documents, data, etc); compare and retrieve different versions (even line by line) as needed; maintain a complete, documented, version history of a project; develop different requirements independently (merging these with the main development only when the work on each requirement is completed); collaborate with others at each stage (design, coding, testing, review, maintenance, etc).

This appendix introduces a widely used version control system known as **Git**, and a related online repository, **GitHub**. Used together, these tools are equally effective when managing small, one-person, applications (even textbook exercises!), and extremely complex development that involves large teams, sometimes thousands of professionals collaborating worldwide. The basics are easy to learn and master, and the textbook Web site provides **two hands-on tutorials**. The first tutorial demonstrates how to: install Git; create a sample Git repository on your local computer; and use Git to track changes while you simulate the development of a simple application. The second tutorial more or less repeats the same procedures as the first, but this time takes advantage of the resources available in GitHub. Together these two tutorials will introduce key terminology and procedures, and provide you with a working knowledge that you can put to immediate use in your work.

Git and GitHub

Git is a widely used, open source, and freely available VCS that runs on **Windows**, **macOS**, and **Linux** platforms (the Git system was created by Linus Torvalds in 2005 when he was engaged in developing the Linux kernel). **Git** tracks changes across your entire application development, taking a "snapshot" on request. These snapshots constitute a history of your work process, and among other things, allows you to return to any previous stage of your work whenever it suits your purpose. Once Git has been installed, you can define any work folder to function as a Git **repository** or **repo**, which allows you to apply Git commands to the files in the folder.

While Git functions very well as a standalone tool for local development, it is often used in conjunction with a cloud-based hosting and version control service called **GitHub**. GitHub is founded on Git tools, and facilitates code sharing, project planning and management, version-based documentation, collaborative development, remote storage, and product distribution. It is very common practice to use Git and GitHub together; a standard approach is to maintain your application's "home" repository in GitHub while downloading (**cloning**) a version to your local git repository, which is the version that you work on. This practice ensures that your modifications are developed separately from the "production" version in GitHub. Your local work can be uploaded (**pushed**) back to GitHub at any stage, as often as needed, and, once in GitHub, may optionally be shared, reviewed and tested by others before being merged into the production version of the application. This production version can be public or private; you may have already used GitHub to download publicly available software, or other resources, provided by other developers.

While GitHub is a proprietary product (owned by Microsoft), and offers a number of priced plans, you can sign up for a free account that provides a comprehensive set of features at no cost. GitHub is extremely popular among developers: at the time of writing GitHub has over 40 million users, and is the largest host of source code in the world.

Using the Tutorials

No previous programming experience is required to use the tutorials, except that you will work from the command line and will need to change directories (a quick read of Appendix C will provide everything you need to know). You can work through the tutorials at any point while working through the textbook, or simply download them for future reference. You should probably allocate about four hours to complete the tutorials and absorb the information.

These and other tutorials can be found on the textbook Web site, under the **Students** menu:

```
https://www.mikeokane.com/textbooks/wbip/support.php
```

The remainder of this appendix describes basic Git procedures and terminology, and explains some common commands (this material is also included in the tutorials).

General Procedure and Terminology

Once a folder has been initialized as a Git **repository**, or **repo**, you can issue Git commands to track and manage changes made to the files within the repository (this includes changes within files, creation of new files and deletion of files). These files may contain code, documentation, media, data files, style sheets, notes and references; all that matters is that the files are stored within the repository (which includes any subfolders). The Git **init** command must be used to initiate a folder as a Git repository.

The Git version control process is based on a series of "snapshots" of your application development: each snapshot records the changes you have made since the previous snapshot. These changes may include: code additions, modifications, and deletions; file additions, deletions, and renaming; media development; documentation and research; data acquisition, etc. When you wish to preserve the latest changes you have made to your repository you simply take a new snapshot. These snapshots are called **commits** in Git terminology, because each snapshot commits your most recent changes to the repository.

Since you are likely to be working on multiple files between commits, and since you may not necessarily want **all** changes to **all** files to be included in the next commit, Git provides a **two-step process**. Before issuing a commit, you must first **add** file names to a "staging area", to indicate that the modifications made to these files since the last commit are to be included in the next commit. Once you have listed all of the files to the stage with changes that you wish to be recorded, you can issue a **commit** command. Git will then compare the content of these files at the time the file name was added to the staging area with their content the previous time they were committed, and any changes will be recorded in the commit.

This process of committing versions as you work allows you to easily maintain a clear history of your development, and the staging requirement means that you can commit versions that reflect changes made for a specific purpose, such as adding a new feature, or completing a task. A commit can also simply capture all of the changes you have made before heading off to lunch, or finishing work for the day, just like making a backup for peace of mind. Git makes it easy to review your history of commits, compare different versions, and go back to a previous version if needed.

(It is not unusual to add a file to the stage and then realize it needs some more work before it's ready for the next commit. That's not a problem: you can add the **same** file to the stage multiple times, in which case only the changes that appear in the latest version will be included in the next commit.)

A unique ID is generated to identify each commit, and you are invited to provide a description as documentation (which can be a few words or more extensive). Once a commit is executed the stage is cleared so you can start adding files for your next commit.

Imagine a sequence of these commits, forming a version history of changes to your application. The entire sequence is called a **branch**, and every repository includes a **main** branch that tracks changes that have been applied to your core application. A pointer called the head points to the latest version (commit) on a branch. If you are not happy with your most recent commit(s) and want to revert to a previous commit in the branch you can **reset** the head to point to an earlier commit.

A single repository can contain multiple branches. A **main** branch may be all you need for a small application, but it is often useful to develop different components, or experiment with your code, on separate "side" branches. You can commit changes on each branch, and then **merge** these changes into the main version if and when you are ready to do that.

A new branch is created with the Git **branch** command and, once created, you can switch to the branch using the **checkout** command. Remember that the **main** branch contains the history of changes (commits) that have been made to the main version of your application, and that the head points to the latest commit. When you first create a new branch, its head will initially point to the same head as the main branch. Once you checkout the **new** branch, your future commits will be added to the new branch, until you checkout a different branch. You can checkout different branches as needed, just remember that your commits are always applied to the branch that you have currently checked out. This may sounds confusing; let's say you're working on a film ratings application, and you've added a branch to develop a new feature that allows users to add new films; you checkout the new feature branch and make commits on it as you work on this new feature; while you're working on this you notice a minor bug in the code, unrelated to the new feature; since you don't want this to be recorded as a commit in your new feature branch you checkout the main branch, fix the bug, commit the change on the main branch, then you checkout your new feature branch again to continue working on the new feature. When (and if) you are satisfied with your new feature, you can tell Git to **merge** the branch commits with the main branch. If any conflicts are found Git will report these to you so you can resolve them. Once the merge process has been successfully completed, you can delete the new feature branch since the commits that tracked this work are now merged into your main branch development.

Don't worry if this is a bit confusing when you first read it. The hands-on tutorial will clarify the process and demonstrate how easy it is to issue Git commands and work between branches, while developing your application.

Summary of Common Git Commands

Here is short summary of the Git commands mentioned above, and a few others that you will use in the tutorial:

git init to establish your project's working directory as a Git repository.

git add to add files to the Git staging area, in preparation for the next commit.

git status to see a list of the files that have already been added to the staging area, and also a list of files that have been modified but not yet added to the stage.

git commit to create a snapshot of all the changes made to the files that are listed in the staging area at the time that each file was added.

git branch to create a separate branch for your development work, allowing you to commit changes to the new branch instead of the main branch.

git checkout to switch to a different branch. When you do this, your future commits will be associated with this branch, until you checkout a different branch.

git merge to merge your commits on one branch into another branch (usually the main branch). If Git discovers a conflict (changes made to the same lines in both files) it will stop the merge and alert you of the conflicts so you can resolve them.

git diff command to compare differences of all kinds (for example, to view the changes you have made to a file since it was added to the stage, or to view differences between two different commits).

git reset to return to (restore) a previous version of your application. This command includes an option to remove all changes made in your application files since that previous version.

git log to view a history of your commits. The history includes the ID and description of each commit, which is useful since you may need this information when issuing other Git commands.

Each of these commands have many options and arguments allowing a great deal of customization, and there are also a number of other Git commands available for your use. For a full list of Git commands and their options, see:

```
https://git-scm.com/docs/
```

Note also that a number of Git GUI clients are available, removing the need to work at the command line, and providing additional development support.

Introducing GitHub

You may have already used **GitHub** to download software or other materials. GitHub is a Web-based hosting platform designed to provide a global resource to support code development, version control, collaboration, code-sharing, and project management. Whereas Git is open source and freely available as a local resource, GitHub is a cloud-based Microsoft product and service. At the time of writing the basic GitHub service, including storage, is available at no cost, with additional services available at different fee levels. Anyone can create a GitHub account, and GitHub works very well in combination with local repositories. There are other online Git-based platforms, but we will focus on GitHub since it is currently the most popular world-wide.

Once you have a GitHub account you can create, maintain, update, and manage your repositories online, while continuing to modify and update the content in a local Git repo, working with a downloaded (**cloned**) copy. This work model is very common: the stable version (often production version) of an application evolves on the main branch of the GitHub repository, and whenever work is to be undertaken, a branch is created for that purpose. The branch is usually cloned to a local repository for development, and when the work is complete it is **pushed** back up the GitHub branch, and "pull requests" are issued, inviting review, testing, and modifications, until the work on the branch is approved for merging with the main branch. This model works just as well for solo development as for larger projects involving teams, even projects that are open to anyone who wishes to become involved. Access to a GitHub repo can be kept private, shared with selected users, or made fully public. Collaboration is at the heart of modern application development and GitHub provides a range of collaboration and shared project management tools.

In Conclusion

Learning Git and GitHub is a sound investment, well worth the small amount of time and effort that is required. A good approach is to start simply, using these tools to keep track of your changes, and to back up your work, and then extend your use, and reach out to other developers, as you gain experience. It is a very good idea to list your experience with Git, and any involvement in collaborative work on GitHub, on your professional resume.

For more about Git and GitHub see:

https://git-scm.com/

https://github.com/

Conclusion

Appendix H

Working with phpMyAdmin

(Note: this appendix is also available as a handout on the textbook Website.)

In **Chapter 14** you learned how to develop PHP code designed to connect to, and work with, **MySQL** databases. This is necessary when your Web application needs to interact with a database to meet a requirement, but what about your own need to work with databases as a developer? How can you issue MySQL commands directly, without coding queries in PHP?

phpMyAdmin is a freely distributed, Web-based interface to your **MySQL** and **MariaDB** databases, that provides a complete MySQL management environment. phpMyAdmin allows you to: create, configure, and drop databases, tables, views, and indexes; execute SQL queries and other statements; manage users and privileges; perform back ups and other house-keeping; and much more.

phpMyAdmin is included in your **xampp** distribution and can be accessed under your **http://localhost** URL. If you use a Web hosting site, your service package will almost certainly include phpAdmin, allowing you to work with your remote databases.

The following tutorial is just intended to introduce the phpMyAdmin interface. For a comprehensive overview and documentation see:

```
https://www.phpmyadmin.net/
```

Before You Start

Before you start this tutorial you should have already worked through **Chapter 14, Connecting to a Database — Working with MySQL**, so that you are familiar with some basic MySQL queries and have already created a user account (**wbip** with password **wbip123**), as well as two database tables, named **personnel** and **timesheet**, in the default **test** database.

Connecting to phpMyAdmin

First start your Web server and MySql if these are not already running. Open a Web browser and use the following URL to connect to phpMyAdmin:

```
http://localhost/phpmyadmin
```

This opens a Web page that displays the home page of the phpMyAdmin interface. On the left you will see a list of available databases. These should include the test database that you worked in Chapter 14, and should include 2 tables, named **personnel** and **timesheet**.

At the top of the main window you will see a row of tabs that provide different options. Let's examine your **test** database: click the **Databases** tab. You will see a list of databases. For now you should only work with your test database, and any other databases that you create yourself.

Click **test** to choose this database. Notice the new set of tabs at the top of the page that give you options to work with the database and its content. The **Structure** tab is open and the page lists the **personnel** and **timesheet** tables that are included in the test database.

Click the **personnel** table. You are now viewing a page under the **Browse** tab that displays a listing of the rows in this table. Note that this page allows you to **edit**, **copy**, or **delete** individual rows and fields, **export** any number of rows, **print** rows, etc.

Issuing SQL Commands

The **SQL** tab provides a page that allows you to submit SQL queries. Click the SQL tab and type the following query in the query box:

```
SELECT * from personnel
```

Now press the **Go** button and your query will be executed. You should see the results of your query Since your query requested **all** of the fields of **all** rows in the personnel table this is the same listing that you saw under the **Browse** tab except that the number of rows that were returned is indicated. Once again you have options to work with any or all of these rows and fields.

Let's try a more specific query, such as the following:

```
SELECT firstName, lastName FROM personnel WHERE jobTitle
='accountant' ORDER BY lastName
```

This time only two rows are displayed, and only the content of the **firstName** and **lastName** fields are included, ordered by lastName.

You can run any of the queries that you learned in Chapter 14, including queries to create. configure, and drop databases and tables, insert, update and delete records, etc.

Using the phpMyAdmin Interface

You can also perform many of these operations with no need to issue SQL commands. For example to use an online form to conduct the last query, click the **Search** tab, type **accountant** in the value field of **jobTitle**, and, under options, select **firstName** and **lastName**.

Similarly the **Insert** tab allows you to add new records, and the **Privileges** tab allows you to add new users, modify the privileges of existing users, and more. Go to the **Export** tab to **export** your tables or query results in a number of different formats, including **SQL, CSV** (plain text with comma separated values), **CSV for Excel**, JSON, **Open Document, Open Document text**, PDF, XML, etc. Go to the **Import** tab to **import** records from one of these formats.

This is just a brief introduction to phpMyAdmin and describes some basic operations. Check the textbook Web site for any additional material.

Index